Appalachia

Appa

lachia

A History

John Alexander Williams

The University of North Carolina Press

Chapel Hill and London

Designed by April Leidig -Higgins
Set in Ehrhardt by Copperline Book Services, Inc.
Manufactured in the United States of America

The paper in this book meets the guidelines for permanence
and durability of the Committee on Production Guidelines
for Book Longevity of the Council on Library Resources.

A longer version of "Introduction: Ghosts, Boundaries, and
Names" was published as "Appalachian History: Regional
History in the Post-Modern Zone," *Appalachian Journal* 28
(Winter 2001): 168–87. Used by permission.

Parts of Chapters 2, 3, and 4 appeared in the author's earlier
works, *West Virginia and the Captains of Industry* (Morgantown: West Virginia University Press, 1976; reprinted 1997)
and *West Virginia: A History* (1976; 2nd ed., Morgantown:
West Virginia University Press, 2001). Used by permission
of West Virginia University Press.

Library of Congress Cataloging-in-Publication Data
Williams, John Alexander, 1938–
Appalachia: a history / John Alexander Williams.
p. cm. Includes bibliographical references and index.
ISBN 0-8078-2699-5 (cloth: alk. paper)
ISBN 0-8078-5368-2 (pbk.: alk. paper)
1. Appalachian Region—History. I. Title.
F106.W68 2002   974—dc21   2001052761

Cloth   06 05 04   5 4 3 2
Paper   06 05 04   5 4 3

Again for Sander, Jared, and Matthew,
and for Claudia and Wallace,
and Lara, Rachel, and Robyn
—Appalachian migrants, once removed—
and for Mike, who stayed

Contents

Illustrations

Maps and Tables

Maps

Tables

Acknowledgments

All books are collaborations, even those with only one name on the spine. The names of my foremost collaborators can be found in the notes and the bibliography. In fact, the first draft of this book read like a historiographical essay, but as one reader pointed out, this genre lacks charm for readers outside of the history profession. So I hope that my collaborators won't mind being consigned to the endnotes and accept this seeming ingratitude as the price of bringing their ideas to the attention of a broader public.

The I. G. Greer Distinguished Professorship in History at Appalachian State University facilitated the writing of this book by providing research assistance, travel funds, and—most important of all—a semester's leave in which to write without interruption. Among my colleagues in the Department of History at Appalachian, Tim Silver read parts of the manuscript and Karl Campbell and Jonathan Sarris provided guidance in their areas of expertise. Mike Wade was a supportive departmental chair, and Brenda Greene and Donna Davis, the department's estimable support staff, provided numerous forms of assistance. Appalachian's College of Graduate Studies and Research provided support for the acquisition of illustrations.

Fred Hay, Dean Williams, and Kathy Staley of the William L. Eury Appalachian Collection in ASU's Belk Library were patient with my requests and helpful with my inquiries. I am also grateful to other custodians of research materials, such as John Cuthbert at West Virginia University, Fred Armstrong at the West Virginia Department of Archives and History, and a number of former colleagues at the American Folklife Center in the Library of Congress: Jennifer Cutting, Judith Gray, Ann Hoog, Mary Hufford, and David Taylor. Among other librarians, I want to acknowledge the helpfulness of the staffs at the public libraries of Huntsville (Alabama), Scranton (Pennsylvania), Fayetteville (West Virginia), and Whitesburg (Kentucky); of archivists at WVU, the universities of Kentucky, Louisville, and North Carolina at Asheville, and at the Hagley Museum and Library; of government archivists at the Library of Congress, National Agriculture Library, National Archives, Great Smoky Mountains National Park, Smithsonian Institution, and the Georgia, North Carolina, and West Virginia Departments of Archives and History. A summer as scholar-in-residence at the Pennsylvania State Archives was invaluable in educating me about the importance of Pennsylvania in Appalachian history. I want especially to recognize Linda Shopes for helping me to make the most of this opportunity. Merle Moore and Jerry Herndon of the National Mine Health and Safety Academy Library in Beckley, West Virginia, made sure that I was up to date on the coal industry. Al Goldberg of the historian's office in the Office of the Secretary of Defense, Department of Defense (DOD), and Roger Jorsted of the DOD Washington Headquarters Services Directorate for Information Operations and Reports, both in Arlington, Virginia, helped me cut paths into the voluminous records of military installations, procurement, and service in Appalachia.

I owe special thanks to the people of Appalshop, including Michelle and David Reynolds, Elizabeth Barret and Herb E. Smith, Mimi Pickering, Will Dodson, Maxine Kenny, Jim Webb, and Tom Hansel. Among my students at Appalachian, David Reynolds, David VanHoy, Bob Hutton, Ralph Lentz II, and Alythea McKinney taught me much that I needed to know about our region's history, while Jennifer Stertzer was a helpful research assistant. I am also indebted to Dave Arnold, Chris Dragan, Jack Gannon, Rebecca Kimmel, and David Dauphiné for informing my view of whitewater history; to Bud Hill, Brian Levine, and Virginia Price of Fayetteville, Stanrod Carmichael of Galax, Ani Kortekaas and Joe Stegmaier of Huntsville, and Jimmy Neil Smith of Jonesborough for helping me to understand their communities' transformations; and to Marye Hacker, Annabel Harrill, Topper Sherwood, and Cecilia Wankel for assorted forms of assistance.

Among scholars at other universities, I owe special thanks to Gordon McKinney of Berea College for his review of the manuscript and for helpful suggestions. Ron Eller of the University of Kentucky shared with me his unpublished research on the Appalachian Regional Commission. My intellectual debt to Altina Waller is, I hope, adequately acknowledged in the notes, but here I also want to express gratitude for her friendship. I am also indebted for friendship and food to my former neighbors, Maïte and Paul Clyatt. After a hard day at my desk, I was always happy to hear Maïte's lilting voice on the phone, inviting me down the hill for another memorable meal.

I was fortunate to have Sian Hunter as my editor at the University of North Carolina Press. I want also to thank Pamela Upton, April Leidig-Higgins, Rich Hendel, and Adrienne Allison.

Within my extended family, my son Jared M. Williams provided legal advice and, with his bride Jessica, tolerated a tourist in New York with a peculiar interest in Appalachia-in-Gotham (e.g., *Bat Boy: The Musical*). His brothers and their families provided places of refuge from the cares of writing, as did Claudia and Mark Krasnoff. Wallace Colyer brought to his critique of the manuscript the eye of someone who reads history for pleasure and so was helpful in spotting some of the more excessively academic passages of the book; his mother, Norma Colyer, provided, as always, aid, comfort, a computer, and a place to sleep in the nation's capital. My thanks to them all.

After all debts are acknowledged, my name is the one on the spine and I alone am responsible for errors and defects.

Flannery Fork, near Blowing Rock, N.C.
August 2001

Abbreviations

AEP	American Electric Power
ARA	Area Redevelopment Administration
ARC	Appalachian Regional Commission
ASA	Appalachian Studies Association
ASU	Appalachian State University
AT	Appalachian Trail
B&O	Baltimore and Ohio Railroad
BEA	Bureau of Agricultural Economics, USDA
C&O	Chesapeake and Ohio Railway
CIO	Congress of Industrial Organizations
CSM	Council of the Southern Mountains
DOD	Department of Defense
ETSU	East Tennessee State University
FPC	Federal Power Commission

FSA   Farm Security Administration

GSMNP   Great Smoky Mountains National Park

HUD   Housing and Urban Development

ICC   Interstate Commerce Commission

L&N   Louisville and Nashville Railroad

LDD   Local Development District, ARC

MFD   Miners for Democracy

MIT   Massachusetts Institute of Technology

MSHA   Mine Safety and Health Administration

N&W   Norfolk and Western Railroad

NASA   National Aeronautics and Space Administration

NIRA   National Industrial Recovery Act

NPS   National Park Service

NRA   National Recovery Administration

NSF   National Science Foundation

OEO   Office of Economic Opportunity

PARC   President's Appalachian Regional Committee

PRR   Pennsylvania Railroad

TCI   Tennessee Coal and Iron Company

TVA   Tennessee Valley Authority

UMWA   United Mine Workers of America

USGS   U.S. Geological Survey

UTW   United Textile Workers

UVA   University of Virginia

VISTA   Volunteers in Service to America

WPA   Works Progress Administration

WVU   West Virginia University

Appalachia

What a place to conjure.

—Robert Morgan, *Blowing Rock*

Ghosts, Boundaries, and Names

There's no better place to begin a history of Appalachia than the bus station outside Wytheville, Virginia. Here travelers stand at one of the crossroads of American history, its arms stretching out like a lazy X laid across the eastern third of the country. The crossroad briefly unites Interstates 77 and 81, one road extending north and south, the other from northeast to southwest. I-81 gives modern form to a famous and historic highway that threads the great central valley of the Appalachian mountain system. This path funneled much of the westward movement of Euro-American settlers to the South and Southwest, following a natural corridor that comes within a few dozen miles of the Atlantic in the hinterlands of Philadelphia and New York and that reaches far into the interior at its southern end. This corridor distributed much of the immigrant population of the middle and later eighteenth century to the Carolina Piedmont, the Ohio country, Tennessee and Kentucky, and, after independence, to the interior plains that lay beyond the mountains along the Mississippi and the Gulf. Heading north on I-81 today, the traveler can reach all of the important colonial gateways to Anglo-America within a day. South and west of Wytheville, the options are even grander: Florida, New Orleans, Texas, the Grand Canyon, L.A.

The other arm of the crossroads is neither famous nor historic, for before the building of the interstate this pathway was much less distinct. There have always been paths between the Ohio valley and the South Atlantic seaboard, but nature did not gather them into a single route, as in the Great Valley. One of several routes known as the Carolina Road (or, at its southern terminus, the Philadelphia Road) branched off from the Great Valley through a gap in the Blue Ridge near modern Roanoke, some seventy-five miles northeast of Wytheville. Southbound I-77 converges with this old route today near the city of Charlotte, after a precipitous and scenic crossing of the Blue Ridge, and more or less follows it to Columbia, South Carolina, where the highway merges into routes carrying travelers to Charleston (South Carolina), Savannah, and Florida's east coast. To the north and west of Wytheville, however, colonial travelers confronted the long, steep-sided Allegheny ridges that border the Great Valley and, beyond them, the broken tablelands and ravines of the Appalachian Plateau. The New River, flowing north from the Blue Ridge toward the Ohio, looks like a natural corridor on the map—an especially inviting one, since the Ohio, like the Great Valley, served as a pathway of empire during the eighteenth century, and this section of Virginia is where the two corridors are closest together. But this proximity of the river and valley paths, so enticing on a two-dimensional map, is illusory. On the ground, the traveler who wanted to bridge this distance faced a choice of numerous paths, all of them difficult. The New River cuts rocky canyons across the ridges bordering the Great Valley and then crosses the inner Appalachian Plateau through the thousand-foot deep trench of New River Gorge, creating a paradise for adventurous recreation, but confronting practical travelers with an "awful and discouraging" journey, as an official party that traversed the gorge reported in 1812.[1]

The builders of I-77 have handled the obstacles in their path with engineering aplomb, tunneling under the mountains north of Wytheville, climbing the Allegheny Front along the eastern edge of the plateau, and then drawing the highway northwest through breadknife cuts and over three-story bridges across the plateau's hills and ravines to the Kanawha River some thirty miles east of the other Charleston, West Virginia's capital city. The interstate bypasses the New River Gorge, except for a spur that crosses the canyon on a spectacular high-level bridge. North of Charleston the highway traverses the gentler hills and wider valleys of the western Appalachian Plateau, crosses the Ohio River, and descends by imperceptible stages to the lake plains in the suburbs of Cleveland. In contrast to the numerous historic sites that beckon to travelers through the Great Valley, there are few monuments today that testify to the significance of I-77's ancestor routes, but while this corridor was indistinct, it too played an important role in the history of the territory now known as Appalachia.

The sign at the highway exit that leads to the bus station says "Max Meadows" and "Fort Chiswell." Max Meadows can be found less than a mile north of the highway. As a name on the map, it is one of the oldest landmarks in this part of Virginia. William (Wilhelm?) Mack was a German-born settler from Pennsylvania whose cabin was found at a location along Reed Creek by John Buchanan, a land company surveyor, in October 1745. Mack had recently died and the surveyor's notes record his effort to recruit appraisers of his estate and someone to get in his crops from among other German-speaking settlers nearby. Despite his brief occupancy, Mack's name—in a corrupted form—clung to the place, and one can still see meadows occupying a spacious bottomland next to the creek. The surrounding landforms, broad fertile fields and a meandering stream, both framed by forested parallel ridges, are typical of the ridge-and-valley province of the central Appalachians. So was the land transaction that followed Mack's death. Buchanan, a native of Northern Ireland and the son-in-law of the largest land speculator then operating in southwest Virginia, ended up owning Mack's land, making it part of a 1,200-acre estate to which Buchanan gave a name that has also survived locally in the name of a church: "the Anchor and Hope." However, his notes also refer to the surrounding neighborhood as "ye Valley of Contention and Strife," a label that probably reflects the tension between settlers like Mack and speculators like Buchanan and perhaps also tensions between Germans and Ulstermen. A parcel of land adjoining the mouth of Reed Creek on New River was entered under the label "Bigottrey."[2]

The railroad came chugging into this bucolic setting in October 1854. It was completed to Wytheville in December and to Bristol on the Tennessee border in 1856. On it rode antebellum Virginia's hope of channeling the Great Valley corridor's southwestern trade toward its tidewater ports at Petersburg and Norfolk. The railroad was called the Virginia and Tennessee at that time, then after the Civil War—when Yankee raiders tried but mostly failed to destroy it—it became the Atlantic, Mississippi and Ohio and then the Norfolk and Western. Today it is part of the Norfolk Southern system. A major flurry of activity occurred around 1890, when developers projected several factories and a resort hotel at Max Meadows. But little came of these plans and, judging by the disused loading docks that border the tracks today, Max Meadows has attracted little other business of importance. But much like the frontier-era names that survive in the area, the rusty sidings at Max Meadows serve as a reminder of the extravagant hopes and frequent disappointments that accompanied Appalachia's development in the industrial era.[3]

Even more interesting is what you *don't* see at Max Meadows. Looking south from the mostly empty parking lot that is now the dominant feature of the village center, all that comes immediately to the eye is a single-wide house trailer. If you had visited before 1990, you would have seen an earlier structure: a log house with an interesting history—so interesting, in fact, that in 1989 a team of foreign experts came over to inspect the house and then came back a year later to disassemble it piece by piece and to carry the pieces across the Atlantic, in order to erect it anew in an outdoor museum in the county of Omagh in the province of Northern Ireland. The Ulster American Folk Park was founded initially to preserve the birthplace of the American financial dynast Thomas Mellon, but it is now promoted by the British government as a monument to the considerable contributions of Ulster and its emigrants to American history. Called the McGavock House, after the Ulsterman who erected it in Max Meadows in 1779 or 1780, the house will serve to teach British, Irish, and continental visitors about American log architecture and the roles played by the people of Northern Ireland in the settlement of the colonial backcountry 250 years ago.

When it stood in Max Meadows during its last years as a residence, the McGavock House was not called that but was known by the name of its occupants, who did not own the house but had rented it for at least two generations.[4] Some of the immigrant James McGavock's descendants had moved west, while he himself failed to develop the lands he acquired from John Buchanan into a commercially successful site. Still he prospered sufficiently to leave a patrimony and family that were long prominent in Wythe County's annals.[5] The people who owned and rented out McGavock's log house had acquired it from McGavock's heirs.

These owners traded the log house to the Ulster museum for the trailer, which they continued to rent to the same occupants. The tenants do not seem to have had much say in the transaction but are reported to have been pleased even though their rent went up; the log house had been leaky and drafty and ineligible for rent subsidies from the county welfare department, whereas the

The McGavock log house in Max Meadows, Virginia, as it was when representatives from the Ulster American Folk Park, Omagh, Northern Ireland, arrived to examine it. In 1990 the house was disassembled and the parts shipped to the park, where it will eventually be reassembled and displayed as part of an exhibit on Ulster's contribution to American culture and history. (Courtesy of Ulster American Folk Park)

single-wide is modern, warm, and eligible. If you were to inquire further about these particular tenants, you might encounter stories of the sort that are frequently told about poor families in Appalachia and which some Appalachian writers (such as the South Carolina novelist Dorothy Allison) will tell you are used to keep such people poor and in their place.[6] Whatever an outsider chooses to believe, what matters is that the exchange of log house for trailer was made—in effect an exchange of one era of Appalachian history for another. The log house is the most enduring symbol of Appalachia. It speaks to the resourcefulness and hard work of pioneer inhabitants and the role that the great Appalachian forest played in the region's development. Along with mountain music, handmade quilts, and other craft objects, log architecture also represents metropolitan America's embrace of mountain people during the twentieth century and the depiction of their culture and lifeways as emblems of what was noble and quaint in the national past and worthy and needful (or degraded and fearful) in the present.

Fort Chiswell, another lost landmark of the Wytheville crossroad, is equally symbolic, a reminder that while the eastern half of Appalachia was settled without notable Native American resistance, the western half—those parts of the Virginias, Kentucky, Tennessee, Georgia, and Alabama that drain through tributaries to the Ohio River—was drenched in blood during the frontier era. Like the log cabin, backcountry warfare endowed Appalachia and its people with much of the region's mystique.

Despite its prominence on maps and highway signs, the name Fort Chiswell now attaches only to three major structures: a handsome brick mansion built by Stephen and Joseph Cloyd McGavock (or, more likely, by slaves working under their direction) in 1839, a high school whose continued existence is threatened by a movement for school consolidation, and an outlet mall tucked into one arm of the interchange where I-77 peels off from its temporary union with I-81.[7] Highway construction obliterated the site of the frontier fort, along with much of the village that clustered about a previous crossroads, the intersections of U.S. Highways 11 and 52. On the north side of the interchange, opposite the outlet mall, a small stone pyramid with a plaque testifies to the fort's former site and frontier importance. What is left of the village of Fort Chiswell, which James McGavock tried and failed to develop into Wythe County's courthouse town, is overshadowed by the usual detritus of a modern American crossroads: motels, truck stops, fast food joints, billboards, and oversized signs, each signaling for the attention of motorists who speed by at 70 mph.

Erected in 1760–61 under the direction of Col. William Byrd III of Westover in tidewater Virginia and named for the discoverer of lead mines in which Byrd had invested, Fort Chiswell was a landmark of colonial Virginia's complex interactions with native peoples who inhabited its western interior and who claimed sovereignty over the New River and Tennessee valleys. Built on a "high barren hill" overlooking Reed Creek near its junction with the river, the fort gave protection to the settlers who had surged into the southwest since the 1740s and also guarded the mines, which were located along the river near the border with North Carolina. Virginia's right to occupy this territory derived—at least to the satisfaction of colonial leaders—from the Treaty of Lancaster (1744). Then the colony had purchased from the Iroquois Confederacy the right to settle on west-flowing waters among its "back mountains." Settlers such as Wilhelm Mack and his fellow Germans from Pennsylvania built their cabins here in advance of this treaty, which is why land speculators officially sanctioned by the colony were able to take the earlier settlers' land or collect rents or purchase money. In 1745 the Virginia assembly awarded a grant of 100,000 acres to James Patton, John Buchanan's father-in-law, to be selected from land in the New River and Tennessee valleys. It is worth noting that Patton had been at Lancaster in an unofficial capacity and seems to have had his eye on southwest Virginia since his first trip there in 1742.[8]

Virginia also chartered another land company—the Loyal Land Company headed by Dr. Thomas Walker, who with Buchanan and Patton and other land prospectors found and named the Cumberland Gap leading toward Kentucky in 1750—to take up and sell land in the upper Tennessee watershed. At the same time, the colony chartered the Ohio Company to acquire and sell land around the Forks of the Ohio (the site of modern Pittsburgh) and the Greenbrier Company, whose territory was the valley of the New River's largest tributary, draining the district adjacent to West Virginia's present border with Virginia. Thus the movement of people into southwest Virginia represented not only a race between settlers and speculators, but also contests among the rival speculators to identify and secure the best land.

The Iroquois later disputed Virginia's interpretation of the Lancaster treaty, while other Indians protested that the Confederacy had no right to dispose of this land on any terms. These views were particularly strong in the Shawnee villages of southern Ohio, which also harbored Delaware and other refugees from their original homelands in the east. The Shawnee claimed as hunting grounds all of Virginia on western waters (including most of present West Virginia and all of Kentucky) and strongly disputed the right of any Europeans to settle there. When several preliminary warnings were ignored, Shawnee war parties struck the New River valley in July 1755, killing James Patton among other victims and capturing Mary Draper Ingles. Her subsequent escape and desperate journey homeward through New River Gorge in the company of an otherwise unidentified "old Dutch [German] woman" helped Virginia authorities to locate the Shawnee towns in Ohio and also confirmed the impassability of the gorge as a route of attack. And so the Sandy Creek expedition, which attempted to reach the Ohio via another stream that flows north from southwest Virginia, marched out in February 1756, with several hundred frontiersmen and Cherokee allies. This effort failed miserably. Steep hills, icy and swift-flowing rivers, and the inability of a Euro-American army to take advantage of the ridgetop paths that Indians used to traverse this area slowed and eventually halted the march far short of its objectives. When starving soldiers began plotting against the officers, the leaders gave up and the army fled in disorder back to the settlements. The Cherokees who accompanied the march watched this outcome with interest and disgust.[9]

The Cherokees also claimed the land in question but, like the Iroquois, did not live there or even hunt there very often. They were interested mainly in trade with Virginia, in order to ease their dependence on South Carolina traders who, the Cherokees believed, overcharged them for the European goods they now depended upon. At the same time, they worried about the Virginian advance into the Tennessee valley. When war broke out between the Cherokees and South Carolina in 1760, Virginia authorities hastened to placate the tribesmen while strengthening their southwestern defenses. Fort Chiswell was completed and occupied by February 1761.

The fort was located near the point where the territorial claims of the Shawnees and Cherokees and Virginia's horde of high-placed land speculators all converged. The various forest paths leading north from the vicinity toward the Ohio could not accommodate the wagons that moved European settlers or armies, but they were adequate to the purpose of Shawnee and other raiders. The Virginians were fortunate that the Shawnees and Cherokees, who spoke unrelated languages and were traditional enemies, never managed to effect an alliance. Even so, the second half of the eighteenth century was an almost uninterrupted period of border warfare in this area, as bloody and unrestrained as any that has been fought in North America. The name Fort Chiswell, prominent on the map although the actual site has been destroyed, offers a reminder of this history, which shaped the collective memory of central Appalachia's early settlers and, through its impact on the land allocation process, the experience of their descendants as they sought to occupy and enjoy the land that warfare and diplomacy eventually won.

It seems particularly fitting that the historic landmarks of this crossroads are ghosts, while its modern structures—the interstate, the shopping mall, the gas stations and other roadside services—are indistinguishable from those we might find in any other part of the country. Fort Chiswell, the McGavock House, and Wilhelm Mack's cabin in the Valley of Contention and Strife can be seen in their original forms only in the mind's eye. This is appropriate, for Appalachia, more than most of the regions into which the United States is customarily divided, is a territory of images—a screen upon which writers, artists, and savants for several generations have projected their fears, hopes, regrets, and enthusiasms about America present and past. The region has been seen as both the essence of America and a place apart, "a strange land

and a peculiar people," as one of the early "discoverers" of Appalachia put it back in 1873.[10]

Interpreters who have immersed themselves in the observation of a specific Appalachian place have rarely challenged this notion of "otherness." Like the museum experts who took apart the McGavock House, scholars who have created ethnographies, community studies, or studies of the folk arts or folk artists have concluded that Appalachia is home to a distinctive and important regional variant of American culture. This assessment has shaped the popular perception of the region and has assumed official form in the interpretation of regional culture put forward by the custodians of popular tourist attractions such as the Blue Ridge Parkway and the Shenandoah and Great Smoky Mountains National Parks. Yet historians who have attempted to see the region as a whole and to isolate whatever it is that sets the region apart from the rest of the country have often ended by doubting that the place even exists as a definable entity.[11] They have concluded instead that it is a territory only of the mind, an *idée des savants*, a place that has been invented, not discovered, an "alternative America" projected onto the mountains and mountain people by reformers whose real purpose is to critique or change things in the nation at large.

One problem with attempting to view the region whole is that Appalachia has no agreed-upon boundaries—nothing comparable to the Mason-Dixon Line or the 100th meridian or the Hudson River, boundaries that are widely accepted as demarcating clear separations between one American region and another. Appalachia is one of the oldest names on North American maps, dating from the early Spanish explorations of the southeastern United States. The name conveys the notion of a regional core somewhere in the highlands, but when we look closely at the natural region, the Appalachian mountain system, we find that its central feature is a trough—the Great Valley—not a line of watershed peaks like those that mark the center of other famous mountain systems such as the Alps or the Rockies. Geologists have marked off five or six distinct physiographic provinces within the Appalachian system: the Piedmont, the Blue Ridge, the Great Valley (and sometimes a separate "ridge-and-valley" province consisting of the Allegheny ridges and valleys that parallel the Great Valley on its northwest side), the Allegheny (or Cumberland) Mountains, and finally the Appalachian Plateau. These provinces comprise all of eastern North America's uplands south of the Adirondacks and extend from the coastal to the interior plains.

Where in this huge territory is Appalachia? Political boundaries do not provide the answer. Geometric lines drawn in London in the seventeenth century to set off Carolina and Pennsylvania from the Chesapeake colonies were abstractions fixed on the Atlantic shore to demarcate the hinterlands of what were then widely separated thresholds of colonization. These lines were subsequently extended inland with little heed paid to the interior's natural features. Thus the New River valley in Virginia is divided politically from the river's headwaters in North Carolina and its outlet in West Virginia, just as the Cumberland watershed was split between Tennessee and Kentucky and the Tennessee River severed from its Virginia headwaters and its tributaries in six other states. These jurisdictional lines drawn in distant capitals slice across the mountains, valleys, and plateaus of Appalachia as if those features had no geometries of their own. The official boundary drawn when the Appalachian Regional Commission (ARC) was established in 1965 both simplified and complicated the problem. The ARC provided for the first time a central data-collecting agency whose purview encompasses the entire region, yet political calculations pushed and tugged the official boundary northward to the southern tier of New York and southwest to a corner of Mississippi while excluding parts of Appalachian Virginia, whose congressman objected to the commission on philosophical grounds.

To appreciate the problem, consider the experience of a traveler flying from Charleston, South Carolina, to Cleveland on a clear day. The boundary between the Piedmont and the coastal plain is marked by a series of waterfalls—the famous "fall line"—now mostly submerged by dams and lakes built to harness the rivers' hydroelectric energy. Farther north, the boundary between the Piedmont and the Blue Ridge is nearly as impressive from the air as it is on the ground, even though there are outliers, such as the South Mountains and Brushy Mountains of North Carolina and the Catoctin Mountains of Maryland and Virginia, that extend east of the Blue Ridge. The continuity and the consistent northeast-southwest trend of the Great Valley is unmistakable as the plane passes over Wytheville; so is the boundary of the Allegheny Front separating the parallel ridges and valleys of the eastern Alleghenies from the high tablelands, steep hills, and deeply incised valleys of the Appalachian Plateau. The plane's gradual descent from Charleston, West Virginia, toward Cleveland mimics the declining altitude and wider valleys of the uplands below. Even though the differences in altitude steadily diminish, the uplands are clearly distinguishable from the plains of central and northern Ohio.

This air journey provides a textbook illustration of Appalachia's varied landforms, yet it also reveals a geography shaped by humans. For example, the sharp-eyed traveler will notice a new geometry as the plane crosses the Ohio River from West Virginia into Ohio, one that has to do with the way that land is divided. Notwithstanding the low, rolling regularity of the Piedmont terrain or the symmetrical progression of ridges and valleys paralleling the Great Valley, the human boundaries visible in those places from the air—the fence lines separating fields and pastures and the pathways of local roads—are highly irregular, reflecting a land-surveying and distribution system that placed a premium on on-the-ground knowledge. Colonial surveyors in the Virginias and Carolinas (and subsequently in Kentucky and Tennessee) followed the lay of the land, excluding rough, steep, or waterlogged places from their surveys, leaving the less desirable tracts for those who came later and creating a crazy quilt of land claims, many of which overlapped. Among other effects, this system placed a premium on land buyers and sellers prospecting the land before settlement, and it stimulated the swift advances into Native American territory that in turn led to decades of border warfare.

In Ohio the boundaries on the ground become more regular; fields are squared off and the byways follow the cardinal directions. The contrast is clearly visible from the air, even in eastern and southeastern Ohio, where these lines cut across the natural trends of upland valleys and hills. The difference testifies to the impact of the federal land survey system first introduced in Ohio in 1788 and carried from there on across the United States until surveyors encountered the Ibero–American land allocation system of Texas and the Far West. Such differences explain why most scholars turn to cultural markers when they try to determine just where Appalachia begins and ends.

The first attempt to define Appalachia systematically was made in 1861 by a Minnesota newspaper. A series of articles published during the early months of the Civil War identified a region that the editor called "Alleghenia": 161 counties in the mountains of Virginia, Kentucky, Tennessee, Alabama, Georgia, and the Carolinas. In this "land of Corn and Cattle, not Cotton," slavery was weak and Union sentiment strong. If Union armies pressed south through Cumberland Gap into the Great Valley, he reasoned, then the "Counter-Revolution" already underway in the future West Virginia would spread throughout the highlands and deal the Confederacy a fatal blow.[12] Differences in highland and lowland economies and in Civil War loyalties were also justifications that Berea College president William G. Frost offered as he reoriented his college's mission to the mountains. In defining "Appalachian America" in 1895, Frost was assisted by a former student who had become a professional geologist, C. Willard Hayes. The 194 counties that Frost and

Hayes included in their version of Appalachia did not follow geological features precisely, but neither did their definition fall back upon state lines.[13]

Most of Appalachia's twentieth-century architects have based boundaries on cultural artifacts—chiefly political borders and especially the Mason-Dixon Line. The literature of Appalachian studies is full of examples, which I have reviewed extensively in another place.[14] What all definitions of Appalachia have in common, though, is that each of them in its way tries to link people and homeland, to find some principle of regional demarcation that identifies both the place and its inhabitants. This book is no different, except in one important respect: It offers a dynamic definition of Appalachia and its people as both have changed through time. Although the traditional approach to Appalachian regionalism originated at least partly in antimodernism, it relied on the modern definition of region as established by geographers at the end of the nineteenth century: a territory set apart from others by an enumerated set of attributes, features that could be mapped in their distribution from regional core to periphery and measured in intensity so that one could say confidently how "Appalachian" (or southern or western or New England-ish) a given place was.

A postmodern approach to regionalism takes a different tack. It recognizes that every place is a zone characterized by the interaction of global and local human and environmental forces and that regional boundaries inevitably shift with the perspectives both of subject and object. From this standpoint, it is possible to see Appalachia as a zone of interaction among the diverse peoples who have lived in or acted upon it, as it is also of their interactions with the region's complex environment. These interactions go further toward defining the region than a specific set of cultural or socioeconomic or environmental markers. Put another way, the modernist tendency to distinguish between "natural" regions defined in terms of environmental features and "artificial" ones determined by political lines is itself arbitrary. All boundaries are vantage points that allow us to make useful and interesting observations about the world, or in this case, a smallish part of it.[15]

Postmodern Appalachia is thus a zone where diverse groups have interacted with one another and with a set of regional and subregional environments over time. Like the Appalachian Regional Commission and a minority of scholarly studies, this book places Pennsylvania in Appalachia, not only because it was by far the most important colonial hearth of Euro-American culture in Appalachia, but because it was also generally from Pennsylvania that industrializing forces spread southward during the nineteenth century, and it was there that the socioeconomic issues raised by deindustrialization emerged

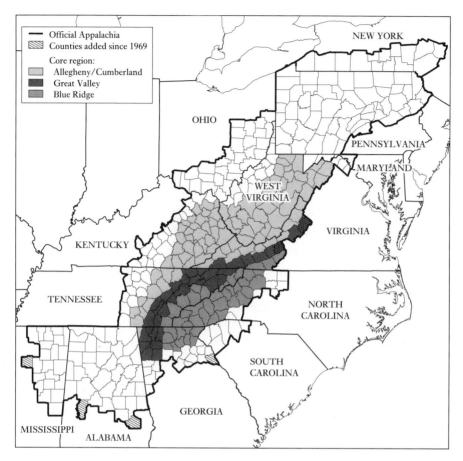

to make the entire region a focus of policy concern in the twentieth. Pennsylvania is also important—along with neighboring sections of Ohio, West Virginia, and Maryland—for contrasts it provides as well as for its similarities with the Appalachian core. At the southern end of the mountains, northern Alabama serves something of the same function.

This book, then, accepts the 1965 boundaries of Appalachia—though readers will find little about New York or Mississippi in these pages—and it also offers a core region of 165 counties that have been included in most of the influential scholarly or government definitions of Appalachia published during the last century. This core spreads over six states—Georgia, North Carolina, Tennessee, Kentucky, and the two Virginias—and is set within an "official" Appalachia comprising the entire ARC territory—which in the year 2000 constituted 406 counties in thirteen states. Where statistics are employed in the pages that follow, distinctions between the core and official regions are indicated appropriately. So constructed, my version of the core region features some anomalies of its own in that it excludes such obviously Appalachian counties as Garrett in Maryland, DeKalb and Jackson in Alabama, Oconee in South Carolina, and a smattering of the Virginia counties whose misfortune it was in 1965 to be represented by Congressman Poff, but since these are all included within the official region they are not completely eliminated. Like all boundary makers, I had to draw the line somewhere.

As if the varying boundaries weren't enough, there is no fundamental agreement even about how to pronounce the word "Appalachia." Residents of southern and central Appalachia pronounce the term with a short a (ă) in the stressed third syllable; further north, the same a is given a long pronunciation (ā), as in "Appal-ay-chia." Most of the experts and bureaucrats who came from Washington and elsewhere to fix the region's problems beginning in the 1960s adopted the northern pronunciation, while resident experts favor the southern—which led to a situation, according to one commentator, wherein "people who said *Appalāchia* were perceived as outsiders who didn't know what they were talking about but were more than willing to tell people from the mountains what to do and how they should do it."[16] Finally, while a majority of both long and short a users crunch the third syllable as though it were spelled *Appal-atch-yuh*, in New England—where the term "Appalachian" first came into widespread use by nongeologists thanks to the Appalachian Mountain Club and the development of the Appalachian Trail—a variant pronunciation uses "sh" rather than "ch," as in *Appal-ay-shuh*.

It sometimes seems that the only things that suggest a natural unity to all of Appalachia are the general northeast-southwest trend of the mountain-valley-plateau system and its progressive narrowing from south to north. Apart from geology, what is most impressive about the region is its diversity rather than its unity. The hardwood forests that covered much of the region are still the most diverse such forests on earth, notwithstanding the numerous extinctions and depletions of the past three hundred years. The species that Appalachia harbored during the Ice Age have spread from the mountains back to their original homes, leaving only a few widely distributed plants or animals whose habitat is exclusively Appalachian. Features created by humans likewise make it difficult to distinguish the region from others. State lines are almost entirely at odds with natural features, while local rather than regional names dominate the map. Thus the Great Valley is named the Lehigh, Lebanon, and Cumberland valleys in Pennsylvania; the Shenandoah, James, Roanoke, and New River valleys in Virginia; the Tennessee valley in southwest Virginia and East Tennessee. The mountains that border the Great Valley on the northwest are called the Alleghenies in Pennsylvania, Maryland, and the Virginias and the Cumberland Mountains in Kentucky, Tennessee, and Alabama. The neighboring Appalachian Plateau is similarly divided on the map between Allegheny and Cumberland.

Among names with a broader currency, "Piedmont" is a term of art based on a confused view of Italian geography, applied to the Great Valley during the eighteenth century but popularized by industrial promoters in the Carolinas during the late nineteenth century; "Blue Ridge" is a designator rarely used north of Virginia, and even in the South the singular term "ridge" is misleading. In Virginia, *the* Blue Ridge is actually a chain of mountains, nowhere exceeding four thousand feet in elevation except near the North Carolina border. In the Carolinas, however, the Blue Ridge escarpment rises above its foothills to heights of over five thousand feet in places, creating an eastern boundary as imposing as anything in North America east of the Rocky Mountains' front range. To the northwest of these peaks lies a high-altitude plateau, up to sixty miles wide, containing the headwaters of the New River and a succession of Tennessee River tributaries. This plateau is bounded in turn on the northwest by a series of mountain ranges—the Stone, Iron, Black, and, most famously, Great Smoky Mountains—through which the headwater streams have cut gorges nearly as spectacular as the canyons further north that the Potomac, James, and Roanoke Rivers carved through the Blue Ridge. These mountain chains form the present North Carolina–Tennessee border and are often included within the bounds of the Blue Ridge.[17] Yet residents of this plateau, surrounded by a multitude of peaks that, as Thomas Wolfe put it, race like hounds across the horizon, typically refer to themselves as living "on *the* mountain" and have even coined the term "off-mountain" to describe less pleasant locations. This almost willful disregard of diversity in favor of unity is echoed in the scholarly and popular literature, providing grist for the analytical mills of such writers as Henry Shapiro and Allen Batteau, who argue that Appalachia does not exist except in the imaginations of people who want it to.

Naming conventions also dictate how one refers to the Appalachian sections of particular states. East Tennessee is a name enshrined in the state constitution, formally recognized with Middle and West Tennessee as one of three "grand divisions," each with its own star in the state flag. It is customary to refer to north Georgia and southwest Virginia but also to east*ern* Kentucky and west*ern* North Carolina; apparently both northern and north Alabama are correct. The mountain district of South Carolina is part of the "upstate," a much larger region. West Virginia has two "panhandles," one extending northward and the other eastward, but before Virginia was divided in 1863 there was only one "Pan Handle." Northeastern Tennessee does indeed lie in that direction relative to Knoxville, but it is more common to hear it described as upper East Tennessee. I have honored these conventions where it could be done without confusion.

A fluid approach to boundaries also affects the division of Appalachian history into time periods. In the first period of postcontact history, extending from the DeSoto *entrada* of 1539–42 to the Cherokee Removal three hundred years later, Appalachia is more or less coterminus with the region that colonial historians call the "backcountry." Colonial Appalachia can be defined by the pathways that linked it to the eastern beachheads of the Atlantic civilization and that led European and African Americans swiftly and deeply into the continent's interior during the eighteenth and early nineteenth centuries. The discovery and exploitation of these paths as routes of settlement and conquest and their subsequent consolidation as transportation corridors binding Appalachia to the commercial and political lineaments of the American nation constitutes the first phase of Appalachian history. The succeeding era, extending variously from the 1760s in the Valley of Virginia to the late antebellum period in the Allegheny and Cumberland plateaus, constitutes the second phase. During this period, Euro-American and African American labor established the farm-and-forest economy of what might be called classical Appalachia and made it the region's most prosperous era relative to other parts of the nation.

The Civil War disrupted the continuity of Appalachian history, as it did that of American history generally, yet the most fundamental trend—the decay of the farm-and-forest economy as population growth came up against a relatively fixed array of environmental resources—was not interrupted, only exacerbated by the violence and impoverishment that occurred during and after the war. Appalachia south of Pennsylvania was devastated by the war. Its wartime experience led the region to be regarded as somehow different from the rest of the South, while at the same time it was visited with many of the same punishments dispensed to the losing side. As the postwar era evolved, Appalachia's differences came to be viewed as markers of cultural peculiarity, an impression deeply engraved on the American imagination and a source of lively and continuing debate among scholars. This was the period when Appalachia was discovered and named by observers for whom the differences that separated Appalachia from the rest of the nation were more compelling than the factors that united them. It was also the time when two defining stereotypes lodged in the American mind: the Appalachian mountaineer, noble and stalwart, rugged and independent, master or mistress of the highlands environment; and the profligate hillbilly, amusing but often also threatening, defined by deviance and aberration, a victim of cultural and economic deprivation attributable to mountain geography.

During the first half of the twentieth century, national institutions—corporations, labor unions, state and federal governments, professions, media, the military, cultural institutions, and the apparatus of tourism—brought Appalachia's economic and cultural resources into the embrace of supraregional systems. This multistaged process included not only the labor struggles to which many historians have been drawn, but also key events in institutional history, such as the origins of the Tennessee Valley Authority, of Appalachia's national parks and forests, of the Council of the Southern Mountains and the Southern Highland Handicraft Guild, of folk schools and festivals and commercial entertainment industries, and of various other federal programs active in the region. This was also an era of town building, and attention must be paid to the gulf that opened between Appalachian towns and cities and their hinterlands in the railroad era and to the gradual closure of that gulf in the succeeding era of automobiles, radio, rural electrification, and consolidated schools.

Finally, there is the postindustrial era of Appalachian history. During and after World War II, Appalachian people in unprecedented numbers poured out of the mountains into military service and into the cities of the surrounding lowlands. For the first time, the region acquired a set of official boundaries, yet any distinctiveness that might be claimed for its history and culture seemed irrevocably compromised. Scholars commonly characterized the region's fate during this era as that of a "colonial economy," but the postwar era featured persistence and resistance as well as acquiescence to exploitation.[18] It was a time of renewal, in other words, as well as of crisis, although the crises attracted most of the journalistic and scholarly ink.

One of the hallmarks of renewal was the emergence of a literary movement that shows no sign of abating, a movement anchored in a rather old-fashioned narrative realism—out of step, perhaps, with the taste for experimentation and irony that characterizes other art in the postmodern age—but one that draws on the ways in which Appalachian people have always used narrative for entertainment and understanding, parsing their experience through Bible stories and folk tales, traditional ballads and country songs, not to mention the everyday parlance of people in small communities who, to borrow a phrase from Eudora Welty, have "a narrative sense" of each others' lives. "Most Appalachian fiction has wanted to depict . . . the specific and concrete world of everyday people and local places," according to the Kentucky writer Gurney Norman: "Our best writers are true heroes to the community because they have been able to take the materials of local life and make something universal from this part of the world."[19] One of the keys to the success of the region's writers is that they have—as educators, folklorists, and missionaries did in earlier eras—continued to hold up to the larger nation an "alternative America," a not-always-welcome image that contrasted with the stress and placelessness that beset "a nation of exiles."

For much of the century, official attention turned on the question of why and how the region failed to keep pace with the material growth of an urbanized consumer society, but at the beginning of the twenty-first century it is reasonable to ask whether Appalachia may have led the nation, not lagged behind, into a future whose outline is only now just coming into view. In the new terrain of globalized market capitalism, the combination of exploitation and per-/re-sistance, of crisis and renewal, that Appalachian history manifests may turn out to be instructive to every dweller in the postmodern world.

To me, this region is the top of the whole world—the land of the Sky People, it was said. The skyline is in all directions and close at hand. It is a land of cold, rushing rivers, small creeks, deep gorges, dark timber, and waterfalls. Great billowing clouds sail upon the mountains and in early morning a blue-gray mist hangs just about the treetops.

—Traveller Bird (Tsisghwanai),
The Path to Snowbird Mountain

CHAPTER ONE

The Roads to Qualla, 1540–1840

Appalachia owes its name to the Spanish empire's search for gold and plunder. The earliest Spanish probes of the New World north of Mexico yielded little but rumors of gold, and initially those rumors pointed to the Apalachee people living in northwest Florida. The Apalachee, having no gold to offer and probably eager to rid themselves of demanding guests, pointed to distant mountains as a potential source. French explorers, appearing in Florida in the 1560s, embellished the story with reports of an inland mountain province where abundant gold was to be found near a lake fed by a waterfall. There was a kernel of fact in these stories: The southern Appalachian mountains were found more or less where the coastal Indians said they were, and these mountains did contain some gold, although the native Americans of the Southeast neither valued nor mined it. In any event, the name "Apalachen" appeared on

European maps as early as 1562, while a 1591 map added a town in the midst of the mountains called "Apalatci." "Appalachians" became fixed as the collective name of the eastern mountain ranges after the American Revolution. "Appalachia" appeared when the writer Washington Irving proposed renaming the United States for its mountains, offering a choice of "Alleghenia" or "Appalachia" in place of "America" in 1839. It is not entirely clear that Irving's proposition was serious, although as the country's leading Hispanist he was certainly aware of Latin American and Spanish resentment of the U.S.A.'s claim to speak for the entire American world.[1]

Members of the Spanish de Soto expedition (1539–43) provided the first European descriptions of the mountains. Following the golden rumors he heard in Florida, Hernando de Soto led his men north and east until he reached what today is called the Carolina Piedmont. Then, somewhere in the Catawba River valley, the expedition turned westward and crossed the Blue Ridge and the Black or Great Smoky Mountains into the valley of East Tennessee, probably following a route not unlike the modern path of Interstate 40. The Spanish had nothing to say about the scenery, even though they traveled in late May and early June—the season of flame azaleas and blooming laurel and rhododendron. The French, English, and American explorers who followed in their wake were likewise silent on such matters: To practical men, bent on finding readily exploitable wealth, mountains were obstacles, full of danger and hardship, lacking the food and shelter required by a numerous company of men and horses. Thus the surviving de Soto records complain about heat in the foothills, cold in the highlands, and difficulty in the crossing but otherwise have little to say about the mountains except as they impeded the expedition's progress or influenced the choice of one route over another. For example, while resting in an Indian village in East Tennessee, de Soto heard reports of a location to the north that held rich villages and auriferous mines. He sent scouts ahead to verify this information, but they reported that "the Indians had taken them through a land so poor in maize and so rough and with such lofty mountains that it was impossible for the camp to march through it; and seeing that the road was getting long and they were greatly delayed, they considered it advisable to return from a small poor village where they saw nothing that might be of use."[2] So the expedition turned south and west, following the contours of the Great Appalachian Valley through northwest Georgia into Alabama and then west toward the Mississippi.

For most of June 1540, the de Soto expedition took its ease in the native village of Chiaha, a pleasant and abundant town located on an island. Situated about thirty miles northeast of the present city of Knoxville, Chiaha belonged to what experts call the Mississippian culture, a prehistoric cultural complex centered in the Mississippi valley that is thought to have introduced agriculture based on corn and bean plants imported from Mexico into the eastern woodlands of North America. This culture profoundly influenced the native people of the mountains, those who came during the next century to be known as Cherokees. "Cherokee" derives from *T'saragi* or *T'salagi*, "people of the cave," but this word derives in turn from the name for Cherokees in other Indian languages. The Cherokees' name for themselves, as with most other native societies, translates as something like "real people," "original people," or simply "Indians," meaning not all natives but only their kind.

The precise degree of relationship between Cherokee prehistory and the Mississippian culture can only be determined by archaeological studies; we do not know, for example, what the people of Chiaha called themselves. But in 1540 the Cherokees were a numerous people, totaling perhaps as many as half of the sixty thousand natives who are estimated to have been living in the southern part of Appalachia when de Soto passed through. They lived in four clusters of towns in or near the Blue Ridge and Great Smoky Mountains in present-day South Carolina (the Lower Towns), North Carolina (Middle Towns and Valley Towns), and Tennessee (Overhill Towns). They spoke related dialects of an Iroquoian language, unlike most of their near neighbors, whose speech derived from the Souian or Muskogean language families. Unlike their distant linguistic cousins, the Iroquois of upstate New York, the Cherokees had no central government or confederation. Each town was self-governing, though both its civil and military leaders consulted with their counterparts in nearby towns. Women played a prominent role in Cherokee governance, to the extent that de Soto thought that one of the women leaders he dealt with was the overall chief or *cacica* of the nation.

According to a Spanish chronicler, the interlude at Chiaha restored the exhausted expedition. "The Indians were with the Christians fifteen days in peace; they played with them, and also among themselves; they swam in the company of the Christians, and in all they served them very well." But then on June 19, de Soto demanded that the village supply his men with women, and the villagers abandoned their island rather than comply. Eventually, after tense negotiations, the village returned, and the Spanish dropped their demand for concubines, accepting instead five hundred *tamemes* or bearers to help the expedition move to its next destination. De Soto departed Chiaha on June 28.[3]

The Spanish evaded confrontations with the mountain peoples, but this option was not open to the British colonies that were eventually established

Mound near Franklin, North Carolina. Mounds constitute the single most important surviving artifact from Appalachia's prehistory. The ancient Adena and Hopewell cultures of the upper Ohio valley left behind large burial and effigy mounds. The mounds of the Mississippian era were often flat-topped, serving as platforms for religious and political structures. In 1776 William Bartram saw such a mound crowned by a "very large dome or rotunda" at Whatoga (as he spelled it), a large Cherokee town located three miles north of Nucasse, the site of the mound pictured above. A National Park Service official photographed the Nucasse (or Nikwasi) mound in 1937, by which time a successor culture was using it as the platform for a billboard. (Photograph by H. C. Wilburn; courtesy GSMNP Archives)

on North America's southeast coast. During the seventeenth century—the planting time for colonial Virginia, Maryland, and Carolina—the interior mountains and their natives were a distant presence on the horizon, known but encountered only by a few explorers and traders as other colonists went about the arduous business of expanding and consolidating their beachheads. But once the English turned their eyes inland, they found their way blocked —not only by the mountains, but by their inhabitants. The easiest southeastern route from the Atlantic into the continent's interior ran from Charleston, South Carolina, around the southern end of the Appalachians—the route eventually taken by railroads and highways.[4] A major trading path developed leading from the Savannah River across central Georgia into Alabama and Mississippi. But this route was always a risky one—exposed to attack by the

Muskogean-speaking Creek peoples whose lands it crossed and to hostile encounters with French or Spanish traders based at Pensacola, New Orleans, and Mobile.

As the deerskin and allied Indian trade became more important in the colonial economy, access to the interior became more and more vital. During the 1670s, Virginia explorers and traders developed a "trading path" linking Fort Wood at the falls of the Appomattox River with Indian villages scattered across the Carolina Piedmont. Traders from South Carolina developed a more direct approach, leading northwest from Charleston via the Santee and Saluda Rivers to the lower Cherokee towns. This became known as the Cherokee Path and the mountains that loomed on the horizon as the Cherokee Mountains. For both colonies, but especially for South Carolina, it became important to prevent an alliance of Britain's enemies with the Cherokees. Although the Cherokees were neither unified nor warlike, mollifying them, maintaining their dependence on British traders for manufactured goods, and ensuring their alliance against rival Indians and Europeans became cardinal points of Carolina diplomacy. As one piece of South Carolina legislation stated, "The safety of this Province does, under God, depend on the friendship of the Cherokees to this Government."[5]

Europeans who looked beyond the Appalachians to North America's interior were similarly deterred from bypassing the mountains to the north. The Mohawk valley of New York, carved by glacial meltwater as a nearly level route dividing the Catskills and the Adirondacks and connected to the great tidal fjord called Hudson's River, was the easiest path between the Atlantic coast and the continent's interior. But this path was available only on sufferance of the Iroquois Confederacy. Here, too, events of the first decades of European contact may have played a role.

In 1534 the French explorer Jacques Cartier encountered Iroquois peoples somewhere on the St. Lawrence River not far from the site of the present city of Montréal. Probably these were Mohawks, who in later centuries were established along the river that bears their name but who may have been living farther north at this time. Not much came of this encounter except to introduce European diseases among the northern Indians and to give France a claim to the St. Lawrence valley and the Great Lakes. When the French returned at the beginning of the seventeenth century, the Iroquois were entrenched in a strategic territory extending from the Mohawk to the Lakes and were firmly resolved to prevent French incursions into their territory, whether by the "eastern door" of the Hudson–Mohawk–Lake Champlain route or the "western door," the portage around the great waterfall at Niagara.

Moreover, at some point during the sixteenth century, the Iroquois had created an ethnic confederacy, a loose alliance of five nations—Mohawk, Oneida, Onondaga, Cayuga, and Seneca—who spoke related dialects and who divided confederate responsibilities among themselves on a permanent basis. Later, in 1722, the confederacy expanded to include the Tuscarora people, Iroquoian speakers who had migrated after losing a war with white settlers in eastern North Carolina. The Tuscaroras were not full members of the Five (now Six) Nations, in that they were forced to speak through the Oneidas in the councils that governed Iroquois politics and diplomacy. They nevertheless outranked the Delawares, Susquehannocks, Nanticoke, Conoy, and other dependent peoples who later came under Iroquois protection. These peoples for the purposes of war and diplomacy were said to have "become women"; that is, they enjoyed the right to be consulted but not to speak in Iroquois councils or to act independently in matters of mutual interest. The Iroquois propensity to incorporate refugee and defeated peoples into the confederacy's structure proved a great strength and a convenience to both the confederacy and the British.

The Iroquois, unlike the Cherokees, were fierce warriors and empire builders, especially during the seventeenth century. In a series of "beaver wars" fought far from the European beachheads along the Atlantic, Iroquois war parties raided as far west as Illinois and as far south as the Carolinas and Kentucky, destroying or subjugating native societies that threatened the Iroquois position as middlemen in the fur trade. Among the victims of these forays were the Susquehannocks and the Lenni Lenape (Delawares) of central and eastern Pennsylvania, who accepted Iroquois overlordship in return for protection against the encroaching English-speaking settlements along the Susquehanna and Delaware Rivers. The Conoy, Saponi, Tutelos, and other groups inhabiting the Great Valley and Allegheny plateau in western Virginia disappeared from history as organized societies at this time; the Conoy lived for a time in a village on the Susquehanna, while other remnant groups were incorporated into the polyglot villages of the Iroquois heartland. Those who retreated south were generally speakers of Souian languages who gradually coalesced as the Catawba Nation centered in the Carolina Piedmont south of present-day Charlotte. Iroquois attacks also scattered the Shawnee people, who had previously lived in loosely confederated villages in the Ohio valley. By the turn of the eighteenth century, Europeans observed bands of Shawnees in such widely separated locations as the French fort at Mobile, the Spanish bastion at St. Augustine, in interior South Carolina, and in southeastern Pennsylvania, where Shawnees took up residence near remnant villages of Delawares, Susquehannocks, and Conoys in the recently established Penn colony.

The Iroquois claimed the lands of the conquered peoples, extending from the Ohio valley eastward across the headwaters of Virginia's and Pennsylvania's rivers, a territory that Iroquois hunted but—except for the Pennsylvania districts closest to their New York homeland—did not occupy. This allowed British authorities, who claimed sovereignty over the Iroquois by virtue of a treaty negotiated in 1685, to claim territorial rights to all of the Iroquois empire, thereby bypassing negotiation with or even recognition of the numerous other native peoples who had originally occupied these lands. The Treaty of Lancaster in 1744 was based on this premise. It gave British subjects the right to settle among "the back mountains of Virginia." Although the Iroquois later disputed the broadest Virginian interpretation of this treaty, the Shawnees and other peoples who had originally inhabited or hunted the lands were given no say in the matter, then or later. The burst of land speculation that followed the treaty and the warfare that followed soon after were the results.

Names on the land memorialize these upheavals. Thus the word "Pekowi," identifying one of the five divisions into which the Shawnees were organized, can be found in one spelling or another on maps of Pennsylvania, Ohio, and West Virginia. "Pocatalico," another Shawnee name, is found on rivers in South Carolina and West Virginia. Lancaster, where the treaty was drawn up in 1744, was built along Conestoga Creek, a name derived from an earlier Susquehannock village that later settlers carried across the continent in the Conestoga wagons developed by German craftsmen who settled there. "Conoy" lives on as the Great and Little Kanawha Rivers of West Virginia. "Catawba," which probably derives from an Algonquian word referring to the Cherokees, came to refer to the Carolina river on whose banks the Catawba villages were clustered, as well as to numerous creeks, mountains, and other landmarks along the routes that their warriors traveled to repay the Iroquois attacks.[6] Other place names mark the brief passage of the Tuscaroras, whose migration from North Carolina to New York proceeded up the Roanoke River valley to its headwaters in the mountains, then northward through the Great Valley to the Niagara area where Tuscarora people can still be found today.

These facts are more than historical curiosities. They remind us that the European and native peoples that collided in Appalachia during the latter half of the eighteenth century were on each side multiethnic, multilingual societies shaped by earlier generations' experience of warfare, migration, and disease. The Appalachian frontier that emerged during the eighteenth century was not a well-defined boundary separating a commercial and agricultural empire from a receding population of stateless hunter-gatherers. Rather it was a zone where the familiar categories of human difference—languages, economic roles, ethnic identities, customs and habits, even the distinctions between men and women and between slave and free—blurred and overlapped. At Shamokin at the forks of the Susquehanna River, the Iroquois established in 1718 an outpost from which they could keep an eye on the whites and on the remnant native peoples who inhabited Pennsylvania on their sufferance. The place afforded many examples of the confusion that the mingling of frontier peoples entailed. "Shamokin was, throughout its life, clearly an Indian town—'The whites have nothing to say here,' Shickellamy once said, 'and no white is allowed to live here'—but which Indians?"[7]

Shickellamy was an Oneida who served as a sort of overseer of eastern Pennsylvania's Indians from 1728 until his death in 1748, but Shamokin was a Delaware town as much as it was Iroquois and also attracted displaced Tutelos from Virginia, nomadic Shawnees, and Indians of various sorts from all over, including warriors painted black on their way to attack southern Indians and survivors of such raids bearing their wounds and stories back home. This meant that at least three Indian languages were spoken in the town, each representing a different linguistic family. Whites who passed through the town included important persons on official business—Conrad Weiser, for example, Pennsylvania's official interpreter and a frequent emissary to and from Iroquoia, a man who spoke German, English, and Mohawk. There were other whites on other forms of business: German pietists came to Shamokin to preach Christianity, white traders came to deal in their wares and to bargain for furs and pelts for sale by the natives, men came looking for missing wives or children who might be captive among the Indians, or for slaves or indentured servants who had escaped. There were French Canadian *métis*, the term for people of mixed-race ancestry, usually of European fathers and Indian mothers. Andrew Montour, whose French Iroquois mother was also a powerful presence in the town, was a man with perfect European features who wore an Indian style of dress (which itself was a mixture of native and European elements). Just as the Indians spoke three languages, the whites who came there might speak English, German, or French. And though it was very much a man's place, women were more prominent in its life than would have been the case in a more settled Indian or Euro-American community.[8] So was drunkenness. The nature of the rum trade, and the Indian male preference for what we would today call binge drinking, made for frequent and uproarious nights among loud, combative, and often abusive men. No wonder that a frightened Moravian missionary called Shamokin "the very seat of the Prince of darkness."[9]

Keowee in South Carolina was a comparable place, a hinge between the Cherokees and the Carolina white settlements. Here the Cherokee Path leading up from Charleston entered Cherokee country, making it another entrepôt of mingling and conflicting cultures. The African American presence was greater at Keowee, as it was in South Carolina generally. To whites who lived along South Carolina's coast, where enslaved blacks outnumbered whites by more than five to one, the idea that escaped slaves might make common cause with the Indians was a recurrent nightmare. In at least one instance the fear was justified, as a party of six African American fugitives sought refuge in Keowee in 1751.[10] The mysteries and confusions of Shamokin were replicated in many other places on the Appalachian frontier—in the embryonic village of Pittsburgh, for example, after the British conquest of that place in 1758, or a generation later at Augusta on the Georgia frontier, or around the Long Island of the Holston River on the Virginia-Tennessee border during the era of the American Revolution, or in the Chickamauga area of southeast Tennessee during the period after 1795. But cultural conflict and exchange was not confined to such crossroads or trading posts. It was present in the home settlements on both sides of the frontier.

Theda Perdue's study of Cherokee women reveals a substantial difference in the ways that native women and men experienced the changes of the frontier era. Traditional Cherokee constructions of gender divided men's and women's lives into "separate categories that opposed and balanced each other."[11] Women lived in the clearing—in the Indian village and its nearby woods, springs, and streams—and men in the forest. Women cared for the community through the crops they planted and the nuts, berries, and herbs they gathered; men were hunters and warriors, supplying meat and protection. Men were raised in the households of their mothers' families and after marriage went to live in the households of their wives; the descent of power, authority, and personal goods was matrilineal. Men led war parties and traveled over long distances to hunt and determine through war or diplomacy the standing of their community vis-à-vis other societies. They dominated the councils that deliberated upon such matters, but women had a voice and frequently institutionalized power. Among the Cherokees, there was a category of "beloved women," postmenopausal women who acquired great prestige and played central roles in ceremonies that renewed communal life and sanctioned male authority in matters of leadership and religion.[12] There were also "war women," women who accompanied male war parties and in some cases participated in battle.

Among the Iroquois, certain older women had the authority to select male civil and religious leaders, though not war leaders. Among the Shawnees and Delawares, women fed the community during the harvest season, men after the fall hunt. At other seasons, women's gathering activities generally brought in more food than men's hunting, which further enhanced women's prestige. Quaker missionaries preaching to the Shawnees on the Susquehanna at the end of the seventeenth century were astonished at the authority that women exercised over the community as a whole and chided the Indian males about it, even though Quakers were themselves far more enlightened about the roles and capacities of women than other Europeans of the day. But when the governor of Pennsylvania visited the Shawnees a few years later, the women politely informed him that they "as well as our men" were included in all his dealings with their community and gave him a present of skins so that he would not forget this point.[13]

Many Europeans who came in contact with the native domestic culture found it appealing. Mary Jemison, a woman captured and held long years among the Senecas, explained why she declined to return to her Euro-American family when offered the opportunity. Indian women worked hard, she stated, but they worked cooperatively and without the supervision or interference of men. Other commentators noted this also; one Englishman resident among the Cherokees commented on the "cheerful and voluntary" manner in which women performed their many tasks. The same commentator also defended Cherokee men against the charge of indolence. Men were expected to perfect their hunting skills, maintain their equipage, and to hazard their lives and die bravely in war if it came to that. Otherwise, apart from very occasional help with land–clearing and certain other domestic tasks, few demands were placed on their time. Just as the autonomy of women appealed across cultural lines to some Euro-American women, Euro-American males, especially young men who in the patriarchal colonial culture labored under the strict supervision of their fathers, were attracted by the freedom that their Indian equivalents enjoyed in the forest. The documents of frontier life are full of examples of Euro-American captives who declined to return to white society when offered repatriation. In contrast to stories of border warfare and horrific accounts of captivity, these stories of cultural exchange did not become part of the lore of colonial Appalachia, but the stories are true and, in their way, often as compelling as the chronicles of war.

An analysis of Cherokee history suggests that cultural exchange between colonial and native societies more profoundly affected Cherokee men. The incorporation of the Cherokees into what one historian calls "a *peripheral fringe*" of a capitalist trading system centered in northwest Europe transformed the male roles of hunter, warrior, and diplomatist, casting all three on a larger geographic scale than previously and increasing the dangers and difficulties of each role.[14] Hunting became an income-producing rather than a food-producing mission. It expanded to cover a larger area and longer periods of time. As hunters and warriors became increasingly dependent upon European weapons, the maintenance of equipment became a matter of negotiated cultural exchanges, as Indians quickly learned to use, but not to make or repair, guns and edged metal weapons. As the Indian demand for manufactured or imported goods such as blankets, kettles, silver ornaments, alcohol, and West Indian or Chesapeake tobacco expanded, diplomacy became for older leaders a matter of preserving the society's autonomy against the need to balance its trade accounts by acquiring presents and selling land, the latter being the only commodity besides furs and pelts that their European and Euro-American trading partners were interested in. Except for the native acquisition of horses, almost all of the cultural change induced by contact with Euro-American societies threatened the status of males, especially young males, in Cherokee society. This is probably why male-centered accounts of Cherokee history during this period interpret it in terms of societal decline, "focused on military defeat and land loss."[15]

For Cherokee women, by contrast, the changes of the contact period left unchallenged and in some cases enhanced the status of women in their society. To be sure, women were generally bypassed by the fur and pelt trade, especially after European markets began to demand raw rather than dressed skins. Moreover, the loss of land ultimately affected women as well as men, although raising crops was easier to pursue in a diminished domain than was hunting. Women's role as providers was enhanced by the acquisition of European food sources such as fruit trees and domesticated animals. Women became the custodians of orchards, chickens, and pigs; they tethered grazing animals and penned hogs to keep them out of their cornfields. The availability of manufactured cooking utensils and clothing reduced their domestic chores somewhat. Perhaps most important, women gained status as the preservers of tradition among the Cherokees. While a few became the wives of traders and the mothers of *métis* families, the majority were insulated from outside presences and pressures. "Europeans, after all, considered women powerless and made fewer demands on them."[16] As conservators of culture, women became the key to Cherokee survival as a separate people.

The era typically defined as the age of frontier and settlement in Appalachia was actually an era of displacement and repopulation.[17] There were four geographic phases of this process during the roughly one hundred years after 1730. The first phase extended from 1730 to 1763 and involved Appalachian Pennsylvania and Maryland, western parts of Virginia, specifically the Great Valley, the adjacent parallel valleys of the Greenbrier and upper Potomac, and a fringe of territory along the Monongahela and Ohio Rivers in what is now West Virginia. The second phase was completed by 1789 and planted Euro-American settlements in upper East Tennessee, northwestern North Carolina, northwestern South Carolina, and the central part of Kentucky. Between 1790 and 1820, repopulation proceeded in the Allegheny and Cumberland plateaus of southern West Virginia, eastern Kentucky, and southeastern Ohio, plus the Great Valley in middle East Tennessee and the Blue Ridge and adjacent foothills territory in western North Carolina. The final displacement and repopulation came between 1820 and 1840, when the Cherokee nation was expelled from its lands in southwestern North Carolina, southeastern Tennessee, north Georgia, and both the Great Valley and Cumberland plateau lands of northeast Alabama.[18]

Appalachia was the *first* American frontier only if we ignore the Spanish thrust across the southern half of North America or the French territories in the north, but the presence of these hostile European powers on either flank—together with the important Iroquois and Cherokee buffer zones—was one of the factors that determined that Anglo-America's first thrust westward would be in the center. Geography decreed that in these circumstances Pennsylvania would be the frontier's gateway, both in terms of Indian displacement and Euro-American repopulation. This Pennsylvania gateway was shaped by nature, giving the Quaker colony better pathways into the interior than those of any nearby colonial jurisdiction. The major rivers of the Chesapeake colonies (Virginia and Maryland) rise beyond the Blue Ridge, but their transit through those mountains is by way of gorges as difficult to navigate as they are scenic.

On the Susquehanna, by contrast, there is no mountain barrier between the Piedmont and the Great Valley, nor in the mid-eighteenth century was there any effective native opposition to a white advance. The Blue Ridge (known in

Pennsylvania as the South Mountain) disappears from the horizon for some seventy miles between, roughly, the present Pennsylvania cities of Reading and Carlisle. In its place are a series of low and easily traversed ridges, permitting easy passage between the Great Valley and ports along the Delaware. This makes possible a number of routes from the tidewater and Piedmont into the valley: The Schuykill River creates a passage northwestward from Philadelphia, a favorite route for German-speaking settlers during the eighteenth century. The Allegheny Path running parallel along ridgetops south of the Schuykill was the principal route of the Indian trade and diplomacy, while an east-west road—later widened into the nation's first paved highway—connected the town of Lancaster (founded 1730) with Philadelphia. A branch of this road connected Lancaster with the Brandywine valley leading to the Delaware ports of New Castle and Wilmington, where ships carrying emigrants from the north of Ireland frequently disembarked. Still another route followed the east bank of the Susquehanna northwest from the river's mouth at the head of Chesapeake Bay. Lancaster served as a collecting point for migrants heading west across the river; a favorite point of river passage was Harris's Ferry, the site of modern Harrisburg.

History in the form of the Protestant Reformation launched the waves of migrants who after 1720 surged through this natural gateway. The religious upheavals of the sixteenth and seventeenth centuries peopled western Europe with minorities driven by fear or hope to find havens in the New World. Ironically, the first of these minorities to arrive in the middle colonies were the Roman Catholics of Maryland, who were persecuted in the British Isles. Here the proprietary Calvert family, headed by the lords Baltimore, established in 1632 a colony flanking both sides of Chesapeake Bay. Initially the Maryland colony developed along the bay's middle reaches and eastern shore, but by 1699, when the port of Baltimore was founded, Maryland's leaders were looking west across the Blue Ridge and north along the Susquehanna to the Pennsylvania gateway. The neighboring Delaware colony harbored ethnic rather than religious minorities—a smattering of Dutch and Swedes and a larger number of ethnic Finns transplanted from the Scandinavian forests under Swedish auspices beginning in 1638. The western part of New Jersey received its first religious refugees in the 1670s. These were Quakers, one of numerous pietistic sects that arose in northern Europe in reaction to the Lutheran and Anglican state churches established in the wake of the Reformation.

William Penn, an aristocratic Quaker and minor investor in the west Jersey Quaker colonies, emerged as the single most important force in middle colony development when he persuaded King Charles II to grant him some thirty million acres of land west of the Delaware River in 1681. For good measure, the king also named the colony in honor of Penn's father, an admiral in the British navy who had been instrumental in arranging the compromise that allowed Charles to assume his throne. Quaker traditions of modesty would not have allowed William Penn the younger to name the colony for himself.

Other large colonial grants originated in much the same fashion: By making large grants of land in America, Charles II could reward loyal followers without upsetting the restoration compromise as it pertained to property in England itself. Besides William Penn and the Calverts of Maryland, two other proprietors—both eighteenth-century heirs of restoration-era royalists—held significant blocks of land extending from the seaboard into the backcountry. These were Thomas, Lord Fairfax, whose lands spread across northern Virginia along the south bank of the Potomac, and John Carteret, the Earl Granville, who owned roughly the northern half of North Carolina. The existence of these proprietaries presented both examples and problems to the American-born elites of the seaboard. The example encouraged them to use their own political influence to acquire large grants of land and to profit from the sale of land to settlers. The problem lay in the locations of the proprietary holdings. The holdings of Penn, the Calverts, Fairfax, and Granville blocked natural routes of expansion from the seaboard; American-born land speculators were thus forced to look far to the west and south to get large tracts of their own. This inducement to distant land speculation was one of the factors that drove the rapid expansion of the Appalachian frontier during the mid-eighteenth century. When William Penn died in 1718, the Anglo-American frontier was still within a day's ride of tidewater. Sixty years later, as the newly independent Commonwealth of Pennsylvania declared the forfeiture of the Penn Proprietary, this frontier extended into western Kentucky and Middle Tennessee, a thousand miles to the west.

Through active recruitment and adroit use of what today would be called public relations, William Penn the younger made Pennsylvania the greatest haven of all for religious minorities and refugees and a beacon for all types of western Europeans looking for a fresh start: "My company on board consisted of many sorts of people," wrote a German Quaker who emigrated in 1682.

> There was a doctor of medicine with his wife and eight children, a French captain, a Dutch cake baker, an apothecary, a glassblower, a mason, a smith, a wheelwright, a cabinetmaker, a cooper, a hatmaker, a cobbler, a tailor, a gardener, farmers, seamstresses, etc; in all about eighty persons besides the crew. They were not only different in respect to age (for our oldest woman

was sixty years of age and the youngest child only twelve weeks) and in respect to their occupations, as I have mentioned, but were also of such different religious and behaviors that I might not unfittingly compare the ship that bore them hither with Noah's Ark.[19]

As this passage suggests, Pennsylvania attracted people who migrated primarily in search of opportunity rather than to escape oppression. These were in the majority even at the beginning; during the eighteenth century economic migrants would constitute over 90 percent of all newcomers, even when they came from lands—such as the Palatinate of western Germany or the northern Irish province of Ulster—that had been deeply scarred by the religious conflicts of the previous century. Economic migrants brought to Pennsylvania orthodox German Lutherans and Calvinists, Scottish and Irish Presbyterians, English and Irish Anglicans. There were even Catholics and Jews. But though the Quakers, Baptists, Mennonites, and other pietistic sects that gave Pennsylvania its reputation for tolerance and religious experimentation constituted a minority, their influence was disproportionate to their numbers. Numerous immigrants converted to a sect after arriving in America. Moreover, the religious ferment centered in Pennsylvania affected the orthodox churches, as for example in the controversy between "new side" and "old side" Presbyterians that broke out in the mid-eighteenth century. Colonial Pennsylvania first exhibited many religious values and practices that would later come to be seen as typical of Appalachia.

Some idea of how diversity influenced individual lives can be seen in the biography of Appalachia's most famous frontiersman. Squire Boone, an English Quaker, migrated to Pennsylvania in 1713. In 1720 he married within the faith but across ethnic lines to Sarah Morgan, whose family was Welsh. In 1731 the couple moved northwest to a newly opened district whose name (Oley, or "valley" in an Algonquian dialect) reflected its location. While in due course a Quaker meeting was established in the neighborhood, in this backwoods area Quakers were surrounded by Germans, Irish, Finns, and Swedes, not to mention the communities of Indians that still lived nearby. The Boone's second son Daniel, born in a one-room log cabin in 1734, would become the most famous embodiment of this diverse cultural environment. At the age of ten, Daniel became the family's herdsman, spending long hours each summer in nearby pastures and woods. Given his first gun at the age of twelve or thirteen, the boy spent increasing amounts of time in the woods, becoming an excellent marksman, ranging longer distances, and mixing in with other white and Indian hunters he encountered along the Schuykill or on the nearby Allegheny Path. By the time he was fifteen, Daniel's family decided to leave Pennsylvania and in its leaving became an example of how that colony's distinctive cultural milieu dispersed across the region we now call Appalachia.[20]

William Penn's "holy experiment," intended to be a place of peace, tolerance, and light in a dark and violent world, was also intended to be a revenue source for the Penn family. Thus land was available to anyone with the price, regardless of religious outlook. William Penn himself saw no contradiction in this, summing up his goals as "the service of God first, the honor and advantage of the king, with our own profit."[21] His experiment produced an almost instantly successful colony, which soon grew into British America's richest province and the home of its greatest city and most enlightened cultural institutions. But it did not make the Penn family rich in Penn's lifetime. When it eventually did begin to pay off, the price of wealth included the sacrifice of peace and, some would have said, of holiness. Still, on most historians' balance sheets, Penn's experiment was a success.

The road that traversed the Great Valley of the Appalachians turned out to be the most important pathway of settlement, but the first Europeans to travel west of the Blue Ridge did not immediately recognize its importance. Thomas Batts and Robert Fallam, traveling from tidewater Virginia in 1671 in search of a path to the Pacific, crossed the valley in the vicinity of modern Salem, Virginia, and ascended the long but gradual slope that separates the Roanoke River headwaters from the New River watershed. It is understandable that they and others who explored westward failed to grasp the fact that the local valleys they traversed were actually links in a chain. North of the Tennessee, there is no great river draining the valley from one end to the other, but instead a series of headwater basins laid end to end, with the ridges separating them like the rungs of a ladder. In places these divides are imposing, as in the Roanoke–New River divide that Batts and Fallam climbed. Elsewhere, as in the ridges separating the chain of valley watersheds between the Potomac and the Delaware or between the New River valley and that of the Tennessee, the ladder's rungs are barely perceptible. What most impressed the Europeans were the high mountains that framed the ladder's sides. "It was a pleasing tho' dreadful sight to see the mountains and Hills piled up one upon the other," wrote a weary Fallam in his journal somewhere on an Allegheny mountaintop.[22] As the geography of Appalachia came more clearly into view during the eighteenth century, colonial geographers borrowed an Indian phrase to describe the rugged Virginia and Pennsylvania hinterlands: "the Endless Mountains."

The Indians knew, of course, that the mountains were not really endless, as they also knew the valley to be a great natural highway. A "Warrior's Path" linked the forks of the Susquehanna at Shamokin with the Great Valley extending southward into Virginia. From Shamokin, a network of paths led north into the heartland of Iroquoia. Some four hundred miles south in Virginia, near what would one day become the city of Roanoke, the path divided into a southwestern branch that continued onward through the valley into the Cherokee country of eastern Tennessee and another branch that cut more directly south through the Blue Ridge into the Carolina Piedmont and the homeland of the Catawbas. The adventurer John Lawson, traveling north from the Catawba villages in the winter of 1701, traversed the lower end of this path, visiting palisaded villages of other Indians who had retreated southward as a result of Iroquois attacks. These were probably the same peoples whose abandoned fields and townsites Batts and Fallam had noticed when they crossed the valley two decades before.

In contrast to Pennsylvania, where the valley path swung close to the open gateway leading to Philadelphia, Virginia's share of the Great Valley, though more extensive than that of any other colony, is located well inland from the coast. Virginia Indian traders remained east of the mountains, competing with Carolina traders in the Catawba country and the Cherokee Lower Towns. Only after Virginians learned to travel the Great Valley path leading southwest to the Overhill villages was a reliable connection established with all of the Cherokees; by that time, the Virginians came often as land hunters and soldiers, not as the traders that the Cherokees so ardently desired. "Virginian," in fact, became a Cherokee designator for the type of Euro-American person who posed the greatest threat to the tranquility and stability of native society.

During the second decade of the eighteenth century, as settlement pushed up into Piedmont locations in view of the Blue Ridge, Virginia authorities became better informed about their mountainous backcountry. Their attention was drawn by the Tuscaroras, retreating up the Roanoke River after their Carolina defeat, as they lingered near that river's Great Valley headwaters in 1713–14. A party of Virginia Indians and traders sent out to check on them found them "dispersed in small parties, in a miserable condition, living like beasts without habitation, and without other provisions than what the woods afforded."[23] Notwithstanding this condition (or perhaps because of it, given

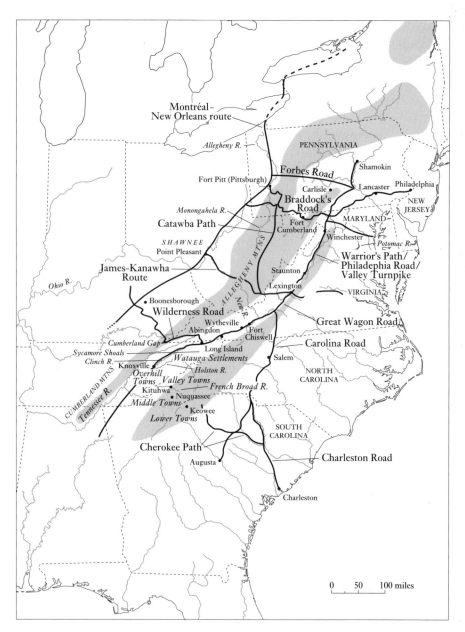

Montréal–
New Orleans route

Allegheny R.

PENNSYLVANIA

Forbes Road

Shamokin

Fort Pitt (Pittsburgh)

Carlisle

Lancaster

Philadelphia

Braddock's
Road

NEW
JERSEY

Monongahela R.

Catawba Path

Fort
Cumberland

MARYLAND

Winchester

Potomac R.

SHAWNEE
Point Pleasant

Staunton

Warrior's Path/
Philadephia Road/
Valley Turnpike

James–Kanawha
Route

Ohio R.

Lexington

VIRGINIA

• Boonesborough

Wilderness Road

Great Wagon Road

Wytheville

Abingdon

Fort
Chiswell

Carolina Road

Cumberland Gap

Sycamore Shoals

Clinch R.

Knoxville

Long Island

Watauga Settlements

Salem

Holston R.

Overhill
Towns

Valley Towns

NORTH
CAROLINA

Kituhwa

French Broad R.

• Nuquassee

Middle Towns

Keowee

Lower Towns

SOUTH
CAROLINA

Cherokee Path

Charleston Road

Augusta

Charleston

Tennessee R.

CUMBERLAND MTNS

ALLEGHENY MTNS

New R.

0   50   100 miles

MAP 2. Long-distance routes of early Appalachia

the Indians' desperate need for food), the Tuscaroras posed a threat to the colony's Piedmont frontier and so their migration northward attracted attention to the path through the Great Valley.

In 1716 Governor Alexander Spotswood led an armed expedition across the Blue Ridge to the Shenandoah River, which he grandly named "the Euphrates." En route, the party got the same view of the broad and inviting valley and the bordering Alleghenies on the west that tourists admire today along the Skyline Drive and Blue Ridge Parkway. While Spotswood's foray was a kind of sporting adventure, it also had to do with land prospecting and gathering frontier intelligence. Within a few years, Virginia made its first land grants west of the Blue Ridge and also made its first diplomatic approach to the Iroquois. In 1722 Spotswood and his Pennsylvania counterpart traveled to Albany to negotiate. The resulting treaty extended to Virginia, Maryland, and Pennsylvania the same standing that New York enjoyed in dealing with the Iroquois, and it also established the Blue Ridge as an Indian boundary west of the Susquehanna. The Six Nations agreed that Iroquois war parties would remain west of the mountains, but *which* mountains became a matter of dispute almost as soon as the Iroquois leaders affixed their signs to the treaty. The Iroquois believed the Blue Ridge to be the line of demarcation, while the Virginians insisted that the ridges west of the Great Valley marked the border.[24] Thus while Iroquois war parties continued to use the Warrior's Path to attack their southern enemies, this practice became a source of increasing difficulty as Virginia's section of the Great Valley began to fill with settlers.

There may have been Virginia settlers in the Great Valley as early as 1719, but the colony did not make its first land grant west of the Blue Ridge until 1730. By 1735 there were at least fifty-four families living on the land included in this grant.[25] In Pennsylvania, settlers spilled into the Lebanon Valley extending northeast from the Susquehanna, forcing the Shawnees who lived there on Delaware and Iroquois sufferance to move farther west. In 1732 Thomas Penn, the third son and eventual heir of the colony's founder, came over from England to sign a treaty with the Delawares officially acquiring this territory. Penn also set in motion the negotiations leading to the notorious Walking Purchase of the Lehigh Valley in 1737 and in 1736 signed a treaty with the Iroquois permitting white settlement west of the Susquehanna for the first time. He also reopened land sales, which had been suspended in the colony for fourteen years following the death of William Penn, worked out a compromise agreement with Lord Baltimore on the Maryland-Pennsylvania boundary (though the definitive line would not be run by Mason and Dixon for another thirty years), and entered into a vigorous competition with Maryland and Virginia authorities for backcountry settlers.[26]

Even so, Pennsylvania actually lost ground to the southern colonies during this period, at least in terms of its proportion of backcountry inhabitants. The reason once again was a blend of geography and history. The natural southward bend of the Great Valley west of the Susquehanna directed the flow of new settlers toward the southern colonies, while history intervened in the form of migrations of unprecedented scope, especially from Ireland and Germany. The Germans arrived first. Some 84,500 German-speaking immigrants came to the British American colonies between 1700 and 1775. Almost all of these settled south of New England, and the majority entered the colonies through the port of Philadelphia.[27] During the peak years of this migration, 1730–55, the influx was so prominent in Pennsylvania that English-speaking residents, such as the transplanted New Englander Benjamin Franklin, became alarmed. "Why should Pennsylvania, founded by the English, become a Colony of *Aliens*, who will shortly be so numerous as to Germanize us instead of our Anglifying them, and will never adopt our Language or Customs?" he wrote, choosing language that he would later come to regret.[28]

A large proportion of these "Pennsylvania Dutch"—so called because their English-speaking neighbors confused the German word for "German" (*Deutsch*) with the English word for Netherlander—remained in the proprietary. But many thousands of them and/or their descendants moved south through the Great Valley, creating neighborhoods in Maryland, Virginia, and the Carolinas that were ethnically distinctive though composed of dispersed rural homesteads. Historians have documented the practice of "chain migration," wherein immigrants from one village or district in Europe tended to cluster near one another in their new American homes, as it pertains to Pennsylvania and Maryland; the practice, though less easily documented, was also followed by newcomers who moved directly south through Pennsylvania as well as by second-generation German Americans who joined them on their journeys down the Great Valley path.[29]

In Virginia, many of the earliest valley settlers called "Dutch" were actually "Switzers," that is, natives of the German Protestant cantons of Switzerland. In South Carolina, some 3,700 German immigrants entered the colony between 1748 and 1759, almost all of them arriving through the port of Charleston. Roughly a third of these came in a single year, 1752, from the southwest German province of Würtemberg. The majority clustered in compact settlements in the Broad and Saluda valleys in the north central part of the province, away from both the Cherokee Path and the road leading north-ward toward Pennsylvania. Once Germans began concentrating in a district, English-speaking settlers tended to avoid it, even when the land and other re-sources of the district were attractive. In contrast with Pennsylvania, there is no record of hostility between English and German speakers in the Carolinas, nor did English settlers already planted in a district abandon it when Ger-mans moved in. Still, newcomers tended to cluster among speakers of their own language.[30] A historical demographer calculated this preference for eth-nic enclaves numerically for four states in 1790 and found it to be most pro-nounced in Pennsylvania and Maryland. Among ethnic groups, Germans and actual Dutch (that is, natives of the Netherlands) had a greater tendency to cluster than did English, Scots, and Scots-Irish.[31]

According to another historian's calculations, less than 10 percent of the eighteenth-century German-speaking migrants belonged to radical religious groups of the sort that had flocked to Philadelphia in the previous century.[32] Nevertheless, these religious minorities were disproportionately prominent in their influence and thus in historical accounts. Two in particular deserve to be mentioned in terms of their later contributions to Appalachian history: the communal settlement at Ephrata near Lancaster, which flourished from 1730 to 1768, and the Unitas Fratrum, more prominently known as the Moravians, who arrived in Pennsylvania in the 1730s and established a second colony in North Carolina in 1753.

Ephrata was the lengthened shadow of one man, Conrad Beissel. He was born in poverty in Germany in 1691 and grew up to be short, talkative, in-tense, and a baker. He loved music, and he had an extraordinary ability to move people, especially women. During the *wanderjahre* that journeyman bakers were expected to take in Germany, he encountered most of the groups and ideas that then made up the German religious underground. In Stras-bourg, he communed with Pietists, who believed in Christian worship guided by inner devotion, and with Inspirationists, who gave themselves up to the Holy Spirit and believed in prophecy, miracles, and speaking in tongues. He also met Theosophists, who searched for visions and ecstasy through mystical exercises, Mennonites, followers of a Dutch anabaptist whose belief in adult baptism had spread through the Rhineland from Switzerland to Holland, and the *Tunkeren* or Dunkards, whose nickname derived from their practice of baptism through total immersion. In Mannheim, Beissel had an affair with the master baker's wife, which led to a hasty departure from the city and a lifelong decision to give up "earthly woman" in favor of a mythical female, the

Virgin Sophia, whom he envisioned as the embodiment of divine wisdom. "But first the days of youth must be well-lived," he would later write, "and then the heavenly epoch is achieved."[33]

In 1720 Beissel found his way to Philadelphia at the age of twenty-nine. He first intended to join a community of cave-dwelling hermits who lived nearby, but, finding that community dispersed, he settled in the village of Germantown, teaching, preaching, and learning a new trade, weaving. Then, in 1722, he resumed his pursuit of solitude, building a lonely cabin in the remote Conestoga frontier region. When followers gathered around him and began to quarrel among themselves, he moved again, this time to an even less appealing area near the headwaters of Cocalico Creek, a name that in the Shawnee language meant "snake hole" or "den of serpents." But followers again drifted in and built cabins of their own near Conrad, who continued to be a seeker. By the early 1730s Beissel's wanderings were over, and the gathering at Cocalico became the place where he wove the varied strands of his religious education into a unique fabric of piety, devotional practice, and frontier creativity. It was about this time that the place began to be known as Ephrata, after the pre-Israelite name for Jerusalem.

Beissel devised Ephrata's mystical religious exercises, and he led its worldly activities of farming, weaving, milling, baking, and printing as it ministered to and provisioned the hundreds of German and other immigrants who thronged into the Conestoga backwoods. But when quarrels arose among the ambitious over the conduct of these missions and the use and control of Ephrata's steadily mounting store of earthly wealth, Conrad stood aside—his focus on things of the spirit, not of this life—and let the quarrelers exhaust themselves or drift away. Among those who drifted were Wilhelm Mack, the settler of Max Meadows, and another group of brethren who established a settlement on the New River in 1745 at a location that has since been known as Dunkard's Bottom.[34] It was probably no coincidence that James Patton, the Virginia land speculator, visited Ephrata while attending the Treaty at Lancaster.[35] Another treaty participant with Ephrata ties was Conrad Weiser, a trilingual frontiersman and from time to time an Ephrata resident, who served as Pennsylvania's chief interpreter in its dealings with the Six Nations.[36]

The Moravians were another immigrant sect that combined simplicity of doctrine with a complicated way of life. Followers of the Czech reformer and martyr Jan Hus, the Unitas Fratrum had been driven out of Moravia into the German province of Saxony during the seventeenth-century religious wars. The decision to come to America followed after they had been taken under the wing of a noble believer, Ludwig von Thurnstein, the Graf (Count) Zinzendorf, a masterful organizer who, after an abortive start in Georgia, brought the Moravians to Pennsylvania in 1741. These pietists believed in the unity of all believers and in the importance of inner peace and spirituality. In contrast to Beissel and his followers, many of them were of upper-class origins, and their clergy was well educated. They did not preach withdrawal from the world but rather hoped by their example to recall all true Christians to the simplicity and purity of the ancient church. Yet years of persecution had bred caution and indirection into their preaching, so that they did not always say what was on their mind. They established "open" congregations at Oley and Philadelphia that purported to be regular congregations of the Lutheran confession, though ignoring or slighting many of the doctrines and forms of worship that set Lutherans apart from other Protestants. Lutheran churchmen bitterly resented this ecumenism, which they saw as a form of empire building, and succeeded in keeping the Moravians from establishing similar congregations among the German-speaking settlers of Virginia.[37]

The Moravians also established missions to the Indians, many of them successful, especially among the drifting communities of Algonquian peoples in northern and western Pennsylvania. Yet Zinzendorf's aristocratic demeanor nearly led to disaster when he went proselytizing in the Wyoming Valley, a beautiful, canoe-shaped basin on the Susquehanna's North Branch. Conrad Weiser, engaged as his interpreter, had stayed behind temporarily in Shamokin, attending to some provincial business with the Six Nations' representative there. When he arrived at Wyoming,

> We found everything in confusion. . . . The Count had made a complete mess of things, and I had all I could do to calm the turmoil [but] If the Indians berated him, he berated them much more. . . . The natives had conducted themselves improperly towards him, showed no respect for his person, used to break wind in his presence in the tent, were always making fun of him, and smoked tobacco beyond all reason, etc. Certainly the poor Indians did not know how to behave with a Reichs Count, and if they had known they would have had no inclination thereto. Neither did the Count know how to behave with the Indians. He is pretty hot-headed and likes to give orders. The Indians on the other hand won't take orders in the least and consider a dictator nonsensical.[38]

At Bethlehem and Nazareth in the Lehigh Valley, Zinzendorf established cloisters not unlike those at Ephrata, with separate living quarters and activities for brethren in "choirs" organized according to gender, age, and marital status. Not surprisingly, he was shocked when he learned how bitterly the Indians resented the Walking Purchase, which is how the Penn proprietary had acquired the land it sold to him. But the Moravians continued building there and when Zinzendorf determined upon another expansion, he turned to another aristocratic proprietor, Lord Granville of North Carolina, engaging to buy 100,000 acres there in 1752. Bishop Augustus Spangenburg, assigned to choose the specific tract later that year, left an absorbing account of one of the first European forays into the Blue Ridge plateau of northwest Carolina. After traveling up the Catawba valley from a point near the limits of Granville's land, Spangenburg and his party approached the high country at the foot of the Blue Ridge escarpment, below the present resort town of Blowing Rock. Scrambling up the 2,000-foot slope ("part of the way . . . on hands and knees"), they then faced the rocky defiles and tangled rhododendron thickets of the Flannery Fork, one of the fountains of the New River, until a lookout spotted an open expanse of meadow in the distance.

> So we cut our way through the bushes to it, reaching it by evening, to the delight of men and horses. We put up our tent, but had barely finished when there came such a wind storm that we could hardly stand against it. I think I have never felt a winter wind so strong and so cold. The ground was covered with snow; water froze beside the fire. What should we do? Our horses would die, and we with them. For the hunters had about concluded that we were across the crest of the Blue Mountains, and on the Mississippi watershed.[39]

This constitutes the first written description we have of the kilometer-high valley that would one day be named for Daniel Boone.

Wisely, Spangenburg chose another location, a square tract just east of the Yadkin River, where in 1753 Moravians assigned by church authorities in Pennsylvania began building the colony they called Wachovia.[40] As they had in Pennsylvania, the Wachovians displayed their usual mix of communalism and cosmopolitanism. Bethabara and Bethania became the more inward-focused of their new settlements, Salem the more worldly. Though it was located in the exact center of the Wachovia tract, Salem was also close to the "shallow ford" where the Trading Path leading to and from the tidewater crossed the Yadkin. The settlement soon acquired flour and saw mills, stores patronized by outsiders as well as believers, and commercial connections overland to Charleston and the Cape Fear region as well as to Pennsylvania. The Moravians also dispatched missionaries to the Cherokees, though with a distinct lack of success.[41]

The Irish Protestant migration to America began just as the influx of Germans was beginning drive up land prices and restrict availability in southeast Pennsylvania. James Logan, the proprietors' longtime secretary of the province, claimed that this new group of immigrants threatened both peace and prosperity. The Irish, as they were generally known, disturbed the Indians and challenged local authorities. Logan stated that they "have overrun all the back parts of the Province as far as Susquehannah and are now to ye further dissatisfaction of ye Indians passing over it and from what I have [said?] in this, you will be sure that a Militia will become unavoidable, for which these men are well fitted." In other words, the Irish influx threatened peace with the Indians, but the newcomers' fighting abilities offered a remedy if war were to come. Some historians have accused Logan of duplicity on this score, noting that he himself was from Belfast, the capital of Ulster, and conceived the notion of importing his "countrey men" as an instrument serving both his personal ambition as a land speculator and the Indian diplomacy he pursued on behalf of the Penns.[42]

Be that as it may, the Irish migration proved one of the formative influences in Appalachian history, though it has created additional problems for historians. If the eighteenth-century southern and northern Irish migrants were counted together, they outnumbered even the Germans, totaling roughly 109,000 to 85,000 for the latter during the period between 1700 and 1775.[43] But tradition demands that the Irish be divided into north and south, which also supposedly amounts to a division between Protestant and Catholic. Modern Irish historians remind us that this tradition imposes the values of nineteenth- and twentieth-century ethnicity in the United States onto an eighteenth-century folk movement and that it overlooks the substantial number of Catholics among emigrants from Northern Ireland and the smaller but still noteworthy proportion of Irish Protestants who came from the southern part of that interesting island.

There is also a problem of nomenclature, since "Scotch-Irish," though current in Logan's day, was rarely used by the migrants from Ulster to describe themselves, "Irish" being the prevailing identifier for both groups. Protestant Irish Americans anxious to avoid being grouped with immigrant Irish Catholics during the nineteenth century popularized the term "Scotch-Irish," which makes it awkward to use for the colonial period. There is the further complication that, while immigration from Germany slowed and then halted before the American Revolution, immigration from Northern Ireland resumed after the Revolution and held steady through the first two decades of the nineteenth century, especially in western Pennsylvania and the upper Ohio valley—which was, with southeastern Pennsylvania, the Great Valley of Virginia and the Carolina Piedmont, one of the four cultural and demographic hearths of the Appalachian region.

In this book, "Irish Protestant" and "Irish Catholic" will be used to identify the two streams of Irish migration, with Ulster and Northern Ireland being used coterminously to identify the majority Protestant counties of the north. It is very difficult to document the influence of the Catholics. Anecdotal evidence suggests that a very substantial number of Catholics came to British America, possibly as indentured servants. The records of the Indian trade are full of characterizations of Irish servants or former servants who worked as packhorsemen on the frontier. And although Catholics in the colonies were predominantly unchurched, in that they suffered under legal disabilities and lacked regular access to Catholic clergy and rituals, there is also anecdotal evidence of frontier Catholics' exhibiting the marks of their faith.[44] It is tempting to believe that Irish Catholics, bearing the burdens of Irish history in the forms of discrimination and economic disadvantage, accounted for the shadowy backwoods population found in the records only as squatters, drifters, and miscreants of various descriptions—the human raw materials, as it were, of the numerous negative stereotypes of frontier and Appalachian people that have dwelt in American consciousness since colonial times. But there is no way to prove—or to disprove—such an association.[45]

That much being said, the Irish Protestants placed a much deeper imprint on the history of the colonial backcountry and of Appalachia. Numbering more than 66,000 during colonial times, they were more dispersed geographically than the Germans, having significant concentrations in New England and New York as well as in Pennsylvania, Maryland, Virginia, and the Carolinas. Nonetheless, their impact on the frontiers of the latter five colonies was significant. Arriving through Philadelphia, the Delaware and Chesapeake Bay ports, and through Charleston, they moved speedily into the less settled parts of the backcountry, located near and sometimes among the Germans and the English, and, as Logan predicted, they became the premier resident aggressors and defenders during the Indian wars. In Pennsylvania, Irish Protestants dominated the east bank of the Susquehanna, from Lancaster townships named Donegal and Derry west through Paxton (or Paxtang) in the vicinity of modern Harrisburg. West of the river, they came to predominate in the Cumberland section of the Great Valley, while Germans prevailed in the triassic lowlands (near modern York and Gettysburg) just east of the Blue Ridge.

In Virginia, Irish Protestants poured into the middle and upper reaches of the Shenandoah Valley, beginning in the 1730s. Leaving German settlers and English Virginians to cope with the quarrels over Lord Fairfax's boundary that affected settlement in the lower (northern) valley, the Irish concentrated in the Borden tract centered on the newly established county of Augusta (1738) and its courthouse town of Staunton and in the Beverly tract centered in the upper valley around the future town of Lexington (founded circa 1740). Beverly and Borden were nonresident speculators, but entrepreneurs among the newcomers soon developed speculative schemes of their own. An elite group from northwest Ireland acquired 50,000 acres in the Greenbrier valley, thousands more in the Roanoke valley, and the two large grants already mentioned that embraced the New River and upper Tennessee watersheds in southwest Virginia. This group included James Patton, a ships' captain who had brought over settlers for Beverly's grant, and his sons-in-law John Buchanan and John Preston—the latter a handsome ferryman from Donegal who captured the heart of a Patton daughter, married her in spite of her father's objections, and became the progenitor of a landed dynasty whose name lived on well into the nineteenth century. There was the Lewis family— father John and sons Andrew, Charles, and Thomas—who acquired wealth as landowners and fame as soldiers on the Virginia frontier. Also among this group was the McDowell family of Lexington, descended from Ephraim McDowell, an early immigrant to Pennsylvania who was a veteran of the siege of Londonderry, one of the military victories in 1689–90 that assured Protestant dominance in Northern Ireland. Two of Ephraim's grandsons, James and Samuel McDowell, both born in Pennsylvania, became the founders of landed political families in Virginia and Kentucky, respectively. In Virginia, James McDowell's son and grandson of the same name became prominent political leaders, with the grandson becoming the second Virginia governor to be chosen from west of the Blue Ridge. Other McDowell cousins moved on to North Carolina and, eventually, to Alabama, Indiana, and Missouri, providing examples of the often-noted tendency of the Irish Protestants to provide leadership throughout the upper South.[46]

A representative Irish Protestant progress might have taken a family from Pennsylvania in the 1730s to Virginia in the 1740s to the Carolinas in the 1750s and 60s, joined at each place by other Ulster emigrants fresh off the boat. Farther south, the most notable Irish Protestant concentration was found at the Waxhaws, a name designating a creek that flowed across the border from North Carolina into the Catawba River in South Carolina and derived in turn from the Waxhaw people who had merged into the Catawba Nation with other Souian-speaking societies. The habitual use of the plural in referring to this district may derive from the fact that it straddled the provincial boundary, which remained in dispute and complicated land titles until a compromise was found in 1764. This is how the most famous scion of this district, Andrew Jackson, came to have two official birthplaces, one in each state, though Jackson's birth in 1770 was obviously a singular event.

Although communal migrations on the scale of the Moravians' did not occur among the Irish Protestants, there is much evidence of group cohesion among them, including the migration of extended families and of substantial portions of church congregations and/or neighborhoods. However, whether they settled in ethnic enclaves or dispersed among other population groups seems to have depended upon local circumstances. In the lower Shenandoah Valley, one study has found, they dispersed among German and English households but maintained their cultural identity through intermarriage and their membership in the Presbyterian Church.[47]

In the Carolinas, the Irish settled in enclaves interspersed among German enclaves in the valleys of the Yadkin and Catawba Rivers in North Carolina as well as in the Waxhaws. One study found a concentration of three or four surnames among the numerous settlers of backcountry districts in South Carolina. The Calhouns of Long Cane Creek in the far northwestern corner of the province provide another example, having migrated as a group of at least five households from Augusta County, Virginia, in 1751. An analysis of names recorded in the 1790 census discloses that 18.9 percent of the population of South Carolina was Scots-Irish, 17.8 percent of Tennessee's, 16.5 percent of Kentucky's, 15.1 percent of Pennsylvania's, 12.2 percent of Georgia's, and 11.7 percent of Virginia's, compared with 10.5 percent of the overall U.S. population.[48] It should be kept in mind that Ulster migration resumed after the Revolution and reached its peak after 1815. The large Irish concentration in the Redstone district of southwestern Pennsylvania developed during and after the Revolution in the midst of Indian warfare. The Redstone Presbytery was created there in 1789. Thomas Mellon, who would provide the model for Irish Protestant leadership in America's industrial revolution, did not arrive in western Pennsylvania until 1818.[49]

At each gap in the Blue Ridge, migrants traversing the Great Valley encountered smaller streams moving west from the Chesapeake Bay colonies. For example, the ancestors of another Appalachian hero, Thomas J. "Stonewall" Jackson, landed in Maryland and moved up the Potomac basin during the 1740s and 1750s. In the Carolinas, the road from Philadelphia crossed the old Indian trading paths leading to the eastern parts of those provinces. Migrants here were more likely to be English than Irish or German, and there were also substantial numbers of Africans. More than twice as many Africans came to colonial America as Germans and Irish Protestants combined; the African influx outnumbered *all* other ethnic groups combined during this period. The great majority were involuntary migrants, kidnapped and sold into slavery in their homelands or transported north from the Caribbean. Comparatively few of this number made their way into the backcountry. Occasionally a free African American could be found among the migrant stream. Such was the case of the first man to establish a land claim on Long Cane Creek in South Carolina: a carpenter named John Chevis, who came with his wife and nine children from Virginia in 1751.[50]

Well-off migrants might acquire slaves in Pennsylvania or in any of the southern colonies, and the presence of blacks on the frontier was noted from the earliest days of settlement. Certain it is that slave labor was used in clearing the land and establishing backcountry mills, forges, and cowpens. The value of this labor is reflected in the concern that white authorities manifested when they demanded the return of escaped or captive slaves on each occasion when native and Euro-American differences were negotiated. But the black people found in Indian country weren't always captives; frequently they stole themselves, escaping into the forest in hopes of a better life than they found on the Euro-American plantations. At the same time, the Indian villages were not always places of refuge. The enslavement of captives was a traditional feature of life in native societies. This form of slavery was not a racial category, as white and red as well as black captives were likely to hold such status and were usually well treated as members of Indian households, though records of mistreatment also survive.

Traders and their *métis* descendants brought African chattel slavery into Indian country as labor for their commercial and household enterprises. The treaty records show that the Indians were usually willing to comply with demands for the return of escaped or captive slaves to the settlements, but not always. In 1775 the Shawnees, in accordance with the terms that ended Dunmore's War, returned all captives who wanted to go home and made those who did not at least go and visit their relatives: "We have Delivered up all your Horses and all your Negroes Except one Negro Man who runaway from the Mouth of Hockhockan Who threatens to kill either White Man or Indian who shall Attempt to Molest him." They also declined to turn over a slave woman's children to the Virginians "as they were Bagat by our People we thought it very hard they shou'd be made slaves of."[51]

The backcountry migration was one of the great folk movements in American history. To accommodate it, the Warrior's Path of the Great Valley became a Great Trail, then a Great Wagon Road connecting Pennsylvania with the South. At its southern end it was known as the Philadelphia Road, in Pennsylvania as the Virginia Road. Where it forked in the Roanoke section of the Great Valley, the southwestern branch became the Wilderness Road, while the southern branch became the Carolina Road. South of the Catawba country, the Great Road merged with the Cherokee Path leading from Charleston to the mountains. When it reached the sandhills and pine barrens that separated the South Carolina Piedmont from the coastal plain, it became the Charleston Road.

East of the mountains another path, also called the Carolina Road, ran parallel to the Blue Ridge and attracted some southbound migrants. The Moravians preferred this route—notwithstanding a number of inconvenient river crossings and a reputation for bandits and horse thieves (which led it also to be known as the Rogues Road)—because at its northern end, east of the Blue Ridge between the Susquehanna and the Potomac, travelers could count on the support of fellow religionists scattered along the way. But the Great Valley road carried the bulk of the migrants. Even in South Carolina, it has been estimated that fewer than 10 percent of backcountry settlers came north from Charleston or other tidewater districts, even though the province officially encouraged such migration with bounties and free land. The majority of backcountry migrants there whose origins can be identified had lived previously in Virginia; the next largest group came from Pennsylvania, and the remainder from Maryland, New Jersey, or North Carolina. Immigrants who came directly from Europe also settled there but were as likely to have disembarked in Pennsylvania or Delaware as in Charleston.[52]

The Boone family traveled this road in 1750 and 1751. Squire Boone decided to leave Pennsylvania after he and his wife Sarah were twice summoned before their Friends meeting to answer for the fact that two of their older children had married outside of the faith, one to a German neighbor, the other to a "worldling" whose ethnicity has not been identified. When he refused to submit a second time to Quaker discipline, Squire was expelled from the meeting and, in the winter of 1749–50, he and Sarah made plans to move away to "Virginia, Carolina or elsewhere." The emigration party totaled at least nineteen members of an extended family, plus son Daniel's best boyhood friend, and it traveled via the Allegheny Path to Harris's Ferry, then across the

Susquehanna to the Virginia Road. Daniel Boone, fifteen at the time, led the way, clutching a new Pennsylvania rifle, with the family's goods following along in Conestoga wagons. These soon-to-be-famous products of the Pennsylvania frontier were of German craftsmanship, but the Boones' cultural baggage also included the Finnish-Irish log cabin, Irish livestock-handling and whiskey-making techniques, English books, Bibles, and newspapers, Native American food crops such as maize and beans, and a male culture of hunting and woodscraft that was also learned from the Indians. In the summer and fall of 1750 and possibly the following year, the Boones squatted on land near the present town of Harrisonburg, Virginia, while Daniel and his friend disappeared into the woods on their first "long hunt." By 1752 the Boone family was established along the Yadkin River in northwest North Carolina, near a Welsh enclave also from Pennsylvania, which was where Daniel Boone found his wife, Rebecca Bryan, in 1756.

"Inhabitants flock in here daily, mostly from Pennsylvania and other parts of America," wrote the governor of North Carolina in 1751; "they commonly seat themselves toward the West and have got near the mountains."[53] In effect, the Boones and thousands like them who followed down the Great Valley Road created a "greater Pennsylvania" in the southern backcountry. Mennonite, Dunkard, Seventh-Day Baptist, Moravian, and even Quaker migrants to Virginia and Carolina added another characteristic Pennsylvanian touch of religious and ethnic diversity—and the political diversity that resulted. A large proportion of southern backcountry leaders during the eighteenth and early nineteenth centuries descended from families that had traveled along the same road from Pennsylvania to the south, among them Andrew Jackson and his great adversary, John C. Calhoun.

One reason for the southward migration was that Pennsylvania's path to its own west was blocked, not just by mountains, but by Indians who had been promised asylum there and by the necessarily long supply lines that were extremely vulnerable to disruption in time of war. And war seemed increasingly likely. As the 1740s wore on, discontent mounted among all the peoples who confronted one another along the Appalachian frontier, and the frustration felt on all sides led to a growing probability of aggressive behavior. The Iroquois, for example, signed the treaties in 1736 and 1737 by which Pennsylvania acquired the remaining lands east of the Allegheny ridges, but they did so reluctantly and with many complaints. "We received from the Proprietors

Folk artist Kenneth Walsh of Wilkes County, North Carolina, calls this carving of Daniel Boone, his dog, and a bear "The Heart of the Blue Ridge." (Private collection)

Yesterday some Goods in Consideration of our Release of the Lands on the West side of Susquehannah. It is true we have the full Quantity according to Agreement but if the Proprietor had been here himself we think in regard to our Numbers and poverty he would have made an Addition to them—If the Goods were only to be divided amongst the Indians present a single Person would have had but a small Portion but if you consider what Numbers are left behind equally intitled with Us to a Share there will be extremely little."[54]

Moreover, white settlers began almost immediately to move beyond the boundaries established in these treaties. At a council in Philadelphia in 1742, Iroquois spokesmen complained about settlers on the upper Juniata watershed, which the Six Nations had given to their Delaware "cousins" to compensate them for lost lands east of the Susquehanna. Proprietary authorities sought out and burned some of these illegal settlements, but that did not end the problem. Meanwhile, the Delawares, angry and sullen over their treatment by the proprietors and by what they regarded as a betrayal by their Iroquois "uncles," moved still farther west into the Ohio valley, where they intermingled with their fellow Algonquians, the Shawnees. The Shawnees themselves had withdrawn from eastern Pennsylvania by 1732 and settled initially near the site of modern Pittsburgh, where the Allegheny, flowing down from New

York, and the Monongahela, flowing north from (West) Virginia, meet to form the Ohio. One of their first actions was to send a delegation to Montréal to hold council with the French governor of Canada, signaling to the Pennsylvanians and others that they too might find it worthwhile to play the European invaders against one another. Later the Shawnees moved farther down the Ohio in the direction of their ancient homes, then, as the traffic of trade and land hunting increased along that river, they moved back from it into the Scioto valley of southeastern Ohio. Here, perhaps for the first time since their dispersal by the Iroquois a century earlier, the five divisions of the Shawnee reunited, and their warriors prepared to make their stand.

The Souian peoples of the Carolina Piedmont who clustered near what came to be called the Catawba Nation remained the implacable enemies of the Iroquois, but they had enjoyed considerable success in manipulating rival European interests, although in their case they played off South Carolina against Virginia, not British against other nationalities. But this success came at a price. Their relative independence carried within it the seeds of dependence, not on any one set of Europeans or Euro-Americans, but on colonial society as a whole.[55] As they began to be surrounded by the white settlers who poured into the Carolinas during the 1750s, their position became more tenuous. Moreover, the hatred of the Iroquois for these old enemies remained intense, thanks to the aid that Catawbas had given to North Carolina and Virginia against the Tuscaroras. Colonial authorities from New York to South Carolina, cognizant of the fact that both Iroquois and Catawbas were valuable British allies, lectured both groups frequently on the need for brotherhood, not enmity, but with little effect.

The Cherokees, distracted by intermittent war with the Creek nations to their south and devastated by a smallpox epidemic in 1739, were under similar pressures. Iroquois and Shawnee raids against their Overhill villages continued to come down the Warrior's Path of the Great Valley, while on the east flank of the mountains, Euro-American settlements grew ever closer to the Cherokee Lower Towns. White settlers were within sixty miles of Keowee, the principal Lower Town, by the early 1750s. These developments, along with losses during the Creek war, increased the importance of the Overhill Cherokee towns. New villages were founded along the Holston River in the upper Tennessee valley, but these locations were uncomfortably close to Virginia settlers moving southwest through the Great Valley. Thomas Walker and James Patton visited these towns during their land-hunting trip to Cumberland Gap.[56] Like the Shawnees, the Cherokees during this period were also testing the advantages of neutrality, pulling back from their alliance with

South Carolina by inviting Virginia and French traders into the Overhill villages to compete with their Charleston competitors and by initiating talks with the French and with both British colonies about the location of forts in the Cherokee country. These initiatives did not flow from a united leadership, however, but rather occasioned much debate and division within Cherokee councils about the wisest course to pursue.[57]

"We know our Lands are now become more Valuable," an Iroquois spokesman proclaimed in the Philadelphia council of 1742. "The white People think we dont know their Value but we are sensible that the Land is Everlasting and the few Goods we receive for it are soon Worn out and gone." Pennsylvania's adroit exploitation of the Six Nations' claim to speak for their Delaware and Shawnee "nephews" flattered Iroquois pride, but flattery by itself could not conceal a multifaceted crisis within Iroquoia at the middle of the century. One crisis grew out of the fur trade, which declined after 1727, both in terms of the proportion that passed through Iroquois hands en route to Albany or Philadelphia and also in terms of a market that was beginning to favor skins over furs and thus southerners over northerners.[58] A second crisis grew out of the renewed aggressiveness of the European empires between which the Six Nations maneuvered, leading to increasing tensions within the confederacy between "anglophile" and "francophile" blocs centered respectively among the Mohawks and Senecas, with neutralists squeezed uncomfortably in the middle.

The Iroquois could not rely on earlier treaties to protect them. This much became clear in 1742, when an Iroquois war party on its way south got into trouble in Virginia. Despite their understanding that the Albany Treaty of 1722 allowed them free passage through the Great Valley, the Senecas had shifted their warpath westward, along what is now the approximate route of U.S. Highway 19 through West Virginia. Southern retaliatory raids along this same route gave it its name, the Catawba Path. However, the war party in question was composed primarily of Onondaga, who descended the Susquehanna and the Great Valley in 1742 as they had done for decades, if not centuries. In Virginia, they had shown their Pennsylvania passes but had been refused food by the settlers they asked, so they killed some hogs running loose in the forest. This action attracted the hostile attention of additional settlers, leading to a confrontation at Balcony Falls, near present Glasgow, Virginia. Nineteen of the Indians were killed and a number wounded. James Patton, an Augusta County magistrate but not an eyewitness to the event, assured the royal governor of Virginia that the Indians had been the aggressors. Pennsylvania authorities, however, hastening to intervene lest the resulting crisis lead to a general war with the Six Nations, believed the Onondaga version. In any event, both Virginia and the Onondagas accepted Pennsylvania's offer of mediation, which defused the crisis and set in motion the negotiations culminating at Lancaster in 1744. The treaty arrived at there compensated the Indians for their losses and also led to further land cessions, although the terms came into dispute almost as soon as the treaty makers went home.

The fact was that neither justice nor the land market determined the fate of the Indians. Rather, it was their need for European trade goods—guns, powder, blankets, pots, axes, whiskey, tobacco, and—increasingly—food. The Iroquois, like all the other native peoples of the woodlands, had become addicted not just to alcohol, but to trade, which they needed to acquire all those implements of daily living that they could no longer provide for themselves. Thus no treaty called to discuss just grievances would turn on principle alone but rather on the volume of goods presented and the Indians' need to receive them. The number of Indians at Lancaster presaged an era when the native delegations at such treaties grew larger and larger, whether convening in Philadelphia, Charleston, or Albany. Since tradition had it that every delegation member would receive presents, the size of the delegation was determined by need.[59]

For the Pennsylvanians, staving off a general war meant putting off a crisis that was building in their own territory, a crisis that would profoundly reshape Pennsylvania politics during the decade after 1744. Alone of the British colonies, Pennsylvania had no militia and no defensive works such as the forts that guarded the coasts and harbors of other colonies' ports. "We have, 'tis true, had a long Peace with the Indians," wrote Franklin, who began his rise to power in Pennsylvania politics by addressing this issue. "But it is a long Peace indeed, as well as a long Lane, that has no Ending. The French know the Power and Importance of the Six Nations, and spare no Artifice, Pains or Expence, to gain them to their Interest."[60] But Pennsylvania since its founding had been guided by the Quaker dedication to pacifism, and although the Quakers had long since become a minority in the colony, they were still powerful in the legislature. The division between Quaker and non-Quaker on issues of defense was complicated by other divisions within the colony, between German and English speakers, between country and city, and between those who supported the proprietary and those who did not. Pennsylvania traders and religious missionaries followed the displaced and unhappy natives west, but otherwise the colony faced the growing crisis in Indian and international affairs in a state of political paralysis.

The two Carolina colonies had problems of their own, not the least of which was the festering border dispute that was finally compromised by a jagged line drawn around the Catawba Nation, leaving the Indians' land entirely within South Carolina but dividing the nearby white settlements between the two provinces. The Cherokee trade remained of critical interest to Charleston officials and businessmen, but not necessarily to the planter elite that dominated the provincial assembly. Nor was any love lost between the coastal aristocracy and the backcountry settlers who, by 1770, comprised the larger share of the white population. With slaves outnumbering whites in the plantation districts by five or ten to one, Carolina planters were terrified by the prospect of servile rebellion, and even more terrified that such a revolt might break out simultaneously with an Indian war. This meant that, in principle, they advocated measures that would attract white settlers and keep the Cherokees dependent upon the Charleston trade. But when it came to accepting specific measures that would bolster these principles—that would make backcountry people happier by giving them a larger say in provincial government, for example, or that would in some way bolster the Cherokee trade— the planter elite was indifferent, if not hostile.

In these circumstances, Virginia took the lead in bringing the various frontier crises to the point of resolution through war. The Lancaster treaty, as we have seen, opened Appalachian Virginia to exploitation—at least by trading and hunting, if the Iroquois interpretation of the treaty were adhered to, and even by settlement, according to the more expansive Virginia interpretation. To settlers like Wilhelm Mack and his fellow German Brethren at Dunkard's Bottom on the New River, or to speculators resident on the Great Valley frontier such as James Patton, the treaty was a signal to move west, into the parallel valleys along the Potomac and New Rivers and into southwest Virginia and the valley of the upper Tennessee. For northern Virginia grandees whose acquisitions of western lands east of the Allegheny Front were stymied by the claims of Lord Fairfax, the treaty invited a great leap westward, across the Great Valley and its hinterland to the land around the Forks of the Ohio.

The Ohio Company, established by the Virginia assembly in 1747, swiftly moved to make good on its claim to 200,000 acres along the Ohio River. In 1749 it established a supply camp on the upper Potomac at the future site of Cumberland, Maryland. In 1751 and 1752, the company sent out Christopher Gist, an experienced hunter and land prospector, to explore the territory across the mountains. Gist also summoned the Indians to a council at Logstown, near the Forks of the Ohio, at which they were promised good trading terms by the Virginians and protection against the French. He found the Indians wary and skeptical of the Virginians' intentions:

While I was at Mohongaly in my return home, an Indian who spoke good English came to me and . . . desired to know where the Indian's Land lay, for that the French claimed all the Land on one side the River Ohio and the English on the other side. After some consideration, "My friend," said I, "We are all one King's people and the different color of our skins makes no difference in the King's subjects. You are his people as well as we. You will have the same Privileges as the White People have, and to hunt You have liberty every where so that You don't kill the White Peoples Cattle & Hogs."[61]

The Ohio valley and its Appalachian hinterland soon became a theater of the European world's first global war. Protestant Britain and Catholic France, dynastic and religious rivals for more than a century, now confronted one another as competing commercial empires, with potential flashpoints scattered around the world from Europe to Asia to the Caribbean and all the seas between. But it was in the North American backcountry that the first explosion occurred. In 1749, having made increasing inroads among the Senecas, the largest Iroquois nation, and among the Shawnees and Delawares recently departed from Pennsylvania, the French royal governor of Canada dispatched an expedition down the Ohio, the purpose of which was to reassert France's claim to the Ohio valley. Within two years, French forts rose on the Pennsylvania shore of Lake Erie and at Venango, the principal portage between the lake and the Ohio watershed. In 1753 twenty-one-year-old George Washington, a militia colonel representing Governor Robert Dinwiddie and accompanied by Gist, the Ohio Company agent, visited Venango with an official warning from Virginia for the French to stay out of the Ohio valley, which the French commander politely refused to accept. In the meantime, Shawnee raids on the southwest Virginia and northwest North Carolina frontiers left behind evidence that the Indians involved had come under French influence.[62]

In 1754 Dinwiddie sent Washington out again with a company of soldiers to build a fort at the Forks of the Ohio, the region's most important strategic location. But the French were already at work there on Fort Duquesne. After a few skirmishes, Washington retreated eastward to a fort of his own, the hastily constructed Fort Necessity, built near the intersection of the Catawba Path and the Nemacolin Path, one of which led south into western Virginia, the other east. The French and their Indian allies invested the little fort on July 3, and after a decent interval, Washington was allowed to surrender on terms that gave him and his men safe passage back across the mountains. A Seneca leader who observed this outcome later stated that "the French had acted as great Cowards and the English as Fools in that Engagement."[63]

British authorities next decided on a major show of force. Fourteen hundred British troops and 450 Virginia militiamen set off from the valley toward Fort Duquesne under Maj. Gen. Sir Edward Braddock in June 1755. Pennsylvania's assembly still refused to undertake warlike measures, but Franklin negotiated a deal whereby Pennsylvania farmers would supply wagons for the British supply train in return for cash payments from Braddock. Twenty-year-old Daniel Boone came back north to serve as a teamster with a North Carolina detachment; other future frontier notables in the campaign included Washington, William Crawford (a future partner with Washington in various land schemes in the west), and Andrew Lewis, land speculator and militia captain from southwest Virginia, who had just returned from the Overhill Cherokee villages, having been allowed to build a small fort there but without the Cherokee allies he had tried to recruit for the Braddock campaign.

Washington and Crawford, among others, scouted land along the route as the army made its laborious way up the Potomac and then overland via the Nemacolin Path, which Braddock's engineers transformed into a wagon road. Ignoring warnings from friendly Indians and the Virginians, Braddock undertook the campaign in European style, leading a four-mile-long column of brightly uniformed troops unschooled in frontier warfare. On July 6, the outnumbered Canadians and "French Indians" ambushed the column at a crossing of the Monongahela River just south of Fort Duquesne. Withering fire from the French in front and the Indians concealed in the surrounding forest shattered the formations of the British regulars, and the column broke up, fleeing in disorder back toward the east. "Its true—we have been beaten—most shamefully beaten—by a handful of Men!" wrote Washington.[64] It was every man for himself in the panicky retreat that followed. Young Boone, cutting loose his lead horse, mounted it and made his way back alone toward his relatives in eastern Pennsylvania. As he crossed the Juniata River, he encountered an armed and drunken Indian who disputed his passage. Though unarmed, Boone managed to best the man in a hand-to-hand struggle. It was the first Indian he had ever killed, and one of only three in his entire lifetime, or so he insisted in his old age. For years afterward the Boone family sang a ballad about Braddock's defeat, which told how Daniel remained

Until that he saw all attempts were in vain.
From sighs and from tears he could scarcely refrain.
Poor Brittons, poor Brittons, poor Brittons remember.
Although we fought hard we were forced to surrender.[65]

General warfare broke out along the Virginia and Pennsylvania frontiers in 1755. The Shawnee raid on Draper's Meadows, Virginia (modern Blacksburg), which claimed the life of James Patton and carried Mary Draper Ingles into captivity, took place in July, even before news of the Braddock debacle became widespread. In the Monongahela valley, an outpost established by a group of Ephrata dissidents was destroyed, as were isolated cabins in the remote valleys on either side of the Allegheny Front. In the Great Valley, war parties struck in southwest Virginia and destroyed the cabins of Lord Fairfax's tenants and purchasers along the upper Potomac. Washington, commanding Virginia's forces along the frontier, had a chain of forts constructed in the back valleys along the present Virginia–West Virginia border. This tactic may have saved from destruction Winchester, Staunton, and other embryonic towns in the Great Valley, but it did not save the more westerly settlers' homes. "I have succeeded in ruining the three adjacent provinces, Pennsylvania, Maryland, and Virginia, driving off the inhabitants, and totally destroying the settlements over a tract of country thirty leagues, reckoning from the line of Fort Cumberland," wrote the French commander at Fort Duquesne. "Thus far, we have lost only two officers and a few soldiers, but the Indian villages are full of prisoners of every age and sex."[66]

In southwest Virginia, Patton's nephew William Preston counted 306 victims of the war between 1754 and 1758. Of these, 113 were killed and 178 captured; the remaining 15 were wounded but without being taken. Every ethnic group, age, and condition on the frontier can be found on Preston's list, including 56 children and several "servants," including "a Negro, 2 young Indians & a servant man" from a single household.[67] Another count claimed 900 lives lost in just one year (1758) in western Virginia, with the overall population cut in half by flight or destruction.[68] And although population growth soon resumed after 1764, many of the settlers who moved south into the Carolinas' surging backcountry carried with them bitter memories that suppressed the differences between friendly and hostile Indians and merged them all into a racial enemy whose eventual removal became a popular goal.

In Pennsylvania, settlements west of the Susquehanna bore the brunt of French and Indian attacks, while those east of the river were full of refugees from the frontier. However, the Carolinas mostly escaped this phase of the war, for Indians from those provinces fought as British allies—the Catawbas in the Braddock campaign, the Cherokees in the successful campaign launched by Braddock's successor, Gen. John Forbes, against Fort Duquesne in 1758. Forbes and his redcoated officers treated the Indians contemptuously, as mercenaries rather than as equals and allies. Thus the Cherokees came home full of resentment, and their mood was not helped by the harassing treatment they received from Virginia settlers as they passed down the Great Valley. French agents and francophile Indians in the Cherokee villages rubbed salt in these wounds, while relations between the Cherokees and South Carolina officials continued to deteriorate.

The South Carolinians had erected two forts in Cherokee country in 1754 and 1756, the first at Keowee, the second (Fort Loudoun) near the Overhill Town of Tellico. Although these were constructed at the Cherokee's invitation, they became on completion a further source of irritation to both sides. The Indians expected the forts to be centers of trade as well as defense and to be populated by the soldiers' wives and children, as stockaded Cherokee villages were, instead of garrisoned only by men. After a series of incidents, including the rape of Cherokee women by a group of white officers, violence broke out on the Carolina frontier in 1759. South Carolina's royal governor, buoyed by British victories over the French in Canada, decided to end his Cherokee problem once and for all by reducing the natives to complete dependency. But a first expedition of South Carolina volunteers led by the governor accomplished nothing but the taking of hostages, some of whom were killed, setting off a new round of Cherokee revenge raids. A second expedition by British regulars fresh from the conquest of Montréal destroyed Keowee and other Lower Towns but was defeated in June 1760 as it passed down the Little Tennessee River toward the Middle Towns of western North Carolina. Finally, a third expedition commanded by James Grant, one of the heroes of the British conquests in Pennsylvania and Canada, broke through the mountains and devasted the Overhill Towns in 1761. The Grant expedition was too late to save Fort Loudoun, which surrendered after a lengthy siege on August 9, 1760.[69] In an incident that became notorious on the frontier, the fort's commander, Paul Demere, had his mouth stuffed with dirt by his executioners, who cried, "'Dog, since you are so hungry for land, eat your fill.'"[70]

Turning aside British demands for the ritual execution of four Indians to atone for the war, Cherokee diplomats successfully negotiated separate treaties with South Carolina and Virginia in the autumn of 1761, both of which looked to the establishment of a permanent boundary line separating Indian lands from white settlers. At this point, violence shifted back toward the northern frontier. Both white and Indian societies were torn by internal divisions as the French and Indian War came to an end. The whites were divided between officials in London and in the colonial capitals who wished to control the cost of war by preventing it—by keeping the native inhabitants and white settlers apart—and speculators and settlers on the frontier who eyed new tracts of Indian land. This disagreement explains the short life of the Royal Proclamation of 1763, which prohibited white settlement beyond the crest of the Allegheny Mountains. It was not as easy to apply such remedies in the field as it must have seemed in London. Washington, his eye on several choice pieces of land west of the mountains, assured his collaborator Crawford that the Proclamation Line would turn out to be only "a temporary expedient to quiet the Minds of the Indians." "Any person," he added, "who neglects the present opportunity of hunting out good lands, and in some measure marking and distinguishing them for his own, in order to keep others from settling them, will never regain it."[71]

In order to keep the cost of the war down, the colonial government had paid Virginia troops in land warrants, promises for free land on the frontier, the precise amounts to vary according to military rank. As an officer who expected to collect thousands of acres by this means, Washington was right about the proclamation of 1763. In order to accommodate the soldiers' warrants, Virginia successfully argued for an extension of the boundary line to the Ohio River. This opened land directly on the Ohio and its major tributaries to settlers and speculators for the first time. Washington offered Crawford a deal that was to be repeated again and again on the Appalachian frontier: Crawford, resident in the newly opened upper Ohio region, would seek out the best parcels of land, and Washington would take care of securing title to them in the colonial capital of Williamsburg, whereupon Crawford would "have such a reasonable proportion of the whole as we may fix upon at our first meeting."[72] In 1770 Washington crossed the mountains again and, guided by Crawford, selected 32,000 choice acres for himself and several thousand more for a syndicate of brother officers.

Settlers moved just as swiftly as speculators; in fact, some speculators—notably Michael Cresap of Maryland—masked their activities by building empty cabins and planting untended cornfields and claiming free land from the colony under the system known as "tomahawk rights," whereby a settler could get free land simply by marking and living on it. Judge Richard Henderson of North Carolina, who had served Earl Granville as Washington had once served Lord Fairfax or Franklin the Penns, stymied because the land immediately west of North Carolina was Cherokee country, began negotiating with the Cherokees for land in Kentucky, notwithstanding the fact that this land fell under Virginia jurisdiction and that neither Virginia nor North Carolina permitted private citizens to buy land directly from the Indians. The Cherokees claimed Kentucky, along with southwest Virginia and much of

Tennessee, as a hunting territory, though it was the Shawnees who actually used it as such most frequently.

Meanwhile, Daniel Boone made his first long hunt into Kentucky in 1769. After six months, his hunting attracted the attention of the Shawnees, and he was firmly but politely told to leave and never return. He made a first unsuccessful attempt to bring settlers into Kentucky in 1773. In 1775 Boone was back, this time on a mission from Henderson to spy out good land. Such a combination—a powerful eastern politician such as Washington or Henderson, allied with an experienced frontiersman such as Crawford or Boone—was to appear again and again in the annals of the Appalachian region. In the face of the machinations that such combinations could achieve, it is no wonder that policies made in far-off imperial capitals dissolved when put into practice in the field.

Native societies were divided between those who wanted to avoid confrontation and those who, by virtue of their temperaments or actions, seemed to promote it. Accommodationists, who sought to achieve peaceful relations with the whites, and militants, who continued to oppose the Euro-American advance, confronted one another throughout Indian country after the French and Indian War. Militant voices grew stronger after 1760, when a religious revival swept the Indian villages. The revival appeared first in a refugee Delaware village on the fringe of Iroquoia, after the villagers beheld a celestial apparition of contending forces struggling against the backdrop of a full moon. The forces from the east won the combat, and the prophets who interpreted the apparition forecast certain doom for all Indian societies unless they returned to traditional ways and cleansed themselves of their degradation by the white peoples' culture. Out of this message grew a second militant initiative: an attempt to create a western confederacy, similar to that of the Iroquois but much broader, reaching out to Shawnees, Delawares, Mingos (Iroquois living outside Iroquoia along the Ohio and elsewhere), Cherokees, and others.[73]

The Shawnees took the lead in preaching the new doctrine, though they were not alone in responding to its appeal. The first fruit of the new militancy was the war of Pontiac's "rebellion" in May 1763, so named for its leader, an Ojibway warrior from southeast Michigan who coordinated a nearly successful attempt to overthrow British rule in the formerly French territories. While the three major bastions acquired from the French—Forts Detroit, Niagara, and Pitt (as the British had renamed Fort Duquesne)—held out through a long siege, smaller outposts fell and the frontier zones of Virginia and Pennsylvania were once again invaded. A British military victory at the Battle of Bushy Run near Pittsburgh in August turned the tide of battle against the Indians, but intermittent warfare continued for a year. A further round of treaties followed between 1768 and 1770. These moved the boundary between white and Indian farther west, this time to the Ohio. Permanent white settlements were established on the river itself, at Pittsburgh and Wheeling, while in the Great Valley settlers pushed farther down the Tennessee watershed toward the Overhill Cherokee territory. While Boone scouted land in the Kentucky interior, Virginia surveyors dragged their chains as far down the Ohio as the falls of the river at modern Louisville.

A new war broke out in the summer of 1774, this time prompted by Shawnee resentment at the land speculators' advance and by a Mingo warrior known by the English name Logan who sought to avenge the slaughter of his entire family by a drunken group of settlers at a place on the Ohio north of Wheeling. This time Andrew Lewis drove yet another road from the Great Valley to the Ohio, linking the James River headwaters with the Great Kanawha, over which he marched 1,100 Virginia militiamen in the fall of 1774, along with supply wagons, flatboats on the Kanawha, and a herd of cattle. Clearly Lewis had learned the lessons of the Sandy Creek campaign. Meeting the Shawnees under their war leader, The Cornstalk, at the junction of the Kanawha and the Ohio, the Virginians prevailed in a pitched battle fought on October 10 in a place that Washington had named Point Pleasant four years before. Governor Dunmore of Virginia, leading a second column down the Ohio from Fort Pitt, hastened to make peace with the Indians on his terms a few days later. This treaty of Camp Charlotte reaffirmed the Euro-Americans' right to travel along the Ohio and to settle along its near bank. Thus Lord Dunmore's War, as it came to be called, closed out one phase of the frontier war for Appalachia and opened another.

During the thirty years that passed between the first intrusions by white settlers and speculators into the Ohio watersheds in the mid-1740s and the end of Dunmore's war in late 1774, the Great Valley north of Tennessee had been secured for Euro-American passage and exploitation, and it had been used as a base from which to secure a second northeast/southwest highway leading into the continent's interior, the Ohio River. That conquest had entailed the building of three east-west wagon roads across the Alleghenies—Forbes's Road, paralleling the Allegheny Path across western Pennsylvania, Braddock's Road, linking the Potomac and the Forks of the Ohio, and the road taken by Lewis's army along the James-Kanawha route. To these would soon

Cherokee ballplayers at Qualla, photographed by James Mooney in 1913–14. The traditional ballgame trained young males to the toughness and discipline required by warfare and was nearly as dangerous. Although the sport of lacrosse developed from this game and attained regional popularity in colleges from North Carolina to New York, Indian players were excluded from intercollegiate competition until federal civil rights laws forced a change during the 1970s. (Smithsonian Institution, National Anthropological Archives)

be added the Wilderness Road, following the trail discovered by Thomas Walker and blazed by Daniel Boone, leading from the Great Valley through Cumberland Gap into Kentucky—a road that, via the Cumberland River, would also extend to the Nashville Basin of Middle Tennessee. Frontier forts guarded the roads, and some of these would grow into Appalachian cities, Pittsburgh being the most obvious example. As the upper Ohio valley attracted settlers to northwestern Virginia and central and northern Kentucky, it became the fourth of the population reservoirs from which the Appalachian region would draw most of its people. All that remained to give Euro-Americans control of Appalachia's future was the elimination of the Iroquois and Cherokee heartlands at the northern and southern ends of the mountains, buffer zones that had forced the white advance into the region's center in the first place. Control of these Indian territories would soon be established as part of the American Revolution.

The Cherokee and Iroquois homelands fell to American armies between 1776 and 1781 in remarkably similar campaigns of the type that later generations would label as "search and destroy." During the first months of the American rebellion against Great Britain, the rebels worked to ensure Indian neutrality while British Indian agents sought to win the native peoples to the imperial side. Cherokee attacks on frontier settlements in 1776 led to a coordinated campaign by all four southern states—Virginia, Georgia, and both Carolinas. "I hope that the Cherokees will now be driven beyond the Mississippi River," Thomas Jefferson stated, "and that this in the future will be declared to the Indians as the invariable consequences of their beginning a war."[74] North Carolina's delegation to the Continental Congress declared it to be among "the duties of a Christian . . . to extinguish the very race of them and scarce to leave enough of their existence to be a vestige in proof that the Cherokee nation once was."[75]

While Georgia forces burned Tugaloo and other villages on the upper Savannah River, columns from the two Carolinas forced the permanent evacuation of the Lower Towns and devastated the Middle and Valley Towns. Virginia forces struck separately down the Warrior's Path to the Overhill Towns. There was only one set battle such as had occurred at Point Pleasant or on the Little Tennessee during the earlier Cherokee War. Otherwise the Indians kept up harassing fire on the expeditions' flanks while withdrawing from their villages into the surrounding mountains. A similar campaign, undertaken at General Washington's direction in 1779–80, devastated the Iroquois heartland. Here, as among the Cherokee, the surprised whites discovered and destroyed orchards and well-ordered croplands, log houses similar to the ones white frontier families lived in, and domesticated hogs, chickens, cattle, and horses.

The American invaders of the Cherokee settlements admired them even as they searched out and destroyed "all things that may be of advantage to our enemies." One Carolina soldier recorded his impressions of the villages he helped burn. There were, he wrote, "curious buildings, great apple trees, and whiteman-like improvements, these we destroyed. . . . We started to another town called Tilicho, a brave plentiful town, abounding with the aforesaid rarities; I may call them rarities; why so? Because they are hemmed in on both sides by or with such large mountains, and likewise the settlements of the soil yielding such abundance of increase, that we could not help conjecturing there was great multitudes of them; the smallest of these Valley Towns, by our computation, exceed two hundred acres of corn, besides crops of potatoes, peas and beans."[76]

It is not hard to understand why the white soldiers, taking note of new surroundings as young men far from home usually do, gave a thought to returning and claiming such inviting spots for their own. Nor is it unimaginable that American authorities, reading such descriptions of native adaptations or approximations of Euro-American culture, fantasized about incorporating native peoples seamlessly into the dominant society. The Cherokees themselves, after the Cherokee War of 1760–61, had adopted a strategy of vesting land and authority near the boundary line in certain *métis* families descended from the unions of white men and native women, seeking in the biculturalism of such families to create a permeable but protective barrier around the core of their society.[77] But at bottom, as the Cherokee leader Corn Tassel reminded negotiators gathered at the Long Island of the Holston River to make peace in 1777, "*We are a separate people!* [The creator] has given [whites and Indians] each their lands, under distinct considerations and circumstances; he has stocked yours with cows, ours with buffalo; yours with hog, ours with bear; yours with sheep, ours with deer. He has, indeed, given you an advantage in this, that your cattle are tame and domestic, while ours are wild and demand not only a larger space for a range, but art to hunt and kill them; they are, nevertheless, as much our property as other animals are yours, and ought not to be taken away without our consent, or for something equivalent."[78]

The victories over the Cherokees and Iroquois during the Revolution were decisive, but not complete, while on the Ohio frontier the war actually ended with Indian triumphs in two cases and, in the last battle, a standoff. The Indian victories came over the Sandusky expedition, an attack across northern Ohio in the spring of 1782 by Pennsylvania frontiersmen commanded by William Crawford. Crawford's capture and subsequent torture and death became a famous episode of frontier lore. At Blue Licks in Kentucky in August 1782 a mixed force of Shawnees and other Ohio Indians, accompanied by British officers, defeated a force of 182 Kentuckians. At Wheeling in September, a force flying the British flag and commanded by Joseph Brant, an educated Mohawk *métis*, invested Fort Henry for three days; though the fort managed to hold them off, the Indians moved on to do damage to other settlements in the Monongahela country.

These still-recent events explain why the Indians north and south of the Ohio were astonished to learn that, in negotiations with the new United States, the British had ceded to the Americans sovereignty over the entire west from the Appalachians to the Mississippi. None of the native societies were immediately stripped of their territory. Rather, the process unfolded over a period of years, extending between roughly 1790 and 1840. The Ohio

Indians would lose their lands completely; the Iroquois and Cherokees lost theirs by degrees, beginning with Cherokee cessions at the Treaty of Hopewell in 1785 but proceeding much more rapidly for the Iroquois, who by 1797 were reduced to a scattering of tiny reservations in upstate New York, Canada, or, in the case of the Senecas, in the hills of northwest Pennsylvania. All native societies were swept by religious and secular movements that sought to reconcile the painful contradictions between accommodationism and the preservation of traditional ways. Followers of the Delaware and Shawnee prophets courted swift and, eventually, total defeats. In the cases of the Seneca reformer Handsome Lake and the Cherokee Sequoyah, their peoples endured, though they did not prevail.

The Cherokees necessarily claim most of our attention here, since their fate unfolded in the heart of Appalachia, whereas the Iroquois on the northern periphery no longer shaped events in the region. In the aftermath of the war, the Shawnees and other Indians now resident in Ohio threw off their former deference to the Iroqouis and assumed the mantle of leadership of a western confederacy. Shawnee and Delaware militants continued to preach resistance to white advances in the Ohio valley and to send out war hatchets to other peoples, including the Cherokees. The Cherokees, having negotiated a peace in 1777, divided and began fighting again in 1779. In that same year, they received Shawnee delegations that came to live in their towns, while some Cherokee militants went to live in Shawnee towns in Ohio. When Virginia militia detachments struck south at the Overhill Towns, they found them once again undefended. Instead, Cherokee militants moved their villages to more easily defended locations and were resupplied by the British.

These developments in turn reflected divisions within native societies, between accommodationists and militants but also between young and old, men and women. A Cherokee's reaction to the unfolding events of the revolutionary era depended in part on where he or she stood within native society. Older men with memories of earlier losses and bloodshed were more of a mind to trade land for peace and trade goods. Cherokee women—the owners, within Cherokee tradition, of the houses, crops, orchards, and domestic animals that were destroyed by the American armies—were likewise inclined toward compromise and peace. But young men depended on hunting and, to a lesser extent, on raiding to support their positions within native society and to validate their existence as men.

The Algonquian prophets who preached a return to the old ways found a ready audience among young men, even if the Cherokees did not respond to the religious message as Shawnees and Delawares had done. Dragging Canoe objected to the selling of land in Kentucky to Richard Henderson and his Transylvania Company, to the toleration of Virginia settlers in the Watauga district of upper East Tennessee, and to the concessions made to the victorious Americans at the Treaty of Long Island of the Holston in 1777. In fact, Dragging Canoe boycotted the latter conference, traveled to Mobile and Detroit to consult with British authorities, and exchanged views with Shawnee militants who were at that time opposing the new Kentucky settlements with fire, gun, and ax. Although Dragging Canoe himself died from smallpox in 1778, his followers remained united and began separating themselves from the rest of Cherokee society, moving southwest along the Tennessee River to the vicinity of Chickamauga Creek, just east of the point where the river breaks through the Cumberland Mountains. Here, as at the Long Island on the Holston, the Warrior's Path intersected with other pathways, roads that connected the Cherokee homeland in both symbolic and practical ways with the larger world in which they exercised their autonomy as a people. This location led the militants to be called "Chickamaugas," but their name for themselves is equally revealing: *Ani-Yun'wiya*, "the real people."[79]

The Chickamauga warriors, together with those of the Shawnees, Delawares and Mingos of the upper Ohio, made the years following the formal peace with Great Britain the bloodiest era of warfare on the Appalachian frontier. While the new United States now had territorial jurisdiction over both of the great natural northeast-southwest highways of the Appalachian region—the Warrior's Path through the Great Valley and the Ohio River from its source to its mouth—none of the east-west roads that linked these two corridors was secure. Forbes's Road, though protected by a chain of forts extending across Pennsylvania from Carlisle to Pittsburgh, remained open to attack from the north by the Senecas. Southwest Pennsylvania and northwest Virginia, where Braddock's and Forbes's Roads converged at the Ohio, and the Kentucky settlements at the west end of the Wilderness Road were subject to repeated attacks by small raiding parties, for after Blue Licks and Fort Henry, the Indians did not offer set battles. Small groups of warriors could slip across the Ohio and thread through the mountains over lesser paths, dodging around the thickened networks of white settlements to surprise settlers in their beds or pen them up in small forts. "The families belonging to these forts were so attached to their own cabins on their farms that they seldom moved into their fort in the spring until compelled by some alarm, as they called it."

[Then] the express came softly to the door, or back window, and by a gentle tapping waked the family. This was easily done, as an habitual fear made us ever watchful and sensible to the slightest alarm. The whole family were instantly in motion. My father seized his gun and other implements of war. My stepmother waked up and dressed the children as well she could. . . . There was no possibility of getting a horse in the night to aid us in removing to the fort. Besides the little children, we caught up what articles of clothing and provision we could get hold of in the dark, for we durst not light a candle or even stir the fire. All this was done with the utmost dispatch and the silence of death. The greatest care was taken not to awaken the youngest child. To the rest it was enough to say *Indian* and not a whimper was heard afterwards. Thus it often happened that the whole number of families who were in the evening at their homes were all in their little fortress before the dawn of the next morning. In the course of the succeeding day their household furniture was brought in by parties of the men under arms.[80]

It is not hard to see why the psychological stress of such circumstances, not to mention the stories of death, torture, captivity, and destruction that were repeated endlessly on the frontier, bred a furious resentment among settlers, both at the Indians and at eastern governments that afforded the settlers scant protection. Meanwhile, the Chickamaugas, sometimes accompanied by Shawnees but at times fighting alone, made travel along the Wilderness Road hazardous and raided white settlements both in Kentucky and along the Cumberland River in Middle Tennessee. They also harassed the Watauga settlements and prevented the American occupation of north Georgia. As the Lower Towns of South Carolina lost their lands to American officers and the Valley and Middle Towns of western North Carolina faced an oncoming tide of white settlers, the Overhill villages became the center of Cherokee society. The Chickamauga command of the paths leading from the Tennessee River east and south across Georgia and Alabama preserved this area to become a new center of gravity of the Cherokee nation.

In 1790 American forces under Gen. Josiah Harmar invaded the militants' Ohio territory, but the expedition ended in defeat and the frontier war continued with renewed intensity. In 1791 a larger American expedition commanded by Gen. Arthur St. Clair met a similar fate. Chickamauga militants were participants in both victories and in 1792 led a combined assault with Creek and Shawnee allies that nearly destroyed Buchanan's Station in Middle Tennessee. However, the attack failed largely because Cherokees from the older towns warned the Americans. This signaled the reemergence of serious internal divisions among the Cherokees and the turning of events in their enemies' favor. In 1794–95, combined diplomatic and military offensives yielded results for the Americans. Jay's Treaty, negotiated in London in 1794, led to British withdrawal from the frontier posts from which Indian militants had drawn supplies and encouragement. The Spanish in Florida also cut back on their support of southern Indians and in 1795 signed a treaty settling outstanding issues with the United States.

In 1794 an expedition of Kentucky and Cumberland militia attacked and destroyed two Chickamauga towns, leading in turn to a treaty at Tellico whereby the Chickamaugas were urged to reunite with the peaceful Cherokees.[81] Meanwhile, U.S. general Anthony Wayne mounted a campaign against the Ohio Indians that led to victory at the Battle of Fallen Timbers in northwest Ohio and the ensuing Treaty of Greenville in 1795. Under terms of this treaty, the Shawnees and their allies in the western confederacy withdrew from the territory now encompassed in the state of Ohio and accepted reservations far from the Ohio River. The Chickamaugas were not part of this treaty, but they understood its implications. Though divisions between accommodationists and militants continued to affect Cherokee society, the Chickamaugan resistance dwindled and most of the militants reunited with the larger Cherokee society.[82] When, a generation later, the Shawnee prophet Tenskwatawa and his militant warrior brother Tecumseh preached pan-Indian unity, few Cherokees responded. In fact, in the Creek War that accompanied the War of 1812 in the southern states, the Cherokees fought on the American side.[83]

Virginia militiamen from the Shenandoah Valley were the first troops from outside New England to join General Washington's rebel encirclement of Boston in the summer of 1775, having marched a "bee line to Boston" covering six hundred miles in twenty-four days. The daring Kaskaskia and Vincennes raids by Virginia militia under George Rogers Clark in 1778 and 1779 drew on frontiersmen from the Appalachian region. During the following year, a lull in Indian fighting permitted a contingent of frontiersmen from southwest Virginia and upper East Tennessee to march over the Carolina Blue Ridge to win a decisive victory over the British at the Battle of Kings Mountain, South Carolina, on October 7, 1780. These are three examples of Appalachia's contributions to the cause of American independence. The victory of the Overmountain Men at King's Mountain has been a favorite staple of the region's historical lore, especially as it involved victory over an opponent who had advertised his contempt for the backcountry men. Loyalism did not prevail, as the British commander expected, but the backcountry records of the time are full of resentment against the considerable number of settlers who remained loyal to the Crown or else refused to take either side in the war. Some families pressed deeper into the woods to avoid the conflict. Thus loyalists or neutrals were among the first settlers of the remote high valleys of the Blue Ridge plateau.

The removal of imperial authority eliminated one of the few restraints on the displacement of Appalachia's Indian peoples. The acquisition of all British territorial claims east of the Mississippi and south of the Great Lakes meant that Appalachia was no longer a frontier that abutted foreign powers. It was surrounded by U.S. territory, containing much land in the Middle West and Gulf South that was more attractive and accessible than land in the uplands. The revolutionary settlement, by vesting sovereignty in the states, meant that future boundary adjustments within Appalachia would be unlikely. Rather, the geometric lines that had divided the colonial beachheads were extended inland, slicing across the mountains and valleys as an invisible grid that ultimately did as much to shape Appalachian society as the natural contours these boundaries ignored. Surveyors' lines became the predominant Appalachian boundary, separating Pennsylvania from Maryland and Virginia and extending Mason and Dixon's line west almost to the Ohio, creating an anomalous sliver of Virginia that extended northward along the Ohio and cut off northwestern Virginia from its natural metropolis at Pittsburgh. Virginia's southern boundary was extended to the Mississippi, lopping off the Watauga and Holston settlements from southwest Virginia and providing, with minor adjustments, the eventual border between Kentucky and Tennessee. North Carolina's boundary with Georgia roughly followed the 35th parallel, which would also be the dividing line between Tennessee and Alabama.

Rivers, which had traditionally been avenues that united rather than divided both banks, were another typical recourse of boundary makers. The Potomac was already established as Maryland's boundary with Virginia, while Georgia's with South Carolina followed the Savannah headwaters up to the North Carolina line. In 1792 Kentucky and (West) Virginia separated along the Big Sandy River and its lesser Tug Fork, which happened to be in flood when the boundary commissioners visited it and so misled them to draw the line here instead of along the main Levisa Fork farther west. The Ohio had been the boundary between Indians and whites for a generation following the Proclamation of 1763. Now it became—with the Mason-Dixon Line—the boundary between north and south, between free labor and slave.

Apart from county boundaries, only four boundaries in Appalachia follow ridgelines, the natural regional subdividers in so many ways. A forty-mile section of the North Carolina–South Carolina boundary follows the crest of the Blue Ridge in the neighborhood of Saluda Gap, following the boundary line drawn after the Cherokee War of 1760–61; this border is thus the only surviving remnant in the United States of the Royal Proclamation Line of 1763. North Carolina's boundary with Tennessee, drawn in 1796, roughly follows the crests of the mountains that define the western edge of the Blue Ridge plateau. A portion of the Virginia-Kentucky boundary follows the crest of Pine Mountain, separating the Cumberland headwaters from those of the Tennessee and Big Sandy. Finally, seventy-five miles of the four-hundred-mile-long boundary drawn between West Virginia and Virginia in 1863 follow the crest of Allegheny Mountain. The net effect of the boundary drawing that took place during this period was to separate numerous hinterlands from their metropolises and to create Appalachia as a nonpolitical region defined as often by what it was not as by what it was. The sectional alignments built into each state by the inclusion of a part of Appalachia was a source of tension in politics and offers a basic reason why Appalachian people were unable to address or even to formulate regionwide problems before the federal government intervened in the region during the twentieth century.

Another impact of the postrevolutionary era was the extension of the social order of the lowland South into the Appalachian region. This was not due solely to the Revolution itself. The process had been well under way since the mid-eighteenth century, but the Revolution consolidated and expanded it, especially through the boost that it gave to land speculation and absentee ownership. The trend began in backcountry South Carolina, where leadership had begun to constitute itself on a hierarchical model at the end of the Cherokee War of 1760–61.[84] In Virginia, the aristocratic leadership that contributed so much to national affairs during the revolutionary era avoided political innovation at home. The state constitution adopted in 1776 was essentially the colonial constitution, minus the king. The powers of royal governors were lodged in the legislature, which remained the creature of the local oligarchies that dominated county government throughout the state. "This was not the government we fought for," Thomas Jefferson complained, but it nevertheless remained in effect throughout most of the antebellum period, forcing ambitious Virginians in the Appalachian half of the state to adapt to it, whether they liked the old constitution or not.

Each of the newly independent states adopted new constitutions in 1776, but all of the Appalachian states except Pennsylvania and Kentucky required property ownership as a condition of voting and holding office. North Carolina and Tennessee permitted otherwise qualified free black males to vote, at least until both revised their state constitutions in the mid-1830s. Pennsylvania abolished slavery in 1780, and even though the process of abolition was gradual, with slaveholding theoretically possible in the state as late as 1840, in fact most slaves were freed by 1800. This action was one of the things that set the Keystone State apart from the southern territories that had comprised Greater Pennsylvania during colonial times. The Northwest Ordinance of 1787, by which the federal government obtained Virginia's cession of its territorial claims north and west of the Ohio River, also abolished slavery in the future states created from this territory. Thus the Ohio valley, like the Great Valley in the east, was divided into slave and free zones. Settlers from New England, seeking western lands but avoiding slave territory, created Ohio's first Euro-American settlement in 1788 at Marietta, across the river from Virginia. The differences that emerged between these Ohioans and their Virginia neighbors or between the inhabitants of the Great Valley north and south of the Maryland-Pennsylvania border offer measurements of just how "southern" Southern Appalachia would become.

The influence of slavery in the southern states was reflected in the allocation of power among the plantation and upland districts of the seaboard states. In North Carolina, the small counties clustered along the tidal bays of the coast continued to dominate the state legislature. Even though new counties were created in the interior to accommodate the influx of settlers into the backcountry, these counties were large in area and were restricted to two votes each in the legislature, whereas the plantation counties, though smaller, were further subdivided so that the east could maintain its majority. In Virginia, tidewater counties elected an absolute majority in the legislature, even though the majority of voters lived west of the fall line and, after 1840, west of the Blue Ridge.

The "federal number" embedded in the U.S. Constitution, which allowed $\frac{3}{5}$ of the enslaved population to be counted in apportioning seats in the House of Representatives, further privileged the plantation counties, both in federal elections and in the apportioning of seats in the state legislatures, which among other powers elected U.S. senators. Not surprisingly, several of the senators elected from the Appalachian portions of their states became ardent defenders of slavery, including John C. Calhoun of South Carolina and Thomas Clingman of North Carolina. Thus underrepresentation in the legislatures encouraged highland politicians with statewide ambitions to find ways of demonstrating loyalty to the slave system, even while continuing to agitate for the "white basis"—that is, apportionment in state elections on the basis of white population only.

In Tennessee, on the other hand, the east-to-west settlement pattern meant that Appalachian Tennessee held some of the same initial advantages as the coastal counties of the seaboard states. But these advantages were quickly eliminated after the state entered the union in 1796. The political rivalry between John Sevier and William Blount, which shaped Tennessee politics during an entire post-Revolution generation, was in many respects a competition between East and Middle Tennessee, even though both leaders lived in the east. When the population of Middle Tennessee outstripped that of the eastern part of the state, apportionment in the legislature and related power arrangements were changed to reflect this fact. Sectionalism, as in other Appalachian states, remained a staple of Tennessee political life during the antebellum period, but here at least the mountainous east did not fight its sectional battles under the handicaps that afflicted its neighbors in Virginia, North Carolina, or Georgia. The contrasting actions of East Tennessee leaders during the ultimate sectional crisis in 1861 may be one of the results.

Led by Virginia and North Carolina, the southern states replicated their hierarchical model of society in their distribution of Appalachian land. This process began before the Revolution, when both Virginia and North Carolina offered warrants for free land in their western territories to men who would fight in the French and Indian War, on terms that gave enlisted men dozens of acres, officers hundreds or even thousands. Military land warrants were also used to reward veterans of the Revolution and the accompanying Indian wars, while treasury warrants were sold directly by state governments to cash purchasers. A detailed study of the subject notes that officers could accumulate warrants for thousands of acres in Virginia and North Carolina, seaboard states that at the end of the Revolution shaped the destinies of three other states—West Virginia, Kentucky, and Tennessee—as well as that of their own Appalachian lands.

By flooding the market with warrants for land by the millions of acres, the seaboard states eliminated much of their revolutionary debt, but they also created a fevered market for speculation. Investors based in Richmond, Baltimore, Philadelphia, and the tidewater plantation districts grabbed up the bulk of the warrants, often for a fraction of their official value. In contrast to the careful surveys that had been run for Washington and other prewar speculators, these new land allocations usually consisted of large blocks whose boundaries ignored natural contours. Tight political control of official survey licenses and the long and difficult distances between frontier locations and the land offices in eastern capitals meant that settlers or small-time speculators—which often amounted to the same thing—competed at a disadvantage with the well connected. Moreover, the acreages claimed by prerevolutionary land companies created complications everywhere for settlers who had occupied and improved their plots but lacked a title that quieted the land companies' overlapping claims.[85]

Even in the best of circumstances, a land buyer—settler or speculator—needed the help of local notables, especially surveyors and lawyers, to obtain a secure title and to manage the land subsequently, if the purchasers did not intend to occupy it themselves. These offices were routes to preferment in the upland districts, leading to possible parity with or even entry into the planter-dominated upper class. A case in point was provided by the Jacksons of northwestern Virginia, the offspring of John Jackson, a wiry and diminutive Irish Protestant who emigrated by way of London, and Elizabeth Cummings, a tall and powerful Londoner who was one of the few women to come to colonial America by herself at her own expense. These two met and married in Maryland and followed the Potomac by stages into and over the Alleghenies to the upper Monongahela valley of northwestern Virginia, producing along the way a family of eight children, one of whom became the grandfather of the celebrated Civil War general.

Stonewall Jackson's background is sometimes portrayed as typically Appalachian: "He was a mountain man [with] the blunt honesty, the firmness, and the self-reliance of a frontiersman from the remote western parts of Virginia," according to one biographer.[86] In fact, Jackson was a scion of a cadet branch of a powerful family, one that had parlayed frontier warfare and land acquisition into positions of leadership and wealth. His great-uncle George Jackson was a lawyer who led the fight in Virginia to override the claims of colonial land companies in the postrevolutionary era in favor of those who held land directly from the state—claims that included 60,000 acres he accumulated for himself. George's brother Edward, Stonewall's grandfather, was a surveyor and state legislator who acquired 73,000 acres on his own and another 52,000 as the local agent for nonresident speculators. George Jackson was a member of the Virginia convention that ratified the U.S. Constitution in 1788 and served three terms in the U.S. Congress during the 1790s; he was succeeded there by his son John George Jackson, who represented northwestern Virginia for six terms before moving on to a federal judgeship in 1819, at which point the congressional seat went to his brother. John George's cousin Jonathan Jackson, Stonewall's father, was a lawyer who won admission to the bar at the age of twenty and soon thereafter entered upon his career as an officeholder, starting near the top as the federal collector of internal revenue for western Virginia, an appointment made by President James Madison, into whose family John George Jackson had married. Meanwhile, the latter built a plantation-style mansion, modeled on Madison's Montpelier, at Clarksburg on the Monongahela, where the family established a number of commercial and industrial enterprises employing slave labor. Political and economic power, then as now, were closely related and flowed from the center, especially in Virginia.[87]

The life of another, unrelated man named Jackson likewise demonstrated that upward mobility on the Appalachian frontier depended on the patronage of the established upper class. Andrew Jackson, born in the Carolina border district of the Waxhaws in 1770, grew up, as Stonewall would later do, as an orphan surrounded by numerous and influential kin. As a young man studying law in Salisbury in Piedmont North Carolina, Jackson came to the attention of William Blount and, under Blount's direction, moved to Tennessee, flourished as Blount's agent there, and eventually succeeded to the considerable economic and political power that Blount had accumulated successively in East, Middle, and West Tennessee. Blount himself was a wealthy planter from the tidewater section of North Carolina, whose western fortunes were based on the accumulation of soldiers' land warrants and of millions of acres of Tennessee land handed out by North Carolina authorities.[88] Thus Andrew Jackson's white-pillared home, The Hermitage near Nashville, like John George Jackson's imitation of Madison's Montpelier in Clarksburg, (West) Virginia, embodied the tribute of ambitious westerners to the plantation elite whose patronage they had earned. The military genius displayed by both Jacksons was doubtless a product of talent, not birth, but in the perfection and expression of that talent, each had had, as his widow's biography of Stonewall Jackson commented about his appointment to West Point, a lot of help from his friends.[89]

The impact of class on the land allocation process may be discerned in the contrasting fates of some other honored names on the Appalachian frontier. Daniel Boone contributed more than any other single individual to the opening of Kentucky to Euro-American settlement. Moreover, his talent and leadership were widely recognized by frontiersmen, and it was by popular demand rather than through official connections that Boone was commissioned an officer of the Virginia militia in 1774. "Boone is an excellent woodsman," wrote another officer. "If that only would qualify him for the Office, no man would be more proper." In the face of impending war with the Shawnees, talent was indeed enough to qualify Boone, and so William Preston, the commander of the militia on the southwest Virginia frontier, using blank commissions provided by Governor Dunmore, appointed him.

Preston was the nephew and heir of the land speculator James Patton and also the surveyor of Fincastle County, which then included all of Kentucky; Preston's nephew-in-law, John Floyd, became his deputy for Kentucky. Preston was a staunch defender of Virginia's authority over Kentucky and an opponent of the North Carolina–based Transylvania Company, in whose service Boone had labored to bring settlers to Kentucky before 1776. Thus the rewards Boone expected as a result of his services to the land company did not materialize, and when Floyd and Boone quarreled over a particular tract of land in 1780, Floyd's arguments carried the day.[90] Floyd himself died fighting the Shawnees at Blue Licks two years later, but his son and grandson of the same name, thanks to family influence and money, established a western Virginia political dynasty whose members were active in Virginia and West Virginia politics into the twentieth century.

Meanwhile, another set of Preston nephews—William, Andrew, and John Breckenridge—and their cousin John Brown established a comparable dynasty in Kentucky. Even though he did not go there to live until the Indian danger was past and Kentucky statehood accomplished in 1793, John Breckenridge already owned thousands of acres of land there thanks to the efforts of his older brothers, both deputy surveyors under the Virginia government; indeed, his decision to move to Kentucky was partly inspired by the danger that the new state government there would take actions unfavorable to non-resident landowners. Even before Breckenridge arrived in the new state, he was elected to represent it in Congress.[91]

Boone, on the other hand, left the state, landless, in 1789, notwithstanding his having filed at least twenty-nine claims on a total of nearly 39,000 acres during his residence there. Boone did acquire enough land to provide for his children who remained behind in Kentucky, but otherwise he shared the fate of at least half of Kentucky settlers who had land warrants but ended up without any land. At the same time, eastern Kentucky, part of the future core of Appalachia, was papered over with speculative claims by absentee landlords, as were neighboring sections of West Virginia and Tennessee. An inquiry into the origins of wealth and poverty in Appalachian Kentucky concludes that "the legacy of colonial Virginia's land laws was a nightmarish pattern of hopelessly overlapping land clams that caused Kentucky to become a 'hothouse of litigation' and frustrated the hopes of many thousands of homesteaders of acquiring property there."[92]

The deleterious effects of land speculation, the commodification of land through the issuance of treasury and military warrants, the difficulty of obtaining correct surveys and clear titles, the shifting tides of settlement caused by the intermittent nature of Indian warfare, the inconsistency of state policies in the taxation of land: All these factors led to shingled claims and to the legal procedures by which thousands of actual residents were later forced to transfer the ownership of their land and/or the rights to the timber on and the minerals under it to nonresident corporations in the industrial era. In preindustrial times, according to one study, inequality in landed property was greater in the Appalachian backcountry than anywhere else in America, notwithstanding the image of volunteer independence and equality among frontiersmen conveyed in the popular histories of the times. Landlessness in the Appalachian states ranged from 51 percent in western Virginia to 36 percent in eastern Kentucky, while absentee ownership of land ranged from 93 percent in the future West Virginia to 33 percent in western Maryland (where veteran officers were awarded only one hundred acres and residency laws limited the acreage that absentee owners could acquire).[93]

It should be pointed out, however, that Pennsylvania—despite the most liberal state constitution of the revolutionary era and a democratic ethos that some conservatives compared to the extremes of the French Revolution—distributed the lands it seized from the Penn family in 1779 and those it acquired from the Iroquois in 1784 in much the same fashion as did Virginia and North Carolina. Large land companies acquired title to millions of acres in northwest Pennsylvania, for example, during the years between 1792 and 1820. The North American Land Company, one of the companies that speculated in Appalachian Virginia and Kentucky, also operated in Pennsylvania. Similar events occurred in New York after that state acquired the bulk of the remaining Iroquois land after 1790.[94] The major difference was that speculators in these states, as in Maryland, were often residents, not on the land in question but in cities such as Baltimore, Philadelphia, and New York.

Worth noting also is the fact that desirable land distributed under more equitable systems often went to speculators as well. This happened in northern Alabama, where land acquired from the Cherokees in 1819 was distributed using the federal land survey system first employed in Ohio, and in Georgia, where the state government used a lottery system to award warrants for free land. In the Huntsville district of Alabama, for example, the best croplands went to planters, many of them migrants from eastern Virginia, while the settlers who competed with them got ridgetop and cove lands in the nearby Cumberland plateau.[95] Moreover, some historians emphasize the widespread availability of land in Appalachia's preindustrial era, notwithstanding the claims of absentee owners and speculators. It is possible that both viewpoints are right, if we distinguish between ownership of land and its use by persons without official title. In the next chapter, this book explores the further ramifications of land and landlessness for Appalachian people in the preindustrial age. At the very least, the many frustrations that would-be settlers encountered in acquiring land on the Appalachian frontier helps to account for the voracious land hunger that prevailed during the late eighteenth and early nineteenth centuries.

Land hunger acquired a new focus in the southwestern part of Appalachia at the turn of the nineteenth century. Georgia, the youngest, most southerly, poorest, and least populous British colony before 1776, grew rapidly during the postrevolutionary decades, its population increasing from 50,000 people right after the Revolution to 162,000 in 1800 and 691,000 in 1840.[96] Leading the migrant stream—which now turned west along the trading path that stretched from Augusta on the South Carolina border across central Georgia through Alabama and Mississippi,—were the sort of people that the Indians called "Virginians," the descendants of the migrants who had earlier filled up the Carolina backcountry. Spilling out across the Piedmont of central Georgia, the tide of settlers provoked new Indian confrontations, culminating in the Creek War of 1813–14. Andrew Jackson's victory over the Creeks and his unauthorized invasion of Florida five years later led to further Indian land cessions and to Spain's withdrawal from Florida in 1821. By 1826, the Creeks and allied peoples had ceded all of their lands in Georgia extending to the Chattahoochee River, which formed the state's western boundary. Meanwhile Congress, reacting to a massive land-jobbing and bribery scandal known as the Yazoo affair, had transferred to the federal government Georgia's territorial claim on the future states of Alabama and Mississippi. In return, Georgia was promised federal assistance in eliminating *all* remaining Indians in the state, awarding their lands to Georgia and removing the people themselves westward. In 1823 Georgia pointedly reminded Congress of this promise, and in 1826, having eliminated the Creeks from its territory, the state turned its attention northward to the mountainous lands still held by the Cherokees.

In 1773, at a treaty held at Augusta, the Cherokees had reluctantly ceded land on the Savannah River in northeast Georgia. In 1805, overriding the fear that if wagon roads were built "then the whites will be among us," they agreed to the construction of a federal road across their territory, linking Augusta with northwest Georgia, where the road branched into other roads leading north to Knoxville and northwest to Nashville in Tennessee. This road was completed in 1807.[97] In a treaty of 1819, the Cherokees made a further land cession of several million acres, giving up their claim to most of East Tennessee, part of Alabama, and about half of their land in western North Carolina. Over half of the remaining Cherokee territory was located in Georgia, running from the Blue Ridge north and west to the Tennessee River just across the state line. The Cherokees also retained the northeastern corner of Alabama and adjacent parts of Tennessee and North Carolina south of the Hiwassee River.[98] At this point the Cherokees determined to hold the line. Their determination was based in part on the confidence born of a remarkable social transformation that occurred after the Chickamaugas were beaten in 1794:

> No other tribe had become so rapidly acculturated, "Christianized," and "civilized." Far from displaying the lack of intelligence, industry, moral discipline, and desire for improvement that [Andrew] Jackson considered innate in the "inferior" red race, the Cherokees, within a single generation, had created a social, economic, and political order so prosperous, stable, and progressive that it rivaled those of most of the frontier regions on their borders. They had given up a hunting economy for a farming economy. They had adopted written laws and a constitution. . . . They encouraged their children to attend mission schools. Their remarkable linguist, Sequoyah, who neither spoke nor read English, had invented in 1821 a simple way to write the Cherokee language and by 1828 they were publishing a bilingual tribal newspaper.[99]

Not the least of the Cherokees' accomplishments was their success in limiting the damage that alcohol inflicted on their society. Thanks to the work of tribal leaders and Protestant missionaries who established schools and training facilities in Cherokee territory after 1801, the drunkenness that had devastated so many Native American societies was not a Cherokee problem. There were, however, class differences among the Cherokees that approximated those of white society. The majority of Cherokees were still traditionalist and "full-blood," illiterate and poor, living simply in remote mountain valleys. Tribal leaders, by contrast, were drawn disproportionately from *métis* families; John Ross, the principal chief elected in 1828, was at most one-eighth Cherokee, and even Sequoyah, despite his thoroughly traditional upbringing, was the son of a white man. The Cherokee elite owned stores, mills, and forges, and several operated large plantations with slave labor. The Nation's new capital, New Echota, was located near the junction of the Knoxville and Nashville forks in the Federal Road; the leading mission school was located on Chicka-mauga Creek, not far from a town that was beginning to emerge at the point where the Federal Road paralleled the Tennessee River. This place was called Ross's Landing in reference to the principal chief's Scottish father, who had established a trading post and tannery near the mouth of Chattanooga Creek in 1800.

Georgia authorities increasingly asserted the state's sovereignty over Cherokee territory during the 1820s, and their Cherokee counterparts just as consistently challenged this assertion. But then in 1829 there occurred two events that from the Cherokee perspective must be counted as disasters. One was the inauguration of Andrew Jackson as president of the United States. A man who shared the Indian-hating outlook that prevailed on the backcountry frontier and whose military reputation was based in large part on Indian war-fare, Jackson determined to complete the process of removing all remaining eastern Indians to territories west of the Mississippi River. The Indian Re-moval Act, passed by Congress at Jackson's urging in 1830, made this goal official United States policy. When the Cherokees successfully challenged Georgia's legal aggressions against them before the U.S. Supreme Court in 1830 and again in 1831, Jackson took no action to enforce the decisions, call-ing the court's rulings "still born."[100]

The second disaster was the discovery of gold on Cherokee land near the present-day city of Dahlonega, Georgia. This set off the first American gold rush, with hordes of goldseekers pushing into Cherokee country in defiance of tribal authorities and of federal soldiers who briefly tried to stem the influx. In 1829 Georgia created ten counties on Cherokee territory, declared the au-thority of the Cherokee government invalid, took steps to punish missionar-ies and other non-Indians who supported the Cherokee position, and pre-pared to hold a lottery whereby Georgia citizens—but neither Indians nor squatters who were already occupying Cherokee land—could compete for a chance to acquire land within the Cherokee boundary. In the drawing held on October 22, 1832, 85,000 citizens competed for 18,309 "land lots" of 160 acres each, while 133,000 competed for 35,000 40-acre "gold lots" in the gold district.[101] Since the winning tickets were transferable, another land market was created for speculators, who ended up with the lion's share of the land made available in this way. In the meantime, Ross and other tribal leaders searched desperately for a way to head off the removal movement in Con-gress, but without success. Under the dual pressures of the gold rush and Georgia's open invitation to whites to defy Cherokee authority, conditions in the Nation deteriorated to the point of chaos, not just in Georgia, but also in

North Carolina and Alabama, where squatters who didn't want to miss out on the upcoming opportunity began to move onto Indian land.

In 1835 the Jackson administration located a cohort of Cherokee leaders, headed by a political rival of John Ross, who agreed to sign a treaty accepting the terms of removal: payment of $5,000,000 for the Cherokee's land and improvements, along with federal absorption of the costs of removal. Ross and his supporters, a majority within the Nation, disputed the validity of this treaty and in a hard-fought battle nearly succeeded in preventing its ratification by the U.S. Senate, where it passed by one only vote. The ratified treaty now had the force of law and called for the removal of all Cherokees within two years. When a majority of Cherokees refused to comply, Jackson's successor, Martin Van Buren, ordered the U.S. army to round them up forcibly, an order that was carried out in the spring and summer of 1838. The poet Ralph Waldo Emerson was one of many prominent Americans who appealed to Van Buren on the Cherokee's behalf: "You, sir, will bring down that renowned chair in which you sit into infamy," he wrote, "and the name of this nation, hitherto the sweet omen of religion and liberty, will stink to the world."[102]

Emerson was right. The Cherokee Removal, both in the racism that underpinned the policy and the brutality with which it was carried out, now ranks as one of the saddest and least honorable events in American history. In October 1838, after having been held in stockades through a hot and disease-ridden summer, the Cherokees started out by river and wagon road to their new home in Oklahoma. Some 1,500 Indians died in the stockades. Another 1,600 died en route along "the trail where they cried," as it was called in the Cherokee language. Added to this toll were hundreds of deaths due to exposure, sickness, and malnutrition among refugees who hid from the federal dragnet in the most remote mountain areas and among those newly arrived in Oklahoma. These 4,000 or more deaths thus amounted to at least a quarter of the 16,456 Cherokees enumerated in a special census held in conjunction with the removal policy in 1835. A Georgia soldier who took part in the expulsion later wrote: "I fought through the Civil War and have seen men shot to pieces and slaughtered by thousands, but the Cherokee removal was the cruelest work I ever knew."[103]

Not all of the Cherokees went west, however. Several hundred Cherokees living in western North Carolina took advantage of a loophole in the removal law by becoming citizens of that state. When other North Carolina Cherokees assisted in tracking down and executing the handful of Indians who offered violent resistance to the roundup, they too were allowed to stay. William H.

Thomas, a white North Carolinian who had been adopted by and raised in proximity to the tribe, began a lifelong crusade to acquire land where the Cherokees could live peacefully and follow their traditional culture. The result was the 73,000-acre Qualla Boundary in the Oconaluftee valley; the Boundary survived thirty years of ambiguous legal status until Thomas managed to secure official recognition by the state and federal governments in 1866 and 1868, respectively.

In the meantime, as the removal crisis subsided, Cherokees who had been hiding out in the Smokies or in remote places in Tennessee, Alabama, and Georgia drifted into Qualla, as did a few returnees from the west, notably the aged warrior Junaluska, who returned in 1846 to die in the land of his ancestors. This Eastern Band of the Cherokee Nation, as it came to be called, numbered 1,517 persons in 1850, and 1,881 persons in 1884.[104] In addition to the inhabitants of Qualla, a number of small mixed-race communities of Indian and *métis* descent survived in remote locations in central West Virginia and in the region where Virginia, Tennessee, and Kentucky converge. Eventually, after most of the real Indians were gone, claiming an Indian ancestor—usually a Cherokee and preferably a princess—became a customary way among whites of explaining dark complexions in a Negrophobic society.[105]

With the tragedy of the Trail of Tears, the first phase of Appalachian history came to a close. Thanks to the rumors of gold that had circulated three hundred years earlier, the aboriginal peoples of the mountains first faced the disease and destruction that accompanied the European invasion of America. Now the actuality of gold in north Georgia gleamed briefly but brightly enough to lead the process of destruction and loss to its logical end. After 1838 Appalachia was "a white man's country," surrounded on all sides by Euro-American settlements. In the course of the nineteenth century, the violent frontier of displacement and repopulation gave way to a different type of frontier, one that blended the culture of the colonial and early republican backcountry with that of an emerging urban-industrial society.

I am of the opinion that it is as hard, or harder, for the people of the west to gain religion as any other. When I consider where they came from, where they are, and how they are, and how they are called to go farther, their being unsettled, with so many objects to take their attention, with the health and good air they enjoy; and when I reflect that not one in a hundred came here to get religion, but rather to get plenty of good land, I think it will be well if some or many do not eventually lose their souls.—Bishop Francis Asbury, near Elizabethton, Tennessee, September 26, 1797

CHAPTER TWO

In the Ocean of Mountains, 1790–1870

In May 1776 the naturalist William Bartram left the border station of Keowee in South Carolina and headed upcountry over the Blue Ridge toward the Cherokee Middle Towns. A Pennsylvania Quaker with a sunny and romantic disposition, Bartram was the son of another naturalist, John Bartram, whom Conrad Weiser had guided twenty years earlier into the Iroquois country and who had later been appointed royal botanist to King George III. William had served an apprenticeship as his father's assistant and now was striking out on his own, mounting two expeditions to the Carolinas and Florida in the years between 1773 and 1776. In 1773 he attended the Indian treaty at Augusta whereby the Creeks and Cherokees made their first substantial cessions of Georgia land. He traveled with a surveying party along the Great Trading Path across Georgia and had then intended to go on north into Cherokee country but judged that Indian anger over the land wrung from them was still too great to risk such a venture.

In 1776 relations with the Cherokees were even worse than before, but Bartram decided to go ahead. Following a ridgetop trail that minimized crossings of the fast-flowing streams of the region, he headed across the northwest corner of South Carolina into Georgia, collecting species and writing in his journal as he went. As he approached the mountains, he could scarcely contain his delight in "this magnificent landscape, infinitely varied and without bound." Passing through "stately columns" of oaks, hickories, maples, and other trees, he recorded the remarkable variety of understory plants and shrubs in the forest. Unlike the Spanish explorers who passed through the Blue Ridge at the same season in 1540, he commented at length on the profusion of blossoming species, especially the flame azalea and varieties of rhododendron. As others had done before him, he likened the mountains rising ahead of him to the waves of the sea, but in the language of an Enlightenment scientist: "The undulations gradually depressing, yet perfectly regular, as the squamae of fish or the imbrications of tile on a roof: the nearest ground to me of a perfect full green, the next more glaucous, and lastly almost blue as the ether with which the most distant curve of the horizon seems to be blended."[1] What might he have said had he known that the Cherokees did not distinguish between blue and green as colors but merged them both into a single blue/green, which they regarded as the color of sadness?

A few days out from Keowee, Bartram came to a cascading creek where the path turned up from the Savannah River headwaters to cross the Blue Ridge into the "vale of Cowee," the uppermost valley of the Little Tennessee River. Here he discovered a new species of magnolia blooming at the base of a waterfall. "This tree, or perhaps rather a shrub, rises eighteen to thirty feet in height . . . ; the wreathing branches arising and subdividing from the main stem without order or uniformity, their extremities turn upwards, producing a very large rosaceous, perfectly white, double or polypetalous flower, which is of a most fragrant scent."[2] Bartram did not publish this discovery for several years, so that in the end the new magnolia came to carry the name of another eighteenth-century naturalist, John Fraser, a Scottish botanist based in Charleston.

Magnolia fraseri is one of the few large species whose range is confined entirely within the southern Appalachians. Its flowers can be glimpsed in the greening forest each May from the mountains of Georgia in the south to those of eastern Kentucky and southeastern West Virginia on the north. In some respects this range constitutes a natural version of an Appalachian core region.[3]

The Fraser magnolia in bloom. (Photograph by the author)

Yet what struck Bartram most about the flora he recorded was not its distinctiveness, but its diversity. As he climbed up and over the Blue Ridge crest in the vicinity of Wayah Bald, he commented often on encounters with plants he had seen in the forests of Pennsylvania or in the lowlands of Georgia and Carolina. The many naturalists who came after him have taken similar note of juxtapositions of northern and southern plants in the mountains. The young John Muir, traversing a similar Blue Ridge path in 1867 and perhaps influenced in his choice of words by the outcome of the recent Civil War, called the mountains "highways on which the northern plants may extend their colonies southward." The twentieth-century naturalist Maurice Brooks found the key to Appalachia's natural diversity in an underlying unity represented by a little bird, the snow bunting, which winters on the Roan Mountain bald along the North Carolina–Tennessee border, feeding on the seeds of the same tiny cinquefoil plant that it finds each summer on the windy beaches of the Gaspé peninsula, whose headlands are the closest junction of the Appalachian mountain system and the sea.[4]

Although Bartram usually managed to keep his feet dry, nearly every step on his journey was accompanied by the music of water. There were cascades "glittering on the sides of the distant hills," mossy rocks dampened by "pearly and crystalline dewdrops collected from the falling mists," a stream that "glides gently with serpentine meanders" through a high-altitude grassland, a charming meadow on the Little Tennessee, where from a distance Bartram watched young Cherokee women gathering strawberries and playing in the river. And there were storms such as the one that came upon him as he crossed the mountain crest: "I approached a charming vale, amidst sublimely high forests, awful shades! darkness gathers round, for distant thunder rolls over the trembling hills; the black clouds with august majesty and power, move slowly forwards, shading regions of towering hills, . . . all around is now still as death, not a whisper is heard, but a total inactivity and silence seems to pervade the earth; the birds afraid to utter a chirrup, . . . every insect is silenced, and nothing heard but the roaring of the approaching hurricane."[5]

Water shaped the mountains as Bartram saw them or as we see them today more than any other force since three Appalachian orogenies laid the foundations of eastern North America's highlands 300–500 million years ago. An orogeny is a mountain-building episode in geological history, caused in this case by the collision of tectonic plates. The mountains at first were the size of Alps, but as a modern naturalist writes, "Erosion's hand is everywhere, sculpting the violence of continental collisions into a landscape of subtle beauty."[6] Whether by seeps, drips, gurgling brooks, or surging storm runoff, water changed the stony, thrusting landscape that only geologists can now see into the wavelike succession of blue-green ridges at which Bartram marveled. Water eroded the tablelands tilting north and west of the high mountains into the steep-sided valleys of the Cumberland and Allegheny plateaus. Near the crests of the ridges and at the headwaters of streams, water ponding behind resistant layers of rock or beaver dams created damp meadows such as the one where the Spangenburg party nearly froze in 1752, but whose grasslands attracted the game that Daniel Boone hunted in 1760 and offered summer pastures for the cattle tended by the slave Burrell, the black man who showed Boone the way.[7]

Floodwaters enabled the rivers of Appalachia to carve their transverse paths across the northeast/southwest grain of the mountains, creating such spectacular rocky exits as the Delaware Water Gap, the Potomac at Harpers Ferry, the New River Gorge, the "Breaks" of the Big Sandy, or the Narrows of the Tennessee. Floods also laid down the bottomlands and terraces on which the Cherokees invariably built their towns and grew the crops that attracted the envious appreciation of white visitors. Water in the form of glaciers gouged out the narrow lakes of Iroquoia, blockaded the proto–Ohio River, changed its direction of flow from north to southwest and turned its more northern tributaries into lakes whose silty deposits later attracted settler-speculators like the Jacksons of Monongahela. The Ice Age is also responsible for driving the boreal spruce-hemlock forest southward along the Appalachian spine and for mingling plants native to Canada with southern species in the mountaintop balds and heaths through which Bartram passed. Appalachia's abundant rainfall, combined with equally abundant sunshine in the southern reaches of the range, created trees whose heights astonished northerners such as Bartram, making southern Appalachia's hardwood forests then and now the richest and most diverse in the world.

To Euro-Americans without a naturalist's eye for abundance, the forests of Appalachia were full of foreboding: dark places, savage, untamed—a "wilderness," to use a word full of horrific meaning to readers of the Christian Bible. Environmental historians point out that our culture today retains some of this feeling; even people who look on wilderness as benign see the woods as "natural," "primitive," and "unchanged by man." These same historians point out, however, that Native American men tended and altered the forest just as women managed the clearings in which they lived. Fire was used to clear the forest understory, which made hunting easier and produced more of the browse on which deer and other game animals fed. Hunters sometimes also used fire as a means of trapping their prey. By the time of Bartram's journey, the forest had been altered by the introduction of new European species and the foraging of hogs, cattle, and horses that had been brought from the Old World but adopted by the Native Americans.[8] The extensive paths he followed were another alteration of the forest ecology, as were the wagon roads that penetrated the Great Valley during the 1730s and 40s, the mountains during the military campaigns and white migrations of the 1750s, 60s, and 70s, and the federal roads built after 1805. The Cherokee hunters whom Bartram met on his journey were all on horseback, as he was, and they could not have proceeded had the forest paths been the narrow parlous ways that the European imagination traditionally assigned to the woods.

The "long hunt," which took men into distant forests for months, even years, at a time, was a by-product of the fur trade of the seventeenth and eighteenth centuries, but historians have been unable to agree as to the source of this innovation. It can be argued that increasingly productive agriculture made hunting ritualistic by the early contact period, meaning that it was less important for producing food or clothing than for the deeds by which males proclaimed their masculinity.[9] Whether or not this was generally true for Native Americans, the fur trade quickly commercialized hunting and turned it into an occupation, first for Indians and then for European men. One theory holds that settlers of Scandinavian descent brought a cultural complex that included the pursuit of distant game to the Delaware valley in the 1630s. Stephen Holston, for example, a Pennsylvania hunter who pursued long hunts during the 1730s and 40s down the Great Valley toward the rivers that now bear his name in southwest Virginia and upper East Tennessee, was of "ancestral Finnish" extraction.[10]

Conceivably, Daniel Boone learned his woodscraft from Pennsylvania neighbors who hailed from the same Fenno-Scandian culture, but he could also have learned from the Delawares and Shawnees who still lived in his neighborhood or who brought their skins to Philadelphia along the nearby Allegheny Path. In any case, hunting was crucial to the colonial economy for both Indians and whites, even though it was also a source of frontier disorder and conflict. Though Boone ended up with a hero's reputation, most professional hunters—that is, those who like Boone depended upon furs and pelts as their principal source of income—were poorly regarded by their fellow frontiersmen. The New Englanders who settled Marietta in southeast Ohio in 1789 regarded the hunters they found already living there as "nothing but a herd of wild Men either read [sic] or white (not much differing except in Collour)." "Hunters" became a generic term among farmers and townspeople for rowdies, drunkards, and thieves.[11] In most places, hunters were surrounded or displaced by farmers within a generation.

Yet even among Euro-Americans who did not pursue it occupationally, the hunt provided a means of occasional income and, during the first years of settlement, an important food source. "It frequently happened that there was no breakfast until it was obtained from the woods," Joseph Doddridge recalled of his youth in northwestern Virginia.[12] In western North Carolina, Elisha Mitchell noted in 1828, "Ashe [County] was first occupied by hunters who came in search of game. When they reported the fertility of the soil to their neighbors—they came in but engaged also much in hunting—and the habits generated in those days still continue even after the game is gone." That is, hunting continued as an avocation, a training ground for boys, and an occasion for the display of manhood, but it produced relatively little food or income. Mitchell found only a few professional hunters left along the upper Watauga, and these mostly pursued their hunts in still unsettled distant places in eastern Kentucky or southern West Virginia.[13]

The forest was also important for the foods that were gathered there. In this regard, white settlers fell heir to the gatherings of Indian women. The first fruit to ripen was the wild strawberry. On Bartram's springtime journey in 1776, he encountered a strawberry field so full of fruit that "their rich juice dy[ed] my horses feet and ancles." Later, at the house of a white trader and his Cherokee wife, he was treated to a bicultural feast of strawberries and cream. However, open-range grazing by cattle and hogs severely reduced the wild strawberry's habitat.[14] Mitchell, in 1828, also found strawberry fields worthy of notice, but only at the highest altitude.[15] After the strawberries came service berries, which ripened in June. Also in late May or early June, the blackberry canes bloomed, often during the spring's last spell of chilly weather, which came to be known as "blackberry winter." This fruit was ready for harvest in July, as were wild raspberries, which like the blackberries grew at the forest's edge or in open places in the woods. The forest also yielded wild plums, cherries, and grapes and the fruit of the hawthorn bushes, a special favorite of children. Medicinal plants and herbs, to be used according to knowledge learned from the Indians, were also gathered.

Autumn brought late-ripening fruit and all manner of nuts: hickory nuts, walnuts, hazelnuts, and chestnuts. These were added to the food and meat stored up during the fall harvest and the hunting time that followed it. Late fall was the season for hunting and hog butchering: Game animals and the half-wild hogs and cattle were easier to track in the open woods after the leaves fell but before the deep snows of winter, and after the weather grew cold enough to preserve the meat for several months. Then in winter and early spring came the time of "sugar camps"—the tapping of maple trees for their sweet sap. Indians had created "groves" or "orchards" of sugar maples in the places where these trees grew best; white settlers added many more like them. Most of the "sugar" was boiled down into syrup, but some might be spilled out on the snow to make a kind of instant candy for children.

Life at the edge of the forest could be a good life, as the poet Louise McNeill —the daughter and sister of avid hunters who was also a trained historian— recorded in her tribute to a German-American backwoods housewife, Katchie [Katje] Verner:

It pleasures her to gather
A hoard when autumn comes:
Of grapes in scroll-worked silver,
Red-streaked and amber plums,
Winesaps and seek-no-farthers,

Green peppers, russet pears,
White roastin'-ears for drying
On frames above the stairs,
Queer handled gourds for dishes
And dippers at the spring,
Long butternuts, fat pumpkins,
Cream-colored beans to string,
Wild meat to jerk and pickle,
Brown chestnuts tipped with cold,
Cranberries from the marshes,
Tree honey dripping gold.

In barrels and crocks and suggins,
In pokes upon the floor
And hanging from the rafters
Is Katchie Verner's store
Against the mountain winter
When sleet-hard drifts will freeze
The deep loam of her garden
And gird her orchard trees.[16]

It should be kept in mind that Verner's fictional husband was an acquisitive man who "counted years by the harvest yield / And wealth by the surveyed line."[17] A real-life backwoods family could just as likely have had different luck with land titles, the weather, illness, accidents, or other misfortunes. Not all men were skillful hunters, or all women industrious wives. Nor were all families intact—widows and widowers had to provide for themselves and their families as best they could until they found another helpmeet. Depending upon the rhythms of nature without the type of communal support that Indian villagers provided to one another could mean a hard life, especially during the hunger and chill of a mountain springtime. Then, the new crops in the fields and the berries and fruits of the forest had not yet matured. There was only meat to depend on; the meat of hibernating bears was a delicacy harvested at this time, by hunters skillful and bold enough to find the bears in their dens. Otherwise, fresh-killed meat tasted worst at this time of year, reflecting the animals' poor forage and lean flanks, and stored meat, unless well-salted and cured, was subject to spoilage. If enough dried vegetables and corn meal had not been set by the previous autumn, a diet that was all or mostly meat caused nutritional problems. This diet left children in particular with an unsatisfied feeling that Doddridge, whose relatively affluent family pioneered in the upper Ohio valley, never forgot. Ramps or wild leeks, wild vegetables that appear in the forest in early spring, often poked their pungent leaves up through the snow. They have a bad odor when cooked but are otherwise wholesome. Children and everyone else looked forward to their coming, and they became a traditional Appalachian food.

Both whites and Indians turned their hogs and cattle into the woods to feed on the mast that covered the forest floor—chestnuts, acorns, beech nuts, hickory nuts, and the "browse" of tender shoots and young leaves. Cherokee males rounded up the cattle they originally acquired from the Spanish by shooting them, just like deer. Settlers' cattle-handling methods came from Ireland and/or Africa and involved rounding up cattle in backwoods cowpens, such as the one Bartram visited in Georgia in 1773.[18] Charles Lanman, a self-described tourist and sportsman who traversed the mountains of Virginia in 1846 and those of Georgia and North Carolina in 1848, concluded that grazing afforded "the principal revenue" for the mountain people. "The mountain ranges afford an abundance of the sweetest grazing food, and all that the farmer has to do in the autumn is to hunt up his stock, which have now become excessively fat, and drive them to the Charleston or Baltimore market."[19] During the first half of the nineteenth century, livestock raised in this manner became the mainstay of the Appalachian domestic economy.

In the upper Yadkin valley of North Carolina in 1828, however, Mitchell heard many complaints about the deterioration of the forest range, which he attributed to two factors. First, an increase in population in this foothills district—and thus in clearings, fencing, and other improvements—inhibited the practice of burning the woods each spring; "The consequence is that small undergrowth is not destroyed as it used to be—the woods become thicker and not like an orchard as they are in the indian country." Second, overgrazing had led to a decline among the most nutritious grasses and plants suitable for cattle. Accordingly, the growing scarcity of forest range led to competition in northwest North Carolina between local cattle and herds driven up in the summer from the Great Valley to the north. In one location near White Top Mountain, Mitchell encountered a stockman who sent boys into the woods beating drums to frighten the invading cattle away.[20] In more thickly settled areas there arose a commercial livestock industry that supplemented wild forage with corn feeding and long-distance livestock drives to urban markets on the seaboard. This industry appeared in the ridge-and-valley country just west of the Great Valley in Virginia as early as the late eighteenth century and spread from there down the valley into East Tennessee and west to central Ohio and the Kentucky Bluegrass region, always combining forest range with corn feeding. In this way, stock raising enabled Appalachia to keep pace economically with the surrounding lowlands until at least 1850.[21]

The importance of game animals and livestock in the early Appalachian economy explains why some early settlers sought locations far removed from the riparian bottomlands that fueled the ambitions of land speculators. Consider the openings known as glades—open and generally marshy grasslands found near the headwaters of streams throughout the region. "It seems very strange that any person should have settled there at a time when the whole country was almost vacant," wrote the son of a man who pioneered in a glade in the Monongahela valley in 1771.[22] Strange it was from the standpoint of a speculator like George Washington, who judged land by its convenient adaptability to commercial field crops and who saw that the surveys that William Crawford ran for him in the 1770s hugged the Ohio and Kanawha river bottomlands closely, avoiding the nearby hills. But for men who had no slaves to clear densely wooded bottoms and who depended on livestock and game for a living, other locations had much to recommend them.[23] Braddock's Road penetrated the Youghiogheny Glades of western Maryland because of their importance in grazing horses and cattle; later the glades became a summer pasture and a waystation for cattle being driven to eastern markets from the upper Ohio valley. Today, only the Cranberry Glades in West Virginia resemble the glades in anything like the condition in which the settlers found them, but the importance of glades is marked by place names on the maps of all but one of the Appalachian states.[24]

The forest through which Bartram passed thus generated the first phase of Appalachia's growth after the Euro-American conquests. How and where that growth developed can be seen in the travels of another itinerant, who during the eventful summer of 1776 began a lifelong mission to the mountains and valleys of Appalachia. His journeying began in August, not long after Indian truculence convinced Bartram to abandon his project to visit the Cherokee Overhill Towns. Francis Asbury, the apostle of Methodism, visited the Virginias as many as 120 times between 1776 and his death in 1816 and steadily widened his mission to include other places as the frontier advanced, embracing the Carolinas, Georgia, Kentucky, Tennessee, and eventually Ohio. The journal he kept, faithfully recorded over a forty-year period, thus became a record not only of the growth of his church and his spiritual concerns, but of the planting and maturing of settlements throughout the Appalachian region.

"O how many thousands of poor souls have we to seek out in the wilds of America," Bishop Asbury wrote in his journal, "who are but one remove from the Indians in the comforts of civilized society, and considering that they have the Bible in their hands, comparatively worse in their morals than the savages themselves." A habitual first stop on his tours through Appalachia was a place that never failed to inspire a gloomy assessment of the region's spiritual prospects. This was Bath, which he first visited on July 18, 1776. Now known as Berkeley Springs, this oldest of mountain resorts was found on Lord Fairfax's land and patronized by the elite of colonial times and the early republic. George Washington, who found relief from his rheumatism in the waters there, persuaded Fairfax to make the springs public property, which they still are: America's first state park, as it were. Asbury—a man who spent as much time in the saddle as any planter or frontiersman—found similar ease from various aches and complaints, even though he disapproved of the carryings-on of most of the clientele. "When I behold the conduct of the people who attend the Springs, particularly the *gentry*, I am led to thank God that I was not born to riches," he wrote in his journal. But even though he referred to the place as "that seat of sin," Asbury visited regularly throughout his life. One reason, no doubt, was the resort's convenience, located as it was in one of the back valleys immediately west of the Shenandoah Valley and the Great Wagon Road.[25]

Over the next several years, Asbury's journeys steadily widened to embrace newer districts west and south of the Great Valley. In 1781 he visited the South Branch valley for the first time, "a country of mountains and natural curiousities." Having shared the pulpit with an African American preacher east of the mountains, he wished for a German-speaking colleague as he traversed the South Branch. The "Dutch people" loved preaching but could not understand English well enough to study and discuss Methodist doctrine, he reported. In 1782 he was back on the South Branch and crossed another mountain to remote settlements along the North Branch of the Potomac. "[A]rriving we found [the people] handing about their stink-pots of mulled whisky. We have, not infrequently, to lodge in the same room with the family, the houses having but the one room, so that necessity compels us to seek retirement in the woods; this, with the nightly *disagreeables* of bugs to annoy us, shows the necessity of crying out to the Lord for patience."[26]

In 1784 Asbury crossed the Allegheny Front to the settlements in the Monongahela valley of northwestern Virginia and western Pennsylvania, traveling as far west as the present site of Washington, Pennsylvania, where he ministered to the Methodists' first circuit west of the mountains, the Redstone Circuit. In 1785 Asbury added North Carolina to his itinerary, visiting the Moravians at Salem and preaching at the home of Morgan Bryan, the patriarch of Rebecca Bryan Boone's family, on the upper Yadkin. He then crossed the Great Valley and headed north through the Greenbrier valley, a beautiful highland basin drained by a New River tributary, and next across the Allegheny Front into Tygart's Valley at the Monongahela headwaters. He followed this route for several years and came to call the rugged mountain passage between the two valleys "the Shades of Death" and the latter settlement "the valley of distress." While making this passage in 1788, he fell in with two women who were also bound for a religious meeting at Clarksburg, one of whom was Mary Hadden Jackson, the grandmother of the future Confederate general. Asbury and his companion gallantly gave up the only bed to the women, and the bishop ended up sleeping on a pile of flea-ridden deerskins. The next night he fared better, lodging at the home of George Jackson, Mary's brother-in-law, a hero of the Indian wars and a companion-in-arms of George Rogers Clark, for whom he had named the village. Jackson himself was not at home; instead he was serving as the northwest's representative at the convention in Richmond by which Virginia ratified the U.S. Constitution.

Also in 1788, Asbury paid his first visit to Tennessee, scrambling across the Blue Ridge plateau in North Carolina from a place called "the Globe" at the base of the escarpment, following the upper Watauga River from its headwaters through the Iron Mountains to the Sycamore Shoals, where thirteen years earlier Richard Henderson had negotiated the purchase from the Cherokees that led to the settlement of Kentucky. When he arrived the next day at Jonesborough, the leading town of the Watauga settlement, Asbury found that "the people are in disorder about the old and new State: two or three men, it is said, have been killed."[27] This was the mini–civil war between supporters of the State of Franklin—organized mostly by settlers who held their land titles under the laws of Virginia and led as its "governor" by a celebrated Indian fighter, John Sevier—and authorities appointed by North Carolina, who declined to recognize the new state and instead organized upper East Tennessee into North Carolina counties. Although the struggle was essentially one between two sets of rival land speculators, it has entered American lore as an expression of frontier democracy. North Carolina won, but once the parent state had secured the right to grant millions of acres of Tennessee land to pay off its revolutionary war debt, Tennessee won its independence, first as the Southwest Territory, then as a state in 1796.

On his 1788 trip Asbury probably conceived his goal of traveling still farther west to Kentucky, but it was not until 1790 that he was able to go there.
The Kentucky "wilderness"—that is, the largely vacant country between the
Bluegrass settlements in the center of the state and the Great Valley east of
Cumberland Gap—was still Indian country at that time; Asbury's party
passed by a site where Chickamaugas and Shawnees had killed twenty-four
whites a few years earlier. Indians also killed or captured some fifteen hundred
travelers along the Ohio River in the decade after the Revolution, while Asbury found Indian alarms in Tygart's Valley as late as 1792. Journeying
through the wilderness, he wrote in his journal, "is like being at sea, in some
respects, and in others worse. Our way is over mountains, steep hills, deep
rivers, and muddy creeks; a thick growth of reeds for miles together; and no
inhabitants but wild beasts and savage men."

Thus in 1790 and again following a second visit to Kentucky in 1792, he returned east by retracing his route through Cumberland Gap and the Great
Valley. In 1793 he pushed down the valley in East Tennessee as far as
Greeneville and in 1796 conceived the desire to visit the settlements on the
Cumberland River around Nashville, although he did not achieve this goal
until four years later. "I shall have ridden nearly one thousand miles on the
western waters before I leave them," he wrote in his journal in 1796; "I have
been on the waters of Nolachucky to the mouth of Clinch; on the north, middle, and south branches of Holston; on New River, Green Brier, and by the
head springs of Mononghela." But he longed for a more direct route: "If I
were able, I should go from Charleston, [S.C.], a direct course, five hundred
miles to Nolachucky; thence two hundred and fifty miles to Cumberland [i.e.,
Nashville], thence one hundred to Kentucky; thence one hundred miles
through that State, and two hundred to Saltville; thence two hundred to
Green Brier; thence two hundred to Red Stone, and three hundred to Baltimore. Ah! If I were young again!"[28]

Over the years, Asbury continued to search for more direct routes connecting his far-flung destinations. Although he visited Georgia for the first
time in 1790, the Federal Road, which would have allowed him to go inland
from Charleston to Augusta and then across Cherokee country and the Cumberland plateau all the way to Nashville, was not finished in time to be of use
to him. In 1800 his probing led him for the first time into Buncombe County,
North Carolina, where he again encountered "too many subjects of the two
great potentates of this Western World, whisky [and] brandy." From there he
went down into South Carolina via the Saluda Gap. Trying an even more direct route east from Buncombe in 1806, he found a less-traveled route

through the Blue Ridge at Mills Gap much rougher: "One of the descents is like the roof of a house, for nearly a mile. I rode, I walked, I sweated, I trembled, and my old knees failed."[29]

It is easy to see that behind this search for more efficient routes was a desire to cover more ground in less time, a goal founded on Asbury's awareness of his aging body and a declining number of years, feelings made all the more urgent by an intensifying atmosphere of religious excitement in the early nineteenth century and the competition offered by other evangelizing faiths. In 1795 Asbury found a route that answered some of these concerns, one that, after he expanded it in 1803 to include the new state of Ohio, gave him an optimum combination of distance and comfort. He developed the habit of spending the coldest months of the winter in Charleston, then moving up the Atlantic coast with the spring weather, from Baltimore and Philadelphia through New Jersey, New York, and New England between May and July, then across Pennsylvania and Ohio and down into Kentucky in August and September, crossing Tennessee from west to east and then traversing the Carolina Blue Ridge during the last fine weather of Indian summer, arriving back in Charleston in December.

This path took Asbury through all of the older districts that served as the population reservoirs of Appalachia, and so his journal became a record of improvement: a new courthouse, "good taverns and stores" in Staunton in the Great Valley in 1793; twenty or more houses, "some neat, and most of them new and painted," in the "pleasant town" of Wytheville in 1800; a "needful and good" bridge over the Holston River at Blountville, Tennessee; a new wagon road across the Cumberland Mountains between Nashville and Knoxville; the new statehouse in the latter town and "an elegant court house" at Lancaster, Ohio, on the far northwest edge of the Appalachian Plateau; the new federal arsenal at the junction of the Potomac and Shenandoah at Harpers Ferry; a turnpike across Tennessee that Asbury termed "a disgrace to the State and to the undertakers, supposing they had any character to lose." On the Ohio north of Wheeling in September 1803, he saw the flatboats of Meriwether Lewis, scraping across the low-water shoals en route to join William Clark at St. Louis. In this and so many other ways, Asbury was a witness to the history of the early republic. Yet his mind was always fixed upon his essential mission: "to civilize, methodize, and spiritualize."[30]

Though in his later years he traveled more by carriage than on horseback and was accompanied by a succession of vigorous young preachers who looked after him, Asbury did not keep to the main roads as they changed into turnpikes but searched out the back valleys where people still lived in log houses and needed comfort and salvation as much as earlier settlers had in the older districts. When his carriage came to an unbridged stream, the horses could be unhitched and swum across while the carriage was floated over on a pair of canoes. If there was no inn or gentleman's house to welcome him, he could still sleep in lofts or on piles of coats before the fire. Traversing the Great Valley in southwest Virginia, he sought out the back valleys in Tazewell and Grayson Counties, whereas the main road traversed Washington and Wythe. Trying yet another route across southwestern North Carolina, he approached the courthouse town of Asheville through the Great Smoky Mountains, crossing one creek on a log and scaling a memorably rugged mountain, "height after height, and five miles over." And while the bishop's journal is full of complaint about hardship and sickness, it is also a record of trust in providence and in human ingenuity and kindness, of one man's acceptance of his calling and of grace.

Typical of his later years was an episode near Wheeling in 1804, when he "was too weak to travel but not to preach." "Were I to charge the people on the western waters for my services, I should take their roads, rocks and mountains into the account, and rate my labours at a very high price," he wrote in 1796. But he did not look for earthly reward. Instead, he said, "I expect a crown." In August 1815, he preached a sermon on the text "the time is short" at West Liberty in the (West) Virginia "Pan Handle," and then the next week he resigned his position as bishop and made his way back east over his usual route through Ohio, Kentucky, Tennessee, and the Carolinas. A few months later he died.[31]

Although Asbury had preached outdoors to audiences large and small since colonial times, his first experience of a "camp meeting" came near Nashville in 1800, shortly before a religious revival based on such gatherings swept through Kentucky and then across all of the Appalachian states. The great Cane Ridge Revival of August 1801, conducted before thousands gathered in a shady grove whose gentle slope provided a natural ampitheater, was organized chiefly by Presbyterians bearing into the new century the "new light" preached by George Whitfield a generation earlier. But there were at least eighteen Baptist and Methodist ministers sharing the pulpit on this occasion, and supposedly it was one of the Methodist preachers whose words set off the behavior that hereafter became a mark of the revival movement.

It might be useful at this point to recall the ancient distinction between people of the Word and people of the Book. All Christians relied on the Bible; if a literate Protestant owned any other books, they were likely to be John Fox's *Book of Martyrs*, a vivid record of persecution under Queen Mary

Tudor and a compelling diatribe against Roman Catholicism, and John Bunyan's *The Pilgrim's Progress*. But the so-called "mainstream" Protestant churches of colonial times were also "liturgical." That is, they emerged from the Reformation with prescribed forms of ritual and with formal doctrines embodied in documents such as the Anglican Book of Common Prayer, the Lutheran Augsburg Confession, or the Westminster Confession that defined orthodoxy for Presbyterians. The organization of these churches, as completed in seventeenth-century Europe, required an educated clergy and a formal structure of authority: episcopal hierarchies in the Anglican and Lutheran churches, synods and councils among the Presbyterians. During the eighteenth century, an admired sermon in these churches could as likely be a learned disquisition on the finer points of doctrine as a stirring appeal to the emotional bases of Christian belief.

The Great Awakening that had swept the colonial seaboard in the mid-eighteenth century was ignited in the backwoods again at Cane Ridge in southern Kentucky a generation later by preachers to whom the emotional basis of religious feeling was as important as doctrine. It was not simply a matter of educated versus uneducated clergy or literate versus illiterate audiences, as authors of institutional histories of mainline churches have sometimes argued. Even such a sophisticated listener as Charles Lanman could prefer a mountain preacher over a more learned one: "They seem to think more of preaching the *doctrines* of Christ than proclaiming their own learning or advocating their own opinions, and it is therefore always a pleasure to hear them," he wrote from western North Carolina in 1848.[32] It was, rather, a contest between head and heart, between the intellectual basis of conviction and the emotional experience of conversion. The latter was an individual's highly personal confrontation with his or her own sense of sinfulness and inadequacy, followed by an emotional turning to God.

In the revival context, this experience could be induced or re-created by the spiritual excitement of extended preaching on the subjects of sin and redemption. This excitement also had physical manifestations, "body exercises" as they were called, including shouting, fainting, convulsions, trances, rolling on the ground, barking, and ecstatic singing and dancing. Such activities were manifestations of the Holy Spirit to believers, "extatic raptures of divine joy and comfort," as one preacher explained it, but to the more conservative such actions were scandalous.[33] The popularity of revivals and the large crowds they attracted also generated other scandals; much of the ecstasy was induced by whiskey, according to critics, and there were lurid reports of seduction and rape in the campgrounds. Kentucky's Presbyterian synod hauled two of the organizers of the Cane Ridge Revival before it to answer charges of heresy in 1803. One of them accepted the established hierarchy's discipline. Another defied it and established the breakaway Cumberland Presbyterian Church in 1810.

Revivals were one of the two great innovations that brought organized Protestantism into the backwoods during this period. The other was the use of decentralized organizational strategies, above all the "circuits" established by Methodists and embodied by Asbury's example, whereby a small number of clergy could serve wider geographic areas. The circuits were in turn linked by larger regional "conferences," such as the Holston Conference in southwest Virginia that Asbury visited in 1783 and which subsequently served as parent to additional conferences spreading into nearby sections of Tennessee, Kentucky, and North Carolina. Baptists also employed circuit riders with even greater success and linked their congregations together in regional "associations." For autonomy-minded Baptist congregations, there was no further hierarchy apart from occasional conventions called to discuss and resolve potentially divisive issues. Methodists, true to their origins as an offshoot of Anglicanism, retained the episcopal hierarchy of "the old church," notwithstanding the decentralization of authority and the enlarged role of laypersons in spreading the church's message through meetings known as "classes" and in exhortations conducted under the hierarchy's license.

Inspired by the revival movement, a relatively simple—the learned might have said simplistic—faith in redemption and salvation by grace spread through the backwoods regions of the South in the early nineteenth century, and from there throughout the nation until it was brought under control by emerging denominational structures during the 1830s. Deriving from an oral culture, the movement depended heavily on preaching, especially on "text interpretation," in which the stories of the Bible were retold vividly and reshaped into parables that applied to the life circumstances of believers. Partly because of the need to save their vocal chords over long hours of exhortation, preachers developed a popular singsong style whose hypnotic effect was enhanced further by a peculiar dronelike style of singing, in which hymns were "lined out" by a song leader and repeated by the congregation in a manner not unlike the call-and-response style of African American work songs. "Shape-note" singing, based on printed hymnals that lined out simple tunes using diamonds, squares, triangles, and other shapes to identify notes in the fashion of medieval plainsong, enabled worshipers untrained in the conventions of musical notation to participate fully in services. The elaborate and elegant church music composed for the European state churches by masters such as William Byrd or Johann Sebastian Bach remained all but unknown in America, with performances confined to a few coastal cities and to enclaves such as the Moravian centers in Pennsylvania and North Carolina. The ecstatic behaviors first manifested at revivals became routine expressions of worship, at least in their more sedate forms of shouting, crying, and falling.[34]

Yet the persistence in Appalachia of the organizational and worship styles of this period of American religious history has occasioned a great deal of scorn and contempt among commentators of the late nineteenth and the twentieth centuries. Writing of the Antimissionary Baptists of eastern Kentucky, a distinguished professor of southern religious history describes "backwater Baptists [who] clung desperately to their traditional faith . . . extremely provincial, defensive, and tenacious in support of their life-style . . . rural and isolated from the mainstream of Kentucky life, [who] saw time passing them by and reacted by clutching their threatened culture more tightly."[35] Some of this reaction can be explained by urbanization, by institutional church rivalries, and by the emergence of a social science perspective that attributed the worship practices common in rural Appalachia to alienation induced by the region's economic exploitation. Only recently have historians begun to examine Appalachian religion *as religion* and not as a manifestation of social and economic patterns, arguing that "mountain religion is the truest mirror reflecting who the mountain people *are*, and apart from which they cannot be understood."[36] Considering the extent to which other forms of Appalachia's expressive culture were readily incorporated into the consumer culture of twentieth-century America, they may have a point.

The faith spread through Appalachia by the circuit riders and their revivals brought together four religious traditions dating back to the Protestant Reformation and the wars and persecutions that followed it. One was the Pietism that can be traced back through Ephrata and Wachovia to the so-called "left wing" of the Reformation, to the small groups of believers in early modern central Europe who defied church and state authority by insisting that the only valid form of religious experience was one grounded in personal conversion and inner feeling and that church organization was more valid the more it emulated the simple rituals and communal bonds that presumably had characterized the primitive church in ancient times. Pietism explains the resistance of Appalachian churches to hierarchical direction and to extrabiblical authority in matters of doctrine. To this were added a set of revivalistic traditions springing from three other roots: sacramental revivals in western Scotland and in northern Ireland during the seventeenth century, the Baptist revivals of the colonial Great Awakening, particularly in eastern Virginia and

Baptism in eastern Kentucky, 1973. (Appalshop photograph by Ben Zickafoose)

North Carolina, and "plain folk camp-meeting religion," especially among the Methodists of Asbury's time, before that church was burdened by the weight of its episcopacy.[37]

Most of the distinguishing marks of Appalachian religion can be attributed to a creative synthesis of traditions drawn from these four sources: the founding of faith on inner conviction derives from Pietism; sacramental rituals such as footwashing, the Lord's Supper, and adult baptism by immersion similarly derives from Pietist and Baptist sources in Germany and the British Isles; preaching as chant derives from Welsh Baptists; camp meetings, sacramental meetings, and "revival culture" from both Scots-Irish Presbyterianism and colonial Baptists; simplified church organization and egalitarianism within congregations has both Pietistic and Baptist roots.

Religion of this type was not "regionally specific" to Appalachia until after 1825, when church hierarchies began an effort to tame revivalism by prescribing regularity rather than spontaneity in the scheduling of revivals and by curbing expressive behavior, especially body exercises, in favor of more sedate styles of worship. "Denominationalism"—that is, the elaboration of church structures dominated by a professional clergy—became the national norm for the evangelical churches (Baptists, Methodists, and Presbyterians, in other words) as it had always been for their liturgical counterparts (Lutherans, Episcopalians, and Roman Catholics). This was true for the North, where professional evangelists like Charles G. Finney used the new style of revival to address the town-dwelling middle class, and in the South, where denominational leaders became more responsive to the needs of the planter elite.

Denominationalism led to schisms among evangelicals over the slavery issue during the 1840s, when Baptists, Methodists, and Presbyterians each split into proslavery and antislavery wings, and parts of Appalachia—especially western (West) Virginia and Kentucky—became battlegrounds over the ownership of church property. But the critical schism, from the standpoint of Appalachian history, was the break between denominationalism and the upland churches who cleaved to "the good old-fashioned way." This schism was widened as denomination-builders adopted such programs as domestic and foreign missions, Sunday schools, and formal participation in nondenominational temperance crusades. "[A]fter an interchange of sentiments among the members of this body," declared a conservative Baptist association in 1827, "it was agreed that we discard all Missionary Societies, Bible Societies, and Theological Seminaries, and the practices heretofore resorted to for their support, in begging money from the public . . . believing these societies and institutions to be the inventions of men, and not warranted from the word of God."[38]

The example just quoted is from the Kehukee Baptist Association of eastern North Carolina, and while it is easy to believe that this statement parallels opinion in the mountain region (for example, in southeastern Kentucky, where dissenters withdrew from the mainstream to form the first "Old Regular Baptist" association in 1825), it points up a difficulty historians encounter when they try to recover the ideas and values of the people of the Word. Oral tradition does not lend itself to precise documentation. The views and actions of those who dissented without building organizations beyond the congregational level must be teased out from fragmentary records or the comments of their contemporary critics or the behavior of their modern descendants. This problem is not confined to the history of the Appalachian religion. It is also a basic problem of Native American history, for example. And it recurs when we examine the region's social structure, particularly in addressing the question of who owned, occupied, and used Appalachian land during the preindustrial period.

While the forest provided the base for Appalachia's regional economy, most people did not live in the woods, or in the emerging towns that provided the region's links with the rest of the nation and the world. They lived in clearings, just as the Indians had done. In 1776 Bartram passed through the Cherokee towns of Echoe, Cowe, Nucasse, and Whatoga—to employ his spellings—and he passed through twice as many abandoned villages en route. All of them were comparably situated in clearings next to a river or large creek, with dwellings and the council house on elevated locations "and the rich level vale and meadows in front, their planting grounds."[39] "They cultivated only the richest bottoms," commented a Georgia man who observed the Cherokee Removal. "An Indian never worked a piece of poor land."[40]

Indian "old fields" were a prime target for land prospectors, and although these were numerous, they were not so plentiful as to accommodate all the settlers who flooded into the backcountry during the frontier era. Nor were there extensive grasslands, notwithstanding the bucolic views to be had of the Great Valley from the crest of the Blue Ridge.[41] Even if there had been, Euro-Americans, like woodland Indians, would not have been likely to choose treeless locations. They needed firewood and logs for construction. They also needed fresh water, more conveniently obtained from a spring than from a large stream, and if commercial considerations were present, as they were with Washington and other speculators, they looked for a potential mill site. This argued for a clearing on land that was somewhat elevated, safe from all but the most exceptional floods, and so as Euro-American farmsteads took shape they were not unlike the Indian villages: croplands and meadows spread along the most level land near a stream, a house and outbuildings on a slope between the fields and the woods, with a convenient spring and orchards planted in places that would not interfere with cultivation. In "the ruins of the ancient famous town of Sticoe," which Bartram saw in the vicinity of present-day Clayton, Georgia, the Cherokee peach orchards—still producing though the town was abandoned—occupied the same elevated location as the council and dwelling houses.[42] These orchards antedated the arrival of the English in Cherokee country, having been adopted from the Spanish a century before. American backcountry people considered orchards to be evidence of a maturing neighborhood, which is perhaps why their armies consistently chopped down orchards when putting Indian villages to the torch.[43]

In 1730 James Logan warned the Pennsylvania proprietors about a land-clearing method that was practiced by squatters from Ireland and others moving across the Susquehanna frontier into the Great Valley. "All your Lands of Value are posses'd and cutt in pieces with Small Settlemt by wch the timber is destroy'd & yet the Land is not clear'd, for they only bark, & thereby Kill ye trees without falling them."[44] This was the practice known as "barking," whereby enough bark was removed from the trunk of a tree to kill it, producing a "dead clearing" in which leafless dead trees were left standing and crops were planted in the sunlit spaces between them until such later time as the trees could be removed or fell from their own dead weight. So common was this method of clearing land in the backcountry that few travelers thought to comment on it, but by the late nineteenth century dead clearings had come to be seen as a mark of backwoods poverty and/or sloth. Fields where stumps remained even though the trees had been cleared away acquired a similar opprobrium. The phrase "back hackings," used by town-dwelling West Virginians in the early twentieth century to connote remote places in the surrounding mountains, may also refer to this practice.[45]

As with other attributes of backwoods culture, there is controversy as to who originated the practice of barking. The Cherokees routinely practiced it, as Bartram observed, both as a technique for obtaining firewood and also for clearing new ground. There are Scandinavian precedents as well, and dead clearings may have been part of the Fenno-Scandian cultural complex that Scandinavian pioneers in the Delaware valley imparted to later arrivals such as the Irish Protestants. Certain it is that the Irish seized on the practice with alacrity, coming as they did from an unforested country and thus possessing few woodland traditions of their own. It is interesting to note that Irish Protestants who settled in New England exhibited little of the woodscraft that those who settled along the Appalachian frontier practiced. This is one explanation for the swift advance of that frontier from Pennsylvania to Kentucky and Tennessee during the last half of the eighteenth century.[46]

In the center of most clearings stood a log cabin. Charles Lanman found them in numerous locations in western Virginia in 1846. "These cabins are almost invariably upon agreeable and appropriate spots: sometimes by a spring in a lonely ravine, . . . sometimes by a rivulet on an elevated hill-side, and sometimes upon the extreme summit of a mountain, with a grassy lawn around, whence may be seen a world of rank and rolling luxuriance, receding to the sky."[47] The log cabin has stirred more interest than any other artifact in Appalachia, both in terms of the emotion attached to it and the amount of controversy it has caused among experts. Where did log cabins originate? we want to know. What can they tell us about the people who built and lived in them, especially about their social status and ethnic origins? Where can we get one? For today log houses are proliferating in suburban and resort areas in or near the mountains, though even the manufactured ones cost more than comparable conventional housing, and a log house that incorporates a historic structure in whole or in part is strictly for people in the upper brackets. One can even buy log-sided mobile homes and recreational vehicles in parts of the region, though of course these logs are plastic, not priceless antiques. It is safe to say that nothing more strongly symbolizes Appalachia to the rest of the nation than this artifact.

Bartram found log dwellings in the Cherokee villages of western North Carolina in 1776, but this building tradition, like the European trade items or domestic animals also to be found there, was borrowed from the invaders. Before the European intrusion, native peoples employed logs mainly for defensive stockades around their villages.[48] Dwellings were made of bark and saplings. Only after they acquired steel axes from the whites did Indians begin to build with logs. Thus log architecture originated in Europe, but in which part? The mostly treeless territories from which Irish, Scottish, and English emigrants came lacked a repertory of log building techniques, although the word "cabin" is Irish in origin, as is also, possibly, the structure's typical plan—a rectangular building with a chimney at a gable end and openings under the eaves rather than the gables.

The most likely places for log construction techniques to have originated are Scandinavia and the Alpine districts of Switzerland and southern Germany. Each of these districts sent emigrants to colonial North America, and people from these homelands mingled in southeast Pennsylvania during the early eighteenth century. German house plans were common enough on the Appalachian frontier, although those of Ireland and Great Britain were prevalent. The argument for log construction's Scandinavian origins points out that although the Alemannic (German-speaking) emigrant homelands had log building traditions, these were mainly tightly built log houses of the sort that succeeded cabins in America as the frontier era passed, whereas Sweden and especially Finland have precedents for both log cabins and log houses, for the variant saddlebag and dogtrot house plans found in Appalachia, and for all the types of log corner notches that experts have argued over so passionately for so long.

Popular usage in the United States tends to ignore the differences between cabins and houses, and many use the term "cabin" when referring to both. But the differences were important. Cabins were temporary structures, thrown up quickly and made of crudely trimmed logs, chinked plentifully with mud, windowless and unfloored, and often with a "wattle-and-daub" (sticks and mud) chimney instead of stone. Houses were more carefully built of trimmed logs fitted together, with window openings and stone chimneys and wooden floors of trimmed and polished log puncheons. A cabin's roof might be constructed of bark or boards, while a house's roof consisted of handmade wooden shingles held in place by boards or stones or, increasingly as the frontier matured, with iron nails. Cabins frequently became outbuildings—kitchens, chickenhouses, stables, corncribs, or other storage areas—after one generation. A log house was built to endure, at least until a family grew affluent enough or embarrassed enough by its implication of poverty to attach it to or hide it within or behind a framed house covered with milled siding painted white.

It is ironic that the log house has come to have such prestige in modern Appalachia, for the "white house" that replaced it during the nineteenth and early twentieth centuries used materials and colors that were intended to proclaim a sharp contrast with log construction. The basic elements of the house form remained the same. Though the white house grew larger, its shape was still rectangular with chimneys at the gables and doors and windows under the eaves, and it was still located at the foot of a hill overlooking the fields and facing the road. The log house, if left standing apart from the new one, would be used as cabins had once been, for storage or for chickens, until at last it became too derelict to allow children to play in it and the caved-in roof and other debris were hauled away. Who could imagine in 1900 that the log house, if cared for and maintained, would one day be worth two or three times the house that replaced it?[49]

Elisha Mitchell, traveling in 1827 and 1828 in his capacity as North Carolina's state geologist and a science professor at the state university, saw the movement from log to frame and/or brick or stone housing as clear-cut evidence of moral and economic progress. A New Englander by upbringing, Mitchell traveled west across the Piedmont to Wilkes County in the foothills, a region he found "raw and countrified." Approaching the Blue Ridge, he followed Reddies River from Wilkesboro to Horse Gap. "These four miles were very pleasant—the steep mountains were on either hand—the river clear as crystal tumbled over its rocky bed, and there were fine fields of corn upon its banks. The farms are small and here, according to some men calling themselves philosophers, in retirement shut out from intercourse with the world by the sides of these streams and hemmed in by these mountains—man may, if he will, be happy."[50] The next day he "clambered" over the crest of the Blue Ridge into Ashe County, surveying the New River valley from the crest of Mount Jefferson, then called Negro (or "Nigger") Mountain:

The air being clear, the prospect delightful. The Pilot [Mountain] could be distinguished clearly, probably at the distance of near a hundred miles. It appeared to be almost exactly east. The Grandfather, or the mountain which we supposed to be the one bearing that name, bore S. 40 west. We had a clear view of the country lying down the New River in Virginia, and also of the part of Surry, Wilkes, etc., lying near the Blue Ridge, for the point on which we were standing was high enough to overlook the Blue Ridge. Nearly the whole county of Ashe lay at our feet, the [meanders] of the river could be traced as on a map. Some of the plantations in view also presented a noble appearance, but oh, what an ocean of mountains.[51]

For two weeks Mitchell traveled through the Blue Ridge plateau, climbing to the top of Grandfather and White Top Mountains, pushing down the Watauga River to the border with Tennessee, taking notes on the district's geology and the commercial potential of its minerals and trees, and preaching on Sundays in his capacity as a licensed minister of the Presbyterian Church. He admired the meadows at Three Forks, where Boone had hunted and Spangenburg froze, and made generally positive comments about the farms and herds he saw along the New River's two branches. "This ride was very pleasant," he wrote of his descent from White Top along the North Fork valley. "A craggy cliff occupied now one side, now the other side of the river, generally overhanging the stream. The other side presented a narrow strip of low ground, fertile, sometimes in a state of nature, sometimes cultivated— the cultivated land extending some distance up the hill side and sometimes an old field, but covered with clover. How different from the old fields of Lower Carolina." The chestnuts were blooming, and the "enchanting" scenery everywhere led Mitchell to empathize with a Baptist preacher who had come up from the lowlands on a missionary errand and who "fell in love with the mountains and removed hither a year or so ago or a little more and soon died." Yet everywhere, he noted with disapproval, people lived in what he called "log huts."

The people lack industry. Some parts of the country—for instance on the three forks and about the Court [i.e., Jefferson, the county seat] are as fine as the good parts of N. England and if the Inhabitants would be industrious and cultivate them in a similar manner they might have painted frame houses instead of the present unsightly log hovels. It is a favorite theory of mine that Ashe has greater facilities for maintaining its soil in a state of productiveness (by means of clover) than any other part of N. Ca. That all the forests will hereafter be cut down and converted into extensive pastures on which will be fed vast herds of cattle and flocks of sheep—that it will hereafter be abundantly more populous than at present and even sought to as an agreeable place of residence.[52]

This turned out to be a fair forecast of Ashe County's future, except that those who now seek out this area as an agreeable place to live are often eager to live in imitations of what Mitchell called "log huts."

Recent studies of folk housing in Kentucky, North Carolina, and Tennessee indicates that the progression from log to frame housing was not as clear-cut an indicator of social and economic mobility as Mitchell imagined. When western Carolinians living in "single pen" log houses wanted more space, they simply attached a duplicate pen to one side or built one across a breezeway (dogtrot) and sheltered the whole with a common roof. This practice continued even among families who could afford to hire carpenters to build a frame center-passage or white house.[53] The true successor to the log cabin was the inexpensive, unframed, unpainted "boxed" or "plank" house of the early twentieth century, built of sawn lumber but within the capacities of traditional cooperative folk construction and requiring neither a professional house carpenter nor storebought paint. In Blount County, Tennessee, log houses continued to be built until the first years of the twentieth century. A woman who grew up in Wayne County, West Virginia, was born in a log house built by her father in the 1920s.[54]

To be sure, the white house appeared first among the most prosperous farmers who owned the best land; it became "the symbol of a developing rural elite" and then, after the Civil War, the common dwelling for highland farmers who adopted and could afford to uphold middle-class tastes.[55] And yet even after they occupied frame houses with more rooms, people who had been reared in log houses lived in the new dwellings in much the same way. One study found that their daily indoor activities were concentrated in one or two rooms, one of which was the kitchen. Sleeping rooms, often unheated or poorly heated, were used only for sleeping, and parlors and guest bedrooms were used mainly for company. For people who spent a large part of their time outdoors, and this included many women as well as most men and boys, a dwelling that afforded many options for activity and privacy was not a high priority.[56] To such people, a log house with its attached porch and kitchen and several outbuildings answered their needs.

Carrie Severt airs quilts on the porch of her hundred-year-old farmhouse near
Sparta, North Carolina, 1978. Although the porch bears more recent ornamentation,
the three-bay façade of this house is the classic front of the white or center-passage
house. Larger or smaller versions were built throughout the Appalachian states.
Over the generations, additions made original "I" footprints into L's and T's, but
the symmetry of the façade's window and door openings remained a constant. The
bearded man at left is Arnold Schofield, a National Park Service intern.
(Photograph by Geraldine Johnson, LC-AFC BR2-20257-36A)

As noted in the previous chapter, the extent of land ownership in early Appalachia is still a matter of debate and may be as difficult to untangle as the
shingled claims and poorly described boundaries that made the region a paradise for land lawyers in the first place. The most pessimistic view argues that
between one-third and one-half of Appalachian households owned no land
and had no hope of inheriting or buying it.[57] On the other hand, given the size
of the region and the character of its terrain, scraps of tillable land and abundant forest access were available to nonlandowners in back valleys and remote
hollows and ridgetops in even the most populous areas. This suggests that
landless white people and even some slaves had access to resources they could
control, if not own.

In the records that document the lives of backcountry people, squatters and slaves lead a shadowy existence. Slaves of course were recorded as property, not as persons, in the censuses and legal documents that illuminate social life in Appalachia before the Civil War. These tell us the numbers of slaves in the Appalachian region, the proportions of free to enslaved persons among African Americans, and the districts within the region that held the greatest numbers and proportions of slaves. This data is summarized for the census years 1790, 1830, and 1860 in Table 2.1. References to slave life appear in the observations of travelers and in the records of slaveowners and their neighbors, but not until late antebellum times do we get much direct testimony from enslaved people themselves.

The recollections of Lizzie Grant, for example, were recorded in Texas during the 1930s, but they tell us something about her life on a Kanawha valley plantation in the years immediately preceding the Civil War. Her owner kept a large garden, giving the slaves "what he wanted them to have out of his garden," which usually meant some greens "and a few potatoes." While many slaves recalled being hungry most of the time or getting only cheap or fatty foods, Grant recalled being well fed. "Yes we had plenty to eat such as it was. We had cornbread gathered right out of the field as we ate it grated by hand, nothing in it but water and salt. We had pork and beef cooked on the open fireplace and . . . it sure was good. We had plenty rabbit, possum and fish, but I never did care anything about such except fish. I sure did like fish fried good and brown on a big flat iron skillet in plenty [of] hog grease. That was all the kind of grease we had back there in those early days." Grant lived with her husband, who was picked out for her by her owner, in a cabin that fell somewhere in between the categories of log cabin and log house discussed above. "All the cracks were daubed with mud to keep out the rain. Our beds were built down on the ground in one corner of our quarters out of moss, shucks, and grass. Yes, we kept real warm in there all the time as we had a big rock fireplace. . . . We kept plenty of wood as that and water was about all we got free."[58]

With squatters, as with slaves, most of what we know comes from the comments of others. Something of their attitude about land ownership comes through in the complaints of James Logan, who contended with Irish Protestants who occupied land that Logan had set aside for the future profit of the Penn family. The squatters "alledg[ed] that it was against the Laws of God & Nature that so much Land should lie idle, while so many Christians wanted it to labour on and raise their Bread."[59] Logan had the squatters removed by force and their cabins burned, but in later periods squatters were not without

Table 2.1. Appalachian Slave and Free Black Populations, 1790–1860

Year/Region	Total Population (%)	Slave Population (%)	Free Black Population (%)
1790			
Official	307,408 (100)	18,224 (5.9)	1,172 (0.4)
Core	86,474 (100)	6,017 (7.0)	562 (0.6)
1830			
Official	2,609,449 (100)	210,837 (8.1)	23,418 (0.9)
Core	531,021 (100)	57,152 (10.8)	5,295 (1.0)
1860			
Official	5,443,287 (100)	516,914 (9.5)	51,330 (0.9)
Core	1,080,189 (100)	102,769 (9.5)	9,395 (0.9)

Source: GAHM.

resources, as George Washington learned with respect to a piece of land that William Crawford had obtained for him on Chartiers Creek, an Ohio tributary not far from Pittsburgh. "As soon as a man's back is turned, another is on his land," Crawford complained in 1772. "The man that is strong and able to make others afraid of him seems to have the best chance as times go now."[60] Crawford began trying to get the squatters off Colonel Washington's land in 1773, but it was not until 1796 that President Washington finally managed to evict them permanently. As he commented about squatters generally, removing them was "a Work of great difficulty; perhaps of equal cruelty, as most of these People are poor swarming with large families, [and] have sought out these retreats on which perhaps their future prospects in likeway wholely depend."[61]

What was true in Washington's day was also true of later periods. Back-country people with modest expectations or poor chances in life could afford to gamble on occupying a piece of land with access to the forest and room for a cabin and a cornfield. They could enjoy its use, employing such delaying tactics as might be available locally against an absentee owner, until finally the sheriff ran them off, at which point they might find another piece of land or move off to the west. Persons who squatted on Cherokee land in the last years before Removal simply moved each time that the authorities came to hassle them and then moved back again when the officers were gone. However, Georgia law made squatters ineligible for the lotteries that carved up the Cherokee domain. Notwithstanding the advantages of access to the forest commons in Appalachia, landlessness and tangled land titles had an effect on the region's future and was probably responsible for the large numbers of people who moved to the north side of the Ohio valley once the Indians had been evicted from the future Middle West.

Ralph Mann's study of Tazewell County, Virginia, in the ridge-and-valley country northwest of Wytheville, throws light on the role that land played in the antebellum Appalachian economy. Mann found that four relatively distinct communities developed there during the period between the American Revolution and the Civil War. One neighborhood endowed with rich land and known simply as "the Cove" developed a middle-class society formed of substantial farms established by early settlers and maintained by their descendants as family holdings throughout the period. This section had few tenants or squatters but a larger proportion of slaves than the other three communities, peaking at 35 percent of the district's population in 1850. A neighboring valley of poorer land was also a domain of family farms, but with no large holdings, much vacant and unclaimed land, and a handful of slaves, each living alone as part of a white household.

A third neighborhood stretching northeast at the edge of the Appalachian Plateau remained 90 percent woodland in 1860. Settled during the frontier wars, this district had been devastated by an Indian attack in 1786. It was not reoccupied until 1798 and was populated mainly by tenants and squatters living on land owned by survivors of the original settler family. This neighborhood demonstrated few signs of commercial activity until the late antebellum period, when a nonresident owner arrived to take over the development of his lands. He and an heir of the original family owned most of the slaves in this section, and more than half of the white households engaged in farming still owned no land. The fourth neighborhood was located in the unique geological feature known as Burke's Garden, a large expanse of fertile and level land almost completely enclosed by Garden Mountain. "Yeoman family farms" accounted for a plurality of landholders in the Garden, but there was also a mix of tenants, landless white farm laborers, and slaves working its increasingly commercial agriculture. Moreover, large landowners with retinues of white and black dependents dominated the district's social life and competed for economic leadership. This included members of the Floyd family, heirs to the colonial Patton-Preston landholdings and by this time prominent leaders in the affairs of Virginia. Most of the Floyds lived elsewhere, but they visited often; their holdings in the Garden were operated by a son-in-law.[62]

The four types of communities in Tazewell could be found in nearly every corner of Appalachia, often in similarly close juxtaposition. There were, of course, many variants and combinations in the mix of old settlers and new-comers, landed and landless, small farmer and large, and tenants, squatters, and slaves. These variations in turn related to differences in the quality and accessibility of land. Tazewell County's affluent Cove community was a case in point. The coves of the Appalachians are linear districts of rich lands along the valleys of headwater streams, opening to the south or southwest or other-wise sheltered by mountains from the prevailing winter storm tracks from the north and west. The term "cove" derived from a maritime term connoting a sheltered harbor, not surprising in view of the proportion of Appalachian set-tlers who came from the sea-girt British Isles. Cove hillsides offered the most abundant hardwood forests. Cherokee towns were almost always located in coves. A cove's combination of favorable environmental resources was bal-anced by relatively difficult access from the roads that followed the Great Val-ley or the Piedmont, a fact that offered the Cherokees a measure of protection against their enemies but that inhibited the commercial potential for cove farmers. The relative proximity of Tazewell's Cove to the Great Wagon Road was undoubtedly one of the reasons for its antebellum prosperity. North Cove, located east of Asheville near Marion, North Carolina, was, in Lan-man's words, a "charming valley . . . twelve miles long, from a half to a mile in width, completely surrounded by mountains, highly cultivated, watered by the Catawba, and inhabited by intelligent and worthy farmers."[63] Cades Cove in East Tennessee, settled around 1818 by whites anticipating the following year's renegotiation of the Cherokee boundary, was a more typical example in its relative isolation, but its occupants still achieved a modest prosperity in an-tebellum times, thanks to the cove's diversity of resources.[64]

Settlers employed another maritime term, "hollow," to connote land that was less desirable but that was still tillable and had access to the surrounding forest. Hollow was originally a term for the U- or V-shaped spaces between the crests of waves in the sea. Applied to Appalachian terrain, it came to mean narrow, small valleys in every part of the region. Hollows were tributary to a cove or another type of sizable valley threaded by a creek or, in Pennsylvania, a "run," and in Virginia, a "draft." The term was used in such a way as to imply finality; once people had moved up into the hollows of a watershed, there was no further hope of tillable land. Actually, this was not quite true. Hollows had tributaries of their own, lateral branches of the main stream along which land could be farmed only at an angle—that is, with crops, pas-tures, orchards, and buildings perched on a slope. The main hollow itself had strips of flat or gently sloping land that served the purposes of subsistence well enough.

The earliest settlers on such land usually established themselves in the mouth of a hollow, near the place where the tributary stream joined the main valley or cove. Later population growth and the division of land among large families drove people up into the branches. "Branchwater" farming came to represent a hardscrabble way of making a living in hill country, especially in the Appalachian Plateau. Overpopulation and the clearing of poor and erosion-prone land in the Allegheny and Cumberland plateaus were basic reasons why Appalachia began to decline relative to other sections of the country in the mid-nineteenth century.[65]

While lucky or well-connected settlers landed in coves in the Blue Ridge or Great Valley, the speculator wanted good land that was close to a road or a river. Washington stated the ideal as well as anyone in his instructions to William Crawford about what type of land he wanted to acquire in the west: "Bottom next to the Water (in most places) is very rich; as you approach to the Hills you come (in many) to a thin white Oak Land, and poor; the Hills as far as we could judge were from half a Mile to a Mile from the River; poor and steep in the parts we see, with Pine growing on them." Generally, in Washington's judgment, the relatively low hills close to the big rivers were fit only to supply the bottomlands with timber for construction and with fuel, and so wherever he could get them, he wanted bottomlands. They were the kind that would sell, that would earn in the long run (as he stated in 1786) a greater return on capital than any other available form of investment. He wanted his land "high, dry, and level," or, if not level, Washington wrote, "at least wavy, that is, in little risings, sufficient to lay it dry and fit for the plough." There should be good timber and meadows, a place for a mill, and, ideally, access to a respectable road or a river without too much danger from floods.[66]

Such descriptions fit the ribbons of Ohio and Kanawha bottomlands that Washington chose for himself in 1770, as they did the limestone valley lands and Tennessee River bottoms that Virginia planters and Georgia speculators chose from Alabama's public lands a half-century later, leaving to small farmers and latecomers the thin soils and rocky ridgetops of the neighboring hills. Getting the best land, however, entailed a combination of on-the-ground knowledge and good political contacts, which is why the office of surveyor was a stepping stone to wealth in the Floyd, Jackson, and other elite families. Those whose prime capital was political, such as the Jeffersonian politicians who overlaid southern West Virginia and eastern Kentucky with speculative claims, compensated for their lack of local knowledge by using land warrants to lay claim to huge surveys embracing thousands of acres, the geometric boundaries of which bore no relation to the natural contours of the district in question.

On the western fringe of the Appalachian Plateau, commercial possibilities were linked to the Ohio and its numerous navigable tributaries, extending from the Monongahela in the north to the Big Sandy, Licking, and Kentucky River basins in the south. In central Tennessee and southeast Kentucky, the Cumberland River, whose navigation extended deep into the plateau of the same name, offered a similar highway. Transportation on the Tennessee River, however, was obstructed by the dangerous narrows west of Chattanooga, where the river's rocky passage through the Cumberlands produced, among other hazards, a celebrated whirlpool known as The Suck; boatmen who made it though that difficulty then had to face the rapids at Muscle Shoals, halfway along the river's loop through northern Alabama.

The quality of the soils in the river lowlands and in the parallel Sequatchie and Coosa valleys compensated to some extent for the difficult transportation. While bottomland farms along the main rivers grew commercial crops in ways that resembled plantation agriculture, nearby ridgetop and tableland farms with gentler angles of slope and relatively good access to a river offered possibilities to stockmen. So did the "back valleys" and highland plateaus of the ridge-and-valley province east of the plateaus. More limited in possibilities were the true plateaus of the region—that is, the high-altitude tablelands immediately to the west of the Allegheny Front in Maryland and (West) Virginia and the intermontane basins of the Blue Ridge plateau in western North Carolina. Although these districts contained much level and rolling land, the streams that drained them passed through rugged, steep-sided canyons, harrowing for travelers. Their native grasslands afforded good summer pasture, as already noted, but only the hardiest crops could withstand the short growing season, and these were hardly worth the price of cartage over the difficult roads that connected them to the Great Valley or the navigable rivers farther downstream.

When Francis Asbury passed through the Watauga headwaters in 1790, he found people anxious because a late frost had killed their crops in the field. Visiting the same area a generation later, Elisha Mitchell found only hunters. When Mitchell judged the value of Ashe County land, he judged by the luxuriant height of the hardwoods, not the length of the growing season. But he noted correctly that livestock, not crops, was the key to wealth in high-altitude country. Anne Royal made in effect the same conclusion about the Greenbrier valley in (West) Virginia. Both Mitchell and Royal commented on the charm and fun-loving character of these regions' young people, and both were sensitive to the delights of the scenery. But both fretted about the locals' lack of ambition, especially when it came to education, and Royal complained about the climate, "their everlasting hills of freezing cold."[67]

A Staunton lawyer, visiting mountainous Pocahontas County, West Virginia, shortly after its formation in 1823, described it in a letter home as "a place as much out of the world as Crim Tartary." And yet, he added, "Pocahontas is a fine grazing county, and the support of the people is mainly derived from their flocks of cattle, horses and sheep, which they drive over the mountains to market. There is little money among them except after these excursions, but they have little need of it—every want is supplied by the happy country they possess, and of which they are as fond as the Swiss of their mountains."[68] Traversing similar country twenty years later, Charles Lanman passed farms that seemed to have been "whittled out of the forest." "The people are ignorant, so far as book-learning is concerned," he continued, "but they are well-supplied with common sense, and are industrious enough to deserve better success than the most of them enjoy."[69]

Traveling in the mountains of Alabama, Tennessee, and North Carolina in 1854, Frederick Law Olmsted came to similar conclusions:

Extreme poverty is rare in the mountains, but a smaller proportion of the people live in a style corresponding to that customary among what are called in New England "fore-handed folks." The number who can be classed as moderately well-informed, using the rural New England standard, is extremely small. . . . The great majority live in small and comfortless log huts, two detached cabins usually forming the habitation of a family. . . . The table is usually abundantly provided. . . . Notwithstanding the ignorance of the people, books are more common than even in the houses of the slave owners of the planting districts. [Mountaineers] seemed fond of reading aloud, those who were able—in a rather doleful and jolting manner.

"The generally open-hearted, frank, and kindly character of the people," Olmsted concluded, "the always agreeable scenery, usually picturesque, and in some parts grandly beautiful, and the salubrious atmosphere, cool at night, and though very hot, rarely at all enervating at mid-day, made this part of my journey extraordinarily pleasant. I would have been willing to continue it for months."[70]

In the greater Appalachian region as a whole—that is, within its official boundaries extending from New York south to Mississippi and from east to west according to the boundaries discussed in Chapter 1—354 out of an eventual 406 counties had been established by 1860, containing a census count of 5,425,719 persons, including 1,304 Indians and 512,929 slaves. (The corresponding figures for the core region defined above were 1,057,887, 1,271, and 98,597, respectively.) The newest of these counties was McDowell in what would become the southernmost tip of West Virginia, established in 1860 with 1,535 people and the only county in all of Appalachia south of the Mason-Dixon Line to record a population with no slaves.

During the middle third of the nineteenth century, eastern Kentucky emerged as a kind of "pan-Appalachian" region. Initially, most frontiersmen bound for Kentucky bypassed the east, heading for the Bluegrass region or northern Kentucky by the two predominant routes of settlement, the Ohio River and Cumberland Gap. Tradition traces the population of eastern Kentucky to persons who dropped out along the way due to poverty or ill luck, but that is a difficult proposition to verify, and in any event the 1820 census recorded only 24,000 people in the core Appalachian portion of the state (4 percent of the statewide total population), compared to 154,000 in western Virginia and 131,000 in East Tennessee. However, eastern Kentucky more than quadrupled its population between 1830 and 1860, drawing a large part of this increase from Virginia, North Carolina, and Tennessee.[71]

Bordering sections of Virginia and West Virginia grew in much the same fashion. For example, Valentine Hatfield and his family migrated north from the Great Valley into Logan County, West Virginia, in the mid-1830s, a dozen years after the county was formed. Not long afterward, two of Valentine's sons moved across the ridge that separated the Guyandotte watershed from the Tug Fork of the Big Sandy and settled on Mates Creek across the river from Kentucky. The families among whom they settled—Vances, Rutherfords, Chafins, and McCoys—had followed a similar path a few years earlier.[72] Dickinson County, Virginia, also on the Kentucky border, attracted overflow population from western North Carolina as well as from the nearby Great Valley.

The attractions that drew settlers into the previously vacant inner reaches of the Appalachian Plateau did not appeal only to the poor and obscure. Members of the Floyd family, for example, which owned land all over southwestern Virginia, knew Logan County from hunting expeditions, but in 1853, George Rogers Clark Floyd came there to settle. The son and younger brother of Virginia governors and the grandson of John Floyd, the surveyor and Indian fighter at Point Pleasant and Blue Licks, Floyd earlier had gone west to Wisconsin with a federal appointment but failed to find his fortune there after the territory became a state. He quickly became Logan's largest resident landowner, patenting some 20,000 acres in the county by 1860, together with other large acreages in nearby Kentucky. He also built a sturdy log house, one of the four rooms of which he lined with books. His family, having converted to Roman Catholicism (though the Floyd males did not advertise this when running for office), was a patron of the new western Virginia diocese of Wheeling and Wytheville. Accordingly, Colonel Floyd sent his daughters to convent school in Wheeling and his sons to colleges in Virginia and Maryland. In due course, the Hatfields became clients of the Floyds, as the Floyds had once been of the Prestons and Pattons, themselves clients, in turn, of the eighteenth-century land grantors who opened western Virginia to settlement. In such fashion, the oligarchical traditions of the plantation aristocracy were extended into the backwoods of Appalachia.[73]

The crop then known as Indian corn unified the diverse agriculture of the Appalachian region during the period between the Indian conquests and the Civil War. Was the application to the maize plant of an English word that originally embraced all forms of cultivated grain a result of colonial ignorance or simply testimony to the plant's importance? "Corn was not only important as a primary foodstuff, it was central to mountain subsistence culture. Corn was ground into meal and made into whiskey; its husks and leaves were woven into hats, dolls, mops, and chair bottoms. Corncobs served as primitive toilet paper, fire starters, bowls for tobacco pipes, and hog and cattle fodder. The harvesting of corn also greatly influenced social relations, bringing neighbors and communities together for annual fall cornshuckings."[74]

The difficulty of getting surplus corn to market was one of the things that inspired the abundant production of whiskey. When the federal government decided to tax the liquor in order to raise internal revenue, an armed rebellion ensued. Although the Whiskey Rebellion of 1794 was centered in the Monongahela country of southwest Pennsylvania and northwest Virginia, protestors throughout the Appalachian region offered resistance in the form of resolutions, tax refusals, and the intimidation of revenue collectors, amounting to one of the few expressions of "perfect unanimity" in the region's entire political history. President Washington and Secretary of the Treasury Alexander Hamilton considered sending troops to western North Carolina but eventually chose the Pittsburgh district as a more convenient target. As federal troops marched across the Alleghenies, the protests subsided and the leaders of the rebellion were pardoned, not hanged as Hamilton had so fervently wished. But though the whiskey tax remained on the books until the 1840s, it was never again collected in Appalachia, as no candidates could be found for the unpopular and even dangerous position of internal revenue collector.[75]

Corn was not the only source of spirits. "Monongahela whiskey," as famous on the frontier as the product of Bourbon County, Kentucky, would become, was made from rye. Surplus peaches, plums, and apples were made into brandy. The knowledge of distilling was widespread among backcountry farmers, especially, tradition holds, among those of Irish extraction, and the equipment needed was simple. However, the skill was perfected among certain families in each neighborhood, and they became the specialists, supplying taverns and ordinaries as well as quenching their neighbors' thirst. Tourists approaching Mount Mitchell in 1857 came across a distiller who specialized in apple brandy, or applejack as it was called. He complained to them bitterly about a recent North Carolina "quart law" forbidding the sale of liquor by the drink at distilleries. "'Formerly neighbors mought come, take a civil drink together, and go their ways; now they can't buy less nor a quart. Now a quart of licker is too much for any man; and a poor man don't like to fling away what he has paid his money for, so he is bound to git drunk, and hits the Legislater's fault.'"[76]

Another popular drug, tobacco, inspired no taxes in this period but followed a path similar to whiskey. Mountain farmers everywhere grew supplies of their own, but commercial tobacco was also available on the frontier in the late eighteenth century as tobacco plantations were developed in the broad bottomlands along the Ohio, Cumberland, and Kanawha Rivers. The richest man in western Virginia in 1860 was probably Albert Gallatin Jenkins, Harvard graduate, congressman, and future Confederate general, who operated a tobacco plantation on the banks of the Ohio. Another Ohio River plantation was located on one of George Washington's surveys and operated by a descendant of Lord Fairfax. Nevertheless, although corn never acquired the prestige of the plantation staples, it was the anchor of the region's antebellum economy. "Corn took up about one tenth of the average farmer's improved land," according to one authority, "but that figure varied across the region, with Ridge and Valley farmers [including the Great Valley] having by far the most acreage in corn production." Tennessee was the greatest corn-producing state by 1840, with nearly equal amounts of the crop coming from the Great Valley and the Cumberland plateau. In spite of its later start, by 1860 East Tennessee became, after western Virginia, the most populous part of Appalachia, comprising nearly 30 percent of the regional core.

Stockmen in the Shenandoah Valley and the adjacent valleys along the Potomac's South Branch began feeding corn to their cattle by 1760 and soon realized the enhanced value of a corn crop that could walk itself to market when consumed by cattle, horses, and hogs. From these districts a commercial livestock industry spread west across the mountains into eastern and central Ohio and the Kentucky Bluegrass, south through the Great Valley into East Tennessee, and southwest into the Greenbrier valley of (West) Virginia. As the industry spread through the region, older centers such as the South Branch and Greenbrier valleys became known for the quality of their livestock.[77] Away from these centers, cattle drovers bought surplus animals in small lots from backwoods farmers and drove them to market. As early as 1742, drovers were observed along the Great Wagon Road driving cattle to Philadelphia. As the industry matured, corn-fed cattle became the norm for urban markets as they fetched higher prices in cities such as Baltimore and Philadelphia in the north and Charleston and Savannah in the south. Lanman observed herds numbering five hundred or more moving east over the turnpikes of western North Carolina and Virginia in 1848; he also visited with prosperous stockmen who moved their own herds to market and others who specialized in one or another branch of the industry, such as operating feeder lots or the drover stands and taverns that dotted the roads over which the cattle passed.[78] The emergence of a corn-fed livestock complex further encouraged experimentation in the breeding of cattle and horses and, eventually, in the hybridization of corn.

The clearing and woodlands of a settler household were gendered spaces. As in the Indian villages, there were places where women's work and men's work were carried on, with tools appropriate to each sex in its territory. Euro-American culture restricted women's sphere more closely than was the case with Native Americans. Men and women spent more time together, for one thing; there was no village council house where idle men gathered to talk and smoke, although country stores sometimes served this function as they became more common. In winter white men spent more time in their family dwellings than native males had. There were also tasks that men and women shared—scraping splits for chair bottoms and baskets by the winter fire, for example, or hoeing corn in the summer. Generally, however, women worked to diurnal rhythms—feeding and otherwise meeting the needs of children and adults, often including elderly parents, entailed tasks that had to be repeated the next day or at least the next week. Men's work was seasonal: plowing and planting in spring, tending crops in summer, harvesting in fall, butchering and hunting in autumn, felling trees, clearing brush, repairing gear in winter, and tending to the requirements of horses and cattle that were likewise seasonal. Women tended to chickens, men to horses, women fed pigs and milked cows, men rounded up the half-wild hogs from the woods and drove cattle, horses, and hogs to market or made deals with the drovers. When cattle or hogs were butchered at home, men handled the heavy work, skinning and stringing up carcasses and quartering the meat, which women then trimmed into smaller pieces and rendered the fat into lard.

Women generally controlled the space inside the house, but men owned the property and almost exclusively were the ones who dealt with strangers and with distant authorities. The porch of a cabin or house—a modification of the East Indian/Caribbean veranda that became popular in the late colonial tidewater and gradually made its way into the mountains—was a sort of neutral zone. An outdoor living and work space in a damp climate, a haven for children above and dogs and chickens underneath, the porch became a ubiquitous feature of mountain domestic architecture over the course of the nineteenth century. Men and women shared it as work space during mild weather, strangers could come up on it without invitation, and business could be transacted there without further hospitality being offered, though this latter case was rare.

The mountain family was patriarchal in a way that contrasted strongly with Native American culture, but otherwise the two societies had much in common. Visitors who looked at both cultures from a distance frequently commented on this and assumed, generously, that the Indians had imparted their knowledge of mountain living to backwoodsmen, or, more typically, that the backcountry induced a kind of reversion to "savagery." Some of the engendering of life among both peoples could be explained by nature: Women bore and nursed children (and suffered the very considerable risks of childbirth); men had larger muscles better fitted to heavy work and generally more endurance on strenuous journeys. In all but a handful of cases recorded by anthropologists, women have been the gatherers, men the hunters, and this was no less true of Appalachia. But most of backwoods life's gendered arrangements originated in culture. Strangers in the mountains both before and after the displacement of the natives noticed the daily demands made upon women and, since these visitors saw things from the vantage point of the clearing—if they were not actually seated before the hearth—they took the idleness of men in domestic space as a sign of their laziness and their enslavement of women. "In a rude hunter's state of society the women become schquaws [sic]," Mitchell observed after his visit to the Watauga headwaters, "very pretty ones, but schquaws notwithstanding."[79] At the houses of men he admired, however, or who provided some service on his tour of the high country, he was silent on the industry of women, though presumably they fed him and he often commented on their looks.

The fact was that most men worked hard also, but out of the ken of visitors. Almost all testimony suggests, however, that males were more prone to drunkenness and to the other forms of abuse to which alcohol often led. Native American traditions of matrilineal descent, easier divorce, and the likelihood that an injured woman's male relatives would take revenge upon the abuser may have kept domestic violence in check among the Indians. In white society, domestic violence was considered a private matter, and the few instances in which it was mentioned in records tended to involve church discipline rather than the law. The notorious case of Frances Stewart Silver, hanged in western North Carolina for the murder of her husband in 1833, testifies to the extremes of this practice, since her lawyer raised neither of the explanations by which plausible legend has explained the crime—Charles Silver's infidelities or his abuse of his wife—and Frances's own father discouraged her from telling her side of the story, urging her on the gallows to "die with it in you, Frankie," which she did.[80]

Women rarely made it into the records by which we reconstruct life in backwoods society. We know that Frances Silver was an accomplished carder and spinner of wool because this was specifically stated in connection with her trial. But we don't know what she did with the product of her spinning— whether she wove it into cloth or traded it, and, if the latter, for cash or barter, and whether she got to keep the proceeds earned from her work. Even after census takers began to collect more details about the residents of the households they counted in 1840, very little about women was recorded if there was a man in the household, even if the male was a widow's teenaged son. Even so, examining the records that do exist shows that "women were actively engaged in a variety of productive strategies that underwrote household subsistence and contributed to the growing commodification of regional economies."[81]

One of the things that served to distinguish eastern Kentucky farms from farms in the Northeast and Midwest was "the remarkably high per-farm values of household manufacturing." Of course, men contributed to this, but as a local commentary noted in 1878, most household manufacturing resulted largely from the labors of women. "They still ply the shuttle, hold the distaff, and chant to the chorus of the spinning wheel . . . and large quantities of home-made jeans, linseys, linens, and cottonade, &c., are manufactured by the old process of hand labor. Besides this, there are produced, for home consumption and traffic, large quantities of butter, eggs, chickens, ducks, geese, turkeys, guineas, feathers, beeswax, honey, ginseng, maple sugar, molasses, shuck and bark collars, leather, home-made, shoes, &c., &c." All were produced by women, with the possible exception of the leather and the shoes.[82]

The Cherokees had honorific titles for women who bent the rules and distinguished themselves as warriors or hunters. In Euro-American society, however, crossing gender lines could produce confusion. Consider the case of Dilly Wyatt, a young woman from the Cheat Mountains of (West) Virginia who astonished the popular mid-nineteenth-century magazine writer Porte Crayon (David Hunter Strother) by her performance as a fiddler at a dance he attended in a backwoods schoolhouse. Crayon learned that Wyatt was accomplished in many other ways. "She could cook and keep house equal to any maid or wife on the fork. She could shear a sheep, card and spin the wool, then knit a stocking or weave a gown with a promptness and skill that were beyond rivalry. Besides these feminine accomplishments, she could fish, shoot with a rifle, ride, swim, or skin a bear, in a manner to challenge the supremacy of the other sex." He could only explain this by relaying a story about the girl's having been courted and jilted by a man from the genteel lowlands, upon which, her heart broken, she had thrown over feminine decorum and practiced her masculine pursuits as a kind of mourning. Yet Strother also reported that she was the only child of a widower, "a stout herdsman and mighty hunter of this wild valley," and so gave us the kernel of a more plausible explanation: that Wyatt's father, as fathers will do, had simply trained his only child in the skills he knew how best to teach. Particularly in the absence of sons, fathers sometimes trained their daughters to do men's work, with or without the presence and cooperation of their mothers.[83] By contrast, there is the case of a North Carolina man who had eight daughters and who therefore hired a neighbor boy to live with the family and share the male work on the farm.[84]

Women were not always confined to the clearing. Rather, the boundaries of gender extended outward to encompass neighborhoods and the schools, churches, and stores of neighborhood crossroads. The schoolhouse dance where Dilly Wyatt performed was a case in point. Teenaged girls and young women, like their brothers, were permitted to visit friends and stay overnight, as well as to attend churches and neighborhood schools. Of these institutions, churches probably had the greatest influence on men and women alike. Religion became one of the identifying marks of Appalachian culture, but a religion that dwelt on the inevitability of sin also preached a gospel of salvation. Dr. Mitchell, a thoroughgoing New Englander and middle class in his values, was taken aback by the relaxed sexual morality he encountered in the moun-

The handwritten caption on the back of this photograph, taken in the Great Smoky Mountains sometime between 1910 and 1920, identifies this bear hunter as "L. H. (Harrison) Moore, son of Big Bill Walker and Mary Ann Moore," suggesting that the Carolina backwoods was still, as Elisha Mitchell termed it a century earlier, a place for domestic "irregularities." (Courtesy of GSMNP Archives)

tains. "Tis a terrible region for these irregularities," he wrote to his wife, with respect to the marital arrangements prevalent among the hunters. This launched him on a lengthy argument about the necessity of female virtue and the inevitability of male predation. "I wish it to be strongly emphasized upon my daughters that *where a woman is concerned, no man is to be trusted—every man is half a demon.*" Farther down the Watauga River, he heard of a family that included an unmarried daughter and her illegitimate child, who were "treated with tenderness and affection by the family, and what is most strange her brother is said to be on the most intimate terms with his sister's seducer."[85]

Preindustrial Appalachia had a farm-and-forest economy, and it differed significantly from the economies of both of its parent regions, Pennsylvania and the plantation South. Appalachia diverged from Pennsylvania in the character and intensity of its commercial agriculture. Although the Quaker colony may have witnessed the creation of the farm-and-forest economy in its colonial backcountry, from the early eighteenth century onward Pennsylvania's most thickly settled areas developed what experts call the "Pennsylvania-midland" system of agriculture—the first half of the name for the system's birthplace, the second for its spread across the Midwest during the nineteenth century to become the predominant form of commercial farming.

Pennsylvania-midland farms produced marketable quantitities of field crops and livestock. During the 1850s, as the superiority of the Midwest for this type of farming became increasingly apparent, ambitious Pennsylvania farmers began to specialize and modernize. Truck gardens, commercial orchards, and dairy farms emerged to supply the cities of Philadelphia and Pittsburgh and the emerging mining and lumbering districts in the northeast and central parts of the state. The establishment of the Pennsylvania Agricultural College (now Pennsylvania State University) in the exact center of the state in 1859 placed it in the vanguard of scientific agriculture. These developments had an impact on the territory immediately south of the Mason-Dixon Line—for example, in the Shenandoah Valley, which was increasingly devoted to wheat production, and the South Branch valley along the upper Potomac, which shared an emphasis on grain-fed livestock with Pennsylvania ridge-and-valley counties just to the north. Similarly, the southwestern Pennsylvania counties bordering (West) Virginia had begun to specialize in sheep and wool production and were drawing northwestern Virginia and southeastern Ohio counties into this orbit. But the backcountry practice of open-range forest farming had nearly disappeared in Pennsylvania; a belt of counties along the Allegheny Front and on the eastern edge of the Appalachian Plateau revealed, in the 1860 census, the low ratios of improved to unimproved land and the relatively high levels of home manufacturing that typified the farms of central and southern Appalachia. But these values, though striking in comparison with other Pennsylvania counties, were low compared to those observed in, say, Clay County, Kentucky.[86]

Just as the farm-and-forest economy set Appalachia apart from ancestral Pennsylvania, so, too, it differed from the surrounding lowland South in its relative lack of reliance on slavery. Shortly before he became governor of Virginia in 1830, John Floyd wrote a lengthy disquisition on southwest Virginia stock raising. One of its chief advantages, in Floyd's view, was its labor requirements. In general, he explained, "slaves are not necessary, very few however to the feeder and still fewer to him who sells from the pasture, and none to those who furnish the store cattle, because they most generally raise them in the range, as it is called, that is by turning [them] in the forest or in the mountains during the winter months."[87]

The slave insurrection of 1831 known as Nat Turner's Rebellion forced Floyd to reflect further on the disadvantages of slavery. "I could not have believed there was half the fear among the people of the lower country in respect to their slaves. Before I leave this government, I will have contrived to have a law passed gradually abolishing slavery in this State, or at all events to begin the work by prohibiting slavery on the West side of the Blue Ridge Mountains." With the governor's encouragement, a group of "talented young westerners" led by his nephews William Ballard Preston and James McDowell moved for the gradual abolition of slavery in the commonwealth, provoking a famous debate that went on in the General Assembly for more than a week. Eventually the motion failed, and the group did not put forward Floyd's fallback position of abolishing slavery only in western Virginia. Two years later, East Tennesseans presented twenty-five petitions for the abolition of slavery to the state's constitutional convention of 1834. However, not only did the convention reject by a 38–20 vote the idea of including a plan for emancipation in the new constitution, but it adopted a Middle Tennessee proposal to require any future act of emancipation to receive the explicit approval of slaveowners. Not long afterward, the tide turned and Appalachian critics of slavery found themselves on the defensive against an aggressive proslavery element that grew more and more influential in southern political life.[88]

There were, however, other aspects of the Appalachian economy that fully reflected the peculiar institutions of the antebellum South. These included all three of the region's principal nonagricultural industries: ironmaking, salt-making, and mountain resorts. With the exception of names connoting the presence of water or streams, the most common names upon the land as Appalachian settlements matured were those indicating the manufacture of iron: bloomery, furnace, and forge. A bloomery smelted iron ore into "pigs" with many impurities. A furnace refined the metal by means of hotter fires and large bellows and created products made of cast iron, while a forge, powered by falling water, pounded the pigs into bars, straps, and other shapes that ironmongers and blacksmiths used to create products of wrought iron.

Edged tools and weapons were the most important metal items in the Euro-American repertory. Most of these were made of steel and generally had to be imported from distant manufacturers, although there were gunsmiths in many Appalachian communities by the 1840s, including a fully qualified Cherokee smith in the Qualla Boundary. Everything else needed around a backwoods home could be cast or wrought from iron, including nails, horseshoes, pots and kettles, agricultural tools, and strap iron for mill and wagon fixtures. Appalachia had abundant supplies of iron ore, found in outcroppings and mines across the region. Limestone, needed as the "flux" that separated melted ore from most of its impurities, was also abundant. Reaching the temperatures necessary to smelt ore required a carboniferous fuel, however. In Britain, smelters were already using bituminous coal for this purpose, or "stonecoal" as it was called to distinguish it from charcoal. In the forests of Appalachia, however, charcoal, in use since Roman times as the traditional fuel for smelting, answered the purpose.

It is estimated that it took around four hundred acres of forest per year to support a single large iron furnace. Felling all this wood and turning it into charcoal required a large force of unskilled workers. Long before coal mining and timbering salted the backwoods districts with industrial villages, there were temporary settlements or "camps" for charcoal burners and ironworkers. Slaves provided much of the muscle power for this work south of Pennsylvania; unskilled immigrant labor also became important as the nineteenth century wore on. In the well-documented case of Buffalo Forge, located on a tributary of the James River southeast of Lexington, Virginia, satellite furnaces and some twenty thousand acres of wood and ore lands located farther back in the mountains supplied the raw materials and fuel required for pig and bar iron production. More than 130 slaves supplied the labor force for the operation in 1858, 70 of whom were owned by the ironmaster, a Pennsylvania descendant of the same Dunkard family that had produced Wilhelm Mack of Max Meadows; the remaining slaves were leased from their masters in eastern Virginia. "Slave workers played a major role in practically every phase of pig iron production . . . throughout the South, from the initial construction of the stack to the completion of a successful blast. Slave masons often quarried, cut, and fitted the heavy blocks of limestone used to build the furnace. Slave carpenters and laborers erected furnace buildings from the timber cut by slave woodchoppers and sawed into lumber at slave-manned mills. Slaves built the extensive dams required to obtain waterpower to run the furnace." For skilled and clerical operations, iron producers relied on a mix of free white labor, free blacks, and hired and owned slaves, but free labor always raised problems of worker reliability and control. The ironmaster at Buffalo Forge "always felt vulnerable in Virginia depending on white workers who had freedom of movement and ready access to alcohol. Hiring skilled slave workers was also a risky proposition. There was no guarantee that their owners would send them to the same ironmaster year after year, and the slaves themselves might decide they did not want to return."[89]

At the southern end of the mountains, furnaces and forges were built in north central Alabama as early as 1818, some of which were fueled by nearby deposits of bituminous coal. Among many such locations in the Appalachian Plateau, Embree's Iron Works on the Holston River in East Tennessee (1808), the Red River iron region of Estill County, Kentucky (1806–8), and the Jackson Iron Works near Morgantown, West Virginia (1830), were places with "a regionally distinct urban-industrial character" that would later be expanded in the mining and timber camps of the industrial era. The factories that made Wheeling the Nail City of the 1840s and 1850s were first established in 1832. In Tennessee, the Embree brothers and their partners formed the Washington Iron Manufacturing Company in 1839, combining the ore, timber, and furnaces from some thirty thousand acres of land in Bumpass Cove in the Black Mountain foothills with a rolling mill and nail factory on the Holston. It is worth noting that the ironmakers who founded these installations usually came from Pennsylvania, the center of American iron manufacturing since colonial times; if they were local, they hired Pennsylvanians and advertised the fact.[90] By 1860 Tennessee was the third-largest iron producer in the nation, behind only Pennsylvania and New York.

There were also other branches of Appalachia's nascent mining industries that relied primarily on free labor. The lead mines established in colonial times on the New River near the Virginia–North Carolina line and a copper mining and smelting operation developed by northern and British investors during the 1850s in southeastern Tennessee were cases in point. Frederick Law Olmsted spent three days in the copper mining district in 1854 and found "several hundred" Cornishmen at work alongside native white miners mostly from North Carolina. He found the British miners complaining about having to drink whiskey rather than ale, and he complained himself about the quality of available public accommodations.[91] The widespread distribution of mining in antebellum times demonstrates that the environmental degradation and labor exploitation for which Appalachia later became noted had ample precedent.

Salt, essential for the preservation of meat at home and in the emerging meatpacking industry of the Ohio valley, was produced in eastern Kentucky, southwest Virginia, and the future West Virginia. In 1829 a Kentucky traveler described the most important salt-producing district along the Kanawha River:

> There are about sixty furnaces. . . . The water is obtained at the depth of about 400 feet, is pumped by horse power, boiled in long rows of 15 or 20 gallon kettles heated by fires made of stone coal dug from the adjoining mountains. Each salt work makes about 10,000 bushels of salt annually, it is principally bought up by a company of Merchants of Kentucky, who give 25 cents a bushel for it at the works, and export it to various towns by means of flat boats. The expense of establishing a Salt work is about 3,000 dollars. They are profitable.[92]

This traveler did not mention that the labor of saltmaking was principally furnished by slaves, perhaps because this seemed so normal to him that a comment was superfluous. Anne Royal, a western Virginia woman traveling through the Kanawha valley at about the same time, left a more vivid description of the working conditions: "These salt-works are dismal looking places; the sameness of the long low sheds; smoking boilers, men, the roughest that can be seen, half-naked; hundreds of boat-men; horses and oxen, ill-used and beat by their drivers; the mournful creaking of the machinery, day and night; the bare, rugged, inhospitable looking mountain, from which all the timber has been cut, gives it a gloomy appearance." "The river," Royal added in a footnote, "which is extremely beautiful, is the only relief to the eye," and even it, she noted in another passage, contained the occasional carcass of a dead horse floating by.[93]

Saltmakers also used slaves in Saltville, Virginia, and in Clay County, Kentucky, where fifteen saltworks flourished near the headwaters of the Kentucky River's South Fork. As on the Kanawha, the Kentucky saltmakers turned to stonecoal as soon as local supplies of wood were exhausted. Elsewhere coal was used for other industrial purposes wherever it lay conveniently at hand;

western Pennsylvania, the Virginia "Pan Handle" around Wheeling, and northeastern Kentucky all had coal-fired ironworks by 1840, as well as forges whose hammers were operated by coal-fired steam engines. In fact, in 1840 Pittsburgh produced more coal-fired steam horsepower than any other place in the United States; Wheeling was second, and both cities were growing into the smoky reputations that identified them for over a century. Even before he reached Pittsburgh, the Kentucky traveler "saw in the distance the dark, lowering & gloomy cloud which eternally rests over this the most filthy of all places which I have ever seen."[94]

In the hope of generating further wealth from their storehouses of minerals, several of the southern Appalachian states, following the lead of Pennsylvania and New York, established state geological surveys during the 1820s, and mountain politicians used the surveys' findings to justify state financing of canals, roads, and railroads that would improve commercial access to the Appalachian region. Elisha Mitchell's journeys into western North Carolina during the 1820s formed one such mission. During the following decade, Virginia's geological survey engaged an even more eminent scientist, William Barton Rogers, later to become the founder of MIT. "What surer foundation of permanent wealth and power of a community can be found than the store of coal and iron embosomed in the rocky strata of [Virginia's] hills and valleys," Rogers wrote in his 1837 report, "and what more efficacious stimulus to the mechanical arts, to industry in general, and to the advancement of all practical and profitable knowledge than the multifarious pursuits linked with the manufacture of iron?"[95] Rogers did not discuss the labor requirements of the envisioned industry, but we may be sure that anyone who read his report at the time understood that those requirements would be met primarily by slaves.

Mountain entrepreneurs did not need science to identify two additional exploitable resources of their region: mineral springs and scenic wonders. The notion of visiting the mountains for reasons of health was well established at the start of the settlement period. The springs of Virginia arose from a conjunction of nature, history, and fashion. After the restoration of Charles II to the British throne in 1660, royal patronage made newly fashionable the mineral hot springs at Bath, a town in southwest England built around the ruins of the extensive Roman baths at Aquae Sulis. During the eighteenth century, Bath became a showplace for wealth and fashion. Virginia's plantation gentry, always ready to emulate those Britons whom it regarded as peers, found the opportunity to do so as settlement broke through the Blue Ridge into the ridge-and-valley province of the central Appalachians. Virginia's own Bath—

Slavery survivor Levi Branham was born in 1852 and was said to have been the first literate freedman in Murray County, Georgia. (Courtesy Georgia Department of Archives and History)

now known by its postal designation of Berkeley Springs, West Virginia—was discovered in the 1730s and became public property in 1776, when Lord Fairfax donated the springs and surrounding acreage to the Colony of Virginia.

Farther south, the Virginia Hot Springs and Warm Springs, both located in what became Bath County in 1790, also remained state property, although private lessees developed the resorts that grew up around these waters. Private developers created the other spas. White Sulphur Springs, which ultimately became the most fashionable of all Virginia spas during antebellum times, was developed by the Bowyer and Caldwell families, heirs of the original settlers; in 1857, a joint stock corporation succeeded these proprietors and in turn became a subsidiary of the Chesapeake and Ohio Railway in 1910. By the time of the Civil War, several dozen similar resorts were scattered through the mountain counties along the present West Virginia–Virginia border and in the nearby Valley of Virginia.

South of Virginia, entrepreneurs in other mountain states also developed spas. In his travels of 1848, Charles Lanman bypassed White Sulphur Springs but visited Clarkesville in northeast Georgia and two resorts—Deaver's Sulphur Springs and Warm Springs—in western North Carolina, where he reported the same mix of hotels, baths, and "a large number of fashionable and sickly people from all the Southern States."[96] The spas also attracted two other types of visitors that would later be important in Appalachian tourism: residential tourists and transients. The wealthiest patrons of such places often built their own summer homes in the mountains, beginning at Virginia's White Sulphur in 1825 and the North Carolina village of Flat Rock in 1837. Flat Rock became especially popular with the Charleston aristocracy because of its convenient access to the Carolina lowcountry via Saluda Gap.

Lanman also reported "elegant country seats" for Georgia nabobs in the Clarkesville district, which afforded not only cool mountain air but access to scenic wonders such as Tallulah Gorge and Toccoa Falls. Access to the region's more remote attractions, such as Mt. Mitchell (Black Mountain) and Grandfather Mountain in North Carolina and the Blackwater wilderness in (West) Virginia's Cheat Mountains, required careful planning and native guides and were generally undertaken only by the hardier males among the tourists. But for vacationers satisfied by generic mountain views and less rigorous outings via carriage or horseback, Asheville became a popular destination. A number of hotels and taverns, developed originally for livestock drovers, and the easy vantage points it offered for admiring the nearby Smoky and Black Mountains made this "busy and pleasant village" more accessible to less wealthy travelers, although resort patrons during the prerailroad age still had to be rich enough that they could afford to spend a month or more away from their workplaces.

Promoters advanced health claims, often backed up by reams of data from medical experts, for nearly all of the resorts, claiming cures of diseases ranging from rheumatism to cancer. Even the dispassionate Lanman reported that the Clarkesville spring "is said to have saved the lives of many individuals."[97] Although these claims were often unfounded, it is easy to conclude that a stay at the waters might improve visitors' health. The remote location of most of the springs enforced at least a week (more commonly a month or two) of idleness and relaxation in preautomobile times. Mountain air brought refreshment and a relative absence of disease-bearing insects. Soaking in the waters eased the aches and pains of men who spent a large part of their lives on horseback and also calmed the nerves of Victorian ladies. If the waters were bubbly as well as soothing and warm, they could also aid in what gentlemen called "rejuvenation."

The custom of visiting the resorts in family groups facilitated courtship in a region where suitable marriage partners for the wealthy young were scattered among the predominantly rural locations of visitors' homes. The resorts provided a venue for the display of wealth and for the exchange of views on fashion and politics. The historian Ulrich B. Phillips noted that White Sulphur Springs amounted to the summer capital of the Old South, since it provided a meeting place for the propagandists of southern independence each summer and an audience of influential planters among whom to propagate their views.[98] Presidents from Jackson through Wilson regularly visited the springs; at White Sulphur, the proprietors provided free accommodations to the Kentucky statesman Henry Clay because of the patronage his presence attracted.

Because their upper-class patronage was drawn mainly from southern plantations and cities, scholars have usually treated the mountain spas as places *in* but not *of* the Appalachian region. This approach not only ignores their importance as seeds of twentieth-century Appalachia's tourism industry, but also two other points of connection between the spas and Appalachian history. As a meeting place, the springs helped to propagate the social values and political outlooks of the southern plantation-owning class among the Appalachian social elite, notwithstanding the differing economic interests of the two groups. Later they performed a similar function in linking the metropolitan rich with coal operators and their retinues of small-town lawyers and bankers. Anne Royal, who before embarking on her journalistic career had passed many years as the unhappy consort of an older man in the mountains bordering the Greenbrier valley, wrote: "This bleak, inhospitable, and dreary country, remote from commerce and navigation, destitute of arts, taste, or refinement, derives great advantages from these springs. Thousands of dollars are left here annually by those wealthy visitors; and in the meantime, as they are mostly people of taste and refinement, they bring a fund of amusement and instruction home to the doors of its inhabitants."[99]

Forming part of the instruction thus received by the mountain elite were the values that passed for civility in a servile society. For, like the iron and salt industries, but unlike mountain agriculture, the resorts depended heavily on slave labor. The wealthiest families brought entire retinues of "house servants" with them, while vacationing bachelors made do with the services of a single valet. Most of the entrepreneurs who owned or managed the mountain spas also owned slaves, though the reorganized White Sulphur Springs Company shifted entirely to free African American labor when it opened its grand new hotel there in 1858. Apart from the institutions of government and politics, there was no factor more effective in committing the Appalachian elite to the defense of plantation slavery than the mountain resorts.

Government and politics in nineteenth-century Appalachia belonged in the male sphere of activity. Women did not vote, and their legal status and property rights were at best ambiguous. Male autonomy was an unchallenged fact in politics, as fundamental as patriarchy was to society and more so even than white supremacy, at least until racial attitudes hardened as the nineteenth century wore on. Powerful men "condescended," as the expression went, to those who lacked power but were regarded, in the law and in politics, as theoretical equals of every other man. Zebulon Baird Vance of North Carolina, born in a log house but heir to the influence of his mother's prominent family, and who had studied at the university at Chapel Hill, admitted in later life to cultivating "the rough and unpolished ways which I so early affected as stepping stones to popularity among a rude mountain people."[100] A Kentucky congressional candidate campaigning in the mountains wrote to friends describing an incident in the mountain courthouse town of Manchester, where he was urged by a crowd to dance to the music of a celebrated fiddler and did so because a refusal might "be ascribed by them to aristocratic pride and seal my destiny in the mountains."[101]

The political culture that produced such attitudes was a paradox: In every Appalachian state, the political system acknowledged in one form or another

the egalitarian traditions of the frontier period, yet the system itself was dominated by the interests of a social elite modeled on the plantation gentry of the
lowlands. Asbury had seen this right away, even in the days when frontier gentlemen wore buckskin and lived in log houses: "The great landholders who
are industrious will soon show the effects of the aristocracy of wealth, by lord-
ing it over their poorer neighbors, and by securing to themselves all the offices
of profit or honour."[102] Historians have tended to agree with the bishop. In
western Virginia, where Asbury made his original observation, "there developed . . . a resident ruling class that, as it emerged to maturity after 1830,
drew its most influential leaders from lawyers who specialized in land litigation and speculation. Based in the larger courthouse towns and plying the
backwoods judicial circuits where they enjoyed a monopoly of legal expertise,
these same lawyers also provided political linkages between and within the
isolated mountain settlements."[103]

Another historian finds "two worlds in the Tennessee Mountains," one a
world of relatively isolated, relatively self-sufficient mountaineers, the other a
world of town dwellers and commerce-oriented farmers fully engaged in the
regional and national economy.[104] In Clay County, Kentucky, later the focus of
influential sociological studies that defined Appalachian poverty in the twentieth century, "early life . . . revolved around two very different systems of
production, the subsistence-oriented system of forest farming, based predominantly on family labor, that was practiced by the vast majority of the
population and a smaller, slave-based [salt] manufacturing and mercantile
economy controlled by a few wealthy families."[105]

In the southeastern section of the same state, "a financially weak landowning and merchant elite [dominated] local political offices and the distribution
of political patronage" and were themselves clients of "the quasi-aristocratic
class of slave-owning planters and lawyers who came to dominate the Bluegrass and, through it, the state as a whole."[106] In western North Carolina, an
analysis of political leadership finds that "the hierarchical order of mountain
society was capped by its slaveowners. Both they and their black property
made up a considerably smaller proportion of the populace than was true for
most of the South, but their dominance of that society was as hegemonic as
that of any Southern planter elite, and had been since the initial settlement of
the region's rich river valleys in the late eighteenth century."[107] In north Georgia, as the dramatist Lillian Smith phrased it, there developed "a chasm between rich and poor that washed deeper and deeper as the sweat of more and
more slaves poured into it."[108]

Social historians have pretty much demolished the old belief that mountain society before industrialization was a manifestation of the Jeffersonian small-holder ideal. They also agree that any attempt to understand the character and impact of the mountain class structure must begin with a fundamental institution, the county. County government in every Appalachian state was both the bastion of male supremacy and an arena whose politics cannot be understood without taking into account the operations of social class in Appalachia between the Revolution and the Civil War.

County government in the South, everywhere but in South Carolina and Louisiana, was derived from the Virginia county as it emerged at the end of the seventeenth century. In Virginia, first of all, counties were "close corporations." That is, like English boroughs, the ruling magistrates—called "justices of the peace" in Virginia and most other states—selected their own membership. Upon the creation of a new county, governors made the initial appointments of magistrates, after which, when one died or moved on, the others selected his replacement, often from among his relatives or, failing that, from among their own. The sheriff—a county's executive, collector of taxes, and enforcer of laws—was selected by the magistrates, sitting collectively as a county court. This was another office often shared out among the justices or their families. Sheriffs set the time and supervised the holdings of elections to choose a county's representatives in the legislature; these representatives frequently were justices themselves, since serving as a magistrate did not preclude the holding of other offices. After 1776 the legislature elected the governor, who selected the justices of new counties, and so on around the circle. North Carolina began implementing this system as early as 1685 as it gradually abandoned the experimental Constitutions of Carolina drawn up by John Locke. Kentucky and Tennessee originated as dependencies of Virginia and North Carolina in 1792 and 1796, respectively, and so adopted the older states' local governments more or less intact, as did Georgia in 1746 and Alabama in 1819.

No state carried the county government to greater extremes than Kentucky, which created 119 counties between 1792 and 1900 and another in 1912. This is second-largest number of counties for any state east of Texas, surpassed only by Georgia with 159. Virginia, before its division during the Civil War, also had 119; North Carolina created 100, culminating with Avery County in 1911; and Tennessee created 95. In the seaboard states, new western counties were both an expression of that section's growth and a response to mounting western demands for a larger say in the affairs of state government. Although eastern representatives subdivided tidewater counties as a means of keeping up with the west's growing legislative strength, western

Virginia had 45 of the 100 Virginia counties by 1840. North Georgia's original 7 counties, augmented by an additional 10 created in anticipation of Cherokee Removal in 1832, expanded to 39 in 1860. By that year, East Tennessee—officially defined in the Tennessee constitution as one of the state's three "grand divisions"—had 31 counties, most of them centered in or bordering the Great Valley, plus another 5 that lay in the Cumberland plateau west of the Grand Division boundary but that are here considered to be part of the Appalachian core.

Kentucky counties were indeed, as their historian suggests, "little kingdoms": "As the exclusive probate courts of the state, county courts annually controlled millions of dollars of property. . . . The court's jurisdiction over guardians and orphans affected thousands of homeless children." The court also had jurisdiction over masters and apprentices; its permission was necessary for a miller to erect milldams; it granted licenses for taverns and ordinaries, dispensed such welfare as was available to the poor, and dealt with health issues such as epidemics. County courts set tax rates and heard misdemeanors and minor civil disputes; their executive arm, the sheriff, collected taxes and supervised the holding of elections.[109]

The creation of a new county was an accommodation to residents. Since cases were tried, militias were drilled, and voting precincts were established at the county courthouse, the ideal size, once a certain threshold of population was reached, was a territory no larger than would permit a man living near the edge of a county to ride horseback to and from the county seat in the course of a single day. This made for an average size of some 335 square miles in Kentucky, with county seats located roughly fifteen miles from a county's borders. Counties in thinly populated districts were much larger in area, especially the mountain counties along the Virginia–West Virginia and North Carolina–Tennessee borders. For example, it was more than forty miles over the Blue Ridge and its foothills from Frankie Silver's home on the Tennessee border to Morganton, the Burke County seat where she was tried and hanged. In the Great Valley or along the Ohio and Tennessee Rivers, county seats such as Winchester, Parkersburg, or Knoxville also played economic roles as they grew into market towns.

But even in small, new, or thinly populated counties, the courthouse and the houses and stores that clustered nearby were prizes worth competing for. On several occasions each year, such places would be thronged with people acting as voters, jurors, lawyers, litigants, militiamen, shoppers, buyers, and sellers, along with loiterers anticipating amusement in the actions of one or more of the other groups. Men who lived part time or year round in the county seat came to have disproportionate influence in the county's political affairs. Although membership on the county court was generally apportioned equally among the leading families of each district of the county, officeholders who provided linkages between the county and regional, state, or federal political institutions or networks tended to take up residence in the county seats, even when they owned farms or other businesses in other locations.

A second institution of fundamental importance was the judicial circuit. The model for this was provided by the U.S. Constitution, under which each member of the U.S. Supreme Court began riding a judicial circuit during the 1790s. This practice soon ended as the federal government created an intermediate level of federal courts, called district courts, between the state courts and the Supreme Court. On the state level, judicial circuits were established by North Carolina in 1777, by Kentucky in 1802, and by Virginia and Tennessee in 1809. In practice, this created a three-tiered system of justice. Sitting as justices of the peace, magistrates of the county court tried misdemeanors and small civil disputes. For this purpose and for some other purposes, such as tax collection in Tennessee, counties were divided into small administrative districts called magisterial districts in Virginia and Kentucky, militia districts in Tennessee, and townships in Ohio and North Carolina. These districts were usually more or less coterminous with neighborhoods and numbered anywhere from four or five to a dozen or more. The magistrates who tried such cases were also members of the county court and usually represented one of the neighborhood's leading families. Once or twice a year these justices also sat as the "county court," but this was an executive session, not a judicial one.

At the county level, circuit courts tried the more serious criminal cases and civil trials involving larger values or nonresident litigants. Trials were held in the courthouse before a judge of the judicial circuit, and thus, although these courts had different names in different states, "circuit court" was the functional if not the official name of these bodies. As the name suggests, the judge, together with most of the lawyers, followed the circuit three or four times a year, holding court every few months in each of several counties. Circuit court days were less frequent than meetings of the county court but were just as important socially and economically and more important politically, since the lawyers who followed the circuit were usually also the politicians who competed with one another for congressional seats, judgeships, and other regional offices. To cite the Frankie Silver case again as an example: At her first trial, the prosecuting attorney was from Charlotte and the judge, on temporary assignment due to a vacancy in the circuit that included Morganton, was from eastern North Carolina.

Militia musters were also held on court days. In all states, able-bodied men between eighteen and forty-five or fifty were required to be militia members and to report for drill twice a year, following the manual created by Baron Friedrich Wilhelm von Steuben after the American Revolution. Militia units were organized on a county-by-county basis, with local companies linked with the militia of nearby counties to form regional units, usually regiments. Because militia companies elected their lieutenants, and these in turn selected their superior officers (who in turn voted on the regional colonels), musters fit right in with the electioneering spirit of court days. The musters became occasions for drinking, brawls, and athletic contests as well as military drill and were notoriously unproductive of military training. Since each man furnished his own weapon, it was not unusual to see antique and defective guns among the marchers, along with rusty swords, farm tools, and even cornstalks, if the more imaginative satires of these occasions can be believed.[110]

The militia laws came to be more honored in the breach than in the observance after the frontier period, but the War of 1812 stimulated a revival, as did the Mexican War of 1846–48 after another period of decline during the 1830s. In most cases, according to a Virginia observer, these "fuss-and-feather parades" offered equal measures of "the honorary and the ludicrous . . . a happy combination of the 'Triumph,' with its martial pageantry, and the 'Saturnalia,' with its license and merriment."[111] In large counties, musters were sometimes held apart from court days and in other locations than the county seat. For example, in 1828 Mitchell tagged along with some officers and candidates bound for an Ashe County muster in the Three Forks community, now a part of Watauga County. En route, he encountered a whiskey seller who eagerly anticipated the number of customers the muster would yield. Later, after each of the candidates made a speech, Mitchell mounted a stump himself and explained the scientific purpose of his visit to Ashe. The next day being Sunday, he forebore from further travel and delivered a sermon. If any of the more exciting events usually associated with musters occurred at this one—that is, fights, foot races, comically inept officers, or drills—Mitchell did not find them sufficiently interesting to record.[112]

In these ways, Appalachian counties became the locus for what might be called a federated oligarchy. Leading families of each neighborhood had representatives on the county court, and some of them began to specialize in other offices—in state or federal legislative offices and in circuit court judgeships and clerkships. More often than not, such specialists were lawyers or merchants; though they might also have agricultural interests, they were rarely just farmers. In Clay County, Kentucky, for example, the resident squirearchy manufactured and sold salt as well as farmed. In the overwhelmingly rural and agricultural world of western North Carolina, the region's leading politicos tended to be town-based merchants or professional men; if they owned farmland, it was rarely their primary place of business or residence. "Of the people who get their living entirely by agriculture," Olmsted informed his readers in 1860, "few own negroes; the slaveholders being chiefly professional men, shop-keepers, and men in office, who are also land owners, and give a divided attention to agriculture."[113]

A detailed study of leadership in Jeffersonian Virginia disclosed ethnocultural differences between those leaders from east of the Blue Ridge and those from the west, representing the greater influence of German and Irish Protestant ancestry and Presbyterian Church membership in the west. But in terms of social-class indicators—whether or not an officeholder was "connected" by blood or marriage to other officeholders, for example, or the proportion of slaveowners—there was little to distinguish the west from the east. Even Thomas Jefferson himself complained about the hereditary privileges of his class, but they persisted in Virginia long after his death. An assessment of western Virginia political leaders in the later antebellum years concluded that the mountain elite's advantages, like those of plantation oligarchs, were "cumulative and hereditary":

> Local offices, which were eligible to nonresidents and (until 1852) appointive, provided sinecures for impecunious relatives and training posts for younger ones. The more successful lawyers developed regional influence and competed with one another for judgeships and seats in the legislature and in Congress. Even after state and local officers became elective in 1852, the viva voce method of voting preserved habits of political deference to local notables, while of course lawyers retained the prerogatives of bench and bar.[114]

At the same time, the emergence of the so-called second American party system had the effect of widening participation in politics. Whigs and Democrats began opposing one another during the second administration of Andrew Jackson; the system was fully matured by the time of the "log cabin" campaign of 1840. Leaders of both parties proclaimed themselves bearers of time-honored party principles. Whigs, though opposed to many actions of the vigorous President Jackson, favored a strong federal government, high tariffs on imported manufactured goods, and federal subsidies for transportation or, as such programs were called in those days, for "internal improvements." Democrats favored a limited government (for practical as well as principled reasons, since a strong federal government might seriously interfere in the institution of slavery) and pledged their devotion to the common man. There were as many exceptions as there were variations on these themes, but the two-party system gradually had an impact on all levels of government. Voter participation increased in Virginia long before the state made most offices elective and removed property qualifications for voting in 1851. In presidential elections, voter turnout increased from 28 percent in 1828 to 63 percent in 1852; participation in elections for the legislature and for Congress increased proportionately. "After years of having one of the lowest rates of participation in the country, the Old Dominion produced turnouts comparable to those of Vermont, Maine, Illinois, Kentucky, and Mississippi and well ahead of Massachusetts and eleven other states."[115]

Initially, the leadership of the mountain districts was more western than southern. This is true whether we are talking about the Shenandoah Valley in late colonial times, Tennessee in the age of Sevier and Blount, or Jacksonian Alabama and Georgia. Apart from the State of Franklin and the intrigues of Aaron Burr's western collaborators with Spanish authorities in New Orleans, the first threat of mountain secession from planter-dominated state governments came from northwestern Virginia. John George Jackson, writing as "A Mountaineer" in 1803, protested Virginia's property qualification for voting and the overrepresentation of tidewater counties in the General Assembly. These threats reached a crescendo in 1816, when westerners met in a convention in Staunton to discuss their grievances, and again in 1830 with western dissatisfaction over the limited reforms adopted by the constitutional convention of 1829–30. Two years later, representatives from eastern Virginia proposed dividing the state rather than submit to western proposals for the gradual abolition of slavery. In 1841 East Tennesseans introduced a bill in the state legislature permitting their section to form a separate state; the bill actually passed the state senate in 1842 but died after failing to win approval in the house of delegates.

Party politics transformed but did not eliminate either the class or the sectional bases of Appalachian politics. The change from western to southern outlooks can be followed in the biographies of two governors: John Floyd, the "independent" father who was governor of Virginia in 1830–32; and his "partisan" son of the same name, governor in 1847–50.[116] The elder Floyd, born in 1783 shortly after his father was killed in Kentucky, grew up under the patronage of Kentucky and Virginia relatives and married a second cousin, Letitia Preston, in 1804. After serving twelve years in Congress, he was elected governor by the legislature; as such, he was both the last to serve under the 1776 constitution and the first under the revision adopted in 1830. Floyd's views on slavery have already been discussed, as have the connections that linked him to the Patton, Preston, Buchanan, and Breckenridge families.

In contrast to his father, John B. Floyd pursued his political career entirely within the party system. The younger Floyd ran as a Democrat, serving in Congress and as governor and, as his father had done, championing the interests of southwest Virginia. Notwithstanding his father's economic critique of slavery, Floyd found increasingly that both his own and his party's success depended upon the strength of their commitment to slavery. As a congressman during the Mexican War, he took the lead in countering the Wilmot Proviso, a proposal to prohibit slavery in territories acquired from Mexico. After his governorship, he served in the cabinets of Presidents Franklin Pierce and James Buchanan. Meanwhile, western Virginia supplied four of the six major party candidates in the first three gubernatorial elections under Virginia's reformed constitution of 1851. Two of these—George W. Summers, the defeated Whig in 1851, and John Letcher, the victorious Democrat in 1859—were forced explicitly to disavow their earlier association with the slavery critics of 1832. Thomas Clingman, a western North Carolina Whig-turned-Democrat, and Zebulon Vance, his successor in Congress after Clingman moved on to the Senate, were other exemplars of a trend that linked programs of economic development in the mountain areas of the South with the mountain elite's allegiance to slavery.

The institutional ties and networks promoted by partisan competition further bound the Appalachian and plantation elites to one another. Balances between Whigs and Democrats were usually determined by national issues and leadership and by rivalries and alliances within each state. As measured by the votes of the region's congressional representatives or the demonstrated preferences in presidential and congressional elections, the most striking region-wide pattern was an extremely close balance between the parties, with the Democratic share of presidential voting in the Appalachian core growing from 44 percent in 1840 to 57.5 percent in 1856. In the three intervening elections, the region's voters were almost evenly split, with Democratic strength in Virginia and Georgia balanced by Whig majorities in Kentucky, North Carolina, and Tennessee. Within the system, members of the elites, both upcountry and lowland, competed vigorously among themselves, but an outlook that has been defined as "deferential democracy" continued to prevail as elite members electioneered among the less privileged voters of their counties and electoral districts.

In all of the Appalachian slave states, the 1850s were a period of intrasectional compromise. As sectional conflict increased nationally, political compromise at home reinforced the social and cultural ties between highlands and lowlands. Slavery in affluent mountain households allowed leaders there to view slavery as a domestic issue, or at best as an economic problem rather than a moral issue. Youthful sojourns in places like Charlottesville and Chapel Hill, or at Washington or Davidson colleges or the new state military academies, reinforced such outlooks. So did personal connections, including marriages with lowlanders whose families, like their own, regularly sent students to the universities or representatives to the legislatures in Richmond or Raleigh. A similar set of ties connected the smattering of elite families in eastern Kentucky with the leadership of the Bluegrass region or those of the Huntsville district of north Alabama with the planter elite of the Black Belt. In the long run, however, the ties that mattered most were railroad ties, which increasingly during the late antebellum decades became the visible bonds that linked the fate of the mountain South to the future of a servile society.

History, the French poet Hilaire Belloc once wrote, belongs to those who control the roads. The road "controls the developments of strategics and fixes the site of battles."[117] And shapes the strategy of development, it might be added, for roads have usually proved as important economically as militarily. As Indian trails were transformed into wagon roads and military supply lines during the eighteenth century, Appalachian towns took root at important junctions. Carlisle, Pennsylvania, originally a trading post at the intersection of the Allegheny Trail and the Warrior's Path, became the base from which General Forbes launched his successful assault on the French in western Pennsylvania in 1758 and has been a military post as well as a courthouse and market town ever since. Winchester, Virginia, was the assembly point for Boone, Washington, Lewis, and the other soldiers who came up from Virginia and Carolina to join the Braddock campaign, while Frederick, Hagerstown, and Cumberland grew up on the sites of Braddock's supply bases in Maryland.

Farther down the Great Valley, Staunton and Lexington emerged as Virginia courthouse towns with economic links to wider hinterlands in the Shenandoah and Greenbrier valleys, Abingdon developed in southwest Virginia at the point where the Wilderness Road turned west from the Great Valley toward Cumberland Gap, and Jonesborough developed near the center of the Watauga settlement in upper East Tennessee. Knoxville began life as a frontier fort near the site where the French Broad and Holston Rivers join to form the Tennessee, while Ross's Landing grew up at the strategic junction of that river and several roads on the Tennessee-Georgia border. Having served as the staging area for Cherokee Removal, the town changed its name and incorporated as Chattanooga not long after the Indians left in 1838. Meanwhile, the former Cherokee lands in southwestern North Carolina were opened to settlement by the soldiers who had campaigned there during the American Revolution. Buncombe County was created in 1790 and its courthouse established in the largest and most fertile of the intermontane basins of the Blue Ridge plateau. The market town that grew up in its center became Asheville in 1797.

Along the Ohio, Wheeling—like its upriver rival, Pittsburgh—began life as a frontier fort, as did Marietta, Ohio, and Charleston on the Great Kanawha. A network of smaller river ports—Clarksburg and Morgantown in the Monongahela valley and Parkersburg, Guyandotte, and Maysville on the Ohio —were established between 1776 and 1810. Along the major rivers, these western ports became the anchors of roads pushed across the mountains from the east, roads that linked the surging trans-Appalachian west with the Great Valley and beyond to the coastal and fall line cities on the east side of the mountains. The Great Wagon Road became the Valley Turnpike in 1834, and the market towns strung out along its length like beads on a wire became the linear urban core of the emerging regional economy. Transportation was the critical variable, both in military and in economic importance. Staunton, Jonesborough, Asheville, and Guyandotte had no military history to speak of, but like towns that did, they provided a node where a productive and overwhelmingly agricultural district was linked to long-distance trade.

Two Appalachias emerged in Virginia between 1790 and 1830, "one based on developing counties with at least one market town and one based on counties lacking an urban component."[118] A number of historians have agreed with this interpretation, applying it to sectional political issues in Virginia and North Carolina and to debates over transportation policy in Virginia and Tennessee. The "two worlds" of East Tennessee were populated by town dwellers, eager for economic development and wider connections to the outside world, and their rural counterparts, relatively poorer and deeply skeptical about the promotional schemes of their urban neighbors. The town dwellers embraced, if indeed they did not originate, many of the negative stereotypes about mountain people that are still popular today.

A literary movement with two centers, one in Richmond and one in Shenandoah Valley market towns, introduced the literary mountaineer to American letters during the 1820s and 1830s in works featuring stalwart backwoodsmen who were worthy descendants of the heroes of Kings Mountain but also impoverished mountain ruffians with German or Scots-Irish names whose only virtue was their willingness to follow the leadership of plantation gentry. Nathaniel Beverly Tucker's *The Partisan Leader: A Tale of the Future* (1836) emphasized the latter type of mountain character in a novel that envisioned a civil war over slavery fought guerrilla-style in the mountains. At the other end of the scale, John Pendleton Kennedy, Philip Pendleton Cooke, John Esten Cooke and William Alexander Caruthers created positive mountain characters equal to the gentry in everything but social polish.

The antebellum decades were also a time of religious schisms between denominationalists, stronger in the towns, and traditionalists entrenched in the countryside. It goes without saying that town dwellers figure more prominently in the historical record, for they after all were mostly people of the Book, and books are made in towns. There was nothing peculiarly Appalachian about this dichotomy, for as another French historian, Fernand Braudel, noted of similar tensions in early modern Europe, "Whether a new arrival or a seasoned visitor, the mountain dweller inevitably meets someone down below who will leave a description of him, a more or less mocking sketch. . . . He is suspected, feared, and mocked. . . . In this way a social and cultural barrier is raised to replace the geographical barrier [between highlands and lowlands] which is always being broken in various ways."[119] Mountain dwellers may be portrayed as both masters and victims of their rural environment, but city folks always control the media.

The urban places in this period of Appalachian history were small by modern standards. Winchester, the largest American town west of the Blue Ridge in 1800, had 2,128 people, while Pittsburgh had 1,565 and Staunton had 1,100. Fifty years later, Pittsburgh, which with its suburb of Allegheny across the river of the same name was by far the largest Appalachian city, counted 68,000 people. Wheeling, the second largest with 11,435, had displaced Winchester as the most populous town in western Virginia.[120] Numbers did not tell the whole story, however. Residing in a county seat, even a very small one, made a western North Carolina leader culturally more akin to a colleague from Asheville than to a constituent from Cove Creek, according to historian John C. Inscoe.[121] Travelers' accounts make similar distinctions between small towns and their rural hinterlands.

Towns provided focuses for the regional economy, and their success before

1850 depended upon the road network that branched out from the Great Wagon Road. The establishment of local roads preoccupied the Augusta County, Virginia, court in its early years, since these roads created a network focused on the courthouse at Staunton. Complementing them were new east-west routes, extending west to Warm Springs and Lewisburg and east through Rockfish Gap to Charlottesville and Richmond. Staunton's position was enhanced by geography—by the lack of alternative gaps to accommodate east-west roads leading to rival centers such as Lexington. The development of Abingdon, Jonesborough, Greeneville, Knoxville, and Chattanooga in the Great Valley and of Morganton east and Asheville west of the Blue Ridge paralleled that of Staunton, allowing for lag time appropriate to their later foundations.

A courthouse town became a market town through the creation of a road network linking its hinterland to a long-distance wagon road, while an increased pattern of specialization and diversification developed within the town's mercantile and manufacturing community. Jonesborough, for example, was established in 1770 and became a courthouse town in 1787 when North Carolina established Washington and Sullivan Counties to serve the residents of its lands west of the Blue Ridge. In this district, the strategic military point of colonial times—the Long Island of the Holston River, where Fort Patrick Henry was built during the American Revolution—failed to develop as a town site before the rise of twentieth-century Kingsport. One reason was that the Cherokees claimed the Long Island as a sacred site and until 1819 exempted it from the many land cessions that enabled white settlement of the district. Another was the effect of Bays Mountain, a ridge that divides the Great Valley in East Tennessee into two unequal parts north of Knoxville. The smaller part, lying northwest of the mountain, carries the main channel of the Holston River and was the route of the Warrior's Path. But the part of the valley lying southeast of Bays Mountain is broader, less hilly, and more fertile. The army of Virginia frontiersmen that assaulted the Cherokees in 1776 established a new road on the east side of the valley, and Jonesborough and a secondary site at the Sycamore Shoals of the Watauga River (present-day Elizabethton) became its central settlements; to these two was added Greeneville after the Nolichucky River was settled in the 1780s. Between 1778 and 1800, the Washington County court ordered the creation of 161 roads, most of them linking the countryside with Jonesborough or the Shoals or linking these two places with Greeneville and the Great Road, as the road north to Virginia and Philadelphia came to be known. The court ordered only one road built southeast across the Blue Ridge plateau, however. Unlike the

Valley of Virginia, the Valley of East Tennessee lacked easy road connections with the tidewater and Piedmont regions, or with the Mississippi valley toward which its rivers drained.

During the early nineteenth century, the federal roads linking Knoxville and Nashville with Georgia, along with the Buncombe Turnpike (completed in 1828 and connecting Greeneville with Charleston via Asheville), provided improved outlets for Tennessee livestock and produce, but the region's landlocked and mountain-bound location continued to frustrate promoters of economic development. Middle Tennessee grew much more populous and much richer. This region had a later start and fewer resources compared with East Tennessee's abundant timber, minerals, water power, and valley land, but the Cumberland and lower Tennessee Rivers afforded good water transportation to outside markets, whereas the upper Tennessee and its tributaries did not. High water in the spring allowed steamboats to move past the obstructions at Muscle Shoals and the dangerous currents west of Chattanooga as early as 1828, when a boat named *Atlas* won a prize offered by the merchants of Knoxville for the first steamboat to dock on their waterfront.[122] However, the shallow rivers north and east of Knoxville and the low water that characterized both tributaries and main stem during the harvest season of late summer and early fall made such outlets unreliable.

Thus, as a speaker in Jonesborough complained in 1831, the east was hemmed in by nature, "aided only by a precarious flood tide to convey our produce to market."[123] "This is the funnel of the universe," cried a Chattanooga booster as the Cherokees languished in their stockades in 1838. "Here is the gate," wrote another, "through which the history of nations must pass."[124] But as long as East Tennessee lacked better outlets to markets, that gate remained partially closed. As it turned out, it took an army to open it.

Along that other great avenue of western expansion, the Ohio River, the source of frustration among urban boosters was the lack of a route across the mountains that could compete effectively with New York's Erie Canal, completed in 1820. George Washington had addressed this problem on his first trip west after laying down command of the victorious Continental Army in 1784, but the elaborate plan he developed for transmontane road and canal networks between the Ohio and Virginia's tidal rivers had yielded only the National Road, completed under federal sponsorship from Cumberland to Wheeling in 1818, and two canals, one extending up the Potomac to Cumberland and the other from Richmond up the James River to a point just west of the Blue Ridge. After President Andrew Jackson killed the hope of further federal responsibility for internal improvements with his Maysville Road veto in 1830, the debates on transportation improvements shifted back to the states, where they were shaped by the political party system as well as by the conflicting sectional interests of the mountain and lowland parts of each state.

Maryland and South Carolina, both of which lacked access to the rivers of the interior, embraced the newly invented railroad. The Baltimore and Ohio (B&O) was the first to be chartered in 1827; the Charleston and Hamburg, extending across the southern corner of South Carolina to a point on the Savannah River opposite Augusta, was the first to be completed, in 1836. Georgia politicians, animated by the fear that Savannah's trade would be thereby diverted to Charleston, responded with an elaborate building scheme involving three state-owned and state-operated railroads that linked Savannah, Macon, and Augusta, with an eventual line planned to extend north through the former Cherokee country into Tennessee. The place in north Georgia where all these roads linked up was initially named Terminus, but J. Edgar Thomson, the Pennsylvania engineer brought south to oversee construction of the Western and Atlantic portion of the network, renamed the junction Atlanta in honor of his railroad.[125]

Meanwhile, back in Thomson's home state, Pennsylvania built a complicated mix of facilities under the rubric of a "main line," linking Philadelphia to Pittsburgh via a railroad, two canals, and an inclined plane to carry canal boats over the Allegheny Front. Virginia proposed a "leading line" of improvements, centered on the James River and Kanawha Canal. But sectional pressures redirected funds to a variety of projects, which left the state with "a grudgingly financed and often ill-planned" system whose most striking features were its incoherence, incompleteness, and a heavy burden of debt.

North Carolina, with the least promising geographical connections to the western rivers, also faced the problem that the western half of the state enjoyed better natural connections with Virginia or South Carolina than with eastern North Carolina's sandy and mostly harborless coast. Consequently, the legislature created a state-owned railroad, the North Carolina Central, to be built across the Piedmont from Raleigh to the courthouse town of Charlotte, with a westward spur across the Blue Ridge to Asheville. Alabama spent no money of its own on railroads but welcomed investors from Charleston and elsewhere who sought to link the emerging Georgia rail network with Memphis via the Huntsville and Muscle Shoals districts in 1857. The prospect of this development in turn spurred Tennessee into action, since Nashville was threatened by an outlet that allowed seaboard and East Tennessee shippers and travelers to bypass Middle Tennessee.

In each of the states, noisy and sometimes angry squabbles occurred over railroad routes and the extent of public control that should follow public investment. For example, in East Tennessee debates concerned which side of Bays Mountain the railroad should follow. There were also delays due to insufficient funding. But eventually a southeastern rail network began to take shape, penetrating and crossing the Appalachians and linking the Ohio valley to the Atlantic seaboard. It was not completed until 1858, when the Virginia and Tennessee Railroad (of Virginia) linked up with the East Tennessee and Virginia road (of Tennessee) at the state border, creating twin terminals at the state line, both of which were eventually named Bristol. Four different lines extending from Atlanta, Nashville, Memphis, and Knoxville linked up in 1854–57 in the new city of Chattanooga. The Pennsylvania Railroad, chartered in 1847, acquired the bits and pieces of the state-owned Main Line, replaced it with an all-rail line from Philadelphia to Pittsburgh in 1853, and brought J. Edgar Thomson back from Georgia to run it. The Baltimore and Ohio beat the Pennsylvania to the Ohio River—but just barely—when it entered Wheeling a few months earlier.

The railroads extending west from Alexandria and Richmond reached Winchester and Staunton, respectively, but did not extend much farther, and so the B&O remained western Virginia's only route to the Ohio, an ominous prospect for the future unity of the state. However, a southwestern branch of this railroad, extending from Grafton to Parkersburg and then across southeastern Ohio to Cincinnati, was completed in 1857. The North Carolina Central Railroad entered Charlotte in 1854, linking the central and western Piedmont of North Carolina with Raleigh and the port of Wilmington, but the westward spur toward the mountains did not quite reach Morganton and would not be completed through to Asheville until 1880.

The success of the seaboard states in building railroads during the 1850s was deeply involved with the debate over slavery. Earlier generations of tidewater planters had resisted western Virginia's and western North Carolina's demands for internal improvements out of the fear that the taxes needed to pay for them would be laid upon slaveowners. But railroad promoters and politicians during the late antebellum decades found a way around this impasse. Emulating France during its second Napoleonic age, each of the southern states substituted governmental for private resources. Georgia, Virginia, and both Carolinas created military academies during this period, not because they were plotting civil war, but because France's École Polytechnique, a legacy of the first Napoleon, provided the best curriculum in the world for the training of engineers, be they civil or military. The French *crédit mobilier* provided a model for state financing of internal improvements, which the rail

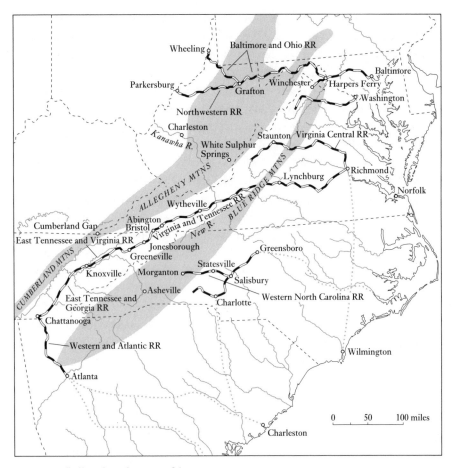

MAP 3. Railroads and towns, 1860

promoters enhanced by a process known as "hypothecation," whereby a state government endowed a railroad company's bonds with its full faith and credit. To these francophile innovations was added a uniquely southern feature—the use of slave labor to construct the roads. The railroads that linked tidewater Virginia and North Carolina with their hinterlands were built with slaves leased from planters along the route as well as with a minority of slaves whom the railroad companies bought outright. As often as not, the lease or purchase price was paid in railroad stock.[126]

Thus, far from being a modernizing element that threatened the archaism of chattel slavery, railroads in the late antebellum South provided an example of the slave system's power to renew itself. Planters competed with one another to lease or sell slaves to the rail companies, and their representatives in the legislature were only too happy to trade such subsidies for western delegates' proclamations of faithfulness to the ways of southern life. Whether the railroad companies supported by such means became state-owned facilities, as was the case in Georgia and North Carolina, or privately owned with a proportion of state directors, as in Maryland, Virginia, and Tennessee, the rail network of the upper South embodied the era of intrasectional good feelings that prevailed in the years immediately before the Civil War.

As in any developmental process, there were winners and losers. Among the biggest winners was Chattanooga, site of a trading post and missionary school in 1838, now in 1860 the most strategic rail center in the southern states. Strategic location was a mixed blessing, however, as Chattanoogans would soon discover. Virginia was a loser, especially in comparison with the states of North Carolina, Georgia, and Tennessee. Georgia had a coherent and integrated state-owned rail system, while Tennessee had a similar system, privately owned. North Carolina's was unfinished, but it also was coherent in that it connected major population centers and compensated for the fact that the state had no natural east-west route linking its six separate southward-draining river basins.

Virginia, on the other hand, had a profusion of east-west routes, and that was the problem. Despite the clarity of the vision that Washington proposed in the 1780s, Virginia dissipated its public investment through two generations of inconsistent transportation policy. Scarce funds were scattered among three different routes—one northern, one central, one southern—and among different transportation technologies. Now, on the eve of civil war, the Old Dominion had a fragmented rail system. Winchester was connected to Baltimore via a spur from Harpers Ferry but only indirectly to Martinsburg on the B&O, thirty miles away. The Manassas Gap Railroad, another uncompleted road, extended from Alexandria west to Mt. Jackson in the Great Valley but did not link up with either Winchester or Staunton. There was no rail parallel to the Warrior's Path and Valley Turnpike. The Virginia Central linked Richmond with Staunton and extended west almost to Allegheny Mountain in 1860. But Staunton had no rail connection with Winchester or with the Virginia and Tennessee Railroad, which connected southwest Virginia with Norfolk via Lynchburg and Petersburg. This fragmented rail path through the Great Valley would have important military implications, as we shall see.

The Appalachian region as a whole was also a loser. The system of state subsidies encouraged the design of railroad systems whose lines ran east-west within the borders of a single state. The classical paths of the colonial and early federal backcountry—the Trading Path, Valley Turnpike, Wilderness Road, and Ohio River routes paralleling the mountains and such transmontane routes as the Buncombe Turnpike—were bypassed in a system that emphasized the funneling of trade within state boundaries to coastal towns such as Norfolk, Savannah, and Wilmington. Forbes Road and the Federal Road of 1805 acquired rail parallels because these two routes lay entirely within Pennsylvania and Georgia, respectively. The Confederate War Department, driven by military exigency, was able to amend the system somewhat by connecting the fragmentary east-west lines into interstate systems during the Civil War.[127] But on the eve of that conflict, the southeastern rail network remained a fragmentary east-west system in a region whose natural corridors of trade ran northeast and southwest.

History belongs to those who control the roads, but the road as it emerged from the first generation of railroad building in Appalachia was not controllable. The Civil War that broke out in 1861 was a war fought mainly for control of railroad junctions, from Manassas to Corinth to Chattanooga to Atlanta to Petersburg. For the most part, the fighting spared the southern seaports that harbored mercantile dreams of southern independence, while destroying the railroads and many of the new railroad towns. Had the Valley of Virginia been threaded by a single railroad, or had Knoxville been within easy reach of Nashville or Kentucky, the war might have been shorter; certainly, as the Union experiences in Middle Tennessee and northwestern Virginia suggest, rail-based supply lines through the valley might have enabled a swifter federal conquest of this region at both its northern and southern ends. Instead, the valley thoroughfare was used by a brilliant native tactician, Stonewall Jackson, to act as a counterweight against federal military pressure on Richmond, while its abundant agriculture served as the Confederacy's granary.

Similarly, the classic road route through the Cumberland Gap alternated as a menace to East Tennessee and to central Kentucky with neither the Union nor the Confederacy able to secure control of the highway until late in the war. The Federals' inability to reach Knoxville until late 1863 or the Great Valley in northeast Tennessee and southwest Virginia until over a year later contrasted sharply with the swift Union advance via the railroads and rivers of Middle Tennessee and northern Alabama. Stalemate in the mountains prolonged the war in that region. The result was a genuine civil war in the Appalachian region—a guerrilla war that contained little of the grandeur of the larger battlefields but yielded a full measure of human tragedy. This was due in no small part to the psychological and political legacy of the era of railroad building.

In effect, the revitalized internal improvements programs of Virginia and North Carolina constituted the price of allegiance to slavery and its defense on the part of the mountain elite. Of course, the transaction was not nearly as bald-faced as this statement implies. Western leaders were already predisposed toward their eventual courses of action by social and cultural ties with their plantation district counterparts. But the railroad-building program, with its twin features of state financing and slave labor, coupled with the actual or promised resolution of outstanding sectional political issues—both purchased with frequent and doubtless sincere protestations of loyalty to the institution of slavery—meant that western leaders confronted a situation whose logical conclusion was their endorsement of the right of secession and the waging of war in slavery's defense.

The contrast with Kentucky, Tennessee, and Georgia is instructive. In Kentucky there was no statewide program of internal improvements, while the official state policy of armed neutrality in 1861 and 1862 paved the way for the comparatively peaceful occupation of the eastern mountains by Union troops in the later years of the war. With battle lines established well south of the state during the first year of the war, Confederate sympathizers were forced to go south, not by Yankee invaders, but by the logic of events. Military action was limited in the region, and although the maintenance of civil authority under the neutralist state government did not insulate eastern Kentucky from guerrilla warfare, it did help to contain its scope. In Tennessee, the railroad-building program of the 1850s was less the product of sectional compromise than of urban imperialism—coalitions of coastal and river ports drawn into competing alliances by the fear that their commerce could be siphoned off by rival towns. The political leaders of East Tennessee thus had no political commitments to slavery of the type that their counterparts in Virginia and North Carolina had traded for railroads, and so they were free to divide on other bases.

With hindsight we can see that the distinctive economy of mid-nineteenth-century Appalachia contained the seeds of its own destruction. Continued population growth in the Allegheny, Cumberland, and Blue Ridge plateaus extended the farm-and-forest economy deeper into those parts of the Appalachian mountain system that were least able to sustain it. The regional economy's limited reliance on slavery was counterbalanced by the political elite's renewed commitment to the slave system after 1832. The transportation system that this commitment helped make possible replaced the backcountry road system focused on the Great Valley and the Ohio River with a fragmentary and incomplete rail network that lacked a regional focus north of Chattanooga. The implications of actual or potential regional unity implied by the traditional term "backcountry" gave way to a divided Appalachia whose economic and political energies were channeled by the geometry of state lines.

In view of the dissent that emerged in Appalachia as the South embarked upon the trial of secession and war, it is possible to imagine other bases of unity in the region, deriving from the interests and actions of ordinary mountaineers rather than the slaveowning elite. But while the Civil War would soon offer abundant evidence of differences between mountain and plantation districts, the mountaineers' resentment of slaveowners and their war was coupled with an even stronger dislike of the slaves themselves and of black people generally. A majority of prominent southern critics of slavery came from places in or near the mountains, but most of them were indifferent, if not hostile, to the fate of African Americans. Three antislavery periodicals were established in Jonesborough and Greeneville in East Tennessee in the early nineteenth century. Their publishers were colonizers—that is, they subscribed to notion that coexistence as free people was impossible for blacks and whites in the United States and so promoted both emancipation and the deportation of freed slaves to Africa.

Among later antislavery leaders, Henry Ruffner and Alexander Campbell of (West) Virginia, Hinton Rowan Helper of North Carolina, and Cassius Clay of Kentucky all came from counties now included in official Appalachia, as did the elder Governor John Floyd and the western Virginia legislators who led the slavery debate of 1832. James G. Birney and John G. Fee came from Kentucky counties adjacent to official Appalachia, as did Daniel Worth in North Carolina. This geographic pattern has sometimes been offered as the basis for claiming antislavery credentials for Appalachia, but such an argument is misleading. First of all, all these critics except Clay were eventually silenced or forced into exile. More significantly, with the exceptions of Fee and Worth, who grounded their opposition to slavery in religion, Appalachian critics of slavery, like their quiescent fellow citizens, were blind to the moral implications of the institution. Ruffner and Floyd in the 1830s and Helper and Clay in the 1850s criticized the slave regime for its negative impact on the region's economy. They saw slavery as wrong because it contravened the interests of white people.

Though Clay claimed in later autobiographical accounts to have been moved by moral indignation, at the time he argued privately to Fee that moralizing was inexpedient: "I have studied the Negro character," Clay wrote. "They lack self-reliance—we can make nothing out of them. God has made them for the sun and the banana." "We desire to be impartial on this subject, being neither in love with slavery nor abolitionism," wrote Alexander Campbell, a prophet of ecumenism and renewal in religion as well as a political leader who spoke for northwestern Virginia. "As a philosopher and a Christian I would say to the North, let the South have their slaves, and throw no impediment in the way. Let them . . . fill up their own territory, or emancipate them, as they pleased; and rather sympathize with them than upbraid them on account of misfortunes which they have inherited."[128] His nephew Archibald Campbell, editor of the *Wheeling Intelligencer* and one of the most ardent advocates of separate statehood for northwestern Virginia in 1861, saw the opportunity to break with Virginia as a chance also to avoid "the miserable one-idea negro policy that has cursed us all the days of our lives. . . . We have had enough of it and want to get clear of negroes."[129] The men who created West Virginia presented it to Congress as a slave state in the midst of the Civil War; when Congress rejected the proposal, the statemakers amended their constitution to end slavery with compensation to slaveowners and to prohibit *all* black people, slave or free, from settling within the borders of the new state. Cassius Clay rested his personal political ambitions on the hoped-for support of nonslaveowning white men, especially the mountaineers of eastern Kentucky. "If we seek liberty for the blacks, it is . . . that the white laborers of the state may be men and build us all up by their power and energy."[130]

John G. Fee, on the other hand, preached immediate emancipation and racial equality on moral and biblical grounds. He attracted a small but courageous Kentucky following in the Ohio River county of Lewis and later in southern Madison County, where Clay induced him to settle in 1854 at a place called "the Glade," a transitional point between the Bluegrass and the mountains to the east and south. Not long afterward, the group moved to a ridgetop location where Clay was not the only landowner; at Fee's suggestion, they called it Berea, after a biblical town whose inhabitants were described in scripture as enlightened and open-minded. The Clay-Fee alliance did not long survive, however, and broke out into open enmity in 1856 when each man publicly criticized the other's views at a Fourth of July gathering. The importance of Berea, however, endured both as a symbol and as a place uniting mountains and lowlands, north and south, white and black.

"We were, so to speak, on the fence, and could see the great question from both sides," wrote Rebecca Harding of the years just before she made her literary reputation with an exposé of the living and working conditions among workers in Wheeling's iron industry. "Abolitionism was never a burning issue in our part of Virginia."[131] Yet John Brown's raid on Harpers Ferry in October 1859 ended even the mildest forms of dissent. Brown had farmed briefly in northwestern Virginia—one of the many unsuccessful stops he made on his path to immortality—but more important, papers captured with him made clear that he expected to use the southern mountains as a redoubt for liberated slaves and that he expected mountaineers as well as blacks to rally to his cause, although in Brown's case this referred less to native mountaineers than to various "free-labor" colonies that had been planted in western Virginia under New England auspices.

The furious reaction to Harpers Ferry ended most manifestations of Appalachian dissent. A mob took over Berea and forced Fee and other leaders of the colony to flee with their families across the Ohio. A free-labor colony at Ceredo, West Virginia, was forced to disband and its members to move north to Ohio or Wheeling. Daniel Worth was indicted in four separate North Carolina counties for incendiary activities and convicted by his home county of Guilford. Sentenced to a year in prison, he wisely departed for New York while his case was under appeal. A second wave of Kentucky mob actions forced another group of Bereans into exile in April 1860. No fewer than ninety-four antislavery men, women, and children were forced out of Kentucky at this time, according to Clay's count. Clay himself resisted expulsion by means of his aristocratic name, his imposing physical presence, and two cannons mounted at the door of his office in the town of Richmond. The school that Fee and his colleagues had founded was forced to close its doors. When they reopened six years later, it was to a very different world.

The people here in Florida

Seem to think the mountain folks are fools

They claim we are poorly equiped for churches

And poorly equiped for schools.

They seem to think we make a living

By running moonshine stills,

But thank God we have a more excellent way

    to live,

In our dear old mountains and hills.

—Aunt Molly Jackson, untitled poem,

    [1907?], in Romalis, *Pistol Packin' Mama*

CHAPTER THREE

Blood and Legends, 1860–1920

On the morning of election day, November 6, 1860, Lizzie Hardin found her-self atop a hill near Abingdon in southwest Virginia, "overlooking one of the fairest portions of that fair land." White Top Mountain could be seen in the distance, and the nearer hills displayed their fall colors. Twenty years old and the inheritor of a name famous in Kentucky history, Hardin normally took a lively interest in politics, but as a woman, "having only a boy's privilege of 'hollering' for my candidate, . . . I determined to leave the country in the hands of the men, and take a ramble over the hills. So, persuading several young ladies to be my companions, I started off, . . . meeting all along the 'Lords of Creation' and amusing ourselves with guesses as to whom they would vote for."[1] The men they passed were argumentative but good-humored, debating the merits of Stephen Douglas and John Breckenridge, representing the northern and southern wings of the divided Democratic party, and the Constitutional Union candidate, John Bell, the favorite of Lizzie Hardin and other conservators of the Whig tradition. No one in this part of Virginia spoke up for Abraham Lincoln, the Republican candidate, although nearly everyone expected that he would be the one elected, as indeed he was.

The six months that followed Lincoln's election are known to historians as "the secession crisis." If we rely on the records of politics and politicians, "crisis" seems an appropriate word for a period that saw the withdrawal of seven Deep South states to form the Confederate States of America and an increasingly polarized debate in the Upper South states whose backyards constituted Appalachia. But from the standpoint of Lizzie Hardin and most other citizens, the crisis was at best a rumble of distant thunder. Through a mild winter and an early spring, most people busied themselves in their seasonal tasks. For an upper-class young woman like Hardin, this meant an extended round of visits and parties with her Abingdon relatives and friends. Rebecca Harding, a young woman of the same age but of very different interests and outlook, recalled these same months as the prelude to personal triumph and national tragedy. In 1860–61, Harding was still living in her parents' home in Wheeling, about to embark on a literary career. "[T]he great mass of the people took no part in the quarrel" during the secession crisis, she recalled; "busied with their farms or shops, the onrushing disaster was as inexplicable [to them] as an earthquake." On the other hand, Nathaniel Southgate Shaler, a Kentuckian who like Harding would also eventually find his destiny in New England, recalled later that he had been warned by a grandfather as early as 1854 that the slavery debate would eventually come to war and that Shaler should choose the Union side in the quarrel, which eventually he did.[2] "Women, everywhere," Rebecca Harding added, "neglected their sewing, housekeeping, and even their love affairs, to consult and bemoan together. They were usually less devout and more radical in their methods than the men; demanding that somebody should at once be hanged or locked up for life. Whether the victim should be Buchanan, Lincoln or Jefferson Davis depended upon the quarter of the Union in which the women happened to live."[3]

The crisis mounted steadily day by day and eventually closed in on ordinary people, forcing hard choices on individuals who were by and large reluctant to make them. The drumbeat of events began just before Christmas, when South Carolina enacted its ordinance of secession. Alabama and Georgia followed on January 11 and 19, respectively, with delegates from the mountain districts of each state casting most of the votes recorded against secession. In early February, representatives of seven seceded states met in the capital of Alabama to create the Confederacy, and Virginia voters approved a ✗ special secession convention to meet at the end of the month in Richmond. However, Virginians also elected a Unionist majority to this convention and required that the results of its deliberations be submitted to the voters for approval in the regular spring elections scheduled for May. North Carolina, voting in late February, also elected a Unionist majority, but on the separate issue of whether to hold such a convention, the "no's" narrowly prevailed.

Tennessee, voting on April 12, decided by a large majority not to hold a convention, with East Tennessee voting overwhelmingly in the negative. But on that same day, Confederate forces in Charleston Harbor attacked Fort Sumter, and three days later President Lincoln issued a call for volunteers to suppress this "rebellion." Governors of all the Upper South states indignantly rejected the call. The Virginia convention voted 88–55 in favor of secession on April 17. Tennessee's governor bypassed the convention process and called the legislature into a special session, which voted to ally with the Confederacy on May 7, subject to ratification by the voters in an election scheduled for June 8. In North Carolina, a special legislative session called for the election of a convention on May 13; a week later the convention met and repealed the ordinance by which North Carolina had joined the Union in 1789. Kentucky, however, adopted a policy of armed neutrality, resolving not to "take up arms for either of the belligerent parties, but [to] arm herself for the one purpose of preserving tranquility and peace within her own borders." Meanwhile, Unionist leaders in northwestern Virginia and East Tennessee met in conventions in Wheeling and Greeneville, respectively, organizing to oppose secession in the referenda scheduled in their states and proposing steps toward the division of each state should a majority of voters statewide approve secession, as they did on May 23 in Virginia and June 8 in Tennessee. State authorities in Richmond and Nashville rejected overtures for the peaceful division of their states on the grounds that the Unionist conventions were unrepresentative of the will of the people. Thus, by the time that fighting began in earnest, the Appalachian backyards of the southern states were theoretically part of the Confederacy.

From a strategic standpoint, however, Confederate Appalachia was no longer a backyard. The mountains held critical reserves of resources and manpower. Saltville, Virginia, for example, was the Confederacy's major supplier of salt once the saltworks of the Kanawha valley, eastern Kentucky, and the coastal districts were put out of reach by federal troops. Southwest Virginia's lead mines and the ironworks of the Great Valley, extending from Virginia down into Alabama, were also crucial suppliers of war matériel. The

Valley of Virginia and East Tennessee contained some of the South's most productive farmland, from which came much of the foodstuffs needed to sustain a war effort. In terms of manpower, Appalachian Tennessee, with more than 380,000 people, had a larger white population than many other Confederate states and thus a larger potential reservoir of fighting men. Appalachian Virginia was even more populous and, like the less-peopled sections of Appalachia in other states, had a relatively small slave population, meaning it was beset by fewer worries of the sort that haunted plantation districts when white males of fighting age marched off, leaving behind black-majority populations.

Appalachia was also geographically strategic; though the Blue Ridge on the east and the Cumberlands and Alleghenies on the west separated the Upper South's richest plantation districts, the Great Valley threading the mountains provided a vital link between the Confederacy's rich southwest and its threatened northeast. The recently completed railroads running through this corridor from Chattanooga to Lynchburg were especially important. Lizzie Hardin and her sisters passed their last weeks in Abingdon going down to the railroad station to cheer troops passing through from the south and west toward the anticipated battlefields of northern Virginia. To Hardin's great satisfaction, the first unit to come along was a Kentucky regiment, but it was soon followed by a unit from Alabama and then dozens from other states. "[T]here seemed to be a continual stream of soldiers pouring along the railroad and at every train the ladies were there with provisions and flowers and flags."[4] Passing through East Tennessee in late May on her way home to Kentucky, Hardin saw little evidence of that region's militant Unionism along the railroad, although she heard reports that the display of rival flags in some places had already led to bloodshed.

Unionism in northwestern Virginia and East Tennessee created the impression among the newly installed Republicans in Washington that the ordinary people of the South were still predominantly loyal and Union-loving. The Confederacy, in their eyes, was the creation of a minority "slave conspiracy." Abraham Lincoln was especially fond of this view, and it was reinforced among later historians by subsequent events such as the success of the West Virginia statehood movement, the outbreak of irregular warfare in the mountains, and postwar propaganda that supported mountaineer claims on the federal treasury and northern philanthropy. But recent research has shown that Appalachian Unionism was much more complicated and its expression much less unified than initially seemed to be the case.

It is true that formal expressions of Unionism in the various referenda, plebiscites, and convention votes that punctuated the secession crisis rejected

secession, at least before shots were fired at Fort Sumter. The problem was
that too few mountain Unionists were prepared to accept the ultimate logic of
their views. Outside of northwestern Virginia and East Tennessee, the mountain elite who represented the region in the various deliberations on secession
consisted for the most part of "conditional Unionists"—that is, they opposed
both secession and the use of force ("coercion," in the parlance of the day) to
prevent it. Thus, when President Lincoln called for troops, their Unionism
vanished and they rushed to defend the Confederacy, at least in rhetoric if not
in arms. "At the beginning of the rebellion I sympathized with the Union
cause," a North Carolina mountaineer told the Southern Claims Commission
after the war. "I first voted in favor of the Union, and the next time in favor of
the States going out of the Union. The big fellows told me it was obliged to go
out of the Union, and I voted accordingly."[5]

As a congressman and leader of the former Whig Party in western North
Carolina, Zebulon Vance was one of the "big fellows" referred to. He claimed
to have been making an antisecession speech when he learned by telegram of
Lincoln's proclamation. "When my hand came down from that impassioned
gesticulation, it fell slowly and sadly by the side of a Secessionist. I immediately, with altered voice and manner, called upon the assembled multitude to
volunteer, not to fight against but for South Carolina." Following his own advice, he marched out of Asheville on May 4 with a volunteer company he had
raised himself, even before his state had completed the formalities of secession.[6] Then, in August 1862, he was elected governor of North Carolina at the
age of thirty-two. "The late election after sixteen months of war and membership with the Confederacy show conclusively that the original advocates of
secession no longer hold the ear of our people," he bluntly informed Jefferson
Davis in October 1862. "Without the warm & ardent support of the old
Union men No. Carolina could not so promply [sic] and generously have been
brought to the support of the seceding states and without the same influence
constantly and unremittingly given the present status could not be maintained forty-eight hours. *These are facts*."[7]

It was also a fact, however, that the mountain region had plenty of secessionists. Thomas Clingman and William Waightstill Avery, Democratic rivals
of Vance for leadership in western North Carolina, were "fire-eaters" even
before the secession crisis. The representatives of southwest Virginia, including present southern West Virginia, voted as heavily in favor of secession in
the Richmond convention as representatives from the northwest voted against
it. When Unionist delegates returning home from Richmond staged their
first rally at Clarksburg on April 22, 1861, prominent secessionists—includ-

ing the only northwesterner to have been elected Virginia's governor—assembled in the same town a week later, calling for loyalty to the Old Dominion. Most prominent officeholders or recent candidates in the northwest accepted this logic, either following Virginia into the Confederacy or remaining at home in sullen neutrality while their sons and younger brothers marched off to fight for the South.

Rebecca Harding recalled also a generational divide, with older men mostly being for the Union—or at least keeping prudently silent if their property lay in the path of the federal army—while younger men supported secession. The civil war between fathers and sons that postwar sentimentalists like to write about often originated in this way. Thus, George W. Thompson, the solitary Virginia circuit court judge who declined to take an oath to the new Confederate government, saw his son William slip away from Wheeling, along with other young bloods of the town, to join the Confederate forces, telling the tailor who made their matching gray uniforms that the duds were for use in a wedding. Even in East Tennessee, where most established political leaders declared for—and remained steadfast to—the Union, younger, town-dwelling professional men were as likely to go along with secession, constituting, according to Senator Andrew Johnson, "an upstart, gulled headed, iron heeled, bobtailed aristocracy, who infest all our little towns and villages."[8] In southwest Virginia, western North Carolina, north Georgia, and East Tennessee, the late antebellum years produced "a society on the rise led by men on the make."[9] It is not too much to conclude that, given the rosy prospects of southern economic independence held out by secession theorists, ambitious younger men in the courthouse and railroad towns of the region might identify their own future with the prospective advantages of revolt.

When we turn from counting votes to counting enlistments, the situation is equally complex. As the secession crisis resolved into war, young men faced their time of decision, though even the decision of whether to fight or not, and for which side, was not always clear-cut. John Brown's raid had produced a surge of militia enrollments across the Upper South, but for most young men, drilling with the militia was still an excuse to play at soldiering and show off for the girls. Besides, militias were organized on a state basis. It was only gradually that these units and the hundreds of volunteer units that sprang up in the late spring of 1861 coalesced into the Union and Confederate armies. In Virginia, Governor John Letcher, a westerner, summoned the militia to state service on May 1, three weeks before the voters ratified the secession convention's ordinance. Even before this, units acting under the direction of a former governor had seized the federal arsenal at Harpers Ferry and the Norfolk Navy Yard, events that were celebrated by an illumination of houses in Abingdon. Militia units in the Pan Handle district around Wheeling refused the governor's call, but everywhere else young men turned up at the county militia musters and worked on their military skills. "I had to go with the boys,—my neighbors and schoolmates," one mountain boy later recalled, "little thinking, or in the remotest degree anticipating, the terrible hardships and privations which would have to be endured in the four years which followed."[10]

There are numerous recorded cases of mountain men who fought on *both* sides. For example, Henry J. Mugler, an Alsatian immigrant who ran a store in Grafton, West Virginia, turned out with the local militia unit to defend the important rail junction in his hometown. Two years later, returning home as a captured and paroled Confederate, he was drafted into the Union army and served until the end of the war. In East Tennessee and southwest Virginia, there were men who returned home either as Confederate deserters or as veterans whose enlistments had expired, and who then fled over the mountains into Kentucky and the federal army rather than surrender to the Confederate draft. Farther south—in western North Carolina and north Georgia—rebel deserters and Union volunteers enlisted in Tennessee units after the Federals took control there in late 1863. Differences in timing as well as opinion also explain something of the "brothers' war" of Civil War sentimentalists: An older brother might march off with his buddies as the local militia was mustered into Confederate service, while a younger one would face different circumstances and options when he came of age a year or two later. Such innocent logic could lead to decades, even generations, of bitterness within and between families after the war.

Still, for most young men the choice was clear, if not easy: join up during the first months of wartime enthusiasm, then submit to lengthened enlistments or to conscription as the war lengthened and stick it out with the fatalism of veterans. In Kentucky and West Virginia, states whose territories were substantially behind federal lines for most of the war, the ratio of Union to Confederate enrollments was roughly four to one, but this figure has to be interpreted in light of the facts that Union conscription operated more effectively in these states than elsewhere and that an undetermined number of midwestern soldiers joined Kentucky or West Virginia units if their initial enlistments expired while they were serving in these states. East Tennessee supplied 75 percent of all Union enrollments from that state, amounting to 27,400 men, but only 36 percent of Tennessee Confederates, which means that East Tennessee rebels numbered 48,800. The 8,000 rebel volunteers who joined up during the first year of the war came predominantly from the Great

Valley; in the mountains proper, only Polk County supplied company-sized units during the period of volunteering before conscription was introduced in April 1862.[11]

Union men who fled East Tennessee during its Confederate occupation often joined up in Kentucky or other states, and these amounted to at least one in ten of the Union soldiers from the state, raising the federal total from East Tennessee to 30,000. In southwest Virginia, western North Carolina, and north Georgia, state (and thus Confederate) authorities remained in control until the end of the war, whereas northern Alabama was conquered swiftly by the Union army after the rebel defeat at Shiloh in April 1862. The volunteer enlistments from these areas were overwhelmingly Confederate, but anecdotal evidence testifies that at least some men fought for the Union. If northern Alabama resembled nearby East Tennessee in its enlistment patterns, as it does geologically, the sandy ridges of the Cumberland plateau should have supplied most Union men, with Confederates coming mainly from the fertile agricultural valleys that those ridges overlooked. However, Lizzie Hardin and her family, having been expelled by Union authorities in Kentucky for their behavior during the Confederate invasion of the Bluegrass in 1862, found refuge on the Alabama ridgetops as they struggled to reach Confederate lines east of the Tennessee River. "The settlement in which we found ourselves was in a wild little cove of the mountains, very far from the pleasures and annoyances. The houses were mostly of logs. . . . In no place did we ever meet with more kindness and hospitality. There was nothing they would not do for us and nothing for which we could prevail on them to receive any compensation."[12]

How soldiers made their decisions is an easier thing to determine than why. Campaigning in northwestern Virginia during the first weeks of the war, Union colonel Rutherford B. Hayes analyzed the social origins of the conflict. "The Secessionists in this region are the wealthy and educated, who do nothing openly, and the vagabonds, criminals, and ignorant barbarians of the country; while the Union men are the middle-classes—the law-and-order, well-behaved folks."[13] We can accept Hayes's analysis—the rich and poor for secession, the middle class for the Union—only with numerous qualifications. First of all, middle-class, town-dwelling, "law-and-order" folks were just as likely to be good Confederate citizens behind rebel lines as they were good Union citizens on the federal side. Second, poorer mountaineers—where their loyalties can be reliably determined—were as likely to be Union men as rebels, at least as the war progressed. As Hayes and his fellow Ohioans pressed southward through trans-Allegheny Virginia, for example, they found staunch Unionists on "little farms in secluded nooks," such as the Flat

Top Mountain region of Mercer and Raleigh Counties. "They worked their farms but every man had his rifle hung upon his chimney-piece, and by day or by night was ready to shoulder it and thread his way by paths known only to the natives, to bring us news of open movement or of secret plots among the Secessionists."[14]

In Ashe County, North Carolina, Union sentiment was centered in the poorer, more remote districts along the Tennessee border, a situation that also prevailed in Fannin County, Georgia. In Tennessee, the most exhaustive studies of the issue conclude that whether a family owned slaves was a key factor in determining loyalties. Among Union soldiers from East Tennessee, only 11 percent owned slaves, and none owned as many as twenty. Over a third of their rebel counterparts were slaveowners, however, and a sixth of the Confederates owned large numbers of twenty or more. "Among white Tennesseeans, Union soldiers overwhelmingly came from the nonplantation counties. And, in stepwise fashion, the lower their economic standing, the more likely men were to fight for the Union."[15]

Separate studies of widely separated western Virginia counties—Preston, on the Pennsylvania and Maryland borders, and Dickinson, bordering Kentucky in the far southwest—conclude that the longer a man's family had lived in the county, the more likely he was to become a Confederate, while newcomers—even from places farther south—were more likely to declare for the Union. However, anecdotal evidence from Tazewell County suggests that long residence was not in itself a sufficient cause of loyalty to Virginia; it had to be coupled with economic success. For example, members of the Burrass family, early settlers and landowners in the Burke's Garden district, had by 1860 lost their land and become alienated dependents of the powerful Floyd family, whose current scion, former governor John B. Floyd, became one of the more famously inept generals in the southern army. When Yankee raiders passed through Burke's Garden in 1863 in an attempt to cut the railroad at Wytheville, one of the Burrasses guided the Union troops through the mountains, for which deed he was later captured and executed as a traitor in Richmond.[16]

Perhaps, then, the best way to revise Colonel Hayes's social analysis of mountain loyalties is to state that the greater the stake an individual had in the existing order of things, the greater his propensity "to go with his state" into Confederate service, whether as soldier or citizen. Conversely, the lesser the stake, the greater the inducement to Unionism. Although this formulation must allow for many individual exceptions, it accommodates ambitious urban secessionists, cautious older Unionists and their fire-eating sons, and poor mountain farmers who, at some point during the war, turned back from the path down which the "big fellows" had led them.

The most impressive testimony to the strength of Appalachian Unionism was the creation of West Virginia, the only enduring boundary change to result from the Civil War. Creating the state in the midst of war and following procedures acceptable to the Lincoln administration and Congress—which meant that no unvarnished appearance of direct secession from Virginia was acceptable—entailed a labyrinthine political and constitutional process that dragged on for two years before the new state took its place in the Union on June 20, 1863. Like other manifestations of mountain Unionism, the statehood movement was in part an alliance of the alienated. The business and political leaders of the Pan Handle held grudges of long standing over Virginia's banking and railroad policies, on which they blamed the widening gap between Wheeling and its upriver commercial rival, Pittsburgh. The Baltimore and Ohio Railroad, as an instrument of Baltimore's urban imperialism, also blamed Virginia for the long delay in pushing its tracks across the Alleghenies to the Ohio River. Thus, even though Wheeling had been the B&O's third choice for a terminus (the first choices, Pittsburgh and a point on the Ohio near present Huntington, had been thwarted by Philadelphia's and Richmond's influence in their respective state legislatures), the Wheeling and B&O leaders made a potent combination, one that designed the boundaries of the new state to remove every inch of B&O track from the Old Dominion.

Whiggish politicians who had found no home in the shifting realignments of Virginia politics during the 1850s constituted another alienated group. George W. Summers, western Virginia's best-known and most influential statesman of the day, retired from public life after futile efforts to engineer a sectional compromise in 1861. He neither countenanced nor opposed the new state. In his absence, John S. Carlile of Clarksburg, Waitman T. Willey of Morgantown, and Francis G. Pierpoint of Fairmont stepped forward. Pierpoint became governor of a "restored" Virginia government that gave the sanction required by the U.S. Constitution for the creation of a new state from Virginia territory; Willey guided the state-making process in three separate Wheeling conventions and, with Carlile, took over the U.S. Senate seats vacated by Confederate Virginians. Peter G. Van Winkle, a B&O lawyer from Parkersburg, replaced Carlile after the latter turned against the statehood movement midway through the process. Although they had campaigned under a variety of party labels since the Whigs' collapse, the state makers coalesced after 1864 under the Republican banner. Feasting on postwar sour grapes, the Virginia legislature repealed the enabling legislation that had sanctioned the state-making process and sued for the return of West Virginia's two easternmost counties, but rulings by Congress and by the U.S. Supreme Court ensured the permanence of the new state.

A comparison between West Virginia and East Tennessee is instructive. Unionists were just as militant in East Tennessee as in northwestern Virginia. Maybe more so, for while most existing officeholders in western Virginia went along with secession, established leaders in East Tennessee led the campaign against secession and, failing in that, organized conventions in Knoxville and Greeneville that petitioned the Tennessee legislature for a peaceful division of the state. The key difference between the two situations was a geographic one, which in turn had profound military implications. However firmly President Lincoln may have believed that all mountain Unionists were in the same boat, in fact the West Virginians were much more comfortably situated. As the first of the Wheeling conventions began its deliberations, Union troops gathered on the Ohio shore of the river, within sight of its meeting place. Held in check until after the May 23 referendum confirmed Virginia's secession, the Federals moved across the Ohio at Wheeling and Parkersburg on May 26 and headed east along the railroad toward Grafton, led by a volunteer regiment from Wheeling. Shots exchanged between a militiaman posted as a sentry on the railroad near Grafton and two local Union volunteers killed one of the latter, making him the first official Union casualty of the war.

Although Robert E. Lee, at this time the commander of Virginia's forces, stressed the importance of the rail junction to his subordinates, the rebel forces nevertheless retreated southward to Philippi, the site of a strategic covered bridge on the Tygart's Valley River. Here, on June 1, 1861, the two armies fought the "first land battle" of the war (Fort Sumter having surrendered to a barrage over water), with the federal troops victorious. A few weeks later, on July 11, federal forces under General George B. McClellan defeated Confederates in the Battle of Rich Mountain near the point where the Staunton and Parkersburg Turnpike angled up across the high ridges of the Alleghenies. This outcome gave the Union control of northwestern Virginia and its railroads for the duration of the war. On the same day, a second invasion of western Virginia began at Point Pleasant and proceeded by road and steamboat up the Kanawha River to Charleston, which was occupied on July 25. General Lee came out in person in August to reclaim the Kanawha valley, but he was unsuccessful. "The views are magnificent, the valleys so beautiful, the scenery so peaceful," Lee wrote to his wife. "What a glorious world Almighty God has given us. How thankless and ungrateful we are, and how we labor to mar his gifts."[17]

Lizzie Hardin, hearing of this "disastrous defeat" in Nashville while en route to her home in Kentucky, also heard the laments and excuses: "Our forces were not obliged to surrender, but wandering about in separate regiments and companies through the wild mountains of Virginia and Maryland, sometimes almost starving, always barefooted, bare headed, worn out, and with the rain beating upon them, the poor remnant of the command at length reached Monterey, many to die there of fever and the effects of their retreat."[18]

Nashville seemed dull by comparison to what she had experienced in Abingdon, where "the expectation of danger without its horrid realities" lent excitement to everyday life. But early in 1862 the Confederate forts defending Nashville fell, thanks in part to the ineptitude of the same General Floyd who had lost the Kanawha valley. What this meant in practical terms was that proponents of statehood in West Virginia could work in comparative safety behind the cordon of federal outposts thrown up in the first weeks of the war, while their East Tennessee counterparts had to run, hide, or keep silent until Knoxville was finally liberated in September 1863. On the other hand, the swift federal conquest of Middle Tennessee and its capital meant that the Unionist refugees of 1861 became the rulers of the state a year later, when Lincoln appointed Senator Andrew Johnson to be its military governor. As they moved to take over the entire state, East Tennessee Unionists eventually abandoned their dream of countersecession. "Thus East Tennessee remained a geographical expression, while West Virginia became the name of a state."[19]

For two years after the Union conquest of northwestern Virginia, the Civil War in Appalachia remained "an affair of outposts," except in the Shenandoah Valley, where Stonewall Jackson's brilliant "valley campaign" of 1862 forced Union troops under a succession of generals to stick close to the B&O railroad. Later that summer, Confederate general Edmund Kirby Smith, exploiting a new route northward from Knoxville through the Cumberland Mountains, occupied central Kentucky, flanking the Union forces both at Nashville and at Cumberland Gap. This lifted the hearts of Bluegrass rebel sympathizers like Lizzie Hardin and stalled the federal advance across northern Alabama for more than a year. But ultimately Kirby Smith's invasion accomplished little more than to bring Kentucky officially into the war on the Union side; Kirby Smith was back in Knoxville by the end of the year.

Elsewhere in 1862 and most of 1863, the main war—the war of massed armies and set battles and later of battlefield parks and splendid television

Union troops guarding a railroad bridge in the Cumberland Mountains near Chatta-nooga, 1863 or 1864. Protecting vital east-west railroad routes across southeast Tennessee and western (West) Virginia was the principal duty of regular Union troops who served in Appalachia during the Civil War. (National Archives, 165-SC-6)

documentaries—was fought out in the lowlands east and west of the mountains until the fall of 1863. Then federal armies commanded by Ulysses S. Grant and W. T. Sherman moved against the railroad junction at Chattanooga, where—after a series of bloody engagements fought on the most scenic battlefields of the war—they drove the Confederate defenders down the Western and Atlantic Railroad into Georgia. Sherman's Atlanta campaign of 1864, like Grant's simultaneous move against Richmond, reduced West Virginia and East Tennessee once more to the status of military backwaters. The Lincoln administration used Wheeling as a place to stash inept but politically influential generals and Chattanooga as a giant supply dump for Sherman's march to the sea.

West Virginia, as noted, pinned its star to the national flag two weeks before the Battle of Gettysburg. After his selection as Lincoln's vice-president in the election of 1864, Andrew Johnson was succeeded as military governor of Tennessee by William G. Brownlow, a former minister and newspaper editor renowned for his vituperative style and relentless hounding of enemies. Both West Virginia's and Tennessee's Unionist governments enacted a stringent series of penalties and "test oaths" designed to prevent Confederates and their sympathizers from taking part in the political process. Their actions reduced voting totals to absurdly low levels in several elections held under their auspices; Congress even threw out Tennessee's electoral vote in 1864, though it counted West Virginia's and accepted the Tennessean Johnson as the nation's new vice-president.

Civil government of a sort was restored in Chattanooga and Knoxville and in northern West Virginia counties within the cordon of federal outposts in 1864, while northern Alabama with its strategic railroad remained under military rule. Elsewhere in Appalachia, local authorities held office by virtue of prewar constitutions, which meant that Confederates were nominally in control of county governments in some parts of West Virginia, in all of Appalachian Virginia south of a fluctuating line around Winchester, in a few counties of East Tennessee, and in all of western North Carolina and north Georgia. Lee's retreat after the fall of Richmond was in fact headed for this zone of Confederate safety, but Grant's pursuit kept the rebels away from the Virginia and Tennessee Railroad and forced their surrender at Appomattox Court House on April 9, 1865, three days short of the fourth anniversary of the official beginning of the war.

Three of the more memorable incidents of the last months of the war occurred in Appalachia. In February 1865, some sixty Confederate raiders swept down the South Branch valley into Cumberland, Maryland, where they captured a couple of Yankee generals relaxing in a hotel. The following month, federal general George Stoneman led some six thousand cavalrymen on a raid through the northwest quadrant of North Carolina with orders "to destroy but not fight battles." In fact, the destruction was less than it might have been, considering that a number of western North Carolina soldiers were among the federal ranks. There was bloodshed and destruction in Boone, Statesville, and Morganton, communities that resisted the raiders, while Asheville was ransacked by the Federals on April 28. One of the war's oddest episodes occurred at Waynesville on May 7, when painted and whooping Cherokees commanded by William H. Thomas, the patron of the Eastern Band, surrounded a federal detachment on the hills above the town and frightened them into a truce, notwithstanding the fact that all other rebel troops in the state had already surrendered. After a night of ridgetop bonfires and war dances, Thomas attended the next day's negotiation "with 20 of his largest and most warlike looking Indians, stripped to the waist and painted and feathered off in fine style." This costume drama could not stave off the inevitable, however, and Thomas's men and two other Confederate detachments surrendered on May 9, officially bringing the war in the mountains to an end.

Traditional accounts of the Civil War in Appalachia focus on the creation of West Virginia, the fate of East Tennessee, and the contributions to the larger war effort of such mountaineers as Stonewall Jackson, Andrew Johnson, and Zebulon Vance. But Appalachia was the scene of a dual war. On the one hand, there was "the Civil War, the war which is spelled in capital letters and read about in textbooks highlighted by names like 'Gettysburg' and 'Chancellorsville' and 'Shiloh.'" On the other, "for the people of mountain Georgia the war was not on these fields, but in their towns and on their farms and homesteads."[20] The same statement could be made about the war in the other Appalachian states, especially the Virginias, North Carolina, and Tennessee. This other war was a genuine civil war that split and bloodied neighborhoods and families and that featured all the hardships and atrocities with which irregular warfare has always been associated. The incidents of this war made only a slight imprint on the official histories and produced no famous engagements, only a fragmented record of raids and counter-raids, ambushes and murders, robbery, arson, and rape. The roots of this conflict lay in the region's class structure and divided loyalties, in its complex geography, and in the fact that both of the regular armies penetrated the region sufficiently to unsettle it but not enough to control it.

Virginia's border with Kentucky and North Carolina's border with Tennessee created theaters of potential conflict along natural mountain barriers that were remote from the regular armies. In each case, Confederate local authorities and home guards on the east side of the state lines confronted a territory on the west that was formally (Kentucky) or heavily (East Tennessee) Unionist. In both districts, rumor and fear added to tensions, and alarms of invasion from one side or the other of the boundaries were compounded by the certain knowledge that each side harbored dissenters or refugees from the other.

In western North Carolina, authorities were haunted throughout the war by the possibility of invasion from East Tennessee—a fear that intensified after the federal occupation of Knoxville in September 1863. In southwest Virginia, Confederates were equally afraid of disloyalty among the mountaineers whose homes flanked both sides of the Great Valley and of incursions by federal troops from Kentucky through Cumberland Gap or from West Virginia via the roads paralleling the New River. Such fears were well grounded, for federal authorities were continually looking for ways out of the stalemate of 1861, with two overriding objectives: to provide military relief to oppressed Unionists in upper East Tennessee; and to sever the Virginia and Tennessee Railroad, "the jugular vein of Rebeldom," according to Hayes.[21] "It was easy," recalled one general, "sitting at one's office table, to sweep the hand over a few inches of chart showing next to nothing of the topography, and to say, 'We will march from here to here'; but when the march was undertaken, the natural obstacles began to assert themselves, and one general after another had to find apologies for failing to accomplish what ought never to have been undertaken."[22]

Thus, there were Union raids south from West Virginia against Wytheville, from Kentucky through Cumberland Gap into upper East Tennessee, and even, in late 1864, a brief incursion that destroyed the New River bridge of the Virginia and Tennessee Railroad. Confederates raided in the other direction, sweeping north of the B&O to burn bridges and gather horses, or north from the defenses of Chattanooga to besiege Knoxville after the Yankees occupied that city in late 1863. All told, however, these actions accomplished little except to raise the level of paranoia among local authorities and to escalate the general level of violence. The stalemate between the regular armies continued until the last weeks of the war. This left both armies with their outposts in central Appalachia but gave over the rest of the territory to guerrillas and marauders.

The hidden civil war in Appalachia began in a way as resounding as the Confederate attack on Fort Sumter. On the night of November 8, 1861, Union sympathizers in East Tennessee assaulted nine of the twelve bridges on the railroads that threaded the Great Valley between Bridgeport, Alabama, and Bristol. Five of the bridges were destroyed. During the days that followed, Union men appeared in arms in numbers as large as one thousand at Elizabethton, Strawberry Plains, and other locations, expecting (wrongly as it turned out) to be supported by a Union army advancing through Cumberland Gap. This was the first signal to Confederate authorities that political opposition to secession had now become military resistance. The reaction was swift and harsh. Felix Zollicoffer, the rebel general commanding at Knoxville, proclaimed martial law and curtailed civil liberties throughout East Tennessee. Seven of the bridge burners were rounded up, and four were executed. On orders from Richmond, their bodies were left hanging by the railroad as a warning to Unionists and a morale booster for loyal Confederates. Those who escaped the roundup either fled north through the Cumberlands into Kentucky or east into mountains along the North Carolina border, from which they would emerge to do further damage in due course.

Central, southern, and eastern West Virginia provided another front for this war, except that here the combat pitted federal regulars against rebel guerrillas. These parts of western Virginia had yielded a great many more votes for secession than had the Unionist heartland north of the B&O, while the railroad itself presented a tempting and convenient target. As the most direct route between the eastern and western theaters of the war, the B&O was of vital importance to the Union, and repeated raids by Confederate irregulars forced the Federals to fortify practically every bridge along the road between Parkersburg on the Ohio and Harpers Ferry on the Potomac. Romney, a South Branch valley town ideally located as a jumping-off place for raiders, changed hands fifty-six times in the course of four years. Since many of the militiamen who answered Virginia's summons in 1861 were subsequently cut off from their home counties by the federal conquests of that year, they made good recruits for such units as the Moccasin Rangers and the Black-Striped Company that operated in the central and southern parts of the state.

Thus, Ohio troops such as those led by Colonel Hayes, who had passed weeks in the summer and early fall of 1861 as "a giant armed blackberry picking party" untroubled by opposition, found themselves increasingly beset by bushwhackers in the winter of 1862, when guerrillas appeared in the Flat Top region in bands as large as fifty men. On Hayes's initiative, his command at Raleigh [modern Beckley] adopted the "search and destroy" tactics that traditionally characterized the United States' Indian and imperial wars. They patrolled the Flat Top region "to ascertain the hiding places of the bushwhackers and when found . . . all houses and property in the neighborhood which can be destroyed by fire will be burned, and all men who can be identified as of the party will be killed, whether found in arms or not."[23] "We do not take prisoners if we can help it," one soldier wrote home to Ohio a few months later.[24]

In central West Virginia, Colonel George Crook, a veteran Indian fighter, took over command of the Thirty-sixth Ohio, and the take-no-prisoners rule became all but explicit. Crook's soldiers, recruited in the Marietta district and thus schooled in a long history of contempt for their neighbors south of the Ohio River, enthusiastically applied the policy and became known as "snake hunters," playing on the Mocassin Rangers' name and thereby endowing West Virginians with a nickname ("snakes") that Ohioans would employ for generations to come. "Well mother . . . if we ant out here to kill Bushwhackers what are we for?" wrote a Marietta soldier, John Palmer.[25] If for some reason prisoners were taken, they were usually sent in chains to Columbus or Wheeling. Summary executions were not unheard of, however. Usually a small group of soldiers escorted the prisoner into the woods where, it was said, he "fell off a log," breaking his neck. The body of one such victim, killed in Monroe County, West Virginia, in 1864, was later strung up by the roadside, with a note pinned to the chest warning other guerrillas that they could suffer a similar fate.

In southwest Virginia, western North Carolina, and north Georgia, Confederate authorities were nominally in control, and regular units of both armies were concentrated in distant places. Thus, although authorities in these localities fretted incessantly about possible incursions by Unionists from East Tennessee, the real threat to order came initially from local dissidents. During the first year of the war, those who had responded to the Confederate call to arms had marched off, and those who did not were able to keep quiet and go about their business. "I have no negroes to defend and will not take up arms for the South," one such individual informed the governor of North Carolina in August 1861. But the circumstances of such dissidents changed with the introduction of conscription in April 1862. "Except it be in the army of the Union, you will not again see this conscript," wrote an Ashe County soldier to Jefferson Davis, whom for good measure he addressed as the "bastard President of a political abortion."[26]

Most men who refused the draft did not do so out of Unionist sympathies, however. They wanted no part of either army but rather, as a Georgia draft evader put it, "to stay home and take care of their families."[27] And so they "laid out" in the woods, attempting as best they could to carry on their family responsibilities while avoiding the conscription agents. It was an open question "whether the mountain people can subsist after taking out every man between the ages of 18 & 40," wrote a former legislator from Macon County on the Carolina–Georgia border. Family councils had already decided which of their young men could be spared for the war effort and which were needed at home to sustain their households. "You know all about men and their powers of endurance," he wrote Governor Vance in November 1862.

> They can turn away from the graves of comrades and brothers firm in their resolve to die as they have died for the sake of objects coming to their recollections with thoughts of home. But what consolation or encouragement can come to a man's heart in an hour of trial from a home where the helpless are perishing for want of his hand to provide? . . . We are opposed to negro equality. To prevent this we are willing to spare the last man down to the point where women & children begin to suffer for food & clothing.

When these begin to suffer & die, rather than see them equalized with an inferior race, [we] will die with them.[28]

Vance urged the War Department in Richmond to suspend the draft in the mountains, as did successive Confederate generals commanding in East Tennessee, but the authorities were unmoved by their appeals. The Confederacy needed soldiers, especially in view of the mounting rates of desertion, and so the draft was maintained and attempts to round up evaders intensified.

As the war continued through 1862, rebel deserters added another element to the volatile situation in the mountains. North Carolina led the entire South in desertions, with some 24,000 officers and men choosing that route. The next-ranking state, Tennessee, counted 12,000 ex-volunteers. A large proportion of deserters from both states ended up in the mountains.[29] "Deserters now leave the Army with arms and ammunition in hand," a Confederate officer reported in September 1863. "They act in concert to force by superior numbers a passage against bridge or ferry guards, if such are encountered. Arriving at their selected localities of refuge, they organize in bands, variously estimated at from fifty up to hundreds at various points." Loyal citizens, including the militia, were dissuaded from helping authorities to track down and detain such outlaws out of fear that "their esprit de corps extends to killing in revenge as well as in prevention of the capture of each other."[30]

Desertion stemmed from many causes: combat fatigue, homesickness, resentment at the extension of enlistments, appeals from a soldier's loved ones that he was needed at home. Other men deserted when their units were ordered away from their home districts. For example, Company E of the Twenty-first Virginia Cavalry consisted of a former home guard unit from the Sand Lick district of Buchanan County on the Kentucky border, a district that had yielded only six volunteers before the institution of the draft. The Sand Lick company proved perfectly willing to do duty in its own section of the state, but when ordered to other places, even no farther away than southern West Virginia or the Cumberland Gap area, the men deserted en masse. Their willingness to fight locally carried no credit with state military authorities, and so the Sand Lick men were forced to lay out and make common cause with other deserters and draft evaders, including "Yankee jumpers," Union deserters forced to enlist in the Confederate army, from which they soon deserted again.[31]

Not far away from Sand Lick, William Anderson Hatfield of Logan County, West Virginia, had enlisted in the Fifty-fifth Virginia Infantry as a private in 1861 and had advanced to the rank of first lieutenant by 1863. But after Union forces operating out of Charleston sacked the town of Logan and burned its courthouse, Hatfield and his brothers Ellison and Elias deserted their regular unit and went home. Shortly thereafter, they organized a partisan band called the Logan Wildcats, with "Anse" Hatfield as its leader. Not much is known about the operations of this unit, but we do know that one of its victims was a Kentucky Union veteran named Asa Harmon McCoy.[32]

Added to the mix of draft evaders and deserters were escaped Yankee prisoners of war and even runaway slaves heading north through the mountains. The combination of shared peril and opportunities led such men to coalesce into bands as large as fifty to one hundred, gangs that may have originated in the need for self-protection, but that had a predatory and criminal character when viewed from the perspective of the people whose food and livestock they took. In Yadkin County, North Carolina, part of a "Quaker belt" that extended from the Blue Ridge eastward across the Piedmont to Greensboro, militia and bushwhackers engaged in a shootout in February 1863, killing two men on each side before the "desperadoes" made their escape into the foothills of Wilkes County. "The robbers & bushwhackers in Wilkes and Caldwell [Counties] are becoming more insolent & aggressive," wrote a man in November 1864, referring to the mountain counties that were the most consistently resistant to Confederate authority. "We never go to bed without thinking they may come before morning."[33]

South of Asheville, bushwhackers targeted Flat Rock, the summer home of many wealthy South Carolinians who continued to patronize the resort during the war. In the counties along the Tennessee–North Carolina border, the bushwhackers were just as likely to be Confederates preying upon Unionists. In Cades Cove, a remote but once peaceful and productive community in the Great Smoky Mountains, raiders repeatedly descended through the mountain passes from North Carolina, stealing food, horses, and livestock. Most of the young men in the cove had gone off to join the Union army, though there was a minority of Confederates. Older men were forced to work guardedly by day and to sleep out in the woods at night in order to evade beatings and killings. The raiders came from a neighboring county in North Carolina, where as early as 1861 local volunteers had offered to cross into Tennessee to attack Union forces, paying themselves "out of what they may be able to get from our Enemyes by conquest not calling on the government for any thing."[34]

During 1863 the raids on Cades Code intensified to the point where the community was under serious threat of starvation the following winter. When the Union occupation of Knoxville failed to bring relief in the form of federal protection, the older men of the community fell back on their frontier heritage and organized for self-defense. They established an alarm system of women and children stationed in the woods to look out for interlopers, drilled themselves, kept their hunting rifles at the ready, and ambushed their enemies when the raids resumed in the spring. Their success forced the raiders to abandon their practice of daylight attacks on the community, though depredations continued at night. During one retaliatory night raid, the bushwackers murdered the man chiefly responsible for organizing the home guard, but his martrydom only reinforced the boost in morale that self-defense inspired. Charles G. Davis, a Massachusetts soldier escaping from prison in South Carolina, came through Cades Cove not long afterward. "We found all good Union men here. They all have to sleep in the bushes every night, and have for the past two years. They live in continued terror of being killed. At dark we went to the bushes for our night's rest."[35] Self-defense did not end such hardships, but it did guarantee the community's survival.

The chaos of irregular war afforded greater scope for young women, for social rules were often suspended along with the codes of "civilized" warfare. The war contributions of conventional ladies were sewing ("a woman's part in peace or war," as Lizzie Hardin noted), nursing, or rolling bandages. Guerrilla warfare afforded women more active roles, along with greater perils. No fewer than nine female partisans found their way into Union custody at Wheeling at some point during the war. One was Mary Jane Green, arrested initially in August 1861 as a Confederate spy. Later Green was imprisoned at Wheeling, where she insistently annoyed guards and other inmates. The provost marshal reported that "General Rosecrans had her brought before him when she abused him with her tongue and he ordered her back to jail. . . . [Later] General Rosecrans directed me to send [her] to her home in Braxton County with the hope and expectation that some Union troops would shoot her. . . . In a short time she was returned to me having been caught in the act of destroying the telegraph line near Weston, Lewis County. She is an ignorant creature, but at times has the ferocity of a perfect she-devil about her. I cannot advise her release."[36]

Although these women were charged with treason, none was shot as was often the case with male guerrillas, but nevertheless their jailers found them "hard cases." Governor Pierpoint first ordered some of them sent to Camp Chase, a Union prison near Columbus, Ohio, then tried to turn them over to Confederate authorities in Virginia. "Wearing soldier's clothing in camp is not an offense for which they can be sent South," an aide informed him, "and if that is all that is against them, they must be disposed of in some other way." A female Moccasin Ranger, Nancy Hart, rode at the head of one band of irregulars with her boyfriend, Perry Connolly. A teenaged beauty who could charm her way out of tight situations, Hart continued fighting after Connolly was killed in 1862. Later she hooked up with another guerrilla, Joshua Douglas; after the Moccasins were dispersed by federal snake hunters, Hart and Douglas moved to a remote location even farther back in the hills.[37]

The former prisoner Davis, approaching Cades Cove with some fellow escapees, encountered one of the girls stationed in the woods above the Cove as sentinels. "She gave the alarm with a horn. When she blew the horn we were looking down the Cove. In an instant it was alive. The men were driving their cattle before them, and every man had a gun over his shoulder." Later Davis asked the girl what she would have done if he had demanded the horn before she had blown it. "[Her] reply was rather a surprise to me as I had always had a great respect for women, but had met only the kind that used soft words, those who had not been on the 'battle line,' so to speak, those who had lived in pleasant homes and surroundings. Her reply was that she should tell him to go to 'Hell'! And from my knowledge of her as a sentinel on duty, I am very sure that she would have done so."[38] Women and children also undertook to hide and feed the men lying out in the woods, for whatever reason. Lizzie Hardin discovered this in northern Alabama, while she and her mother and sisters were awaiting a chance to slip across the Tennessee River to Confederate lines. The young women of a family that sheltered them habitually went out at night into the nearby mountains, carrying food to Confederate stragglers hiding out from the Union troops that occupied Bridgeport and its railroad. Hardin herself spent a night "in the bushes" until someone could be found to take them across the river safely.

"The warfare between scattering bodies of irregular troops is conducted on both sides without any regard whatever to the rules of civilized war or the dictates of humanity," wrote Governor Vance in August 1864. "The murder of prisoners and non-combatants in cold blood has, I learn, become quite common, and, in fact, almost every other horror incident to brutal and unrestrained soldiery." Vance knew whereof he spoke, for the most notorious and atrocious incident of the war had occurred on his watch. This was a massacre at Shelton Laurel in Madison County on January 18, 1863, when a detachment from the Sixty-fourth North Carolina Regiment summarily executed thirteen prisoners, including a sixty-year-old man and a boy of twelve, after beating and torturing women in the community in an attempt to learn the hiding places of others. Apart from its scope, however, there was little to differentiate Shelton Laurel from other atrocities, such as the actions of the snake hunters who pursued rebel guerrillas in West Virginia in 1862–63, or the execution of deserters in Lumpkin County, Georgia, in 1864, or the fate of local deserters and a Yankee jumper killed in Buchanan County, Virginia, that same year at a place that would later be known as Deadman's Hollow. There are several common elements that link such events besides disregard for the rules of conventional warfare. One is the wariness and contempt that exposure to guerrilla war bred in soldiers in the regular army. "Surrounded by hostile people, moving in terrain known intimately by the invisible enemy, it was easy to surrender to brutality. In guerrilla warfare men can feel that the environment itself is hostile to them, that each tree or hillside is dangerous, and that death stalks them. In regular battle, death terrorizes but not to the same extent [for] there are things in regular combat that a man can do to restrain his fears, to fight back." Another linkage is the antagonism between town and country. The officers deemed responsible for the Shelton Laurel massacre were town-dwelling professional men in civilian life, as were the Ohio and northern West Virginia men who led the federal snake hunters and the Dahlonega merchant who decided the fates of the Georgia deserters. Middle-class culture and peacetime encounters had already conditioned such men to regard country fellows as, at best, "improvident mountaineers" or, more typically, "mean whites" or "ignorant savages." Both Union and Confederate regulars disliked duty in East Tennessee and expressed contempt for its citizens, notwithstanding the fact that the official policies of each government theoretically offered protection to civilians there.[39]

Finally, there was the pervasive localism that everywhere characterized conflict in the mountains. Both sides of the firing line at Dahlonega were staffed by men who had stayed home from the distant theaters of the war to stand guard over their own homes and communities. The men who held the rifles there or at Shelton Laurel or at Deadman's Hollow were duly sanctioned by state authority and the force of law to bring down their antagonists. The men at whom the guns were pointed had resisted that same authority, as deserters or outliers, for the same reason—because they preferred to fight close to home and for causes that did not have to be explained to them by politicians or soldiers coming out from the county seat. In the extreme acts that occurred at these places, and in the much more numerous incidents of lesser notoriety, we have the kernel of antagonisms that would flare up again and again in Appalachian history, in incidents extending from the Civil War well into the middle decades of the twentieth century.

The Civil War, in both its regular and irregular versions, casts a long shadow over Appalachian history. Though there were other causes of the region's impoverishment, the effects of the war were significant. The impoverishment of the defeated South generally hurt Appalachia in several ways. The plantation market for Appalachian livestock and foodstuffs was drastically reduced after the war, as were livestock herds in districts where the armies had foraged. The state-owned or state-subsidized railroad systems were substantially wrecked. Railroad corporations based in the North gradually gathered up the financial wreckage as the roads were rebuilt and thereafter operated most of the roads as subsidiaries of northern systems. Although mountain resorts emerged from the war largely intact, their upper-class southern patrons were damaged beyond the extent that even General Lee, who made a point of visiting White Sulphur Springs during the immediate postwar years, could repair.

Wartime congressional initiatives that granted free land to western railroads and free homesteads to settlers of the trans-Mississippi West in effect subsidized competing producers of the agricultural commodities that had underpinned Appalachia's antebellum prosperity. Although the region's relative prosperity had already been compromised as farmers and herdsmen moved ever more deeply into the Appalachian Plateau, the profits of the antebellum era had borne fruit in the form of several promising local initiatives that were subsequently damaged or disrupted by the war. Two examples are offered by the Burning Springs oilfield near Parkersburg, West Virginia, and the emerging ironmaking districts around Chattanooga and in northern Alabama. When these industries eventually did flourish, it would be as subsidiaries or junior partners of northern firms.

With the impediment of southern congressmen and senators nullified, Congress enacted other legislation that placed the South generally and Appalachia in particular at a disadvantage vis-à-vis the North and West. The National Banking Act of 1863 created a national banking system that dried up credit in the South and West and allowed regional developers to operate only on terms laid down by metropolitan financial interests. Added to lowland resentment at real or imputed mountain disloyalty during the war, the impoverishment of southern state governments meant that the public funding that had financed the canals, turnpikes, and railroads—not to mention the puny educational funding of the antebellum era—was no longer an option for needful mountain communities.

In communities that have been studied intensively, such as Beech Creek, Kentucky, and Cades Cove, Tennessee, the years between 1850 and 1880 were decisive ones in the transition from backcountry to Appalachia, from the region traversed by Lanman and Olmsted that was united by a common culture, a prospering economy, and a satisfying way of life to a postwar society that was fragmented, divided, impoverished, and violent. The demographic transition, whereby undiminished population growth ran up against diminished resources, was perhaps more significant, but since the war was the most important event of the transitional decades and contributed to the decline of Appalachia's prospects, the two causes cannot really be separated. Demography lacks the capacity to claim our sympathy for individuals whose fate it was to be born in such interesting times. Stories of war will always be able to do that.

Among the most prominent Civil War leaders from the Appalachian region, Stonewall Jackson was accidentally killed by his own men near Chancellorsville in May 1863. Zebulon Vance, the most effective of the southern Civil War governors, remained in office until the war ended, at which time he was briefly imprisoned by Union authorities. After his release, he set about rebuilding his career in urban settings, choosing first Wilmington and then Charlotte, where, along with Mary Anna Morrison Jackson, Stonewall's widow, he became one of the leading citizens of that rising town. After his death, Asheville nonetheless built a monument to him that still presides over the city's most prominent public space. Another mountaineer governor, Joseph E. Brown of Georgia, would like Vance play a leading role in post-Reconstruction state politics. Joseph E. Johnston, a native of Abingdon, Virginia, took over command of the Confederates facing Sherman following the rebel debacle at Chattanooga and surrendered his army to Sherman near Durham, North Carolina, on April 17–18, 1865.

Among unionists, Andrew Johnson succeeded Lincoln as president of the United States; after his frustrating and unsuccessful presidential term was up, he became a U.S. senator from Tennessee, in which capacity he was serving when he died in 1875. "Parson" William G. Brownlow, who succeeded Johnson as governor of Tennessee in 1865, also served in the Senate. While the Republican Party he helped to found in the state lost control of it in 1869, those foundations turned out to be an enduring basis for Republican strength in East Tennessee.

The West Virginia state makers also lost control of their state when conservative Unionists deserted them in protest against Republican Party policies on racial issues and more and more wartime Confederate sympathizers came to the polls. Stonewall Jackson's Unionist cousin, federal district judge John Jay Jackson Jr., a Lincoln appointee, struck Republicans a decisive blow in

1870 when he ruled that West Virginia's ex-Confederates were eligible to vote under the federal Fifteenth Amendment. In 1872 a constitutional convention dominated by former Confederates rewrote the state constitution and remodeled state and local government along Virginia lines. The leaders of the statehood movement retired into relative obscurity. For example, Francis J. Pierpoint, who had followed the "restored" Virginia government eastward, first to Alexandria, then to Richmond, served a dispiriting three years as Virginia's Reconstruction governor. Afterward he returned home to West Virginia. While his prewar partner in the coal-mining business became a multimillionaire, Pierpoint never saw his fortunes recover from their wartime neglect. Late in life, he became interested in genealogy and changed the spelling of his last name to Pierpont, which is the spelling used by West Virginia when it erected a statue of him in Statuary Hall of the U.S. Capitol in 1910.

Laura Jackson Arnold, Stonewall's sister and an ardent Unionist, was divorced by her elderly, pro-Confederate husband after the war on grounds of infidelity, allegedly with Union officers stationed at an outpost near her home in Beverly, West Virginia. While the court rejected the scandalous charges as unproven, the divorce was granted and Laura, after living with one of her children for a few years, disappeared into a convalescent home near Columbus, Ohio. Her voluminous correspondence with her brother also disappeared. Late in life, she was honored at Union veterans' reunions in Ohio.

Rebecca Harding, having achieved literary success with the publication of her exposé of the lives of Wheeling ironworkers, published her first novel in 1863. In that same year, she married another writer named Davis and moved to Philadelphia. Between 1862 and 1865, under the pressure of financial hardship, she published a large number of stories of doubtful literary merit that nonetheless portrayed realistically the divided wartime loyalties of Appalachia and the brutal irregular warfare carried on in the mountains. Later, during the 1870s, Davis shifted the locale of her stories to western North Carolina and, with greater literary polish, presented Appalachian mountaineers as mostly Unionists, helping more than any other single writer to establish what a modern scholar calls "the myth of Unionist Appalachia."[40]

Meanwhile, Lizzie Hardin made her way home to Kentucky from middle Georgia, where she and her mother and sisters had found refuge during the last two years of the war. They traveled by foot and by wagon through ruined Atlanta and the devastated villages of north Georgia before reaching a functioning railroad just south of Chattanooga. Riding in railroad cars furnished only with wooden benches, they passed through Nashville, crowded with blue-coated soldiers and vindicated Unionist politicians, and then on to their home, where Lizzie lived out the rest of her life in the genteel routines of an unmarried Victorian lady. Although she touched up her Civil War journal a bit, she did not substantially alter her wartime impressions, but they were not published until 1963, some seventy-one years after her death.

Among those still unknown to fame at the war's end, a nine-year-old former slave boy named Booker Taliaferro Washington walked with his family across the mountains and valleys from Franklin County, Virginia, to the Kanawha valley in West Virginia. Some freedmen were not reassured by the existence of the new state and kept on going until they had placed the Ohio River between themselves and their former masters, but Washington's family found work in the saltworks east of Charleston. Notwithstanding the West Virginia constitution's provision for separate but equal schooling for white and black children, Kanawha County provided no money for the education of African Americans, but a preacher who was also a saltworker organized a school funded by the black community, and the young Booker attended that. In this way he began the educational adventure that led him up from slavery to national fame and influence at the end of the century.

Following the same route—or perhaps a different path leading up from the plantations of the Carolina Piedmont or from the freedmen's camps surrounding concentrations of the victorious Yankees at Knoxville, Chattanooga, Winchester, or Richmond—a former slave who called himself John Henry embarked on the route to fame of a different order. He found work with the construction crews who began the work of physical reconstruction in the Valley of Virginia, and by 1870 he was working steadily with a crew organized by a man from Winchester known as Captain W. R. Johnson. Johnson bid on contracts let by the railroad once called the Virginia Central, now rebaptized by new owners as the Chesapeake and Ohio (C&O) and engaged in extending its line across southern West Virginia to the Ohio. While whites, especially Irishmen, also hired on for railroad construction, the majority of the workers were African American. Somewhere along the line, as the C&O drove west under Allegheny Mountain into the Greenbrier valley (but perhaps also on earlier jobs in other places), John Henry acquired the specialized skill of a steel driver, the worker who hammered into the rock the steel drills that made holes for explosives. In 1870 Johnson won a contract to build a tunnel under Big Bend Mountain, where one-and-a-quarter miles of track through the tunnel would save the C&O the expense of following a ten-mile loop of the Greenbrier River. Work on the east portal of the tunnel began in the summer or early fall of that year. Here John Henry would meet his fate.

Jedediah Hotchkiss, a New York–born schoolmaster who marched off with

Virginia troops and became one of Stonewall Jackson's most trusted aides, returned to Staunton as a schoolteacher but was soon putting the cartographic and surveying skills he had displayed during the war to peaceful commercial uses as a land surveyor and speculator. In the latter role, he ran up against the economic depression of 1873–79 and was further frustrated by suspicion aroused among British capitalists by any development scheme coming from Virginia, since the state's large antebellum public debt remained unpaid while Virginia and West Virginia bickered over their respective responsibilities for repayment. Unable to raise capital, Hotchkiss turned to promotional writings. In *The Virginias: A Mining, Industrial and Scientific Journal Devoted to the Development of Virginia and West Virginia*, Hotchkiss offered a vision of a new industrial region based on the iron ore and foundries of the Great Valley and the rich coal deposits of the Appalachian Plateau, as identified by the earlier research and reports of the antebellum state geologist, William Barton Rogers. Though forced to support his family primarily by mapping, surveying, and holding geographical institutes for schoolteachers, Hotchkiss kept Rogers's vision alive during the hard years after the war.

Anderson Hatfield went back to his father's land on Grapevine Creek near the Kentucky–West Virginia border. Lacking tillable land of his own, he found a way to make a living cutting timber on the hillsides. Anse organized his brothers and other veterans of the Logan Wildcats to work in gangs that felled the timber, trimmed the logs, and gathered them into long "rafts," which could then be floated downstream on flood "tides" of the Tug Fork River to sawmills that sprang up in Catlettsburg and other Ohio River towns. Though the work was hard and the income provided by logging irregular, Hatfield became one of the most prosperous men in his district, accumulating more mountain land and, with the additional acreage, additional enemies.

In North Carolina, the Cherokee veteran A'yun'ini (Swimmer), formerly second sergeant of Company A in Thomas's Legion (Sixty-ninth N.C. Infantry, C.S.A.), made his way back to his home in Big Cove after the surrender at Waynesville. He was about thirty years old at this time. Educated by tribal leaders in the remedies, sacred formulas, and myths by which the Cherokees ordered the human place in the universe, A'yun'ini was literate in his own language, though he spoke no English. Sometime after the war, he began (or perhaps resumed) the task of transcribing sacred rites and formulas in the Cherokee syllabary. For the next twenty-five years, he lived quietly at Big Cove, dedicating himself to antiquarian tasks and playing a prominent role in dances, ballgames, and other activities calling for respect for tradition. He became, in effect, the keeper of legends.

Throughout Appalachia there were other young men who found it difficult, for one reason or another, to settle down after the war. Many of these headed out for fresh starts in new places. Most of the pro-Confederate minority in Cades Cove disappeared in this fashion. So did Hamilton Bower, who returned from Confederate service to Ashe County, North Carolina, and then in 1866 moved his young family north to West Virginia. There Bower settled in Wyoming County, one of the most remote districts of the new state's southern "interior" and home to one of the few districts thereabouts that had stood for the Union rather than the Confederacy during the war. Here Bower carved out a backwoods farm that prospered in his children's day as it came to be surrounded by hungry mining communities. In 1915 Hamilton's son Wiley built an imposing white frame house enclosing his father's original cabin. Fifty years later, workers tearing down the white house to make way for Twin Falls State Park discovered within its walls this original log cabin, which the park now preserves as the centerpiece of a generic "pioneer homestead."

A different sort of immortality awaited another Carolina mountaineer whose love life got him into trouble. Thomas C. Dula (whose surname was pronounced "Dooley" in the mountain vernacular) was twenty-two years old, a veteran, a fiddler, and something of a lothario when he returned home to Wilkes County in the summer of 1865. He soon became involved in a love triangle with an old girlfriend, a married woman named Ann Melton whom he had apparently slept with as a teenager before the war, and a new flame, Laura Foster. Neither woman was a paragon of Victorian female virtue, for medical testimony later disclosed that both had contracted syphilis, as had Dula and a third woman, also named Foster, with whom he was also involved. When Laura Foster disappeared in the spring of 1866 after telling a neighbor of her plan to elope with Dula, suspicion fell upon him and he fled across the Blue Ridge to Johnson County, Tennessee. There a Union veteran named Grayson was instrumental in his capture. Taken back to North Carolina without the formality of extradition, Dula twice stood trial for murder, once in Wilkes County and once in the Piedmont courthouse town of Statesville, where he was retried after the state supreme court threw out his first conviction. Despite a "brilliant" defense mounted by none other than Zebulon Vance, Dula was found guilty a second time. Unlike Frankie Silver, he did not go to his grave silently, but rather exonerated Melton and made a rambling hour-long statement, standing on the cart that served as his scaffold with the rope around his neck. A crowd numbering in the thousands witnessed his execution.[41]

Violence of many kinds plagued the mountain region in the years after the war. Returning Confederate soldiers were assaulted by Unionists in East Tennessee, as were agents of the new West Virginia government in pro-Confederate counties along the southeastern border. There were race riots—which in this context meant attacks on African Americans by white mobs—in Asheville, North Carolina, and in Hinton and Charles Town, West Virginia. Gangs of marauders continued to operate in western North Carolina through the end of 1865, and there were personal grudges to settle. Although most wartime Unionists who claimed damage at the hands of Confederates pursued their claims through the courts, some took more direct action. For example, a member of the Shelton family killed a neighbor who had aided the perpetrators of the Shelton Laurel massacre, while another Madison County man shot down a man who had bragged about his involvement in a wartime killing of the shooter's relatives. The naturalist John Muir, embarked on a thousand-mile walk from Kentucky to Florida in 1867, was twice accosted by bandits in the Cumberland Mountains and escaped being robbed only because he carried very little that was worth stealing.

Folklorist William Lynwood Montell argues that the violence of the Civil War years trained mountain people in the use of force to settle personal and political disputes, and that these effects lasted through at least two generations. Investigating the oral traditions of a district he variously calls "Upper Cumberland" or "State Line Country," two Tennessee and two Kentucky counties on the western edge of what is now official Appalachia, Montell found evidence of at least sixteen killings, the details of which were not documented by official records or printed sources. Even excluding violence during or directly related to the war, folk tradition suggests that there were a dozen such killings during the period 1865–95 and another ten between 1895 and 1915, for a homicide rate two to five times greater than before 1860 or after 1940. After 1915, the documentary record supplements oral tradition and shows an extremely high ratio of homicides to population, even compared with the rest of the South, not to mention the nation at large. Only after the creation of state police systems and the easier access that automobiles gave lawmen to backwoods venues did the district's murder rate subside to southern and then near national levels. Montell concludes: "A tendency for lethal violence in these valley settlements began by virtue of guerrilla warfare, spread across the adjacent countryside, and left a self-perpetuating imprint on local culture."[42] This thesis has not been tested against the experience of other parts of Appalachia, but it is certain that the region acquired a reputation for violence in the postwar decades that it had not had in antebellum times, and that this reputation was sufficiently justified by events to convince writers who did not probe the social dimensions of violence that there was something inescapably "savage" about the culture of Appalachian mountaineers.

Even though violent incidents directly related to the war diminished after 1870, new causes of strife arose, at least one of which had roots in wartime decisions. This was the trouble engendered by the attempt to enforce federal revenue laws against mountain distillers. After the Whiskey Rebellion of 1794, federal taxes on distilled spirits had gone uncollected in the backcountry and were eventually taken off the books. In 1862, however, Congress reenacted the tax as a measure of wartime revenue, though no serious attempt to enforce it against private distillers was made until President Rutherford B. Hayes took office in 1877. Enforcing the liquor tax appealed to Hayes for several reasons. A supporter of the temperance movement, Hayes had prevented the soldiers under his command from obtaining spirits during his West Virginia campaigns, and his wife—known to history as "Lemonade Lucy"—substituted fruit drinks for champagne at White House entertainments.

There was also a political dimension to the new policy. Enforcing revenue laws in the southern backcountry was a way of proclaiming federal supremacy in the South just as federal troops were being withdrawn from the region and black freedmen were left to their fates at the hands of ex–Confederate "Redeemers" and Ku Klux Klan terrorists. Moreover, as part of the deal with southern Democrats that allowed him to assume office after the disputed presidential election of 1876, Hayes had agreed to take a southerner into his cabinet and made former Confederate David M. Key of Chattanooga his postmaster general. Since Key's position controlled the most abundant number of federal jobs, local postmasterships, some other form of patronage was needed to accommodate Republican officeholders who were driven from their posts as Redeemer governments took over all of the southern and border states between 1870 and 1877. Collectors of internal revenue were normally appointed for each state. An expanded number of deputy collectors and revenue agents—known to moonshiners as "revenuers"—provided both offices to fill and manpower for a stepped-up enforcement effort.

The middle-class town-dwelling element of Republicans in West Virginia and East Tennessee also supported the enforcement drive, especially as prohibitionism made headway in the evangelical churches and modernization began to widen the gulf between town and country. George Wesley Atkinson of West Virginia, the chronicler of the antimoonshine crusade in the Hayes and subsequent administrations, was a perfect example of this type. A temperance man and upholder of bourgeois respectability in private life, he was also a Republican postmaster forced to give up that job in 1877 in a state that had gone over to the Democrats in 1870. From his perspective, enforcement of the revenue law was a source of cultural right and personal satisfaction as well as of employment.

The new crusade began as soon as Hayes took office and climaxed with a series of coordinated raids in the mountains from West Virginia to Georgia in January 1880. As Atkinson told the story in a "thrilling, yet truthful narrative" published in 1881, these raids were full of daring adventures on the part of the revenuers, violent resistance and cowardly tactics by the moonshiners, and happy endings wherein lawlessness gave way before the forces of morality and order.[43] In fact, the shootouts and ambushes that Atkinson portrayed were the exception in Appalachia, not the rule. Most gunfights were between individual "blockaders" and revenue agents, not between massed gangs on each side. Distillers caught violating the law dutifully appeared in court, paid their taxes and fines, and went home, usually to resume their production of spirits. The federal district courts in which such cases were tried normally suspended prison sentences for small producers unless they were chronic offenders.

This was the case with Anse Hatfield, who was summoned into court occasionally during the 1870s and 1880s on moonshining charges, and also with his oldest son, Johnson (or Johnse), a high-spirited young man whose first conviction for moonshining was facilitated by an informant, a neighbor from the Kentucky side of the Tug Fork valley named Tolbert McCoy. Throughout the mountains, violent resistance to the revenuers peaked during bad times, when poor farmers turned to distilling to make ends meet, and tended to level off during prosperity. Thus, liquor-related violence was more intense during the initial years of enforcement, which were also years of depression, than during the more prosperous 1880s. In rural areas where respectable, churchgoing people looked askance at the drunkenness and abuse that usually characterized moonshiners' families, there were a few who were willing to step forward and assist the revenue agents, even at the risk of having their barns burned or suffering worse forms of retaliation. This was the case in Cades Cove, for example, although at a somewhat later time period.[44] Moonshiners' wives were also voluntary but secret informers, considered more reliable by the revenue agents than any other kind. Yet the most consistent support for the crusade came from paid guides and informants.

Blockaders fought back with beatings, arson, and sometimes deadly force. In five northwest Georgia counties between 1889 and 1894, night riders resembling the Ku Klux terrorists of Reconstruction committed at least sixty-

A still and the Internal Revenue agents who confiscated it in 1931, at a site now
within the boundaries of Great Smoky Mountains National Park. Today prohibition
officials in Appalachia are more concerned with marijuana growers than with un-
licensed distillers. Allegedly, pot has replaced tobacco as the most important cash
crop in eastern Kentucky, and there and elsewhere its production is often said to be
undertaken by families that specialized in moonshining in earlier generations.
(Photograph by George Grant, courtesy of GSMNP Archives)

six attacks, so far as can be judged by newspaper reports and court records. Of
these, thirty-five—more than half of the total number—occurred during the
depression years of 1893–94, and over half of those incidents whose causes
can be identified derived from moonshining conflicts. Due to the intimidation
of witnesses and secrecy enshrouding membership in the so-called "white
cap" gangs, the attackers went unpunished until 1893, when federal prosecu-
tors took over and hauled the accused into court in Atlanta, "where between
November 1894 and June 1895 twenty-four white caps were convicted."[45]

Even after the violence subsided, the social impact of liquor revenue enforcement lingered on. Revenuers, whether operating openly or in the guise
of land prospectors, cattle and timber buyers, or peddlers, became a standard
if unwelcome feature of the social landscape of the mountain region between
Reconstruction and 1919, when the enactment of the prohibition amendment

greatly expanded the market for moonshine and spread revenuers and block-aders across the nation. Mountaineers once known for their hospitality and openness to strangers now became suspicious and close-mouthed, and travelers were well advised to be cautious in asking questions, approaching houses, or displaying weapons, whether they had business or sport in the mountains or were just passing through.

Appalachia's reputation for violence was further enhanced by a long sequence of events known collectively as "mountain feuds." The most celebrated was the Hatfield–McCoy feud, which began with a court battle in 1878 over a razorback hog that backwoodsmen still ran loose in the forest. A Kentucky jury awarded ownership of the hog to the Hatfield claimant, but the McCoys were unsatisfied. When one of the trial's key witnesses, a Hatfield relative, was found shot to death some time later, the Hatfields accused two sons of Randolph "Old Ran'l" McCoy. A jury acquitted them, but the affair exacerbated tensions between the two families. There was also a romantic dimension to the conflict involving Johnse Hatfield and Rose Anne McCoy, Old Ran'l's daughter, and the birth of an illegitimate child to the couple in 1881.

Screenwriters and such have had a field day with these lovers, who became the Lucia and Edgardo of mountain feud lore. As it happened, Johnse Hatfield's love life was too complicated for opera, much less Hollywood. Rose Anne left him after only a few months, upon which Johnse took up with her cousin Nancy, to whom he was married for seven years until she too left him due to his dalliances with other women. At the time, the sexual angle seems to have been less important than the hog. In any event, tension was high when men from both families encountered one another on August 6, 1882, at a polling place on the Kentucky side of the Tug Fork. Voting was held at the log house of Anderson Hatfield, a Baptist preacher known as "Preacher Anse" to distinguish him from his cousin "Devil Anse," the former rebel guerrilla and current logging entrepreneur who lived across the river in West Virginia. Because campaigning and voting were social as well as political occasions— Johnse Hatfield and Rose Anne McCoy had first gotten together on election day in 1880—it was perfectly natural for West Virginians to come over to the poll in Kentucky, and because there was usually plenty of liquor available, there were usually plenty of fights. On this occasion, a brawl led to the wounding of Ellison Hatfield, Devil Anse's brother, by three of Randolph McCoy's sons, who in turn were captured and taken to the West Virginia side of the river to await the outcome of Ellison's struggle for life. Ellison Hatfield died on August 9. At dusk on the same day, the three McCoy brothers were taken back across the river into Kentucky, tied to some bushes, and shot.

No one ever proved Anse Hatfield's personal involvement in this execution or in any subsequent killing, but the commanding presence of this tall, black-bearded veteran of fifty and his patriarchal status at the head of a large and vigorous clan made him the central figure in the publicity that later attached to the feud. The first round of killings attracted little attention outside of the neighborhood, however. A grand jury in Pike County, Kentucky, returned some twenty indictments against various Hatfields for the McCoy brothers' deaths, but no effort was made to enforce them until the summer of 1887. Then the appearance of a McCoy relative in the prosecutor's office in Pikeville and a new governor in the Kentucky statehouse led to a request to West Virginia for the Hatfields' extradition. West Virginia turned down the request and instead soon issued extradition warrants of its own against Kentuckians who crossed the border in pursuit of the Hatfields. The dispute between the two states, which went all the way to the U.S. Supreme Court, and a series of sensational and bloody raids and counter-raids back and forth across the Tug Fork attracted national attention. As a result, the Hatfields and the McCoys became the most famous feudists in American history, rivaling Shakespeare's Montagues and Capulets in notoriety and surpassing the historical vendettas on which Mark Twain and Sir Walter Scott had modeled their stories of family feuds.

Unlike its fictional prototypes, however, the real-life Hatfield-McCoy conflict had repercussions that the journalists who cultivated the public's fascination with the feud did not bother to report. The political dimension of feuding derived from the complications of post-Reconstruction politics, which varied in details from state to state but generally involved resurgent mountain Republicans allied with white agrarian insurgents and/or African American voters in industrial towns and cities or in the former plantation districts. This resurgence led to a series of hard-fought and extremely close elections throughout the Upper South, which in turn gave increased leverage to local politicians whose support could tip a statewide contest one way or another. Two examples were Perry Cline, the Pike County prosecutor who persuaded Kentucky's governor to renew the extradition warrants against the Hatfields, and John B. Floyd, a West Virginia officeholder who persuaded West Virginia's governor not to honor them.

Cline was a McCoy descendant with personal reasons to hate Anderson Hatfield. Floyd was a backwoods aristocrat—the son of George Rogers Clark Floyd, who had carried his family's name and standing into the southern West Virginia interior. Floyd's relationship to the Hatfields was of the classic patron-client variety. Significantly, when his faction of West Virginia's Democratic Party turned over the governorship to a conservative industrialist in 1890, the Hatfields' immunity from extradition soon came to an end. Anse Hatfield sent word to the press through his son Cap that "the war spirit in me has abated, and I sincerely rejoice at the prospect of peace."

A close examination of the Hatfield-McCoy conflict led Altina Waller to conclude that "the violence associated with this feud was more related to the economic and political modernization of the region than to family animosities or ancient or unknown cause."[46] Her survey of fifteen feuds that attracted national media attention between 1872 and 1895 shows that, in the great majority of cases, these conflicts involved either Republicans shooting at Democrats (or vice-versa) or the combat of intraparty rivals for political influence and office. Except for the Hatfield-McCoy feud and one other that occurred in Tennessee, these conflicts took place exclusively in Kentucky, and all but one of them in counties that this book assigns to the Appalachian core.

The extent to which Kentucky vested power in so many county governments may account for this pattern. Each of these "little kingdoms" was virtually autonomous, and many were small and impoverished, unable to meet the increased demands that economic and demographic growth placed on local authorities. Among a longer list of forty feuds covered by Louisville newspapers, thirteen were located in the Bluegrass or in northern or western Kentucky. The remaining twenty-seven took place within official Appalachia, twenty-two of these in the core. Even so, the identification of feuding as an Appalachian phenomenon, as opposed to a Kentucky one, is questionable, since there were no counterparts to the Kentucky feuds in Georgia, North Carolina, or the rest of West Virginia, and the only Virginia incident to gain notoriety as an example of feuding was a courthouse shooting in Hillsville in 1912 that also had political overtones. Nevertheless, Louisville editor Henry Watterson, a tireless promoter of economic development in Kentucky and the New South, seized upon the West Virginia residence of the Hatfields as evidence that feuding was an Appalachian—not just a Kentucky—problem. Watterson's propaganda perhaps explains why the British historian Arnold J. Toynbee—who became fast friends with an Anglo-American student from Kentucky after he matriculated at Oxford University in 1907—later made his famous characterization of Appalachian mountaineers as examples of a population that had reverted from civilization to savagery.[47]

If the feuds subjected to in-depth investigation by contemporary scholars are any guide, the key variables in explaining feuding are social and economic. Anse Hatfield's land acquisitions and logging activities represented a response to the opportunities presented to Appalachian entrepreneurs by rising market

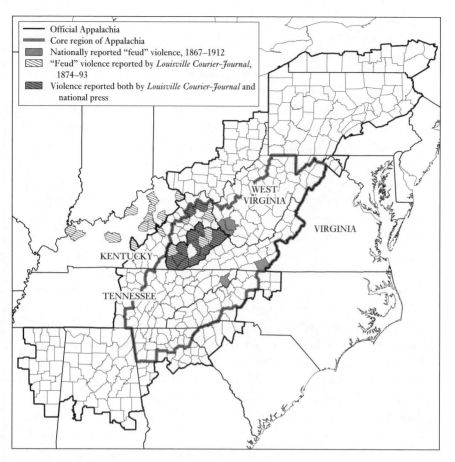

MAP 4. Counties where violence reported as feuding occurred, 1867–1912

demand for the region's timber and mineral resources in the late nineteenth century. It was a modest response, but one rooted in the local community. In fact, Waller found that it was participation in Hatfield's logging activities, not family ties or residence on the West Virginia side of the Tug Fork, that determined who took part in the feud on his side. But Hatfield was not the only entrepreneur in southern West Virginia. In the early 1880s, thanks in part to Jedediah Hotchkiss's long promotional campaign, Philadelphia capitalists acquired control of a heterogeneous collection of Virginia railroads, including the Virginia and Tennessee of Civil War fame, reorganized them into the Norfolk and Western (N&W), and pointed the new railroad northwest toward the Ohio River and the urban-industrial markets of the Midwest. By 1888, as national attention focused on the Hatfields and McCoys, N&W surveyors were busy in the feud region, with land, timber, and coal prospectors swarming alongside them. Construction crews were at work by 1890, and during the next year, a syndicate of West Virginia and Kentucky businessmen laid out the new town of Williamson on the Tug Fork opposite the mouth of Pond Creek, whose headwaters held the McCoy stronghold. By 1893 Williamson had two hotels, a bank, and a newspaper, and smaller towns were springing up all around it, including Matewan near the site made famous by Ellison Hatfield's death and his murderers' execution a decade earlier.

These activities made Anse Hatfield's land holdings more valuable, but the feud also made his economic activities more vulnerable, especially when he decided to move away from the Tug Fork to a fortified log house deeper into West Virginia. Creditors called in the debts he had incurred in financing his logging activities and outfitting his men. In these circumstances, Hatfield lost much—though not all—of his former economic independence. When Cap Hatfield got involved in another election-day shooting in 1896, he found himself spending some time in the new Williamson jail.

The end of the feud thus affirmed that the largest profits to be realized from the N&W's extension through the Tug Fork valley belonged to metropolitan capitalists and their local allies and that local entrepreneurs like Hatfield would have to be satisfied with whatever, if anything, was left. And in fact the Hatfields did make out better during the industrial age than most of their neighbors. Although some of Anse's sons continued to lead turbulent lives, most of the younger generation settled down to respectable modes of existence and tended to wear white collars in the new era. Johnse became a land agent for the Island Creek Coal Company. Willis, after a youthful brush with the law, also went to work for a coal firm. Joe Hatfield became the first Republican sheriff of Logan County in 1924 and, despite the generally scandalous character of his term, was succeeded in office by another brother, Tennyson Hatfield ("Tennis").

Among the sons of Anse's brother Elias, Greenway Hatfield shook off his early reputation as a moonshiner and feudist to become a deputy U.S. marshal and a three-term sheriff of Mingo County, where, during the 1920s, his sons supplied Williamson with its postmaster, jailer, and mayor. Elias's second son, Henry D. Hatfield, won the best terms of all. As a child he became something of a pet of old Colonel G. R. C. Floyd, John B.'s father, who instilled in him ambition and a fondness for learning. Later in life he credited the colonel for inspiring him to go off to college at the age of seventeen and then on to medical school in Louisville. He then returned to the mining village of Thacker, not far from his birthplace on Mate Creek, and embarked on a political career that led him to the West Virginia governorship in 1913.

The Clay County (Kentucky) War of 1898–1901 took place against a similar economic background, though the details were somewhat different. No actual railroad would appear in this county before 1917, but the floating of "paper railroad" schemes and economic growth in adjacent areas of eastern Kentucky set off a land boom in the late 1880s and early 1890s, followed by a collapse of land prices when the nation slid into economic depression in 1893. The land bust in turn put stress on the local political system, which had been the arena of competition for seventy years between the county's two richest families, the Garrards and the Whites, whose fortunes originated in antebellum salt manufacturing and whose competition had burst into violence on two prior occasions, notably during the economic depression of 1837–45.

The Garrards were bankers as well as extensive landowners and had investments in central and urban Kentucky. The White family had also owned salt furnaces, slaves, and timber and farm lands and augmented its wealth by a near monopoly on Clay County's elective offices. The Bakers and the Howards were more modestly engaged in local timbering, milling, and farming and were clients of the Garrards and the Whites, respectively. The Whites and their clients dominated local offices and the county court; the Democratic Garrards had better statewide connections and usually served in regional elective offices such as congressional seats or in local offices subject to gubernatorial appointment. The election of a Republican governor in 1895 upset this balance, however, further exacerbating tensions that had originated in the economic sphere.

When violence between the two factions finally erupted early in 1898, the initial causes were disputes over a logging operation and the site of a sawmill, but the shooting escalated quickly into a full-scale war. The Whites used their control of the county court and the sheriff's office to harass their enemies, while the Garrards used their wealth to cushion these blows for their clients, the Bakers, who did most of the actual fighting on their side. Circuit court judges attempted to impose order and compromise but could find no neutral or institutional basis for imposing peace on the two factions. Finally, the governor was forced to send in troops to quell the situation, but even surrounding the courthouse with militia failed to end the bloodshed, and Tom Baker was assassinated by a sniper as he stood next to his wife while in the soldiers' supposedly protective custody. Another year and a second military occupation was needed before the two parties finally agreed to a truce, followed by an actual treaty of peace signed in 1901. Even so, the trouble flared up again briefly in 1904 and again in 1932.[48]

Still another variant of mountain violence attracted nationwide attention in 1912. This was the so-called Hillsville tragedy that occurred when a trial on relatively minor charges against Floyd Allen, a prosperous member of a prominent Carroll County, Virginia, family, ended (on his being sentenced to prison) in a general courtroom shootout in which the judge, sheriff, and prosecuting attorney were killed, along with a juror and a bystander, and several other persons were wounded, including Allen and his brother Sidna and their principal antagonist, circuit court clerk Dexter Goad. This was the incident that led one metropolitan newspaper to demand that Appalachian mountaineers be confronted with two choices: "education or extermination."

Yet again outside observers overlooked the broader dimensions. The Allens lived in a part of the county located on the southeast slope of the Blue Ridge escarpment; the courthouse at Hillsville was seven miles away from the elegant and modern home and prosperous store that Sidna Allen operated on the Fancy Gap road and fourteen miles from Floyd Allen's store near the North Carolina line. The brothers were Democrats, and their part of the county— foothills and valleys ranging 300–1,800 feet below Hillsville in altitude—was economically oriented more to Piedmont North Carolina than to Virginia; the twin cities of Winston and Salem were less than fifty miles away. Carroll County was ruled by Republicans, however, and the much larger part of the county that lay "on the mountain" was no longer poorer than the Allens' district, thanks to the coming of a Norfolk and Western feeder line and the wood-products town of Galax on the county's western edge.

In 1911 Floyd Allen had organized other Democrats to intervene in an election quarrel in favor of one Republican faction against another headed by Dexter Goad. Goad's faction won narrowly, and so when two of his men illegally arrested two Allen nephews on the Carolina side of the state line on charges growing out of a scuffle with four other young men, they took the opportunity to parade the boys, bound and manacled, back to Hillsville via a route that took them by both of their uncles' stores. Floyd Allen intervened, trying to persuade the deputies to free the boys from their handcuffs. On being refused, he disarmed the deputies and unbound his nephews himself. This led to Floyd's trial on charges of interfering with an officer, at the conclusion of which the shooting broke out.

While it was never proved who exactly fired the first shot, nor were any autopsies held or questions raised as to why so many heavily armed men were allowed in the courtroom, both county and state authorities were determined to punish someone for the slaughter of a judge and two other officials. The wounded Floyd Allen was soon arrested and charged with murder, along with his son Claude, captured after a week of hiding out in the surrounding mountains. After lying out in the woods for several weeks, Sidna Allen and his nephew Wesley Edwards left the mountains and headed west. They were captured in Iowa six months later. The detective agency that tracked them down, headed by a Galax businessman named Felts in partnership with a Roanoke railroad detective named Baldwin, thereby acquired national fame and a boost to its business as private police in the Appalachian coalfields. Meanwhile, Sidna Allen was sentenced to thirty-five years in prison, and Floyd and Claude Allen were sentenced to death. In 1914 they became the first men to die in Virginia's new electric chair.

The Allens were not ignorant hillbillies, any more than the Hatfields and McCoys, much less the Garrards and the Whites, who were wealthy and cultivated by travel abroad and college educations. In his memoirs, Sidna Allen scoffed at press reports that portrayed him and his brothers riding into Greensboro "'roughly-clad [and] mounted on shaggy mountain ponies.'" Allen continued: "When it is remembered that the Allens lived about seventy-five miles from Greensboro and that when they went there they went by train, the reference to shaggy mountain ponies is absurd. So far as I know, no Allen ever did ride a horse of any kind to Greensboro. But had they gone there mounted, I can assure the reader that it wouldn't have been on shaggy mountain ponies. The Allens owned and rode good horses."[49]

The sensational publicity that the Hillsville killings generated nevertheless helped to fix feuding in particular and irrational violence in general as marks of Appalachian culture, along with moonshining and sexual irregularities of the sort that shocked and titillated those who followed Tom Dula's trials. Grafted onto the stock caricatures that town dwellers have traditionally made of country people, the stereotyped Appalachian mountaineer that emerged at the turn of the century would be featured in literally hundreds of cultural productions during the twentieth century.

While journalists and educational and religious missionaries contributed to and exploited the emerging Appalachian stereotype, it was primarily the product of a generation of impressionistic local color and travel writers, beginning in 1873 with Will Wallace Harney's magazine article "A Strange

Land and a Peculiar People," first published in *Lippincott's Magazine* in 1873. Mary Noailles Murfree, a woman who lived variously in Nashville, St. Louis, and a family plantation in Middle Tennessee but who vacationed in the Cumberlands and Smokies, published numerous fictional works in this vein, notably *In the Tennessee Mountains* (1884), published under the nom de plume of Charles Egbert Craddock. Readers accorded her book such popularity that, as Cratis D. Williams wrote, "Writers who have attempted to present a literary mountaineer based on any type of real mountaineer other than the one she selected have met with an indifferent success. . . . Since Murfree created the literary mountaineer and the props that go with him, her archetypes and stereotypes in character, setting and atmosphere have remained standard instruments."[50]

Harney and Murfree had many imitators, but none was more successful in fixing the representation of mountain people in the American mind than the Kentuckian John Fox Jr., whose novels *The Little Shepherd of Kingdom Come* (1903), *The Trail of the Lonesome Pine* (1908), and *A Cumberland Vendetta* (1911) were among the first American best-sellers—or at least the first whose popularity was enumerated when such lists began to be kept. Collectively, Harney, Murfree, and Fox and their many imitators defined Appalachia's people in a new light, cataloging an inventory of behaviors and customs that set the people apart from what was then considered to be the American mainstream.

The inventory invariably began with speech patterns and personal comportment and included both expressive culture (notably vernacular log architecture, folk music and dance, handicrafts, woodscraft, superstitions, and religious practices) and social behavior, with emphasis on such deviance as illiteracy and a propensity for feuding and brawling. The literary props included mountain scenery with stirring contrasts of heights and valleys, light and shade, wildness and tameness, and log houses with puncheon floors and dim firelit interiors, bright quilts on crude beds, and cane-bottomed chairs. Stock characters numbered young women whose beauty was enhanced by coarse garb, shapeless middle-aged mothers, and spare and haglike grannies smoking pipes; young men with athletic builds, blond hair, and gray eyes, "lithe" and "striking" as observed in their variable roles of hunter, moonshiner, a farmer's son, or a young feudist; older men who are still lithe and tough, doltish if prosperous, unsympathetic if poor, but "thoroughly masculine" and kind to animals, especially to their numerous dogs; and children, invariably tow-headed and shy, fleeing from strangers but "grave and respectful" in the presence of elders. The only variations in this type of fiction, as Williams noted of Murfree and her imitators, were the actions that drove the plot. By the end of the century, blue-gray romances involving the sons and daughters of Unionists and rebels gave way to feuds as the most popular plot device.

To a significant extent, the Appalachian image so constructed was a Manichean one: a positive set of attributes associated with the quaint but stalwart mountaineer and a negative set identified with the ignorant and impoverished hillbilly. (The latter term first appeared early in the new century with specific reference to the sandhill districts of Alabama and Mississippi, but the label was soon applied to Appalachian mountaineers generally.) The feuding stereotype can in fact be divided in this fashion, understood either as evidence of depravity, induced by genetic inheritance or geographical isolation, or as affiliation with an admired but obsolete culture descended from—but not evolved beyond—the clan warfare of late medieval England and Scotland.

Appalachia's image as a territory of cultural deviance was reiterated in dozens of popular magazine articles in the early twentieth century and by numerous two-reel "mountain melodramas," some filmed on location in the Blue Ridge Mountains and shown in movie theaters all over the country. Eventually came talking films and Hollywood epics, not to mention more books and articles, comic strips and cartoons, Broadway musicals and television comedies. Admittedly, mountaineers were not the only rural stereotypes served up to the urban masses in this fashion. The same media generation that produced the feuding and whiskey-running hillbilly also produced the grizzled prospector, the midwestern hayseed, and, above all, the cowboy. But thanks to the feudists and the moonshiners, none of the other stereotypes had quite the capacity for violence and evil-doing as the Appalachian mountaineer. While a mountain character might not always wear a black hat, he (or she) was still in need of redemption. Unlike the good cowboy, the stalwart mountaineer had to be saved to be worthy. For fictional mountaineers, the savior usually appeared in the form of a Yankee engineer or a Bluegrass or tidewater aristocrat. As for the real mountaineers, by 1900 several distinct groups had assigned to themselves the work of their salvation.

During the Civil War, evangelical churches in the northern states dedicated themselves to the moral as well as the political reconstruction of the postwar South. Moving south in the wake of the Yankee army, missionaries established schools and churches to minister to the freed slaves and also, or so they hoped, to southern whites, whom they believed had been betrayed by the native proslavery ministry and whose churches therefore needed reconstruction on a "non-caste" basis. These missionaries laid the foundation for the South's system of African American colleges and seminaries. In Appalachia, Storer

College in Harpers Ferry, West Virginia, a site made sacred by the blood of John Brown and his men, and Lincoln Memorial University in the hills of East Tennessee were institutions that grew out of this impulse. At Berea, the school founded by John G. Fee and his followers reopened in 1866 under its original motto: "God hath made of one blood all nations of men."

As time wore on, however, southern white resistance and the waning of northern radicalism eroded the nonsectarian and integrationist ideals of these early efforts. By 1890 northern missionary activities in the South had become denominational and segregated, in practice if not in theory. The northern Methodists approved of segregation in principle as early as 1876 and in 1882 moved two predominantly white circuits from the theoretically integrated South Carolina Conference into its all-white Blue Ridge Conference. Other churches followed with similarly segregated arrangements. Even at Berea, the number of southern white students dropped to fourteen in 1890, and the number of northern radicals who were willing to send their children there to be educated on a noncaste basis was dwindling.

In these circumstances, the Appalachian region presented an inviting field for missionary activity. From the perspective of mainstream northern denominations, mountaineers "were southern. They were white. They were unchurched." In addition, "they were sympathetic to the ministrations of northern missionaries."[51] They were also worthy, according to the myth of wartime Appalachian Unionism, which made mountain missions fundable in the eyes of northern congregations and philanthropists. The only problem, as Henry Shapiro has pointed out, was that this turn to the mountains—in contrast to the earlier ministry to freedmen—did not grow out of the needs or appeals of the mountain people, but rather met the needs of the missionaries for new beginnings in a new field. Later, in some cases, the founders of mountain schools or settlement houses thought to arrange an invitation from the locals, but such invitations were based on classic client/patron relationships, not on popular demand.

Northern clergymen coming to western North Carolina for health reasons founded the first two schools specifically dedicated to "mountain whites" (as the clients came to be known). The Rev. L. M. Pease, exhausted by his work as a Presbyterian minister in the slums of New York City, founded the Home Industrial School for Girls in Asheville in 1877; a "farm school" for boys followed in 1886–87. Meanwhile, in 1879, the Rev. Luke Dorland, a veteran of freedmen's education in Piedmont North Carolina and subsequently moved by "the low and degraded condition of the mountaineers," founded the Dorland Institute in Hot Springs, not far from the Madison County site of the

Shelton Laurel massacre. In 1882 Dr. Edward O. Guerrant, a former Confederate cavalryman who had prospered as a physician in Bluegrass Kentucky before becoming a lay missionary of the Southern Presbyterian Church, founded the first of thirteen schools he would establish in eastern Kentucky. The Presbyterians organized sixty-five schools in Appalachia between 1885 and 1905.[52] In the atmosphere of competitive denominationalism that prevailed in these years, the Methodists and Baptists, both northern and southern varieties, soon followed suit, along with Episcopalians, who began their work in the mountains in 1889.

This religious and educational movement acquired its most influential spokesman in 1892, when William Goodell Frost became the third president of Berea College. From this pulpit, Frost would preach the most widely resounding call for the redemption of the mountaineers, a famous essay published in 1895 under the title "Our Contemporary Ancestors." Frost defined "Appalachian America" as one of "God's Grand Divisions" and proclaimed its people to be the inheritors of the culture of Elizabethan England and colonial America. Frost thus grounded the worthiness of mountaineers not only in wartime Unionism but in racial and ethnic identity. Mountain people were not just white, but the right kind of whites: bearers of "Anglo-Saxon blood." In this they stood apart from other exceptional populations among whom missions had been planted: African and Native Americans and foreign-born slum dwellers. The highly publicized feuds and revenuer-moonshiner incidents that might be thought to contradict this appeal Frost offered as evidence of the need for educational as well as moral redemption. "The cure of the feud must lie in that moral progress which is called education," he told a Chautauqua Assembly in 1903. "We are proposing not merely to prevent the mountain people from being a menace, but to bring the people of Appalachian America over from the ranks of the doubtful classes and range them with those who are to be the patriotic leaders and helpers of the new age."[53]

Berea embraced the stereotypical view of mountain violence by promising to cure it. Thus, a 1913 issue of the *Berea Quarterly* featured a photograph of armed young men, "proud of being dangerous," on the cover and an article inside explaining "How to Make Something Out of This Fighting Stock." From the standpoint of Berea's survival, the turn to the mountains paid off, especially after a 1904 Kentucky law forced the college to drop its nonracial admissions policy. Nevertheless, Frost's formulation was primarily based on images established by the creators of the literary mountaineer, not an assessment of mountain realities. Clay County, Kentucky, for example, had twenty churches and eighty schoolhouses at the beginning of its decade of feuding notoriety; in 1900 its literacy rate was 84 percent for men, 70 percent for women. How one interpreted such data depended on one's perspective, of course. An illiteracy rate between 16 and 30 percent could be seen as alarming or hopeful, a glass half empty or half full. For Frost and his imitators, the glass was empty.

Also in 1895, a modified version of the missionary impulse yielded a new kind of educational mission, the settlement school, inspired by the work of Charles Booth in the slums of London and his American emulators in the immigrant neighborhoods of New York and other big cities. The Log Cabin Settlement in Asheville was the first of this type, while a group of upper-class Louisville women, after scouting out possible locations in eastern Kentucky in 1898, established the most influential of the settlement schools at Hindman in Knott County in 1902. Similar efforts followed in other Kentucky locations and in Tennessee, Georgia, Virginia, and North Carolina. The Berry Schools (1902) of Rome, Georgia, the Pi Beta Phi Settlement School (1912) in Gatlinburg, Tennessee, and Penland School (1923) near Spruce Pine, North Carolina, were influential examples that still flourish today as mountain training grounds for artists and artisans.

The crafts revival movement in Appalachia repesented yet another variant of the salvationist impulse. Allanstand, a crafts school and outlet established in Asheville in 1895, was the pioneer in this movement. Berea established its Fireside Industries program in that same year. Biltmore Industries, also in Asheville, followed in 1901, finding its market among the upper-middle-class vacationers and residents attracted by the completion there of George W. Vanderbilt's spectacular 220-room French chateau, Biltmore House, in 1895. Among the settlement schools, the Hindman and Pine Mountain settlement schools in Kentucky, the Berry Schools in Georgia, Pi Beta Phi in Tennessee, and Crossnore School in Cranberry, North Carolina, mingled educational and crafts-revival programs, while other establishments, such as Tryon Toy Makers and Penland in North Carolina and Pine Burr Studio near Chattanooga, specialized in the actual production of crafts.

Behind the crafts revival was the same mix of English and New England influences that inspired the settlement schools. John Ruskin, William Morris, and other critics of the crudeness and injustices of everyday life in British industrial society had stimulated an international "anti-modernist" crusade to revive the folk arts and craftsmanship of preindustrial Europe. In New England the movement attracted reformers seeking alternative work for women who would otherwise become factory workers; it also appealed to nativists who saw the crafts revival as a means of sustaining the anglophone culture of preindustrial—and preimmigrant—days. Crafts schools, like settlement schools, also provided an alternative to marriage for educated upper-middle-class women who were still barred by patriarchal custom from most professional careers. Married women of the same class sustained the movement, both as financial backers of the crafts schools and as consumers of the products that they brought to market. Appalachia had been a region of home manufacturing in the mid-nineteenth century, but—agents of the crafts revival noted with alarm—as stores and cash incomes expanded in the mountains, consumers there showed a distinct preference for store-bought goods, and the looms, kilns, and other tools that had sustained home manufacturing fell into disuse.

Rural New England had experienced a similar transition in the early nineteenth century; in this sense, then, Frost was right when he spoke about "contemporary ancestors" in Appalachia. But New England in the early nineteenth century had lacked a cadre of literate observers standing by to register their concern at the transition, as happened in turn-of-the-century Appalachia. Although home manufacturing was a means of self-sufficiency in the subsistence agriculture that most Appalachian farmers followed, it was also part of an exchange system that operated more by barter and credit than by cash. This system had always encouraged specialization. There were individuals and families who specialized in certain types of handicrafts and who exchanged their products with producers of other goods or of food products. Such persons survived at the turn of the century, some of them in remote locations that were still governed by midcentury circumstances, but mostly among families and individuals who were by inheritance or temperament tradition bearers. The revivalists seized on such persons wherever they could find them and made them the centerpieces of exhibition and instructional programs that served two purposes: Their example convinced metropolitan supporters and consumers that Appalachia was indeed a repository of authentic preindustrial American culture; and they had skills that could be shared with other persons, mostly women, who could be induced to attend the crafts schools. However, revivalists did not set the craftswomen to producing the homely and utilitarian pots, baskets, weavings, and carvings of their ancestors. Rather, the schools and workshops produced items that were adaptable to mostly decorative uses in middle-class and upper-middle-class homes. Pots became vases, weavings became place mats and table runners, carvings became toys and *objets d'art*. The schools also preserved the gendered structure of traditional home manufacturing, with women specializing in weaving and sewing, men in furniture making or in other products involving wood or leather.

In effect, the crafts movement succeeded in making "Appalachian" one of the leading brands in twentieth-century neotraditional home fashions and decorative arts.[54] And while it is appropriate to note the limitations of such an achievement from the standpoint of Appalachia's many other needs in the early twentieth century and to criticize the ethnic biases, pseudo-traditionalism, and class condescension that characterized the revival movement, it is useful also to remember that this was a movement led primarily by and for women. That is, by orienting Appalachian craftsmanship to an economic niche controlled by wealthier women, the revival generated incomes for mountain women who had few other sources of cash and, to that limited extent, increased their personal autonomy within patriarchal households. At the same time, the revivalists set in place a definition of Appalachian artisanry that was at once so elastic and so limited that a scholar in 1990 could only half-jokingly offer a definition of Appalachian crafts as "objects of wood, clay or fiber that are guaranteed to fit in the back of your car."[55]

A growing interest in Appalachian folk music accompanied the crafts revival and lent it credence, while the mission schools provided bases for folklorists as they began to comb the region for "survivals" of its traditional culture. So persistent and successful were these collectors that Appalachia came to be considered folklore's "natural habitat." "Of all the distinctive regions in the United States," wrote a twentieth-century authority, "the one most customarily linked with folklore is the southern Appalachians."[56] The idea that Appalachia is a reservoir of American folk culture originated with the local-color movement and persisted through the development of folklife studies as a professional enterprise. Today the centrality of Appalachia in the definition and study of folklife has receded, but folklife forms still provide icons that set apart the region from other parts of the United States. In fact, if Appalachia is represented by anything in popular culture other than the violent stereotypes bequeathed by moonshiners and feudists, it is nearly always by some sort of reference to folklife, usually folk music or crafts.

As with the crafts revival, serious interest in Appalachian folklife derived from English precedents. Thus the Folk-Lore Society in Great Britain inspired the creation in 1888 of the American Folklore Society, centered in New

England. A decade later Francis James Child published a canonical collection titled *English and Scottish Popular Ballads*, consisting of 295 texts of broadsides and other printed materials from the sixteenth and seventeenth centuries that had become the bases of popular songs. Ballad hunting—identifying variants of the Child ballads that had been imported to America during colonial times and transmitted orally to later generations—became a favorite avocation among a small but dedicated group of antiquarians. Thanks to the publicity generated by writers and educators, Appalachia soon became a favorite hunting ground. State folklore societies established in Kentucky and North Carolina in 1912, Virginia in 1913, and West Virginia in 1915 grew out of the collectors' focus on folksongs, as did the establishment of the first folk festivals in the region, at Asheville in 1928 and White Top Mountain, Virginia, in 1931.

Meanwhile, academic interest in ballad texts made the second and third decades of the twentieth century a "golden age" of folksong collecting in the mountains, with some of the more active collectors being C. Alphonse Smith and Arthur Kyle Davis in Virginia, Frank C. Brown in North Carolina, E. C. Perrow, Josiah Combs, and Hubert G. Sherin in Kentucky, and Louis W. Chappell and John Harrington Cox in West Virginia. Combs, a native of eastern Kentucky who completed his education in France after fighting there in World War I, published his collection in French as a doctoral dissertation at the University of Paris. Cox's *Folk Songs of the South* (1925) established a model for the academic publication of folksongs in the United States.[57] The work of the folklorists established a twentieth-century trend perhaps best labeled "competitive representation," whereby academic professionals and allied groups of enthusiasts challenged the fiction writers, journalists, and mission school fundraisers who had constructed the concept of Appalachian "otherness" for the right to speak for the region and its people.

Geologists and geographers also contributed to this trend. John Wesley Powell, the intrepid explorer who established the U.S. Geological Survey (USGS) in 1878, was the first American expert to use and articulate the idea of "region" as a territory whose human institutions and outlooks were (or should be) derived from the environmental features that set the territory apart from other regions. A parallel system of regional theory developed in French and German universities during the late nineteenth century. The German variant, which argued that environmental factors not only influenced but determined the culture and institutions of a given region, made its way to the United States in the baggage of Ellen Churchill Semple, an upper-class Louisville native who was the first woman to receive a doctorate from a German university. In 1901 she published in Europe an influential essay, "The Anglo-Saxons of the Kentucky Mountains: A Study in Anthropogeography," that earned her an invitation to become a founding member of the Association of American Geographers in 1904. "A glance at the topographical map of the region shows the country to be devoted by nature to isolation and poverty," Semple wrote. The region's people, she added, were prime examples "of the influence of physical environment, for nowhere else in modern time has that progressive Anglo-Saxon race been so long and so completely subjected to retarding conditions."[58] Semple was also a social acquaintance of some of the women who established the Hindman Settlement School and established her authority on the basis of fieldwork as well as theory, traveling over 350 miles "on horseback" through eastern Kentucky. "The author is not a natural scientist but a student of history," wrote a professional reviewer. "In any case, it is evident that the study has had its strong appeal, not from scientific explanation nor from broad generalization, but from eloquent and colorful local description of people in their habitat and way of life."[59]

Semple was not the only Kentuckian studying Appalachia. The first American to hold an academic appointment in geology, Nathaniel Shaler of Harvard, was a student when the Civil War broke out, and after brief service as a Union volunteer he returned to Cambridge to complete his studies. After the war, without surrendering his academic appointment, he served briefly (1873–76) as director of the Kentucky geological survey, which he devoted to mapping the state and identifying its commercially exploitable resources, such as eastern Kentucky's iron ore and coal. In 1875 Shaler established Camp Harvard at Cumberland Gap as the first geological summer field camp in the United States; the graduate assistant who ran the camp for him was William Morris Davis, who in turn became the first American to hold an academic appointment in geography, also at Harvard.

Shaler's students, and Davis's and Semple's in the subsequent generation, made Kentucky a center for the study of earth sciences, which sharply increased awareness of Appalachia among scholars who were advancing the conceptual and practical frameworks of regional studies. Yet it is also true that, at least in those early days, scholars in the earth and social sciences relied more on popular images than on their own fieldwork in constructing their view of mountain people and culture. C. Willard Hayes, the Oberlin graduate and former USGS geologist who helped Berea's Frost define "Appalachian America" geographically, clearly took his cues from Frost when he described Appalachian people in a professional geographical treatise. "In some of the more remote mountain valleys the mode of life does not differ essentially from that which prevailed throughout the country during colonial times," he wrote. "[Mountain people] are perhaps the purest stock in the United States. Curious archaic customs and forms of speech are preserved among them which have entirely disappeared elsewhere."[60]

The sociologist George Vincent also derived his views from Frost, as reflected in an article published in 1898 in the *American Journal of Sociology*, while Semple apparently lifted her characterization of mountain feuding directly but without attribution from the pages of a magazine writer.[61] These and other examples of scholarly representation of Appalachia tended to reinforce images of Appalachian otherness established by popular writers. The scholars may have had different interests at stake in the competitive representation of Appalachia, but they did not offer competing viewpoints.

The first book-length studies of the region both codified and challenged cultural stereotypes. Emma Bell Miles, Horace Kephart, and John C. Campbell were all outsiders who settled in the mountains and became intimately involved with their neighbors and informants. Their books offered many correctives to the distortions and oversimplifications of earlier writers, but essentially they confirmed at least the positive aspects of mountain culture and reiterated the folklorists' preservationist concern that the attractive features of the culture would be overwhelmed and destroyed by the advance of urban-industrial society into the mountains.

Miles's *The Spirit of the Mountains* (1905) offered a sympathetic and contextual portrait of mountain people, with emphasis on the expressive culture of religious, social, and domestic life and on the role of women as "repositories of tribal lore—tradition and song, medical and religious learning."[62] Horace Kephart's *Our Southern Highlanders* (1913) elaborated upon Miles's portrayal of men as the bearers of outdoor traditions associated with farming, hunting, and woodcraft. A former librarian and a refugee from middle-class domesticity in the Midwest, Kephart relished the "manliness" of his neighbors in the North Carolina mountains, even when their conception of manhood precipitated violent behavior. Nevertheless, he attempted to balance the sensationalism that journalists had attached to the subjects of moonshining and feuds.

John C. Campbell's *The Southern Highlander and His Homeland* (1921) offered a magisterial survey of Appalachian geography, history, and culture, into which was incorporated the folksong researches of his wife (and posthumous editor), Olive Dame Campbell. In contrast to most other writers, Campbell emphasized the diversity of Appalachia, both in its class structure and its geographic features. Had scholars followed up his observations on the differences between town and country in the region, or on the class differences between bottomland, cove, and branchwater farmers, the social dimensions of Appalachian history would not have remained unexplored for the next fifty years. But Campbell died before his book was published, and his wife devoted her energies to folksong researches and to creating a secular mission, the John C. Campbell Folk School, as a monument to her husband. Through her agency, the leading English folksong collector of the day, Cecil Sharp, was persuaded to come to Asheville, which he used as a base for collecting expeditions totaling forty-six weeks during the years 1916–18. Sharp gathered some 1,600 folksongs in North Carolina, Virginia, West Virginia, Tennessee, and Kentucky during this period and introduced to American collectors the practice of "catching" and noting the tunes of the ballads as well as recording their texts. *English Folk-Songs from the Southern Appalachians* (1917) was the initial product of these efforts, followed in 1932 by the posthumous publication of a two-volume opus that took its place alongside Child as a canonical work.

Sharp pursued his work with an urgent attention to authenticity and purity, certain that the expressive culture he was documenting was on the verge of degradation and destruction. In letters to his English family and the New England sponsor of his work in the United States, he privately expressed doubts that the missionaries and educators who often served as his hosts and guides in the mountains were really doing the mountain people any good. "I don't think any of them realize that the people they are here to improve are in many respects far more cultivated than their would-be instructors. Take music, for example. Their own is pure and lovely. The hymns that these missionaries teach them are musical and literary garbage. For my part, I would leave them as they are and not meddle. They are happy, contented, and live simply and healthily, and I am not at all sure that any of us can introduce them to anything better than this. Something might be done in teaching them better methods of farming, so as to lighten the burden of earning a living from their holdings; and they should certainly be taught to read and write—at any rate, those who want to, ought to be able to. Beyond that I should not go."[63]

"Although the people are so English they have their American quality . . . [in] that they are freer than the English peasant," Sharp told his wife. "They own their own land and have done so for three or four generations, so that there is none of that servility which unhappily is one of the characteristics of the English peasant." Approached by a magazine to write an article about mountaineers, Sharp replied disdainfully, "I always thank my stars I am not a literary man having to note characteristics of my friends and acquaintances and turn them into copy." Berea he found a poor spot for collecting, and he rejected out of hand the premise that sustained President Frost's appeal to supporters. "A case of arrested development?" Sharp wrote. "I should prefer to call it a case of arrested degeneration."[64]

Yet despite their sympathetic views of informants, Sharp and his fellow codifiers amplified three tendencies that shaped the twentieth-century perception of Appalachia as a cultural region. One was the habit of generalizing about the entire southern Appalachian region, regardless of the geographic limits of a given investigator's research. Kephart, for example, spent almost all of his time in the mountains in or near Swain County, North Carolina, but he did not hesitate to echo Miles's claim that "throughout the highlands . . . , our nature is one, our hopes, our loves, our daily life the same."[65] "The mountaineers are homogenous so far as speech and manners and experiences and ideals can make them," he wrote, an assertion that belied careful distinctions drawn elsewhere in his and Miles's work between prosperous "valley people," "the average hillman," and impoverished "branch-water people."[66]

This tendency toward generalization reinforced the presumption that, no matter how carefully a researcher's conclusions were qualified or how sharply the research might be focused upon a particular genre or on the folklife of a particular locality or even of a particular family, they would be interpreted as documentation of a regional folk culture. This was true even of Sharp, whose expeditions through several states seem to justify the regional breadth of his book titles. In fact, Sharp and his amanuensis, Maud Karpeles, spent at least five of their forty-six weeks in Asheville and another eight in neighboring Madison County and adjacent districts in Tennessee. They also spent a month in Burnsville, North Carolina, and an unspecified number of days in Waynesville. Elsewhere, they stayed two months in Virginia, working primarily out of Charlottesville, and visited other parts of Tennessee mainly in transit between Asheville and Kentucky. The team spent a week each in Berea, Barbourville, Manchester, Hazard, Hyden, and the Hindman and Pine Mountain settlement schools in Kentucky, but they visited West Virginia for only three days, Georgia and Alabama not at all.

Four hundred of the 1,612 tunes Sharp "caught" from 281 singers were gathered during his initial forays around Asheville; 70 of these (comprising 40 of the songs that he eventually published) came from a single informant, Jane Hicks Gentry. A member of the Hicks family of Watauga and Avery Counties in North Carolina, and—along with her many cousins and heirs who became folk performers—the possessor of a rich store of traditional music and lore through both the Anglo-American and German-American branches of her family tree, Gentry had moved with her husband to Hot Springs in Madison County in 1898 so that their children could get an education at the Dorland Institute. "She scrubbed floors, did washing, boarded teachers, and wove coverlets to pay tuition," according to her biographer; she also ran a boarding house and worked with her husband in the fields, sometimes hoeing corn by moonlight.[67] And she sang while she worked, which in due course brought her to the attention of ballad collectors. Olive Dame Campbell introduced Gentry to Sharp during his first trip to the mountains in 1916. It is worth noting that while Sharp appreciated Gentry's balladry, he ignored her equally large repertory of folktales, inherited through the German-American side of her family. These remained to be collected by another folklorist some years later.

John C. Campbell's more systematic approach to regional analysis led him to emphasize the importance of "constant qualification" in generalizing about the mountains.[68] But he and particularly Olive Dame Campbell contributed to a second tendency—an instrumental view of folklife, valuing it in relation to its usefulness in advancing other projects, such as the "folk school" Campbell established in her husband's memory in 1925 as the centerpiece in a program of rural uplift. This habit had ample precedent in the crafts programs that Berea and the settlement schools had established and grounded the value of folklife in its efficacy as an adjunct of moral instruction and vocational education. Even Cecil Sharp, who had no particular ax to grind in the form of a specific project (other than folksong collecting), was part of a larger antimodernist movement by which a minority of the intellectual elite in countries such as Britain and the United States sought to establish alternatives to the mass culture of urban-industrial society. Robert Winslow Gordon, a Harvard-trained collector who gathered folksongs in Appalachia and elsewhere and who founded the Archive of Folk Song in the Library of Congress in 1928, saw folksong collection and dissemination as an instrument of Americanization: "Personally, I frankly believe that the whole project of reviving and making known our true American folk stuff is one of the most worthwhile things to be done today. From the point of view of true Americanism. That stuff is the very soul of our past, of pioneers, of the men who made America. It's not modern Hebrew Broadway jazz."[69]

Gordon's barb may have been a dig at George Gershwin and other denizens of Tin Pan Alley during the Jazz Age, but it is also an expression of resentment against the larger social forces of urbanization and pluralism. In either case, his comment leads us to a third tendency in the representation of Appalachia that Miles, Kephart, Sharp, and the Campbells all codified in the first decades of the century: its whiteness. All of the codifiers paid little or no attention to the region's social diversity. John C. Campbell commented at length on the multiple strains of Euro-American ethnicity that characterized the colonial and early national periods of Appalachian history, but this observation had little impact on his colleagues or, for that matter, on his own writing about later periods. He noted that the fact that African Americans comprised as much as 12 percent of the population of Appalachia (as he defined it) would "surprise" some readers, but he took steps to insulate that fact from influencing his conclusions. There were "some slaves" present during the frontier era, he acknowledged, but in the twentieth century "the Negro population is largely in the cities of the Highlands, in the Greater Valley, and in the larger accessible valleys of the Blue Ridge Belt."[70] In other sections of the book, he speculated about the possible negative impact that the black population had on the region's literacy and mortality statistics. In a table illustrating the former, he included industrial West Virginia, where literacy rates were high, but excluded it from a regional compilation of homicide rates, noting that "where the miners form the largest per cent of the population the homicide rates are highest." In connection with pulmonary diseases, he lamented that data on their incidence were not broken down by race, which prevented him from using the data as a "basis for conclusions as to the strength of Highland blood."[71]

Sharp, of course, came to the mountains looking for British border ballads from Child and other canonical repertories, and that is all that he found. He ignored topical song, even such later favorites of folklorists as the nineteenth-century ballads about Frankie Silver and Tom Dula. As much as the ballads of Barb'ry Allen or Lord Randall and Fair Elinor, these too were "love songs about murder," sanctified by the passage of time and oral transmission, but Sharp, if he encountered such ballads at all, left them for later collectors.

Sharp regarded the mining districts of the region, along with the cities, as being hopelessly bankrupt of traditional survivals. After "a tiresome journey into West Virginia," Karpeles explained, "we found that the continuity of rural life had been disturbed by the coal industry." "Primitiveness in custom and outlook is not, I am finding, so much the result of remoteness as bad economic conditions," Sharp wrote after a visit to Clay County, Kentucky. Even this locality, a former hotbed of feuding whose courthouse town had no sewerage or water systems or paved streets when Sharp and Karpeles visited, "was quite sophisticated; . . . and the inhabitants received my remarks about the old songs with a superiority of air that was almost contemptuous."[72]

In avoiding the coal camps and railroad towns of the Virginias and Kentucky, Sharp was of course eliminating the possibility of collecting labor or occupational songs, but these were not yet part of the canon. In the same fashion, he avoided the foreign-born and nonwhite populations; even native white townsmen were suspect. "[W]e are too close to Waynesville," he wrote to his New England patron from North Carolina, "and the inhabitants have been partly spoiled, that is from my point of view. The log-cabins are primitive enough, but their owners are clean, neat and tidy. . . . It is sad that cleanliness and good music, or good taste in music rarely go together. Dirt and good music are the usual bed-fellows, or cleanliness and rag time!"[73] Such attitudes conveyed to succeeding generations of Appalachian scholars, and to the general public, the impression that whatever was of cultural interest in Appalachia was exclusively rural and predominantly white. Even after the canon of collectable folklife broadened, these strictures on the social context continued to hold true.

The other codifiers also tended to ignore the region's town-dwelling and nonwhite populations. Sharp traveled the railroads of the Upper South oblivious to the African American blues and banjo and gospel music that must have been all around him, suffering no epiphanies such as the one that had started his collecting career many years before, when he chanced to hear a gardener singing while at work on the greenery of an English country parsonage. Miles, though living in Chattanooga or on Walden Ridge twenty miles away at a time when the black share of the city's population was around 40 percent, makes no reference to African Americans in *The Spirit of the Mountains*. Kephart refers to "a casual Jew peddler or two, and one stray Italian who had been jailed on a charge of assassination" while the writer was living at a boarding house in Bryson City, North Carolina.[74] He also accompanied—unwittingly at first, or so he says—a revenue agent named Quick on a search for moonshiners on the Cherokee reservation and on a manhunt through the Smokies after an accused *métis* distiller whom Kephart called Buck Ruff broke out of the Bryson City jail. "Man-hunting is the finest sport in the world," he quoted the revenuer as saying, and apparently Kephart agreed.[75] Otherwise, he published what he knew and thought about Native Americans in another place. He devoted 2 pages out of 469 in *Our Southern Highlanders* to African Americans, and then only in the context of explaining that mountaineer antipathy to blacks was not a by-product of poor-white resentment against slavery. "Their dislike of negroes is simply an instinctive racial antipathy, plus a contempt for anyone who submits to servile conditions."[76] Even though Campbell, Miles, Kephart, and Sharp were none of them native-born southerners, it is perhaps unfair to expect them to have transcended the racist values of their times, but there is no question that they contributed further to the whitened image of Appalachia already established by the missionary educators and the writers of local-color fiction.

Fortunately, two additional canonical works devoted to Appalachian peoples of color appeared during the era of legend making, though neither was incorporated into the canon of Appalachian otherness. James Mooney's *Myths of the Cherokee* appeared in 1901, the product of an extended period of living in the Qualla Boundary in 1887–90, just as Cherokee history had passed the nadir of the post-Removal era and population was beginning to rebound. Mooney came to the mountains as a representative of the Bureau of American Ethnology of the Smithsonian Institution, another of the influential Washington scientific organizations founded by John Wesley Powell. Having no formal training in anthropology, Mooney nonetheless was a tireless and skilled fieldworker and had learned the Cherokee language. Making connections among the veterans of the Thomas Legion, he soon met and was accepted by Swimmer (A'yun'ini), who became by far his most important informant, credited by Mooney with over three-fourths of the material published in *Myths of the Cherokee* and about the same proportion of his other material. Swimmer also turned over his 120-page journal of the shamanic songs, prayers, and prescriptions he had transcribed in written Cherokee, and other medicine men contributed another 400 transcriptions. From these Mooney published *The Sacred Formulas of the Cherokees* in 1891.

Mooney intended his publications to be preliminary and planned an expanded and more definitive work on Cherokee traditions. To that end he returned to Qualla for additional fieldwork in the summers of 1913–16. His health failed, however, and he died in 1921, his magnum opus unwritten. The Swimmer manuscript collected during his early fieldwork was lost, and though it was later reconstructed by an anthropologist working with Cherokee elders and Mooney's notes, *Myths* and *Sacred Formulas*—along with Mooney's sketch of Cherokee history—alone have survived as the canonical works in Cherokee studies and as monuments to the memories of both men. Mooney's personal tribute to Swimmer appeared in the preface of *Myths*:

A genuine aboriginal antiquarian and patriot, proud of his people and their ancient system, he took delight in recording in his native alphabet the songs and sacred formulas of priests and dancers and the names of medicinal

A Cherokee homestead, photographed by James Mooney in 1888. Swimmer, Mooney's principal Cherokee informant, can be seen standing behind the woman grinding corn. (Smithsonian Institution, National Anthropological Archives)

plants and the prescriptions with which they were compounded, while his mind was a storehouse of Indian tradition. To a happy descriptive style he added a musical voice for the songs and a peculiar faculty for imitating the characteristic cry of bird or beast, so that to listen to one of his recitals was often a pleasure in itself, even to one who understood not a word of the language. He spoke no English, and to the day of his death clung to the moccasin and turban, together with the rattle, his badge of authority. He died in March, 1899, aged about sixty-five, and was buried like a true Cherokee on the slope of a forest-clad mountain. Peace to his ashes and sorrow for his going, for with him perished half the tradition of a people.[77]

While Mooney was conducting his fieldwork at Qualla, another classic work was passing in musical form among the African American railroad hands, construction workers, and miners of Appalachia. This was the ballad of John Henry, a work song that combined African voices with the high-pitched tones and Dorian modes of Anglo-American balladry. A North Carolina collector first published the song in a folklore journal in 1909, but it was heard long before then by working men. W. C. Handy, the blues composer, first heard it as a child in northern Alabama, sung by workers digging a canal around the Tennessee River obstruction called Muscle Shoals. A Virginian first came across it while working in an oyster house in Norfolk. A Carolina man heard it in Georgia in 1888, where it "was being sung by all the young men. . . . In those days I knew all the words but can't remember all of them now, but it was that he would die with the hammer in his hand before he would be beat driving steel. . . . He was a negro and a real man so I was told."— A West Virginian who had worked "all over the South [and] South West" noted, "I have heard [the song] mostly in the same section of the country that is, West Virginia, Virginia, Kentucky, Tennessee, and North Carolina, seldom elsewhere except by men from one of the above states." N. A. Brown, a sailor on the USS *Pittsburgh* stationed in Shanghai, China, wrote to folklorist Louis Chappell:

I've heard the song in a thousand different places, nigger extra gangs, hoboes of all kinds, coal miners and furnace men, river and wharf rats, beach combers and sailors, harvest hands and timber men. Some of them drunk and some of them sober. It is scattered over all the states and some places on the outside. . . .

The opinion among hoboes, section men and others who sing the song is that John Henry was a negro, "a coal black man" a partly forgotten verse says, "a big fellow" an old hobo once said. He claimed to have known him but was crying drunk on "Dago Red," so I'm discounting everything he said. I have met very few who claim to have known him.[78]

Chappell, a West Virginia University professor, began trying track down the details behind the John Henry story during the 1920s, in strained but polite competition with another scholar, Guy B. Johnson of the University of North Carolina. There was no confusion about the ballad itself. The song tells with rhythmic conviction the story of a steel driver of prodigious strength and skill who competes with a steam-operated drill and wins, only to die shortly thereafter. The protagonist has a wife, Polly Ann (or Julie Ann, Sary Ann, or Mary Ann), and perhaps also a girlfriend, "Ida Red," who got her red dress from a railroad man and her shoes from "a man in the mines." The song also refers to John Henry's boss, the "Cap'n," and to a fellow worker, the shaker whose job it was to swiftly turn and place the steel bits between blows of the driver's hammer.

Given the nature of the song's hard-driving rhythm and imagery, Chappell took note of suggestions that the song is not really about work but about sex and the battles of men and women rather than men and machines. However, his conclusions and those of most scholars and enthusiasts over the years were that the verses of the ballad may be taken at face value, although perhaps the bawdy subtext accounted for the song's great popularity. John Henry was first and foremost a steel-drivin' man who promised his captain to best the machine drill and did, thus affording satisfaction everywhere to men and women who take pride in the work of their hands and encouragement to those whose lives and jobs are threatened by the work of machines. It is also a sad song, for, as in most other traditional ballads, the hero dies in the end, either from his exertions against the steam drill or from some other cause in what was in those days an extremely hazardous occupation.

Through the work of Chappell, Johnson, and others, certain facts have been established, at least as firmly as is likely ever to be the case. We know that John Henry was a real person, that he was African American, and that, according to most sources, he was large, well proportioned, and dark complexioned. Certainly his size and strength and the fact that he could earn a steady living as a steel driver would have made him attractive to women. It is reasonably certain that John Henry worked on the Big Bend Tunnel, and it is also reasonable to conclude that he may have died there, if not from a stroke induced by his contest with the steam drill, then from a roof fall, the mishandling of explosives, breathing rock dust, or one of the many other hazards that tunnel workers faced.

We know also that steam drills were coming into general use after 1865 but that their efficacy depended on geological conditions at the site as well as on the machine's design. Salesmen usually had to stage a demonstration of their machine to close a sale. Such a demonstration might well have taken the form of a contest and, given the kind of rock that the Big Bend Tunnel had to go through, a skilled hand driller might well have beaten the machine most likely to have been used. The variant forms of the ballad don't tell us what inducement other than pride might have occasioned John Henry's participation in the contest, but at wages of a dollar or less for a twelve-hour day, it is not hard to imagine a man responding to a relatively modest incentive. With the right machine fitted to a given set of conditions, steam drilling could move rock at one-third to one-quarter the cost of hand drilling, however; with improvements in the drills, it displaced hand drilling in tunnel construction by the 1880s.

John Henry said to his Captain
A man ain't nothing but a man.

The ballad of John Henry is also an anthem for a society in transition. Appalachia at the end of the nineteenth century was a society of farmers and herdsmen on the verge of becoming industrial workers. It was a society governed by custom and case law about to enter the age of bureaucracy. It was an age of wood about to become an age of iron and steel—and paper. The psychological distance to be covered was enormous, and so were the changes in everyday life.

Agricultural labor was as physically demanding as almost any industrial job, but the work was more varied than industrial labor. Agricultural tasks changed with the seasons. Women worked to diurnal rhythms year in and year out, but men had time to go fishing on hot summer days while the crops matured. After the harvest, crisp autumn days were perfect for hunting and butchering. Midwinter was a time to work indoors, mending and fixing equipment and tools. This was also the time when farmers such as Anse Hatfield and his crew became part-time lumbermen, felling trees and dragging the logs to stream banks with teams of oxen and horses so that the logs could be floated down to Catlettsburg or Frankfort or Knoxville on the spring tides.

Rural life had its own kind of routine and drudgery. The isolation of farm life in the mountains often led to boredom, and cash was a rare commodity for families on subsistence farms. Industrialization in the Northeast and Midwest, meanwhile, had created a growing stream of consumer goods—everything from bicycles and cameras to pianos and fishing reels—that were increasingly available to rural people in expanding numbers of crossroads stores. Poorer people were cut off from this new wealth of goods. Many, perhaps most, of them could get by on what they grew or made for themselves, but that didn't mean that they wanted to. Like the Indians of the previous century, they had become addicted to trade goods.

Especially among young people, whether black or white or Native American, there were plenty of people in Appalachia who were ready for change. They were eager for new kinds of work and for the cash incomes that "public work" (i.e., work away from the farms of family members or neighbors) made possible. John Henry represented a class of people for whom *any* change was likely to be an improvement. Most African Americans after the Civil War still worked hard on other people's land. The relatively small number of immigrants who arrived in Appalachia during this period came from rural areas in Europe where landless peasants lived at the edge of starvation. The maturing of the grandchildren and great-grandchildren of the original settlers of the Blue Ridge and Appalachian plateaus led to the extension of clearing and plowing onto slopes formerly reserved as woodlots or pastures and pushed settlement up hollows and coves to the point where spring and fall frosts and summer droughts threatened crops, while rain in any season carried off valuable topsoil. The "Beech Creek" neighborhood in Clay County, Kentucky, for example, held twenty-six relatively prosperous people in 1850, "all of them located near the mouth of the stream." By 1880, "forty-nine people in seven households lived along the creek from its mouth almost to its headwaters. . . . Population on the creek increased further from 86 in 1900 to 164 in 1920, after which it remained almost stationary until 1942 because of the outmigration of 95 people."[79] The same pattern can be said to have occurred throughout the Appalachian region, except in the Great Valley, where the growth of towns and cities absorbed the surplus rural population, and the mining and other industrial districts, where industrialization in one form or another provided the subsistence that mountain agriculture alone could no longer provide.

Traditional ways of getting by in the farm-and-forest economy were also coming under pressure. The advance of railroads and the growth of towns and of tourism called "fence laws" into being, meaning that the owners of livestock were liable for damages done by wandering animals. This imposed restrictions on the traditional habit of treating the mountain forest as open range for cattle and hogs, while environmental changes restricted the value of free-range grazing anyway when the growth of underbrush eliminated grasses that had nourished cattle. Timbering also restricted access to land and increased the number of lawsuits for trespassing. Another traditional practice that came under pressure during these years was hunting. West Virginia adopted its first modern fish and game laws in 1887, and although these were poorly enforced for many years thereafter, backwoods hunters suffered from the same conditions that had called the new laws into being: the depletion of game and fish stocks due to overhunting, the pollution of streams, and the destruction of forests.

Industrial work offered Appalachian laborers a way out of the demographic dead end they were facing, just as it had done for the third and fourth generations of New Englanders seventy years before. Migration out of the region was another alternative, as had also been the case in New England. Seasonal migration—wherein men left home to find work during the agricultural off season or worked away from home for longer periods to earn cash to buy land or pay store or tax bills—offered a transitional possibility, just as part-time logging had done before industrial logging and its retinue of timber cruisers (prospectors) and buyers took over. But shuttle migration was rarely more than a temporary expedient. By whatever route, agricultural workers who left the farm sooner or later had to face the matter of industrial discipline. However much they needed cash, they weren't born knowing how to pull start and stop levers, how to rotate or strike a drill bit so as to advance the drill hole the farthest distance in the least time. Above all, rural people were not used to working by the clock.

Industrial work also had its seasonality, but it was different from the seasonal patterns of farm and forest. Times were "good" whenever there was "plenty of work." During these times, employers wanted workers on the job all day, every day, month after month. A working day could stretch to as long as sixteen hours. For iron and steel workers in Wheeling or Chattanooga or the new mill towns then building in northern Alabama, drawing the swing shift meant a workday of twenty-four hours. On the other hand, industrial workers might face long months when there was little or no work at all. One of the reasons why Captain Johnson's crew was pushed to the limit was that the C&O was tottering financially as it pushed its tracks across West Virginia. The postwar economy was slowing down, heading for a full-scale depression in 1873; if the railroad collapsed, contractors like Johnson would then have to wait years before they got their money, if they got it at all. Thus an abstraction called the business cycle ruled the lives of industrial workers as firmly as winter, spring, summer, and fall had governed the working lives of their farmer ancestors.

Industrialization increased the speed and regularity of work. The new American system of manufacturing, which had first been tried out in Appalachia in the Harpers Ferry rifle factories in antebellum times, required that employees work as steadily and reliably as their machines. Standardized parts, in other words, meant standardized production, and standardized production meant standardized behavior. Very often a worker had to perform the same task over and over again, hour by hour, day by day. Thus John Henry worked with a shaker or turner,

> whose unenviable job it was to shake the drill after each blow to rotate the cutting edge and prevent rock dust from impacting around the point. Depending on whether the driver was hammering up, down or sideways, the shaker might lie flat on his back, holding the drill between his legs, or plaster himself against the rock face with the drill crooked in his arm or close to his chest. Shakers needed very steady nerves and profound faith to steady the drills as hammers flashed by them in the tunnel's dim light: if they slipped or the drivers missed they might easily find their flesh mangled or their bones crushed.[80]

People brought up on on farms had trouble getting used to industrial discipline. There are few cases on record where such people actually enjoyed doing tasks in a regular, predictable, day-in-and-day-out manner without being told what to do each time. When the New England factory owner John Hall introduced machines into his privately owned rifleworks in Harpers Ferry, the nearby federal armory tried to do the same, only to be frustrated when the artisans who worked there went on strike, used their numbers to stir up a political row, and thus retained control of their working conditions. A superintendent who backed the mechanization effort was even murdered. The workers continued to control the pace and length of working days. Older, skilled craftsmen worked shorter hours than young, inexperienced hands. The pace of work was irregular. Workers took time off for personal errands, card games, fights, and drinking. Absences and tardiness were common, and any attempt to impose change in this regime met with stiff resistance. Then in 1841 the army took over direct management of the armory. The officer in charge banned drinking on the job and other irregular practices. He also installed a clock and required each worker to put in a ten-hour day. This led to the "clock strike" of 1842, but on this occasion the workers were unsuccessful. During the next fifteen years, the armory was fully mechanized. Skilled craftsmen steadily lost ground to unskilled "operatives." The furious local hatred that greeted John Brown's raid on the federal arsenal in 1859 was partly due to lingering worker resentment against the innovations and inventions of other Yankees such as John Hall.[81]

Whenever they could get away with it, new industrial workers offered resistance to their employers' demands for regular and steady work. This was hard to do in cities, for there were usually other unemployed workers ready to take their jobs. But in more isolated locations, such as the lumber and coal-mining camps that began to spread through Appalachia during the 1880s, employers had more trouble finding workers to fill vacant posts. Before 1865 the owners of industries such as the saltworks in Kentucky and the Virginias or the iron foundries there and in northern Alabama and East Tennessee solved their labor problems by using slaves. Some of the enslaved workers were the property of the industrialists, but many more were hired or leased from owners in Bluegrass Kentucky or the Great Valley. Construction crews at work on canals and railroads also included hired or leased slaves. Both apologists for and antagonists of slavery in late antebellum times argued that the conflict between North and South was one of labor systems—not of industry versus agriculture, but of systems based on free labor versus an alternative system based on worker enslavement, a system that, as the 1850s prosperity of the Upper South demonstrated, could be based on industrial slavery as much as on the more familiar plantation variety.

After emancipation the recourse to slave labor was no longer possible for

Appalachian capitalists, although something close to it was achieved by the use of convict labor in the postwar era. North Carolina used convict labor to repair and extend its state-owned railroads into the mountains. Official statistics acknowledged the deaths of 120 convicts in the construction of the Western North Carolina Railroad from Morganton to Asheville and then southwest through the Blue Ridge plateau between 1875 and 1891. Nineteen died in a single incident when shackled men were spilled into a turbulent mountain river after the boat ferrying them across it capsized. Estimates of the actual—as opposed to the official—number of deaths range as high as 500. Rebecca Harding Davis described the living conditions of those who survived: "[T]he gorge swarmed with wretched blacks in the striped yellow convict garb. After their supper was cooked and eaten [over campfires], they were driven into a row of prison cars, where they were tightly boxed for the night, with no possible chance to obtain either air or light."[82]

Virginia permitted the leasing of convicts to contractors working on its half of the C&O, but as West Virginia did not, we can be fairly sure that the men among whom John Henry worked were free laborers. Tennessee leased its convicts to the operators of coal mines in the Cumberland plateau, as Alabama did to the mines around Birmingham. And although it was possible for white lawbreakers to get caught up in the system, the overwhelming majority of convict laborers was black. A study of the system in Tennessee shows that the proportion of whites to blacks among male convicts changed from 150 out of a total of 200 convicts in 1865 to 300 out of more than 1,400 in 1892; until the late 1880s, the largest single category of crime for which Tennessee prisoners were convicted was petty larceny.[83] In Alabama the overwhelming majority of convict laborers was black, many convicted for minor infractions that in some cases seem to have been placed on the books for the purpose of ensuring a steady supply of convicts to be leased. The system was, in effect, a postbellum extension of slavery.[84]

The role of slaves in the antebellum farm-and-forest economy—providing labor for clearing the best agricultural land and herdsmen for the livestock industry, for example—though unquantifiable, needs also to be remembered in this context. Thus, whatever other meanings we may attribute to the legend of John Henry, it serves to remind us of how much of the wealth and the infrastructure that made possible the industrialization of Appalachia was extracted from the coerced or underpaid labor of African Americans. This was not a fact that many white Americans wished to acknowledge in the early twentieth century, and so it is not surprising that legend makers turned a white mountaineer into the greatest American hero of World War I. Alvin

Daniel Boone Pridemore of Leburn, Kentucky, in 1918, ready to defend his country in the spirit of Sergeant York. (Courtesy Alice Lloyd College)

York was a thirty-one-year-old farmer and former religious pacifist from Fentress County, Tennessee, who captured 132 Germans single-handedly in the Argonne Forest on October 8, 1918. This was not the most astonishing feat of its type by an American soldier: Mass surrenders were not uncommon during the last weeks of the war.[85] Yet York was the one singled out for attention by journalists and military propagandists during the months immediately following the war.

"York was never simply an American hero," Henry Shapiro has commented. "He was first and last a mountaineer, and no less a mountaineer because his virtues were the virtues of the native American folk. Tall and lanky, stolid, loyal, simple, choosing duty over his Christian convictions and his pacifism, his sinewy muscles developed by splitting logs on the hillside farm, his marksman's eye trained in squirrel hunting, Alvin York was the mythic mountaineer come to life."[86] By practicing his mountaineer virtues as readily in France as in Tennessee, York validated the notion that these virtues derived from a *culture*, not just an environment. His legend reinforced the widespread belief in Appalachian exceptionalism while confirming at the same time the essential Americanism that was at the core of the mountaineer image.

J. W. Williamson's study of Hollywood mountaineers reminds us that the national psyche was not wholly comfortable with the notion that there might be a little bit of hillbilly in all of us: "He's the shadow of our doubt," Williamson writes. But Sergeant York's version of the mountaineer character was entirely reassuring.[87] His war heroism represented a wholesome, indeed an all-American, form of violence that contrasted sharply with the threats implied by feudists and moonshiners—not to mention the insurgent coal miners who were making headlines during these same years. His personal demeanor in the face of adulation and the attempts of others to capitalize on his fame provided a dignified alternative to the comedic hillbillies who were beginning to cavort across the comic strips, air waves, and movie screens. The fact that York's wife and mother appeared to be entirely subordinate to him further strengthened his appeal. The lives of other legendary figures might better approximate the diverse realities of Appalachian life during a complex transitional era, but the iconic Sergeant York posed no threat to white supremacy or male prerogative or middle-class respectability and striving. His example thus ensured that the positive image of the mountaineer—stalwart, worthy, and manly—would flourish alongside the needful and degraded hillbilly into the new century.

The first class passengers all sit still,

Second class passengers walk up the hill,

But the poor third class have fallen behind.

[They?] push like the devil on the Coal and

Coke Line.—"The Coal and Coke Line,"

sung by Addison Boserman, recorded at

Tygart Valley Homesteads, April 1939

CHAPTER FOUR

Standing the Times, 1880–1940

When Ernest Stoneman was born in a log cabin in Carroll County, Virginia, in 1893, his family was well along on the downward spiral to rural poverty that many Appalachian families traveled during the late nineteenth and early twentieth centuries. Stoneman's ancestry faithfully reflected the population history of the Blue Ridge: It included Quakers who came from Pennsylvania via the Carolina Piedmont, Germans (also from Pennsylvania), and an ancestor who according to family tradition came to Virginia as an indentured servant after having been kidnapped in his teens from a village near London. All of these forebears obeyed the biblical injunction to multiply. Within three generations, they ran up against the limitations of farming in the Blue Ridge plateau.

Martin Stoneman, Ernest's grandfather and himself the grandson of the original settler, was forced to leave the family's first neighborhood along the headwaters of Chestnut Creek and move to an unpromising location called Iron Ridge in the county's northwest corner, not far from the gorge where the New River forces its way northward into the Great Valley. Martin's son, Ernest's father, made a living there as a hardscrabble farmer and "hard-shelled" Baptist preacher, but by the time that Ernest and his younger brothers and sisters were coming up, it was clear that they would have to find other kinds of work. In this the Stonemans' fate was the same as that of thousands of other young people who came of age in the mountains during the first decades of the new century. The only difference is that one of the options Ernest Stoneman chose made him famous and attracted a biographer, and so we know in some detail what those options were and how they reflected the choices faced and made by others who lived their lives more obscurely.

The choices that people like Stoneman faced were for the most part determined by decisions made far from the localities in which they lived. In 1900, for example, the Norfolk and Western Railway (N&W) extended a branch line up the New River from the bridge that Yankee soldiers had tried so often to destroy to a promising hydroelectric site just west of the Carroll-Grayson county line. A bit later, the railroad built a spur off the new branch leading twelve miles up Chestnut Creek to a townsite straddling the county line. The Washington Weaving Corporation of North Carolina built a textile mill next to the hydroelectric site, along with a dam and a power plant. Above the mill, along streets carved out of the ridge rising above the river, the millowners built a company town which they named Fries in honor of an investor, a Moravian banker from Salem. In 1903 other investors laid out another townsite called Galax at the end of the Chestnut Creek spur and turned it into a center for wood processing and furniture making.

Ernest Stoneman, who sometimes listed his address as Galax, sometimes as Fries, continued to live on Iron Ridge but found carpentry work in both locations. He never worked as a millhand, however, nor did he go into the mines as his brothers Ingram and Talmer did. They went north to the N&W's new main line through the coalfields of West Virginia. Talmer was killed in a McDowell County mine in 1916; Ingram continued to work underground, but Ernest never did, though he found occasional carpentry work around the mines, especially after his marriage in 1918 necessitated a steadier source of income. He developed what in the aggregate social context would be called a pattern of shuttle migration, leaving his wife and children back on Iron Ridge while he worked as a carpenter anywhere he could along the N&W. He built houses in Max Meadows, for example, during one of its brief stirrings as an industrial center, and he found work in Bluefield, the railroad town that the N&W built on the Virginia–West Virginia line near the point where the railroad crossed from the New River valley into the coalfields.

It was on a Bluefield street in 1924 that Stoneman encountered his larger destiny. Walking past a furniture store that also sold phonograph machines and records, as most furniture stores did in those days, he heard a familiar piece of music sung in a familiar voice. The sound came from a recording, and the voice was that of Henry Whitter, whom Stoneman had known as a millhand in Fries and a musician with whom he had played in country dances and other occasions around the Galax-Fries area. "I know that I can outsing Henry Whitter any time—if I couldn't, I'd quit," Stoneman told his wife on his return home. Since Whitter had gone at his own initiative and expense to a recording session in New York, Stoneman resolved to do the same and was soon traveling there often, not at his own cost but at that of the record companies, for Stoneman quickly became a "star" in the rapidly emerging field now known as country music.

His earnings were small by later standards but were still more than a mountaineer could earn as a miner or millhand. In the year 1927, when Stoneman and his band, the Dixie Mountaineers, were the featured performers at a historic RCA Victor recording session held in Bristol, he earned around $5,000, five times the annual income of a factory hand. His children recalled the 1920s as a time of prosperity: a new frame home on Iron Ridge that Ernest built himself, a car, a telephone, a gasoline-powered electrical generator, and two kinds of electric curling irons—one to curl, one to wave—for their mother, Hattie Frost Stoneman, an attractive and talented woman who often accompanied Ernest on fiddle. They also had "hired girls" to help out around the house. Fortunately, a carpenter can nearly always find work, for these were the peak years of Stoneman's good fortune. Other musicians recorded at Bristol—notably Jimmie Rodgers, "the singing brakeman" from Mississippi, and the Carter Family trio from southwest Virginia—introduced new fashions in country music that made "the Galax sound" of Stoneman and Whitter seem obsolete. It was not until his rediscovery as "Pop" Stoneman during the 1950s that the family would again live so well.

The musical culture that Stoneman, the Carters, and numerous other Appalachian performers helped make popular during the 1920s and 1930s derived, like the people themselves, from numerous sources. The Stoneman family heritage included musicians of both German and British origin. Ernest's grandmother sang ballads. He had a cousin who "caught" tunes from the county's most celebrated nineteenth-century fiddler. Another cousin made musical instruments. Hattie's family had a similar history. There are family traditions about fiddles made from gourds, a banjo made from a Civil War soldier's canteen, and another whose head was made from the tanned hide of a cat. But as Ernest came into his own, there were also autoharps from Montgomery Ward, mail order mandolins and harmonicas, and a store-bought banjo that Ernest picked up during his stay at Max Meadows.

Similarly, the musical repertory included traditional ballads and fiddle tunes, but the bulk of the Stoneman recordings consisted of sentimental parlor songs and religious music published during the Victorian period. Though some of this repertory may have reached mountain musicians through the traditional form of oral transmission, most of it derived from printed forms, from newspaper poetry or hymnbooks. There were also "event songs," or ballads inspired by specific incidents. Noticing that one of Henry Whitter's first two recorded songs was "The Wreck of the Old '97," about a locally celebrated train wreck near Danville, Virginia, Stoneman went Whitter one better and set to music a poem about the doomed *Titanic*, the chorus of which— "It was sad when the great ship went down"—is still sung by people who have no idea that this is a product of so-called Appalachian culture. Stoneman also composed a song, "Claude Allen," about the Hillsville tragedy and another about Stonewall Jackson, and he borrowed the ballad of John Hardy, a black West Virginia gambler who is often confused with John Henry, from *Folks Songs of the South* by John Harrington Cox. Whether Cox, who as a good folklorist worried about the corrupting influence of popular entertainers like Stoneman on the mountains' traditional musical life, was ever aware of this debt is not known.

From these details in Ivan Tribe's biography, we can discern the factors that transformed life in the mountains during "Pop" Stoneman's lifetime. There were, first of all, the railroads and, nearly as important, the new towns the railroads called into existence: Bristol, Bluefield, Fries, Galax, and Keystone, for example (the last-named being the West Virginia town where the coal miner Ingram Stoneman pursued the enjoyments of gambling, drinking, and cockfighting that made his life seem much more exciting to his nieces and nephews than the soberer ways of his brother, their dad). The railroads, towns, and coal and lumber camps presented opportunities for public work. Towns also had electric lights, movie theaters, department stores, daily newspapers, paved streets, high schools, country clubs, and a dozen other features that introduced newcomers to the pleasures and debts of a consumer society. During the years between 1880 and 1920 a gulf opened up between town and country that was wider and deeper than anything seen before or since. But in town, people like the Stonemans also encountered the things that would start to close that gulf: the automobile and the radio. Mountain people contributed to this new world as much as they took from it, but except for a privileged few, mostly what they had to contribute existed only within the space of their bodies: their talent, in the case of the musical Stonemans, or their labor, the contribution of almost everyone else.

Most of the capital that went into the modernization of Appalachia came from elsewhere and returned to its owners in the form of the lion's share of the profits. Musicians were as familiar with this pattern as anyone else, and occasionally their productions referred to the social context of the changes they and everyone else were experiencing. In a ballad about a young man from Grayson County killed on a railroad in West Virginia, Ernest Stoneman made reference to the Johnson law, a statute that exempted corporations from the consequences of accidents that occurred on their property. Blind Alfred Reed of Princeton, West Virginia, another musician present at the Bristol sessions of 1927, contributed a song called "How Can a Poor Man Stand These Times and Live?" which was revived by a new generation of musicians during the radical 1960s. Reed, a streetcorner preacher as well as a musician, also wrote a song heaping scorn on women who wore pants and bobbed their hair. This song was *not* revived, but it demonstrated at the time of its original issue that Appalachian people were not isolated by their rugged environment, as the folklorists and geographers and missionaries insisted they were. Mountaineers, for better or worse, were fully integrated during these years into the nation's urban-industrial culture.

Foremost among the elements that transformed Appalachian life was the railroad. Appalachia's first trunk-line railroad, as noted earlier, was the Baltimore and Ohio. The railroads converging on Chattanooga constituted a second east-west route, although unlike the B&O they were not managed as a single line; the Chesapeake and Ohio (C&O), which John Henry helped build, was a third such route; the Norfolk and Western a fourth. The Wabash Railroad, which built an extremely expensive line crossing the hilltops of eastern Ohio and northern West Virginia into Pittsburgh, then linking that city to Baltimore via the West Virginia Central and Western Maryland railroads, constituted a trunk line of sorts before it crashed into receivership in 1915. The Virginian Railway, connecting the interior of southern West Virginia to the seaports of Hampton Roads, though not exactly a trunk line in that it did not

Many of the early country music stars were women. Lily Mae Ledford and the Coon Creek Girls performed on a popular radio "barn dance" show during the 1920s and 1930s. Her music was revived during the 1970s when she became the subject of an Appalshop film. (Courtesy of Berea College)

extend from the seaboard through the mountains to the interior plains, represented the climax of ambitious railroad development when it was completed in 1914.

The Shenandoah Valley Railroad extended southwest from Hagerstown, Maryland, to the new town of Roanoke, Virginia (formerly a hamlet called Big

Lick), where it crossed (and was merged by its owners into) the new N&W in 1881. This development finally created a rail parallel to the Valley Turnpike, while the Clinchfield Railroad (formally the Charleston, Cincinnati and Southern) brought to completion in 1908 an old ambition to create a rail parallel to the classic wagon routes through Cumberland and Saluda Gaps. The Clinchfield crossed the Great Valley in upper East Tennessee—helping to create two new towns, Kingsport and Johnson City, that would eventually merge with the two Bristols into a sprawling, three-cored, bi-state urban area—and then crossed the Blue Ridge through a series of tunnels and loops paralleling mountain streams that enabled it to climb and descend over 2,000 feet at an average grade of 1.2 percent.

Neither the Virginian nor the Clinchfield roads would play a role in economic change as significant as that of the trunk lines, but their modern engineering and avoidance of the jury-rigged financing and construction that plagued roads like the Wabash during the late nineteenth century made them generally more profitable than the trunk lines. By contrast, the Louisville and Nashville Railroad, which penetrated the Cumberland plateau from the north and west, and the Southern Railway System, which sent branches into the mountains from the Virginia, Carolina, and Georgia Piedmont, both played major roles in Appalachian development, even though their main lines were centered elsewhere. For example, the new industrial city of Birmingham, Alabama, was laid out where the main line of the L&N crossed a line extending from Chattanooga toward New Orleans that eventually became part of the Southern system.

Appalachia's railroad history can be divided into four periods between the Civil War and World War II. During Reconstruction, the emphasis of railroad managers was exactly that: reconstructing the existing war-damaged roads physically and financially. Much of the indebtedness incurred by Reconstruction state governments was expended on railroad needs, and although northern lenders became a source of capital, those roads that had initially been built or controlled by state governments continued to have a large public involvement in their management. After rebuilding, the railroads concentrated on strategic objectives, competing with one another for rights-of-way, alliances, and acquisitions that would connect existing termini to distant ones or at least prevent rival railroads from siphoning away long-haul traffic at regional "gateways," points of origin or destination for traffic between the Atlantic or Gulf seaboards and the river ports of the interior. Thus, the Louisville and Nashville Railroad, expanding southward from its namesake cities, eventually reached Mobile, New Orleans, Memphis, and Chattanooga but was unsuccessful in preventing the rival Cincinnati and Southern and Richmond and Danville systems from entering East Tennessee.

The Chesapeake and Ohio was the only new trunk line actually completed during this second phase, thanks to the effects of the Panic of 1873, which further eroded the financial strength of southern railroads and led to even more privatization in the management of state-financed railroads. The Western North Carolina Railroad, however, remained under state ownership, although along with other state-owned lines it was leased and operated by private corporations. The use of convict labor enabled it to reach Asheville in 1879; it then turned southwestward, threading the mountain counties along the Tennessee border, reaching Murphy in 1891. The Richmond and Danville system, pieced together from formerly independent lines across the Piedmont from Virginia to Georgia, and the L&N emerged as multistate systems, one centered east of the Appalachians, one west, both fighting each other as well as other rivals for dominion in the crossroads region extending between Knoxville, Chattanooga, Atlanta, and the new industrial zone of northern Alabama. One long-term impact of this second phase of railroad building was the founding of numerous new towns and cities: Huntington, Hinton, and Bluefield in West Virginia; Roanoke in Virginia; Birmingham, Talladega, and Anniston in Alabama; and Andrews in North Carolina all date from these years.

The third phase of the railroad era was the critical one for Appalachia, for after the depressed years of the 1870s, the roads began to concentrate more on increasing traffic along their existing lines. The Norfolk and Western was the first to focus primarily on the development of local traffic. In the nature of things in Appalachia, this meant coal traffic, since local farmers produced little volume and had few incentives to market their products in distant locations. The N&W's turn northwest through southern West Virginia was not the product of farsighted strategy, but a practical adaptation to circumstances. Having finished a poor third in the battle for control of East Tennessee's railroads, the N&W abandoned its former strategy of trying to reach the Mississippi via Chattanooga or Nashville. Only in hindsight was the decision to concentrate on coal traffic instead endowed with the logic of inevitability. In any event, as the N&W began to build its Ohio Extension, it also sent another branch line from Bluefield through the back valleys of southwest Virginia, reaching Wise County on the Kentucky border in 1883, opening another new coalfield. The C&O, originally completed by Collis P. Huntington as part of a transcontinental strategy, also became a major coal carrier at this time.

The last decade of the nineteenth century and the first of the twentieth constituted an era of feeder railroads, built outward from the trunk lines into the mountains and linking the resources of Appalachia—including its workers along with its minerals and trees—to the factories of distant cities. This too was an era of town building, although generally the new towns were smaller places than those that had been created during the battle over the long-haul lines. In addition to Johnson City, already mentioned, Kenova, West Virginia, and Hickory, North Carolina, are two of the towns that developed at new railroad junction points; Waynesboro, Clifton Forge, and Pulaski, Virginia, and Erwin, Tennessee, developed as railroad yard and maintenance towns; Elkins and Marlinton, West Virginia, started life as the termini of feeder lines, as did Fries and Galax, Virginia, also mentioned above. The transforming effect that even a modest feeder line could have is illustrated by the L&N branch that reached Manchester, the county seat of Clay County, Kentucky, in 1917. "The cars swayed to and fro and creaked like an old sailing-ship riding out a severe storm," Cecil Sharp wrote of this line shortly after its completion. "They say it is safe because they travel so slowly—about nine miles an hour—but I don't look forward to the return journey."[1] Creaky and slow it may have been, but this particular road did what its promoters had hoped for: Within a few weeks of its completion, Clay County coal mines— confined to local markets since the antebellum saltworks had finally closed down—were shipping coal to urban and industrial markets.

The integration of Appalachia into the national rail system was disrupted during the 1890s by another economic depression. Every major railroad in the South except the L&N fell into bankruptcy; even the venerable B&O collapsed in 1895, and its management passed for the first time into the hands of bankers and officers who did not live in Baltimore. The rickety Richmond and Danville system also collapsed and was replaced in 1895 by the Southern Railway System organized by New York financier J. P. Morgan. The Southern system also incorporated the leased state-owned railroads of North Carolina and Georgia. Morgan and Alexander J. Cassatt, president of the Pennsylvania Railroad (PRR), also formed a "community of interest" among the coal-carrying trunk lines, with each of the other major coal carriers—B&O, C&O, and N&W—coming under the control of the PRR. Congressional reaction to this consolidation—which took the specific form of new laws sponsored by a West Virginia senator who was also an owner of coal mines and feeder railroads—mitigated these anticompetitive arrangements somewhat by giving the Interstate Commerce Commission more control over freight rates and the distribution of coal cars.

After a brief period of complete government control during World War I, the railroad industry entered into its fourth phase, the years of its maturity. During the 1920s and 1930s, the carriers reduced their track mileage slightly, modernized their rails, roadbeds, and equipment, adopted an advertising strategy that emphasized the glamour of railroading, and began their confrontation with their eventual nemeses, automobiles and truck carriers. Not until another era of heroic and patriotic service had passed did they enter upon their definitive decline following World War II.

It is difficult to think of anything in Appalachian life that the coming of railroads did not change. I was reminded of this in 1979 in a country cemetery near Adrian, West Virginia, where my maternal grandparents are buried. There are people at rest there who shouldn't have been sleeping next to each other, if we believe the ethnic template of William Goodell Frost and others among Appalachia's nativist discoverers. For example, there are Irish Catholics buried in a Methodist churchyard; even more unusual is to find them there in large numbers. Still more surprising are the numbers of New England names on the tombstones—Phillips, Gould, and the like—names of families from Hampshire County, Massachusetts, who had settled before the Civil War on land that local speculators realized no Virginian could be persuaded to buy and who later had provided stern and vigorous support for the West Virginia statehood movement during the Civil War. New England militants, Irish immigrants, and southern yeomen with English and Scots-Irish names—three groups not noted for mutual admiration, much less mingling. How did they come to rest together near a secluded country church?

The answer is as clear as a train whistle. The Coal and Coke Railroad, later a part of the B&O, passes under this particular churchyard through a tunnel that connects different valleys in the Monongahela watershed. There is even a folksong about this railroad that can be found in the collection of the American Folklife Center in the Library of Congress; the song is full of unflattering references to the man who built it, Henry G. Davis, a power in West Virginia politics for fifty years after the Civil War.

The men [hit?] for wages, then Henry said
"What a darn foolish notion you've got in your head!
I may run this railroad till the devil goes blind
But I won't raise your wages on the Coal and Coke Line."[2]

The New Englanders, Irish Catholics, and mountain Methodists buried in the churchyard on the Coal and Coke Line had been born among their own kind in separate and isolated valleys, but they had come down to the railroad as adults to work in the towns or industries that the railroad created or on the

Prosperous African Americans established homes in Appalachian cities during the late nineteenth and early twentieth centuries, among them the C. C. Dodson family of Knoxville, photographed here in 1900. Like many town dwellers with roots in the country, the Dodsons grew food as well as ornamentals in their urban front yard. (Library of Congress USZ62-49479)

railroad itself, and there they had intermarried and mingled in life as they would in death. The little churchyard at Adrian is an example of how the railroad became an agent of change throughout Appalachia.

A catalog of such changes could elicit many thousands of similar anecdotes, illustrations of how the railroad changed the way people lived—*how* they lived and *where* they lived. In addition to establishing new towns, railroads made some old towns more important (Clarksburg, Martinsburg, Staunton, Abingdon, Knoxville, and Asheville, for example) and sharply reduced the importance of some older towns that they bypassed (Lewisburg and Guyandotte, West Virginia; Lexington and Salem, Virginia; Wilkesboro, North Carolina; Elizabethton, Tennessee). Railroads created new counties in several states. In old counties, courthouses moved from old towns to new towns. Birmingham even expected to become Alabama's state capital and set aside land at the edge of the business district that was known for decades as Capitol Park.

Railroads changed the conditions of life in every place they touched. Martinsburg, (West) Virginia, a Shenandoah Valley market town founded in 1772 and named for a relative of Lord Fairfax, became an industrial town when the B&O located its shops there in 1842. Soon it acquired woolen factories, flour mills, and other agricultural processing industries as well as a notable concentration of railroad workers. This is where the nation's first great railroad strike began in July 1877, when the B&O's management, responding to the economic depression of those years, cut wages while increasing the workloads of its employees. Martinsburg workers walked off the job, intercepted trains, and convinced the trainmen to join them. The Redeemer governor of West Virginia—ignoring the fact that politicians of his type across the South had denounced the military interventions of Reconstruction—nevertheless requested that federal troops be sent to Martinsburg. The situation there calmed down, but the strike spread along the rails throughout the nation, in particular to Pittsburgh, where three days of riots, gunfire, and arson thoroughly frightened property owners everywhere.

Although the 1877 strike eventually sputtered out, and union membership fell back proportionately with cuts in wages and in the numbers of railroad jobs, the embers of labor militancy did not die out completely. The railroad brotherhoods would rise again, and their militancy would ride the rails into other industries along the lines. Identifying themselves to other union men by red bandannas (one of the sources of the term "rednecks"), railroad workers became the sponsors and protectors of union organizers in other industries. The relatively high wages and prestige of railroad jobs made them the glamour jobs of their day. Yet railroad towns were full of one-armed and one-legged men who had been disabled in train accidents.

Railroads transformed politics. It has even been said that the Baltimore and Ohio Railroad created the state of West Virginia. This is an exaggeration, but indirectly the railroad exerted great influence in the state's creation, from the determination of its borders to the design of its constitution. Railroads hired the first lobbyists, and their statehouse representatives remained powerful political figures in most states from the 1870s through the 1930s. The roads were large property owners and taxpayers in most counties, which meant that they always had work for lawyers, especially lawyers who were active in politics. They also bankrolled newspapers and bribed editors and legislators with free transportation until public outcries put a stop to the practice. The pervasive political influence of railroads added more weight to the inertia of state governments when it came to dealing with the problems that came along with industrialism.

Not every town became a citadel of labor militancy, but the railroad shops and yards that were scattered through the region distributed Appalachian industry on a wider scale than accounts focused only on coal and timber camps lead one to believe. Johnson City, for example, grew up around a crossroads initially called Johnson's Tank, where a single eponymous entrepreneur had established himself at a point where the railroad met a wagon road. In 1882 the settlement acquired its first industry—a tanyard, an enterprise that converted bark harvested from the chestnut-oak forests of the mountains into the acids required to tan leather. Within a year, the Johnson City Foundry and Machine Works was established, the first of many that drew upon the coal and iron resources found on opposite sides of the town's Great Valley location. Also in 1883, the town acquired a second tanyard, its first newspaper, and its first real-estate company. A second railroad, a narrow-gauge line known formally as the East Tennessee and Western North Carolina but soon nicknamed the Tweetsie, extended southward in 1881 from Johnson City to the iron-ore beds of Cranberry, North Carolina; in due course a third railroad, projected in 1887 and eventually expanded into the Clinchfield Railroad in 1908, made the town a yard and maintenance town as well as a distribution center for upper East Tennessee and adjacent parts of Virginia and North Carolina. The presence of lumber yards and foundries in turn attracted fabricators, not of the high-end durable goods that put northern towns such as Schenectady or Toledo on the economic map, but of humbler items such as plow handles and bed slats. These industries entailed lower costs, wages, and profits than more elaborate manufacturing processes, but they were still sufficient to attract new residents and to raise local land values. By 1888 Johnson City had an electric company and a street railway.

In this fashion, railroads greatly enhanced the profits from urban real estate, both in the towns that they founded and in the older ones whose growth they stimulated. Collis P. Huntington's Central Land Company, created to develop the namesake city where the C&O located its shops, yards, and transshipment facilities on the Ohio, paid a far higher return on invested capital than did the railroad itself, though of course the town depended on the railroad for its growth. The purchase of 437 shares in the Elyton Land Company, formed in 1870 to promote the new town of Birmingham, eventually made a Montgomery banker the richest person in Alabama. His story was repeated on a more modest scale in dozens of smaller places. The Norfolk and Western combined several types of railroad-related development when it built a handsome resort hotel across the tracks from Roanoke's new downtown. In Kingsport, where the Clinchfield Railroad brought to life an ancient cross-roads known as the Long Island of the Holston in colonial times and as Boat Yard during the nineteenth century (after the flatboats built there to transport salt and agricultural products on upper East Tennessee's shallow rivers), am-bitious local entrepreneurs raised money to finance an entire new town laid out according to the principles of progressive town planning. They attracted a cement factory, a book printing firm, and Eastman Kodak, which created Tennessee Eastman in 1920 to manufacture methanol and other wood by-products used in the manufacture of photographic supplies.[3]

The progressive planning ideals embodied in the development of Kings-port were the exception rather than the rule among Appalachia's new towns. Fries and Galax typified the two more common approaches to town building. Fries was a company town, with a company-owned general store and com-pany houses climbing the hillside behind the Washington Weaving Com-pany's mill. In its physical layout and social structure, it differed little from the captive communities then being created throughout Appalachia by coal, lumber, and textile mill operators. Galax, like Kingsport, was the creation of real-estate speculators who sold lots to individual businesses and home-builders and worked to convince industrialists in other locations to build or expand operations in the new town.

The history of Spencer, West Virginia, reflects the ways in which railroads affected life in smaller and older towns and influenced as well the relations be-tween town dwellers and country folks. Spencer became the terminus of a B&O feeder line in 1892. Until that time, it had differed from the other crossroads settlements of its county only on court days, since it was the Roane County seat. After the railroad came, the number of merchants in Spencer multiplied, and they were able to offer customers both cheaper prices and larger selec-tions of goods. Spencer became a supply center for the oil and gas industry that boomed in the Ohio valley at the end of the century; it also became a communications center by virtue of a newspaper and its position as the cen-tral distribution point for rural free delivery of mail and mail-order packages. By 1910, Spencer had gas heating and lighting, paved streets, water and sew-erage service, fire hydrants and sidewalks, telephone service, and a movie the-ater. A high school was established in 1911 and an electric utility company in 1914. After 1910 the population of Roane County as a whole began to decline, as rural young people began moving north to the factories of Akron and other industrial cities. Spencer itself continued to grow, however. Between 1890 and 1920, Spencer's share of the total county population tripled. It became rou-

The so-called second Ku Klux Klan of the 1920s was an urban and national movement. Its antipathies embraced not only blacks in cities like Asheville, where this Klan funeral took place, but Catholics, Jews, and immigrants generally. In northern Appalachia, the foreign-born, especially those with roots in southern or eastern Europe, were the principal victims of Klan intimidation. (Ewart M. Ball Collection, Ramsey Library Special Collections, University of North Carolina at Asheville)

tine for newspaper editors and others to make firm distinctions between "country people" and those who lived in the towns. That distinction was dramatized for Spencerites by the actions of a local doctor's daughter, who deliberately courted arrest in a rural village that had once been Spencer's equal in prerailroad days by driving her father's roadster there while wearing slacks, a mode of dress strictly forbidden to women by a local ordinance. The arrest made national as well as local headlines and, further, made hayseeds and hillbillies seem hopelessly outmoded during the Jazz Age.[4]

The coming of a railroad invariably led to population shifts: from farm areas to mining areas; from north to south in the cases of some entrepreneurs and skilled workmen, from south to north in the cases of African American miners and railroad men; from southern black belts and immigrant ports to lumber and coal camps. The location of railroads determined or reorganized the spatial organization of cities. Railroad companies or their subsidiaries built new resorts (Deer Park, Maryland, and Highlands and Linville, North Carolina, for example), rejuvenated old ones (Hot Springs, Virginia, and White Sulphur Springs, now in West Virginia), and bypassed others, which soon died (Sweet Springs, West Virginia, and the Sweet Chalybeate Springs in Virginia). They brought access to information via the telegraph lines that ran alongside every track. They brought amenities like the barrel of fresh oysters that Harrisville, West Virginia, epicures received every Tuesday from Baltimore.

Railroads also led to cultural changes. It was not just railway men and construction crews who sang about John Henry. The folk and country music songs that were sung in the Bristol sessions of 1927 included three train songs; two of them were about wrecks and the third, "The Longest Train I Ever Saw," testified to the power of railroad imagery in other areas of life. Later came "Waiting for a Train," "Working on the Railroad," "Orange Blossom Special," "Lonesome Whistle Blues," "This Train Is Bound for Glory," "Midnight Special," and "New River Train," to name only the best known. Also in circulation were folk songs such as "The Coal and Coke Line."

Townspeople who drifted down to the railroad station to see who came in on the local or to wave at the express would find fresh stacks of city newspapers to keep them up to date with the nation and the world. Like their brothers across the nation, Appalachian men developed the habit of turning to the sports pages, following the exploits of big-time spectator sports: baseball, boxing, horse racing, and college football. A national football powerhouse emerged in Appalachia at the University of Tennessee, while Pitt, Penn State, and West Virginia developed a triangular rivalry in the northern part of the region. Radio enabled Kentuckians to follow Cincinnati Reds baseball each summer, while northern West Virginians followed the Pittsburgh Pirates, except in the Potomac valley where the favorite was the Washington Senators.

The region's larger towns supported minor league teams. Asheville's team started out as the Moonshiners, then became the Mountaineers, before settling in as the Tourists in 1915. During the following season, it had the honor of playing in the shortest game in professional baseball history, a thirty-one-minute, 2–1 loss to Winston-Salem; the game was notable also for the participation of a fifteen-year-old batboy, Thomas Wolfe. The Birmingham Barons —originally the Coal Barons—established legends of their own, as did the Pittsburgh Crawfords and the Birmingham Black Barons of the segregated Negro League. The Appalachian League, founded in 1921, at various times planted franchises in nearly every small city or large town between Bluefield and Cleveland, Tennessee; eventually it found its destiny on the bottom rung

Although most states restricted girls' interscholastic sports before the 1970s, Kentucky permitted girls' basketball to flourish until 1932, when the legislature banned it. In *Girls' Hoops* (1998), Appalshop filmmakers Stephanie Wagner and Justine Richardson (seen here against the right rear wall, under the word "ain't") documented this history and the sport's resurgence after the ban was lifted in 1974. The Whitesburg team depicted in this still from the film went on to win the state championship. (Appalshop photograph by Jeff Whetstone)

of the professional ladder, becoming a rookie league where many a big-league hero established himself in the game.

While men and boys continued to display their individual prowess in wrestling, foot races, and shooting matches, baseball became the game of choice at the community level during the early decades of the century, with most every coal camp and mill village fielding a team. As the number of high schools grew, however, boys' interscholastic sports gradually displaced baseball as the prime locus of community pride. Basketball allowed even the smallest schools to field teams, including girls' teams that, in Kentucky, followed the same rules and played on the same courts as the boys until 1932, when the legislature banned girls' interscholastic sports, supposedly for financial and health reasons. Women's athletics made a full-scale resurgence only after federal and state laws banned such discrimination after 1972.

Notwithstanding its enhanced access to the amusements of urban America, Appalachia remained overwhelmingly a rural region. Town dwellers counted for only 30 percent of the population in official Appalachia in 1910, and for 11 percent in the core, at a time when the country as a whole was rapidly urbanizing. It was for good reason that the kind of music "Pop" Stoneman and the others recorded at Bristol became known as "country" music. However, a rural settlement was no longer necessarily an agricultural settlement. To a significant extent, Appalachia's industrialization took place in hollows and hamlets, where the census measure of population density obscured the actual conditions of life. The reason for this is that Appalachian industry was primarily extractive in character. It extracted minerals from the ground and harvested trees from the forest, sending them off to markets with only a minimum of processing. These resources—especially wood and coal—were essential to the expansion of American cities and industry that took place between 1880 and 1930, but the wealth that grew from processing the resources and combining them with other materials and human factors to create finished products became more concentrated than ever before in urban areas. The railroads made it possible to add Appalachia's natural resources for the first time to this complex of inputs, but at the same time they made it profitable to extract Appalachia's raw materials in their most socially and environmentally destructive forms.

The completion of the rail network and its role in developing Appalachia's extractive industries decisively concluded the reshaping of the region's economic geography that had begun in the antebellum era. During colonial and early antebellum times, the Great Valley and its Great Wagon Road had been the focal points of the region's farm-and-forest economy, which, it will be remembered, constituted the region's principal alternative to the rival agricultural systems represented by the Pennsylvania midland mixed-farming regime and the plantation South, neither of which suited the mountains. While the east-west turnpikes of Virginia, the Federal Road in Georgia, and the Buncombe Turnpike in the Carolinas and Tennessee had in due course siphoned traffic away from the valley thoroughfare, the emerging market towns scattered through the valley from Hagerstown to Chattanooga provided central places for more complex development in agricultural processing and related industries.

The role of antebellum state governments in railroad development began the disruption of Appalachia's economic unity by fostering east-west rail connections whose determinants were state lines and the ambitions of rival seaboard cities; the Civil War and its troop movements further fragmented the region. The rail network that emerged around 1910 reinforced the economic importance of the east-west trend of state lines drawn diagonally across the region's natural boundaries. Freight and travelers along the N&W could move more cheaply and easily from Columbus to Norfolk than they could retrace their ancestors' paths from Tennessee to Philadelphia or Baltimore; only the larger profits flowed in the traditional southwest/northeast direction. Freight traversing the Great Valley along the routes of colonial warriors would encounter divergent management objectives and the expenses of interchange at at least three, more commonly four, locations. In the cases of products such as pig iron and coal, in which the value of the product was low proportionate to its weight and bulk, the economics of the long haul encouraged both producers and carriers to ship these products with little or no processing; shippers attempted to keep the merchandise on the same carrier for as long a distance as possible, until consuming manufacturing industries or cheaper barge transportation were accessible at the coastal or river ports.

A vision of unified regional development remained clear in the minds of such persons as Jedediah Hotchkiss, who continued to champion the antebellum dream of a Great Valley–centered iron and steel industry built upon mineral resources of the surrounding mountains. To the extent that the upland South retained and even expanded its role as a center of the iron industry, this vision had a basis in fact. Although steel was the glamour product of late nineteenth- and early twentieth-century industrialism, in terms of its technological complexity and profitability, the iron age lived on as the expanding nation consumed vast amounts of cast-iron pipe for sewerage and water systems and cast plate for stoves and boilers, fire plugs, bed frames, radiators, fencing, store fronts, and dozens of other components of residential and commercial construction. Even after coke replaced charcoal as the fuel of choice for iron smelting, there remained a market for charcoal iron of the sort that had been produced in Blue Ridge iron plantations since antebellum times and continued to be produced at places like Cranberry, North Carolina. Charcoal iron from Cranberry, for example, was used for the wheels of mine and railroad cars built in urban factories in Knoxville, Johnson City, and Huntington.

The South's share of national foundry-iron production actually rose during the last decades of the nineteenth century, at the expense primarily of the Northeast, although this was hardly noticed at a time when the much more widely chronicled growth of steelmaking began to dominate markets for rails, pipes, and the structural shapes and plate used in building bridges, tall buildings, and battleships. And because southern iron production was heavily concentrated in the uplands from Alabama northward, the ongoing strength of iron-age industrialism was primarily an Appalachian contribution. Steel production remained the goal of both promoters and producers, however. When the Tennessee Coal and Iron Company (TCI) finally managed to produce the alloy commercially at Birmingham in 1899, boosters were ecstatic. "It was a great day for Birmingham and Alabama," declared the *Birmingham Age-Herald*, "and presages the coming of that greater day when this district will control the steel as well as the iron trade of the world."[5] That day never came, however; the absorption of TCI by the U.S. Steel Corporation in 1908 and the subsequent stifling of its potential in favor of northern steelmaking centers such as Pittsburgh and Bethlehem have remained potent symbols of Appalachia's place in the New South's "colonial economy."

In terms of official boundaries, of course, a steel industry centered in the upper Ohio valley was still an Appalachian industry, for several major centers of northeastern production—Pittsburgh and its suburbs, plus Johnstown and Wheeling—fall within the region's official bounds, while the mills of Youngstown, Bethlehem, and Buffalo lie just outside of them. Apart from the limited steel production of southeast Tennessee, however, the Appalachian core provided the raw material for steel but few of the manufacturing or fabrication facilities. The so-called "smokeless" coalfields of southern West Virginia and adjacent parts of Virginia and Kentucky yielded coking fuel as well suited— or better suited—to steelmaking as that of western Pennsylvania, as the numerous "captive mines" developed by steel companies in central Appalachia would eventually testify. Yet the role that Pennsylvania played in supplying capital, entrepreneurs, experts, equipment, and tools to Appalachian extractive industries generally suggests that, in the Appalachian South, the colonial economy assumed the aspect of an updated version of the "greater Pennsylvania" of colonial times.

Consider the example of Bramwell, a West Virginia town established in 1883 along the Norfolk and Western approximately twelve miles northwest of Bluefield and just four miles away from the initial mining development in the region at Pocahontas, Virginia. Jedediah Hotchkiss and Isaiah Welch had discovered and promoted the rich Pocahontas coal measures, which offered bituminous coal with high thermal values and few impurities in easily accessible, ten-to-fourteen-foot-high "seams" in the hollows sloping eastward from Flat Top Mountain. Philadelphia investors already experienced in the coal business of their home state bought up the land (or rights to the minerals underlying it) that Hotchkiss and Welch identified. The N&W, now owned by a related Philadelphia-based syndicate, extended its line into the area and built spurs into the coal-bearing hollows. An N&W civil engineer named Bramwell laid out the town inside a horseshoe curve of the Bluestone River, bought the land, sold lots, named it for himself, and became the first postmaster. Bramwell became the nation's first "bedroom community" and achieved its highest per-capita proportion of millionaires, according to local tradition, since it served as a convenient and pleasant location for mine owners to house their families while managing their nearby mines. Of the thirty-five men identified by local historians as founders of "pioneer families," eleven came to Bramwell from Pennsylvania.

When we look more closely at the history of these families, however, a more intricate pattern emerges. Of the twelve pioneers who came in as mine owners or soon rose to that position, ten had started their American careers in the anthracite coalfields of northeast Pennsylvania, but of these, five had been born in England, four in Wales, and one in Pennsylvania of Welsh immigrant parentage. Nine of the twelve had started out as ordinary miners, but at least four had had managerial or other white-collar experience before coming to the Virginias. Four had owned or managed mines in the New River coalfield before coming to Bramwell, and two had done so in western Pennsylvania bituminous mines before moving south.

Of eight pioneer professional men in the town, the three who had direct connections with mining were all Pennsylvanians, while those who practiced medicine, dentistry, or pharmacy came from nearby sections of the Virginias or Kentucky. The three bankers among the pioneers were all West Virginia–born, as were all five of those who held political offices or patronage appointments worth mentioning. Of fifteen who held white-collar positions related to mining, but who did not become mine owners, four were from Pennsylvania, eight from Virginia or West Virginia. The latter two states also furnished the town's livery man, freight agent, postal workers, insurance salesmen, and—most probably—the Baldwin-Felts detective who later became the Bramwell police chief, though he was the only one of the thirty-five pioneers whose birthplace was not identified.[6]

Interestingly, eight of the twelve mine owners started out in working-class families, while many of the other men who wore white shirts and lived in two-story houses came from landowning families in the Greenbrier and similar highland valleys located east of the coalfields, areas that had also produced more than their share of Confederate soldiers and Redeemer politicians during the Civil War and Reconstruction. Isaac T. Mann, who became the richest and most powerful of the mine owners, was also the only one with local connections. A Greenbrier County youth who parlayed his position as the first cashier of the Bank of Bramwell into a multimillion-dollar fortune, he was also the only one of the operators to become a political power with statewide influence. An overlapping study embracing both the New River and Pocahontas coalfields finds a similar pattern—roughly equal numbers of operators native to Pennsylvania, Virginia, West Virginia, and the British Isles. However, most of the British immigrants passed through Pennsylvania on their way south, while most of the West Virginians had "distinctly 'Virginian' connections."[7]

The material culture of mining was even more strongly Pennsylvanian. The firms that produced mining and haulage equipment did not move south with the industry, and so everything from locomotives to electrical machinery to picks and shovels came from Pennsylvania, while the better-paying jobs and more abundant profits to be made from such products remained there. Mining law in Appalachia drew on Pennsylvania's pioneer legal codes pertaining to mining, as had, for that matter, the mining law of the California goldfields and the metal-ore mines of the upper Great Lakes. Since Pennsylvania capital, personnel, and experience went into Appalachian timbering and ironmaking in similar proportions, industrial Appalachia became once again a province of Greater Pennsylvania.

Pennsylvania's imprint was also apparent in the Appalachian timber industry, which like coal mining expanded in a general southward direction between 1890 and 1920. A case in point was that of William M. Ritter, a native of the Williamsport region of north-central Pennsylvania who became known as "the father of southern hardwoods."[8] Beginning with $1,700 in capital and a single sawmill on the Norfolk and Western near Bluefield in 1890, Ritter rapidly expanded his company through the forests of five Appalachian states: West Virginia, Virginia, Kentucky, Tennessee, and North Carolina. Pennsylvania lumbermen also opened the spruce and hardwood forests of the White Top Mountain district along the Virginia–North Carolina border and created Ritter's two next-largest rivals in the Great Smoky Mountains: the W. B. Townsend Company, which operated in Tennessee, and the Whitmer-Parsons Company, which like Ritter operated in West Virginia before expanding into North Carolina.

An allied industry, the misnamed West Virginia Pulp and Paper Company, operated in Maryland and Virginia and was owned by the Luke family, also of central Pennsylvania. As with the coal business, however, Appalachian lumbering offered some scope for locally based operations and attracted experienced capitalists from other areas of the Northeast and Midwest. A Maine lumberman established one of the first logging operations in western North Carolina, while Michigan capitalists were attracted to eastern Kentucky. A Cincinnati firm established the Champion Fiber Company at Canton, North Carolina, to produce brown paper, while the midwestern firm of Cole and Crane bought up timberlands in West Virginia that turned out to be even richer in coal measures than in trees, thus generating a real-estate trust that still earns money from coal leases. Some of these funds made possible the support of a musically gifted grandson. It may seem a stretch to hear echoes of Appalachia in the sophisticated throb of Cole Porter's music, but it was in- — come from coal and timber that helped make possible his translation from Indiana to Yale, London, Paris, and Broadway.

Logging had long provided Appalachian men with an opportunity for public work and cash incomes during slack periods on the farm. That is how Anderson Hatfield recruited the men and boys who rode the spring tides of the Big Sandy down to the sawmill town of Catlettsburg on the Ohio, but this form of traditional logging—dependent largely on muscles of men, horses, and oxen and by necessity seasonal in nature—had a much lighter impact both on backwoods communities and on the forest environment. The railroads freed lumbermen from the necessity of confining their operations to locales near a navigable stream, and a succession of technological breakthroughs increased the range of logging crews both in terms of the distances and slopes they could master and the rapidity with which they could cut through a forest.

As happened in mining, the new industrial timber corporations established company towns, some of which were stable enough to last one or two generations. These included Cass and Maben in West Virginia; Konnarock in southwest Virginia; Stearns, Kentucky; Ravensford, Proctor, and Judson, North Carolina; and Townsend, Tennessee. Other new towns were devoted to allied products: pulp and paper towns such as Luke, Maryland, Covington, Virginia, and Canton, North Carolina; Rainelle, West Virginia, built by yet another Pennsylvania company to produce hardwood flooring and shoe components; Richwood, West Virginia, which made wooden clothespins. Tanneries clustered along rail lines in western North Carolina, East Tennessee, and eastern West Virginia. Established urban communities like Charleston, the West Virginia capital, attracted wood-products manufacturers, while Asheville, Morganton, and Knoxville attracted tanneries.

The Little River Lumber Company's Camp 18, on the Three Forks Prong of Little River, now within Great Smoky Mountains National Park. Although the timber industry created a few permanent towns to house management and railroad and mill workers, loggers themselves usually lived in temporary camps in the woods. These camps often took the form of a "stringtown," boxcar-shaped houses strung out along the railroad tracks. The one shown here is located within a switchback and displays the typical landscape of such places, set down within the stumps and culls left behind by the logging operation. When the woods here were logged out, the camp could be moved by rail to a new location. (Courtesy GSMNP Archives)

Chemical process manufacturers whose raw material was cellulose were also drawn to the region. American Enka Corporation, named for the Dutch initials of its European parent company, built a rayon factory and company town near Asheville in 1928. Two German manufacturers of rayon—Bemberg and Glanzstoff—built textile mills near the old town of Elizabethton, attracted by the water power of the historic Sycamore Shoals of the Watauga River as well as by abundant supplies of wood in the surrounding mountains. Kingsport was not, strictly speaking, a company town, but as Tennessee Eastman expanded its operations there, it came to feel like one.

"The entire community was elated at the coming of the saw mills," wrote the labor organizer Fred Mooney of his youth in a rugged section of the Kanawha valley. "'There will be plenty of work,' was the general expression."

But this enthusiasm soon turned to "bitterness and chagrin," as Mooney put it.[9] Notwithstanding the larger towns growing up throughout the region, the typical home for loggers was a lumber camp, hastily built of green timber or mounted on railroad cars deep in the woods—a rough, damp, smelly, and crowded place whose inhabitants acquired a deserved reputation for rowdy behavior on the occasions when they came into town to spend their paychecks. Women sometimes found jobs in these places cooking and doing laundry. Maggie Wachacha, a Cherokee woman born in 1892, washed and cooked for a gang of Indian loggers near their reservation in North Carolina—three meals and all their laundry for $1.50 a day. "It's hard work," she later remembered; "I wouldn't wash a pair of socks now for a dollar and fifty cents."[10]

By and large the lumber camps were masculine preserves, noted for fights and brawls and also for injuries, for loggers in the southern mountains suffered accidents at roughly three times the rate of their counterparts in the Pacific Northwest.[11] When respectable citizens mobilized to incorporate Cass and to threaten its saloons and whorehouses, these services simply moved across the Greenbrier River to an unincorporated zone, which inevitably became known as "Brooklyn" and the swinging bridge that connected it to Cass as "the Brooklyn Bridge." Not until a middle-class temperance crusader disguised herself in men's clothes and gathered evidence that implicated local lawmen were the cribs and blind pigs of Brooklyn closed down.[12]

In further contrast to the Northwest, there were no labor unions to contest corporate dominance of the Appalachian timber industry. Even if there had been, they would have enjoyed even less public support than miners' unions would come to command. In each of the extractive industries, the county elites of old-time Appalachia welcomed the new investors, smoothing their way in return for very junior partnerships. An arrangement with Michigan lumber companies gave J. C. C. Mayo, eastern Kentucky's leading native entrepreneur, his first breakthrough, for example. The small middle class of the mountains also benefited from the coming of the loggers and sawmills, either directly through jobs as timber cruisers, clerks, and purveyors of professional services to the companies and their crews, or indirectly through the stimulation that population growth and the availability of logged-out land gave to local farmers. The apple-growing industries of western North Carolina and West Virginia's South Branch valley blossomed along with the sawmills, while the value of locally produced livestock went up with the loggers' demand for food.

Moonshiners had a field day, notwithstanding the growing strength of prohibitionism; so did the "distinguished land attorneys" who presided over the transfer of land and/or timber rights from local landowners to speculators and industrial corporations. A study of the industry in West Virginia finds that judges and lawyers bent statutes and even the state's constitution in order to protect railroad, mining, and industrial timber organizations from liability for the devastation their activities wreaked on the bodies and property of farmers, workers, and others.[13] Incipient radicals such as Mooney soon moved on to the coal industry.

In a generation that saw rapid change, the greatest change of all was the disappearance of the Appalachian forest. As late as 1870, two-thirds of West Virginia was covered by old-growth forest, amounting to at least 10,000,000 acres. By 1900 this figure had been reduced by half; in 1910, by more than four-fifths. The virgin forest was gone, except for the pathetic remnants of a few hundred acres, by 1920. Along the North Carolina–Tennessee border, Ritter and his competitors harvested some two billion board feet of lumber from the Smokies, a product acquired at an incredibly low price in terms of payments to landowners and the wages of workers. Ritter himself became a business hero of the Jazz Age, an exemplar of "Christian principles" in entrepreneurship. "The more service one renders, the greater and more certain will be the reward flowing back to him."[14]

The idea of stewardship among such men did not embrace the environment. Cutover land brought new pastures to some places, but more typical was a stubble of stumps and culls that naturally gave birth to a less valuable and less attractive second growth. The diversity of the Appalachian forest that had so astonished William Bartram and every other naturalist who set foot in it was reduced by the loss or diminution of the habitat required to support its huge number of biologically interdependent communities. Throughout the region, visitors saw blackened wastelands in the unluckiest places. Here the fires that nearly always followed the lumbermen and their locomotives swept through the cutover debris and burned down through the ages' accumulation of humus to the rocky subsoil beneath. Each of the Appalachian states in due course took steps to foster protection against fire, to control the further exploitation and destruction of fish and wildlife, and to restrict the pollution of streams. But the burden of these efforts fell largely on individual citizens and sportsmen, not on the corporations whose industrial activity was the root cause of the devastation.[15]

Many mountaineers were themselves implicated in the disaster in one way or another, but an equal number felt deeply about the fate of their homeland. "The true mountaineer has no respect for a tree, feeling merely that the timber is there to be exploited," wrote a presumably authoritative observer of western North Carolina in 1928; "he is glad for the lumber operations that afford employment." On the other hand, a New Englander, writing of the Smokies in 1916, reported, "Indians and white mountaineers alike have an affectionate regard for their forests I have not found in the North. . . . They regard with a certain melancholy the invasion of the lumbermen, who since my first visit . . . have hacked their way to the top of the Balsams, and peeled off great areas of spruce." "It seems as if they just naturally tear up everything," a mountain herdsman lamented. "Soon there'll be no more big woods."[16]

The Pennsylvanian cast of Appalachian industrialism is not enough in itself to distinguish the region's industrialization from that of the New South generally. According to W. David Lewis, the very term "New South" is misleading, for it suggests a departure from the economic and social contours of the antebellum plantation regime that he finds unjustified by the experience of industrializing Alabama. The South in the industrial age, Lewis argues, pursued an economic strategy similar to that of the Old South, in that it created a system dependent upon labor-intensive production, exploited labor, favorable environmental factors, and export markets. Labor-intensivity, as opposed to capital investments in technological change, did not mean that the South was technologically backward by necessity; when required to, southern managers could come up with native or imported Yankee inventors to address problems of production that would not yield to the cheap-labor prescription. Thus northern Alabama, because of the impurities in its raw materials, originated coal- and ore-washing technologies that eventually became nationwide standards in the mineral industries.

The environmental advantages that promoters like Hotchkiss and his Alabama counterparts ceaselessly trumpeted were the close geographic juxtaposition of industrial raw materials, especially coal and iron. Coerced labor, in the form of the convict-lease system, was minuscule in proportion to slavery, but—Lewis argues—it was not coercion as such but the threat of competition from convicts and draconian forms of suppression and exploitation in captive communities such as coal camps and mill towns—all reinforced by a virulent racism that kept black and white workers divided—that allowed southern factory and mine owners to keep free labor cheap enough to give the region competitive advantages in distant markets.

Finally, reliance on export markets flowed from other elements in the strategy. The northern model of free labor and relatively high wages meant also relatively high levels of consumer demand, which in turn made the Northeast and Midwest the centers of the nation's emerging consumer-durables industries. Living at the edge of subsistence, southern miners, millhands, and sharecroppers did not provide much of a durable-goods market, which led southern industries oriented to home markets to produce low-end goods such as "gray iron," "gray goods" in textiles, coke from beehive rather than by-product ovens, bed slats, ax-handles, and clothespins rather than office furnishings and white paper. This divergence between northern and southern capitalism was not simply a matter of southern adaptation to postwar conditions flowing from the Confederacy's defeat, but was rather a product of continuity between antebellum and postbellum industrial leadership. One aspect of this continuity in Alabama was the importation of capital and management personnel and outlooks from Virginia planter-industrialists who had somehow managed to keep their capital insulated from the effects of the war and from northerners, especially New Yorkers, whose businesses were rooted in antebellum ties between northern mercantile and southern agricultural interests.[17]

If we accept this model of diverging northern and southern economic strategies, then Appalachia was a borderland between the two systems, as it had been between the Pennsylvania-midland and plantation systems of agriculture. The divisions already noted in the smokeless coalfields, with roughly equal numbers of Pennsylvanian and Virginian mine operators and Pennsylvania-owned railroads leading to Virginia ports, are cases in point. The antebellum Appalachian economy, in creating a successful agriculture based on animal husbandry, the use of the forest commons for grazing, and the harvest of other forest products such as pelts, nuts, honey, and herbs, had created a viable alternative to both the Pennsylvanian and the plantation systems. Can the same be said for the industrial era? Was there an Appalachian third path to industrialization? As the farm-and-forest economy of the mountains foundered in the late nineteenth century on the shoals of overpopulation and environmental depletion, did Appalachian families like the Stonemans have only the northern and southern models of industrialization to turn to? To explore these questions fully, we must look at the history of the Appalachian coal industry and the unique communities and violent labor confrontations that characterized it during the first years of the last century.

Coal was the chief source of energy during the iron age. Coal-fired boilers provided the steam power that drove locomotives and factory spindles and lathes. Other boilers heated homes, generated electricity, and ran steam shovels and logging equipment. Coal-fired smelters produced most of the pig iron from which foundries made household fixtures and building products, along with stoves and storefronts, machine tools, and marine fittings. Everything seemed to be made of iron around 1900, from sewing machine treadles to the cast-iron dome of the U.S. Capitol. And increasingly, things that could not be made of iron were made of steel: the rails that extended and modernized the nation's railroads, or the structural shapes that made possible tall skyscrapers and daring bridges. Semibituminous coking coal from Appalachia was one of the essential resources for steelmaking; as the twentieth century wore on, by-product coke ovens also produced raw materials for a new chemical process industry based on German patents seized during World War I. Steel was also the key to military power on land, naval power at sea. None of this would have been possible without abundant supplies of bituminous coal.

Thus it was natural for leaders such as William A. MacCorkle, West Virginia's outgoing governor in 1900, to expect that mineral resources would guarantee Appalachia a rich and prosperous future. Yet at the turn of the century changes were under way that dimmed this promise in unexpected ways. Coal remained an important component of industrial growth, but after 1910 the market for bituminous coal did not expand as rapidly as overall national economic growth—alternative fuels, more efficient boilers and steam engines, campaigns against air pollution, the end of railroad expansion, and the subsequent switch to diesel locomotives, along with an increasingly competitive export market, were all factors that constricted potential markets for coal, while other factors that had once seemed advantageous to Appalachian producers encouraged expanded production regardless of fluctuations in demand. The demand for coal was inelastic: Lower prices did not lead to more consumption, just to lower profits as coal operators scrambled to hold their own in a general atmosphere of decline. Producers sought to offset lower profits with lower wages; the fledgling United Mine Workers of America (UMWA) sought to defend wage levels while working politically for federal intervention into the industry's stormy labor relations. The result was an almost continuous crisis in the coalfields after 1910, interrupted only by booms during and following World Wars I and II.

In 1900 experts spoke knowledgeably about "coal fields," although the agricultural metaphor embedded in the term could hardly have been less appropriate. Coalfields were the products both of the railroad network and of geology. In the broadest terms of economic geography, it was possible to speak of six large coalfields in eastern North America, four of which were in the region we now know as Appalachia. In northeastern Pennsylvania lay the anthracite region, containing most of the world's deposits of anthracite coal, which consists of nearly pure carbon and yields the greatest amount of heat per unit of weight; it also burns with very little smoke, which made it so desirable as a domestic fuel that its use was required by law in most cities. Farther west, extending across the Allegheny plateau of central and western Pennsylvania, western Maryland, northern West Virginia, and southeastern Ohio, was a coal region that had no commonly used name but whose greatest resource was the Pittsburgh seam of bituminous coal, so named from the city in which it lay exposed and was first exploited; this seam dipped to deeper levels south and west under the rolling hills of the upper Ohio valley.

Along the Kanawha and New Rivers in West Virginia and the Ohio and Tennessee River tributaries in southwest Virginia, eastern Kentucky, and a small corner of East Tennessee lay deposits of mostly semibituminous coal, freer of sulfur and other impurities than Pittsburgh coal but far less accessible to river and rail transportation before the late nineteenth century. The fourth of the Appalachian coalfields extended southwest of Knoxville through the Cumberland plateau of East Tennessee and northern Alabama. This coal had higher levels of sulfur than semibituminous coal; it was also deposited in relatively thin seams that made for dangerous working conditions and a high volume of slate and other noncombustible matter mixed with the coal as it exited the mines. But it lay in closer proximity than any other coal deposits to the two other essential ingredients for making iron and steel: iron ore and limestone. In Jefferson County, Alabama (greater Birmingham), the three raw materials were practically within sight of one another, abundantly available within a thirty-mile radius, compared with the fifty miles that separated Pittsburgh from the Connellsville coking coal of western Pennsylvania and the thousand miles over which iron ore had to be transported to Pittsburgh from the iron ranges of the upper Great Lakes.

The existence of two non-Appalachian coalfields east of the Mississippi influenced the prices that Appalachian coal producers could command. The Central Competitive Field, so called from the price-fixing pool that operators organized during the 1880s, comprised mines found in a lower Ohio valley region extending through western Indiana, southern Illinois, and western Kentucky. The chief advantage of coal from this region was its proximity to the most lucrative midwestern industrial markets centered in St. Louis, Chicago, Louisville, Cincinnati, and Indianapolis. Coal operators from West Virginia, Tennessee, Alabama, or eastern Kentucky who sought to compete in the same markets had to ship their coal across the Central field and fought with particular bitterness to maintain the compensating advantage that lower wages gave them in the face of higher transportation costs. Operators in the Central field knew this and were the first mine owners to collaborate with the UMWA— founded in 1890 and headquartered in Indianapolis for the first forty-five years of its existence—to raise wages and thus the costs of production in the competing Appalachian fields.

Finally, there was the Cape Breton coalfield of Nova Scotia. Geologically part of the greater Appalachian mountain system, Cape Breton enjoyed the advantage of a seaside location, meaning that its products could economically be shipped to New England, a heavily industrialized region that produced no coal of its own. However, Cape Breton was also on the wrong side of an international border, meaning that its coal was subject to tariffs that could negate or minimize its impact in American markets. Even when tariff reduction held out to American producers the prospect of competing in the potentially lucrative coal markets of southern Ontario, most Appalachian producers south of Pittsburgh remained devoted to the notion of tariff protection for bituminous coal. (Anthracite coal needed no such protection, since it was a unique American resource, little used for industrial purposes outside its home region of central and northeastern Pennsylvania.)

The pattern of railroad development created subregions within the great Appalachian coal regions that were, confusingly enough, also known as "fields." Thus, the anthracite region was subdivided by geology into upper, middle, and lower fields. With regard to markets, it was divided between operators and railroads oriented toward New York, as in the Scranton–Wilkes-Barre region, and those oriented via the Reading Railroad to Philadelphia and the smaller industrial cities of southeastern Pennsylvania. The Clearfield coalfield referred to the north-central Pennsylvania district served by the Pennsylvania Railroad. The Georges Creek coalfield lay on the B&O just west of Cumberland, Maryland, and adjacent to the Elk Garden field across the Potomac River in West Virginia. The New River and Pocahontas fields were the first to be exploited along the C&O and N&W, respectively, but as these railroads developed their rail-borne coal traffic to the west, marketers came to speak of the Kanawha, Logan, and Big Sandy coalfields along the C&O and the Elkhorn, Tug Fork, and Williamson coalfields on the N&W. In eastern Kentucky, the L&N opened coalfields in Bell and Harlan Counties in the upper Cumberland basin and in Perry and Letcher Counties in the Kentucky river headwaters, while the C&O penetrated Floyd and Pike Counties from the north via the Big Sandy watershed.

Where Kentucky, Tennessee, and Virginia converged, the L&N, N&W, and Clinchfield Railroads each fostered mining districts in close proximity. The Kanawha coalfield of West Virginia had the further advantage of access to water transportation along the Kanawha and Ohio Rivers; so did the Fairmont field of northern West Virginia, as the Army Corps of Engineers gradually turned the Monongahela and upper Ohio Rivers into canals. In Alabama, three distinct coalfields—the Cahaba and Coosa fields east and southeast of Birmingham and the much larger Warrior field to the city's northwest—provided fuel for their home markets and also shipped coal by rail and barge to the ports of the Gulf Coast. The great cost advantage of water as opposed to rail transportation also led coal marketing analysts to speak of "river," "lake," "gulf," and "seaboard" coal "trades," referring respectively to coal barged to cities along the Ohio and Mississippi Rivers, the Great Lakes, the Gulf and South Atlantic coasts, and the mid-Atlantic and New England coasts extending between Norfolk and Boston.

A mine operator in central Appalachia—southern West Virginia, eastern Kentucky, and southwest Virginia, in other words—found it necessary to keep track of all these market factors, all the while competing for customers—located far to the east, west, north, and south of his mines—with operators in other fields in intervening geographic locations, and at the same time negotiating for favorable terms with whichever railroad held a monopoly of shipments from his particular district. The social origins of self-made coal operators and their middle-class dependents also need to be considered in assessing the furious opposition that efforts to unionize the coalfield workforce aroused in the first decades of the twentieth century. So does the connection of mining with the business cycle. Each downturn of the cycle in Pennsylvania mining led to intensified competition, bankruptcies, and eventually consolidation into larger firms, with those who were forced out or bought out of older mining districts frequently turning up in new ones farther south.

Five of the ten Bramwell coal operators who came from Pennsylvania came specifically from the western edge of the anthracite fields following an expansion of the Reading Railroad's coal-mining operations, which in turn followed the economic depression and labor violence of the late 1870s. The opening of mines by Connellsville, Pennsylvania, investors in the Norton–Wise–Big Stone Gap area of far southwest Virginia during 1882–83 was an echo of the consolidation of Connellsville coke production under the auspices of H. C. Frick and Andrew Carnegie a short time earlier.[18] Twenty years later, as large mining firms such as Baltimore's Consolidation Coal Company and the Mellon-owned Pittsburgh Coal Company expanded in the older coal-producing areas, smaller mine operators from these districts opened new mines in central Appalachia. As the *Engineering and Mining Journal* commented in 1902, "Our bituminous fields are far too extensive and too widely scattered to make it probable that they can be controlled by a single trust or combination."[19] This factor added to the instability of the coal industry, to its endless oscillation between boom and bust.

The ease with which Appalachian coal could be mined once rail connections were established, along with the region's lower wage scales, compensated for the operators' greater distance from northern and midwestern industrial markets, but these factors, in turn, intensified the environmental and human impact of the industry. Coal measures lying exposed on the hillsides of the Allegheny and Cumberland plateaus could be readily exploited by drift mines instead of the costlier shafts, while the surrounding forests provided abundant lumber for mine timbers and general construction purposes. The N&W's tunnel under Flat Top Mountain between the Pocahontas field and the Elkhorn coalfield of McDowell County, West Virginia, even paid for itself from the coal that was mined out during tunnel construction. These conditions made it relatively easy for operators forced out of northern fields by consolidation to reopen farther south, often with more modern and productive equipment than before. But deforestation on the mountain slopes greatly increased the danger of flooding in the narrow valleys, and the initial assault on the lower and more accessible coal measures sometimes led to fractures of the measures above, causing wastage or increasing the temptation to strip-mine when that technique became feasible after 1940.

Some operators sought to protect themselves against the power that railroads held over them by virtue of their ability to set freight rates and to control the distribution of coal cars. Justus Collins, an Alabama mine superintendent who reversed the usual pattern by migrating northward to West Virginia, opened mines along the C&O, N&W, and Virginian Railroads and used his ability to increase the volume of production at one or another of his mines as a means of exerting leverage on freight rates and car distribution. This option became less relevant as railroad consolidation increased and the Interstate Commerce Commission (ICC) asserted its control over the ratemaking and car distribution processes after 1910. The greatest advantage of southern Appalachian operators remained their lower labor costs, which they believed essential to balance higher transportation costs and the expense of building towns and opening stores and other services in remote mountain locations. The operators' determination to retain this advantage was another causal factor in the violent upheavals that came to be known as the mine wars.

The coal operators who fought the UMWA in central Appalachia were themselves men who had a relatively limited space in which to maneuver. The re-

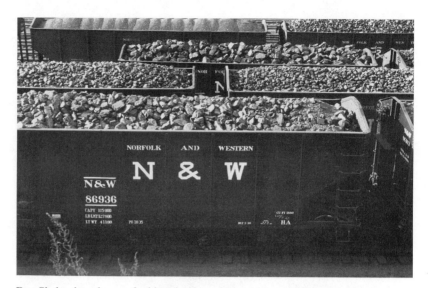

Ben Shahn, later known for his painting and his pronounced left-wing views, was one of a number of talented photographers hired by the New Deal's Farm Security Administration to document rural poverty during the 1930s. However, in this 1935 photograph of the Williamson, West Virginia, N&W marshalling yards, the play of light upon textures captured the artist's eye. The different sizes of coal, ranging from "pea" to "lump," were sorted at the mines in tipples and shipped according to customers' requirements. (Library of Congress USF33-006197-M2)

ally big money was not in Bramwell, but in the large cities of the Northeast and Midwest. This much was demonstrated when Henry H. Rogers, a Standard Oil Company partner based originally in Cleveland, built his own railroad, the Virginian Railway, after being denied favorable freight rates for the coal that he mined at Glen Rogers in the Winding Gulf field. The Virginian was one of the engineering marvels of its age, designed so as to take advantage of the fall in altitude in moving coal from the mountains to tidewater ports. Although several West Virginians, notably I. T. Mann of Bramwell, made money on the Virginian's development, it could not have been built with local capital only. Its completion in 1914 closed out the era of railroad building and led instead to an era of consolidation and eventual decline in coal transportation. Through a series of mergers supervised by the ICC, the number of competing coal carriers in Appalachia declined from ten in 1920 to two in 1998. It is significant that the nuclei around which the two modern-day systems are organized were both profitable coal carriers—the C&O in the case of CSX and the N&W in the case of Norfolk Southern. There was money to be made in coal, and the railroads figured out how to make and keep more of it than did operators or miners. It should be borne in mind, however, that of all three groups, the railroads had the weakest identification with the welfare of local communities.

Coal mining is a distinctive branch of a distinctive industry. Although it shares many practices with the mining of other materials, its occupational culture is unique to coal. Like most forms of culture, it was learned informally by miners who came into the mines as children and young adults, working alongside older family members. As a result of this informal folk system of learning, coal mining inspired an extraordinary volume of occupational lore and music, a culture that continues to flourish and adapt, even though the technology and the formalized system of training for new miners have changed drastically over the last fifty years.

The miners' traditions best known to the public stem from the long struggle for unionization of the mines, a struggle that, in central Appalachia, lasted from the 1890s into the 1940s, to be revived anew between 1978 and 1999. Whereas operators viewed their industry from the perspective of higher shipping costs and lower profit margins compared with northern competitors, miners saw it from the perspective of the company town. The remote and thinly populated character of the Appalachian coalfields virtually dictated the building of company towns to house the workforce, while the marginal position of many operators increased their temptation to lower overhead costs at the mines by exploiting these captive communities.

Enumerators of the 1909 census of manufacturers found that "not a few" operators admitted to selling their coal at a loss and making up the difference in their mercantile and real-estate profits. In northern Alabama and East Tennessee, such profits carried many coal companies through bad times and good; in fact, until 1902, when a decision was made by Sloss Furnaces' management to specialize in foundry iron, the company's most profitable enterprise had been coal mining, and the mercantile and real-estate earnings of coal mining subsidiaries was what today would be called the company's single greatest profit center. By the 1920s, some 80 percent of West Virginia miners lived in company towns, as opposed to 64 percent in Kentucky and 9 percent in Indiana and Illinois. The U.S. Coal Commission, surveying 708 of these towns in 1922, near the end of a prosperous period, found generally unwholesome living conditions existing in most of them, with the worst examples in central and southern Appalachia. The violent confrontations between miners and operators that punctuated Appalachian history during the last decade of the nineteenth century and the first half of the twentieth were essentially struggles for control of these unique communities.

There were, to be sure, model communities scattered here and there through the hills. Holden, built by the Island Creek Coal Company in Logan County, West Virginia, was a model town with all the appurtenances of what was called "welfare capitalism," whereby the company tried to blunt the appeal of the UMWA by providing good working and living conditions. After U.S. Steel took command of the Tennessee Coal and Iron Company in Alabama, it built the model steel-making community of Fairfield, with the satellite mining communities of Edgewater and Bayside in the nearby hills. U.S. Steel also built the model mining towns of Gary in West Virginia and Lynch in Kentucky to supply metallurgical coal to its new Chicago-area steel mills. Such communities, however, were "captive" mines, somewhat insulated from market forces by virtue of the fact that they were owned by steel companies that produced coal for their own use. Other model towns like Coalwood and Tams, West Virginia, and Wheelwright, Kentucky, were paternalistic towns, firmly in the control of authoritarian operators devoted to the care of "their" people. But, as the Coal Commission put it, "in the worst of the company-controlled communities, the state of disrepair at times runs beyond the power of verbal description or even photographic illustration, since neither words nor pictures can portray the atmosphere of abandoned dejection or reproduce the smells." The evils of company towns were less glaring where larger and more stable firms controlled. A West Virginia state commission headed by the Roman Catholic bishop of Wheeling condemned company towns generally but had warm words of praise for the model towns it encountered. Still, one of the towns singled out for praise was Monongah, where the greatest mining disaster in American history occurred in 1907, claiming, at a minimum, 361 lives.

Somewhere in between the best and worst of the company towns were towns like Justus Collins's Winding Gulf in Raleigh County, West Virginia, and the nearby town of Tams. Collins was an absentee owner, living in Cincinnati or Charleston; Walter P. Tams spent his entire life in his town. Collins insisted upon an "absolutely nonunion" operation and employed Baldwin-Felts detectives to watch and infiltrate his workforce. Tams had no love for the union, but he also disliked the brutality of the guards and kept them away from his town. He governed the town directly, taking a paternal interest in the personal and social lives of his workers and providing them with the area's best recreational facilities. Collins built saloons or, after Prohibition took effect in West Virginia in 1914, "thirst parlors." It was his policy to ignore personal matters that did not directly impinge upon the company's economic functions.

From the standpoint of the people who lived there, the common features of Tams and Winding Gulf were as important as their differences. Both towns were nestled in isolated wilderness valleys and built largely from green lumber sawn on the spot. The houses here, as in nearly every coal camp, had open-post foundations, board-and-batten siding, and tarpaper roofs; even Collins called some of his houses "shanties." Tams painted his houses white; other operators preferred yellow; some houses were painted red or green; but whatever the color scheme, the towns were monotonous in appearance and always begrimed by the gritty black mud that seemed a special curse of coalfield communities. Each town was divided into distinct clusters, one for blacks, one for foreign-born workers, one for native whites. Even if there were no guards, the local constables and other county officials were usually involved with the coal companies in some way or another. Allowing for the very best of circumstances, miners still enjoyed none of the privacy and few of the options that other classes of industrial workers enjoyed.

The mine guards were the most visible and the most fiercely resented symbols of the captive character of company towns, and the most notorious supplier of guards was the Bluefield firm of Baldwin-Felts. To judge from the reports that this firm passed on to Collins, the undercover men were often as preoccupied by gossip, grumbling, and Saturday-night sprees as by the real or imagined doings of union men, but the guards who openly exercised their authority were easily the most hated men in the camps. At best, they were symbols of the miner's almost complete lack of control over his working and living conditions. At worst, they were swaggering bullies who tyrannized the camps. After the Paint Creek mine war of 1912–13, Baldwin-Felts men became so controversial that some operators, particularly in northern West Virginia, began to hire and train their own guards, while others switched to deputy sheriffs commissioned by the counties but paid from company funds. The more enlightened mine operators pressed West Virginia to emulate Pennsylvania by establishing a state police. Despite the bitter opposition of labor leaders, the legislature established a state constabulary in 1919, but it was too poorly organized and patronage-ridden to be very effective in the mine wars, which resumed in that year.

From the perspective of the coal regions' small middle class—the people who lived in two-story houses, as one journalist put it—the union representatives were "outside agitators."[20] In Alabama, an emerging African American middle class led by Birmingham ministers and professional men actively preached against unionism among black coal miners and steel workers; echoing the accommodationist philosophy of Booker T. Washington, "don't bite the hand that feeds you" became their watchword, although the same leaders raised their voices in favor of improving some of the most objectionable features of the coal camps surrounding the city.[21]

Throughout the coalfields, comfortably situated people in the railroad and industrial towns simply couldn't believe that conditions in the company towns were as bad as critics insisted, and, as usual, the mountainous terrain shielded uninquisitive eyes from uncomfortable truths. The miners themselves knew better than to accept the outside agitator line. Many of their demands antedated the UMWA's formation in 1890. "Screen" and "scrip" laws, both having to do with the way wages were calculated and paid, first went on the books in West Virginia in 1887, but the companies ignored them. It was the same with mine-safety legislation, which dated back to 1883. Periodic mine explosions kept pressure on the legislature, and the device of appointing mine inspectors afforded a harmless way to relieve it, for though Tennessee's first mine inspector was a qualified man serious about his mission, it was an open secret among politicians in West Virginia and Alabama that the inspectorships were intended to pad the patronage rolls and only incidentally to promote safety in coal mining.

Another grievance that became the subject of legislation was the appointment of mine guards as deputy sheriffs and the subsidization of deputies' salaries by coal operators. This became illegal in West Virginia in 1913 by virtue of a law that lacked an enforcement clause. The convict-lease system, exploited by coal companies in Georgia, Alabama, and Tennessee (and in Kentucky until Knights of Labor agitation led to its abolition in 1886), provided southern miners with another grievance. Outside of Georgia's few coal mines, which were worked almost entirely by convicts, prisoners constituted a small proportion of the mining workforce, but operators could deploy convict labor strategically, using prisoners as strikebreakers and working them full time during periods of slack demand, when free miners were lucky to get more than one or two days of work in a week. In the absence of effective governmental action to remedy these grievances, miners turned to the unions. The union organizers, venturing into the coal camps often at great personal risk, did not create discontent. They tapped it, gave it voice, and shaped it into goals that related in concrete ways to the miners' working and living conditions. With the union, men felt less alone. Company recognition of the union was an important psychological breach in the isolated and autocratic character of the mining towns.

The struggle to establish miners' unions began, like so many other aspects of Appalachian mining, in Pennsylvania. From the 1850s through the end of the century, the anthracite region was the scene of several notable "wars" between labor and capital, the best known of which was the Molly Maguire uprising of 1877–78, which culminated in the hanging of eight Irish American union members in Carbon County in January 1879.[22] A 1902 strike by anthracite miners led to a breakthrough in labor relations: the first federal intervention into a labor-management dispute that could fairly be described as neutral (earlier interventions having been clearly aligned with the interests of the capitalists involved). President Theodore Roosevelt convened a meeting of labor and coal company officials in Washington and lent his authority to a settlement that forced anthracite operators to grant recognition to the UMWA.

Meanwhile the union and its predecessors in the earlier political movements led by the Greenback Labor Party in the 1870s and the Knights of Labor during the subsequent decade were active in the bituminous coalfields of the Midwest and the Appalachian states. It was largely men from the Central Competitive Field, initially gathered into a miners' assembly within the Knights of Labor and a rival independent union, who came together in Columbus, Ohio, in 1890 to found the UMWA, but the new union soon expanded into the coalfields of the Virginias, Kentucky, Alabama, and Tennessee. Within months of their creation, the UMWA's District 19, then embracing the mines of eastern Kentucky and Tennessee, and District 20, in Alabama, were involved in strikes over wages and union recognition. Although these walkouts failed to meet their objectives, they were followed in short order by miner "rebellions" in both states that amount to some of the most remarkable episodes in American labor history.

In Tennessee, the dispute focused on the convict lease system. Initially, union leaders sought to eliminate the system through legislative action, encouraged by the example of Kentucky and by the populist rhetoric used in Tennessee by Democratic gubernatorial and legislative candidates during the 1890 election campaign. When the politicians failed to live up to their promises, the miners took matters into their own hands in July 1891, marching on a stockade holding convicts in the Coal Creek district and placing the prisoners on a train to nearby Knoxville. A few days later, armed miners intercepted a train carrying replacement convicts, turned them away, and emptied another stockade of 125 prisoners at another Coal Creek mine. A truce followed while a special session of the legislature met in Nashville to consider abolishing the lease system, but when lawmakers again failed to act, miners responded in an even more dramatic fashion. This time they freed the convicts and set fire to the stockades, leading the governor to order state militia from Memphis and Nashville into the coal districts, since local units from East Tennessee had shown too great a disposition to fraternize with the protesting miners.

This second rebellion was also notable in that it spread from Coal Creek in East Tennessee, where most miners were white Tennessee natives and the coal companies were small, to the Tracy City and Sequatchie Valley mines located on the southwest margins of the Cumberland plateau between Nashville and Chattanooga. Here a single company—the Tennessee Coal, Iron and Railroad Company (TCI)—dominated production and also had an exclusive lease with the state allowing the company to sublease convicts that it did not employ directly to other mining and manufacturing companies. A three-way battle ensued in which TCI pressed the state for military protection and reimbursement for its losses, the miners continued their agitation against the lease system and turned their anger increasingly against the soldiers who patrolled the coalfields, and the state government—dominated by agrarians but committed to the Bourbon Democratic regime of economy in government— sought to find the least expensive way out of the conflict. Finally, a compromise was reached in April 1893 when the legislature voted to abolish the lease system within three years, meanwhile committing itself to build a state prison on coal lands purchased for that purpose and to pay for it by using convicts to develop and work a state-owned mine. Thus, Tennessee miners did not entirely escape wage competition from convicts, but no longer did they have to work side by side with them. The Brushy Mountain Prison opened on schedule and proved a profitable investment by the state, producing coal for the open market from 1896 to 1938.[23]

The UMWA opposed convict leasing in Alabama and, as in Tennessee, was disappointed by the gap between the rhetoric of the agrarian insurgents who challenged the state's reigning Bourbon Democrats during the early 1890s and their actual willingness to take action in support of union goals. Here again, opponents of the lease system faced the powerful TCI, which had expanded southward to become Alabama's largest coal and iron producer by 1890, and a penurious state government, which now depended upon the profits from convict leasing for roughly 10 percent of the entire state budget.[24] District 20's leadership, carefully constituted to reflect the biracial composition of the Alabama workforce, also sought higher wages, union recognition, and remedies to the grievances engendered by company housing and stores, by the hazards of mining, and by the ways in which wages were calculated and paid.

In 1894 and again in 1904 and 1908, the union enrolled a majority of the district's miners and led them on strike, sustaining strikers with food supplies and moral support from the national union, only to come up against the collaborating forces of state and local government and the coal companies. In particular, TCI would give no ground on the issue of union recognition, even when market circumstances forced it to compromise on wages and related issues. After its merger with U.S. Steel in 1908, TCI became the New South's foremost proponent of corporate welfare in the model towns that it built around Birmingham, but even then it steadfastly withheld union recognition. "The welfare programs of U.S. Steel," writes a modern scholar, "were designed to create a labor force socialized in the values of efficiency, diligence, rootedness, obedience, and aversion to unionism."[25]

The Alabama state government, led by "progressives" whose programs included the disfranchisement of black voters as well as fiscal reforms and an expanded role for bureaucratic experts, joined with coal operators to crush the union during the 1908 strike. At this time, the national union, strengthened by the 1902 anthracite settlement and growing political influence and coal company recognition in the northern states, worked hard to sustain the Alabama miners, building tent colonies for strikers evicted from company houses and supplying food and clothing and other necessities. Its opponents replied with an array of tested expedients: strikebreakers, mostly black farm laborers transported from the state's former plantation districts; white soldiers, also drawn from the Black Belt, to enforce martial law in the coal region; and the extravagant use of racist rhetoric, the purpose of which was to stir dissention within the miners' ranks and to convince the middle-class public that the biracial composition of the UMWA represented a threat to what was termed "southern civilization."

Finally, in September 1908, Governor Braxton Bragg Comer ordered soldiers to destroy the tent colonies and threatened to convene the legislature to pass a vagrancy law that would permit authorities to arrest strikers and return them to the mines as convicts rather than as free workers. The strike collapsed soon afterward, and union membership, which had peaked at fourteen thousand in 1904, again contracted to a few hundred. While corporate welfare programs improved the lot of miners lucky enough to work at the model towns that TCI and a few other companies established, most of Alabama's miners continued to live in conditions of squalor and deprivation. In 1911 the state's worst mining disaster occurred at the Banner mine operated by a TCI subsidiary; 129 men were killed, all but 8 of them African American and all but 5 of them convicts.[26]

The weakness of the progressive impulse in Appalachia was amply demonstrated during the first of West Virginia's four "mine wars." The UMWA first appeared in northern West Virginia during the 1890s and by 1902 had established itself there and in the Kanawha coalfields extending along that river east of Charleston. Operators resisted union recognition, however, in the two easternmost districts of this coalfield, each of them a characteristically narrow valley winding northward to the Kanawha and lined with coal camps and mines. Paint Creek miners went on strike in 1911 and were soon supported by the miners of nearby Cabin Creek. As the strike wore on, it grew increasingly violent. Wholesale evictions from company houses began along Paint Creek in May 1912, accompanied by the importation of strikebreakers and of heavily armed mine guards to protect them and to police the towns. By midsummer, the surrounding hills routinely echoed with the crack of gunfire and even the rattle of machine guns, which the guards posted in ironclad forts they built near some of the company towns. Miners took to the woods, where they lay in wait to draw beads on the guards or to fire down into the towns and at trains carrying strikebreakers. The guards manned their forts, patrolled the surrounding woods and pathways, and even armored a train from which they blazed away at one of the tent colonies established by the union on the few scraps of "public" (that is, noncompany) land in the valley. State authorities sent National Guard units into the strike zone in July and proclaimed martial law there in September. These measures stemmed the violence as the soldiers confiscated thousands of weapons and set up military courts to deal summarily with persons—usually strikers—accused of violating the governor's proclamations. As the fall elections approached, the National Guard was withdrawn but returned as violence flared anew. By the time Dr. Henry D. Hatfield took office as West Virginia's governor in March 1913, the soldiers were still deployed along the valleys, and so were the tent colonies. At least twenty, and perhaps as many as fifty, men had been killed in the mine war by this time.

Governor Hatfield was the nephew of Devil Anse Hatfield, but if he retained many memories of the time when his father and brother and cousins went everywhere armed and always sat where they could face a room's windows and doorways, he had little to say about it except to claim for himself "all the courage of his feudist kinsman [sic] of an earlier day." Instead, he presented himself as a professional man, a doctor as well as a politician, and thus well suited to bridge the many divides that preoccupied voters during the so-called Progressive Era—divides between conservatives and progressives, between town and country, and above all between capital and labor. The combination of his professional status and his celebrated family name made Hatfield an appealing candidate and so, besting two more experienced politicians in the state's first primary election in 1912, he went on to victory as a Republican in the fall, becoming, at the age of thirty-seven, the first West Virginia governor to have been born in the new state.

On March 5, 1913, his first full day in office, Hatfield visited the strike district, traveling alone and carrying the small black bag that identified him as a medical man. The doctor's kit came in handy, for the governor found "small pox, diptheria [*sic*], measles and every other conceivable form of disease" in one of the tent colonies along Cabin Creek. As he told the story in later years, he spent two days in the strike zone, treating the sick, consoling the bereaved, and spreading the promise of social as well as medical healing. One of the patients he treated was the strike's most famous participant, Mary Harris ("Mother") Jones. At the age of eighty-three, Mother Jones was a grandmotherly figure with a sweet face and a salty tongue that delighted working-class audiences as much as it offended the guardians of "law and order." Although she had ranged widely across the country during forty years of labor struggles, West Virginia—"Medieval West Virginia!" as she called it—came as close as any place to being her adopted home. When she had visited the state in support of earlier UMWA organizing drives, corporation lawyers hired stenographers to follow her around, hoping to hear something incendiary. They were not disappointed. But Mother Jones's forte was her ability to dramatize the miners' plight, creating solidarity among the workers and their families and winning support from the world beyond the hills. West Virginia military authorities gave her an even more expansive stage to tread in February 1913, when they seized her on the streets of Charleston and hauled her before a court-martial sitting at Pratt, a railroad junction at the mouth of Paint Creek, where military trials were held in a makeshift courtroom in the local Odd Fellows Hall.

Pending trial on charges of conspiring to murder, Jones was held either in "a pleasant boarding house . . . on the banks of the Kanawha River," as Governor Hatfield told inquisitive congressmen in 1913, or in a "plank cottage," as Senator Hatfield recalled the story while running for reelection in 1932. In any case, when the governor visited her on March 6, he found her dangerously ill with pneumonia and had her taken to Charleston and placed under medical care. But he did not set her free as soon as she recovered, as he sometimes claimed in later years. Instead, she went back into custody at Pratt, where she helped fan a growing national controversy over the arbitrary means of her seizure and the obviously trumped-up character of the charges she faced. "I can raise just as much hell in jail as anywhere," she told a visiting journalist, and she proved true to her word by generating widespread attention in the press and provoking a debate in Congress over the character and causes of the West Virginia war. Under pressure of this publicity, Hatfield released her from custody on May 8. Jones then embarked on a speaking tour of eastern cities and a lobbying trip to Washington, whence she returned to Charleston a month later, bringing in tow an investigating subcommittee of the U.S. Senate Committee on Education and Labor.

In common with many American public figures in the Progressive Era, Hatfield believed that it was government's duty to search out and hold the middle ground between the contending interest groups of modern industrial society. But he soon found that middle ground in the Appalachian coalfields was as narrow as the valleys where the bitterest conflicts were fought. Observers who saw him in action in the strike zone were impressed by his personal goodwill toward the miners and his desire to deal fairly with both sides in the dispute. But like many progressives, he tended to pressure the weaker contenders when he was unable to translate his personal goodwill into effective social policy. He initiated negotiations between operators and the UMWA in Charleston on March 13, serving as a go-between because the operators refused to sit down face to face with union representatives. When these talks failed to produce an agreement, Hatfield issued a unilateral "compromise proposition," wherein he proposed to give the miners a nine-hour workday, the right to employ "checkweighmen" to safeguard the calculation of wages, the right to spend wages at places other than company stores, and an amorphous "right to organize" unsecured by contract or by any other formal recognition of the union on the operators' part. He also condemned, but provided no sanctions against, the employment of mine guards and made known his disapproval of the military courts and the numerous and lengthy sentences they had imposed on the strikers.

Since these proposals offered no real gains for the union, the operators promptly accepted them. Rank-and-file miners, especially members of the Socialist Party, which had flourished in some coalfield districts in recent years, openly scorned the governor's propositions, but Hatfield refused to negotiate further. Instead, he issued an ultimatum on April 25, telling the UMWA to accept his program or to face draconian measures against the union. Putting the best face they could on this "Hatfield Agreement," the union leaders capitulated. On May 1, the governor was once again touring the strike zone, leading a brace of intimidated union leaders and proclaiming an end to the strike. In fact, dissatisfaction with the agreement among rank-and-file workers was one of the factors that brought a more militant union leadership to the fore in West Virginia in subsequent years, setting the stage for a renewal of the mine wars soon after World War I.

The UMWA succeeded in realizing many of its goals during the war years. The boom in coal production and the attendant labor shortage enabled the union to negotiate from strength, while the friendly attitude of wartime federal agencies inhibited antiunion activities. In Alabama, 23,000 of 25,000 coal miners signed union cards during the war. A new, militantly socialist leadership led by native-born mountaineers such as Fred Mooney emerged in West Virginia and pressed wartime advantages forcefully. As a result, union membership grew from 6,000 to 53,000 during the war, incorporating over half of the state's miners. The Pocahontas, Winding Gulf, Logan, Tug Fork, and Williamson fields remained unorganized, however, and it was here that production had expanded most rapidly during the war. The UMWA was as anxious to organize these districts as the operators were to defend them. By mid-1919 conditions for a new mine war were brewing, with the battle line now located south of the Kanawha River along the ridges that defined the Guyandotte watershed.

The UMWA recognized, it should be added, the chronic instability of coal prices and offered the industry a solution: put a uniform floor under wages, and prices would firm up on this base. It was an unspoken but obvious corollary that marginal producers would go out of business if uniform wage scales were the rule. The problem was, who was marginal? Was it the older, less efficient operators or those most distant from markets? No matter how the question was answered, a significant proportion of Appalachian producers, especially those south of the Kanawha, felt that the UMWA program treated them unfairly. In fact, operators habitually insisted that the union was the pawn of its competitors, that it represented a conspiracy between operators and miners in Pennsylvania and the Midwest to put southern competitors out of business and their miners out of work. This argument had a sufficient kernel of truth to persuade many middle-class people who might otherwise have remained neutral or supported the union. The "conspiracy" thesis reinforced the "outside agitator" argument and cast the UMWA program as a plot aimed at Appalachia's general prosperity by inhibiting the exploitation of its premiere resource.

The progressive impulse faded after 1916 with the election of public officials who felt it their patriotic duty to defend the coal industry against union inroads. State and local judges routinely granted coal company requests for blanket injunctions against union organizers, making it illegal for them even to mention the existence of a strike in some mining counties. The search for middle ground gave way to a conservative determination to hold the line. Neither the union nor its opponents regretted this situation, since neither was much interested in compromise during the postwar years. The UMWA was anxious to expand and consolidate its gains. Nonunion operators were equally anxious to draw the line, while some who had submitted to unionization during the war hoped to go back to prewar conditions. The result was an almost continuous struggle as the union sought first to break into the nonunion fields and, failing that, to defend its position north of the Kanawha. A central figure in determining this strategy was John L. Lewis, a dynamic midwesterner of Welsh ancestry who became the UMWA's national president in 1919.

In Alabama, the waning of wartime demand and federal influence led to wage cuts and strikes, beginning in the summer of 1920. While commercial coal operators signed individual contracts with their union locals, the iron and steel companies that owned mines around Birmingham remained resolutely antiunion and began wholesale evictions from company housing, leading eventually to tent colonies holding as many as 48,000 people. In September, Lewis dispatched the UMWA's most effective organizer, Van A. Bittner, to take charge of the strike in Alabama, while at the same time the governor ordered four companies of the Alabama National Guard into the coalfields. The results were predictable. "As the strike dragged on into winter, the miners' prospects grew dim. A sharp industrial slump late in the year depressed markets for coal, while production at the hands of strikebreakers gradually rose. Violence, intimidation, and repression of union meetings incapacitated the strike. Public opinion grew increasingly hostile to the miners' plight." In February 1921, Bittner capitulated and the UMWA's District 20 formally ended the strike, accepting a proposal that Governor Thomas E. Kilby impose a resolution to the dispute. Kilby's terms, unsurprisingly, were almost identical to those of the operators. The strike had been "illegal and immoral," in Kilby's view; any resulting distress was the union's responsibility. "Once again, the Alabama UMW lay in ruins."[27]

In West Virginia, the struggle produced some of the most dramatic episodes in American labor history. On four separate occasions in 1920–21, West Virginia governors asked for federal troops to patrol Mingo and Logan Counties, where they joined an already impressive array of police agencies that included Baldwin-Felts men, deputy sheriffs, the new state police force, and a host of "special police"—the latter being vigilantes recruited from among businessmen and white-collar workers in towns such as Williamson and Bluefield. The Matewan Massacre of May 19, 1920, was the first of several noteworthy explosions all this firepower produced. It involved Baldwin-Felts agents, including two of the three founding Felts brothers, natives of Galax, Virginia, and already famous nationally for their role in the Hillsville tragedy of 1912. These were pitted against union men and prounion local officials, one of whom—"Two Gun" Sid Hatfield—became the miners' most prominent hero. A tough, diminutive character, Sid lived up to all the romantic potential of the Hatfield name, even though he was not actually a blood relative but rather had been born out of wedlock to a woman who later married a man of that name. He survived the shootout in Matewan, which claimed the lives of both Felts brothers along with Cabell Testerman, the mayor of the town, but fell himself on August 21, 1921, shot down on the steps of the McDowell County courthouse by a Baldwin-Felts man who claimed self-defense.

Hatfield's assassination aroused an angry reaction in the coalfields, culminating in an armed march of some three thousand miners from the Kanawha River to Blair Mountain in northern Logan County. Here, on the border between union and nonunion territory, the miners skirmished for five days with a private army assembled by Logan sheriff Don Chafin until federal soldiers forced the two "armies" apart on September 4. One of the more bizarre features of this March on Logan was the participation of a squadron of army airmen who came down from Washington to see how air power could be deployed in civil disturbances. The army planes never made it to Blair Mountain. Six of them got lost and crashed in the mountains, leaving the remainder grounded in Charleston with nothing to do. However, Chafin's force borrowed a plane and dropped a homemade bomb near the battlefield, startling two women who were hanging out their wash, and thus made airborne history anyway.

The aftermath of the Logan march was scarcely less remarkable. A Logan County grand jury indicted nearly six hundred alleged participants, fifty-four of them for murder and treason. The "treason trials" that followed in 1922 took place under changes in venue in the agricultural Greenbrier and Potomac Counties, including the Jefferson County courthouse where John Brown had been tried on similar charges in 1859. These trials resulted in few convictions and generated much favorable publicity for the union cause. But press clippings could not roll back the tide of unfavorable economic circumstances that pitted miners against their employers. As postwar "normalcy" returned and European mines began again to serve their home markets, American coal mines had a capacity to produce nearly twice as much as the U.S. market could absorb. Notwithstanding a national business boom that continued until nearly the end of the decade, the fortunes of the coal industry turned downward early, and mine owners scrambled fiercely to hang on to a share of an unstable market.

Wage cuts were the only competitive weapon that Appalachian mine operators actually controlled. In October 1922, the UMWA formally abandoned the Mingo County strike that had led to the March on Logan and began a long and unsuccessful rearguard action to retain its bases in the Kanawha, New River, and northern West Virginia fields. John L. Lewis insisted that existing wage rates be maintained in the unionized districts. When West Virginia union leaders protested this policy in hopes of saving more local jobs, Lewis replaced them with "provisional" district officials of his own choosing in 1924 and placed Bittner in charge of a new strike in the Fairmont coalfield in the northern part of the state. Here a long and violent war, fought mainly with dynamite and midnight bombings, sputtered on into 1927.

In 1925 the Consolidation Coal Company, the region's largest employer, abrogated its union contract, claiming that coal could no longer be sold at prices that the union wage scale required. The union leaders widened the strike and worked valiantly to sustain it, but in the end union miners had to scramble to fill a declining supply of jobs, just as the operators competed for shares of the shrinking market. Even C. E. Lively, one of the most notorious of the Baldwin-Felts spies and the accused assassin of Sid Hatfield, was desperate for work by 1927. "Coal business here is very bad and I have eight little kiddies," he wrote to an antiunion journalist. "If you can get me located it will be appreciated and I will gladly pay for your time and trouble."[28] By 1930 the bituminous coal industry throughout Appalachia was sliding toward bankruptcy as the national economy caved in on top of an already depressed market. The UMWA was down to a few hundred diehard members in West Virginia, even fewer in Kentucky and Alabama. "In nineteen hundred an' thirty-two / We wus sometimes sad an' blue," wrote Uncle George Jones, a blind African American singer and former miner whom the union employed as a kind of minstrel-organizer around Birmingham.

Travelin' roun' from place to place
Trying' to find some work to do.
If we's successful to find a job,
De wages wus so small,

We could scarcely live in de summertime—
Almost starved in the fall.[29]

Unlike the bituminous coal industry, the textile industry of the South was not centered in Appalachia. Each of the southern Appalachian states had textile factories of some sort, but those of Kentucky and West Virginia had a minuscule impact on overall production, and those of the remaining states were concentrated in a belt of Piedmont counties extending from Virginia to Alabama, with a much smaller concentration in the Great Valley. Of the 21 southeastern counties whose factories contained more than 200,000 spindles in 1929, only 8 were located within the bounds of official Appalachia, and none in the region's core. Similarly, of counties containing between 50,000 and 199,000 spindles, fewer than a third (64 of 194) were in official Appalachia – and less than a sixth (29) were in the regional core. There were notable concentrations of textile factories in the foothills counties of the Carolinas and in the urban counties of the Great Valley, but the output of these districts was modest compared to that of the Piedmont.[30]

Appalachia's great contribution to the textile industry came in the form of cheap labor—entire families that left worn-out mountain farms in great numbers to seek work in the mills. It is impossible to be precise about the proportion of millhands who were former mountaineers, for census takers did not distinguish between mountain and lowland birthplaces within the same state, nor could they take into account the high rate of geographic mobility among younger families who frequently moved from place to place within the industry looking for a mill with wages they could live on and a mill village that they liked. The proportion must have been high, however. The heaviest concentrations of textile mills were in Piedmont or foothills counties bordering the Blue Ridge in the Carolinas and in the intermontane urban districts (Huntsville, Anniston, Chattanooga, Knoxville, and the Tri-Cities) of Alabama and Tennessee. Stories of mountain homeplaces figure largely in the reminiscences of millhands that were collected by reformers and scholars during the twentieth century. One of the factors that drove the efforts of Olive Dame Campbell and others who sought to strengthen farm life in the mountains was a desire to stem the flow of mountain families to the textile mills.

Lots of people with a good free will
Sold their homes and moved to the mill.

We'll have lots of money they said.
But everyone got hell instead.
It was fun in the mountains rolling logs,
But now when the whistle blows we run like dogs.[31]

A poignant feature of the collective oral history of the millhands was the number of people who remembered pining hard for their mountain homes. Many families traveled back and forth between homeplace and mill village several times before settling; some people never did make the adjustment. Shy people of both genders found mill-village life noisy and jarring. Men who were used to the autonomy and variety of farm work often had trouble adjusting to the work routines of a mill. Ernest Stoneman might have fallen into this category, shuttling between jobs at factories in Fries and Max Meadows and the mines in southern West Virginia while his family remained at home, had not his carpentry skills and then his musical earnings freed him from the necessity of submitting to factory routine. More typical was the story of a man named Hickum, a western North Carolinian whose son's recollections were recorded by oral historians. "He got around that machinery and he never seen nothing like it," recalled the son. "You know what a racket machinery makes. I think the machinery scared him too much to try to run a job. He'd been around old sawmills and stuff, outside, but a lot of difference in that. Now when all [the food the family had brought with them from the farm] was gone, we had to start going to the store and living out of a tin can. That's what hurt. My daddy didn't like that. He couldn't work in no cotton mill, so he went back to the mountains."[32]

Other men sent family members into the mills while working themselves at a mix of odd jobs, including hauling and gardening that approximated the kind of work they had done on the farm. Observing them from the vantage point of mill offices and probably unaware of the variety of ways such men worked to earn income, a mill owner scornfully called them "gentlemen" and advocated public flogging or putting them to work on the chain gang. Men missed the sense of accomplishment that farm work brought. "'I'm going back to the farm,'" one millhand recalled a fellow worker's telling him. "'I don't like this. I work all day and I look back and I can't see a thing I've done.' At that time he was laying up roping, and they'd take it down as fast as he'd lay it up. He didn't like that. In about a couple of weeks he was gone, sure enough."[33] The nostalgia for rural life that became an enduring theme of country music songwriters had an ample basis in individual lives.

There were similarities in structure between the coal and textile industries.

Both were decentralized, both were prone to cycle between boom and bust, and both were labor rather than capital intensive, although during and after World War I the same split developed in textiles between producers with obsolete but still functioning facilities and modernizers who made investments in improved machinery and electrification. The proportion of southern-born mill owners to those who originated in the North was roughly comparable to the coal industry, though the textile industry was rooted in New England rather than in Pennsylvania. Above all, the mill villages were remarkably similar to the coal camps. In fact, an even higher proportion of millhands lived in company housing than coal miners in coal camps, and although most mill villages were located near larger, more diversified towns, psychological and social factors rendered them nearly as isolated as coal camps were in the preautomobile age.[34]

Both industries, too, showed a similar pattern of labor militancy, at least up through the early years of the Depression. Textiles, like coal, had enjoyed boom times during World War I, with corresponding gains in wages and union membership, followed by a difficult postwar adjustment characterized by falling demand, falling wages, and a rising level of labor militancy. A wave of strikes in 1919 in Georgia and the Carolinas led to hopeful compromise settlements, but when a more serious downturn in the industry in 1921 led to more strikes in the Charlotte area of North Carolina, the strikers lost, although their militancy probably prevented deeper wage cuts. "Quietly, efficiently, ruthlessly, the union has been blotted out," wrote a friendly journalist in 1921. "There never was a hint of compromise, never even a suggestion of negotiation. The mill owners simply waited until the strikers' resources were exhausted, and then called on the governor for troops to prevent any resort to violence."[35]

Even more than the Kentucky and West Virginia politicians who deferred to coal operators, state authorities in the textile states were intensely hostile to union activity and used both legal and violent means to suppress it. Yet militancy flared again in the mill villages as the mine wars subsided during the late 1920s, with the most notable outbreaks occurring in Elizabethton, Tennessee, and in Marion and Gastonia, North Carolina. Elizabethton and Marion were located in the Appalachian core and had left earlier marks in regional history, Elizabethton as the home of the musical Taylor brothers who enlivened Tennessee politics during the 1880s and both towns as sites where the Overmountain Men of Revolutionary times had rendezvoused on their march to Kings Mountain in 1780. Gastonia lies on official Appalachia's eastern boundary and was, in 1929, the county seat of the Piedmont's leading textiles county, a place where former mountaineers worked alongside radical labor organizers from New York and New England.[36] To a far greater extent than earlier textile organizing efforts, the Elizabethton, Marion, and Gastonia strikes captured national attention.

One of the notable features of these strikes was the prominence of young mountain women among the strike leaders. In Elizabethton, "rebel girls" like Trixie Perry and Flossie Cole Grindstaff emulated Mother Jones in exploiting the conventions of genteel femininity to confound courtroom officials and National Guardsmen, while at the same time rousing and delighting fellow workers by their defiance of the limits on ladylike conduct. In Gastonia, one former mountain girl in particular—Ella May (the name she went by, though she was known to others by the name of a long-gone, ne'er-do-well husband named Wiggins)—combined independence and militancy with mountain traditions. Born in 1900 into an itinerant mountain family that followed the logging industry, May came to Gastonia as a single mother of seven children (four of whom died in childhood) for whom she was the sole support. She was also a musician, and when a strike broke out in April 1929, led by the communist-dominated National Textile Workers Union, May gained prominence among the strike's leaders by her organizational skills and by adapting traditional ballads to militant purposes. Her best-known song, "The Mill Mother's Lament," was based on a ballad about the 1915 lynching of Atlanta mill superintendent Leo Frank and was popularized originally by Fiddlin' John Carson, one of the first country music recording stars. May's revision, stripped of the anti-Semitic overtones of the original, combined an adroit mix of conventional sentiment and union militancy:

> We leave our homes in the morning,
> We kiss our children goodbye.
> While we slave for the bosses,
> Our children scream and cry.

> And when we draw our money
> Our grocery bills to pay,
> Not a cent to spend for clothing,
> Not a cent to lay away.

> And on that very evening,
> Our little son will say:
> "I need some shoes, dear mother,
> And so does sister May."

How it grieves the heart of a mother,
You every one must know.
But we can't buy for our children.
Our wages are too low.

It is for our little children
That seems to us so dear,
But for us nor them, dear workers,
The bosses do not care.

But understand, all workers,
Our union they do fear.
Let's stand together, workers,
And have a union here.[37]

When May was killed during an assault by local thugs on union leaders, her immortality was assured.

Like the mine wars, the 1929 textile strikes attracted sympathetic attention but won few gains for the strikers. Instead, the mill owners prevailed through a combination of official repression and violence. The mills brought in strikebreakers and obtained injunctions; state authorities sent in troops, brushing aside the objections of local authorities in the case of Elizabethton. An attack by National Guardsmen on unarmed strikers in Marion led to six deaths, while in Gastonia violence led to the killing of the local police chief and to the martyrdom of Ella May. The deaths were followed by a series of well-publi- — cized trials wherein a brace of labor leaders were convicted, on dubious evidence, of the police chief's death while the locally well-known killers of May got off.

Notwithstanding the sputtering ineffectiveness of labor militancy during this period, events in the coalfields and mill towns led to a notable transformation in the popular understanding of Appalachian culture. Before the mine wars, folklorists had presented industrialism as a threat to traditional culture. "Where there is coal and good wages to be earned," Cecil Sharp wrote from Kentucky in 1917, "the families soon drop their old-fashioned ways and begin to ape town manners, etc."[38] Labor organizers, on the other hand, usually came from outside Appalachia, and so when they turned to music to rouse their followers they usually coupled verses composed for the occasion with tunes from well-known Protestant hymns. During the Paint Creek–Cabin Creek mine war of 1912, for example, the composer-organizer Ralph Chapin set the lyrics of a satirical view of Christian otherworldliness, "There'll Be Pie in the Sky," to the music of the well-known hymn "In the Sweet By and By." In Walker County, Alabama, miners rallied to the verses of another "good old song," "We Will Overcome Some Day."[39]

Ella May's balladry in Gastonia drew instead from traditional and country music, while left-wing intellectuals venturing into Kentucky in support of a 1930 strike organized by a communist-led rival to the UMWA also heard striking miners and their families making music in the traditional Appalachian style. Soon "Aunt Molly" Jackson and other members of her musical family were traveling to New York, where they entertained radical supporters with songs of labor militancy performed in traditional style and with traditional ballads that—in order to accommodate cosmopolitan notions about folk culture—they had learned from published folksong collections specifically for this purpose.[40] Meanwhile, in West Virginia, another rival union, this one organized by socialist leaders who had been driven out of the UMWA, attracted a radical New York organizer who drifted north with his guitar from the textile mill strike in Gastonia. While in Gastonia, this organizer had heard a recorded lament, "The Death of Mother Jones" (an event that occurred in 1930), made by a young country music performer from Texas named Gene Autry and produced in a commercial studio in New York. Arriving in West Virginia with his guitar but not the record, the aforementioned organizer performed the song for striking miners. A few years later, a folklorist from Pennsylvania collected the song from a miner in Fairmont, West Virginia, and published it as an example of spontaneous folk responses to the labor turmoil of an earlier age.[41] Thus was born the identification of Appalachian folk music—and folk culture generally—with liberal and left-wing struggles for social justice, an identification that persisted through the twentieth century.

Of more immediate concern to most miners, not to mention politicians and union leaders, was the swift revival of union militancy under President Franklin D. Roosevelt's New Deal. In textiles, this agitation led first to an industrywide agreement under the New Deal's National Recovery Administration (NRA) that seemed to promise relief from the starvation wages and "stretchout" tactics of the 1920s and then, when this promise remained unfulfilled, to a "great uprising," a general textile strike in 1934 that idled factories throughout the South. This strike led to another round of violence and repression in Virginia and the Carolinas and to a general collapse of textile union militancy that would haunt southern labor organizers for generations to come.

One of the questions that emerged from this debacle asks us to account for the different fates, after 1933, of coal and textiles, industries whose labor histories had been so similar in earlier years. One possible explanation lies in the different impacts on these two industries of mechanization and electrification, which led to changes in the organization of work that left textile workers much more subject to direct supervision and control than was the case with coal miners, who retained much of their former autonomy over the pace and organization of work routines. Another difference was the absence of women from the miners' ranks, although the militant female textile workers of the 1920s could surely have held their own in comparison with the all-male UMWA. Another explanation is the caliber of union leadership:

> To most UTW [United Textile Workers] officials, the South was a foreign land; they paid attention to southern workers only sporadically and then primarily as a low-wage threat to the union's stronghold in the Northeast. Although women made up a large percentage of the textile work force, the union sent few female organizers into the region, framed its strategy around the demand for a "family wage"—that is, a wage that would enable a man to keep his wife and children at home—and made no attempt to address working women's needs.[42]

The mine workers, on the other hand, were led by John L. Lewis, a stormy and overbearing figure who left a controversial imprint on American history during a career that extended from 1919 to 1961. The UMWA, like the UTW, originally looked southward to counter low-wage threats to higher-waged northern workers, but Lewis—who replaced independent leaders with loyal minions and who eliminated or outmaneuvered rivals in the UMWA hierarchy—moved the union's headquarters from Indianapolis to Washington, suggesting more of a national outlook. Perhaps most important of all, his leadership not only was guided by a drive for power, but was also informed by a genuine concern for miners and their welfare and by a program that aimed to reconcile their needs and desires with remedies for the industry's chronic instability.

Lewis owed his opportunity during the 1930s to friendly federal legislation sponsored by Roosevelt and his liberal allies. "The President wants you to join the union," UMWA organizers told the miners, and once again the union rolls swelled to record numbers. Coal industry leaders, in Appalachia as elsewhere, caught momentarily off balance and willing to try anything to alleviate the industry's desperate situation in 1933, at first submitted tamely to Lewis's whirlwind organizing campaign. Only Harlan County, Kentucky, dominated by a bloody-minded coalition of coal operators and county politicos, along with a few less notorious bastions, held out. Elsewhere, UMWA Districts 19

An unidentified photographer captured these coal-camp children along Scotts Run near Morgantown, West Virginia. The plight of Scotts Run families inspired Arthurdale, the New Deal's most famous "subsistence homestead" community, but only native-born white families were accepted as Arthurdale residents. (Courtesy West Virginia Department of Archives and History)

(Kentucky/Tennessee) and 20 (Alabama) signed up close to 85 percent of potential members. Total West Virginia union membership rose from a few thousand in 1931 to nearly 300,000 a decade later. On September 21, 1933, the UMWA signed the first of a series of industrywide contracts known as Appalachian Agreements, which, among other features, provided for the gradual narrowing and then the elimination of the regional wage differentials that had kept the region's miners' earnings near the bottom of earlier wage scales.

By the time operators began to regroup in opposition to these changes, Lewis confronted them with other achievements, notably the Wagner Labor Relations Act of 1935, which he then used to establish the Congress of Industrial Organizations (CIO) to organize the nation's mass-production industries. When the Supreme Court struck down the National Industrial Recovery Act (NIRA) of 1933, which had been the basis of the UMWA's initial organizing breakthrough, Lewis and his political allies maneuvered the Guffey Coal Acts of 1935 and 1936 through Congress. These enacted in separate and somewhat different form the bituminous coal price-and-wage-stabilization features of the NIRA. During subsequent years, the union took on successively and successfully the goals of establishing "closed shop" agreements that required UMWA membership as a condition of a miner's employment, organizing the mines of U.S. Steel and other industrial corporations that operated captive mines, and breaching the walls in Harlan County, where coal operators capitulated to the union in 1939. In 1941, Lewis negotiated his most successful Appalachian Agreement yet, ending the regional wage differential and planting the seeds of an extensive union-run health and welfare benefits program. To drive home the extent of his victory, he staged the signing of the agreement at the Greenbrier resort in White Sulphur Springs, a shrine of Old South nostalgia that had long been a favorite among coal operators.

Labor's advance in the coalfields thus represented another major trend in Appalachia's history during the 1930s—the growing importance of the federal government. Heretofore, state governments had been more important in the region's history, even though—apart from West Virginia—Appalachian counties constituted "backyards" of lesser political importance in the Appalachian states, even in East Tennessee. With the imposition of Bourbon Democrat rule at the end of Reconstruction and the defeat of the agrarian insurgencies of the late nineteenth century, southern state governments adhered to a low-taxation regime that complemented the low-wage standard of New South industrialization. "Economy in government" became an excuse for inaction on all sorts of issues and the chief excuse for the convict-lease system in those states that exploited it.

After the turn of the twentieth century, circumstances forced the states into a more expansive role. Modernization and urbanization stimulated demand for government services throughout the nation: Thanks to population growth and an expanding economy, states were forced to cope with more court cases, more convicts, more school students, more banks and professional practitioners to be examined and licensed, more personnel in every job category from archivist to fire warden. In West Virginia between 1902 and 1916, expansion led to a struggle over tax reform that threatened to shift a larger burden of taxation to the state's extractive industries, but aggressive lobbying and political intervention by petroleum and coal corporations turned the reformers aside. Progressive governors like West Virginia's Henry D. Hatfield

(1913–17) and North Carolina's Thomas W. Bickett (1917–21) briefly brought a more evenhanded approach to labor issues, but by the 1920s the prevailing conservatism channeled the reform impulse into what has since been called "business progressivism": programs of education and infrastructure improvement that ignored the social conflicts that had absorbed the attention of earlier reformers. Typical of the era were the "good roads" movements that appeared in every state during the second and third decades of the century. Whether financed on a "pay-as-you-go" basis, as in Virginia, or by bond issues, as in the other states, the popularity of road-building programs represented one of the first impacts of the automobile on public life.

Automobiles also changed private life, at least for those who could afford them. Cars changed the look and shape of cities and towns. Riverside cities like Wheeling, Charleston, Huntington, and Chattanooga had originally spread out along the level ground bordering their historic centers, but now middle-class families began to build homes in the surrounding hills. Previously the hills had been home only to the rich, who had carriages and horses to haul them up to the hilltops, or to the very poor, who walked to ramshackle homes near the mouths of the hollows below.

Residential bottomlands gradually turned into business districts or government centers, such as the one that grew up around the imposing new state capitol building erected during the 1920s in Charleston's East End. When Ernest Weir built his new steel-making town along the Ohio River during this era, he placed the country club and houses for his managers on a hilltop from the outset, leaving the workers' houses to share the smoky bottomland below with the mill. In Chattanooga, elite homes climbed the slopes of the mountaintop battlefields south of the city. In Birmingham, foundry owners and their professional retainers followed new boulevards across Red Mountain to the hillside suburbs of Mountain Brook and Homewood, leaving only handsome, stone-built Episcopal and Presbyterian churches as monuments to their earlier residential precincts near Capitol Square. Renamed in honor of President Wilson, the square itself became the focus of a typical urban manifestation of business progressivism, the civic center, wherein government buildings and civic institutions such as libraries and auditoriums were grouped in a monumental core expressing civic ambition. There was nothing regional about this movement. Civic centers less complete but just as ambitious as Birmingham's can be found today in places as diverse as Charlotte, Harrisburg, San Francisco, and Denver.

The family car freed farmers, town dwellers, and miners alike from dependence on nearby crossroads, neighborhood, and company stores. But these changes depended upon highways, since in areas without paved roads cars were useless for much of the year. It was, in fact, customary for farmers who owned cars to keep them up on blocks during the winter and much of the spring, when the condition of local roads made driving impossible. As the highway lobbies succeeded in their objectives, however, their focus remained on intercity connections. By concentrating funds there instead of on local networks tying farms to county and market towns, the road-building programs served the interests of town dwellers and in particular members of urban elites, thus contributing to the era's gulf between town and country. U.S. Highway 19, for example, took shape as an intercity route, cutting across Appalachia from north to south, carrying tourists and trucks from Pittsburgh to Atlanta via such towns as Clarksburg, Bluefield, Bristol, and Asheville. A parallel route, U.S. 21, extending from Ohio to South Carolina via Charleston, West Virginia, Charlotte, and Columbia, was promoted as a Lakes-to-Florida route for the benefit of tourists, an elite group at this stage in history whose stray dollars local merchants and promoters hoped to capture en route.

U.S. 11, threading the Great Valley from eastern Pennsylvania to Birmingham, brought the Great Valley Road back to life as part of an intercity route extending from Montréal to New Orleans. To be sure, paved highways did begin to inch out of the cities toward rural areas; prosperous or ambitious families unwilling to wait for the roads to reach them could escape the confinements of country living by moving into town. Blanche Lazell, a budding artist from a comfortable West Virginia farm family, urged her relatives to move into Morgantown so that her younger sister, nieces, and nephews could enjoy "the educational advantages." "None of us are much use on a farm any more," she wrote; in fact, most of the family's income by this time came from leases on coal lands. Lazell herself moved on to Paris in 1912, and then, when war broke out, to Provincetown on Cape Cod. "The scenery is not any more beautiful than W. Va. but it's the artistic air about it."[43] For similar reasons, Jane Hicks Gentry and her husband left Beech Mountain, North Carolina, for the resort town of Hot Springs, where their children could get an education and where Gentry became the prime informant of the folklorist Cecil Sharp.

Two of Appalachia's greatest writers, James Agee and Thomas Wolfe, grew up in towns during this period. In *A Death in the Family*, Agee's haunting autobiographical novel of his childhood in Knoxville, the automobile is a link to the father's mysterious and disturbing family up in the hills, but the fictional child Rufus's life, like Agee's, orbits around his mother's family in the city. Wolfe parodied the "boomers" of 1920s Asheville in *You Can't Go Home Again.*

His characters, as Wolfe himself had done, look out from town toward the surrounding mountains but do not inhabit them. Written in a somewhat later period, Mary Lee Settle's West Virginia stories unfold against a background of parties in Charleston's East End and South Hills and of forays by the prosperous inhabitants of these precincts through the mountains to White Sulphur Springs, which during the interwar years became a golf mecca and a place where well-heeled people could sample the era's prohibited joys.

Trains sped these writers toward their destinies in New York and Europe, but the Appalachian urban life they left behind and chronicled in their writings increasingly revolved around the private car. Meanwhile, out in the countryside and in the mill villages, coal camps, and crossroad hamlets, mountain people who were prosperous enough to own cars remained "stuck in the mud." Even when federal funds became available in massive quantities, as they did for road building after 1916, state treasuries became the primary fiscal points of entry for federal dollars and the primary sources of funding for county governments. These funds greatly enhanced the patronage jobs available to politicians who commanded newly expanded school and highway systems but had no appreciable impact on government's willingness to address social issues. North Carolina's "good roads governor," Cameron Morrison, was also the one who sent troops to end the 1921 textile strike, just as his West Virginia counterparts summoned federal military forces to intervene in the mine wars.

Nor did business progressivism bring an end to earlier abuses. The communist labor organizer Fred Beal, heading for Charlotte and Gastonia by motorcycle, congratulated a local man on the quality of North Carolina highways. "All of these here good roads you sees spread all over Carolina is the doin's of chain gangs," the fellow replied, adding that he himself had put in six months on a road gang in Cabarrus County.[44] Joseph A. Holmes, the state geologist who later achieved national prominence as an advocate of industrial safety, was also an enthusiastic advocate of convict labor, calling it "the basis of the modern road building in the southern states."[45]

The advent of the New Deal in 1933 changed the balance between state and federal governments in the affairs of Appalachian localities. For one thing, alliances with the New Deal enabled liberals in some states to bring to heel Democratic politicians who did not share the national party's support for labor goals. Labor support helped to elect U.S. senators Matthew M. Neely and Harley Kilgore in West Virginia, Lister Hill in Alabama, Alben Barkley in Kentucky, and Olin D. Johnston in South Carolina; Neely and Johnston also served terms as governors of their respective states. In Alabama, labor votes helped to elect Governor Bibb Graves, while in Georgia, a "little New Deal" centered in Atlanta under governors Ed Rivers and Ellis Arnall achieved something of a standoff with "an incongruous coalition of moguls and rustics" led by Senator Eugene D. Talmadge.[46] In Tennessee, a statewide machine based in Memphis accepted Roosevelt's leadership and sent to Washington representatives who generally supported his initiatives. Alben Barkley of Kentucky, who with presidential and labor backing narrowly won the Senate Majority Leader's post in 1937, proved a loyal lieutenant, adept at forging compromises between opponents and supporters of the New Deal. Even in seaboard states dominated by old-fashioned conservatives such as Virginia's Harry Byrd and an "aggressive aristocracy" of textile magnates and lawyers in North Carolina, mountain districts sometimes elected liberals or at least moderates who supported the New Deal. Western North Carolina's Congressman Robert Doughton was one example.

Political change in turn led to dramatic reversals in labor relations, as in Alabama in 1938, when Governor Graves declined to deploy the usual mix of state troops and legal harassment against a textile workers' strike in Huntsville. Instead, mill operators there were forced to play by the new rules laid down by federal legislation, resulting in a union victory by the end of the year.[47] A breakthrough in West Virginia labor history took place in 1941, when Governor Neely intervened in a strike at U.S. Steel's captive mine at Gary, disciplining state policemen involved in violence at a picket line rather than jailing the picketers, as would have been done in previous years.

Appalachia also provided homes for leadership to the left of mainstream politics. The Council of the Southern Mountains (CSM), organized in 1913 to provide a forum for missionaries, educators, and reformers in the mountains, was liberal in intent and in the personal views of many of its leaders, though it steered carefully away from labor disputes and other economic issues during this period. However, the Highlander Folk School, established at Monteagle, Tennessee, in 1932, became a training ground for labor organizers, first for East Tennessee and then, after receiving a CIO mandate in 1937, for the entire South. Two native mountaineers, Myles Horton of Tennessee and Don West of Georgia, forged Highlander's mission: "In residence terms of four to six weeks, or in briefer 'workshops' and weekend conferences, the students received instruction in labor history, economics, strike tactics, public speaking, current events, and parliamentary law. By 1947 Highlander had trained more than 6,900 and had reached more than 12,300 through field or extension classes."[48]

The Southern Highland Handicraft Guild, established in 1929 and made prominent by the patronage of Eleanor Roosevelt and other New Deal notables, did not address labor issues and in fact quarreled with the Women's Bureau of Frances Perkins's U.S. Department of Labor, whose investigators insisted that the making of craft items by mountain women was an aspect of production, not tradition, and thus subject to federal regulations on wages, hours, and benefits. The guild, on the other hand, adopted the position that the workers who stocked its inventory of consumer items were expressing cultural traditions, not producing for the market, even though its own tightly controlled policing of what was marketed as Appalachian crafts would today be classified by experts under the rubric of brand management.[49]

Black Mountain College, established in 1933 in the North Carolina mountains, offered a home for radical experimentation in the arts and in personal lifestyles. During its heyday between 1933 and 1948, Black Mountain faculty and students had relatively little direct impact on their immediate neighborhood, and the cultural activities that engaged them had no connection with Appalachian culture as it was traditionally defined. But like the apolitical reformism of the CSM, the savvy government relations of the Handicrafts Guild, and Highlander's forthright radicalism, Black Mountain's very location in the mountains reinforced the image of Appalachia as a region of alternatives to the conservative repression of the industrial New South.

It is appropriate to return here to the question: Did industrial Appalachia differ in significant ways from the lowland South? If so, was it simply a Yankee peninsula extending into the New South and coexisting there with New South social arrangements, much like the plants that William Bartram saw growing side by side in the Blue Ridge and separately in Carolina and Pennsylvania in late colonial times? Or was Appalachia different from *both* of its parent regions, as exemplified by its farm-and-forest economy in preindustrial times?

The answer to the last question is a heavily qualified "yes." Evidence on the point is fragmentary, but there is too much of it to be ignored, especially in the realm of labor history. First, the persistent interracialism of union organizing drives, especially among mine workers, is one thing that sets Appalachian labor history apart from both the industrial North, where race was a much less divisive factor than ethnicity during the first half of the twentieth century, and the New South, where race was the touchstone of almost all public issues and a powerful tool in the hands of the business and political leaders who enforced the oppressions of the labor-intensive and exploitative New South regime. Second, notwithstanding the distortions and fantasies incorporated into the popular understanding of "Appalachian culture," the disproportionate role played in labor and other social justice struggles by native mountaineers also seems significant. This point is related in turn to the issue of continuity between industrial Appalachia and the preindustrial farm-and-forest economy. One reason for the rise of labor militancy in Appalachia during the first third of the twentieth century is that the preindustrial economy of the Appalachian Plateau could not by itself sustain the continued prosperity of the region after the Civil War. But it subsidized the first generation of industrial workers to the extent that they could accept the low wages initially offered by the region's extractive industries.

As a new generation grew to maturity after 1900, however, miners and other workers could no longer fall back, when they needed to, on the resources of farm and forest and so turned to labor movements out of sheer necessity for survival. A similar pattern was at work in textiles, where a new generation of workers came of age after 1918. It is worth noting that local leadership in the Elizabethton, Marion, and Gastonia strikes was drawn disproportionately from workers with mountain roots. In Elizabethton, the striking rayon workers enjoyed the support of crossroads merchants and of residents in the hilly farmlands surrounding the town, and also of the Carter County sheriff, although town officials and professionals supported the mill owners. In Gastonia, Ella May was the only member of the local leadership to organize among African American employees of the mill. A collective biography of miners and local residents involved in the violence at Matewan, West Virginia, shows that, while foreign-born and black workers were involved in the strike, all of those identified as perpetrators of the Matewan Massacre by Tom Felts, the surviving founder of the detective agency whose brothers were killed in the shootout, were native mountaineers. They were acquitted of charges by a local jury, notwithstanding coal company dominance in Williamson, the county seat.[50]

Much more research is needed on Appalachian industrialization and its impact than I have been able to do for this volume, but the evidence available to date is enough to suggest that the issue of regional distinctiveness is worth exploring. One of the most suggestive areas for investigation is religion. A distinctive characteristic of coal camps and mill villages alike was the company-sponsored church, usually representing the mine or mill owner's preference among mainstream Protestant denominations. Catholic churches were not directly susceptible to company control, and they were also less common south of Pennsylvania, but a word from the company owner to the local bishop could have a restraining effect on the activities of a prolabor priest.[51]

The practices of lay exhortation and congregational control that prevailed among traditional Protestant churches in Appalachia rendered them less amenable to outside manipulation, for preachers in these churches were by custom unpaid ministers who gathered a flock from among their neighbors and fellow workers; their congregations could flourish in ordinary houses and outdoor meeting places, thus bypassing company control of church buildings. Some preachers in traditional sects might scorn the issues that unions raised as too "worldly" to merit worshipers' attention, but there were others, equally religious, who made no such distinction. John Welborn, a preacher who exchanged his Bible for a rifle during the West Virginia mine wars, was one of the few miners convicted in the treason and murder trials that followed the March on Logan. There was also a "cowboy preacher" in southern West Virginia coal camps whose "good news" represented a potent combination of the Bible and the UMWA; his activities can be followed, as through a glass darkly, in the reports that Baldwin-Felts agents delivered to mine owner Justus Collins.

The emergence of new Protestant sects in Appalachia during the early twentieth century brought new religious voices into the coal camps and mill villages. The Church of God, which traces its origin to four small congregations in the mountain region where Tennessee, Georgia, and North Carolina converge, and the Pentecostal movement, which developed as a traditionalist offshoot of Methodism, jointly precipitated a revival of the "highly emotive, nonrational religious experience" that had typified Appalachian mountain religion since colonial times. One study of Gastonia found that twenty-six new congregations of these or similar traditional churches were established between 1910 and 1939, each drawing its membership from among millworkers. Known collectively to outsiders as Holy Rollers, these congregations engaged in emotional worship practices that, as had been the case a century earlier, stirred up mixed reactions among middle-class observers. By directing the energies of workers inward to the rewards of the afterlife—"pie in the sky," in the agnostic lexicon of the socialist organizer Ralph Chapin—the sects could act as a stabilizing force among workers, but the emotionalism of their worship carried with it an implication of empowerment that made some employers nervous. "There is no use letting them get all stirred up emotionally," a Gaston County mill president explained. "I'm a Methodist, but I don't like the old type of revivals."[52] To the extent that religious revival contributed to the sense of militancy that surrounded union organizing movements, here too was a potentially powerful contribution of traditional Appalachian culture to the region's industrial mix.

Finally, while federal intervention into the economic and social crises spawned by the Great Depression took place on a state-by-state basis, other interventions were either unique to Appalachia or strongly focused there. Appalachia, like every other part of the country, experienced the impacts of Social Security, wages-and-hours legislation, and relief programs such as the Works Progress Administration (WPA). Paul Salstrom has argued that these New Deal programs, though they inhibited further environmental destruction by curbing the expansion of subsistence farming, also completed the "addiction" to cash incomes that had begun with the movement of the Appalachian working class from the farms into public work in the mines, mills, and lumber camps. Thus, in the long term, the last vestiges were destroyed of the communal features of the farm-and-forest economy: that informal part of household regimes that depended upon cooperative labor within and among families and neighbors, the bartering and borrowing that substituted for cash, and the recourse to the forest commons for grazing and the harvest of wild products. New Deal transfer payments—while certainly humane on their face and justified in terms of the immediate relief from suffering that government cash provided—meant that when the next crisis hit the region, mountaineers would have no alternative but migration. From this perspective, the contours of postindustrial Appalachia took shape in the industrial crisis of the previous generation.[53]

It should be added that the character of federal intervention into the postindustrial crisis of the 1950s and 1960s was also influenced by the nature of federal intervention during the years between the two world wars. The experience of three federal agencies in particular—the U.S. Forest Service, the National Park Service, and the Tennessee Valley Authority—cast a long bureaucratic shadow over Appalachia.

Appalachia's national forests (today numbering sixteen with 7.4 million acres in the official region, eight of which, totaling 5.8 million acres, are in the core) originated in the concern aroused by the excesses of industrial logging in the early twentieth century. An alternative approach to the harvest of timber, grounded in Progressive Era's respect for efficiency and expertise, in fact established its "cradle" in western North Carolina in 1892, when forester Gifford Pinchot assumed management of the 100,000-acre tract adjoining George W. Vanderbilt's Biltmore Estate near Asheville. A wealthy Pennsylvanian who had been educated in Germany and at Yale, Pinchot became the prophet of "scientific forestry" in the United States. His main critique of the lumber companies did not derive from their destructiveness, but from the wastefulness of their methods. Their cutover and abandoned lands, properly managed by persons trained in scientific silviculture, could yield new harvests of wood for future generations and prevent downstream flooding and navigational problems by protecting the forested headwaters of rivers. Pinchot and his followers thus advocated greater selectivity in timber cutting, both as to species and the size of trees taken, and the protection of watershed resources against the hazards of erosion and fire.

The industry's elimination of old-growth forest and the consequent reduction of the mountains' biodiversity were not among Pinchot's concerns, as scientists did not yet understand the importance of such matters to human welfare. Having demonstrated the profitability of his methods in North Carolina, at least to Vanderbilt's satisfaction, by 1898, Pinchot soon moved on to Washington, where he became chief forester in the Department of Agriculture's Division of Forestry during the administration of Theodore Roosevelt. In 1911, after a noisy public fight between Pinchot and the succeeding administration's secretary of agriculture, the principles of scientific forestry were established by the Weeks Act, which authorized the federal purchase of both forested and cutover lands in the name of watershed protection.

The Forest Service's purchase of lands began almost immediately, amounting to more than 1.4 million acres of southern Appalachian land in the first fifteen months of the Weeks Act's operation. These purchases concentrated initially on land in remote watersheds that had not yet been cut over, but in 1924 the service's mandate was broadened by further legislation to include lands unrelated to navigation and flood control. Meanwhile, in 1916, President Woodrow Wilson proclaimed the establishment of Appalachia's first national forest, Pisgah in North Carolina, where initial federal purchases embraced nearly 90,000 acres of the original Vanderbilt estate. A second tract, now part of George Washington National Forest in Virginia, followed in 1918, and in 1920, five new Appalachian forests were proclaimed, extending into Georgia, West Virginia, Tennessee, and both Carolinas. Three others were added to the system during the 1930s. In 1930, when Forest Service land buying shifted from the purchase of large tracts from lumber companies to the acquisition of hundreds of small individual properties, total national forest acreage in the region exceeded 4,000,000 acres.[54]

Fire prevention was one of the immediate goals of the Forest Service and its backers. The Weeks Act provided money to states that passed fire safety laws and provided machinery for their enforcement. Kentucky, Virginia, West Virginia, and North Carolina each created a state forestry office and established fire patrols by 1915; Tennessee, Georgia, and South Carolina followed in 1921, 1925, and 1928, respectively. The new laws posed a challenge to traditional practices: Following Native American custom, backwoods farmers traditionally set "light" fires in the spring, burning away leaves and underbrush and creating forage for both domestic and wild animals in the form of new grass and tender shoots; another objective of traditional burning was the control of snakes and insects. The practice must have very ancient roots, for there are tree species in the mountains that are specifically adapted to fires of this type. Only when such fires got out of control or fed on the debris left behind by industrial logging were productive forest soils and hardwood species such as oak, chestnut, and poplar threatened.

From the standpoint of the new scientific forestry, however, *all* fires were dangerous. Forest Service regulations and the new state laws and agencies created another class of local miscreant, the "firebug," who became the object of law enforcement efforts as vigorous as the renewed drive against moonshiners during the dry twenties and early thirties. Following the practice of revenue agents, the Forest Service hired local men as rangers and to fill other positions where possible, thereby recruiting more effective allies in the drive to stamp out traditional burning. The Forest Service's fire prevention mission also became an educational hallmark of the era, reaching into the schools and into the network of county agents and farm demonstration clubs promoted by other branches of the U.S. Department of Agriculture. Appalachian children learned the tenets of forest fire prevention long before the advent of Smoky the Bear.

The Tennessee Valley Authority (TVA), like the Forest Service, was rooted in progressive concern over the efficient use of natural resources, in this case water power from the nation's rivers. In 1920 Congress passed the Water Power Act, creating a Federal Power Commission (FPC) and vesting in it control over hydroelectric uses of the nation's navigable rivers. Meanwhile, as a war emergency measure, the Muscle Shoals project in northern Alabama submerged the Tennessee River's greatest navigational obstruction under the impoundment behind Wilson Dam, which was built to generate the huge amounts of electricity needed to "fix" nitrogen from air, an essential requirement in the production of explosives—and of fertilizer. The war ended before the dam was finished, but a handful of progressive Republican senators led by George W. Norris of Nebraska prevented the privatization of Muscle Shoals during the 1920s and held out its potential use as a publicly owned facility whose hydroelectric production would serve as a "yardstick" by which to measure the real costs and appropriate levels of profit due to regulated private electrical power and fertilizer producers.

At the same time, private appropriation of hydroelectric sites on Appalachian rivers proceeded rapidly. The small hydroelectric dams like the one that powered the Fries textile mill where Ernest Stoneman and Henry Whitter worked during the 1910s were absorbed by regional electric utility holding companies such as Appalachian Power, while these same companies built larger dams and reservoirs after the war. The Aluminum Company of America (ALCOA), the Pittsburgh-based firm that held the patent on the electrolytic production of its namesake metal, built three dams in the Little Tennessee River basin between 1919 and 1930 to power its manufacturing facility at Alcoa, Tennessee. Duke Power, founded by James Buchanan Duke after federal trustbusters forced the breakup and sale of his American Tobacco Company, absorbed the small power companies and hydroelectric sites of the Carolina Piedmont, then moved into the mountains with the construction of Linville Dam and Lake James at the foot of the Blue Ridge escarpment in 1916–23.

Soon afterward, Union Carbide Chemicals Corporation, a war-born conglomerate that absorbed much of West Virginia's new chemical-process industry, engaged the same Virginia firm that built Duke's Lake James facility to build a hydroelectric dam, tunnel, and generating station at Hawks Nest near the lower (northern) end of New River Gorge. Racing to complete the project before the FPC could declare the gorge navigable and thus subject to federal oversight, Union Carbide gave its contractor incentives to hurry, with tragic results. The rock through which the Hawks Nest Tunnel was drilled had a silica content of up to 99 percent—so pure, in fact, that Union Carbide was able to use it without further refining to make ferrosilicon, a steel alloy. Safe drilling methods would have slowed the work, and so the contractors provided the tunnel workers with none of the known precautions against breathing silica dust. At least 764 men died of silicosis after working in the tunnel, some quickly, some after subsisting in a debilitated state for years. The nearby town of Gauley Bridge became famous briefly as "the town of the living dead." At least three-quarters of the victims were African Americans. Many of these are likely to have been veterans of the Lake James project who were brought up from North Carolina not only because of their experience but because the interracial union militancy previously demonstrated by southern West Virginia mine workers made the contractors leery of hiring locally. The Hawks Nest Tunnel disaster still stands as the worst industrial "accident" in American history. The contractor paid some $130,000 to settle damage suits brought by tunnel workers or their survivors in 1933; half of this sum went to the victims' lawyers.[55]

Public power could prevent such abuses, according to its advocates, but the main argument of Norris and his colleagues was that public ownership represented greater efficiency and equity. Publicly owned facilities could be built larger and could produce energy more abundantly and cheaply than any single private corporation; also, because the distribution of power would be subject to public authority or influence, utility companies could be forced to serve rural as well as urban areas, notwithstanding higher rural distribution costs. The principle of public power was well established in New York when Franklin D. Roosevelt took office as governor of that state in 1929, but Roosevelt also introduced a new element into the dialogue that eventually led to the TVA—the idea of regional planning. As Roosevelt came to advocate it, planning was an integrative public policy mechanism, allowing power development to be designed in tandem with the requirements of navigation and flood control, watershed protection, soil and forest conservation, and the restoration of cutover forests and depleted or marginal land.

Roosevelt's experience with planning in New York was augmented by his attendance at a "roundtable on regionalism" at the University of Virginia in July 1931. Here Roosevelt was exposed to the regionalist ideas of such thinkers as Lewis Mumford, Benton MacKaye, and Howard Odum. At the same time, the governor gave the visionaries lessons in the realities of politics: "I do not know what 'Regionalism' means. I do have certain fairly clear ideas in respect to the relative spheres of government of states on the one hand and Federal government on the other hand. . . . I think we are apt very often to run after false gods in this country, to take up some 'ism' and assume that in a generation or two that they are going to be so different that we must scrap everything tried and familiar."[56] Nonetheless, the legislation that Roosevelt submitted to Congress soon after assuming the presidency suggested that he had absorbed more of the regionalists' ideas than his comments at Charlottesville seemed to indicate.

The TVA Act was an amalgam of regional and progressive ideas. The Muscle Shoals power project became the lynchpin of a multipurpose development embracing the entire Tennessee valley, from the river's headwaters in Appalachia to its mouth on the Ohio, with initial development focused on the upper valley upstream from Wilson Dam. The TVA would be a "grassroots" bureaucracy, headquartered in Knoxville rather than Washington, but supposedly insulated from state and local politics by a unique administrative structure that, in effect, created a publicly owned corporation; it would be subject to congressional oversight in the appropriation of its capital budgets and the appointment of its three-person directorate, but otherwise the do-

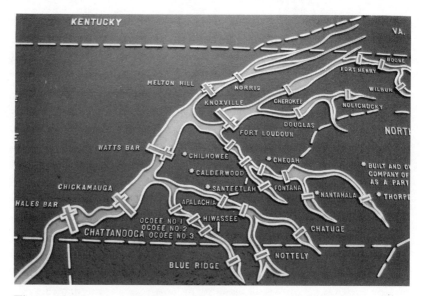

The completed TVA hydroelectric system, as portrayed by a plaque at an overlook near Norris Dam. (Photograph by Carroll Van West)

main of experts who would be guided less by political concerns than by the requirements of efficiency and justice. That justice would include the needs of the region's poor rural inhabitants as well as its urban and landowning elites—or so it seemed in 1933.

Sections 22 and 23 of the TVA Act embodied the regional planning principles Roosevelt had articulated in his formal remarks at the Charlottesville roundtable. He expanded upon the TVA's promise in a speech delivered in Montgomery, Alabama, after a postelection visit to Wilson Dam in January 1933: "We have an opportunity of setting an example of planning not just for ourselves but for the generations to come, tying in industry and agriculture and forestry and flood prevention, tying them all into a unified whole . . . so that we can afford better opportunities and better places for living for millions yet unborn, in the days to come." The TVA was not simply "initiated or organized for the purpose of selling electricity," Roosevelt told his National Emergency Council in 1934. "The work proceeds along two lines, both of which are intimately connected—the physical land and water and soil end of it, and the human side of it." Referring specifically to the mountain inhabitants of the Tennessee headwaters, the president stated, "We are going to try to bring him some of the things he needs, like schools, electric lights, and so on. We are going to try to prevent soil erosion, and grow trees, and try to bring in industries. . . . And when you build a dam as an incident to this entire program, you get probably a certain amount of water power development of it."[57] From the standpoint of many mountaineers, however, it was they and not the dams that turned out to be incidental.

The idea of eastern national parks originated in the debate over forest policy, but by 1920, proposals for an "Appalachian national park" had taken on a life of their own, especially in Tennessee—where Knoxville promoters advocated a park that would stimulate automobile tourism—and in Virginia, where Governor Harry Byrd and a coalition of fellow Great Valley businessmen advocated the creation of Shenandoah National Park in the Virginia Blue Ridge. Park advocates in North Carolina initially focused on Linville Gorge and Grandfather Mountain, but in 1925 Asheville tourism promoters joined forces with their Knoxville counterparts to press for a national park in the Great Smoky Mountains along the border between their two states. In order to compete with the tourist appeal of the Cherokees living in or adjacent to the proposed park in North Carolina ("though the school children and younger inhabitants may be transferred to a western reservation," a park booster explained), Knoxville promoters insisted on incorporating Cades Cove, a picturesque and beautiful but inhabited Tennessee district entirely circled by mountains. Since the federal government lacked the power of eminent domain, it was up to the states to obtain the necessary land, through purchases or condemnations, before turning the tracts over to the National Park Service (NPS). All three states created public commissions to identify and acquire the desired land.

Neither the inhabitants of the proposed parklands nor most of the timber companies who were the largest landowners were eager to have the parks there. In North Carolina, where lumber companies owned most of the proposed park area, the Champion Fiber Company of Canton led the opposition. Small landowners—263 in North Carolina, 879 in Tennessee—either sold out quickly or stood on the sidelines, hoping for the best but fearing the worst. However, John Oliver of Cades Cove, a community leader and descendant of the cove's first settler, contested Tennessee's seizure of his land through a series of legal challenges between 1929 and 1935. Oliver was finally forced to yield, moving the last of his household goods on Christmas Day in 1937. Meanwhile, the two states each put up $2,000,000 for the park, raised another $1,000,000 privately, and in 1928 topped the initial funding with a $5,000,000 donation from John D. Rockefeller Jr., the son of the controversial oil baron. The Rockefeller money quieted opposition among the lumber companies, which began lining up for their share.

Great Smoky Mountains National Park (GSMNP) came under federal management in 1931 and was open for business as a unit of the National Park Service in 1934, by which time a new set of federal officials had taken office under Roosevelt. Promoters also wanted to build a parkway to compete with Shenandoah National Park's Skyline Drive, but this idea was shelved until 1935, when it reemerged in somewhat different form as a New Deal work relief project under the National Industrial Recovery Act. From the standpoint of its sponsors, the Blue Ridge Parkway was designed to relieve hardship and unemployment in the mountain counties along its route, but its designers also took the opportunity to create a masterpiece of landscape architecture, an automobile route following the crest of the mountains from the southern end of the Skyline Drive to the Great Smoky Mountains National Park entrance near the Cherokees' Qualla Boundary reservation. Although parkway construction was mostly finished by 1967, the entire route was not completed until 1987, when the spectacular Linn Cove Viaduct around the flank of Grandfather Mountain closed the final five-mile gap. Meanwhile, North Carolina highway builders launched another scenic highway across the mountains, bisecting Great Smoky Mountains National Park via Newfound Gap, where Roosevelt himself unveiled a dedicatory marker on the state line in 1940.

Newfound Gap was a point of access to another institution forged during this era, the Appalachian Trail (AT). Though the AT was established under private auspices, it encountered many of the same obstacles that confronted the builders of the national parks and parkways: negotiation with hundreds of local landowners along its 2,100-mile route and a potential for cultural conflict between its recreational users and the mountaineers through whose backyards it passed. New England hiking enthusiasts, organized in the Appalachian Mountain Club and similar groups, provided a model for the trail with the well-marked paths and open-air shelters for overnight hikers that graced such attractions as New Hampshire's Mt. Washington.

Beginning in 1921, the planning visionary Benton MacKaye promoted the creation of a footpath extending from Mt. Washington to Mt. Mitchell as a means of teaching eastern city dwellers about the importance of mountain watersheds and the joys of wilderness experience. As summarized by the travel writer Bill Bryson, MacKaye "saw the AT as a thread connecting a network of mountaintop work camps where pale, depleted urban workers in the thousands would come and engage in healthful toil in a selfless spirit and refresh themselves on nature. There were to be hostels and inns and seasonal study centers, and eventually permanent woodland villages" not unlike the "resettlement" communities created by Roosevelt's New Deal. But MacKaye withdrew from the project in 1935 in angry opposition to the Skyline Drive, which crisscrosses the AT along the Blue Ridge crest through Shenandoah National Park.

The Appalachian Trail Conference, founded in 1925, brought the AT to completion in 1937, in a longer but simpler form, under the leadership of a Washington lawyer named Myron Avery. Today the trail extends from Maine to Georgia and offers the 2,000-plus hikers who attempt to hike its full length each year less a communal experience than a test of individual mettle. Those who complete this challenge number in the few hundreds, but the AT also brings satisfaction to the uncounted thousands who trek along it for shorter distances. Maintaining the trail by means of volunteer labor, the conference, headquartered in Harpers Ferry, is in Bryson's words "the largest volunteer-run organization on the planet, . . . gloriously free of commercialism."[58]

By advertising the mountains as a place of recreation and renewal for city folk, the AT nevertheless contributed to Appalachian commerce in the new age of mass tourism. In terms of numbers, the new park and parkways had a much greater impact. Almost 41,000 people visited GSMNP during its first month of federal operation in June 1934; in June 1935 this figure rose to 128,533.[59] Today it is the most popular national park in the United States. Shenandoah, less than seventy miles from Washington, D.C., and thus even closer to the most populous cities and most-traveled highways, was also a success, while visitors to the Blue Ridge Parkway rose in proportion to the expansion of automobile tourism and family vacations in the post–World War II era. What historians notice most about these parks today, however, is not their institutional success but their roles as cultural artifacts. The Appalachian parks became, each in its own way, monuments to the cultural forms of other parts of the nation, while their expansion at the expense of local landowners and forest users was often justified in terms of the ways in which Appalachian people were thought to depart from national cultural norms.

National parks were among the first institutions to reverse the traditional progression of cultural norms from east to west in this country; instead, the parks expanded from west to east. They were supposed to preserve wilderness and natural wonders for future generations. Yet the Blue Ridge and the Smokies offered no Old Faithfuls or El Capitans; the wonders they did hold were less spectacular—an admirer might have said subtler—than those of the West. The eastern parks were wilderness areas only in a very incomplete sense of that term. Above all, they were inhabited, by nearly six thousand people in the case of the Smokies, about half as many in Shenandoah, plus a few dozen families that had to be moved out of the path of the Blue Ridge Parkway.

What the Appalachian mountains offered was an amazing biodiversity still largely unstudied and unappreciated during the 1930s, and that diversity included the imprint of human alterations—the celebrated "balds" of the Smokies, for example, and the introduction of exotic animals and plants such as the European wild boar (introduced by sport hunters around the turn of the century), Japanese honeysuckle (which Cherokee women learned to use to make the baskets that they sold to tourists), and rainbow trout (called "California fish" by locals), which drove the native brook trout further back into the headwaters. The most nefarious introduction of all was the chestnut blight, which first appeared in New York on infected nursery stock in 1904; by 1919 it was in the Virginia Blue Ridge, and it reached the Smokies in 1925. The blight, perhaps the most notorious ecological disaster to occur in the United States, destroyed one of the mainstays of the Appalachian forest, a tree whose role in human, animal, and plant ecology was irreplaceable. Chestnuts provided lumber and bark for construction, nuts that were unusual in their abundance and that were savored by humans and by domestic and wild animals alike, and a place in the forest canopy that was only gradually refilled by oaks and hickory trees. For the mountain people who lived through these years, "the cumulative changes—logging, national park removal, the blight— all ran together in people's consciousness."[60] "When families moved out, their hearts were broken," a native of the Cataloochee valley in North Carolina remembered. "Most of them left crying," a Tennessean recalled. Forced expropriations endowed all three parks with a legacy of bitterness, one that—at least in the case of Shenandoah National Park—still lingers on both sides, with descendants of expropriated landowners demanding fuller accountings of the expulsions and Park Service officials still employing legal technicalities to resist these demands.[61]

"The history of the Great Smoky Mountains is not the simple story of preserving a wilderness," Margaret Lynn Brown writes, "but rather the complex narrative of restoring—and even creating—one."[62] Although J. Ross Eakin, the first superintendent at GSMNP, was a West Virginian by birth, his Park Service career took him to Glacier and Grand Canyon National Parks before he came to the Smokies in 1931. Even he was unprepared for the extent to which tourists expected to find western scenes and experiences replicated in the Smokies. Eakin introduced horseback trail riding, a favorite activity in western parks, to GSMNP, but he was prepared to let Cades Cove as well as the cutover timberlands he inherited grow back into "wilderness." But tourists enjoyed the charming contrast that the abandoned fields of the former inhabitants presented against the surrounding wooded hills, and so the landholdings were consolidated into broad grasslands, mowed by park employees and dotted by grazing cattle, just like meadows in the Rockies.

As the park's services and administrative needs expanded, park structures took on the rusticated look of their western counterparts. Not far away, at Linville, North Carolina, the architect Henry Bacon had designed a resort for the lumber company that owned Grandfather Mountain by combining Adirondack twig ornamentation with local materials such as chestnut bark siding. The chestnut blight ensured that this experiment would spread no further. Following the lead of the parks, derivative architecture from the West or, worse, a bastardized form of central European mountain architecture became the norm in Appalachian resorts. Meanwhile, in Cades Cove, all traces of modernity, including numerous white frame farmhouses, were destroyed. On the Blue Ridge Parkway, officials developed a roadside attraction at Mabry's Mill, Virginia, by pulling down frame houses, removing the gasoline-powered electrical generator and lighting system the mill owner had installed, and moving log structures to the site from other locations. The result was a quaintly flattering view of "pioneer life" and its hardships, with an even more flattering subtext that invited tourists to celebrate the modern consumer society to which both they and the parkway's designers were heirs.

Western parks also featured human attractions in the form of Indians who clustered around hotel lodges and railroad stations, offering souvenirs and crafts. Although only a few Indians were allowed to live in western parks—notably, the Hopi deep in the Grand Canyon—tourists expected to find them there, and the Eastern Band of Cherokees was only too happy to provide counterparts in GSMNP. Cherokee, North Carolina, at the edge of the Qualla Boundary, acquired its first paved road in 1927, but the new parkway and the highway through Newfound Gap to Tennessee soon made tourism a major source of income for the reservation. Although a small museum was organized to display authentic Cherokee artifacts, the souvenirs that sold best were those that met tourist expectations of how Indians should look and act. In place of the sturdier cane and white-oak materials and utilitarian styles of traditional Cherokee basketry, basketmakers resorted to vine and other light materials that could be worked more quickly into the decorative items preferred by tourists. Cherokee men discovered a lucrative sideline in "chiefing": dressing up in Plains Indian costumes, including full war bonnet regalia, and charging a fee for tourists who wished to photograph them. The scenic overlooks on the Newfound Gap highway became an especially popular spot for such transactions.

On the Tennessee side of the mountains, there were no Indians to bring the

While FSA photographers dramatized the plight of impoverished farmers and miners and folk enthusiasts like Bayard Wootten and Doris Ullmann dressed young people in their grandparents' clothes or sought out the elderly to construct images of Appalachian quaintness, the self-taught eastern Kentucky "pictureman" W. R. Mullins placed his subjects squarely in the American mainstream. Here he experiments with an image that probably owes its inspiration to the drawingroom comedies of 1930s Hollywood. On his next shot, Mullins managed to get himself and most of the flash out of the mirror. (Courtesy of Appalshop)

Hollywood West to life for park visitors, and so park officials gingerly encouraged interaction between tourists and the small numbers of native mountaineers who remained in the park. These were mostly elderly people, who continued living as they had, as best they could without the support and companionship of an intact community. Especially popular with visitors were the Walker sisters, five women who elected to remain on their homeplace in the Little Greenbrier section of GSMNP. Visitors followed directions in printed travel guides in order to visit the sisters and observe their daily routines. "They are one of the park's greatest assets now," according to one reporter. The sisters did not enjoy being placed on exhibit, however, and eventually asked the Park Service to remove the signs directing visitors to their place. It was not until the new town of Gatlinburg, just outside the park entrance, developed its full touristic potential that visitors were able to see the Hollywood version of Appalachian culture brought to life.

Before the rise of the Forest Service, the Park Service, and the TVA, the federal government's role in Appalachia had been remote or had achieved its impact through state and local government or, in wartime, through the military. Now the "feds" were established throughout the region as employers, landowners, and developers. As much as the educators who established settlement schools and promoted the spread of public education in the mountains, these three government agencies acted as catalysts for modernization. Admittedly, the TVA had a unique administrative structure, while both the Forest Service and NPS were units of larger federal departments (Agriculture and Interior, respectively). Each agency had its distinctive mission, bureaucratic routines, and career paths. Yet their commonalities better define their role in Appalachian history. Each resisted the demands of state and local politicians for patronage opportunities; Tennessee senator McKellar was especially bitter in his denunciation of "outsider" experts like GSMNP superintendent Eakins and the host of "Yankee" lawyers and engineers that the TVA imported to Knoxville. Each agency demonstrated something of the missionary spirit of William Goodell Frost and the Campbells; many of the agencies' staff members were openly appalled at the living conditions that they observed among the most impoverished mountaineers and had not the slightest doubt of their duty to bring mountain life up to twentieth-century standards, whether the mountaineers involved wanted this or not.

The commonalities are revealed most strongly, however, in their roles as landowners, charged with expropriating and relocating the people who lived on the territory that they claimed. The TVA, profiting from the experience of the Park and Forest Services, enjoyed an explicit power of eminent domain, granted by Congress, from the very beginning; the agency also had the force of logic behind its actions, since the construction of a dam could not begin until the lands it would drown had been secured, and construction jobs were the most immediate benefit that local people expected. With five dams in East Tennessee and northern Alabama (Norris, Wheeler, Pickwick Landing, Guntersville, and Fowler's Bend) scheduled for completion during the 1930s and a fifth (Little Tennessee, later renamed Fontana) beginning construction in North Carolina in 1940, the displacements created by the TVA dwarfed those of the national parks. Some 6,600 families had to be removed from lands involved, 3,500 from the Norris Basin alone. As with the parks, TVA relocations were complicated by the impact of the Depression and by the fact that the lands to be drowned constituted a large proportion of the valley's best farmlands—bottom and terrace lands whose fertility had best withstood the destructive soil-mining practices of traditional farming. A lack of alternative land hampered the relocation process from the outset.

Internal dissention within the agency exacerbated these problems, for the TVA's three directors quickly fell out over how best to implement their planning goals. The Norris area was a test both of the TVA's broader ambitions and of the impact of its internal confusion. As envisioned by Arthur E. Morgan, the engineer/educator whom Roosevelt named as the senior TVA director, the town of Norris was to be a model village, housing both construction workers and families from the area's drowned and marginal farmlands. Instead, it became a "suburb in the wilderness," a white-collar enclave housing professionals who commuted via a new freeway to Knoxville, thirty-six miles away. Wielding its condemnation power so effectively that few landowners challenged either its authority or the prices it offered, the TVA compensated owners for their property but provided only limited emergency support for the landless tenants and laborers whose families constituted more than a third of those removed from the area.

Morgan, though full of ideas as to how the agency might help to provide opportunities for improvement for such people, was clumsy in his advocacy of new programs and ineffective in dealing with his fellow directors, David Lilienthal, a public-power lawyer who favored this aspect of the TVA's mission above all others, and Harcourt E. Morgan (no relation to Arthur), a former president of the University of Tennessee who pursued an ultimately successful policy of forming alliances with local politicos and the landowning elite represented by the American Farm Bureau. In 1938 Lilienthal and Harcourt Morgan succeeded in forcing Arthur E. Morgan's removal. Meanwhile, although the relocated families had been studied elaborately by social scientists and caseworkers, the TVA made very little help available to them apart from information about available land elsewhere.

The historians who have studied the Norris project most closely estimate that some 60 percent of the people whose homes were taken ended up leaving the area to seek work in Knoxville and Nashville or the manufacturing cities of Ohio, Indiana, and Michigan. They also note that "the Authority's legal minds, so innovative and energetic in the struggles with the power companies, were . . . timid in the face of social reform." Morgan and other TVA planners who put forward creative solutions to the problems of relocation and welfare grew accustomed to having their proposals turned down, of being handed "the old story of emphasizing how something cannot be done rather than how it can be done."[63]

The relocation issues raised by TVA projects gave rise to much discussion about the "resettlement" of people living on marginal agricultural land into new communities, or, as Arthur Morgan phrased it, "new towns created on principles which will insure diversity of employment, garden space for every home, and good community organization." The idea of "subsistence homesteads" emerged from a succession of agencies within the U.S. Department of Agriculture as part of a program to develop government-financed communities where displaced families could live simply and decently while growing their own food and earning cash through combinations of part-time work and the sale of handicrafts.

First Lady Eleanor Roosevelt was the strongest advocate of such schemes. Her interest was piqued in 1933 when she ventured into the Scotts Run mining district near Morgantown, West Virginia. Here relief workers from the Red Cross and religious charitable organizations had come to aid the families of unemployed miners who were stranded in this coal-blackened valley on the verge of starvation. In addition to addressing the urgent human needs of Scotts Run, the relief workers had also taught some of the miners to make simple wood furniture, which a Quaker organization distributed to consumers under the label Godlove. Mrs. Roosevelt had acquired a Godlove chair and came to West Virginia to see what could be done about the plight of its makers. She would return several times, bringing her husband in tow in 1937 to inaugurate a new model community built on a mountain plateau east of Morgantown and christened Arthurdale. This was the first and best known of the subsistence communities developed by Roosevelt's controversial Resettlement Administration, which acted on the assumption that industrial growth had reached its apogee in the United States and thus that the surplus members of both the urban and rural work force needed to be provided with other means of supporting themselves. In Arthurdale, this meant subsistence gardening and craft production, even though few if any of the miners from Scotts Run had backgrounds in farming or handicrafts. Cumberland Homesteads near Crossville, Tennessee, was another of these communities, one on which TVA relocation officials briefly fixed their hopes of improving the lives of their charges.

The publicity that the first lady helped generate for the resettlement program was augmented by cultural programs inaugurated by the WPA's Roy Stryker, who hired talented young photographers to canvass the country for images of rural hardship, and by Charles Seeger, a musicologist now best known for being the husband of the composer Ruth Crawford and the father of entertainer Pete Seeger. The elder Seeger headed a "special skills" unit in the Resettlement Administration, composed chiefly of folklorists who fanned out across the country, tape recorders in hand, with instructions to record and preserve folk music. John A. Lomax, a Texas folklorist who became head of the Library of Congress's Archive of Folk Song in 1933, reinforced Seeger's efforts. In 1941 the even more radical children of these left-leaning administrators—Pete Seeger, Alan Lomax, Elizabeth "Bess" Lomax, and Bess's future husband, "Butch" Hawes—joined with the knockabout Oklahoma performer Woodie Guthrie to create the Almanac Singers, considered to be the ancestral seed of what became known after World War II as the folk music revival.[64] Thus, out of the agony of the miners, millhands, and mountain farmers was born a movement that would have much to do with shaping the Appalachian region's postindustrial identity.

Roosevelt himself appealed to traditional Appalachian imagery in justifying the TVA's nobler ambitions. The program's benefits would start in the headwaters, in "a shack on the side of the mountain where there is a white man of about as fine stock as we have in this country who, with his family of children, is completely uneducated—never had a chance, never sees twenty-five or fifty dollars in cash in a year, but just keeps body and soul together—manages to do that—and is the progenitor of a large line of children for many generations to come. He certainly has been forgotten, not by the Administration, but by the American people."[65]

The fact that the president, along with the tourists, was attracted to the more positive images of Appalachian culture did not prevent authorities from resorting to negative stereotypes when it suited them. In varying degrees, each of the federal agencies or their apologists summoned lurid images of depravity and deprivation to justify the seizure of homes and land. Roy Stryker instructed his photographers to focus on subjects that enhanced demand for his agency's program: "[W]atch out for poorly constructed school houses. The purpose here is to show that the taxpayers' money could better be spent on larger centralized schools if we could resettle these people on better lands."[66] "They didn't want something that looked good," a Tennessee man recalled of the photographers who documented living conditions in the Norris area. "They wanted to show the worst side. They took pictures." Another man complained that the photographers "showed the Henry Stooksbury family with the old ladies out in front of the big log cabin with their bonnets, washing their clothes. And people up there felt that they were being portrayed as ignorant mountain people."[67]

When TVA caseworkers approached Proctor, North Carolina, one of the Ritter Company lumber towns that would be drowned by Fontana Lake, they reported "a unique picture of community decadence and disorganization," populated by "residue of the more prosperous periods of lumbering and mining." Progress had made some inroads, the social workers admitted, since "feuds have practically disappeared."[68] Feuds, of course, had never been a feature of life in this part of Appalachia, except in the imaginations of writers. In Virginia, a park promoter justified the Shenandoah removals by portraying the communities concerned as rife with illiteracy, immorality, inbreeding, moonshining, and lawlessness. These communities lacked schools and churches, according to the promoter, and were so isolated that local men had never heard of the Civil War or World War I.

Modern scholars who have investigated these charges as they apply to one section of the park have refuted them point by point. Literacy had declined in this district, but at least a third of the people were literate at the time these charges were made; 91 percent of couples were legally married, although common-law marriages were not uncommon in a couple's early years together. A local doctor who examined half of the people in question in 1936 reported only three cases of venereal disease. The oldest church in the community dated to 1778. Fourteen men from the community had served in the Civil War, five in World War I. Names from the community appeared on voter registration rolls, and so on; only the allegations of moonshining had a basis in fact.[69]

Caseworker investigations of the families removed from the Norris Basin disclosed similar facts. To cite only a few examples, the 239 square miles of land that the federal government acquired in this district held 204 churches.

The illiteracy rate was 5 percent for tenants and 3 percent for landowners, although 25 percent had no more than a third-grade education. Relatively few people had electricity; fewer still a radio. But 476 owners and 132 tenants owned automobiles (26 and 16 percent, respectively); 726 (39 percent) and 196 (24 percent) owned phonographs. Although the area undoubtedly was impoverished and overcrowded, its physical and cultural isolation was clearly a relative thing.[70]

The fact that such calumnies were self-interested and refutable did little to help the victims of expropriation. Expulsion from mountain homes during the 1930s was a catastrophe, especially for poorer mountaineers. Those who owned land received compensation, but the deflationary spiral that accompanied the Great Depression reduced its value, and in any event there was little land available elsewhere at comparable prices. Appraisals did not take into account that a mountain farm, however ramshackle, provided a viable sustenance at a time when few alternatives were available, much less the psychic trauma of being thrown off of family homeplaces and out of shattered communities. Younger workers took jobs with the new federal agencies and settled down in houses closer to the new paved roads, or they drifted into mill or factory towns or nearby cities to look for work. Destitute older people went on relief.

If he had cared to, the president could have found an exemplar of most of the characteristics he attributed to mountain people not far from the White House. Ernest Stoneman moved his family to the Washington area in 1932, after a futile effort to sustain the life his musical earnings had brought him in the previous decade. As his music career collapsed after 1928, Stoneman reverted to his earlier strategy of temporary migration, leaving the family back in Galax while he went to places such as Roanoke or Winston-Salem, trying to earn money either by playing music or, increasingly, by competing with the army of other unemployed fathers for laboring jobs. His children remembered this period of their lives by the disappearance of things as times grew harder: first the hired girls, then the furniture, then the house that Ernest had built, along with property that Hattie Stoneman had inherited from her family and even Ernest's father's hardscrabble farm up on Iron Ridge. The father went north to live with his miner son Ingram, who still had a job in West Virginia.

Ernest managed to keep a rattletrap car by outwitting the sheriff who came to repossess it, and by this means the family, now numbering nine children, joined the trickle of migrants who abandoned the mountains altogether. In terms of net migration—that is, the ratio of people moving out to those moving in—parts of Appalachia had been losing population since early in the twentieth century; a high birthrate had disguised the loss in aggregate terms, and Stoneman certainly did his best to illustrate this, fathering a total of fifteen children, thirteen of whom survived. The Appalachian region actually experienced a slight gain from migration during the thirties, as migrants who had left during the twenties returned to their parents' farms after being laid off from northern factories. But as the experience of the Norris Basin illustrated, migration remained an option to those who had been uprooted from their inherited ways of life.

The choice was not an easy one, nor were the rewards of city life what they had been during the prosperous 1920s. The Stonemans lived in a succession of tumbledown rented houses in the nation's capital and its suburbs, always short of money and food, as Ernest and his older children earned what they could through odd jobs and the occasional musical gig. Although the welfare and relief programs of the New Deal were the recourse of many Appalachian families, others fell through the cracks, including the Stonemans. Whether through pride or ignorance or because of their frequent changes of residence, the Stonemans never received government aid during the 1930s, except incidental help that materialized from firemen when the family once rented a house across the street from a firehouse. Meanwhile, in West Virginia, "Blind Alfred" Reed, Stoneman's fellow veteran of the historic Bristol sessions of 1927, was driven from town to town by authorities who worried about the image he created by performing for pennies on street corners. "How can a poor man stand these times and live?" ran his plaintive refrain. How, indeed?

By 1940 things were getting better. The European war that broke out in 1939 and the American military buildup that ensued made more jobs available. Ernest Stoneman and his older sons and daughters found permanent work in Washington; miners returned to work in the Virginias, Kentucky, and Alabama. The TVA placed the building of a second generation of dams on an expedited schedule, beginning with Fontana on the southern edge of Great Smoky Mountains National Park. The people who were forced off their land for this project found plenty of work in Alcoa or nearby Knoxville.

In 1942 Alan Lomax persuaded the Office of War Information to fund a recording trip to the Fontana region, whereby the inhabitants might record their views on patriotic sacrifice for dissemination by military propagandists. Instead of support for the government's action, however, Lomax found the same mix of confusion, regret, resignation, and resentment that interviewers had found in the Norris Basin eight years earlier. People leaving their mountain homes might eventually be better off, as many claimed in later decades, but in return for these long-term gains—quite uncertain from the perspective of 1940–41—they traded short-term upheaval and the permanent loss of their physical and emotional connections to viable communities. "Even while modernization may create better aggregate standards, better socioeconomic indices, more mobility, more advantages, and more opportunities, there was a very radical trade-off involved for many of these [Appalachian] families. And that trade-off was in the loss of a closeness and an identity not easily replaced in most modern societies. . . . [W]ithin this sense of modernization runs the desire for the retention of old cultural values associated with a poorer, harder way of life."[71]

The country music to which Appalachian migrants listened in their new homes and in urban bars and roadside taverns expressed a nostalgia for this way of life that gradually eroded the stinging memories of hardship, replacing them with a sentimental view of country living that belied the manner in which most mountaineers of the mid-twentieth century would live. An equally sentimental, though classier, view of Appalachia's past premiered in Washington when the Library of Congress's Music Division presented the ballet *Appalachian Spring* in 1943. The composer Aaron Copland, a native of New York City, teamed up with the Los Angeles–born dancer Martha Graham to create a modern classic. Originally titled "Ballet for Martha," Copland's score drew on old hymns and folk tunes that were not specific to Appalachia, while Graham's choreography created archetypical ballet characters: a pair of mountain sweethearts, a "Pioneer Woman" as a kind of fairy godmother, and a villain in the form of a menacing preacher. As much as any cultural production of its day, *Appalachian Spring* fixed the mountain region indelibly in American minds as a territory of images, a place apart from the mainstream, with timeless ways of life divorced from hard realities. Written for a chamber orchestra, Copland's music in due course became a kind of regional anthem, scored for symphony orchestras and even for marching bands, identifying a place at once haunted and beautiful, a place that always will be—and never was.

In the dead of the night,

In the still and the quiet

I slip away like a bird in flight

Back to those hills, the place that I call home.

—Hazel Dickens, "West Virginia, My Home"

I was so hell-bent on leaving. They tell you
you're going have to go, there are no jobs here.
There aren't a lot of jobs here, but you must
make some choices. You have to get on one side
or the other. Why should county people leave
the county to the tourists?

—Julie Colvard, Ashe County, N.C., 1975,
in *The Past Is Another Country*

CHAPTER FIVE

Crisis and Renewal, 1930–2000

Helen Matthews was born in Jackson County, Georgia, but when she was ten her parents moved to Cumming, the Forsyth County seat, and she always considered herself a "north Georgia girl . . . one of the hill people." She was not the first of her family to live on the southern edge of the mountains. One set of ancestors had come down from Virginia as part of the Calhoun colony that settled Long Cane Creek in the South Carolina backcountry in the 1750s. Another had founded the town of Auraria in the antebellum Georgia gold field. Her own family, in 1934, was modestly prosperous. Her father was a rural mail carrier, and the home he found for his family was just off Highway 19, one of the Lakes-to-Florida highways that southern states had stitched together in hopes of capturing Yankee tourists, at least for a night or two.

Locally, Highway 19 was celebrated for other reasons. It was at that time one of the only paved highways in north Georgia and thus a favorite route for whiskey haulers making their runs from the mountains into Atlanta. Helen recalls that on warm evenings she and her playmates would listen for the distinctive sound of souped-up engines and hope that they would get to see the cops chasing the bootleggers. "Some of the kids could recognize whose car was being chased: Roy Hall or Parker Seay," Helen recalls. "They were like folk heroes for they were also race car drivers on their days off," racing other drivers on a dirt track just outside Dawsonville in the next county north. Along with similar young men in similar places in Tennessee and the Carolinas, these guys were helping to create the sport of stock-car racing, the upland South's unique contribution to the sports entertainment culture of the American century. The Dawsonville Pool Room is still maintained as a shrine to these "good ol' boys with bad ol' reputations," while Helen Matthews has never forgotten the day when a girlfriend of Seay's drove down in his convertible and gave the Cumming kids a ride.[1]

There were few other connections between this part of Georgia and Atlanta at this time. The Chattahoochee River had not yet been dammed and there was no Lake Lanier flooding the county's best bottomlands. There were no weekend retreats and certainly no commuters. But lots of rural Georgians were moving into Atlanta, and Matthews, after college in Milledgeville and a year of graduate school at Duke University, became one of them. Georgia was the first state to give eighteen-year-olds the vote in 1945. Helen Matthews became a youth organizer for a progressive Democratic coalition led by Ellis Arnall, the state's wartime governor and a hero of southern liberals in those days, in its struggle with Eugene Talmadge, Georgia's contribution to the roster of southern demagogues who flourished during the first half of the twentieth century. Her candidate to succeed Arnall won the popular vote in the 1946 Democratic primary but lost the election because of the county-unit system, an extreme Georgia version of an electoral college.

Talmadge died before he could take office, however. His son, Herman, disputed the incoming lieutenant governor's right of succession, but after the state supreme court sided with the latter, Matthews got a job in the governor's office. In 1948 she was arrested for participation in an interracial meeting in the Atlanta CIO office. Meanwhile, she married Judd Lewis, whom she had met at Duke, and in due course went off with him to the University of Virginia (UVA) so he could study for his doctorate. Though women were not admitted as undergraduates at "Mr. Jefferson's university," they could take graduate classes. Helen Lewis got her master's degree in sociology from Virginia in 1949, writing her thesis on "The Woman Movement and the Negro

Movement: Parallel Struggles for Rights." She taught a few undergraduate classes, worked in various research capacities, and then moved with her husband to Richmond, where she worked two years as a social worker.

Lewis hated Charlottesville, with its genteel pretensions and cultivated conservatism that contrasted so strongly with the postwar ferment she encountered on campuses in North Carolina and Georgia. But it was her UVA connection that led her to her ultimate vocation as a scholar-activist in Appalachia. Under pressure to serve more people without diluting its special brand of Virginian elitism, UVA created a series of campuses around the state, most of which eventually grew into a system of regional universities. Clinch Valley College in the far southwest corner of the state, however, remained a UVA branch, serving coalfield communities that had been hit hard by the mechanization of mining and the consequent unemployment. Helen and Judd Lewis both got jobs at the college and moved to Wise in 1955. A decade later, Helen won a National Science Foundation fellowship and went off to the University of Kentucky, from which she received her doctorate in sociology in 1970.

Lewis could have taken her fellowship money elsewhere, including Berkeley, where she had begun the continuation of her graduate studies at a summer institute in 1962. She chose Kentucky in 1964 because that was the best place to study a subject that had already begun to fascinate her: the social order of the Appalachian coalfields. Elsewhere, although regionalism was a prominent intellectual strain in history, English, and social science departments, Appalachia did not appear on most regionalists' academic maps. At a conference of prominent academic regionalists funded by the Rockefeller Foundation at Madison, Wisconsin, in 1946, neither the name nor the concept of Appalachia came up for discussion.[2] The University of Kentucky had a cadre of sociologists whose research was focused on eastern Kentucky, though even there Lewis found "a very traditional program, not one Appalachian course of any kind," and a distance between professors and students that she found hard to take as a mature woman. "I got through that program as fast as I could," she remembers. Despite the alienating experience, her work at Kentucky provided a foundation for the sort of activist research that she helped to call into being in Appalachia.[3]

Sociologists were not the only ones illuminating the trials of Appalachian families during the postwar years. This period saw the emergence of a literary movement that combined the social realism of earlier writers with the narrative traditions of Appalachian folktales and balladry. Harriette Arnow, Davis Grubb, Wilma Dykeman, and Don West all came to the attention of critics and readers during this time. But they were not the first Appalachian writers, at least in the geographical sense. Louise McNeill of West Virginia had achieved modest success as a poet with *Mountain White* (1931) and *Gauley Mountain* (1939); James Still and Jesse Stuart began publishing their stories of eastern Kentucky at the same time that Thomas Wolfe, in short stories published late in his brief life, turned his gaze outward from Asheville toward the surrounding mountains. The special circumstances of mountain people and life were at the center of the postwar generation's fictional universe. Like the data turned up by the Kentucky sociologists and other investigators, the fiction of the narrative realists illuminates the contours of Appalachian history during the second half of the century.

It has been said that all mountain regions must import capital or export people. During most of the twentieth century, Appalachia did both. During the first third of the century, as in the last third of the nineteenth, most of the capital came from private sources in the Northeast and Midwest. Beginning with Franklin D. Roosevelt's New Deal in 1933, the federal government became a major new source of investment in Appalachia. The motivation for federal investments varied according to time and project, but generally they sought to stem the tide of migrants whom the failures of market-driven development intermittently washed out of the region. With only their labor to invest and in numbers that exceeded the region's capacity to support its population through agriculture, forestry, and mining, most Appalachian migrants had little choice but to go wherever work could be found. The many experts who traversed the region from the 1930s onward saw depopulation as an obvious solution to many problems, but the receptivity of migrant destinations and the approval of Washington bureaucrats varied according to the rate of urban unemployment. Local leaders never willingly embraced a solution that deprived mountain localities of workers and voters. Nevertheless, migration remained a fact of Appalachian life throughout the twentieth century.

The Appalachian core sustained a net population loss through migration as early as 1910, but such losses were disguised, up until the 1950 census, by a relatively high birthrate and by the seemingly temporary nature of war-related migration during the two world wars. It now seems clear that population losses would have occurred even earlier and certainly would have cut deeper without industrialization, for as we saw in the previous chapter, Appalachian families already confronted a demographic crisis as smaller and less productive mountain farms were subdivided repeatedly among the members of large families. During World War I, military service and opportunities for work in booming northern cities drew still more people out of the mountains. "Money is plentiful but people scarce," wrote a West Virginia observer in 1917. "There is a restless flocking hither and thither, to the towns in the first case and afterward to the big cities. . . . They sell their farms for what they can get; or even where they can get nothing they abandon them."[4]

It was during this period that the tire-making city of Akron became "the capital of West Virginia" and the beachheads of Kentucky migration were established in Cincinnati, Dayton, and other industrial cities in southwest Ohio. During the 1920s, although the populations of both the core and the official regions grew on the whole, a belt of agricultural counties in Kentucky and West Virginia actually lost population, notwithstanding high birthrates. This pattern reversed itself during the 1930s, as agricultural counties drew unemployed industrial workers back home and mining counties grew or remained static. Thus the total population count of the region continued to increase during the Depression decade, by 7 percent in the official region, 14 percent in the core. The number of black mountaineers showed a much smaller increase, however (2.5 percent and 1.3 percent, respectively), forecasting a trend that would increase dramatically after 1940, whereby African Americans moved out of Appalachia in much higher proportions than whites.[5] Among the most significant changes that migration brought about in the second half of the twentieth century, the outflow of black residents made the Appalachian region decidedly whiter.

The connection between official policies and the Appalachian diaspora was obvious in the cases of those expelled from their homes to make way for TVA lakes or national parks or the secret military reservation that the government built near Oak Ridge, Tennessee, during the Second World War. But the great majority of migrants left home voluntarily, under no compulsion save their own circumstances. Moreover, people from Appalachia—or at least the southern two-thirds of the official region—were part of an even larger exodus that headed north and west from the upland South. Appalachian migrants comprised the majority of those white southerners who moved north and received the lion's share of attention from officials and experts who considered the matter.[6] Official responses to the exodus varied according to timing and circumstances. It seems clear, however, that although many federal programs in Appalachia ostensibly tried to halt the flow of people from the region, the

—overall federal impact tended to stimulate it. The twinned topics of migration and federal policies in Appalachia must be sorted out for the sake of discussion, but these topics are really two sides of the same coin.

Understanding the sources, volume, and flow of Appalachian migration and documenting the rural society from which it issued became the life's work of Helen Lewis's mentor at Kentucky, the sociologist James S. Brown. A native Kentuckian and Berea College graduate, Brown had studied at Harvard with Pitrim Sorokin and Talcott Parsons, two of the leading American social theorists of the day. Parsons directed Brown's doctoral dissertation, "Social Organization of an Isolated Mountain Neighborhood," based on fieldwork carried out in Kentucky between 1942 and 1944. Brown called his study area Beech Creek, although in fact the actual research site was a different watershed several miles distant from the Clay County stream of that name; the pseudonymous geography served to protect the privacy of informants who confided personal information, family histories, and community gossip and lore during Brown's interviews.[7] Even though it wasn't published until nearly forty years after its completion, Brown's study, in dissertation form, circulated widely among scholars, along with a followup study published in 1971 that traced migrants from Beech Creek to their new homes in the Midwest. Beech Creek joined Middletown, Yankee City, and Southern Town among the classic pseudonymous locales of this genre.

The Beech Creek project produced a complex and nuanced portrait of an Appalachian community at a turning point in its history. Settled in the early nineteenth century, Beech Creek had become poor and crowded in its fourth generation. Migration seemed the only solution, and in fact had been under way for a generation before the sociologists came around. The regional survey that the federal Bureau of Agricultural Economics (BAE) completed in 1935 concluded that migration was both inevitable and desirable.[8] More intensive followup studies in two Kentucky and two North Carolina mountain counties agreed. The Great Depression, however, had sent many of the early Appalachian migrants home, where they "doubled up" in parental households or searched out scraps of available land to establish new farms of their own. The BAE reported that, in some mountain counties, the number of new farms and new farmers surged by as much as 51 percent between 1929 and 1934, with no appreciable increase in the amount of available farmlands.[9] This meant that already small homeplaces were being further subdivided among family members or leased out to tenants or sharecroppers.

Even within the context of southern poverty, Appalachian farms were poor. Farm incomes in eastern Kentucky averaged less than a tenth of similar incomes in the nearby Bluegrass. The southern Appalachian region contained fifty-two of the sixty-four U.S. counties with per-capita farm incomes of less than $100 in 1929.[10] Thus, even if the new farms managed to keep people fed, which for the most part they did, the cost was high in terms of both human and environmental degradation. Under the New Deal, an expanded U.S. Department of Agriculture (USDA) developed programs (such as the Soil Conservation Service and the Agricultural Conservation Program) to protect and restore abused mountain land. But what about the people who scratched out a subsistence from this land? The most consistent answer during the 1930s was relief, either direct through cash payments or indirect through employment by CWA, PWA, FERA, WPA or some other among the new "alphabet agencies."

These "transfer payments," as they are called on national economic balance sheets, were essential, even for what was by national standards a very low level of living. In 1935, Appalachia contained twenty-one of twenty-nine U.S. counties in which the number of persons on relief exceeded 36 percent or more of the 1930 population: eleven counties in Kentucky, five in West Virginia, two each in Alabama and Pennsylvania, and one in Tennessee. The study that came up with these figures concluded that, while the region's mining counties were in bad shape, in the agricultural counties things had gone from bad to worse and that these were "areas marked either for 'permanent poverty' or for a drastic reduction of population."[11]

The Depression-era studies demonstrated that the Appalachian crisis was not so much a crisis in agriculture, for mountain farms had reached the limit of self-sufficiency long before 1929, as the pattern of migration from farm counties demonstrated. Rather, the crisis stemmed from the loss of "public work" in mines, mills, and forests on which the majority of rural families had come to depend. The Appalachian region had the nation's greatest concentration of so-called self-sufficient farms in 1930, plus an even larger concentration of part-time farms, where people got by through a combination of agricultural and nonagricultural work.[12] With opportunities for part-time work off the farm limited, and with little or no reserves of suitable agricultural land—indeed, with vast amounts of land that had been abused past its ability to support pastures or crops—there was little that agricultural experts could recommend apart from "rehabilitation" and "resettlement." Both of these terms became controversial and were replaced by euphemisms, but the formulas remained. Rehabilitation promoted improved farming practices, better stocks of working animals and seeds, and soil, water, and forest conservation. Resettlement meant moving "stranded" families (like the former miners who moved into the model village at Arthurdale) and those who occupied marginal land into settings where they could use their farming skills to feed themselves while depending on some kind of nonfarm work for a minimal but necessary cash income.

"Marginal," in practice, meant mostly landless families living as tenants or laborers. Notwithstanding changes in nomenclature from "resettlement" to "farm security," relocation programs usually aroused furious opposition from the American Farm Bureau and conservative politicians, owing to the threat that resettlement posed to the supply of cheap agricultural labor. The price-support programs of the agricultural New Deal—subsidies for commercial field crops that a majority of market-oriented farmers and their spokesmen also managed to embrace—had the long-term effect of promoting farm mechanization and benefiting landowners and agricultural productivity but throwing thousands upon thousands of tenants, sharecroppers, and agricultural laborers off of the land. Although this particular impact of federal policy was greater in the staple-crop producing areas of the plantation South than in Appalachia, those who opposed New Deal programs designed to cope with the human dimension of the problem drew no distinction between mountains and lowlands.

Also of some concern was the matter of what the people at whom these programs were directed might prefer, though this never became a basis of policymaking. Fieldwork by the BAE in 1936 revealed that mountaineers were much more willing to change occupations than locations, an indication that "to many people a stable environment, although achieved at the expense of an occupational readjustment, seems preferable to the unstable environment which allegiance to a particular calling sometimes entails."[13] Although we have no record of resentments as bitter as those voiced by people forced off their land by the TVA or the national parks, we can safely assume that attachment to mountain homes and communities was a factor in individual decisions about whether to leave or to stay. Permanent migration frequently followed a lengthy experience of "shuttle migration" or "sojourning," moving back and forth in response to specific needs and opportunities with no conscious intention of making a permanent move. More than half of the migrants from Beech Creek, for example, returned at least once to Kentucky before making their final "big move."[14] Such practices made it easier for some migrants to postpone a final decision until they reached a point at which their lives had become centered elsewhere and permanency became a matter simply of accepting the fact that they were never going home. But even the most realistic migrant approached her or his circumstances with a "divided heart."[15]

Even in the best of circumstances, resettlement meant finding adequately remunerative and reliable nonfarm work for the migrants, and, since relocating them to industrial cities was clearly out of the question during the 1930s, there seemed to be no official solution that did not involve larger and more permanent federal subsidies than the political climate of the late thirties was likely to support. Among the New Deal crop-support programs, only one had any relevance to mountain agriculture: the tobacco price-support program. The increase in cigarette smoking—itself a product of urbanization and the accompanying shift of tobacco users from outdoor to indoor work—created a greater demand for burley tobacco, a beautiful but (as we now know) carcinogenic plant whose desirable smoking qualities flourished in the stressful ecological conditions of small patches of mountain land. The BAE and Farm Security Adminstration (FSA) experts who surveyed Appalachia included expanded tobacco production in their recommendations for improvement wherever possible, and in fact tobacco spread steadily as a cash crop among mountain farmers able and willing to negotiate the web of subsidies and regulations that comprised the price-support program. Otherwise, migration was the only answer to the problem of too many people on too little good land, even though in the 1930s no one was able or willing to articulate, except in the most abstract terms, exactly who should leave for which destinations, and at whose cost.

Appalachian migration resumed with the return of prosperity during World War II. Of the 399 persons living in the Beech Creek neighborhood in 1942, 251 were living elsewhere ten years later; another 149 left during the following decade.[16] Thanks to natural increase and some in-migration (mostly to urban areas), the population of Appalachia as a whole grew between 1940 and 1950, by 4.5 percent in the official region and 8.2 percent in the core, but the overall loss from net migration during this decade exceeded 700,000.[17] In agricultural counties with few opportunities for mining, logging, or industrial work, emigration outran natural increase and population declined. Clay County's population decline of 3.3 percent during the 1940s was modest in comparison with the sixteen other Kentucky mountain counties whose decline ranged from 4 to 24 percent.[18] In other states, Gilmer, Braxton, Tucker, and Pocahontas Counties in West Virginia all suffered population losses greater than 15 percent, as did Highland, Virginia, Swain, North Carolina, Hancock, Tennessee, and Dawson, Georgia, in the core region, along with several counties in Georgia, Alabama, and Mississippi located on the official region's southern edge. Birthrates also fell during the postwar period, making the total population loss from farming counties even more drastic. By contrast, urban counties grew rapidly during this decade, though none so dramatically as Anderson County, Tennessee, the home of Oak Ridge, where population increased 124 percent.

Miners, loggers, and millhands soon followed the farmers as wartime demand on their industries waned. After protracted negotiations culminating in a bitter strike in 1950–51, the United Mine Workers and the coal operators' association entered into an agreement that traded union acceptance of mechanization and the resulting loss of jobs for high wages and a health and welfare fund that promised comfortable retirements and good medical care for both retirees and active miners. At about the same time, the coal operators began a massive selloff of company-owned property, allowing miners to acquire their own homes but forcing local governments in the coalfields to assume responsibility for many of the services that company towns had heretofore provided. Nothing in the agreement addressed the needs of young people coming of age in the coal towns, since the number of new jobs was expected to decline slowly but steadily.

As events unfolded, however, the productivity gains and consequent job losses came quickly, the promised benefits more slowly if at all. The UMWA health and welfare fund, financed by royalties on coal output, was depleted within a few years and its commitments sharply cut back or passed along to public welfare agencies. These developments led to a "great migration" from Appalachia's mining counties and the further impoverishment of many of those who were left behind. During the 1950s, the mining counties of Kentucky, the Virginias, Tennessee, and Alabama suffered population losses of between 15 and 30 percent; the Pennsylvania anthracite counties lost smaller percentages, mainly because they had already started exporting people during the 1940s. The official Appalachian region lost more than two million people during the 1950s, just under a million of them from the core; even though metropolitan areas such as Charleston, Asheville, Knoxville, and Chattanooga expanded, they failed to grow as fast as comparable areas in other parts of the nation.

Writing in 1961, James S. Brown remarked that he was "just thunderstruck by how many people have left that part of the country" and noted, "There are many more people . . . that I knew 15 years ago on Beech Creek in Clay County now in South Lebanon, Ohio, than there are on Beech Creek itself today."[19] The Beech Creek studies revealed some of the dynamics of migration as it affected—and was shaped by—Appalachian communities. The influence of class structure was one of Brown's most surprising discoveries. Whereas mountain communities seemed homogeneous to most outside observers, Beech Creek had a class structure that ordered family standing in the

Appalshop filmmakers Elizabeth Barret and Frances Morton pose with a coal miner in 1982. Although women had worked around the mines during both world wars, their right to regular employment underground was established during the 1970s by the Coal Employment Project and the persistent demand among Appalachian women for access to what were still the best-paying jobs available in many communities. (Courtesy of Appalshop)

community according to conformity with behavioral and cultural norms as well as relative wealth. Higher-class families revealed different migratory patterns than lower-class ones. They were under less pressure to leave, took more resources with them to ease their passage when they did leave, and were less likely to cluster in low-income communities or low-paying jobs after reaching their destinations. Lower-class families were just the opposite; having fewer options and resources, they were more likely to cluster near other Appalachian migrants and more likely to end up in low-skilled, low-paying jobs.

From the standpoint of other aspects of social structure, the migration experience cut across class lines. Migrants tended to be young adults, with very young children, if any. Single men were more likely to establish their own households at the new destination, whereas single women were more likely to move in with relatives or friends. Temporary migration often preceded a permanent move, especially among more mature households where the breadwinner was in the twenty-five-to-forty-five age cohort. Chain migration linked specific communities of origin to specific neighborhoods and employment patterns in destination cities; broader regions were linked as parts of "migration systems." Thus, Kentuckians and western West Virginians moved to Ohio, Indiana, and Michigan; Virginians and eastern West Virginians moved to Washington-Baltimore; Georgia, Alabama, and the Carolinas absorbed more of their own Appalachian migrants than did other states, thanks to the postwar growth of such cities as Atlanta, Birmingham, Charlotte, Winston-Salem, and Greensboro.

Within these broader patterns migration wove connections between specific communities of origin and destination: between the Little Kanawha valley of West Virginia and Akron, for example, or between Cocke County, Tennessee, and Cleveland or Harlan County, Kentucky, and Detroit. The link between Ashtabula, Ohio, and the White Sulphur Springs area was established in 1938 when a patron at The Greenbrier, White Sulphur's luxury resort, offered his caddy a job at his Ohio factory. Eventually some fifty mountaineers followed the caddy's path. Another migrant path connected Ashtabula with Tucker County, West Virginia, but migrants from the dying mining and lumber towns there could also make for beachheads established by kin and former neighbors in Washington and Baltimore.

Often, migrants from Appalachia tried more than one destination before settling down. This was the case with Lawrence Elmo Brown, an African American from Wytheville, Virginia. Brown saw action in Korea and was wounded there, but when he returned home from the army in 1953 he found only menial jobs available to him. At first he and his wife tried Detroit, but in 1956 they moved on to Ashtabula where an uncle had established himself. Blacks faced segregated housing in Ohio just as they had in Virginia, but at least some factories would hire them at the same wages as whites.[20]

Ties even linked Appalachian places and specific employers in the destination localities. The connection between Ashtabula and Wytheville, for example, originated because Union Carbide, a major employer in northeast Ohio, had a calcium carbide processing plant at Ivanhoe on the New River. At Armco Steel in Middletown, Ohio, the boundary between two departments was humorously (but not unrealistically) denoted as the line between two adjacent Kentucky counties, Morgan and Wolfe.[21] Further research in Beech Creek and in the destination cities of Ohio and Indiana where Beech Creekers settled enabled Brown and his colleagues to document these patterns in fine detail, coupling personal histories to statistical overviews. The fieldwork that supported this project was nearing completion as Helen Lewis arrived at the University of Kentucky.

Brown and his colleagues argued also that migration patterns were shaped by cultural values, and that these too functioned as part of the rural community's class structure. The data they collected confirmed the social theories of Talcott Parsons, who emerged in the postwar period as one of American social science's leading theorists of modernization, defined as the successful adaptation of groups and individuals to the social structure and economic patterns of the postwar world led by the United States and its western European and Japanese allies. Today we recognize that modernization theory was shaped at least in part by the ideology of liberal American scholars and politicians during the Cold War.[22]

Parsons's theory posited "modern" as a complex of social attitudes and behaviors opposed to another complex called "traditional." Modern behavior was rational, purposeful, and optimistic, devoted to individual achievements in wealth and well-being in a world ordered by advanced industrial capitalism and the social welfare state. Democratic politics shaped specific government policies within a broad consensus that abjured extremes of wealth and poverty and promised all competitors for government power and economic success fair access under well-understood and enforced rules—a Fair Deal, in other words, as President Harry S Truman promised in his successful campaign for reelection in 1948. Under this system, individuals or groups whose needs were unmet by the system were expected to band together in "interest groups" in order to change it. Those whose needs could not be met by the system—for example, the sons and daughters of Appalachian farmers or miners who found no hope of prosperity in their native communities—were expected to rethink their aspirations and to change their goals. In other words, they were expected to adjust.

The promotion of adjustment was a goal of most welfare and educational agencies during the Cold War era, as it was at the core of the bitter experience of Gertie Nevels, the fictional migrant heroine of Harriette Arnow's *The Dollmaker* (1954). Well-adjusted persons were said to be "functional," in that they were able to negotiate effectively the social pathways that led them toward their goals. People who did not adjust were "dysfunctional" in their social contexts. Any reluctance or inability to undertake adjustment was, in and of itself, evidence of not being modern. Traditionalism was one of the brakes on contemporary social development that modernizers expected to overcome.

The traditionalism of Beech Creek at the time Brown initiated his fieldwork manifested itself in several ways. "Familialism" was the most pervasive value he documented. Family members cooperated within a strict patriarchal hierarchy and gendered division of labor and supported the family against all perceived external threats. Depending on circumstances, familial expectations extended to cousins and in-laws as well as stem-family kin. More important, those who did not uphold their assigned roles met with community disapproval—for example, fathers who did not support their children or husbands who beat their wives, but also wives who dominated their husbands and dissolute sons or daughters who "got in trouble" through sexual transgressions or crime. These expectations were enforced by a second pervasive value that Brown labeled "puritanism," though "fundamentalism" frequently stood in for this term in his writings and those of other social scientists.

Fundamentalists belonged to "sects" as often as to churches; they enforced a strict code of conduct based on a rigorous adherence to biblical injunctions as interpreted mainly by unlettered preachers. Moral transgressions not followed by quick and usually public contrition were grounds for withholding fellowship and lowering the status of the transgressor and his or her family in the community. The occupational and economic status of individual families had a lesser impact in determining the family's position in the social structure than did its standing in a fundamentalist moral order. In place of the educated clergy and programmatic support of social adjustment typical of mainstream Protestant and liberal Catholic religionists, fundamentalist congregations were led by untrained and typically part-time preachers whose gospel emphasized Old Testament justice and the punishments of hellfire.[23]

Fundamentalism among Appalachian mountaineers was in turn related to another pervasive value: fatalism, which outside observers variously explained as passive acceptance of one's earthly state in expectation of a better life in the hereafter, disdain if not outright hostility for the social-gospel activism of mainstream churches, and an indifference to the instrumentalities for social change and individual advancement presented by the welfare state and democratic politics. And yet, as Brown was careful to point out, Beech Creekers were democratic in their outlook as far as social equality was concerned. All men and their families were figuratively if not literally equal according to the community value system; in fact, one of the causes of passivity in the face of so many problems was the anxiety among potential leaders to avoid the appearance of "putting on airs."

Modernizers from the BAE and New Deal relief agencies had earlier encountered this pattern of community values in Appalachia but had not made general statements about it, preferring instead to attribute variations in individuals' responsiveness to modernizing programs or opportunities to personal attributes such as "shiftlessness."[24] The Beech Creek studies systematized such observations and imbued them with the credibility of social scientific theory and methods. Brown and his colleagues also identified connections between community values and social structure, pointing out that before and after migration and during the transitional period of adjustment in between, higher-class Beech Creekers, whether at home or north of the Ohio River, were more successful in terms of modernization. Brown approvingly cited the example of a high-class Beech Creek family whose status was rooted in their reputation for intelligence and industriousness, clean living, and intermarriage with other "good livers" with equal standing but larger amounts of property. When Brown entered the community, husband and wife

were respected as unusually hard-working and thrifty. They bought a farm which was as good as any place in the neighborhood . . . [with] a nice four-room house, not new but well taken care of. The house was kept immaculately clean, the yard neatly mowed. For years [the husband] went out during the winter to Louisville, Hamilton, and other industrial cities to work, leaving his family behind. By 1942, their children had migrated from the creek, and the father and mother were alone. They had a fine garden, canned much food, raised hogs for meat and lard, and were relatively self-sufficient. . . . Their five children had "turned out well." All finished the eighth grade; one was a trained nurse. Another went to Ohio to work and married an engineer. A third daughter had recently gone to work in a defense plant in Ohio. One son lived in Hamilton, Ohio, and another was in the army.[25]

"Low-class" families in the neighborhood, on the other hand, were much less likely to be descended from the Creek's original settlers than families of the high class; they were half as likely to own no land of their own, to live in tumbledown, ill-cared-for houses with trash-filled yards, to commit sexual transgressions and get in trouble with the law, and to depend on government handouts and irregular work for cash incomes. "Low-class people in general did not have the drive to 'amount to something' like high-class people. They were usually less interested in education and were less educated than people of [higher status]"; by way of further contrast, they seemed to "live more for the present and less for the future." However, they also "seemed more happy and contented than any other group in the society. They appeared more relaxed and less restrained, in the way the low-class Negro in the Deep South seems more relaxed and less restrained."[26]

In terms of the popular stereotypes through which most twentieth-century Americans identified the Appalachian mountaineer, low-class Beech Creekers brought to life Li'l Abner, while their high-class neighbors reminded folks of Sergeant York. Thus, the Beech Creek studies linked social theory with popular stereotypes and embedded both linkages in an engaging web of careful participant observation and telling anecdote. Other case studies of specific communities—John B. Stephenson's *Shiloh* in the North Carolina Blue Ridge, for example, or Jack Weller's book, *Yesterday's People: Life in Contemporary Appalachia*, set in Lincoln County, West Virginia—extended the influence of this approach to understanding Appalachian life.[27]

As John C. Campbell had done for an earlier generation, Brown and other social science investigators elaborated on a full range of social types, including many "intermediate-class" families who displayed traits of both the higher and lower classes of mountaineers. Other writers who took up the cultural and social dimensions of the postwar Appalachian crisis were less careful. Harry M. Caudill, a lawyer from Whitesburg, Kentucky, published *Night Comes to the Cumberlands: The Biography of a Depressed Area*, which became a nonfiction best-seller in 1962. A skillful writer whose book was suffused with love for his native land and indignation at its fate, Caudill addressed general readers—that ill-defined but influential segment of the audience that paid less attention to Appalachian social reality than Talcott Parsons or James Brown but more than Al Capp, Li'l Abner's creator.

This audience was already prepared to believe the worst about mountain people, thanks to Arnold J. Toynbee, whose magnum opus, *A Study of History*, published in a 600-page abridgment in 1947, became a surprise success in the United States, selling over 200,000 copies in hardcover and helping to renew in the postwar generation the notion that "the Appalachian 'mountain people' to-day are no better than barbarians . . . a people who have acquired civilization and then lost it."[28] Toynbee attributed this barbarism largely to the persistence and decay of the mountaineers' Irish Protestant inheritance. Caudill—not surprisingly, given his own genealogy—looked elsewhere for an explanation of the deplorable cultural traits he found in eastern Kentucky, reviving an obsolete and unproven thesis of the Social Darwinist historian John Fiske, to the effect that Appalachia's original settlers came from the ranks of indentured servants brought to the Chesapeake and Delaware colonies during the eighteenth century as the dregs of English society and the refuse of London's jails. Once in the mountains, Caudill argued, geography isolated these settlers, leading to a "depleted gene pool" among their descendants, which in turn explained the unambitious and socially dysfunctional character of Appalachian people today.

Appealing directly to policymakers, Caudill described the bleak prospects of eastern Kentucky and argued in his concluding chapter for an Appalachian regional agency modeled on the TVA. At the same time, he provided a damning indictment of the TVA for ignoring the social and environmental consequences of its purchases of low-cost, strip-mined Kentucky coal. In *Night Comes to the Cumberlands* and a series of later books, he identified and condemned the resident and nonresident exploiters who created Appalachia's colonial economy and the shortsighted and corrupt local politicians who starved education and other public services in order to keep taxes low for coal and timber companies while monopolizing courthouse and schoolhouse jobs for themselves. Yet Caudill's musings on population history and genetics tacitly gave readers permission to blame the mountain people themselves for their circumstances.

Jack Weller also addressed policymakers, and although he came up with a more realistic and fairer view of history—arguing that Appalachian people were trapped within a culture of traditionalism and poverty that he attributed to the deficiencies of the region's agricultural and industrial economies—he also concluded his volume with a helpful thirty-four-item "comparative summary" of "middle class American" and "Southern Appalachian" values. Under the personal traits of mountaineers, Weller listed individualism, traditionalism, fatalism, anxiety, inadequate savings and budgeting, a preference for anecdote, action, and personal interests over abstractions, long-range planning, and group goals, a disinclination to follow the advice of experts, and "stress on traditional masculinity." Under family life, he described Appalachian families as being adult centered and male dominated, with permissive —

childrearing habits, strictly gendered work roles and social lives, and "separation of family and outside world" (contrasted with the middle-class family as a "bridge" to the world). As for "relationships with others," Weller contended that mountain people were person- rather than object-oriented, did not seek status, preferred "leveling" to middle-class "striving" in society, did not join groups generally, and, when in groups, were able "to function only on a personal basis." "Detachment from work; little concern for job security or satisfaction," "ambivalence toward education," "fear of doctors, hospitals, those in authority, the well-educated," antagonism and suspicion of government and the outside world generally, and "rejection of organized amusements, cultural activities, etc." rounded out the list.[29]

It is useful at this point to recall that the generation of academic social scientists led nationally and regionally, respectively, by men like Talcott Parsons and James S. Brown laid claim to the credibility and prestige accorded to physical sciences during the postwar era. The access their disciplines were given to the National Science Foundation (NSF) when it was created in 1947 was one mark of their success. So was increasing access to private foundations and other Washington funding agencies. The original Beech Creek fieldwork was financed by Harvard University and by Brown's personal resources, for example; the followup study on migration and adjustment was funded by the National Institute of Health. The Ford Foundation invested $250,000 in a regional survey launched at the University of Kentucky in 1958 and another $20,000 in a workshop on "urban adjustment of Southern Appalachian Migrants" held at Berea in 1959 and followed by a weeklong bus tour of mountain counties between Berea and Knoxville.[30] The Rockefeller Foundation had funded migration studies during the prewar era, but federal agencies generally sent their own experts into the field, sometimes taking academics along with them, but usually with the expectation of giving rather than receiving advice.[31]

Postwar academics, however, expected to make their impact on the world by offering expert guidance without surrendering their university posts, except perhaps on a temporary basis, as happened during World War II. The election of John F. Kennedy in 1960 and the subsequent inclusion in his presidential administration of prominent university faculty such as McGeorge Bundy, John Kenneth Galbraith, and Arthur Schlesinger Jr. of Harvard and W. W. Rostow of MIT made government more receptive than ever to the application of academic expertise to matters of public policy. Modernization theory had wide applicability to the Third World, where the United States was engaged in global competition with an alternative statist and socialist model of economic development sponsored by the Soviet Union. As Brown pointed out in his contributing chapter to the Ford survey, the lessons to be learned from the confrontation of modernity and tradition in Appalachia were potentially applicable to other "transitional" societies at home and abroad.[32] Similarly, the struggle for "hearts and minds" that America waged during the Cold War in Africa, Latin America, and Southeast Asia might have applicability in Appalachia.

Closer to home, the experts confronted the issue of what state and local governments should do to alleviate the Appalachian crisis. A leading folklorist, for example, received a grant to teach health-care workers in Detroit how to get Appalachian migrants to make better use of their services. In Georgia, a team of sociologists investigating Appalachian childrearing practices discovered that the "verbal inaccessibility" of mountaineers—that is, their inability or unwillingness to express themselves in the abstracted language of professionals during interviews or in answering questionnaires —impeded useful strategies for adjustment. This study, in turn, became a Forest Service history's excuse for relying only on official documents in compiling a history of that agency's role in the mountains.[33]

The authors of the Ford survey applauded an array of postwar achievements—new state parks and tourism promotion efforts, for example, or a profusion of new community hospitals, mostly funded by outside money from federal agencies or the United Mine Workers, that brought regional access to health care closer to national standards. The survey mapped hopeful progress and the distances still to be traveled between regional and national standards in social services, public libraries, highway transportation, and so on. Additional federal funding was justified in nearly every aspect of organized regional life. Yet in confronting the topics of the regional economy and public education, the survey's contributors were forced to confront the question of purpose. Mass migration during the 1950s and 1960s was now an established fact, not a potential solution. But then what? Should the exodus simply be allowed to continue until population fell to the level that postwar agriculture, mining, forestry, and tourism were able to support? Should Appalachian officials join in the hunt for branch plants and low-wage manufacturing that animated Mississippi and other southern states that wanted to "balance agriculture with industry?" (Actually, most already had, with disappointing results.)

The recessions of the Eisenhower years revived the concerns of destination cities about the large numbers of mountaineers moving into their towns; this consideration waned during the prosperous 1960s, but it remained a long-term worry. Throughout world history, mountain regions, with their traditionally high birthrates and generally healthful climates, have produced population surpluses that eventually invaded the lowlands in one manner or another. Even though birthrates in Appalachia fell after 1940, they still remained high by national standards. Where did Appalachia fit into the national scheme of things?

The question was particularly relevant in connection with education. When it was launched in 1958, the Ford Foundation survey was able to draw on a number of recent assessments of Appalachian schools conducted under state auspices. These found that, during the twenties and thirties, thanks to the impacts of business progressivism and the financial exigencies of the Depression, public schools in most Appalachian states had come under the direction of state education agencies. Kentucky was a partial exception; local authorities remained in control or at least continued to exercise strong influences in most eastern Kentucky localities, where they used the schools above all else as a source of political patronage. One result was that illiteracy rates in Kentucky remained relatively high throughout the first half of the twentieth century, exceeded among native whites in only two other states, New Mexico and Louisiana, both of which had large non–English-speaking minorities. The 1935 BAE study of 205 Appalachian counties disclosed that the highest rates of illiteracy were to be found in twenty eastern Kentucky counties and in thirteen others adjacent to Kentucky in Virginia and Tennessee.[34]

But even West Virginia, whose statewide rates of educational attainment were generally higher before 1950 than those of other southern Appalachian states, lagged significantly behind national standards. During the 1950s, all of the states moved closer to national norms, but national standards themselves were rapidly upgraded during the postwar era. Thus, while the average number of years of schooling for West Virginians moving to Ohio was roughly equal to that of Ohio natives, a child who transferred from an Appalachian to a non-Appalachian school was two or three years behind in educational achievement compared to northern urban schoolchildren in the same grade. Not surprisingly, teachers and administrators in the destination districts concluded that Appalachian children were dumb and that their low educational standing reflected inherited cultural outlooks.[35]

As we now know, expectations of educational failure have an impact on performance, and so it is no wonder that school failures and dropout rates in the destination communities of Appalachian migrants were higher than among comparable populations of native white midwesterners. One contribution to the Ford survey, Roscoe Griffin's "Appalachian Newcomers in Cincinnati," observed that, with respect to educational achievement and other measures of social adjustment, there were no significant differences between high-class and lower-class mountaineers and native white Ohioans of the corresponding class. But it also concluded, "Since a large proportion of the numerous Southern Appalachian newcomers in Cincinnati are among those of the lower social class, we must certainly conclude that professional workers associated with schools, churches, business, recreation, law enforcement, health, and welfare have not been engaging in sheer fabrication in reporting them a problem group."[36]

This being the case, experts were hard pressed to define the purpose of educational reform in the various Appalachian states. Orin Graff, a University of Tennessee professor who surveyed the region's schools for the Ford study, found it easy to map educational deficiencies in terms of per-pupil, per-teacher, and capital outlays and to call for "at least doubling expenditures for educational purposes." He also called for further school consolidation in conformity with the influential reform proposals of James B. Conant, the former Harvard University president, whose book *The American High School Today* "was found in 90 percent of the offices visited" in the course of Graff's research.[37] Graff found little evidence that the region's colleges and universities had an impact on primary or secondary education, even though most of them had been steadily turning out schoolteachers trained "to survive if not prosper in isolated districts and to spread genteel middle-class values in rural hardscrabble coal country."[38] (This was written about Fairmont State but was equally pertinent during the 1950s to Marshall, Appalachian State, East Tennessee State, Morehead State, or the region's dozens of small, mostly church-related colleges.)

The inculcation of middle-class norms along with a smattering of liberal learning was an extension of efforts begun by northern missionaries and educators at the turn of the century. The spread of high schools and of teachers' colleges augmented this sort of missionary work, along with the growing standardization of state curricula and graduation requirements. Yet, as Graff pointed out, existing curricula had little to do with the practical needs of Appalachian students. "The programs of most high schools in the Region offer little for the pupil who does not go to college," he stated—in other words, 55 percent or more of graduating seniors at the time of the survey, "not to mention the 44 to 63 percent of the pupils who had already dropped out." The

Smith-Hughes Act of 1917 had made federal funds available to schools for vocational agriculture programs, an effort that now seemed misplaced in view of the decline of farming in the region. Graff concluded with a call for vocational technical education, along with more money, better buildings, and consolidated schools.[39]

There was general agreement among experts that education should prepare students for effective participation in urban-industrial society, but in terms of Appalachia's postwar realities, this meant preparing students to leave. The students at the time were under no illusions in this regard. "Ozzie Stroud," interviewed in Chicago's Uptown migrant neighborhood in 1970, came from Mingo County, West Virginia, where his family had lived comfortably until his coal-miner father was disabled in 1959, forcing the family onto welfare. "As I remember most you either worked in the coal mines, or you was a schoolteacher, school bus driver, or you was on welfare. . . . It was a trend there that once you graduated from high school you went off to Chicago, Cleveland, Columbus, Baltimore, Detroit. I graduated at two o'clock on Sunday, June the fourth, 1967. Two o'clock Monday afternoon I was sitting in Columbus." When job hunting in Columbus didn't pan out, Stroud moved on to Chicago, where a married sister and her husband had relocated in 1964.[40]

Whether education prepared students to leave or to live better lives at home depended on the region's economy. It was one thing to call for more manufacturing jobs, quite another thing to create them. The spread of manufacturing into the cities of the Great Valley initially seemed a harbinger of the future, when the valley would once again be the economic core of Appalachia, as it had been in prerailroad times. And yet, while Roanoke kept pace with national growth during the fifties and sixties and the cities of Bristol, Kingsport, and Johnson City grew together into a new metropolitan area, Knoxville and Chattanooga each lost ground relative to national trends, as did Birmingham relative to Atlanta and Charleston and Huntington-Ashland relative to the cities of Ohio, Indiana, and Michigan. In fact, migrants from Ashland developed their own little corner of transplanted Kentucky in urban Cincinnati.

Chattanooga grew modestly, notwithstanding the appearance of a new industrial hinterland in the adjacent counties of northwest Georgia. "Tuftland," as boosters called the area that grew up around Dalton, originally developed as a center for making tufted bedspreads, rugs, and robes, first by hand methods that developed directly from traditional craftsmanship, then through the use of mechanized tufting machines. After World War II, local tinkerers figured out how to apply mechanical tufting to the manufacture of carpets.

The Dalton area boomed as tufted carpeting grabbed a larger and larger share of the nation's postwar market for "soft flooring," gaining population at a time when other north Georgia counties were still in decline. Chattanooga machine shops developed sidelines related to carpet manufacture, but the industry's financial and managerial sectors tended to migrate toward Atlanta or New York. In addition, despite its local origin and management, the tufted-carpet industry adopted the low-wage and antiunion policies that had traditionally characterized the southern textile industry. Although a shortage of workers and the impact of federal wages-and-hours legislation mitigated the worst abuses of this approach, the Dalton area maintained generally a nonunion, low-wage workforce at a time when the midwestern manufacturers of other consumer durables were providing the wages and benefits that made the American manufacturing worker's living standards the boast of what was called the "free world."[41]

"Tuftland" and Appalachia's major metropolitan areas aside, Appalachia in 1960 was still preponderantly rural (two-thirds of the 1960 census count, and even more if Asheville, Charleston, Chattanooga, Huntington–Ashland, Knoxville, and Bristol–Kingsport–Johnson City are subtracted from the regional core).[42] The region seemed likely to continue exporting people for the foreseeable future. In these circumstances, Rupert B. Vance, the North Carolina sociologist and dean of the surviving interwar regionalists, advised other experts to assign "area development" to the federal government while leaving "human development" to the states and localities.

The logic of the postwar economy prescribed metropolitan growth—boosting the region's cities and bolstering their ability to compete with the growing cities of the lowland Southeast and Midwest and thus their ability to absorb the surplus labor of rural Appalachia. "The tendency heretofore has been to speak of the Appalachians as an underdeveloped area, the implied assumption being that a high stage of development is a natural order to be achieved by all American regions," Vance noted. Yet the fact had to be faced that "certain developments should be fostered on the basis of the higher per capita income of a sparser population." Local authorities could hardly be expected to collaborate in seeking regional depopulation, however rational that goal might be from a planner's point of view. "What banker, what real estate owner, what school administrator wishes to aid in the depopulation of his community and thus weaken the basis of his business and of the community's social institutions?" For this reason, Vance advised separating the planning functions, reserving to regional and federal entities the hard choices to be made concerning the region's economic redevelopment and leaving to subre-

Both Appalachian State University and West Virginia University are "Mountaineers" in intercollegiate athletics. During the 1940s, not long after WVU adopted a buck-skin-clad frontier hero as its official mascot, rebellious students at Appalachian State traveled in the other direction, creating a hillbilly mascot named Yosef ("yourself"). In the summer of 1999, ASU administrators decided to "update" Yosef and hired a New York graphic design firm to work up a more contemporary image. The result caused an uproar among students and alumni: a kind of slicked-up "country chic" mascot, clean-shaven and garbed in a cowboy hat and L. L. Bean clothes. With-drawn after only one appearance, the new Yosef eventually got his beard back, though it's trimmer than before, but hiking boots cover his feet and he now wears suspenders instead of overalls. The unexpurgated Yosef is shown on the facing page. (Photographs courtesy of WVU Publication Services and by the author)

gional authorities the matter of sorting out the educational, cultural, and social implications. To a significant extent, such a divided responsibility was built into the organization and program of the Appalachian Regional Commission.[43]

Academic regionalists may have ignored Appalachia in 1946, but twenty years later the region was on every well-informed American's map. Much of the credit for this second discovery of the region belongs to social scientists like Brown, and to writers like Arnow and Caudill who popularized many of their findings. And yet these same people—writing as regional advocates and with the best of intentions—tended to define the region and its people negatively. Their problematic approach overlooked the fact that a large proportion of Appalachian migrants were successful in achieving personal goals of economic improvement and in adjusting to the requirements of life in destination communities. In fact, a quantitative study of white families who left the South for the Northeast, Midwest, or West Coast between 1940 and 1970 finds no significant long-term differences between their living standards or metropolitan places of residence and those of white natives of the industrialized regions.[44] Yet social science and popular writing about Appalachia's "Great Migration" strongly emphasized its pathologies.

In particular, an emphasis on "low-class" migrants and the cultural basis of their social maladjustment in both their communities of origin and their destinations gave new life to the hillbilly half of the twinned Appalachian stereotype. Stalwart mountaineers were present, perhaps even predominant, in the exodus, but the academic experts focused more attention on the dysfunctional hillbillies who accompanied them. Popular culture reinforced this focus, for cartoonists and scriptwriters of the postwar era populated stage, screen, and the funny papers with an unusually large assortment of comedic hillbilly characters.[45] Moreover, Hollywood and the Atlanta-based writer James Dickey collaborated to revive the demonic hillbilly, a more sinister character who first populated the lurid pages of yellow journalism at the time of the Hatfield-McCoy feud. The novel (1970) and film (1972) *Deliverance* offered a distorted view of mountain society in the outraged opinion of many experts. But it must be admitted that their studies, no less than the caricatures that Dickey, Capp, and others provided, helped make the hillbilly the dominant image of Appalachia at this time.

The political response to the Appalachian crisis originated in Pennsylvania, where even as World War II drew to a close it was apparent to some observers that the state was about to enter a period of relative decline. The anthracite region of northeast Pennsylvania had not shared in the wartime boom to the extent that other parts of the state had, while the wartime construction of pipelines carrying oil and natural gas to northeastern markets promised under peacetime conditions to hasten the decline of coal as a fuel for domestic heating, factories, and railroads. A leading demographer forecast a drop in the Scranton–Wilkes-Barre area's population, and the *Wall Street Journal* chimed in with predictions that the wartime growth of industry in southern and western states would hurt Pennsylvania's position as the nation's leading manufacturing and second-most-populous state. Some local economists hotly disputed these projections, arguing that southern and western growth was temporary, based on ephemeral military needs, while Pennsylvania produced basic products such as coal and steel, essential to the nation's postwar prosperity. But the gloomier forecasts turned out to be right.[46]

Pennsylvania leaders responded with an active program that concentrated on the state's two biggest cities. Urban renewal, as it came to be called, expanded older programs of slum clearance into complex schemes of downtown revitalization, expressway construction, historic preservation, and the building of new civic facilities such as parks, museums, sports arenas, and concert halls. In Pittsburgh a powerful alliance of Republican businessmen and Democratic machine politicians overrode the objections of coal producers and labor unions to create a smoke abatement policy that speeded the decline of western Pennsylvania coal production. The same coalition prodded the Pennsylvania legislature to enact laws that permitted the condemnation through eminent domain of private land and its resale by the city to other private owners whose plans conformed to the renewal program. As the new law successfully made its way through the courts, Philadelphia adopted a similar program, and Pennsylvania precedents formed the basis of new federal housing and urban renewal legislation passed by Congress in 1949 and 1954.

Meanwhile, the Pennsylvania Turnpike, completed between the suburbs of Pittsburgh and Philadelphia in 1941, expanded after the war by means of expressways extending into the heart of each city and a northeast extension to Scranton and Wilkes-Barre. It became the model for the interstate highway system that Congress created in 1956. David Lawrence, Pittsburgh's erstwhile "boss" who became mayor of the city in 1945 and governor of Pennsylvania in 1959, stepped onto the national stage in 1960 as a backer of John F. Kennedy's presidential bid and a member of Kennedy's administration after completing his gubernatorial term. The advocates of bold action to address Appalachia's problems on a regional basis made sure that Lawrence was kept abreast of their plans.

Maryland, like Pennsylvania, embraced both impoverished mountain districts and cities coping with the problems of metropolitan growth. Governor J. Millard Tawes, elected as a Democrat in 1958, took a lively interest in regional planning as a means of addressing both kinds of problems. Accordingly, he issued an invitation to the governors of nine Appalachian states to meet in Annapolis in May 1960 to discuss the region's crisis and to formulate a collective response to it. Kentucky governor Bert Combs, a native of eastern Kentucky, hosted a followup meeting in Lexington that October. These gatherings provided the political platform for the creation of the Appalachian Regional Commission (ARC). Later Combs shared credit with Tawes for launching the program, but credit also belonged to a pair of gubernatorial aides, Lawrence Grossman of Tawes's staff and John Whisman of Combs's. Both were from Kentucky and were well versed in the theory of regional planning as well as in the ways of practical politics. The unusual structure of the ARC, as Congress eventually created it in 1965, was grounded in politics, but its program for regional renewal was put forward in the language of economists and planners.[47]

Regional economics, like other aspects of interwar regionalism, swiftly fell out of favor in the postwar era, but a new synthesis emerged that had important implications for Appalachia's future. Keynesianism—the doctrine that the federal government bore ultimate responsibility for managing the national economy through its fiscal and monetary policies—became so dominant among professional economists that by the 1960s they were claiming the ability to "fine-tune" the national economy with this or that adjustment of resource flows. Appalachia's economy clearly needed a tuneup. There were two overlapping schools of thought from which solutions to the region's problems might be drawn.

W. W. Rostow provided one set of solutions in his influential book *The Stages of Economic Growth* (1960), which outlined in clear and easily digested terms a sector theory of economic growth.[48] Based on his understanding of British and American economic history, Rostow traced the origins of growth to an economy's "primary" sector—in other words, extractive industry, which under commonly accepted definitions included agriculture and forestry, fisheries, and mines, or all activity that extracted wealth more or less directly from the earth and contributed to the basic transport and processing of the extracted materials. The second stage of growth was one of "secondary" activity: the manufacture of more complex products in locations determined more by transportation efficiencies than by proximity to raw materials; the growth of mass production and consumption and of cities as distribution, manufacturing, and service centers; the creation of labor unions and of a cadre of professional managers, all of which was capped by the emergence of government as a kind of economic umpire, making sure that everyone followed the rules and that no one got away for very long with passing off the economic inefficiencies of their particular line of work at the public expense, unless the underwriting of such "externalities" was a part of the democratic consensus. The third economic sector encompassed services ranging from education to finance and real estate to entertainment and culture. Just as the profits from primary industries financed the move to the secondary stage, the profits from manufacturing and profitable infrastructure underwrote banks, schools, sports franchises, and ballet troupes. Once all three stages were in place, economic growth became self-sustaining, able to generate from its internal resources of savings and investment new industries in each sector to replace old ones that became obsolete.

The sector theory accommodated both Keynesianism and modernization, since in the first place it assigned general guidance and oversight of the economy to the welfare state and, in the second, marked out a path toward modernity that could compete with the Marxist path sponsored by the Soviet Union. Indeed, Rostow—who regarded himself and his fellow experts as "the junior officers of the Second World War come to responsibility"—sub-

titled his book *A Non-Communist Manifesto*.[49] The theory enabled modernizers such as the administrators of American aid to Third World countries to
point out to local clients the economic inefficiencies of traditional forms of
behavior—for example, the use of bribes to grease the skids of economic
transactions, or nepotism and other forms of political corruption, or the manipulation or monopolization of economic resources by influential family or
ethnic groups—even though, as historians have showed, all these had also
been part of Britain and America's early modern history.

Another source of ideas was the field of "regional science," an amalgam of
regional geography, economics, sociology, and planning that emerged in the
late 1930s. Experts in this area busied themselves in mapping the imbalances
that existed within all Western democracies and in advancing and debating
proposals for their amelioration. Britain had Clydeside and Tyneside, impoverished northern industrial districts, along with the Midlands and Welsh
coalfields. France had its grimy northeast, Italy its sun-baked and somnolent
south. Each of these presented quandaries comparable to Appalachia in the
United States: how could the government promote prosperity in districts
beset with surplus workers and obsolete economic sectors in a way that would
not require either massive dislocations of people or long-term mortgages on
the national treasury? European politicians came up with some solutions that
were not politically viable in the United States—state ownership of basic industries and utilities in Britain, for example, and their use to bolster regional
economies, or the massive subsidies that Italy provided to industries that located in the *mezzogiorno* region south of Rome. It has to be said that these European solutions did not work very well or for very long; most such responses
were abandoned during the 1980s. In any event, alternative solutions in the
U.S. had to take into account both federalism and capitalism. There were limits to the extent that American public officials would sustain industrial subsidies, and there were constitutional and political barriers to the operation of
regional programs of the sort that Harry Caudill proposed.

One of those barriers was the history and reputation of the TVA itself. During the presidential administration of Dwight D. Eisenhower, TVA supporters
stymied Republican attempts to curb the agency's growth and trim back its
influence. Accordingly, having built dams at nearly all of the practical hydroelectric sites of the Tennessee basin, the TVA turned to coal-fired and nuclear
power generation, setting the stage for new controversies during the 1970s,
when the agency would be assaulted from the left instead of the right. The
agency also became an American model of regional planning to be held up before the Third World, notably Iran, where David Lilienthal himself headed a

development project designed and funded by the United States, and Southeast Asia, where in 1965 President Lyndon Baines Johnson offered TVA-style development in the Mekong River basin in return for peace in Vietnam.

The TVA was no model on its home turf, however. Among state governors and the federal bureaucrats who ran rival development agencies, the TVA inspired the sentiment "never again!" During the 1940s, an alliance of state governors, the federal Bureau of Reclamation, and the Army Corps of Engineers successfully fought the establishment of a Missouri Valley Authority in the midwestern and plains states. The states did not wish to be invaded by a powerful federal agency that operated independently of local politics, as had been the case in Tennessee, while the federal bureaucrats spied a threat to their agencies' autonomy and their own career prospects. The defeat in Congress of a proposed Columbia Valley Authority in 1948 drove home the lesson. Similar forces could be expected to coalesce again should Caudill's proposal for Appalachia or anything like it become a political possibility.

For these reasons, congressional advocates of federally sponsored regional redevelopment, such as Senator Paul Douglas of Illinois, a professional economist, sought to open up other avenues to this goal. One was the Area Redevelopment Administration (ARA), which was passed by Congress only to meet with Eisenhower vetoes three times but was enacted again and signed into law by President Kennedy in May 1961. This legislation provided for development districts to be set up within each state that were eligible for federal funding on the basis of two criteria: the unemployment rate and the poverty level. The criteria used made a third of U.S. counties eligible for ARA funds; Appalachia received 29 percent of this money, with West Virginia getting over half of the ARA's Appalachian funds. Legal obstacles and the protests of competing industries prevented the ARA from funding the development of hydroelectric power or other natural resources, and so most of its money went to tourism projects.[50]

The entire nation was eligible to participate in the ARA program, and there were some like John Whisman who thought this the first step toward a national policy of "wall-to-wall" regionalism. But the modest level of funding available and the piecemeal character of the ARA program meant that there still remained a need and a growing demand for a regionwide approach to Appalachia's problems. These problems, as Lawrence Grossman outlined them in the briefing book for the first conference of Appalachian governors, were greater than could be addressed by existing state and federal agencies. A comprehensive program of much larger scope was called for. The articulation of this demand and its ultimate translation into action came when Appalachia and its crisis moved to center stage on the national political scene.

The Appalachian governors' conferences met twice in 1960, once in Annapolis and once in Lexington, but more significantly, the meetings came at the twin peaks of the national election season, the first during the presidential primaries, the second at the height of the fall campaign. The conferences invited all presidential candidates to put forward their ideas for dealing with the Appalachian crisis. Only one candidate responded, but he was the one who counted most: John F. Kennedy. Early in 1960, Kennedy and his campaign managers determined that the West Virginia primary scheduled for May 10 represented a major opportunity to strengthen his bid for the presidency. The campaign's public pronouncements portrayed Kennedy as an underdog, a Roman Catholic from urban Massachusetts running in a rural and overwhelmingly Protestant state. Privately, campaign advisors concluded that Kennedy could win West Virginia and that such a victory was needed to balance an expected win by his chief rival, Senator Hubert H. Humphrey of Minnesota, in the Wisconsin primary to be held the preceding week.

Kennedy's chances in West Virginia were buttressed by a quiet but effective alliance with a Democratic statehouse machine that had controlled state government since 1940, with the exception of a single gubernatorial term. W. W. Barron, a corrupt but shrewd politician who was the machine's candidate for governor, ran alongside Kennedy in the primary, fueled by copious amounts of Kennedy money and the machine's equally impressive array of campaign workers drawn from the ranks of state and local government employees.[51] The alliance won a substantial majority of the primary votes, creating a momentum that led to the election of Kennedy as president and Barron as governor in November. As Tawes and Combs made plans for further gatherings of the Appalachian governors, they made sure that Barron, along with David Lawrence, was in agreement with their plans.

Kennedy later identified the West Virginia primary as the most important single milestone on his road to the White House, and the same might be said of its importance in the emergence of Appalachia's crisis as a national issue. Kennedy himself was touched by what he saw in the state's farming and mining districts, while the television cameras that followed him and Humphrey through the state broadcast haunting images of regional poverty amid national affluence, scenes that soon became a staple of national news programs during the 60s. Although Kennedy and his entourage arrived in Charleston by air, they traveled through West Virginia by bus and car in the early spring,

A road cut near Pound Gap on the Kentucky-Virginia state line, where Appalachian Development Highway corridors B and G (U.S. highways 23 and 119) intersect. (Photograph by the author)

when nature had not yet hidden in greenery the abuse of the land by mining and farming practices. The politicians and reporters following the campaign trail were less impressed by the state's scenic beauty than by its environmental scars and miserable roads. Even without the sanction of regional theory, it was not surprising that Kennedy's proposals for healing Appalachia concentrated on improving the roads.

Shortly after his election, Kennedy appointed a President's Appalachian Regional Committee (PARC), composed almost entirely of West Virginians, to make recommendations for federal action.[52] But though Barron and others in his state began compiling their wish lists, and though Kennedy added benefits that could be achieved through executive order (such as expanded eligibility for federal welfare programs and the addition of a new interstate, I-79, paralleling U.S. 19 from Charleston north toward Pittsburgh and Erie), the program that the administration eventually presented to Congress more closely followed the ideas advanced at a third gathering of Appalachian governors held in Cumberland, Maryland, in 1962. As it was eventually established, the

Appalachian Regional Commission would have regional scope but pursue its program through the agency of the states. A federal administration based in Washington and headed by a presidential appointee would share authority with state officials reporting to each governor. Governors would share overall authority with the federal "co-chairman" on a rotating basis, and gubernatorial approval was required for any ARC project carried out within a particular state. There were also state matching requirements for ARC projects.

The commission was thus designed to prevent it from acting independently of state and local authorities. Advocates made much of this unique federal-state partnership, but the long-run implication was that the ARC was more a regional consulting than a coordinating body. The contrast with the TVA's independence, or that of the numerous urban-renewal authorities modeled on Pittsburgh precedents, was striking and revealing. In effect, it represented the determination of the region's political echelons and local elites to enjoy the benefits of income redistribution between regions—that is, the transfer of tax monies from more prosperous parts of the country to Appalachia via the ARC—without loosening their control over the region's social structure.

Even with these safeguards, Congress turned down Appalachian proposals the first two times that Kennedy presented them. Still under the sway of an alliance between conservative Republicans and southern Democrats that had formed during the later administrations of Franklin D. Roosevelt, Congress looked skeptically on the program. Moreover, there were objections from within the region itself, from civic officials and boosters in Roanoke and Knoxville who resented being lumped with poor rural folks in an Appalachia defined as a national problem, for example, or from Congressman Richard Poff of Virginia, a Shenandoah Valley Republican who had his district cut out of official Appalachia as a protest against government activism. Even in West Virginia there were those (such as the Charleston country club members whom Mary Lee Settle caricatured in her novel *Charley Bland*) who resented the "bad publicity" that Kennedy had brought to the state or who worried about the impact of too much government activism on local power structures.

After a devastating flood struck Appalachia in March 1963, Kennedy moved the region to the top of the ARA's agenda. By executive order he created an expanded PARC and renamed it a commission under the chairmanship of Franklin D. Roosevelt Jr. In June 1963, the president returned to West Virginia to preside over the state's centennial celebration and to renew his commitment to regional redevelopment. Still, Congress did not act until after Kennedy's assassination in 1963 and Lyndon B. Johnson's landslide victory in the presidential election of the following year. In March 1965, at the climax of his "honeymoon period," Johnson signed the Appalachian Regional Development Act (ARDA) establishing the commission. Even then, Congress stripped the proposal of most of its natural resource development features, prohibited the ARC from undertaking hydroelectric projects, and limited other water resource development to a survey to be made by the Army Corps of Engineers.

Meanwhile, determined to advance his own program as well as carrying on Kennedy's legacy, Johnson declared "war" on the causes of poverty in America and made Appalachia a central theater of that war by launching his crusade from the porch of a former miner's house in Martin County, Kentucky, on April 24, 1964. While the region's politicians dutifully signed on to the crusade during audiences such as the one Johnson held at the Huntington airport on the day after his declaration, the practical effect was to make Appalachia a two-war front: the first being a drive, led by the ARC, to redevelop the region from the top down; the other an effort by the Office of Economic Opportunity (the War on Poverty's action agency) to remake it from the bottom up.

The centerpiece of the ARC's redevelopment strategy as it emerged during the late sixties was a 3,025-mile system of "development corridors": modern four-lane highways designed to augment the interstate system, which according to law had to follow established paths of commerce between major cities. The ARC highways were designed to tie those cities to "growth centers" within Appalachia: places such as Asheville, Knoxville, and the Tennessee-Virginia Tri-Cities and smaller centers such as Beckley, West Virginia, or Pikeville, Kentucky. In these places new industrial development stimulated by the highways and other forms of infrastructure investment would absorb the surplus population now pouring out of the region. The strategy promised to remedy deficiencies caused by the failure of Appalachia's extractive stage of development to yield the tax revenues that should have funded better roads, schools, and so on, thus hampering the region's ability to develop secondary and tertiary sectors.

Although government funds might properly remedy these infrastructure defects, further development would be left to the private sector; American aid that flowed into developing countries overseas followed a similar strategy. In point of fact, the ARC directed over two-thirds of its funds into highways. Other forms of infrastructure funded by the ARC included clinics and hospitals, sewerage, trash collection and water systems, airports, and industrial parks. The commission confined human-resource development projects mainly to vocational education and health care. Apart from the "vo-tech" schools ⟶ that soon began to dot the region, the ARC did not directly address the educational issues raised by the Ford survey, though it was allowed to provide supplemental funds to local projects funded by grants from other federal agencies. Its approach to human resources thus remained piecemeal, determined on a project-by-project basis by means of proposals sent forward by the governors' offices and sixty-nine "local development districts" (LDDs).

The LDDs were multicounty planning units established in numbers ranging from three in Appalachian Ohio and New York to eleven in West Virginia. Some were inherited from the ARA; others went back to state-sponsored redevelopment programs in Pennsylvania and Kentucky. But most were prodded into existence by the commission. In 1975 LDDs gained a power that guaranteed their future importance: the authority to certify that federal grant applications from an LDD's district were coordinated with other locally operating federal programs. Thus, supplemental funds and the certification process allowed the ARC to leverage its nonhighway expenditures, though the leverage involved depended in large part on the receptivity of a given governor's office and the specific federal agencies involved. Long-established agencies such as the TVA, the Army Corps of Engineers, the Forest Service, and space and military agencies tended to ignore this function of the LDDs. Newer agencies whose programs, though national in origin, were generally more local in scope were more cooperative. These included the Environmental Protection Agency (EPA), the Department of Housing and Urban Development (HUD) and various offices charged with development planning and activities in the departments of agriculture and commerce.[53]

State and local authorities disliked the growth-center strategy, which forced them to prioritize in ways that they found difficult to explain to local constituencies. And in fact, this aspect of the ARC program, much trumpeted and criticized in theory, had little impact in practice, apart from the concentration of jobs and population around the nodes where ARC highways linked up with the interstates or with each other. Governors and LDDs alike tended to disperse nonhighway projects geographically, trumping regional science theory with traditional logrolling. Both at the regional and local levels, ARC review of project proposals became less a function of coordination than one of brokerage. A 1990 study showed that nonhighway projects tended to concentrate in a few areas of activity, mainly water and sewer projects, health-care delivery, and child-development programs. But the range of funded activities was considerable: "access roads and airport facilities in [northern] Alabama, Upper Cumberland (Tennessee) and Northeast Pennsylvania districts; industrial park facilities in East Tennessee; and libraries and recreational facilities in [the Kanawha Valley of] West Virginia."[54] More recently, small-business incubators have been popular, along with such distinctive projects as a professional football practice facility in upstate South Carolina, a documentary film on West Virginia history, and the International Storytelling Center and the Encyclopedia of Appalachia projects in East Tennessee.

Although the ARC grew under the Republican presidencies of Richard Nixon and Gerald Ford and flourished under Democrat Jimmy Carter (the first governor from an Appalachian state to become president of the United States since Andrew Johnson), from 1981 to 1990 it confronted hostile Republican administrations. Ronald Reagan "zeroed out" the agency by eliminating it from the executive budgets submitted to Congress; his successor relented to the extent of proposing an appropriation of $50,000,000 for 1990, compared with the nearly $400,000,000 the commission had received in its best pre-Reagan year.

The Democratic Congresses that sat throughout this period could be expected to reinsert the agency's funding, ranging from $162,000,000 in 1983 to $110,000,000 in 1989. The impact of the Reagan-Bush strategy was nonetheless demoralizing, especially to the ARC's Washington staff, forced to become ever more cautious in its approach to Appalachian problems. Why, critics asked, should Appalachia get special funding in a time of budgetary stringency, when no other part of the country had such a claim on the treasury? Yet when Jesse White, President William J. Clinton's appointee to the federal cochairmanship, proposed in 1993 to redirect the commission's mandate—cutting loose those Appalachian counties whose socioeconomic parameters now approached or exceeded national norms while incorporating new areas in the South and West whose levels of economic distress equaled that of the impoverished counties of central Appalachia—he ran into a political stone wall. The thirteen state governors and the U.S. senators and congressional representatives from Appalachia had no intention of surrendering their exclusive claim to federal largesse. In effect, the ARC has become another government agency preoccupied with the perpetuation of its existence, while its supporters constitute an interest group like most of the others that contend for preferment in Washington. Appalachia's hefty bloc of senators and representatives seems to guarantee the commission's permanence, although to exactly what purpose is becoming increasingly unclear.

A full evaluation of the ARC program must await the completion of its highway system. By the end of the century this was 82 percent complete, but since the remaining mileage traversed some of the region's most rugged mountains, the part remaining to be done was expected to cost more than the completed part.[55] Of course, the agency did not have to wait this long to hear from critics, and a number of preliminary evaluations have been made. A survey by a Pittsburgh newspaper disclosed in 2000 that 111 of the 406 counties now included in official Appalachia were still "distressed" in that their levels of poverty and unemployment exceeded 150 percent of the national average, with per-capita income at two-thirds or less of the national norm, and others were "transitional" in that one or two of these socioeconomic indicators reached similar levels.[56]

The distressed counties—concentrated in eastern Kentucky but also represented in significant numbers in southern and central West Virginia, northeast Mississippi, southeastern Ohio, and East Tennessee—made up slightly less than half the number of counties similarly identified in 1965. But the total was up by 25 percent since 1980, thanks to the decline of the region's previously prosperous manufacturing districts and a renewal of out-migration. This time the migrants were abandoning Appalachian cities and rural industrial districts, thanks to deindustrialization in iron and steel, chemicals, and textiles, along with a new surge of unemployment in the coalfields. In terms of net migration, Allegheny County (Pittsburgh) and two other nearby industrial counties lost 120,000 people at the peak of this exodus between 1980 and 1986. The counties containing Birmingham, Chattanooga, Charleston, West Virginia, Binghamton, and the Pennsylvania cities of Johnstown, Erie, and Wilkes-Barre lost between 9,000 and 18,000 each. A belt of industrialized counties extending through the upper Ohio valley, plus coalfield counties in the Virginias, Kentucky, and Alabama, furnished most of the remaining migrants.[57]

A brief surge in coalfield prosperity during the "energy crisis" of the 1970s gave way during succeeding decades to the return of high levels of oil imports and the quickening of two other trends that continued through the end of the century: the increasing reliance by midwestern utility companies on strip-mined western rather than deep-mined eastern coal, and the decline of Appalachian coal employment in both surface and underground mines due to the increasing scale and technological sophistication of mining equipment. In addition, the Clean Air Act of 1990 reduced the marketability of high-sulfur coal from the upper Ohio valley, while the entire industry felt threatened by the emergence of global warming as a political issue. One measure of the social change induced by these trends was the number of miners in West Virginia: more than 150,000 in 1945, but just over 17,000 in 1999, by which time there were fewer miners in the state than there were nurses or telephone so-

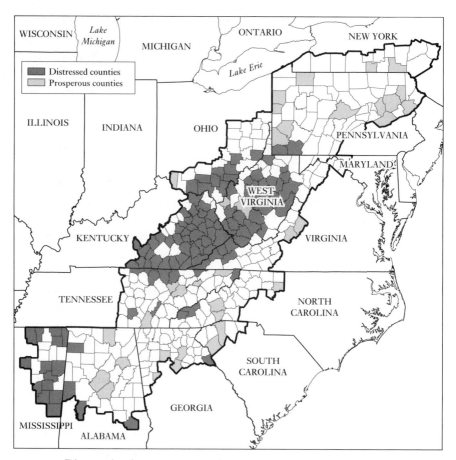

MAP 5. Distressed and prosperous counties, 2001

licitors. WalMart now has more employees in West Virginia than any coal company, although coal industry apologists still insist that "five thousand people working at Wal-Marts in this state don't equal 400 coal jobs."[58]

Somewhat balancing the exodus, in-migration surged in a belt of urban and suburban counties on the southern fringe of the official region, and smaller gains were registered in a tier of mountain counties located within range of urban tourists and commuters and extending through the highlands of eastern Appalachia along the Blue Ridge and the Allegheny Front to the Pennsylvania Poconos. Appalachian counties on the fringe of metropolitan Atlanta gained almost as many people through migration during the early 1980s as the Pittsburgh area lost. In-migrants to Madison County (Huntsville, Alabama) exceeded out-migrants from Birmingham, while Berkeley and

Jefferson, the two West Virginia counties closest to Washington–Baltimore, gained people at roughly the same rate that traditional mining counties such as Fayette or McDowell lost them. Although there were still pockets of poverty tucked into various corners of these counties, here the problems associated with Appalachia's underdevelopment gave way to those associated with growth.

One Kentucky study attributes a direct connection between a given county's relative prosperity and the amount of ARC spending in that county.[59] Because highway construction greatly exceeded any other form of ARC expenditure, this should not be surprising; the highway program by its very nature concentrates investment, and thus population, at strategic nodes in the region. Elsewhere, the relative prosperity of northern Alabama, north Georgia, western North Carolina, and much of East Tennessee may be said to constitute a success story, but the success can hardly be ascribed to the ARC alone. The TVA and Cold War defense spending were greater influences in Alabama and Tennessee, while the resort districts of Georgia and North Carolina (along with western Maryland, eastern West Virginia, and the three Pocono counties of northeast Pennsylvania) have prospered in tandem with the growth of the adjacent metropolitan areas from which their tourist and commuter businesses derive. The rest of Appalachian Pennsylvania, New York's southern tier, and adjacent areas in eastern Ohio, northern West Virginia, and western Maryland present the case of stabilization after significant outmigration to more prosperous areas. Since these areas never manifested the levels of distress found within the mining and rural counties of central and southern Appalachia, the region's northern districts now demonstrate the benefit of roughly the same resources distributed among a sparser population.

Regardless of what critics have thought of the ARC program, it is hard to assign the agency too much credit or blame for the region's continued uneven development. The roughly $8.3 billion spent by the agency from 1965 to 2000 was never more than a modest percentage of overall federal expenditures in Appalachia. The highway program (which accounts for $5.4 billion of this total) leveraged the impact of ARC funds by improving access to—and egress from—the region. Although new roads seem to have benefited Appalachian growth centers somewhat less than they did those metropolitan areas bordering the region (Lexington, Columbus, Greensboro–High Point–Winston-Salem, Charlotte, Atlanta, and Baltimore-Washington, in other words) that became more accessible to consumers and workers from the mountains, the same roads speed tourists the other way and help to account for at least part of the prosperity of some areas.

Assessing the ARC's impact also involves considering some issues that academic experts avoided before the 1970s. "We are not commissioned to pass judgment on the capitalistic system as a whole, to predict its degree of permanence, or to analyze the entire range of proposals for increasing its stability," wrote a team of scholars including Rupert Vance in 1936.[60] How could society address the problem of Appalachia without addressing the problems of capitalism, specifically the types of economic and social exploitation that seemed to flow not just from the margins of the market system, but from its very nature? Vance and his colleagues backed away from this question, while to postwar modernizers the issue was not the deficiencies of capitalism as a system but merely the challenge of tuning it up so as to produce more desirable social outcomes.

During the ARC program's first decade, however, there appeared in Appalachia a number of individuals and groups who were not shy about raising fundamental issues and who gave the modernist approach to regional redevelopment and the ideological assumptions on which it rested a searching critique. These critics came to believe that capitalism and the social structure it had created in Appalachia were the problem, not the solution. Foremost of those who came to share this belief was Helen Lewis, who returned from Lexington to her southwest Virginia campus more determined than ever to ask basic questions about Appalachian problems. The publication of her *Colonialism in Modern America: The Appalachian Case* (1978), an anthology edited with two other scholars, brought to the fore a growing body of opinion that it was the system, not its victims, that deserved the blame for Appalachian poverty.[61]

The War on Poverty in Appalachia officially lasted a little more than five years, from its opening declaration in Kentucky by LBJ until it was phased out by the Nixon administration. Its impact on the region's history was much greater than this brief official tenure would suggest, however. Partly this was because the OEO was part of a larger vision—Johnson's Great Society—that led to several more durable new programs: Medicaid, Medicare, VISTA (Volunteers in Service to America, a domestic equivalent of Kennedy's Peace Corps), and Head Start were all begun in 1965, while eligibility and coverage for established programs such as Social Security and federal urban and rural housing subventions were expanded. Moreover, Nixon's program of "revenue sharing," although undertaken in a very different spirit than that of the Great Society, placed unprecedented sums of federal money under the direction of state and local governments.

To the contentions of modernizing experts and local elites over how to deploy these resources were added the alternative visions of five overlapping groups that were attracted to Appalachia during these years. First, there were "community organizers" who came into the region as part of the official War on Poverty. They were abetted and often joined by young white activists, many of them veterans of the civil rights movement in the lowland South, who mobilized in Appalachia under the banners of VISTA or of the Appalachian Volunteers (AVS), an equivalent group funded by the Council of the Southern Mountains (CSM) and other nongovernment sources. A resurgence of labor militancy developed in the coalfields after 1968 in opposition to the corrupt UMWA leadership that succeeded John L. Lewis. Environmentalism emerged in Appalachia, as in the nation, during the early 1970s and found irresistible targets in the practices of strip-mining and clear-cutting. At the same time a small but significant number of in-migrants came to the region as permanent settlers, seeking to establish a simpler and more purposeful way of living than seemed possible in the nation's cities and suburbs.

Poverty warriors, AV and VISTA volunteers, civil rights and labor militants, environmentalists, and settlers may be identified as distinct groups for purposes of discussion, but their programs and personnel often blended, and they all drew upon the cultural values and forms of the suburban youth culture that emerged nationally during the adolescence of the postwar baby boom. Collectively they represented a very different way of looking at the Appalachian crisis than the outlooks of those politicians and experts who marked out the official path to regional redevelopment.

Partly in reaction against some of the excesses of the top-down social programs that accompanied urban renewal, guidelines for federal antipoverty action included a requirement for "maximum feasible participation" in the design of specific programs by the communities involved. Just what this might mean in practice was pretty much up to OEO agents, under the general supervision of the home office in Washington. Courthouse politicians throughout Appalachia, but especially in southern West Virginia and eastern Kentucky, happily anticipated the jobs and money that federal programs promised, but they were not eager to share these spoils with newcomers whose idea of community was different from their own. To this source of tension was added cultural conflict, for many of the poverty warriors displayed the long hair and other personal adornments and mannerisms of the suburban youth culture that evolved during the sixties as a bohemian "counterculture." "They are dirty, nasty; they won't shave," a West Virginia politician complained. Throughout the region, the poverty workers' advocacy of radical changes in the way power was exercised in Appalachian communities left them open to accusations that they were teaching communism.

The poverty warriors were augmented and in many cases joined by another group of young white activists, veterans of the civil rights struggle in the lowland South who found themselves shouldered out of leadership positions there by the rise of the Black Power movement. Arriving in the mountains much as northern missionaries had done at the end of Reconstruction a century earlier, these activists soon learned that controversy was inherent in any program that involved better service to poor people whose prior access to government programs had been through gatekeepers tied into local power structures.

This was true even where the activists were locals, not outsiders. A case in point was Mingo County, West Virginia, where Huey Perry, a young schoolteacher with roots in the county, took on the job of OEO administrator. The Mingo program started out modestly enough by sponsoring some twenty-six local "community action" groups with small-scale objectives having to do with school bus service and road repairs. But these activities soon led to confrontation with the county's notoriously corrupt political structure headed by state senator Noah Floyd, representing the latest generation of his powerful and historic family. In 1967 the community action groups organized a biracial political action league. "The strategy was to direct the energies of the poor away from development and implementation of federal programs, which usually treated only the symptoms of poverty, toward the building of a political base from which the poor could attack poverty itself."[62] Floyd had powerful friends in Charleston and in Washington, but the reformers nevertheless managed to purge the voting rolls of several thousand dead and other illegally registered voters (not a few Appalachian counties had actually registered an increase in voters as their populations declined) and set in motion a series of investigations and political realignments that led to Floyd's defeat in the 1970 Democratic primary.

The civil rights movement provided a model as well as personnel. Although West Virginia, Maryland, and Kentucky moved to comply voluntarily with the 1954 Supreme Court decision outlawing school segregation, there were pockets of resistance in these states, while mountain counties in Tennessee, Alabama, Georgia, the Carolinas, and Virginia were dragged along by racist state officials determined to defy the decision. The result was a decade of turmoil in these states, particularly Alabama, and painfully slow progress toward school integration after formal resistance ceased. Many younger

African Americans found the snail's pace of desegregation unacceptable and so, in 1960, turned to the "direct action" tactics that had been effective in other southern locations such as Montgomery and Greensboro.

Although the Deep South remained the primary civil rights battlefield throughout the 1960s and 1970s, Appalachia witnessed many skirmishes. "I stopped being Negro, turned black, and grew the first Afro in Piedmont, West Virginia," Henry Louis "Skip" Gates Jr. recalled of his high school years in a paper-mill town on the upper Potomac. Gates, who later became an Ivy League professor and one of the nation's foremost authorities on African American literature and history, recalled the late sixties and early seventies as a time of "glorious black awakening," to which his personal contributions included organizing a school boycott in Piedmont on the day of Martin Luther King Jr.'s funeral, an unsuccessful attempt to integrate a local student hangout, and a successful attempt to shut the place down when the owner refused to obey West Virginia's new human-relations laws.[63]

Further south, the Highlander Folk School began training civil rights workers and promoting interracial education even before the Supreme Court decision. As its integrationist activities became more prominent, the state of Tennessee moved to revoke the school's 1932 charter and, after a protracted series of court battles wherein it was portrayed as a "Communist training school," succeeded in doing so in 1962. Reconstituting itself as the Highlander Research and Education Center, first in Knoxville, then after 1971 in a rural setting near New Market, Tennessee, Highlander turned to training community organizers and increasingly focused on the problems of Appalachia: "strip mining, land and mineral ownership, and occupational and environmental health hazards." Helen Lewis joined the Highlander staff in 1978 and remained affiliated there until 1997, serving briefly as the center's interim director after the retirement of its founder, Myles Horton.[64]

Direct action, which in labor relations dated back to the days of Mother Jones, also became the strategy of choice when activists confronted the corrupt and violent men who ran the United Mine Workers between 1961 and 1972. The Miners for Democracy (MFD) movement—triggered by a coal-mine explosion at Farmington, West Virginia, in November 1968 and the UMWA leadership's complacent reaction to it—swept through the coalfields, especially after the movement's leader, Joseph "Jock" Yablonski, was murdered along with two members of his family at his Pennsylvania home in December 1969. Coupling union reform with demands for recognition of "black lung" (pneumoconiosis) as an occupational and thus compensable disease and for better mine health and safety regulation generally, the MFD placed one of its own in the UMWA presidency in 1972. Meanwhile, an overlapping Black Lung Association, through a series of demonstrations and wildcat strikes, forced improved compensation legislation through the West Virginia legislature and then the U.S. Congress in 1969.

The federal Mine Enforcement and Safety Administration, established in 1969, evolved after 1977 into the Mine Safety and Health Administration (MSHA), holding regulatory jurisdiction over all forms of mining. The annual number of accidental deaths in coal mines declined from an average of 220 annually during the 1970s to less than 40 per year after 1993, when the Clinton administration renewed the drive against unsafe mining practices under Assistant Secretary of Labor J. Davitt McAteer, a former MFD activist. In 1998 the number of mining deaths fell to 29, the lowest level ever, which was reported to have made coal mining, at least for that year, a safer mode of employment than banking.

The poverty, civil rights, and union democracy crusades also helped introduce into Appalachia such innovations as legal aid for poor people, public-interest law firms, women's rights organizations, and environmental activist groups such as SOCM (Save Our Cumberland Mountains, 1972), KFTC (Kentuckians for the Commonwealth, 1981), and the Western North Carolina Alliance (1983). Each of these groups had a particular cause that spurred it to action: In the SOCM's case this was strip-mining, in the KFTC's the notorious broadform deed that permitted the owners or lessees of mineral rights to adopt practically any means to get at the mineral, including the destruction of surface property. The Western North Carolina Alliance organized to stop oil and gas drilling in the state's western national forests and in 1985 initiated a nine-year drive against clear-cutting in national forests.

To conservative critics, environmentalism appeared to be an attack on property rights, but its main thrust was to assert, in law and in public opinion, a higher order of rights possessed by communities in protecting their quality of life against industrial spoliation and by other species and nature generally against destruction in the name of profitable enterprise. Battlefields on this front opened in all of the Appalachian states, notably in the form of crusades against strip-mining in the coalfields. The Buffalo Creek disaster of 1972 claimed 125 lives and 4,000 homes in a narrow West Virginia valley when an improperly constructed wastewater dam burst. The Pittston Company, whose subsidiary built the dam, termed the disaster "an act of God," but for everyone else it united environmental concerns with the many other grievances people held against absentee coal corporations.

In the Pigeon River watershed adjacent to Great Smoky Mountains National Park, controversy over stream pollution pitted environmentalists against the Champion International Paper Company and the upstream state of North Carolina against the downstream state of Tennessee. At the same time, a North Carolina state administration that expressed outrage at Tennessee's refusal to accept Champion's waste in the Pigeon River took on Virginia and West Virginia interests to protect the New River headwaters. The New River controversy involved a proposed dam and pumped storage project that would have flooded prime farmlands in Ashe County, North Carolina, in order to generate electrical power reserves for the Appalachian Power Company and water supplies to help flush out stream pollution in the industrial Kanawha valley. The interstate complications allowed North Carolina officials to pose as protectors of the environment in this case, causing the project to be abandoned in 1976 and the New River to be declared a national resource under a federal "wild and scenic rivers" program (although in fact the New River was a good deal less wild than it was scenic). Another controversy of the era pitted the TVA and an array of business clients against defenders of the snail darter, a tiny but unique fish whose Tellico River habitat was threatened by a TVA dam project of doubtful public utility. The snail darter became famous, but its habitat was nonetheless lost when a powerful U.S. senator, Howard Baker, slipped a measure through Congress exempting the TVA from the requirements of the Endangered Species Act.[65]

Still another movement among young people augmented the ranks of Appalachian environmentalists and activists. This was the back-to-the-land movement. Writing of his parents, who settled on a hardscrabble farm in Calhoun County, West Virginia, in 1974, the year of his birth, Jedediah Purdy writes, "They meant to live with few needs, to raise as much of their own food and do as much of their own work as possible, and to share what they could not do themselves with like-minded neighbors. As my father once said to me, they intended 'to pick out a small corner of the world and make it as sane as possible.'"[66] Settlers like the Purdys tended to drift in small clusters into agricultural counties where land prices were cheap, thanks to the Appalachian exodus. One hundred and fifty Appalachian counties had smaller populations in 1970 than they had had in 1920, so there was plenty of room for people who planned to live modestly. The newcomers tended to avoid coal country, however, as well as those southern hill counties that had been part of the civil rights frontier. Rather, they settled in the interior hill counties of the Ohio valley, and in the back valleys that flank the borders of the Virginias and of North Carolina and Tennessee, and in those few counties in north Georgia not already staked out by Atlanta exurbanites.

Another subset could be found near Appalachian college towns like Athens, Ohio, Morgantown, West Virginia, Boone, North Carolina, and Blacksburg, Virginia. Their numbers too small and scattered to be called colonies, the settlers nevertheless formed rural enclaves ranging from a handful to a few dozen households. Nearly every community exchanged stories of its encounters with the locals, for like the poverty warriors and other activists, these newcomers held allegiance to the counterculture, at least in its less commercial forms. This made jeans and chambray work shirts obligatory costumes for both genders, along with "granny dresses" for women and long hair and beards for men.

The roster of Purdy's boyhood community was not atypical. It included "a charismatic born poet, a construction worker by trade and motorcyclist by vocation . . .; a Manhattan-trained ballerina who settled in West Virginia to teach dance and art to rural children . . .; a couple, educated at Yale, she now a small-town lawyer and he, among myriad community projects, a farmer and an amateur blacksmith, who lectured me on radical economic theory and American labor history as we put up loose hay with his horses."[67] Such people established homes that were environmentally friendly, though even where they heated with wood and read by kerosene lanterns, stereo phonographs were one electrical appliance that few settlers could do without; these could be run off of old car batteries. They also tolerated, if they did not indulge in, recreational drug use and alternative sexual partnerships and household formations. Yet while these outlooks did not endear them to the people among whom they settled, nearly every settler household had exchanges with native farm men who shared their expertise or tools and with farm women who treated them according to the custom of rural hospitality.[68] Perhaps the ultimate badge of acceptance for male newcomers was an invitation to join the local rescue squad or volunteer fire company. Rescue squads had originated in Roanoke earlier in the century and spread throughout the region, typically with the help of state or federal funds for equipment and training. As more and more people commuted into town to work and shop, the rural buildings housing rescue and firefighting equipment became centers for male socializing, displacing the crossroads store (or the company store in the coalfields).

In due course, the settlers sorted themselves out into those who were merely sojourning in the mountains and who soon returned to conventional life in the cities and those who put down roots. Some former back-to-the-landers became urban homesteaders in Asheville, for instance, fixing up old houses in rundown districts and helping to give the city of Vance and Wolfe a portion of countercultural dash. Those who stayed in the country often found themselves replicating the gender divisions of traditional farm labor, with the men doing seasonal farm work and construction while women assumed responsibility for day-to-day chores.[69]

"Do we *have* to stay?" the wife of a craftsman-settler asked when life on a backwoods place a mile from the hard road began to get to her. No, he replied; they could leave if she wanted. Given permission to consider leaving, she found it possible to stick it out, though later when the children were older she went off to law school and returned to become an attorney in the county seat. Even without law degrees, settler women often found it easier to get local jobs than men did. The decline of farming, mining, and logging diminished the number of traditionally male jobs, while the expansion of service jobs in the postindustrial economy had a feminizing effect on the work force. Educated women in particular had an edge where local governments sought to fill white-collar positions with people who could meet qualifications mandated by state or federal grants. Competition for such jobs was fierce, however, in the districts surrounding college towns. "I know it looks like I'm overqualified," a Boone woman was overheard stating as she interviewed for a clerical position, "but I really need this job."

In one fashion or another, settlers became "neonatives" who developed strong attachments to the communities they adopted. Indeed, as the sociologist John Stephenson observed of his pseudonymous community, Shiloh, "The newcomers may now have a stronger sense of place than do the natives, who are uncertain what is happening to their place."[70] Settler-native relations, while remaining problematic in that the cultural gaps that separated the two groups never entirely closed, were strengthened by mutual distaste for another class of neonatives who came into the Blue Ridge in increasing numbers during the 1970s. These were residential tourists: part-time residents and retirees who built new homes in the mountains, often perching them in unaccustomed places on ridgetops, driving up land prices, and polluting the night sky with high-wattage floodlights either because their contractors sold them on the idea or because they found the quiet, dark mountain nights unsettling.

Eventually those settlers who had been part of experimental households grew more conventional. Settler families began raising children and either schooled them at home, as Purdy's parents did for him and his sister, or packed them off to public schools whose deficiencies led some of them to run for the county school boards, setting up yet another test of their local acceptance.[71] The most famous settler was a rich man, John D. Rockefeller IV of New York, who came to Appalachia as a poverty worker and eventually became West Virginia's governor and later a U.S. senator. Less prominent set-

Historic preservation is, in many respects, an urban counterpart of the back-to-the-land movement. Here, Capitol Street in Charleston, West Virginia, exhibits the charm that develops when disused central retailing and warehouse structures are transformed into professional offices, bookstores, cafés, and boutiques. The tall building in the right center was once the headquarters of Carbide and Carbon Company, a component of Union Carbide; behind it, "Sunrise" displays its pillared façade in the hills south of the Kanawha River. Built by governor William A. MacCorkle (1893–97), a promoter of extractive industry and a lawyer for nonresident corporations ("I smiled, and the money came," he wrote in his autobiography), Sunrise is now part of the city's art museum. (Photograph by the author)

tlers still included a proportion of "trust-fund babies," but for most the checks from home eventually ceased to arrive in the mailbox—if they had ever done so—and the newcomers found ways to support their families, although like the natives they were rarely able to do this without some kind of income earned off the farm.

One of the attractions that drew metropolitan young people to Appalachia, apart from cheap land and the opportunities to put ideals into practice, was a growing interest in Appalachian culture—not the dysfunctional social traits identified by older experts, but traditional folklife and crafts. Music was one of the badges of identity in the commercial youth culture in which most young Americans had grown up. The counterculture sustained this interest but encouraged rebellion against conventional popular music in preference of more "authentic" musical forms. People who had grown up playing in or listening to self-taught rock 'n' roll bands as teenagers now searched for more complex and personal musical identities in the mountains. The folk music revival of the 1950s—having made Tom Dula a household name among college-age listeners—paved the way for further explorations in folk, traditional, bluegrass, and old-time music, as well as a host of innovations that mingled and blurred these genres.

Appalachian virtuosos like North Carolina's Arthel "Doc" Watson, the Stanley Brothers of Virginia, and the Bluegrass Boys featuring Bill Monroe, Lester Flatt, and Earl Scruggs (of, respectively, Indiana, Tennessee, and North Carolina) were all discovered by larger audiences during this period. Their fame in turn inspired a new generation of fiddlers and guitar and banjo pickers who self-consciously revived the rural tradition of homemade entertainment. Some young musicians went further, seeking out and sitting at the feet of an even older generation, performers of old-time or early country music such as the Stoneman and Hammons families or the fiddlers Clark Kessinger and Melvin Wine of West Virginia or Tommy Jarrell of North Carolina. At the new Highlander Center, folk performers Guy and Candy Carawan made Appalachian music a centerpiece of the school's program of community organizing. The musical culture produced by this ferment became a bridge between activists and settlers and the natives of their local communities. For example, a Festival of the New River, featuring bluegrass and country music performers, helped rally the diverse coalition of natives, neonatives and nonresident activists fighting to save the upper New River from Appalachian Power's dam project in 1975.[72]

The same ethic of personal creativity that transformed musical culture also attracted graphic and decorative arts craftspersons to settle in the mountains and inspired new interest and respect for traditional folk arts such as quilting, pottery, basketry, and woodcarving. This in turn attracted the interest of tourism development and promotion authorities and led to a new crafts revival that displayed both innovation and elements of continuity with the revival of the New Deal era. In 1980 the Southern Highland Handicraft Guild opened an exhibition and sales facility on the Blue Ridge Parkway near Asheville, built partly with ARC funds, with a sales branch in the Moses Cone mansion, the summer home built by a textile magnate on the parkway near Blowing Rock and acquired by the Park Service in 1947. Plans to build a comparable center for folk music on the Virginia–North Carolina line near Galax were soon under way. The state of West Virginia, through its travel and tourism authority, created twin arts-and-crafts fairs at Harpers Ferry near Washington and at Ripley just off I-77, while in Kentucky, the work of a folk carver, Edgar Tolson of Wolfe County, became the object of a three-way tug-of-war between the Lexington artists who "discovered" him, an antipoverty agency that wished to make his work a centerpiece of redevelopment strategies based on crafts production, and the folk art dealers who merchandised his work to metropolitan collectors.[73]

Other developments during the 1970s illustrated the continuing appeal of Appalachian images to broader publics. The Foxfire program began as a class project for high school students in Rabun County, Georgia, who collected folk materials from relatives and other informants. Gathered into anthologies and published by the students' teacher, Eliot Wigginton, the materials filled a series of books that became national best-sellers between 1973 and 1986 and that served to counteract the hillbilly image conveyed by *Deliverance* and its host of imitators. (Ironically, one of the movie's more ominous scenes was filmed at the log house of the Foxfire series's best-loved informant.) Featuring "ways of life and crafts of pioneer America still surviving in Appalachia," Foxfire reached audiences through a magazine, a Broadway play, a Hollywood film, and an assortment of products, with royalties and sales going to fund an educational foundation for mountain youth. Moreover, as this project faded from view, a new generation of Appalachian writers matured who melded the narrative tradition of the mountains with realistic stories of social crisis. They included Gurney Norman of Kentucky, Jo Carson of Tennessee, Breece D'J Pancake and Denise Giardina of West Virginia, Lee Smith of Virginia, Dorothy Allison of South Carolina, and Fred Chappell, John Ehle, Robert Morgan, and Charles Frazier of North Carolina.

Even *Deliverance* helped draw national attention to some positive regional images through its portrayal of virtuosic banjo playing and its advertisement of whitewater adventure. Hitherto the challenge of pitting minds, bodies, and boats against the foaming rapids of the Cheat, Youghiogheny, Nantahala, New, Gauley, Ocoee, and Chattooga Rivers had been the private sport of a handful of young professionals from big cities—not unlike the fictional Atlantans who come to grief in *Deliverance*. For instance, Sayre Rodman, a chemical engineer from Cleveland, came with his wife Jean and fellow daredevils to the Gauley during the 1950s, applying skills they had learned in the mountain West to careen through rapids in military-surplus inflatable rafts that sometimes closed up around their occupants like clamshells.

In 1972, however, the Munich Olympics popularized a new style of white-

David Dauphiné (bearded, sitting high in the stern of the raft) guides a raft through Seven-foot Falls on the Chattooga River on the Georgia–South Carolina state line in 1978. His future wife, Posie, is in the left front, leaning to her right. The Dauphinés, both New Englanders, settled permanently in western North Carolina. (Courtesy of David and Posie Dauphiné)

water kayaking among enthusiasts, and a new European technology for molding fiberglass kayaks soon became available in places like Cincinnati, Columbus, Ohio, and State College, Pennsylvania, all now within easier reach of Appalachian rivers thanks to the new highways. Also in 1972, two Georgians —Horace Holden and Peyton Kennedy—founded the Nantahala Outdoor Center near Bryson City, North Carolina, and began running the Nantahala and Chattooga Rivers with members of an Atlanta Boy Scout troop. These developments created a class of young experts who provided the guidance that untrained recreationists needed in order to avoid whitewater disaster. Some of those who came as recreational users stayed on to become river guides and to found rafting companies of their own. After a period of rapid growth during the 1980s, firms like Class VI River Runners—which four college buddies from Ohio founded in 1978 to guide paying customers through the Gauley and New River Gorge rapids—now serve thousands of visitors annually, bringing millions of dollars into the mountains. After rafting came rock climbing, mountain biking, skiing, hang gliding, and diving, all sports whose participants thrived on the personal challenges presented by Appalachian waters and terrain.

Crisis and Renewal | 359

"My mother cried when we told her we were moving to West Virginia," recalls Chris Dragan, who with his older brothers Jon and Tom established the first commercially successful rafting company in New River Gorge. But the Dragans, along with many others like them, settled into new homes, started families, and even ran for the school board.[74] These adventurous neonatives were not always environmentalists in the activist sense of the term. But through their stewardship of the rivers they plied and the demonstration they offered of an entire new tourist market developing on the basis of scenic resources, they strengthened by example the arguments of those activists who argued that Appalachia's future would be better if only the spoliations of the extractive industries could be abolished or curbed. Business development experts engaged by the "Dead Pigeon" River Council, for example, drew on Nantahala whitewater veterans to identify rafting as an alternative source of income if Champion Paper could be forced to end its dumping of effluents. Champion countered by becoming a corporate sponsor of the U.S. Canoe and Kayak Team and staging a "whitewater shootout" on the river in 1994, to which critics responded by invading the competition course and festooning it with slogans about the water's carcinogenic properties.[75]

Some of the activists and settlers who came to Appalachia during this period subsequently went off to graduate or professional schools and then returned to the region as experts in their own right. One of the more distinctive centers of expertise developed in Whitesburg, Kentucky, Harry Caudill's hometown, where a recent Yale graduate, Bill Richardson, arrived in 1969 as a poverty worker. By this time, Appalachian poverty had become a fixture of network television, largely because the image of impoverished white mountaineers lent weight to the liberal assertion that poverty was "color-blind" and not the exclusive province of urban minorities, as the big city crises of these years might otherwise have led viewers to assume.

Fathoming the resentment that these images engendered among the ordinary citizens of places like Whitesburg, Richardson helped local young people start the Appalachian Film Workshop, whose declared purpose was to give mountaineers power to determine how the region's image was projected to the larger society. Operating as a collective in the experimental tradition of the counterculture, the organization evolved into Appalshop, which by the mid-1990s had become one of the largest employers in Letcher County and a magnet that offered training and practice to young filmmakers from all over the country in what came to be called community-based media. Appalshop established a radio station, a cable television service, a record company, an arts-and-crafts gallery, and a theater troupe that offered performances to school and community groups throughout eastern Kentucky and surrounding states.

Its greatest outreach, however, was through an expanding roster of documentary films, created in a style that avoided television conventions such as narration by older males with upper-class accents and distinguished mien. Instead, Appalshop films let people tell their own stories by means of video interviews and oral history. The Appalshop catalog (as of 2001) includes nearly one hundred films on a variety of subjects such as *Strip Mining in Appalachia* (1973), *Coal-Mining Women* (1982), traditional craftsmanship (*Chairmaker* [1975], *Quilting Women* [1976], and *Waterground* [1977]), *The Big Lever* (1982, depicting political competition and corruption in eastern Kentucky), *Mud Creek Clinic* (1986, portraying the establishment of a community-based clinic in the face of opposition from the local medical establishment), *Chemical Valley* (1991, raising issues about air pollution and public health in the Kanawha valley), *Ready for Harvest* (1993, portraying the interlocking interests and outlooks of the Forest Service and the forest-products industry in western North Carolina), and biographies of such Appalachian musicians as Ralph Stanley, Hazel Dickens, and Sarah Ogun Gunning. The collective's most ambitious project—a film history of Appalachia initiated in 1979 under the general direction of Helen Lewis—had produced three episodes by 1995. In 1991 Appalshop made its first venture into fiction with a production of *Fat Monroe*, based on a short story by Gurney Norman and starring the Academy Award–winning actor Ned Beatty, who appeared in the film gratis in expiation of his earlier performance as the victim of a sodomite hillbilly in *Deliverance*.

Activists, settlers, and experts, including some individuals wearing all three hats, attacked the ARC program in earnest during its early years, especially its emphasis on road building and its avoidance of the social issues laid bare by the War on Poverty. An opposition PARC (People's Appalachian Research Collective) flourished briefly in Morgantown during the early 1970s, sustained by the interest stirred by the MFD movement and by the patronage of the Institute for Policy Studies, a radical Washington, D.C., think tank. Its *People's Appalachia* was one of several small journals established in the region to keep up a barrage of anti-ARC criticism and to provide alternative visions for redevelopment. New energy suffused older organizations such as the Council of the Southern Mountains during these years, sometimes to the point of sparking fierce arguments over whose visions to support—the activists' plans to generate change through direct action and community organization or the more conservative schemes favored by foundations and government agencies.[76]

In 1977–78 activists and experts came together in Boone and Berea to create the Appalachian Studies Association (ASA). Rotating their annual meeting among the six core states of the region, ASA members developed a critical view of Appalachian society and history that stressed the exploitative nature of capitalism as the main source of regional problems. Emphasizing Appalachia's colonial economy and its identity with similarly exploited places in the Third World provided a fruitful basis of criticism, but the vision of redevelopment from the bottom up drew more on the poverty war's ethic of community action as embodied in dozens of small successes and some stirring defeats. Community studies undertaken from this perspective found values that an older generation of social scientists had thought dysfunctional to be, instead, valid expressions of tradition and/or appropriate responses to the corrosive impact of capitalist social relations. This positive valuation of regional history and culture led to an educational alternative to the genteel middle-class values enshrined in the public schools. Members of the ASA created outreach programs for high school students and schoolteachers, and ASA meetings provided numerous opportunities to hear and play Appalachian music and to celebrate the achievements of regional writers.

As the ASA reached maturity during the 1990s, it came more and more to resemble conventional scholarly associations, thanks to the aging of the original activists and the tendency of annual meetings to attract more participants from colleges and universities outside of the region. In the interim, its members compiled an impressive body of work. John Gaventa's *Power and Powerlessness* (1980) identifies the power of absentee economic interests to manipulate, through legal and extralegal means, the political agendas of local communities as a better explanation of supposed quiescence in the face of exploitation than the conventional wisdom about fatalism. David Corbin's *Life, Work, and Rebellion in the Coal Fields* (1981) and Denise Giardina's *Storming Heaven* (1987) provide, respectively, scholarly and fictional views of the mine wars as the struggles of ordinary people, not just episodes in the institutional histories of labor and capital in the coal industry. Henry D. Shapiro's *Appalachia on Our Mind* (1978) and Rodger Cunningham's *Apples on the Flood* (1987) laid bare the diverse origins of Appalachian stereotypes in American and European culture. Ronald Eller's *Miners, Millhands, and Mountaineers* (1982) provides a synthesis of regional history that emphasizes the colonial nature of Appalachia's industrialization, while Wilma Dunaway's *The First American Frontier* (1996) depicts the era of Indian wars and removal as a stage in the creation of a capitalist "world system." Deborah Vansau McCauley's *Appalachian Moun-*

tain Religion (1995) and Loyal Jones's *Faith and Meaning in the Southern Up-lands* (1999) rescue that topic from the modernist critics of fundamentalism.

This list includes only books that won the W. D. Weatherford Award given since 1970 by Berea College (and, after 2000, by the ASA) for the best book of the year published on Appalachia. A complete list of groundbreaking works in Appalachian studies—covering at most a couple of dozen books in 1975—would now number in the hundreds, with most of them challenging the basic premises upon which the official diagnoses of and responses to the Appalachian crisis rested. The transition to academic respectability did not come smoothly in all cases. Helen Lewis brought her new Ph.D. to East Tennessee State University (ETSU), only to be fired after one year for "nurturing radical students."[77] This launched her on a peripatetic career that eventually took her to most of the colleges and universities that were launching Appalachian studies programs in the 1970s and 1980s, including Appalachian State, Berea, Clinch Valley, the University of Kentucky, West Virginia University, and Virginia Tech. Even ETSU joined the movement, although under somewhat more conventional leadership.

The overall impact of the Appalachian Studies movement was the creation of a body of scholarly work that complements the documentary view of regional history and culture put forward by Appalshop. By the end of the century, Appalachian scholarship had matured sufficiently to merit codification. This came in the form of an Appalachian encyclopedia project based at ETSU's Center for Appalachian Studies and Services, a project that achieved official recognition and funding in 1995 from the revitalized Clinton version of the ARC.

As for the natives, the supposed beneficiaries of the changes envisioned by the ARC and its activist and academic critics, their response to the developments of the years after 1965 was at best ambiguous. A minority managed to benefit directly from the capital projects, tourism development, cultural revivals, and expanded welfare and social services that descended upon the mountains during these years. Many beneficiaries formed effective alliances with outside sponsors of change, creating groups of "inside outsiders and outside insiders" who mediated conflicts between natives and newcomers.[78] But other natives experienced a sense of loss or threat that, in the aggregate, created an atmosphere of unfocused resentment, feelings that rarely affected personal transactions between natives and neonatives but that often flared into angry public debate when issues involving control over local schools or the regulation of land use or of alcohol sales and consumption were at stake.

Whether welcome or uninvited, social change challenged natives' sense of place and identity. "If you grew up on the land, knowing everyone within twenty miles of where you are, you also know where they live, you know their kin and their kids, their dogs and cats. It's a matter of being practical," Julie Colvard, an Ashe County, North Carolina, woman explained to a scholar investigating the New River controversy. A native's sense of identity derived from family and community narratives that shaped everyday discourse without being written down or otherwise transmitted formally; having to define and proclaim this identity to outsiders inevitably transformed it. Similarly, an unspoken code of reciprocity governed routine interaction among neighbors and kin. Intrusion from the outside—whether by bureaucratic invaders like Appalachian Power or its parent company, American Electric Power (AEP), or by government agencies in Raleigh or Washington, or by the infiltration of neonative settlers and tourists—forced natives to defend their communities either by articulating (and thus oversimplifying) rules and practices that had traditionally been embodied more in acts than in words or by redefining local identity as a kind of Appalachian ethnicity.

Neither alternative was satisfying, nor was the choice between the dam promoters' plan to drown the county's best land *or* the opposition scheme to turn the New River into a federally protected river and state park. The scenic river would attract tourists, some of whom would end up buying rescued farms for retirement or summer homes, reducing local economic autonomy while driving up land prices for everyone else. Both threat and rescue forced natives to form alliances with outside groups bereft of local knowledge and to discourse in abstract legal-bureaucratic terms rather than the highly specified actions or narratives through which mountain people customarily articulate opinions and values. And though most settlers made the effort to fit into the networks of neighborhood reciprocity, tourists—whether residential or transient—expected to find the same transactional styles in the mountains that they knew in cities and suburbs. The results were a "monetization" of many exchanges that had once been reciprocal and a "subtle power of cultural domination" by the newcomers. Colvard concluded that Ashe County was really no better off than the coalfields. "I have come to support the idea that the Appalachian region is a colony," she wrote in Appalachian State's student newspaper. "The same system of colonialist exploitation which is at work in the strip mines of Kentucky is at work in the land/ski/condominium debacle in the mountains of North Carolina. The system is simply couched in prettier terms."[79]

A similar situation occurred in several southwest Virginia counties during the 1990s, when AEP announced another large project, an electrical transmission line supported by thirteen-story towers and running through a large

When the owner of Grandfather Mountain stymied the National Park Service's original plan to blast its way across the Linn Cove boulder field, the NPS turned to a European technology to build this roadway with less environmental damage. One hundred and fifty-three precast reinforced concrete panels, no two of them alike, were lowered from above into place atop seven piers, creating the beautiful S-shaped Linn Cove Viaduct, one of the signature landmarks of the Blue Ridge Parkway and the last part to be completed when it was finished in 1987. (Photograph by the author)

swath of land from the coalfields to Roanoke. In the Giles County village of Newport, both natives and neonatives opposed the project but did so in contrasting styles. The natives expressed their sense of communal solidarity through the Newport Agricultural Fair, an annual event—part festival, part community homecoming—that involved traditional rural displays and amusements and offered a sense of connection with the community's past, even though the number of residents who make a living by farming is now far fewer than those who work in industry or commute to jobs in nearby Montgomery County, the home of Virginia Tech. The neonatives, including Tech professors and students and a number of other settlers, mobilized formally through COPE (Citizens Out to Protect Our Environment), an advocacy group that held monthly meetings in the community center next to the rescue squad. Although a few inside outsiders and outside insiders crossed the cultural boundary to work with their opposite numbers, for the most part the boundary remained in place, weakening the community's position against AEP in the view of neonatives but reflecting among natives the same sense of threat on two fronts that surfaced in Ashe County twenty years before.[80]

There was another dimension to the Appalachian crisis that both the modernizing experts and their left-wing critics generally overlooked. This was the forty-year international struggle known as the Cold War, a global conflict with profound domestic implications. In effect, the military-industrial complex that emerged after 1948 amounted to "a kind of underground regional policy," one with vastly larger resources and carrying a greater impact than the TVA, the ARC, and urban renewal combined. Defense-related spending accomplished all of the goals set forth by formal redevelopment efforts: it served "to reduce income disparities between regions, to transfer industries to or promote new ones in lagging regions, to encourage infrastructure investments in backward regions, and to promote training and education policies in order to improve the quality of the regional work force."[81] Unfortunately, Appalachia was not among the regions favored in this regard.

Among its other impacts, the Cold War created the Sunbelt, transforming the South from "the nation's number one economic problem," as a presidential commission had stated in 1938, into an economically dynamic region fifty years later.[82] Yet the upland sections of the southeastern states, with the striking exception of the Huntsville district of northern Alabama, were largely omitted from this transformation, as were the Appalachian sections of Maryland, Ohio, Pennsylvania, and New York. In terms of manpower, Appalachia seems to have been a net contributor to the Cold War, but the region did not receive anything like a proportional return in terms of military bases, payrolls, and contracts. A complete assessment of the Appalachian crisis must take these facts into account.

When *The Dollmaker*'s Gertie Nevels encounters the outside world as a first step on her fictional migration to Detroit, the outsiders are soldiers bound for Oak Ridge. They could hardly have been headed anywhere else, for the large and secret nuclear facility that the Manhattan Project built in Anderson County, Tennessee, during 1943–45 was the only major military installation that the federal government placed in the Appalachian core during World War II. After 1946 Oak Ridge, now under civilian control, remained one of the few components of the military-industrial complex to be found in the mountain region. The Redstone Arsenal at Huntsville became a second focus of Appalachia's Cold War during the 1950s, especially after the National Aeronautics and Space Administration (NASA) located its principal engineering research and development facility there. The location of Redstone, like that of Oak Ridge, could be justified by the abundant availability of cheap TVA power, but there were many other factors, as we shall see. In any case, no other places in either official Appalachia or the regional core ever acquired the stimulus that an Oak Ridge or a Redstone gave to their local economies.

Military spending helps to explain why West Virginia, which had a higher per-capita income than its mother state of Virginia in 1940, became a steadily poorer relation during ensuing decades, along with the rest of Appalachia. Beginning with the completion of the Pentagon in 1941, eastern Virginia prospered on the payrolls of major military installations and contractors, only one of which—the Radford Arsenal—could be found west of the Blue Ridge. Radford's defense payroll averaged around $5 million during the last decade of the Cold War, quite a contrast with a $4 *billion* payroll in the cities surrounding Hampton Roads.[83] West Virginia's biggest military contractor during this period was sometimes the phone company, presumably because of the communication links among the various recruiting offices that helped to channel the flow of migrants from the state.

A comparison of the Appalachian and non-Appalachian portions of Georgia, Kentucky, Maryland, Mississippi, New York, North Carolina, Ohio, Pennsylvania, South Carolina, and Tennessee reveals similar patterns. In fact, no military bases or significant private contractors were to be found in the Appalachian portions of five states (Ohio, Maryland, Kentucky, North Carolina, or Georgia), although soldiers and airmen based elsewhere sometimes conducted training exercises in the Carolina and Georgia mountains. Only in Alabama did Appalachian counties receive a larger share of statewide defense-related expenditures relative to their population or area. Table 5.1, based on data from years when the Department of Defense tallied complete inventories of military installations, illustrates the scope and persistence of this pattern.[84]

An analysis of all federal expenditures after 1983—when consolidated reports on federal spending first became available—reveals similar patterns. Table 5.2 compares the basic categories of federal expenditures for West Virginia and the U.S. at large for the fiscal years 1983, 1985, 1990, and 1995. Since West Virginia is the only state located entirely within official Appalachia, it can fairly stand in for the Appalachian sections of the other twelve ARC states. Just to be sure, however, Table 5.3 uses county-level data from two

TABLE 5.1. Distribution of Military Installations, 1955–1990

Year/Region	Population (% of U.S.)		Military Bases (% of U.S.)	
1955				
U.S.	151,325,798	(100.0)	691	(100.0)
Appalachia (ARC)	17,612,887	(11.6)	11	(1.6)
Appalachia (core)	5,010,126	(3.3)	2	(0.3)
1960				
U.S.	179,323,175	(100.0)	786	(100.0)
Appalachia (ARC)	17,987,234	(10.0)	14	(1.8)
Appalachia (core)	4,810,837	(2.7)	5	(0.6)
1970				
U.S.	203,211,926	(100.0)	607	(100.0)
Appalachia (ARC)	18,485,460	(9.1)	14	(2.3)
Appalachia (core)	4,828,581	(2.4)	5	(0.8)
1980				
U.S.	226,545,805	(100.0)	574	(100.0)
Appalachia (ARC)	20,452,820	(9.0)	15	(2.6)
Appalachia (core)	5,609,808	(2.5)	6	(1.0)
1990				
U.S.	248,709,873	(100.0)	370	(100.0)
Appalachia (ARC)	20,819,324	(8.4)	6	(1.6)
Appalachia (core)	5,621,124	(2.3)	1	(0.3)

Sources: GAHM (regional population data)*; Statistical Abstract of the United States* (national population data); U.S. Department of Defense, *State Maps of Major Military Stations* and Washington Headquarters Services, DIOR, *Atlas/State Data Abstracts.*

other states—Kentucky and North Carolina—for the same years, showing the same contrast between the Appalachian and non-Appalachian portions of these states as that revealed by a comparison of West Virginia and the United States as a whole. Table 5.4 provides another point of comparison, this time between the Appalachian and non-Appalachian portions of Virginia and Georgia in fiscal year 1995, not long after the collapse of the Soviet Union confronted the military-industrial complex with demands for a "Cold War dividend" in the form of lower military spending. Eastern Virginia gains, of course, from its proximity to the nation's capital and from the numerous naval installations that surround the Hampton Roads anchorage, while Georgia's military payrolls and contracts owe more to the influence of politicians like Richard B. Russell and Sam Nunn, each of whom served as chairman of the

U.S. Senate's Armed Forces Committee, and Carl Vinson, who occupied a similar position in the House. Again, the pattern is striking and instructive.

The social implications of these numbers are considerable. A high level of defense employment and procurement, for example, tends to go along with a larger volume of federal loan guarantees, an indicator of housing expansion and small-business formation. A higher level of direct payments to individuals indicates a larger proportion of people dependent upon pension, disability, and welfare payments. Thus, although West Virginia's figure of $5,601 in per-capita federal expenditures in 1995 surpassed the national per-capita figure and trailed only Virginia and Maryland among the statewide averages for Appalachian states, a closer examination of Table 5.2 shows that the Mountain State remained more dependent on grants than on contracts and more on transfer payments than payrolls. In *The Watches of the Night* (1976), Harry Caudill worried that the expansion of social programs that accompanied the War on Poverty had turned Appalachia into a giant welfare reservation.[85] The fact that, twenty years later, West Virginia exceeded the national per-capita average and led all other Appalachian states in per-capita transfer payments suggests that he had a point.

Appalachia's humble place at the military-industrial trough was not totally disadvantageous, however. A Highlander study published in 1983 detailed the problems that flowed from defense procurement in eight southern states: West Virginia plus seven others with counties included in official Appalachia. These problems included the boom-and-bust cycles that followed changing defense weapons priorities, ground, water, and air pollution, low wage rates, discriminatory policies toward unions and nonwhite workers, indifference to worker health and safety, and a variety of scams by which large corporations, usually northern-based, managed to scoop up contracts reserved for small businesses or "surplus labor areas." The study concluded that the procurement programs that fueled high-technology booms in New England, Texas, and California were "anomalies" in the South, apart from the Huntsville district, Atlanta's suburbs, and Virginia installations around Washington or Hampton Roads. Elsewhere southern contractors chiefly supplied textiles, tobacco, coal, and food to the military. Apart from Huntsville, Oak Ridge, and the two ordnance works at Radford, Virginia, and Kingsport, Tennessee—all of which earned Highlander's censure on environmental and labor issues— Appalachia's share of defense spending conformed to the overall southern pattern. Only one major defense contractor was based in the region: Kentucky's Ashland Oil, which sold mainly fuel oil, rocket propellants, and coal to the military.[86]

TABLE 5.2. Federal Spending in West Virginia and the U.S., 1983–1995

Year	Population	Direct Federal Spending		Grant Awards	Salaries & Wages	
		Total	DOD		Total	DOD Payroll
1983 — U.S.	235,234,026					
Total ($ millions)		701,649	195,660	102,961	102,598	53,702
Per-capita $		2,983	832	438	436	228
1983 — W.Va.	1,950,254					
Total ($ millions)		4,845	240	967	397	68
% of U.S.	0.83	0.69	0.12	0.94	0.39	0.13
Per-capita $		2,484	123	496	204	35
1985 — U.S.	239,845,161					
Total ($ millions)		788,793	230,797	111,998	115,490	59,400
Per-capita $		3,289	962	467	482	248
1985 — W.Va.	1,952,181					
Total ($ millions)		4,995	244	890	474	78
% of U.S.	0.81	0.63	0.11	0.79	0.41	0.01
Per-capita $		2,558	125	456	243	40
1990 — U.S.	249,367,300					
Total ($ millions)		1,010,376	225,767	784,609	146,095	69,103
Per-capita $		4,213	941	3,271	609	288
1990 — W.Va.	1,877,000					
Total ($ millions)		6,726	417	1,142	600	96
% of U.S.	0.75	0.67	0.18	0.15	0.41	0.14
Per-capita $		2,158	482	1,676	312	148
1995 — U.S.	264,188,106					
Total ($ millions)		1,368,571	227,200	242,598	168,151	71,192
Per-capita $		5,180	860	918	636	269
1995 — W.Va.	1,822,640					
Total ($ millions)		10,209	459	2,338	797	125
% of U.S.	0.69	0.75	0.20	0.96	0.47	0.18
Per-capita $		5,601	252	1,283	437	69

Source: CFFR (CD), February 1994, August 1995.
Note: Rounding may affect some totals.

| Direct Payments to Individuals | | | Procurement | | Other Federal Obligations | Other Federal Assistance | |
Total	Retirement & Disability	All Other	Total	DOD	Total	Direct Loans	Loan Guarantees
325,876	231,299	94,577	158,929	127,017	11,287	16,192	154,249
1,385	983	402	676	540	48	69	656
3,287	2,399	888	184	104	9	23	678
1.01	1.04	0.94	0.12	0.08	0.08	0.14	0.44
1,685	1,230	455	94	53	5	12	348
348,986	256,182	92,804	197,054	154,188	18,264	11,275	112,533
1,455	1,068	387	822	643	76	47	469
3,374	2,582	791	217	90	10	5	536
0.97	1.01	0.85	0.11	0.06	0.05	0.04	0.48
1,728	1,323	405	111	46	5	3	275
502,889	334,228	168,661	188,531	135,259	24,867	9,999	247,494
2,097	1,394	703	786	564	104	42	1,032
4,519	3,175	1,344	325	223	139	47	707
0.90	0.95	0.80	0.17	0.16	0.56	0.47	0.29
1,074	714	360	403	289	53	21	529
729,776	452,083	277,692	202,209	126,004	25,838	25,923	461,250
2,762	1,711	1,051	765	477	98	98	1,746
6,312	4,135	2,177	708	203	54	166	890
0.86	0.91	0.78	0.35	0.16	0.21	0.64	0.19
3,463	2,269	1,194	388	112	30	91	488

TABLE 5.3. Federal Spending in the U.S. and Appalachian Kentucky and North Carolina, 1985–1995

Year	Population	Direct Federal Spending		Grant Awards	Salaries & Wages	
		Total	DOD		Total	DOD Payroll
1985—U.S.	239,845,161					
Total ($ millions)		788,793	230,797	111,998	115,490	599,400
Per-capita $		3,289	962	467	482	2,499
1985—Ky.	1,243,455					
Total ($ millions)		2,506	283	639	197	30
Per-capita $		2,016	227	514	158	24
1985—N.C.	1,269,916					
Total ($ millions)		2,413	213	273	181	15
Per-capita $		1,900	168	215	143	12
1990—U.S.	249,367,300					
Total ($ millions)		1,010,376	225,767	784,609	146,095	69,103
Per-capita $		4,213	941	3,271	609	288
1990—Ky.	1,084,400					
Total ($ millions)		4,271	132	728	191	20
Per-capita $		3,939	121	671	176	18
1990—N.C.	1,313,900					
Total ($ millions)		3,964	288	483	237	18
Per-capita $		3,017	219	368	181	13
1995—U.S.	264,188,106					
Total ($ millions)		1,368,571	227,200	242,598	168,151	71,192
Per-capita $		5,180	860	918	636	269
1995—Ky.	1,074,100					
Total ($ millions)		5,257	148	1,035	230	46
Per-capita $		4,894	138	964	214	43
1995—N.C.	1,371,648					
Total ($ millions)		5,066	258	941	275	19
Per-capita $		3,694	188	686	200	14

Source: CFFR.
Note: Rounding may affect some totals.

Direct Payments to Individuals			Procurement		Other Federal Obligations	Other Federal Assistance	
Total	Retirement & Disability	All Other	Total	DOD		Direct Loans	Loan Guarantees
348,986	256,182	92,804	197,054	154,188	18,264	11,275	112,533
1,455	1,068	387	822	643	76	47	469
1,695	1,500	439	347	218	12	7	355
1,363	1,206	353	279	175	10	5	286
1,777	1,384	430	172	124	9	7	123
1,399	1,090	338	135	97	7	6	97
502,889	334,228	168,661	188,531	135,259	24,867	9,999	247,494
2,097	1,394	703	786	564	104	42	1,032
2,451	1,830	600	1,261	56	18	41	417
2,260	1,687	554	1,163	51	17	38	384
2,453	1,883	579	214	177	15	23	326
1,867	1,433	441	163	135	11	17	248
729,776	452,083	277,692	202,209	126,004	25,838	25,923	461,250
2,762	1,711	1,051	765	477	98	98	1,746
5,423	2,312	1,011	632	41	9	53	497
5,049	2,152	941	589	38	9	49	463
3,628	2,631	1,016	181	114	13	29	398
2,645	1,918	740	132	83	9	21	290

TABLE 5.4. Federal Expenditures in Mountain and Nonmountain Counties
of Georgia and Virginia, 1995

State/Region	Population (%)	Direct Federal Spending	
		Total (%)	DOD (%)
Georgia	7,055,235 (100)	33,414,551 (100)	7,753,446 (100)
Mountain (ARC)	1,751,899 (25)	4,611,994 (14)	350,763 (5)
Nonmountain	5,303,336 (75)	28,802,557 (86)	7,402,683 (95)
Virginia	6,550,826 (100)	51,490,236 (100)	23,315,130 (100)
Mountain (ARC)	649,314 (10)	2,684,816 (5)	231,824 (1)
Nonmountain	5,901,512 (90)	48,805,420 (95)	23,083,306 (99)

Source: CFFR.

These concerns notwithstanding, it must be recognized that "the military and its surrogates acting in the name of national security . . . nurtured leading industries, steered migration, financed physical infrastructure, expanded higher education, and promoted the births and deaths of regional economies."[87] Moreover, federally funded defense or aerospace research led to commercial spinoffs comprising whole new industries: semiconductors, computers, a range of electronic communications applications, and civilian nuclear power, for example.[88]

When we inquire as to the reasons for Appalachia's Cold War fate, certain answers seem obvious. An inland eastern mountain region is not a likely site for naval bases or a useful staging area for Pacific wars. On the other hand, in the face of nuclear threat, remote locations are desirable under the doctrine of "industrial dispersion," which many American strategists advocated during the early years of the Cold War (and which became official policy in the Soviet Union). A team of regional scientists that investigated the matter closely concluded that such factors as climate, terrain, and geographical convenience or remoteness cannot in themselves account for the locational impacts of defense spending. "Gunbelt" is a more appropriate shorthand for the favored regions than is Sunbelt, they argue, for the complex of military installations, prime military contractors, and "high-tech" electronics and communications firms constitutes a band slung loosely around the nation's perimeter from key concentrations in California and southern New England, with a cluster in the states of Arizona, Colorado, Utah, New Mexico, and Texas that might be imaginatively described as a holster. Not all of the favored places enjoy the benign climate implied by the term Sunbelt. "[I]t is not the passive attributes of places that determine the location of defense-related activity in the economy,

Salaries & Wages		Procurement	
Total (%)	DOD (%)	Total (%)	DOD (%)
5,800,507 (100)	3,174,575 (100)	4,314,721 (100)	3,513,236 (100)
313,871 (5)	27,293 (1)	297,690 (7)	196,620 (6)
5,486,636 (95)	3,147,282 (99)	4,017,031 (93)	3,316,616 (94)
12,016,238 (100)	8,864,853 (100)	16,598,065 (100)	12,119,771 (100)
110,766 (1)	18,940 (0)	445,817 (3)	166,289 (1)
11,905,472 (99)	8,845,913 (100)	16,152,248 (97)	11,953,482 (99)

but the active involvement of many participants, each with distinctive motivations, choosing among a number of potential sites. Whether boosters, colonels, generals, firm managers, or elected representatives, selected groups have mattered a great deal in shaping America's military-production geography."[89]

Politics also played a part in military location decisions, including not only electoral politics, but the politics of military planning and interservice rivalries, plus, of course, the informal politics of lobbying at the Pentagon and on Capitol Hill. The modern United States inherited a geographic spread of military installations that reflected nineteenth-century Indian warfare, the insecurity of the Mexican border, and, after 1890, a fear of urban mobs that led to the creation of new bases close to big cities. The major wars of the twentieth century saw departures from these patterns, chiefly through the distribution of new training and logistical facilities across the Southeast and Far West—for strategic reasons in the case of California during World War II and the Korean and Vietnam Wars, but for less obvious ones in the cases of numerous bases strewn across the southern Piedmont and coastal plain from Virginia to Texas. Our twentieth-century wars were fought under liberal Democratic presidents whose successes depended in part upon alliances with conservative southern Democrats (Georgia's Russell or Nunn, for example) who headed key committees in Congress.[90] This dependency was certainly not irrelevant in the distribution of military installations, but we are entitled to ask why the Appalachian constituents of these same committee chairmen fared so poorly at the military-industrial trough.

Consider the cases of several influential Appalachian members of Congress. Senators Sam Ervin of North Carolina, Howard Baker of Tennessee, John Sparkman of Alabama, and Matthew M. Neely, Harley M. Kilgore, and

Robert C. Byrd of West Virginia were all powerhouses in Congress in their days. Kilgore, Neely, and Sparkman in particular invite attention, for all three were among the most consistent supporters of an assertive foreign policy and aggressive military posture during the inaugural years of the Cold War. Most politicians reacted to Cold War issues on the basis of constituent interests; a given senator's response reflected the relative importance in his or her state of trade with those parts of the world where American and Soviet interests clashed. Kilgore, Neely, and Sparkman were "liberal" exceptions to this rule, however.[91] Sparkman and his senatorial colleague Lister Hill headed the South's most liberal congressional delegation, one that grew increasingly vulnerable to race-baiting Alabama rivals after the Supreme Court ruled against segregated schools. Kilgore and Neely were among organized labor's chief congressional allies, with their liberalism—like Sparkman's and Hill's—grounded in support of the New Deal's labor and welfare programs. Yet the West Virginians did not steer defense installations to their state the way the Alabamians did. Neely was distracted by party and patronage battles at home. Kilgore took a vigorous and prominent interest in postwar reconversion policy and was also a close personal friend of President Harry Truman; however, he invested his influence on postwar reconversion issues mainly in matters of primary interest to organized labor.[92]

Similarly, Ervin took pride in his mastery of constitutional issues in Congress and left "case work" and related economic chores to his senatorial colleagues from eastern North Carolina. Unlike Sparkman, he had no race baiters to distract with patronage and defense contracts, since he was an ardent segregationist himself.[93] Tennessee's Baker built his considerable reputation on national rather than regional issues, although, as we have seen, he did in the snail darter and, according to the Highlander study, made his East Tennessee hometown the center of body bag production during the Vietnam years.[94] His Democratic predecessor and successor as Senate Majority Leader, Robert C. Byrd, followed a similar statesmanlike role during the first three decades of his senatorial career; only after he stepped down as Majority Leader in 1989 did Byrd devote himself to sowing federal jobs, installations, and contracts among his constituents.

Beginning as early as 1950, the liberal Truman and Kennedy administrations attempted to direct at least part of the flow of defense dollars to areas of persistent "labor surplus," such as Appalachia, but the military resisted this move, while southern congressmen led a successful effort to block implementation of the plan.[95] Congress also blocked implementation of industrial dispersal, while Kilgore's proposal for a centralized federal agency directing scientific, industrial, and military research gave way to a competitive and decentralized model of private research contracts funded through a set of independent federal agencies: the NSF, NASA, the National Institute(s) of Health, the Atomic Energy Commission—all of them put in place between 1946 and 1957—plus the army, navy, and air force.

During the Cold War's initial decades, defense-related procurement and research were "privatized"—carried out by corporate contractors rather than by government operations. This meant that locational decisions, like so much else about the military-industrial complex, were mediated by informal political relationships among lobbyists, military brass, and elected officials and by service rivalries as much as by the formal concerns of policymakers.[96] Consequently, Appalachia remained below the salt at the military-industrial table. Byrd's mentor in the Senate, Richard B. Russell, helped to make Lockheed, based in Los Angeles but with a concentration of branch plants in metropolitan Atlanta, the largest industrial employer in the Southeast during the 1960s and 1970s. Lockheed employees could be found in 55 of the state's 159 counties, but none of them worked in the Appalachian core of north Georgia.[97]

The difference that political influence could make is further illustrated by comparing Scranton, Pennsylvania, with Huntsville at the opposite end of official Appalachia. Scranton, with 125,000 people in 1950, was the anthracite region capital whose bleak postwar prospects led to calls for federal assistance as early as 1944; Huntsville (population 16,000 in 1950) might with equal justice have been described then as a textile-mill town facing a likely renewal of labor troubles.[98] Scranton's leadership was divided, with the local congressional seat seesawing between Republicans and Democrats throughout the 1940s and 1950s. Huntsville, on the other hand, had Sparkman, first as its local congressman, then as a senator. The army had established Redstone Arsenal, along with an ordnance works, in Huntsville during World War II, giving the South its first federal arsenal since the destruction of Harpers Ferry at the beginning of the Civil War and Huntsville its first significant alternative to textile mill payrolls. Sparkman worked hard to protect these installations from postwar cutbacks. After the army transferred its cadres of military ballistic missile experts and German rocket scientists from Fort Bliss, Texas, to Redstone in 1951, Sparkman helped to guide the arsenal through the shoals of army–air force rivalries over national missile development to become one of the capitals of American space technology and exploration. The Germans proved to be the army's trump cards in the competition, but though army ascendance allowed the continued operation of Redstone as a traditional arsenal under government control, the army was also forced to modify its distaste for air force–style privatized procurement; NASA followed that policy from its creation in 1961.

Thus, although NASA's installation in Huntsville is named for George C. Marshall, the army general who as Truman's secretary of state was one of the architects of Cold War policy, and the John Sparkman Center for Missile Excellence is found on the Redstone property next door, privatized procurement also brought facilities of major private military contractors to Huntsville. Ironically, when a pause occurred in defense and space-related growth in the late 1970s, the ARC stepped in with planning assistance that helped Huntsville use the talent that NASA and the army had brought to the city to lay the foundation for a more diverse private economy.[99] Many of the scientists, engineers, and high-tech entrepreneurs who today lead the city's growth were surprised to find themselves living in Alabama, much less Appalachia. Yet their presence made the Huntsville district one of the region's rare success stories during the crisis years.

Scranton, on the other hand, mobilized private investment, state and local government funds, and federal ARA and urban redevelopment grants to reinvent itself as a manufacturing center. When deindustrialization disrupted this path to renewal during the 1980s, redevelopment became more dependent than ever on federal funds, but not the kind that generate the multiplier effects seen in Huntsville. Republican Rep. Joseph M. McDade wrangled a seat on the House Appropriations Committee in 1965 and managed to accumulate enough clout over the years to earn a national reputation for pork-barrel "piggery." McDade helped the city piece together expressway construction, historic preservation, and downtown revitalization projects, sweetened by an occasional military contract such as the one that established an army ordnance works in a disused corner of the Lackawanna Railroad shops. In 1986 he inspired the addition of the phrase "park barrel" to the political lexicon when Congress passed legislation requiring the National Park Service to take over a collection of mostly Canadian locomotives and passenger cars acquired from a Vermont collector and to use it as the basis of Steamtown—a museum and equipment menagerie housed in a rebuilt Lackawanna roundhouse. An adjacent shopping mall built as the centerpiece of downtown renewal serves as an adjunct to this federally operated tourist attraction.[100]

The relative value of Scranton's and Huntsville's paths to renewal is illustrated by Tables 5.5 and 5.6, which compare the population histories of the two cities since 1940 and the scope and character of federal spending in each

TABLE 5.5. Population Change, 1940–2000

	1940	1950	1960	1970	1980	1990	2000
Lackawanna County, Pa. (Scranton)	301,243	257,396	234,531	234,107	227,908	222,300	213,295
Madison County, Ala. (Huntsville)	66,317	72,903	117,348	186,540	196,166	236,700	276,700

Source:GAHM; Bureau of the Census, *American Factfinder,* <www.factfinder.census.gov>.

since the early 1980s. As was true of West Virginia vis-à-vis the U.S. or the mountain versus the lowland portions of other Appalachian states, these data illustrate Scranton's greater dependence on grant awards, Social Security, and welfare payments and its relative dearth of defense payrolls and small-business and housing loan guarantees. Huntsville grew somewhat less dependent upon NASA and the defense department over time, but the payrolls and contracts from these two agencies still account for roughly half of all federal spending there, compared with less than 10 percent in Scranton. Huntsville's level of transfer payments is less than a third of that found in Scranton, while an expanding volume of loan guarantees indicates dynamism in the private economy.

Clearly, if federal funds had been invested in other Appalachian places on a scale comparable with that in Huntsville, there would have been no Appalachian crisis. This fact is important, because politicians and the public evaluate the developmental benefits that accompany defense dollars very differently than they do those that come through federal grants and transfer payments. Studies of social welfare programs since the New Deal show that programs originally intended for the support of men and male-headed households (such as unemployment compensation and retirement benefits) quickly became invested with the aura of entitlement, whereas those aimed at the support of single women and female-headed households (such as aid to families with dependent children) soon came under a cloud of opprobrium and were eventually, during the 1990s, disconnected from the claim of entitlement.[101]

Similar attitudes stick to distressed areas like Appalachia. Claims on the federal treasury in the name of defense generate a patriotic aura that even the most antigovernment conservative can embrace, and the same is true for the array of agricultural price-support programs, small-business loans, and home-mortgage guarantees sanctioned in the name of family farms and middle-class enterprise. On the other hand, Appalachia's transfer payments acquired the opprobrium of handouts and pork barrel, though they might just

TABLE 5.6. Federal Spending in Lackawanna County, Pennsylvania (Scranton), and Madison County, Alabama (Huntsville)

Year	Population	Direct Federal Spending		Grant Awards	Salaries & Wages	
		Total	DOD		Total	DOD Payroll
1983						
Lackawanna	227,908					
$ (millions)		629	121	20	31	5
% of total direct federal expenditures		19.2	3.2		4.9	0.8
Madison	196,966					
$ (millions)		1,321	729	22	531	374
% of total direct federal expenditures		55.2	1.7		40.2	28.3
1985						
Lackawanna	223,977					
$ (millions)		710	104	66	34	5
% of total direct federal expenditures		14.6	9.3		4.8	0.7
Madison	210,020					
$ (millions)		2,044	1,110	101	596	425
% of total direct federal expenditures		54.3	4.9		29.2	20.8
1990						
Lackawanna	222,300					
$ (millions)		841	54	73	43	5
% of total direct federal expenditures		6.4	8.7		5.1	0.6
Madison	236,700					
$ (millions)		3,565	1,676	87	712	485
% of total direct federal expenditures		47.0	2.4		20.0	13.6
1995						
Lackawanna	216,011					
$ (millions)		1,281	87	296	61	10
% of total direct federal expenditures		6.8	23.1		4.8	0.8
Madison	258,036					
$ (millions)		3,209	1,581	149	691	453
% of total direct federal expenditures		49.3	4.6		21.5	14.1

Source: CFFR.

Direct Payments to Individuals			Procurement		Other Federal Obligations	Other Federal Assistance	
Total	Retirement & Disability	All Other	Total	DOD		Direct Loans	Loan Guarantees
467	364	103	109	99	1	19	18
74.2	57.9	16.4	17.3	15.7	0.1		
274	239	35	510	318	4	10	88
20.7	18.1	2.6	38.6	24.1	0.3		
511	381	131	97	91	2	0	14
72.0	53.7	18.5	13.7	12.8	0.3		
320	272	48	1,020	642	7	3	62
15.7	13.3	2.3	49.9	31.4	0.3		
664	448	216	58	40	2	1	45
79.0	53.3	25.7	6.9	4.8	0.2		
483	404	78	2,278	1,126	5	8	194
13.5	11.3	2.2	63.9	31.6	0.1		
832	536	296	89	66	84	1	83
64.9	41.8	23.1	6.9	5.2	6.6		
652	519	142	1,705	1,042	3	24	248
20.3	16.2	4.4	53.1	32.5	0.1		

Two familiar sights that owe nothing to the counterculture of postindustrial Appalachia: Coffindaffer crosses and a trailer park. West Virginia businessman-turned-evangelist Bernard Coffindaffer, after recovering from a health crisis, began planting these crosses in his home state during the 1980s and eventually branched out, setting up 1,773 crosses—each group featuring two blue crosses flanking a central one in gold—in twenty-eight states before his death in 1993. Mobile homes are popular in Appalachia for three reasons: absentee ownership by extractive industry and government agencies restricts the amount of buildable land; home mortgages are not available on leased land, but mobile home loans, structured like automobile loans, put this form of housing within range of most working people; and finally, trailers reflect gendered preferences, in that Appalachian men still spend much of their time outdoors and are as inclined to invest in cars and recreational equipment as in larger houses, while women can obtain a full suite of modern appliances with the purchase of a mobile home. (Photograph by Frank P. Herrera)

as fairly be characterized as reparations for the damages done to the region through its contributions of energy and raw materials to the national economy. Thus, the Reagan administration mounted an effort to zero out ARC funds at precisely the time it also launched a large and costly military buildup. With gulps from the defense budget and sips from the ARC trough, Huntsville thrives on the achievements of its military-industrial economy, while Scranton, in common with the many less fortunate places in Appalachia, continues to slide.

Although Appalachia was not invited to the developmental feast served up by the Cold War, it seems to have supplied its share of manpower for the conflict—possibly more than its share, although this is difficult to prove. Intuitively, one suspects that military service played an important role in the migration of Appalachian young people, that military recruiters targeted Appalachia's surplus manpower, and that local draft boards granted deferments and other considerations more often to middle- and upper-income town dwellers than to young men from farming and mining communities. The "daycoach migration" of World War II—so called from the hot and crowded passenger trains that carried men and women from the mountains to defense plants and military bases in places like Norfolk, Baltimore, and Detroit—is well documented.[102] Military service during the war gave thousands of Appalachian soldiers and sailors a chance to sample the possibilities of life and work in distant parts of the nation. A new policy of mingling recruits from different places in military units rather than organizing them in geographically based divisions further broke down resistance to leaving home.

The social disruptions of World War II occurred on a larger and more visible stage than those of later Cold War conflicts, but it seems safe to assume that defense-related migration continued. Moreover, while coal miners and certain classes of farm workers could get war-work deferments during World War II, the later conflicts coincided with the Appalachian crisis that encouraged young people to look outward for their opportunities. At least one military manpower specialist saw the coalfields as prime recruiting territory. Brig. Gen. Charles R. Fox, a Pacific war veteran who became head of the West Virginia National Guard after the war, made it his particular task to tout the advantages of military service to high school assemblies in coal country. His success in West Virginia during the 1950s led him eventually to Washington, where he became a Selective Service System manpower specialist on the eve of the Vietnam War.[103]

The revival of the peacetime draft in 1948 led to the reconstitution of local draft boards that exercised considerable influence on the way the draft affected particular communities. Under Gen. Lewis B. Hershey, who headed Selective Service from 1940 until the elimination of the draft in 1973, these volunteer boards represented a locality's respectable leadership, "the county seat folks" of a rural district, not a sample of its social diversity.[104] The system's potential for abuse is obvious, although the extent to which it occurred cannot readily be documented, thanks to Hershey's effort to place Selective

TABLE 5.7. Congressional Medal of Honor Winners

	World War II			Korea		
Region	No. of CMOH	% of U.S.	% of U.S. Males 14+, 1940	No. of CMOH	% of U.S.	% of U.S. M 14 +, 195(
United States	440	100		131	100	
Appalachia	58	13.2	12.4	26	19.8	11.4
West Virginia	10	2.3	1.4	2	1.5	1.2

Sources: U.S. Army Center for Military History, <http://www.army.mil/cmh-pg/mohiia1.htm>; GAH.

Service records in military hands after his retirement, rather than in the National Archives.

Available data does not allow us to identify recruitment patterns at the county level, nor is there data available that identifies veterans' postdischarge locations. In North Carolina, a detailed study of the draft during World War II makes it possible to determine the proportion of Appalachian to non-Appalachian recruits, and this proportion was almost—though not quite—identical to the distribution of population: 23.9 percent of males in the eligible age range were drafted or enlisted between 1940 and 1946 in counties later included in official Appalachia, compared with 22.3 percent for non-ARC counties. Otherwise there is little evidence that the experience of mountain men was any different than that of men from eastern North Carolina or the Piedmont. Three mountain counties were able to meet their initial draft quotas entirely or mostly through voluntary enlistments, while six Appalachian states (North Carolina, Kentucky, South Carolina, Georgia, Tennessee, and West Virginia) were among the top seven in the nation in this regard. Collectively, however, western North Carolina counties lagged slightly behind the statewide proportion of volunteers in 1940–41, while the ratio of enlistments to drafted recruits for the entire period (1940–46) in the mountains was nearly identical to that in the state at large. The same is true with respect to those who served in the military without ever having registered for the draft—a total that includes women in uniform as well as those men who served in the armies of allied nations.[105]

At the height of the Cold War, Walter B. Miller, a cultural anthropologist whose studies of the "upward diffusion" of "lower-class culture" among middle-class teenagers pioneered the culture-of-poverty theory, warned that programs designed to curb the violent tendencies of lower-class males, though reducing the risk of juvenile delinquency, might also compromise

	Vietnam		All Wars, 1941–1976 Totals	
No. of CMOH	% of U.S.	% of U.S. Males 15–34, 1970	Number	%
239	100		810	
32	13.4	8.7	116	14.3
7	2.9	0.8	19	2.3

their usefulness as soldiers.[106] This observation was not specific to Appalachia, but it dovetails with a widespread belief in the region that mountaineer traditions of markmanship and other soldierly skills produced a disproportionate number of Congressional Medal of Honor winners. This belief is perhaps a legacy of Sergeant York, but as Table 5.7 suggests, there is evidence to back it up. Rural men everywhere displayed more soldierly qualities as recruits, but in general such differences did not persist through training and combat experience. Yet Appalachian men gave the last full measure of devotion in larger numbers than the region's share of the national adult male population would indicate, but this is true only if we define Appalachia in terms of its official boundary rather than its core.

It should also be pointed out that, if western North Carolina in World War II is any indication, this record may owe something to the slightly larger proportion of mountain men who served in the military, rather than to any Appalachian edge in valor or duty. In any event, these data establish that Appalachia did indeed do its share in the nation's defense, even if it got a poor economic return in the bargain. It seems somehow fitting that the best-known Appalachian recruit of the Cold War era was not a Stonewall Jackson or a Sergeant York, but a fictional GI, Pvt. Will Stockdale. Brought to life on Broadway and in a film by actor Andy Griffith of Mt. Airy, North Carolina, Stockdale became one of the most popular comic hillbillies of the postwar years. Griffith followed up with a television series in which he shared the limelight with another comic hillbilly, West Virginia's Don Knotts. So enduring was the popularity of *The Andy Griffith Show* that, during the 1990s, Mt. Airy reinvented itself as its fictional locale, Mayberry, becoming a tourist attraction and, as such, one of the few Appalachian places to gain a developmental return on its manpower contribution.

As with a pine cone that requires a forest fire in order to germinate, the Appalachian crisis planted seeds of renewal, but whether these originated in official or unofficial responses to the crisis, the end results were relatively modest. In any process of social change, there are winners and losers. Sometimes it is hard to tell which is which. A Pittsburgh reporter who sought to assess the region's overall progress at the end of the twentieth century started her assessment in Martin County, Kentucky, at the home of the former miner whose front porch had provided the backdrop for President Johnson's pledge to end poverty in 1964. The house is still ramshackle, she found; its yard is still trash strewn and the owner is still out of work, having never found a full-time job since the mines where he worked shut down before LBJ's visit.

Martin County crawled briefly out of the ARC's "distressed" category during the energy boom of the 1970s, went back on the list during the 1980s, and remained there at the century's end, when it again made headlines thanks to the collapse of a 250-million-gallon coal slurry impoundment near the county seat of Inez. In contrast to Buffalo Creek in 1972, no lives were lost in the Inez disaster, but numerous homes were damaged, and the inundation covered streams and land with a coating of gooey black sludge. The usual investigations were mounted, though experienced observers of the coal industry expected them to end in a whitewash. Meanwhile, the National Academy of Sciences established a blue-ribbon committee to investigate the safety of such impoundments—a committee then noticeably deficient in experts who were not employed by or otherwise affiliated with the industry.[107]

Over in West Virginia, Huey Perry, a poverty war veteran from Mingo County who is now a developer of historic properties in Huntington, is philosophical. "We had some small victories, and then there was a tendency to let down. In some ways, things look bleaker now. The only way you can really fight poverty is to give people the power, and no politicians are willing to take the risk."[108] However, a recent assessment suggests that Appalachian success stories are numerous enough to be encouraging. Richard A. Couto counts more than twenty community-based projects that mitigated "the savage side of market capitalism" in one fashion or another.[109] These projects ranged from statewide mobilizations of schoolteachers and senior citizens in West Virginia to the victory of tiny Brumley Gap, Virginia, in fighting off another Appalachian Power pumped-storage project and the Western North Carolina Alliance's success in forcing the Forest Service to moderate its enthusiasm for clear-cutting.

Yet most of these victories, modest though they were, depended on some kind of outside subvention, in the form of grants from foundations or government agencies, or on unenforced laws intended to curb the abuse or neglect against which the communities mobilized. In the area of social capital, no less than in economic terms, Appalachia has yet to reach the stage of self-sustaining growth. And it faces a future wherein the forces of globalization and political conservatism seem likely to discourage the larger society from providing the kinds of subventions and legislation upon which mobilized mountain communities must be able to draw.

Contrasted with coalfield and rural communities, the town of Jonesborough, Tennessee, looks like a winner. "Tennessee's oldest town" and its frontier capital, Jonesboro—as the Post Office insisted on spelling it until forced to change as part of the town's renewal program—fell on hard times during the 1950s and 1960s. A drape of neon signs and tangled utility wires disguised the latent charm of its nineteenth-century storefronts, while local retailers steadily lost customers to the shopping malls of nearby Johnson City. Although Johnson City had problems of its own in the decline of its railroad yards and foundries, it managed to reinvent itself as a service center, thanks to federal funds for highway construction, the expansion of East Tennessee State University, and a new Veterans Administration medical school housed on the grounds of an old soldier's home built originally for Union Civil War veterans. Some of the doctors discovered that Jonesborough's charming old houses were within easy commuting distance and became historic preservationists as well as homeowners.

These neonatives joined hands with natives worried about the town's survival to launch a renewal program based on Jonesborough's architectural heritage and financed through a succession of state and federal grants. The grants made it possible to update the town's infrastructure and refurbish the downtown streetscape with buried utility lines, brick sidewalks with stone curbs, and Victorian street furniture. These changes helped to transform the main street into a specialty shopping district that attracted tourists and recreational shoppers. Seasonal festivals were established to lure shoppers away from the malls. One of these, a fall event organized by Jimmy Neil Smith, a high school teacher and history buff who served as mayor during a critical phase of the renewal process, grew into the International Storytelling Festival.

Although it started out modestly, the Jonesborough storytelling festival quickly became the center of a national movement. The storytelling revival was part of the counterculture's general shift during the 1970s away from politics and toward the inner frontiers of spirituality and personal growth.[110] Related movements such as the folk music revival or the back-to-the-land movement never acquired a capital like Jonesborough, however. The festival, growing in attendance from a few dozen in 1973 to 10,000 in 1997, made a star out of Ray Hicks, a master of traditional folktales and a member of the tradition-bearing North Carolina family that had provided singers and storytellers to earlier generations of folklife collectors. It also became a career-building focus for a new breed of professional storytellers, revivalists who found that they could make a living performing at schools and public libraries, campuses and special events. And it became an object of contention among storytellers for whom such a singular focus was constraining or inconvenient and among those who suspected that Smith's first loyalty was to Jonesborough, not to them.

At the end of the century, Smith—having survived a political assault by Jonesborough natives who resisted the community's transformation by outsiders like the medicos and storytellers—accommodated critics by assisting at the division of the National Storytelling Association into two parts: one offering membership services to professionals and the other an organization that sponsors education and performance programs for both professionals and the general public. A new International Storytelling Center, designed by a famous New York architect to blend in with Jonesborough's antique streetscape, provided a year-round performance venue and tourist attraction beginning in 2001. A new ordinance prohibiting "demolition by neglect" of historic properties whipped recalcitrant native property owners into line, while the town acquired its first neonatives of the seasonal variety.[111]

Fayetteville, West Virginia, is another Appalachian courthouse town undergoing transformation. When C. R. "Bud" Hill came home from law school in 1954, the only job he could find was in a local bank. Fayette County lost 25 percent of its population during the 1950s, another 20 percent during the 1960s, and 17 percent during each of the two ensuing decades. This population implosion left behind empty houses and vacant storefronts—two of the factors that helped in the growth of whitewater rafting and other recreational activities that have changed the New River Gorge from a transportation barrier into a tourist attraction.

Cheap housing made it possible for rafters and other sportspeople attracted to the gorge to become settlers, while the fine old houses in the center of town, once the homes of bankers and coal company lawyers, became bed-and-breakfast inns serving recreational tourists. Only the law firms fronting the courthouse square remain from the old days. Otherwise, hardware and drug stores have given way to shops selling recreational gear, crafts and art galleries, an organic grocery, and—between 1994 and 1999—a restaurant, the Sedona Grille, that served southwestern-style food so good that it attracted not only the whitewater crowd but also local diners from as far away as Charleston and Beckley. Started by a Pennsylvania couple, Virginia Price and Brian Levine, who came to Fayetteville mainly because of the low cost of starting up their own place there, Sedona supplied a flashpoint for native reactions to change when it applied for a liquor license in 1995, and again in 1999 when the owners tried to expand from their crowded storefront into one of the nearby inns. Price and Levine won the first contest after a lengthy and dispiriting court battle but lost the second, moving instead into another location on the outskirts of town. Sedona is still popular, even with some natives who may resent the fact that they must choose from what seems to them an exotic menu, but who eat there anyway because the food is so good. New flashpoints have emerged in controversies over school consolidation and the enforcement of preservation regulations in the recently established Fayetteville Historic District.[112]

On one level, we can see in Jonesborough and Fayetteville the importance of the maturing counterculture, with its emphasis on authenticity, preservation, and alternatives to mass consumption as represented by fast food and motel chains, shopping malls, and look-alike suburbs. However, we can also observe in both places the pervasive influence of the federal government— not the huge infusions of aerospace dollars that transformed Huntsville, but smaller investments made on a project-by-project basis and the expansion of welfare services that came with the Great Society. As far as Bud Hill's bank was concerned, the turnaround came after 1969, when miners and ex-miners got their first black lung checks and the bank's deposits tripled within two to three years. A further bank expansion occurred when nonfarm rural housing became eligible for federally guaranteed mortgages previously reserved for farms.

Dave Arnold, one of the founders of Class VI River Runners, sees the new federal highways as the key factor in renewal; without the interstates, U.S. 19 (transformed by the ARC into the Mountaineer Expressway), and the New River Gorge Bridge (so spectacular that it serves as a tourist attraction in its own right), he finds it hard to imagine weekend visitors driving to Fayetteville from Washington or Cincinnati, or even from Charleston for dinner at the Sedona Grille. (The Mountaineer Expressway, it should be pointed out, also carries local shoppers to Beckley's Crossroads Mall near the junctions of U.S. 19 and I-77.) "Park barrel" in the form of the New River Gorge National River, created at the prodding of Senator Byrd, placed the National Park Service brand on the gorge and its recreation businesses, although the coming of professional park managers introduced another element of social friction between natives and neonatives on one side and NPS "frogs"—so called for their green uniforms—on the other.

The typical mix of state and local funds matching federal dollars made possible a complex new water system engineered to bypass the groundwater problems caused by the honeycomb of abandoned coal mines under Fayetteville and the adjacent north rim of the gorge, just as a similar mix financed Jonesborough's new streetscape and sewerage system. Even the Army Corps of Engineers, whose Bluestone and Summersville dams affect the quality of recreation on the New and Gauley Rivers, has come around to cooperating with the rafters, although it took years of pressure from state and congressional leaders to achieve this.

Traveling south on U.S. 19 today, motorists will find an ARC-funded expressway parallel to or merged with interstates nearly all the way from Pittsburgh to Atlanta. Four hours south of Fayetteville, this route passes through the sprawling Tri-Cities metropolitan region, with pretty Jonesborough caught in its ganglia like a bird's nest in a charmless tree. Here the route divides into eastern and western paths on either side of the North Carolina–Tennessee border, uniting again as it approaches Asheville, the largest center of residential tourism in Appalachia, also polished now with eleven historic district neighborhoods ringing a countercultural downtown. Beaucatcher Mountain, one of nineteenth-century Asheville's most romantic landmarks, is now disfigured by a U-shaped highway cut as deep and ugly as can be found anywhere, but this is the price of having one's cake and eating it too: being able to browse at lunchtime or on weekends through the city's refurbished center while living and shopping for most of life's necessities in automobile suburbs perched on the sides of more distant hills.

Crossing into Georgia, U.S. 19 has been displaced by an expressway (Georgia 400) carrying Atlanta commuters and weekenders nearly to the North Carolina line. When Helen Lewis finally retired in her mid-seventies, she decided to go back home, but home was no longer Forsyth County, now a metropolitan bedroom community, and so she finally settled in Morganton, near the point where the Georgia, Tennessee, and North Carolina state lines meet. Every north Georgia county included in Appalachia now approaches or exceeds national norms in social indicators. The peril in this prosperity is that the entire region may become an appendage of the nearby metropolis, although a Mountain Area Management Plan, sponsored by a mountaineer governor, Zell Miller, imposes some restraint on the excesses of development.

Most people living in the coalfields of Kentucky or the Virginias would gladly exchange the problems of metropolitan encroachment for those of continuing social distress, but one may fairly doubt the accuracy of labeling Fayetteville, Jonesborough, Asheville, and Morganton as winners and the still-distressed counties as losers in the Appalachian crisis. The former places have recovered from one Appalachian crisis only to face a new one, with natives losing control of their communities to neonative settlers and both of these groups confronting an influx of residential tourists and the corporate developers and consumer enterprises that follow such affluent market segments. Place has become a commodity in these communities—the product of commercial techniques such as packaging and branding, rather than of cultural resources accumulated over generations.

The colonial nature of a tourism economy is less obvious than was the case with the extractive industries whose exploitative character Lewis and others documented during the 1970s, but development of this sort still represents the loss of local control over a community's resources and future. In 1998 the Cherokees' new casino at Qualla brought new jobs and an average profit of $4,000 per tribal member, but its management is lodged with a corporate partner, Harrah's Entertainment, Inc., of Las Vegas. On the Tennessee side of the Smokies, the singer Dolly Parton may think that the Dollywood theme park in her native Sevier County is "kind of a culture thing, . . . a way to preserve the Smoky Mountain heritage" and to employ her local relatives.[113] But it is also a corporate venture no less than the outlet malls and entertainment venues that have made Pigeon Forge a tourist destination in its own right rather than just a pit stop on the way to the national park. Pigeon Forge and Gatlinburg represent the more likely fates of Appalachian tourist places than does "Aspenization"—the threat that affluent visitors and residential tourists will drive prices so high that natives and neonative settlers can no longer afford to live there. Still, it is well to remember that in 1950 Aspen was a remote and rundown former mining town.[114]

Most places have come through the Appalachian crisis with a mix of winners and losers, the exact proportion of the mixture often determined by the extent to which outside investment, in one form or another, was available. In Ivanhoe, Virginia, a community that grew up near the lead mines discovered by Colonel Chiswell back in colonial times, a Highlander project led by Helen Lewis failed to bring in new payrolls after the mines and processing plants shut down for the last time in 1981. After that, Ivanhoe workers either had to move away or commute sixty miles or more each day to Wytheville or other employment centers. Yet the mobilized community did succeed in preventing county officials from selling off an unsuccessful industrial park, turning it instead into a recreation center. They also developed adult education programs and wrote a community history that won the Weatherford Award in 1990.

In nearby Galax, where Congress has finally provided funding to create the National Folk Music Center on the Blue Ridge Parkway, the parkway and an annual old-time music festival remain staples of the tourism economy, along with a recreational trail along the New River that replaced the Norfolk and Western branch lines leading to Galax and Fries. The festival is held in Felts Park, named for the Baldwin-Felts founder who survived the mine wars, and the Felts mansion near the center of town is its showplace of historic preservation. Some of the furniture and wood-products factories that provided Galax's livelihood in Pop Stoneman's day have shut down, along with the textile mill in Fries, and those industries that survive do so with the help of a low-wage, nonunion workforce drawn increasingly from Mexican and Central American immigrants. Enough Spanish-speaking people now live in the Galax area to give the town a distinct ethnic flavor, and these newcomers also have a showplace: Tlaquepaque, a successful Mexican restaurant named for the village in Jalisco state from which the owners and many of the original restaurant workers came. Once housed in a recycled fast food joint, Tlaquepaque has tripled in size, moved into new quarters, and attracts a multicultural clientele from at least four counties in Virginia and neighboring North Carolina. And though it now has Anglophone as well as Latino members of its waitstaff, it remains something of a Latino community center, its lobby placarded with Spanish-language flyers advertising *curanderos* and local professionals who speak Spanish.

Spanish can now be heard on the main streets of many Blue Ridge and Great Valley towns, although immigrants into the impoverished coalfields have been understandably few. A case in point is Spruce Pine, North Carolina, located near the Blue Ridge Parkway in a county named for Elisha Mitchell and the mountain on which he died. Called into existence by the Clinchfield Railroad near the point where it tunnels under the Blue Ridge crest and starts its winding descent down the mountain, Spruce Pine in its heyday was home to loggers, miners, and railroad men, while the nearby Penland School of Handicrafts became a landmark of an earlier generation's approach to regional renewal. The town's twin main streets—one at the level of the railroad, the other at the level of the highway bridge that carries old U.S. 19E over the railroad tracks—are still home to a few retailers and two restaurants. But mostly the streetscape features empty windows interspersed with a feeble array of the sorts of shops and galleries that line the main streets of Fayetteville and Jonesborough, along with signs revealing the impact of the social welfare economy. The marquee of the former Carolina Theater now advertises church services, and former stores house externally funded good works such as a food bank. Across the tracks, a recreation grant has made possible some ballfields and a three-block-long walking and biking trail along the Toe River. A modestly successful conference center housed in a former high school climbs the hillside beyond, while a new bypass has collected some fast food places and a few other businesses on what was formerly the edge of town.

One of Spruce Pine's restaurants features Mexican food, but unlike Fayetteville's Sedona Grille or Galax's Tlaquepaque, this one serves a mostly Latino clientele rather than locals or tourists. Workers from Mexico and Central America have become a mainstay of two Blue Ridge industries—the mining of mica and feldspar and the growing of Christmas trees. Western North Carolina is the nation's leading producer of mica, which is used in electrical insulation, while the native Fraser fir—or mountain balsam, to give it its traditional name—grows in an almost perfect conical shape, perfect at least for bringing to life the image of Christmas as it is planted in most American minds. And so the chatter of Spanish is heard in Spruce Pine in the early morning as Latino workers emerge from apartments above the empty storefronts that face the tracks. Mitchell County, like all but two western North Carolina counties, experienced a net loss through migration during the 1980s, but in terms of overall population growth it broke even. During the 1990s, total population increased nearly 9 percent.[115]

The extent to which the growing number of Latinos in the mountains figure into these numbers is difficult to ascertain, owing to the shyness that these immigrants feel around census takers and any other officials that might draw them to the attention of *la migra*, the U.S. Immigration and Naturalization Service. Census takers counted 311 Latinos in Mitchell County in 2000, up from 50 in 1990, which means that 2 percent of the county's population is officially Hispanic. This is less than half of the statewide proportion and less than a fifth of the Latino percentage officially counted in Galax. In other western North Carolina counties, the Latino share of the 2000 count ranges from 1 percent or less in southwestern counties along the Georgia and Tennessee borders to around 6 percent in three foothills counties and in the apple-growing mountain county of Henderson. The number of Latinos not counted remains elusive. It is nevertheless clear that the Latino population of Appalachia is increasing, mostly in the southern and highland counties where there are jobs and few English-speaking workers who will now take them at the wages offered. Mexicans and Central Americans provide construction labor, service workers for highland hotels, resorts, and conference centers, and harvesters of apples, vegetables, and other mountain crops as well as Christmas trees. This new in-migration is no more exotic, in the Appalachian context, than were Italian or Slavic coal miners at the turn of the last century or countercultural settlers during the 1970s. One test of whether Appalachia retains its distinctive image in the twenty-first century will be whether the children and grandchildren of Spanish-speaking immigrants find their identities as Latinos or as mountaineers.

Tourism—soon to become, if it is not already, the world's largest industry—is today the leading economic force in the Blue Ridge and Allegheny highlands. Its growth has generated problems for those communities that already have plenty of tourists and envy among distressed counties that want them. Residential tourism and Latino migration have brought new energy and new social friction into local debates about the future. Many Appalachian communities now experience the phenomenon of "place exchange," wherein "people who have lived in the mountains for generations move away because there are not enough jobs worth having or enough money in mountain farming, while new families move in with trust funds, portfolios, and pensions to live in more satisfying ways than they think possible in the cities where they made their money and to which ironically the migrant Appalachians have gone to look for jobs."[116]

Out-migration is still a factor in the coalfields, but the hillbilly highway has turned south toward Sunbelt cities where persons with Appalachian accents are not classified as culturally exotic. Thus, mountaineers who moved north constitute part of an official ethnic group in Ohio and Michigan, whereas those who move to Charlotte or Atlanta are labeled according to the classic southern calculus: They are either black or white. Statistical analysis of those who moved between 1985 and 1990 from Appalachian core counties of West Virginia and North Carolina to off-mountain counties in North Carolina or to Florida indicates a tendency of migrants to cluster closer to home. Western North Carolinians who moved "off the mountain" were more likely than not to remain west of I-77 or to move to the eastern counties that contain the state capital and flagship public universities. Former West Virginians cluster in the industrial Piedmont along both sides of the interstate. Charlotte is their principal mecca, but Lincoln County—the most rural county in the Charlotte Metropolitan Statistical Area—has a larger proportional concentration of former mountaineers. This is the only county in "Metrolina" where zoning permits the siting of house trailers. It is also on the west or less developed shores of the hydroelectric lakes that Duke Power strung along the Catawba

River. As Gurney Norman says about his male cousins who have moved south from eastern Kentucky, they get themselves jobs, buy a bass boat, and eventually forget that they ever carried a union card in the coalfields.[117]

While we await the outcome of these social changes, it is difficult to be optimistic about the survival of Appalachia as a distinctive environment, for postindustrial society now has the tools to reshape the land in ways that would have been unimaginable a century or even a few decades ago. The ARC highways will be completed by "blowing through mountains," at an estimated cost of $7 to $9 billion.[118] The same engineering and equipment that conquer mountains to build roads, augmented by giant hundred-ton "drag lines," now make possible the strip-mining method known as "mountaintop removal." Thus, in the coalfields of Ohio, Kentucky, and the Virginias, the familiar razorback ridges of the Appalachian Plateau are giving way to sere tablelands resembling desert mesas in the intermontane West. Secretary of the Interior Bruce Babbitt, a former governor of Arizona, even welcomed this development in 1996, terming a decapitated mountain "in some ways a better landscape than it was before."[119]

In underground mining, increased reliance on the long-wall method of coal removal has further improved productivity and workforce supervision, at the expense of an increased risk of mine subsidence at the surface. Soaring expressway bridges are matched by deep broadside cuts that lay bare a mountain's geological secrets (except at Cumberland Gap, where even the road builders recognized that the surface is too historic to be sliced up and built a tunnel instead). Bulldozers and blasting powder have made possible the building of shopping malls and airports in coalfield towns once confined to narrow floodplains; in Pikeville, Kentucky, the ARC and other federal agencies actually financed the relocation of a river from one side of a mountain to the other. Other machines have scraped ski runs on the higher slopes of Blue Ridge and Allegheny peaks and have carved out golf courses on the gentler hillsides below. Landscape designers in north Georgia and western North Carolina have created resort towns in the image of prosperous Atlanta suburbs, with security features modeled on those that guard the island enclaves of Miami. Thanks to its casino and new highways, the Cherokee reservation at Qualla now enjoys express bus service to both Atlanta and Charlotte.

Appalachia is thus no longer a strange place for visitors who find comfort in the familiar landscapes of metropolitan America, but the region's "pecu-

Strip-mining, begun with steam-powered equipment during the late 1930s, accounts for a growing proportion of the coal mined in Appalachia, thanks to diesel-
powered earthmoving and haulage equipment of vastly increased scale and capacity.
The result is the controversial technique of mountaintop removal, shown here in an
aerial view near Racine, West Virginia. The technique not only flattens ridgetops but
pours "spoil" into adjacent valley "fills," such as the terraced and landscaped con-
tour shown at the right margins of the photo. Opponents argue that such fills inevitably lead to stream pollution and loss of animal habitat and usually disrupt the
lives and damage the homes of people living in the valleys nearby. (Photograph by
Lyntha Scott Eiler, LC-AFC 1999/008CRF-LE-C0033-08)

liar" people still fascinate. The Manichean image of mountain people remains
a staple of American culture, with hillbillies contending for space in our imagination with stalwart mountaineers. *The Beverly Hillbillies* and *Deliverance*
gave way to *Foxfire* and *The Waltons*, and the actress Jodie Foster did a star
turn in the 1990s as a simple mountain girl who lived in a remote location that
was nonetheless somehow adjacent to a TVA lake. "In the normative heart of
the economy, where the middle class strives and where cartoon hillbillies and
other comic rural characters have entertained us on a regular basis since at

least the mid-1800s, we take secret pleasure in the trashing of hallowed beliefs and sacred virtues—not to mention hygiene. Secret pleasure is guilty pleasure, and guilt begs containment. So we have made the hillbilly safely dismissible, a left-behind remnant, a symbolic nonadult and willful renegade from capitalism."[120]

The comedic hillbilly's demonic cousins, descendants of the mountain rabble whom Virginia cavaliers led to partisan warfare in the fiction of Nathaniel Beverly Tucker and who glowered from the pages of newspaper stories about Hatfields and McCoys, threaten not only social pretension but social tranquility. *Deliverance* was followed by a succession of popular hillbilly demons whose crimes of murder, incest, and rape were sometimes made more awful by their being bound up with the sensational though rare Appalachian religious practice of snake handling. Notable examples are 1991 remakes of two 1950s film classics, *Cape Fear* and *Night of the Hunter*, and Pat Conroy's 1995 novel *Beach Music*—all of which featured gratuitous insertions of demonic hillbilly characters into plots that had little or nothing to do with the mountains. *The Kentucky Cycle* (1993), a nine-act West Coast production that became the first play to win the Pulitzer Prize before having opened in New York, featured a cast of stalwart mountain women but also depraved males in such numbers that it took two full evenings to parade them across the boards.

The twentieth century ended, as it began, with Americans reading bestselling books about Appalachia. Charles Frazier's *Cold Mountain*, combining folk and ethnographic materials with harrowing accounts of backcountry violence during the Civil War, achieved both literary acclaim and a mass readership and won the National Book Award in 1997. Robert Morgan's *Gap Creek* won a similarly large audience in 2000, demonstrating along with the more modest successes of other Appalachian writers that positively drawn mountain characters have as much mass appeal as the depraved characters of *Deliverance* and *The Kentucky Cycle*. Among nonfiction best-sellers, Homer Hickam Jr., a retired rocket engineer living in Huntsville, captivated readers with *Rocket Boys*, a memoir of youthful intellectual adventure set against the 1950s backdrop of a dying West Virginia coal town. This book reached an even wider audience as a Hollywood film, *October Sky*, although it is worth pointing out that the producers chose to avoid unionized West Virginia as a location and filmed the story in nonunion Tennessee. Hickam followed his success in 2000 with an elaboration of his memoir, entitled *The Coalwood Way*.

Whereas *Rocket Boys* views the nadir of the Appalachian crisis through an optimistic lens, Jedediah Purdy's *For Common Things* suggests that the worst may be yet to come. The son of back-to-the-landers who schooled him at home before sending him off to prep school and Harvard, Purdy uses his home state of West Virginia as one of two touchstones—the other being the former Soviet satellite nations of east-central Europe—by which to argue against his generation's ironic detachment from politics. "When I think of responsibility or foolishness, preservation or destruction, generosity or greed, they take the forms of Appalachia. They come to me as green slopes and shattered hills, good and poor farms, faces firm with practiced concern, contorted with outrage, or slack and ruddy with indifference." In the context of environmental degradations such as mountaintop removal, Purdy's book is, above all else, a stand against indifference. "The destruction of Appalachia is a terrible symptom of a blinkered economic logic that needs changing," he concludes.[121] Whether or not this message gets through will determine much of Appalachia's future and also shape the historical reputation of Purdy's peers.

Each of these books establishes a dialogue between past and future, hardship and endurance, evil and good, and their Appalachian settings reinforce the tensions that these dualities invoke. In turn, we are reminded that Appalachia is both a real place and a territory of imagination, and that social reality there lends credence to both aspects. If we need the example of the ignoble hillbilly to remind us of where we've been and what we could become, even more do we need the noble mountaineer. Whether fictional like Gertie Nevels or real like Ralph Stanley and Ray Hicks—or both, like John Henry—the mountaineer reminds us that to be truly civilized people must live in nature, not against it, that expressive culture is not simply the sum of urbane refinement, and that genuine community is purchased through respect. Most of all, the mountaineer reminds us of what we will lose if the consumer culture of advanced industrial capitalism is allowed to wreak its unchecked havoc on the special places of the earth. Appalachia lives on divided in our minds because we need it to.

Notes

Abbreviations

CFFR	U.S. Department of Commerce, Bureau of the Census, *Consolidated Federal Funds Report*
DOD	Department of Defense
GAHM	ePress Project, *Great American History Machine*
HSP	Historical Society of Pennsylvania
LC-AFC	Library of Congress, American Folklife Center
NA	National Archives, Washington, D.C.
NSA	National [now International] Storytelling Association
PBF	Franklin, *Papers of Benjamin Franklin*
PSA	Pennsylvania State Archives, Harrisburg
USDA-BAE	U.S. Department of Agriculture, Bureau of Agricultural Economics
WVU	West Virginia and Regional History Collection, West Virginia University Library, Morgantown

Introduction

1. "Report of the Commissioners," in Cometti and Summers, *Thirty-fifth State*, 194.

2. Kegley, *Kegley's Virginia Frontier*, 116–22, 128; Spiker, *Max Meadows*, 8–9, 64–65; John Buchanan, "Memorandums Relating to Sundrey Passages with Respect to My Journey to Wood's River Commencing ye 4 of Octobr 1745," in Quaife, *Preston and Virginia Papers*, 4; Kegley, *Wythe County*, 19–20.

3. Noe, *Southwest Virginia's Railroad*, 29; Spiker, *Max Meadows*, 16–47.

4. The account that follows is based on interviews conducted in Ireland in March 1992 and in Max Meadows on August 11, 1992.

5. Gray, *McGavock Family*, 1–2; Spiker, *Max Meadows*, 3–9.

6. Allison, "A Question of Class."

7. Spiker, *Max Meadows*, 188–89.

8. Kegley, *Wythe County*, 16.

9. Williams, *West Virginia: History*, 96; William Preston, "Diary of the Sandy Creek Expedition [February–March 1756]," in Quaife, *Preston and Virginia Papers*, 10.

10. McNeil, *Appalachian Images*, 45–58.

11. Shapiro, *Appalachia on Our Mind*; Thomas, *Alternative America*; Batteau, *Invention of Appalachia*.

12. Taylor, *Alleghenia*, 14. I am grateful to my colleague Fred Hay for calling this source to my attention.

13. Hayes, *Southern Appalachians*, and Willis, *Northern Appalachians*; Frost, *For the Mountains*, 97–98, 102–3, and "Educational Pioneering," 556.

14. Williams, "Appalachian History." See also Williams, "Counting Yesterday's People."

15. This approach is similar to that which has emerged among historians of North American frontiers (as in, for example, Clayton and Teute, *Contact Points*) or in British studies that take the interactions of the varied peoples of Britain as their focus rather than the more traditional London-centered "Crown and Commons" approach (see Raphael Samuel, *Island Stories: Unravelling Britain* [London: Verso, 1998], and Norman Davies, *The Isles: A History* [New York: Oxford University Press, 2000]).

16. Puckett, "On the Pronunciation of Appalachia," 28.

17. See, for example, Brown, *Wild East*, 4.

18. Couto, *Making Democracy Work Better*; Fisher, *Fighting Back in Appalachia*.

19. Norman and Olsen, "Frankenstein in Palestine," 94.

Chapter One

1. Milanich, *Florida Indians*, 94, 118; Walls, "On the Naming of Appalachia," 56–59.

2. "Account by a Gentleman from Elvas," in Clayton, Knight, and Moore, *De Soto Chronicles*, 87–89. For the most recent scholarly conjecture on De Soto's route, see National Park Service, *De Soto Trail*, frontispiece (map).

3. "Account by Rodrigo Rangel," in Clayton, Knight, and Moore, *DeSoto Chronicles*, 282–83; for the location and culture of Chiaha, see Davis, *Where There Are Mountains*, 14–23.

4. A city known as Charles Town in colonial times but for convenience referred to here by its modern name.

5. Quoted in Meriwether, *Expansion of South Carolina*, 14 (n. 30).

6. Hudson, *Catawba Nation*, 27–28; Merrell, *Indians' New World*, 109–13. Hudson disputes the cultural and prehistorical significance of the Catawbas' Siouan lan-

guage affiliation, documented only after 1800. Merrell (118–21) documents the process of amalgamation among the remnant Piedmont "hill tribes" during the eighteenth century and describes the continuing warfare between Catawbas and their enemies to the north.

7. Merrell, "Shamokin," 23.

8. Ibid., 27.

9. Ibid., 18.

10. Hatley, *Dividing Paths*, 74–75.

11. Perdue, *Cherokee Women*, 17.

12. Ibid., 36–37.

13. Pennsylvania Council of State, *Minutes of the Provincial Council*, 2:404.

14. Dunaway, *First American Frontier*, 10–11.

15. Perdue, *Cherokee Women*, 10–11.

16. Ibid., 186.

17. Dunaway, *First American Frontier*, 51.

18. Ibid., 51–56, esp. map 3.1.

19. Pastorius, "Positive Information from America," 355.

20. Faragher, *Daniel Boone*, 9–15.

21. William Penn to William Blathwayt and Francis Gwin, November 21, 1682, in Soderland, *William Penn and the Founding of Pennsylvania*, 190.

22. Robert Fallam, "Journal," in Lewis and Hennen, *West Virginia*, 25.

23. "Minutes from a Letter Written by Governor Spotswood to the Board of Trade, November 16, 1713," in Hawks, *History of North Carolina*, 2:438.

24. Richter, *Ordeal of the Longhouse*, 241, 258 (map).

25. Mitchell, *Commercialism and Frontier*, 27–30.

26. Approached by a Swiss promoter who sought land west of the Susquehanna to settle German-speaking immigrants, Thomas Penn reiterated his father's policy: "We will not pretend to dispose of any lands before they are fairly purchased of the Indians" (Thomas Penn to James Logan, February 10, 1731, Thomas Penn Papers, HSP, [microfilm copy in PSA], roll 3). Instead, the promoter in question acquired land in Virginia.

27. Fogleman, *Hopeful Journeys*, 2, 4–6.

28. Benjamin Franklin, "Observations Concerning the Increase of Mankind, Peopling of Countries, Etc." [1751], in *PBF*, 4:232, 234.

29. Fogleman, *Hopeful Journeys*, 11, 60–63, 74–76.

30. Ibid., 155–56.

31. These figures are collected from scattered articles by Thomas L. Purvis in Fogleman, *Hopeful Journeys*, 80–83, esp. tables 3.1 and 3.2.

32. Ibid., 102–3.

33. Beissel, *Confidential Writings*, xii.

34. Fogleman, *Hopeful Journeys*, 8.

35. Kegley, *Wythe County*, 16.

36. Wallace, *Conrad Weiser*, 60–64, 107–11, 185–95.

37. Fogleman, *Hopeful Journeys*, 107–13; Wallace, *Conrad Weiser*, 116–17.

38. Quoted in ibid., 140–41.

39. Fries, *Records of the Moravians*, 1:55–56.

40. A Latinized form of Wachau, the name of one of Zinzendorf's German estates.

41. Hatley, *Dividing Paths*, 234.

42. Jennings, *Ambiguous Iroquois Empire*, 248, 271; Cunningham, *Apples on the Flood*, 85.

43. Fogleman, *Hopeful Journeys*, 2.

44. See, e.g., Hatley, *Dividing Paths*, 42–51, and Cresswell, *Journal*, 87, 92–93.

45. In 1992 David Taylor, of the American Folklife Center in the Library of Congress, and I traveled to Northern Ireland with the objective of developing a method of identifying Irish Catholic survivals from the eighteenth-century Appalachian frontier on the basis of contemporary folklife research such as has been carried out to identify *converso* (Jewish) survivals from the Spanish frontier in New Mexico. This effort foundered on the insufficiency of eighteenth-century Irish emigration records, which are too few and/or imprecise to link specific points of departure in Ireland with destinations in the future United States.

46. McDowell Family Papers, Ulrich Bonnell Phillips Collection in Southern History, Yale University Library, New Haven.

47. Keller, "What Is Distinctive about the Scotch-Irish?," 72–75, 81–82.

48. Purvis, "European Ancestry," 98.

49. Briscoe, *Thomas Mellon*, xxix.

50. Meriwether, *Expansion of South Carolina*, 133; Hatley, *Dividing Paths*, 86.

51. "Treaty with the Western Indians at Fort Pitt, 1775," in Thwaites and Kellogg, *Revolution on the Upper Ohio*, 104–5.

52. Meriwether, *Expansion of South Carolina*, 117–61.

53. Quoted in Faragher, *Daniel Boone*, 37–39.

54. "Speech of Canasatego [Onondaga] to the Governor and Council of Pennsylvania, July 7, 1742," quoted in Wallace, *Conrad Weiser*, 127–28.

55. Merrell, *Indians' New World*, 59.

56. Hatley, *Dividing Paths*, 82–83.

57. Ibid., 92–95.

58. Richter, *Ordeal of the Longhouse*, 269–70.

59. Conrad Weiser counted 390 Indians at the Easton Conference, while others counted more than 500 (Wallace, *Conrad Weiser*, 524–35). See also Richter, *Ordeal of the Longhouse*, 255–79.

60. "Plain Truth" (pamphlet, 1747), in *PBF*, 3:193.

61. "Christopher Gist's Journals," in Cometti and Summers, *The Thirty-fifth State*, 31.

62. Faragher, *Daniel Boone*, 35.

63. Extract from Weiser's journal, quoting Tanacharison ("the Half-King"), in Wallace, *Conrad Weiser*, 366–67.

64. Washington, *Papers*, 1:356.

65. Faragher, *Daniel Boone*, 39.

66. Dumas to the Minister of the Marine, July 24, 1756, quoted in Wallace, *Conrad Weiser*, 395.

67. "A Register of the Persons Who Have Been Either Killed, Wounded or Taken Prisoners by the Enemy in Augusta County, as Also of Such as Have Made Their Escape," in Cometti and Summers, *The Thirty-fifth State*, 51–56.

68. Hatley, *Dividing Paths*, 168, 184.

69. Ibid., 107–33.

70. Quoted in ibid., 133.

71. Washington to Crawford, September 17, 1767, in Washington, *Papers*, 8:27–29.

72. Washington to Crawford, September 21, 1767, in Washington, *Writings*, 2:469.

73. Dowd, *Spirited Resistance*.

74. Quoted in O'Donnell, *Southern Indians*, ix, and Hatley, *Dividing Paths*, 193.

75. Quoted in Hatley, *Dividing Paths*, 193.

76. Quoted in ibid., 195.

77. Ibid., 205–8.

78. Ibid., 213–14.

79. Ibid., 222–23.

80. Doddridge, *Notes on the Settlement and Indian Wars*, 95.

81. Dowd, *Spirited Resistance*, 109–10, 112.

82. Hatley, *Dividing Paths*, 228.

83. Dowd, *Spirited Resistance*, 185–90.

84. Hatley, *Dividing Paths*, 173–75, 183–87; Klein, *Unification of a Slave State*.

85. Dunaway, *First American Frontier*, 51–72.

86. Vandiver, *Mighty Stonewall*, 2.

87. Williams, *West Virginia: History*, 26–27, 40–41; see also Davis, *John George Jackson*.

88. Dunaway, *First American Frontier*, 57, 345 (n. 15).

89. Jackson, *Memoirs of Stonewall Jackson*, 14.

90. Faragher, *Daniel Boone*, 105, 242–44.

91. On the Breckenridge migration to Kentucky, see Garcia, *To Western Woods*, 75–93, 100–101, 170–71.

92. Billings and Blee, *Road to Poverty*, 38; see also ibid., 35–37 and references on 356–57.

93. Dunaway, *First American Frontier*, 57, 75, 66–67.

94. Ann Marie Dykstra, "Land Policy," in Muller, *Concise Historical Atlas*, 82–83.

95. Dunaway, *First American Frontier*, 72–73; Hamilton, *Alabama*, 11.

96. Lane, *People of Georgia*, 91, 93.

97. Govan and Livingood, *Chattanooga Country*, 53–54.

98. All cessions by the Cherokees and other Indian peoples after the establishment of U.S. independence are described in detail in Royce, *Indian Land Cessions*, 648–879, plus referenced maps.

99. McLaughlin, *After the Trail of Tears*, 6–7.

100. Robert Remini argues convincingly that Jackson never made the more famous

statement—"Mr. Marshall has made his decision, now let him enforce it"—attributed to him on this occasion (*Andrew Jackson*, 275–76).

101. Williams, *Georgia Gold Rush*, 53.

102. Quoted in McLaughlin, *After the Trail of Tears*, 2.

103. Quoted in Williams, *Georgia Gold Rush*, 115.

104. Finger, *Eastern Band of Cherokees*, 49, 143.

105. The origin of these communities remains a subject of debate, but the most convincing scholarship argues that West Virginia's "Guinea" people probably combine Delaware, African, and Euro-American descent, while the "Melungeons" of southwest Virginia and upper East Tennessee, also of mixed race, derived originally from Saponi and other small native societies found in the Virginia and North Carolina Piedmont in colonial times. See especially Gaskins, "Introduction to the Guineas"; Everett, "Melungeon History and Myth" and "Everett Answers Killebrew and Kennedy."

Chapter Two

1. Bartram, *Travels of William Bartram*, 212. The editor's commentary tracing Bartram's route on this expedition is found on 384–92.

2. Ibid., 215.

3. Compare the core region identified in Map 1 of this book with the map of the Fraser magnolia's range found at <<http://www.wildwnc.org/trees/Magnolia_fraseri.html>>.

4. Muir, *Thousand Mile Walk*, entry of September 23, 1867; Brooks, *The Appalachians*, 3–4.

5. Bartram, *Travels of William Bartram*, 216–17, 225–26.

6. Weidensaul, *Mountains of the Heart*, 15.

7. Faragher, *Daniel Boone*, 53–54.

8. Perdue, *Cherokee Women*, 25, 118.

9. Ibid., 25.

10. Jordan and Kaups, *American Backwoods Frontier*, 218–19.

11. Andrew R. L. Cayton, "Marietta and the Ohio Country," in Mitchell, *Appalachian Frontiers*, 188–95.

12. Doddridge, *Notes on the Settlement and Indian Wars*, 98.

13. Mitchell, *Diary of a Geological Tour*, 54.

14. Bartram, *Travels of William Bartram*, 219, 221.

15. Mitchell, *Diary of a Geological Tour*, 26.

16. McNeill, *Gauley Mountain*, 24.

17. Ibid., 32.

18. Bartram, *Travels of William Bartram*, 196–97; Otto, *Southern Frontiers*.

19. Lanman, *Letters from the Alleghany Mountains*, 152.

20. Mitchell, *Diary of a Geological Tour*, 25–26, 40.

21. Salstrom, *Appalachia's Path*, xii–xxiii, 11–19, 41–59. See also MacMaster, "Cattle Trade."

22. William Haymond to Luther Haymond, February 18, 1842, Haymond Family Papers, WVU.

23. Williams, *West Virginia: History*, 6–7, 13.

24. Based on an examination of the DeLorme *Atlas and Gazetteer* for Alabama, Georgia, Kentucky, Maryland, North Carolina, Ohio, Pennsylvania, Tennessee, Virginia, and West Virginia. The exception is South Carolina.

25. Asbury, *Journal*, 1:427 (July 5[?], 1782), 1:607 (August 8, 1789), 1:760 (June 7, 1793).

26. Ibid., 1:404 (June 7, 1781), 1:406 (June 11, 1781), 1:427 (July 5[?], 1782).

27. Ibid., 1:571 (May 7[?], 1788).

28. Ibid., 1:715 (May 26, 1792), 1:636 (May 11, 1790), 2:88 (May 20, 1796).

29. Ibid., 2:262 (November 6, 1800), 2:518 (October 1, 1806).

30. Ibid., 1:759 (June 1, 1793), 2:250 (September 18, 1800), 2:251 (September 24, 1800), 2:614 (August 30, 1809), 2:795 (November 1, 1815), 1:709 (March 18, 1792).

31. Ibid., 2:654 (December 1, 1810), 2:444 (October 27, 1804), 2:84 (May 7, 1796), 2:787 (August 6, 1815).

32. Lanman, *Letters from the Alleghany Mountains*, 81.

33. Quoted in McCauley, *Appalachian Mountain Religion*, 193.

34. Boles, *Religion in Antebellum Kentucky*, 25–27.

35. Ibid., 134–36.

36. McCauley, *Appalachian Mountain Religion*, 53.

37. Ibid., 36, 156–61, 168–94, 201–37, 238–46.

38. Ibid., 122.

39. Bartram, *Travels of William Bartram*, 219.

40. Quoted in Govan and Livingood, *Chattanooga Country*, 93.

41. Mitchell, *Commercialism and Frontier*, 22–24.

42. Bartram, *Travels of William Bartram*, 218.

43. Davis, *Where There Are Mountains*, 46–49; French, "Journal," 18–19.

44. James Logan to Thomas Penn, October 19, 1730, Thomas Penn Papers, HSP [microfilm ed., PSA, roll 4].

45. See Strother, "The Mountains," passim.

46. Jordan and Kaups, *American Backwoods Frontier*, 94–99.

47. Lanman, *Adventures in the Wilds*, 500; for a similar description of Georgia and North Carolina backwoods homes, see Lanman, *Letters from the Alleghany Mountains*, 153–54.

48. Davis, *Where There Are Mountains*, 30–31.

49. Williams, *West Virginia: History for Beginners*, 248–57; Morgan, *Log House in East Tennessee*; Montell and Morse, *Kentucky Log Architecture*, 1–51, 91–94; Williams, *Homeplace*, 1–113. My use of the term "white house" derives from family tradition and refers to frame center-passage houses that replaced log houses for my maternal great-grandparents in Braxton County, West Virginia, in 1899 and for my paternal great-grandfather in Pocahontas County sometime between 1900 and 1910. I am grateful especially to my late great-aunt, Bridget Greene Lang, and to my late cousin, Ann Denison Fisher, for their responses to my curiosity on such matters.

50. Mitchell, *Diary of a Geological Tour*, 15, 18.

51. Ibid., 20,

52. Ibid., 26, 27, 53–54.

53. Williams, *Homeplace*, 47–49, 93–113. Williams (161, nn. 1, 3) rejects, as I do, the scholarly term "I-house" (coined by the cultural geographer Fred Kniffen, who first encountered these farmhouses in Indiana, Illinois, and Iowa) in favor of "center-passage house," since a central hall was an almost invariable feature. So was white-painted siding, however, and "white house" seems likely to have been more widely used in everyday parlance than technical architectural terms such as "center passage."

54. Starr and Perry, *Blaze Starr*, 4.

55. Williams, *Homeplace*, 89–92, 94–100.

56. Though I am no relation to Michael Ann Williams, I can testify personally to the truth of her observations, having grown up in Greenbrier County, West Virginia, in a 1906 colonial revival house built for a great-aunt, who had lived until the age of nineteen in a log house that was then succeeded by a center-passage house painted white. Though the 1906 house was large and spacious, family life was lived almost exclusively in two rooms—the kitchen and dining room, the latter of which had a large fireplace that became the center of activities until the acquisition of a television set in 1954. The twin parlors that flanked the center hall were used only for company, piano practice, and the Christmas tree. Bedrooms were used only for sleeping. However, cold-storage areas attached to the rear of the house, a pantry between the kitchen and dining room, and, in warm weather, the house's extensive verandas were heavily used.

57. Dunaway, *First American Frontier*, 78–79, esp. tables 3.6 and 3.7.

58. Lizzie Grant, interview by B. E. Davis, Madisonville, Tex., March 6, 1938, in Rawick, *American Slave*, 1553–55.

59. James Logan to John, Thomas, and Richard Penn, April 2, 1731, Thomas Penn Papers, HSP, roll 3.

60. William Crawford to George Washington, March 15, 1772, in Butterfield, *Washington-Crawford Letters*, 25.

61. George Washington to Lord Botetourt, December 8, 1769, in Washington, *Writings*, 2:530.

62. Mann, "Diversity in the Antebellum Appalachian South."

63. Lanman, *Letters from the Alleghany Mountains*, 142.

64. Dunn, *Cade's Cove*, 9–97.

65. Salstrom, *Appalachia's Path to Dependency*, 11–26.

66. Washington, *Diaries*, 1:428–29, and *Writings*, 3:31, 28:436–37; Cook, *Washington's Western Lands*, 43.

67. Royal, *Sketches of Life, Manners, and Society*, 55.

68. Quoted in Phillips, *Life and Labor*, 342–43.

69. Lanman, *Adventures in the Wilds*, 500.

70. Olmsted, *Journey in the Back Country*, 230–32.

71. Moore, "Economic Development in Appalachian Kentucky," 223.

72. Waller, *Feud*, 34–35.

73. Williams, *West Virginia: History*, 123–24.

74. Davis, *Where There Are Mountains*, 137.

75. Slaughter, *Whiskey Rebellion*, 99, 119–20, 151.

76. Strother, "A Winter in the South," 732.

77. MacMaster, "Cattle Trade in Western Virginia," 128–30.

78. Lanman, *Letters from the Alleghany Mountains*, 68–69, 123, and *Adventures in the Wilds*, 481–84.

79. Mitchell, *Diary of a Geological Tour*, 34.

80. Anglin, "Lives on the Margin," 185–86.

81. Ibid., 187–98.

82. Billings and Blee, *Road to Poverty*, 168–69; the quoted material is from Kentucky's first state report on agriculture.

83. Strother, "The Mountains," July–November 1872, 508–15.

84. Williams, *Homeplace*, 55–56.

85. Mitchell, *Diary of a Geological Tour*, 32–34.

86. Billings and Blee, *Road to Poverty*, esp. table 5.5 (180–81), compared with Pennsylvania data from Kennedy, *Agriculture of the United States in 1860*.

87. Ambler, "Life of John Floyd," 79–81.

88. Ambler, "Diary of John Floyd," 166 (November 21, 1831); Lacy, *Vanquished Volunteers*, 100–101.

89. Dew, *Bond of Iron*, 3–4, 38–39, 99.

90. Hsiung, *Two Worlds in the Tennessee Mountains*, 84–84, 120–21.

91. Olmsted, *Journey in the Back Country*, 242–44.

92. Scott, *Footloose in Jacksonian America*, 21.

93. Royal, *Sketches of Life, Manners, and Society*, 40–41.

94. Scott, *Footloose in Jacksonian America*, 93.

95. Quoted in Roper, *Jedediah Hotchkiss*, 136–37.

96. Lanman, *Letters from the Alleghany Mountains*, 31, 117, 125.

97. Ibid., 31.

98. Phillips, *Life and Labor*, 365–66.

99. Royal, *Sketches of Life, Manners, and Society*, 57.

100. Vance, *Papers*, xxvii.

101. Quoted in Billings and Blee, *Road to Poverty*, 303.

102. Asbury, *Journal*, 1:577 (July 15, 1788).

103. Williams, "Class, Section, and Culture," 217.

104. Hsiung, *Two Worlds in the Tennessee Mountains*, xii, 1–19.

105. Billings and Blee, "Agriculture and Poverty," 237.

106. Pudup, "Social Class and Economic Development," 241.

107. Inscoe and McKinney, *Heart of Confederate Appalachia*, 18. See also Table 2.1.

108. Quoted in Inscoe, "Race and Racism," 114.

109. Ireland, *County in Kentucky History*, 18–26.

110. Strother, "Virginia Militia Training," 243–44.

111. Strother, "Old Time Militia Musters," 212–13.

112. Mitchell, *Diary of a Geological Tour*, 29–30.

113. Olmsted, *Journey in the Back Country*, 226.

114. Williams, "Class, Section, and Culture," 218.

115. Shade, *Democratizing the Old Dominion*, 109–10.

116. Ibid., 174.

117. Hilaire Belloc, writing in 1924, quoted in Wallace, *Indian Paths*, 1.

118. Mitchell, "Introduction: Revision and Regionalism," 21.

119. Braudel, *The Mediterranean*, 1:44, 46.

120. U.S. Bureau of the Census, *Seventh Census of the United States*, 221, 258, 308, 366, 422, 574–75, 612–13, 850.

121. Inscoe, *Mountain Masters*, 34–37.

122. Govan and Livingood, *Chattanooga Country*, 120–21.

123. Quoted in Hsiung, *Two Worlds in the Tennessee Mountains*, 131.

124. Quoted in Govan and Livingood, *Chattanooga Country*, 99, 100 (n. 2).

125. Ward, *J. Edgar Thomson*, 40–42.

126. Nelson, *Iron Confederacies*, 11–29. Although Nelson's important work emphasizes the role that state subsidies and slave labor have played in southern railroad development, it ignores the French connection that inspired this strategy and that accounts for the creation of engineering schools such as the Virginia Military Institute, the Citadel, and the North Carolina and Georgia military academies modeled on the École Polytechnique.

127. Ibid., 29–45.

128. Campbell, "Slavery and the Fugitive Slave Law," 263–65.

129. Williams, "Birth of a State," 229.

130. Quoted in Sears, *Kentucky Abolitionists*, 16.

131. Davis, *Bits of Gossip*, 165–66.

Chapter Three

1. Hardin, *Private War*, 1–2.

2. Shaler, "Border State Men," 251.

3. Davis, *Bits of Gossip*, 110–11.

4. Hardin, *Private War*, 19.

5. Quoted in Inscoe and McKinney, *Heart of Confederate Appalachia*, 85; see also Groce, "Social Origins," 31, 35.

6. Quoted in "Biographical Sketch" in Vance, *Papers*, xxxviii.

7. Zebulon B. Vance to Jefferson Davis, October 25, 1862, ibid., 276.

8. Quoted in Fisher, *War at Every Door*, 31.

9. Inscoe and McKinney, *Heart of Confederate Appalachia*, 27.

10. Johnston, *Story of a Confederate Boy*, 28.

11. Groce, "Social Origins," 34. See also Wallenstein, "'Helping to Save the Union,'" 15–16.

12. Hardin, *Private War*, 197.

13. Rutherford B. Hayes to Samuel Birchard, August 17, 1861, in Hayes, *Diary and Letters*, 4:68.

14. Cox, *Military Reminisences*, 1:221.

15. Wallenstein, "'Helping to Save the Union,'" 16–18.

16. Mann, "Diversity in the Antebellum Appalachian South," 154–55.

17. Quoted in Zinn, *Lee's Cheat Mountain Campaign*, 69.

18. Hardin, *Private War*, 25.

19. Williams, "Birth of a State," 233.

20. Sarris, "Execution in Lumpkin County," 149–50.

21. Rutherford B. Hayes to Lucy Hayes, January 12, 1862, in Hayes, *Diary and Letters*, 4:184.

22. Cox, *Military Reminiscences*, 1:145.

23. Rutherford B. Hayes to Jacob D. Cox, March 14, 1861, in Hayes, *Diary and Letters*, 4:208.

24. William Ludwig to George Ludwig, July 29, 1862, Brooks Collection, Box 2, WVU.

25. Quoted in Noe, "Exterminating Savages," 117.

26. Quoted in Inscoe and McKinney, *Heart of Confederate Appalachia*, 113.

27. Quoted in Sarris, "Execution in Lumpkin County," 144.

28. D. W. Siler to Zebulon Vance, November 3, 1862, in Vance, *Papers*, 302–3.

29. Paludan, *Victims*, 70–71.

30. Quoted in Inscoe and McKinney, *Heart of Confederate Appalachia*, 125.

31. Mann, "Sand Lick Company," 78–103.

32. Waller, *Feud*, 31–32. Like "snakes," the Wildcat name lived on in the mascot of Logan High School's powerful twentieth-century athletic teams.

33. Quoted in Inscoe and McKinney, *Heart of Confederate Appalachia*, 105.

34. Quoted in ibid., 108.

35. Quoted in Dunn, *Cades Cove*, 137–38.

36. Hardin, *Private War*, 19. See also Williams, "Birth of a State."

37. Quoted in Williams, "Birth of a State," 226.

38. Quoted in Dunn, *Cades Cove*, 138.

39. Inscoe and McKinney, *Heart of Confederate Appalachia*, 137; Paludan, *Victims*, 94–95.

40. Noe, "'Deadened Color and Colder Horror.'"

41. Quoted in West, *Lift Up Your Head*, 122.

42. Montell, *Killings*, 146, 158, 164.

43. Atkinson, *After the Moonshiners*.

44. Dunn, *Cades Cove*, 234–47.

45. Holmes, "Moonshining and Collective Violence."

46. Waller, "Feuding in Appalachia," 364.

47. William H. McNeill describes Toynbee's lifelong friendship with Robert Shelby Darbishire (*Arnold J. Toynbee*, 25, 26, 31–34).

48. Billings and Blee, *Road to Poverty*, 281–306.

49. Allen, *Memoirs*, 42.

50. Williams, "Southern Mountaineer," 660.

51. Shapiro, *Appalachia on Our Mind*, 46.

52. Ibid., 55.

53. Quoted in Billings and Blee, *Road to Poverty*, 311.

54. Jane Becker documents this phenomenon conclusively, although she does not employ the concept of "brand" and "brand management" to characterize the movement's goals (*Inventing Tradition*, esp. 73–92).

55. Williams, "Cultural Intervention in Appalachia," 36.

56. Dorson, *Buying the Wind*, 163.

57. Pages xv–xxx of Cox's book describe the collecting movement with specific reference to West Virginia.

58. Semple, "Anglo-Saxons of the Kentucky Mountains," 147, 174.

59. Quoted in James, Bladen, and Karan, "Ellen Churchill Semple," 31.

60. Hayes, *Southern Appalachians*, 335.

61. Billings and Blee, *Road to Poverty*, 9, 307–8.

62. Miles, *Spirit of the Mountains*, 37.

63. Karpeles, *Cecil Sharp*, 153.

64. Ibid., 146, 148.

65. Miles, *Spirit of the Mountains*, 200.

66. Kephart, *Our Southern Highlanders*, 384–85, 428–29, 443–47.

67. Smith, *Jane Hicks Gentry*, 7.

68. Campbell, *Southern Highlander*, 328.

69. Quoted in Kodish, *Good Friends and Bad Enemies*, 134.

70. Campbell, *Southern Highlander*, 74, 94–95.

71. Ibid., 117, 210; also compare table 5 (115) and table 14 (263).

72. Quoted in Karpeles, *Cecil Sharp*, 160–61, 166.

73. Quoted in ibid., 158.

74. Kephart, *Our Southern Highlanders*, 192–93.

75. Ibid., 205.

76. Ibid., 453–54.

77. Mooney, *James Mooney's History*, 236–37. See also Ellison, "James Mooney and the Eastern Cherokees," on which much of the preceding two paragraphs is based.

78. Williams, *John Henry*, 18–23.

79. Billings and Blee, *Road to Poverty*, 196.

80. Williams, *John Henry*, 7.

81. Smith, *Harpers Ferry Armory*.

82. Abrams, "Western North Carolina Railroad." The Harding quote is from Poole, *Railroading in Western North Carolina*, 6.

83. Shapiro, *New South Rebellion*, 252–53.

84. Lewis, *Sloss Furnaces*, 152–54, 478–79.

85. Lee, *Sergeant York*, 65.

86. Shapiro, *Appalachia on Our Mind*, 262–63.

87. Williamson, *Hillbillyland*, ix, 207–24.

Chapter Four

1. Cecil Sharp to Mrs. James Storrow, August 26, 1917, quoted in Karpeles, *Cecil Sharp*, 159.
2. Sung by Addison Boserman and collected by Gordon Barnes, Tygart Valley Homesteads, Elkins, W.Va., April 1939, American FolkLife Center, Library of Congress, accession no. 3571B1.
3. Lay, *Industrial and Commercial History*, 69–101.
4. Mylott, *Measure of Prosperity*.
5. Lewis, *Sloss Furnaces*, 237.
6. The foregoing analysis is based on data from Becker, *Diary of a Millionaire Coal Town*, 71–119.
7. Sullivan, *Coal Men and Coal Towns*, 114.
8. Brown, *Wild East*, 67.
9. Mooney, *Struggle in the Coal Fields*, 5–6.
10. Quoted in Brown, *Wild East*, 71.
11. Ibid., 57.
12. Clarkson, *On Beyond Leatherbark*, 181–82, 188.
13. Lewis, "Railroads, Deforestation, and the Transformation of Agriculture," 304–10.
14. Quoted in Brown, *Wild East*, 67.
15. Ibid., 114–17.
16. Quoted in ibid., 69, 72.
17. Lewis, *Sloss Furnaces*, 1–3, 30–38, 82–96, 103–29, 293–95, 474–508.
18. Eller, *Miners, Millhands, and Mountaineers*, 75–76; Warren, *Triumphant Capitalism*, 23–38.
19. Quoted in Williams, *West Virginia and the Captains of Industry*, 189.
20. Quoted in ibid., 141.
21. Letwin, *Challenge of Interracial Unionism*, 164–71; Lewis, *Black Coal Miners*, 61–62.
22. Palladino, *Another Civil War*, 3, 146–62. Two of the victims were hanged for a killing that had occurred in 1863, when mine owners collaborated with conscription officials to draft union leaders and other "agitators" into the Union army during the Civil War.
23. Shapiro, *New South Rebellion*, 244–46.
24. Lewis, *Black Coal Miners*, 26.
25. Letwin, *Challenge of Interracial Unionism*, 162.
26. Ward and Rogers, *Convicts, Coal, and the Banner Mine Tragedy*, 1–25, 123–25.
27. Williams, *West Virginia: History*, 130–48; Letwin, *Challenge of Interracial Unionism*, 184–88.
28. C. E. Lively to C. E. Smith, November 8, 1927, C. E. Smith Papers, WVU, Box 34.
29. Quoted in Alexander, "Rising from the Ashes," 62.

30. This paragraph is based on Hall et al., *Like a Family*, xxvi (map 1), xxviii (map 2), 4–43.

31. Dave McCarn, "Cotton Mill Colic No. 3," quoted in Whisnant, *All That Is Native and Fine*, 7.

32. Hall et al., *Like a Family*, 38.

33. Ibid., 153–54.

34. Ibid., 114–20; Hanchett, *Sorting Out the New South City*, 95–114.

35. Gerald Johnston, quoted in Hall et al., *Like a Family*, 195.

36. Salmond, *Gastonia 1929*; Hall et al., *Like a Family*, 212–36; Beal, *Proletarian Journey*, 158–59.

37. Quoted in Hall et al., *Like a Family*, 226–27.

38. Quoted in Karpeles, *Cecil Sharp*, 159.

39. *Famous Labor Songs from Appalachia*; Letwin, "Early Years," 37.

40. Aunt Molly Jackson, interview by Alan Lomax, May 1939, LC-AFC; Greenway, "Rejoinder" and "Folksong."

41. Green, *Only a Miner*, 249–64.

42. Hall et al., *Like a Family*, 219.

43. Blanche Lazell to "My dear Mr. Post," n.d. [1905–9?], and Blanche Lazell to "My dear Sister," July 22, 1917, Blanche Lazell Papers, reel 1 [microfilm reel 2988], National Museum of American Art, Washington, D.C.

44. Beal, *Proletarian Journey*, 109.

45. Quoted in Lichtenstein, *Twice the Work of Free Labor*, 164–65.

46. Tindall, *Emergence of the New South*, 617.

47. Ibid., 519–52.

48. Ibid., 633.

49. Becker, *Inventing Tradition*, 73–92.

50. Salstrom, *Appalachia's Path to Dependency*, 60–82; Hall et al. make a similar point in *Like a Family*. My conclusions about Matewan have been shaped by unpublished research kindly made available by David Reynolds.

51. For example, the actions of James Cardinal Gibbons of Baltimore in disciplining a pro-labor priest in Westernport, Maryland, in response to a request from mine owner and railroad builder Henry G. Davis (Henry Gassaway Davis Papers, WVU).

52. McCauley, *Appalachian Mountain Religion*, 259–75; Hall et al., *Like a Family*, 179.

53. Salstrom, *Appalachia's Path to Dependency*, 94–121.

54. Mastran and Lowerre, *Mountaineers and Rangers*, 23–28, 35.

55. Cherniack, *Hawk's Nest Incident*.

56. "Excerpts from Charlottesville Talks," Howard Washington Odum Papers, box 12, folder 255, Southern Historical Collection, Chapel Hill, N.C.

57. McDonald and Muldowney, *TVA and the Dispossessed*, 12, 263–64.

58. Bryson, *Walk in the Woods*, 28–30. Bryson's bibliography (275–76) is a useful guide to the literature of the Appalachian Trail.

59. Brown, *Wild East*, 138.

60. Ibid., 101.

61, *Washington Post*, March 6, 2000, B1.

62. Brown, *Wild East*, 10.

63. McDonald and Muldowney, *TVA and the Dispossessed*, 170, 193.

64. I have dealt with these developments at greater length in "Radicalism and Professionalism in Folklore Studies." See also Romalis, *Pistol Packin' Mama*, 1–18, 89–126.

65. Quoted in McDonald and Muldowney, *TVA and the Dispossessed*, 263.

66. Roy E. Stryker to Arthur Rothstein, May 23, June 6, 1936, Stryker Papers, ser. 1, box 1, folder 2, University of Louisville Library, Louisville, Ky.

67. McDonald and Muldowney, *TVA and the Dispossessed*, 50, 57.

68. Quoted in Brown, *Wild East*, 161.

69. Perdue and Martin-Perdue, "Appalachian Fables and Facts."

70. McDonald and Muldowney, *TVA and the Dispossessed*, 110–11, 114, 119.

71. Ibid., 161.

Chapter Five

1. Author's conversation with Helen Lewis, Beckley, West Virginia, August 25, 2000; e-mail message, Helen Lewis to author, March 7, 2001; Chapin, *Fast as White Lightning*; Wilkinson, *Dirt Tracks to Glory*.

2. Jensen, *Regionalism in America*.

3. Lewis, "You've Got to Be Converted."

4. Father Thomas Quirk to Father Weber, January 23, 1917, quoted in O'Donovan, *Rock from Which You Were Hewn*, 208.

5. Changes in some areas forecast later population declines. For example, nonwhite population fell in the 1930s to between 6.8 percent and 21 percent in the mining districts of Pennsylvania, Ohio, northern and central West Virginia, western Maryland, and Tennessee, while increasing in similar districts in southern West Virginia, southwest Virginia, and eastern Kentucky. It also declined in nonmining areas such as north Georgia and northeast Alabama and in Great Valley counties in both Virginias, while increasing in western North Carolina. Among the region's cities, Altoona, Scranton, Wilkes-Barre, Wheeling, Huntington-Ashland, Asheville, and Knoxville lost nonwhite population, while Charleston, Chattanooga, Birmingham, Pittsburgh, and Winston-Salem gained (see Bogue, *State Economic Areas*, table A, 12–32).

6. Berry, *Southern Migrants, Northern Exiles*, 11–18.

7. While several University of Kentucky scholars have collaborated in a "Beech Creek group" following up on Brown's studies, Beech Creek's real name has never been published, although Dwight Billings and Kathleen Blee revealed Clay County as the general location of Beech Creek in *The Road to Poverty*. Historians and others who wish to assure themselves that it is a real place can do so easily by comparing the geographical information in Brown's dissertation with a topographical map of Clay County.

8. USDA-BAE, *Economic and Social Problems*, 5.

9. Dodson, "Living Conditions and Population Migration."

10. Goodrich, Allin, and Hayes, *Migration and Planes of Living*, 10–11, 43, and maps following p. 10; this is per capita farm, not total population.

11. Ibid., 51.

12. Ford, *Southern Appalachian Region*, fig. 4, p. 6.

13. Dodson, "Living Conditions and Population Migration," 5.

14. Schwarzweller, Brown and Mangalam, *Mountain Families in Transition*, 99–102, especially Table 5.1.

15. Berry, *Southern Migrants, Northern Exiles*, 16–17.

16. Schwarzweller, Brown, and Mangalam, *Mountain Families in Transition*, 74–77, esp. table 4.2.

17. Ford, *Southern Appalachian Region*, 58, table 8.

18. Calculations based on data files found in *GAHM*, files c952_13, "Percent Population Increase, 1940–50."

19. Quoted in Berry, *Southern Migrants, Northern Exiles*, 104.

20. Feather, *Mountain People in a Flat Land*, 23, 65–75, 128–30, 193–222, 223–31.

21. Ibid., 122–24; Berry, *Southern Migrants, Northern Exiles*, 119–21.

22. Latham, *Modernization as Ideology*, 1–68.

23. Brown, *Beech Creek*, 173–96.

24. Dodson, "Living Conditions and Population Migration," 84–87.

25. Brown, *Beech Creek*, 162–63.

26. Ibid., 168–69.

27. Stephenson, *Shiloh*; Weller, *Yesterday's People*. See also Pearsall, *Little Smoky Ridge*.

28. Toynbee, *Study of History*, 149.

29. Weller, *Yesterday's People*, 161–63.

30. Berry, *Southern Migrants, Northern Exiles*, 181.

31. For example, the series of "traveling conferences" held under the joint auspices of the Farm Security Administration and the Bureau of Agricultural Economics in 1939 (USDA-BAE, "Traveling Conference," NA (mimeographed itinerary).

32. Brown and Hillery, "Great Migration," 78.

33. Stekert, "Focus for Conflict"; Polansky, Borgman, and De Saix, *Roots of Futility*, esp. 75–84, 166–77, 191; Mastran and Lowerre, *Mountaineers and Rangers*, v, ix (n. 1).

34. Bowman and Hayes, *Resources and People in East Kentucky*, 214–15.

35. Berry, *Southern Migrants, Northern Exiles*, 196–97.

36. Griffin, "Appalachian Newcomers in Cincinnati," 84.

37. Graff, "Needs of Education."

38. McCormick, *This Nest of Vipers*, 17.

39. Graff, "Needs of Education," 196, 199.

40. Quoted in Berry, *Southern Migrants, Northern Exiles*, 192.

41. Halperin, *Livelihood of Kin*; Patton, *Carpet Capital*.

42. This figure was arrived at by eliminating core counties containing the cities of Asheville, Ashland (Ky.), Bristol (Tenn.-Va.), Charleston, Chattanooga, Johnson City, Kingsport, and Knoxville. If these counties are included, the rural percentage in core

counties drops to just under 60 percent. Official Appalachia, including all its metropolitan areas, was 53 percent rural in 1960.

43. Vance, "Region's Future."

44. Berry, *Southern Migrants, Northern Exiles*, 178–80; Gregory, "Southern Diaspora and the Urban Dispossessed."

45. Newcomb, "Appalachia on Television," 155–64.

46. *Wall Street Journal*, August 16, 1943; *Philadelphia Inquirer*, October 31, 1944; Commonwealth of Pennsylvania, Department of Commerce, press release, January 18, 1944; The Pennsylvania State College, "News for Evening Dailies" (press release), May 16, 1945; all in Clipping Files, War History Program, PSA.

47. I am grateful to Ronald D Eller of the University of Kentucky for sharing with me his research on the history of the Appalachian Regional Commission in advance of its publication.

48. Rostow, *Stages of Economic Growth*.

49. Rostow, *Diffusion of Power*, 215.

50. Bradshaw, *Appalachian Regional Commission*, 31; Whisnant, *Modernizing the Mountaineer*, 72–91.

51. Chafin and Sherwood, *Just Good Politics*, 130–50; Ernst, *Primary That Made a President*.

52. *New York Times*, December 5, 1960, sec. 1, p. 8.

53. Bradshaw, *Appalachian Regional Commission*, 80–81.

54. Ibid., 77.

55. Jones, "Appalachia's War," *Pittsburgh Post-Gazette*, November 26, 2000.

56. Ibid.

57. *GAHM*, 1988 City County Data Book, file c988_10.

58. Quoted in Jones, "Looking for Life after Coal."

59. Wharton School Industrial Research Unit, *Migration and Economic Opportunity*, 494.

60. Eller et al., *Kentucky's Distressed Communities*, 33–38.

61. Lewis, Johnson, and Askins, *Colonialism in Modern America*.

62. Perry, *They'll Cut Off Your Project*, 135, 145.

63. Gates, *Colored People*, xvi, 184–88.

64. Glen, *Highlander*, 3, 207–81; Helen M. Lewis to author, March 7, 2001.

65. Bartlett, *Troubled Waters*; Schoenbaum, *New River Controversy*; Wheeler and McDonald, *TVA and the Tellico Dam*.

66. Purdy, *For Common Things*, ix.

67. Ibid., 90; see also Beaver, *Rural Community*, 121–22.

68. Purdy, *For Common Things*, 115–37.

69. Ibid., 128–29.

70. Quoted in ibid., 237. The concept of neonativity is developed in Rothman, *Devil's Bargains*, 26, 77–78, 98, 137, 208.

71. For example, Jedediah Purdy's mother, whose school board activity eventually led to involvement in state politics and then law school (Purdy, *For Common Things*, 189–91).

72. Schoenbaum, *New River Controversy*, 114–19.

73. Ardery, *The Temptation*.

74. Author's interviews with Dave Arnold, Chris Dragan, C. R. "Bud" Hill, and Jack Gannon, Lansing, West Virginia, January 31–February 1, 2001; *Fayette Tribune*, December 3, 2000.

75. Bartlett, *Troubled Waters*, 288–91.

76. Whisnant, *Modernizing the Mountaineer*, 18–39.

77. Lewis, "You've Got to Be Converted," 252.

78. Quoted in Foster, *Past Is Another Country*, 119. This paragraph and the following one are based on this book and on conversations with Appalachian State students and colleagues who were engaged in the New River controversy.

79. Ibid., 154–55, 179, 195.

80. Carlisle, "Insiders, Outsiders and the Struggle for Community."

81. Markusen et al., *Rise of the Gunbelt*, 244–45.

82. Schulman, *From Cotton Belt to Sun Belt*.

83. Based on 1983, 1985, 1990, and 1995 data in *CFFR*. These data are updated annually and were also printed through fiscal year 1995. After 1996, they are available on CD and online at <http://www.census.gov/govs/www/cffr.html>.

84. The data on which this paragraph and Table 5.1 are based come from DOD, Office of the Secretary of Defense, *State Maps of Major Military Stations*, and DOD, Washington Headquarters Services, Directorate for Information Operations and Reports, *Atlas/State Data Abstract for the United States*.

85. Caudill, *Watches of the Night*.

86. Schlesinger et al., *Our Own Worst Enemy*, 9–11, 26–41, 58–73, 123–38, 187–93, 197–223.

87. Ibid., 55–57.

88. Schulman, *From Cotton Belt to Sunbelt*, 137.

89. Markusen et al., *Rise of the Gunbelt*, 46, 48, 187–90, 247–49; Friedberg, *In the Shadow of the Garrison State*, 325.

90. Markusen et al., *Rise of the Gunbelt*, 3–4, 239.

91. Schulman, *From Cotton Belt to Sunbelt*, 135–52.

92. Fordham, "Economic Interests, Party, and Ideology."

93. Maddox, *Senatorial Career*; Rogers et al., *Alabama*, 524–25, 532–38.

94. I am indebted to my colleague Karl Campbell, who is at work on a biography of Ervin, for information on this point.

95. Schulman, *From Cotton Belt to Sunbelt*, 143–47.

96. Friedberg, *In the Shadow of the Garrison State*, 212–35, 306–15.

97. Schulman, *From Cotton Belt to Sunbelt*, 141.

98. "Scranton Seeks Aid in Job Crisis," *Philadelphia Record*, April 13, 1944, in War History Program, PSA; Rogers et al., *Alabama*, 511, 522.

99. Bradshaw, *Appalachian Regional Commission*, 82, 85.

100. Clemensen, "Historic Resource Study"; O'Malley, "United States of America vs. Joseph M. McDade," Scranton Public Library, Scranton, Pa.

101. Gordon, *Pitied but Not Entitled.*

102. Edwin Kemp, "Kentucky Emigrants Making Good Farm Hands in Pennsylvania," *Philadelphia Record*, April 6, 1943, in War History Program, PSA.

103. Charles R. Fox Collection, West Virginia Department of Archives and History, Charleston. Fox's diaries from 1952 through 1956 are found in Box 2 and reveal the locations of his speeches to high school students. His personnel record can be found in Box 1.

104. Davis and Dolbeare, *Little Groups of Neighbors*, 54–99; King, *Selective Service in North Carolina*, 50–74. Comparing the occupational categories of the men who served on draft boards (p. 64) with the overall occupational structure of the state's 1940 male workforce (table 9, pp. 142–43), it is easy to imagine that these boards represented the same "county seat folks" who were enemies of the FSA and other New Deal programs aimed at the rural poor. My personal experience in Greenbrier County, West Virginia, in 1957 is relevant on this point. When I appeared to register at the draft board with a friend who, like me, was town dwelling, middle class, and college bound, we were advised not to apply for student deferments. Since the board always filled its quota from the mining and lumber districts in the western end of the county, we were unlikely to be drafted, we were told, whereas a student deferment increased the likelihood of being called up after graduation. It was good advice.

105. King, *Selective Service in North Carolina*, 20, table 46 (pp. 294–95), and app. E, table I (pp. 406–9).

106. Kvaraceus and Miller, *Delinquent Behavior*, 79–84; see also Williams, "Politics of Urban Decay."

107. Jones, "Appalachia's War"; "A Tale of Two Successes," *Pittsburgh Post-Gazette*, November 27, 2000; Tom Loftus, "Mine Expert Fears Whitewash," *Louisville Courier-Journal*, April 10, 2001.

108. Jones, "Appalachia's War."

109. Couto, *Making Democracy Work Better*, 3; app. A (pp. 303–5) contains a list of the projects examined.

110. Tennessee State Planning Office, "Summary Plan—Jonesboro, Tennessee" (June 1977), copy in NSA Records, LC-AFC (I am grateful to David Taylor of the LC-AFC for informing me that these records would soon be transferred to Washington and to Jimmy Neil Smith for allowing me to examine them before they were boxed up and shipped off); Sobel, *Storytellers' Journey*, 20–26, 33–63, 77–117, 212–39; author interview with Jimmy Neil Smith, Jonesborough, Tennessee, January 5, 2001.

111. Author interview with Jimmy Neil Smith; "Town of Jonesborough, Directions 2000," "1989–1990 Report to the Town," "Revenue Sources, July 11, 1995," and "National Storytelling Center, Total Funding—by Source," copies in NSA Records, LC-AFC.

112. Author interview with Virginia Price and Brian Levine, Fayetteville, West Virginia, February 1, 2001; *Fayette Tribune*, March 29, April 12, 21, May 17, 31, August 30, September 23, December 6, 1999, January 17, April 18, August 21, October 9, 2000, January 15, 2001.

113. Casino data from <http://www.cherokeemuseum.org/HTML/archives_FAQb.html#7>; "Daisy Mae in Hollywood," *Interview*, July 1989, 36, 37, 40, 85, excerpted in *Appalachian Journal* 17 (Fall 1989): 19–20.

114. Rothman, *Devil's Bargains*, 247–86.

115. Daw et al., *1990 Census Atlas of North Carolina*, maps 6, 7. The figures in the following paragraph are drawn from <http://factfinder.census.gov>, tables QT-PL, "Race, Hispanic or Latino, and Age, 2000."

116. Williams, "Unpacking Pinckney in Poland," 165. (The concept of place exchange comes from Stephenson, "Place for Sale," 117.)

117. Williams and Kelley, "Other End of the Hillbilly Highway," and Williams and Hooker, "Southbound on the Hillbilly Highway."

118. Jones, "Appalachia's War."

119. Purdy, *For Common Things*, 129–30.

120. Williamson, *Hillbillyland*, ix.

121. Purdy, *For Common Things*, 132, 149, 159.

Bibliography

Manuscript Collections

Chapel Hill, North Carolina
Southern Historical Collection, University of North Carolina Library
  Howard Washington Odum Papers

Charleston, West Virginia
West Virginia Department of Archives and History
  Charles R. Fox Collection

Harrisburg, Pennsylvania
Pennsylvania State Archives
  Thomas Penn Papers (microfilm)
  War History Program

Louisville, Kentucky
University of Louisville Library Special Collections
  Roy E. Stryker Papers

Morgantown, West Virginia
West Virginia University Library
  West Virginia and Regional History Collection
    Brooks Collection
    Henry Gassaway Davis Papers
    Haymond Family Papers
    C. E. Smith Papers

New Haven, Connecticut
Yale University Library, Archives and Manuscripts Division
  Ulrich Bonnell Phillips Collection in Southern History
    McDowell Family Papers

Philadelphia, Pennsylvania
Historical Society of Pennsylvania
  Thomas Penn Papers

Scranton, Pennsylvania
Scranton Public Library
  O'Malley, Scott. "The United States of America vs. Joseph M. McDade."
  Unpublished seminar paper, Syracuse University, 1999.

Washington, D.C.
Library of Congress, American Folklife Center
  Aunt Molly Jackson, interview by Alan Lomax, May 1939, tape LWO-4872,
  reel 162B
  National Storytelling Association Records
National Archives
  U.S. Department of Agriculture, Bureau of Agricultural Economics, "Traveling
  Conference of the Department of Agriculture in the Southern Appalachian
  Region, October 30–November 4, 1939, Kentucky Section" (unpublished
  mimeographed itinerary)
National Museum of American Art, Smithsonian Institution
  Archives of American Art
    Blanche Lazell Papers

Books, Articles, and Theses

Abrams, William Hutson, Jr. "The Western North Carolina Railroad, 1855–1894."
Master's thesis, Western Carolina University, 1976.

Alderer, E. G. [Everett Gordon]. *The Ephrata Commune: An Early American Counterculture*. Pittsburgh: University of Pittsburgh Press, 1985.

Alexander, Peter. "Rising from the Ashes: Alabama Coal Miners, 1921–1941." In Brown and Davis, *Its Union and Liberty*, 62–83.

Allen, J. Sidna. *Memoirs of J. Sidna Allen: A True Narrative of What Really Happened at Hillsville*. Madison, N.C.: Allwith Publishing Co., 1929.

Allison, Dorothy. "A Question of Class." In *Skin: Talking about Class, Sex, and Literature*. Ithaca, N.Y.: Firebrand Books, 1994.

Ambler, Charles H. "Life of John Floyd." *John P. Branch Historical Papers of Randolph-Macon College* 1–2 (June 1918): 5–117.

———. *Sectionalism in Virginia from 1776 to 1861*. Chicago: University of Chicago Press, 1910.

———, ed. "Diary of John Floyd." *John P. Branch Historical Papers of Randolph-Macon College* 1–2 (June 1918): 119–233.

Anglin, Mary K. "Lives on the Margin: Rediscovering the Women of Antebellum Western North Carolina." In Pudup, Billings, and Waller, *Appalachia in the Making*, 185–209.

Ardery, Julia S. *The Temptation: Edgar Tolson and the Genesis of Twentieth-Century Folk Art*. Chapel Hill: University of North Carolina Press, 1998.

Asbury, Francis. *The Journal and Letters of Francis Asbury*. Edited by Elmer T. Clark, J. Manning Potts, and Jacob S. Payton. 3 vols. Nashville, Tenn.: Abingdon Press, 1958.

Atkinson, George Wesley. *After the Moonshiners: By One of the Raiders: A Book of Thrilling, Yet Truthful Narratives*. Wheeling, W.Va.: Frew and Campbell, 1881.

Bartlett, Richard A. *Troubled Waters: Champion International and the Pigeon River Controversy*. Knoxville: University of Tennessee Press, 1995.

Bartram, William. *The Travels of William Bartram: Naturalist's Edition*. Edited by Francis Harper. Athens: University of Georgia Press, 1998.

Batteau, Allen. *The Invention of Appalachia*. Tucson: University of Arizona Press, 1990.

Beal, Fred E. *Proletarian Journey: New England, Gastonia, Moscow*. New York: Hillman-Curl, 1937.

Beaver, Patricia Duane. *Rural Community in the Appalachian South*. Lexington: University Press of Kentucky, 1986.

Becker, Jane S. *Inventing Tradition: Appalachia and the Construction of an American Folk, 1930–1940*. Chapel Hill: University of North Carolina Press, 1998.

Becker, Martha Jane Williams. *Diary of a Millionaire Coal Town*. Logan, W.Va.: The Printers, 1988.

Beissel, Conrad. *Confidential Writings of Conrad Beissel*. Edited and translated by Elder Russell Yoder. Snow Hill, Pa.: N.p., 1994.

Berry, Chad. *Southern Migrants, Northern Exiles*. Urbana: University of Illinois Press, 2000.

Billings, Dwight B., and Kathleen M. Blee. "Agriculture and Poverty in the Kentucky Mountains: Beech Creek, 1850–1910." in Pudup, Billings and Waller, *Appalachia in the Making*, 233–69.

———. *The Road to Poverty: The Making of Wealth and Hardship in Appalachia*. Cambridge: Cambridge University Press, 2000.

Billings, Dwight B., Gurney Norman, and Katherine Ledford, eds. *Confronting Appalachian Stereotypes: Backtalk from an American Region*. Lexington: University Press of Kentucky, 1999.

Bladen, Wilford A., and Pradyumna P. Karan, eds. *The Evolution of Geographic Thought in America: A Kentucky Root*. Dubuque, Iowa: Kendall/Hunt Publishing Co., 1983.

Bogue, Donald J. *State Economic Areas: A Description of the Procedures in Making a Functional Grouping of the Counties of the United States*. Washington, D.C.: Government Printing Office, 1951.

Boles, John B. *Religion in Antebellum Kentucky*. 1976; Reprint. Lexington: University Press of Kentucky, 1995.

Bowman, Mary Jean, and W. Warren Hayes. *Resources and People in East Kentucky: Problems and Potentials of a Lagging Economy.* Baltimore, Md.: Johns Hopkins University Press, 1963.

Bradshaw, Michael. *The Appalachian Regional Commission: Twenty-five Years of Government Policy.* Lexington: University Press of Kentucky, 1992.

Braudel, Fernand. *The Mediterranean and the Mediterranean World in the Age of Philip II.* Translated from the French by Sian Reynolds. 2 vols. New York: Harper Colophon Books, 1972.

Briscoe, Mary Louise. *Thomas Mellon and His Times.* Pittsburgh, Pa.: University of Pittsburgh Press, 1994.

Brooks, Maurice. *The Appalachians.* Boston: Houghton Mifflin, 1965.

Brown, Edwin L., and Colin J. Davis, eds. *Its Union and Liberty: Alabama Coal Miners and the UMW.* Tuscaloosa: University of Alabama Press, 1999.

Brown, James S. *Beech Creek: A Study of a Kentucky Mountain Neighborhood.* Berea, Ky.: Berea College Press, 1988.

Brown, James S., and George A. Hillery Jr. "The Great Migration, 1940–1960." In Ford, *Southern Appalachian Region,* 54–78.

Brown, Margaret Lynn. *The Wild East: A Biography of the Great Smoky Mountains.* Gainesville: University Press of Florida, 2000.

Bryson, Bill. *A Walk in the Woods: Rediscovering America on the Appalachian Trail.* New York: Broadway Books, 1998.

Bulger, Peggy A., ed. *Promoting Southern Cultural Heritage: A Conference on Impact.* Atlanta: Southern Arts Federation, 1991.

Butler, Lindley S., and Alan D. Watson, eds. *The North Carolina Experience.* Chapel Hill: University of North Carolina Press, 1984.

Butterfield, C. W., ed. *The Washington-Crawford Letters.* Cincinnati, Ohio: Robert W. Clarke and Co., 1877.

Campbell, Alexander. "Slavery and the Fugitive Slave Law." *The Millenial Harbinger,* ser. 4, vol. 1 (July 1851): 386–92. Quoted in Cometti and Summers, *The Thirty-fifth State,* 262–65.

Campbell, John C. *The Southern Highlander and His Homeland.* With a new foreword by Rupert B. Vance and an introduction by Henry D. Shapiro. Lexington: University Press of Kentucky, 1969.

Carlisle, Fred. "Insiders, Outsiders, and the Struggle for Community." *Appalachian Journal* 26 (Spring 1999): 14–51.

Caudill, Harry M. *Night Comes to the Cumberlands: A Biography of a Depressed Area.* Boston: Little, Brown, 1963.

———. *The Watches of the Night.* Boston: Little, Brown, 1976.

Cayton, Andrew R. L., and Fredrika J. Teute, eds. *Contact Points: American Frontiers from the Mohawk Valley to the Mississippi, 1750–1830.* Chapel Hill: University of North Carolina Press, 1998.

Chafin, Raymond, and Topper Sherwood. *Just Good Politics: The Life of Raymond Chafin, Appalachian Boss.* Pittsburgh, Pa.: University of Pittsburgh Press, 1994.

Chapin, Kim. *Fast as White Lightning: The Story of Stock Car Racing*. New York: Three Rivers Press, 1998.

Cherniack, Martin. *The Hawk's Nest Incident: America's Worst Industrial Disaster*. New Haven, Conn.: Yale University Press, 1986.

Clarkson, Roy B. *On Beyond Leatherbark: The Cass Saga*. Parsons, W.Va.: McClain Printing Co., 1990.

Clayton, Lawrence, Vernon James Knight Jr., and Edward C. Moore. *De Soto Chronicles: Hernando de Soto to North America in 1539–1543*. Tuscaloosa: University of Alabama Press, 1993.

Clemensen, A. Berle. "Historic Resource Study: Steamtown National Historic Site, Pennsylvania." Unpublished report, National Park Service, Denver Resource Center, n.d. [1988?].

Cometti, Elizabeth, and Festus P. Summers. *The Thirty-fifth State: A Documentary History of West Virginia*. Morgantown: West Virginia University Library, 1966.

Cook, Roy Bird. *Washington's Western Lands*. Strasburg, Va.: Shenandoah Publishing Co., 1930.

Couto, Richard, with Catherine S. Guthrie. *Making Democracy Work Better: Mediating Structures, Social Capital, and the Democratic Prospect*. Chapel Hill: University of North Carolina Press, 1999.

Cox, Jacob D. *Military Reminisences of the Civil War*. 2 vols. New York: Charles Scribners' Sons, 1900.

Cox, John Harrington. *Folk Songs of the South*. Cambridge, Mass.: Harvard University Press, 1925.

Crawford, Martin. *Ashe County's Civil War: Community and Society in the Appalachian South*. Charlottesville: University Press of Virginia, 2001.

Cresswell, Nicholas, *The Journal of Nicholas Cresswell, 1774–1777*. New York: L. MacVeagh, The Dial Press, 1924.

Crofts, Daniel W. *Reluctant Confederates: Upper South Unionists in the Secession Crisis*. Chapel Hill: University of North Carolina Press, 1989.

Cunningham, Rodger. *Apples on the Flood*. Knoxville: University of Tennessee Press, 1987.

Davis, Donald Edward. *Where There Are Mountains: An Environmental History of the Southern Appalachians*. Athens: University of Georgia Press, 2000.

Davis, Dorothy. *John George Jackson: A Biography*. Parsons, W.Va.: McClain Printing Co., 1976.

Davis, James W., Jr., and Kenneth M. Dolbeare. *Little Groups of Neighbors: The Selective Service System*. Chicago: Markham Publishing Co., 1968.

Davis, Rebecca Harding. *Bits of Gossip*. Boston: Houghton Mifflin, 1904.

Daw, Jonathan, Neal G. Lineback, Arthur Rex, and Mark Heglin. *The 1990 Census Atlas of North Carolina*. Boone, N.C.: Department of Geography and Planning, Appalachian State University, 1992.

Dew, Charles B. *Bond of Iron: Master and Slave at Buffalo Forge*. New York: W. W. Norton, 1994.

Dix, Keith. *What's a Miner to Do?: The Mechanization of Coal Mining.* Pittsburgh: University of Pittsburgh Press, 1988.

Doddridge, Joseph. *Notes on the Settlement and Indian Wars of the Western Parts of Virginia and Pennsylvania from 1763 to 1783.* Pittsburgh, Pa.: John S. Ritenour and William T. Lindsay, 1912.

Dodson, L. S. "Living Conditions and Population Migration in Four Appalachian Counties." Unpublished report, U.S. Department of Agriculture, Farm Security Administration, and Bureau of Agricultural Economics, 1937. National Agricultural Library, Beltsville, Md., catalog no. I.95 S01 no. 3.

Dorgan, Howard. *The Old Regular Baptists of Central Appalachia: Brothers and Sisters in Hope.* Knoxville: University of Tennessee Press, 1989.

Dorson, Richard M. *Buying the Wind: Regional Folklore in the United States.* Chicago: University of Chicago Press, 1964.

Dowd, Gregory Evans, *A Spirited Resistance: The North American Indian Struggle for Unity, 1745–1815.* Baltimore, Md.: Johns Hopkins University Press, 1992.

Dunaway, Wilma A. *The First American Frontier: Transition to Capitalism in Southern Appalachia, 1700–1860.* Chapel Hill: University of North Carolina Press, 1996.

Dunn, Durwood. *Cade's Cove: The Life and Death of an Appalachian Community.* Knoxville: University of Tennessee Press, 1988.

Eller, Ronald D *Miners, Millhands, and Mountaineers: Industrialization of the Appalachian South, 1880–1882.* Knoxville: University of Tennessee Press, 1982.

Eller, Ronald D, with Phil Jenks, Chris Jasparro, and Jerry Napier. *Kentucky's Distressed Communities: A Report on Poverty in Appalachian Kentucky.* Lexington: Appalachian Center, University of Kentucky, 1994.

Ellison, George. "James Mooney and the Eastern Cherokees." In Mooney, *James Mooney's History, Myths, and Sacred Formulas,* 1–30.

ePress Project, Academic Software Development Group. *The Great American History Machine: An Interactive Atlas of Nineteenth- and Twentieth-Century United States Social and Political History.* CD data base. College Park: University of Maryland, 1995.

Ernst, Harry, *The Primary That Made a President: West Virginia, 1960.* New York: McGraw-Hill, 1962.

Everett, C. S. "Everett Answers Killebrew and Kennedy: A Dissenting Voice in the Discourse of Descent." *Appalachian Journal* 27 (Winter 2000): 129–40.

———. "Melungeon History and Myth." *Appalachian Journal* 26 (Summer 1999): 358–409.

Fallam, Robert. "A Journal from Virginia to beyond the Appalachian Mountains in September 1671." In Lewis and Hennen, *West Virginia,* 24–27.

Famous Labor Songs from Appalachia. Huntington, W.Va.: Appalachian Movement Press, 1970.

Faragher, John Mack. *Daniel Boone: The Life and Legend of an American Pioneer.* New York: Henry Holt, 1992.

Feather, Carl E. *Mountain People in a Flat Land: A Popular History of Appalachian Migration to Northeast Ohio, 1940–1965.* Athens: Ohio University Press, 1998.

Finger, John R. *The Eastern Band of Cherokees, 1819–1900.* Knoxville: University of Tennessee Press, 1984.

Fischer, David Hackett. *Albion's Seed: Four British Folkways in North America.* New York: Oxford University Press, 1989.

Fisher, Noel C. *War at Every Door: Partisan Politics and Guerrilla Violence in East Tennessee, 1860–1869.* Chapel Hill: University of North Carolina Press, 1997.

Fisher, Stephen. *Fighting Back in Appalachia: Traditions of Resistance and Change.* Philadelphia, Pa.: Temple University Press, 1993.

Fogleman, Aaron Spencer. *Hopeful Journeys: German Immigration, Settlement, and Political Culture in Colonial America, 1717–1775.* Philadelphia: University of Pennsylvania Press, 1996.

Ford, Thomas R., ed. *The Southern Appalachian Region: A Survey.* Lexington: University Press of Kentucky, 1967.

Fordham, Benjamin O. "Economic Interests, Party, and Ideology in Early Cold War Era U.S. Foreign Policy." *International Organization* 52, no. 2 (Spring 1998): 359–96.

Foster, Stephen William. *The Past Is Another Country: Representation, Historical Consciousness, and Resistance in the Blue Ridge.* Berkeley: University of California Press, 1988.

Franklin, Benjamin. *The Papers of Benjamin Franklin.* Edited by Leonard W. Labaree. 5 vols. New Haven, Conn.: Yale University Press, 1959–96.

French, Christopher. "Journal of an Expedition to South Carolina." Reprinted in Butler and Watson, *North Carolina Experience,* 18–19.

Friedberg, Aaron L. *In the Shadow of the Garrison State: America's Anti-statism and Its Cold War Grand Strategy.* Princeton, N.J.: Princeton University Press, 2000.

Fries, Adelaide L., ed. *Records of the Moravians in North Carolina.* 10 vols. Raleigh, N.C.: Edwards and Broughton, 1922–69.

Frost, William G. "Educational Pioneering in the Southern Mountains." In *National Education Association of the United States: Addresses and Proceedings.* Washington, D.C.: The Association, 1901.

———. *For the Mountains: An Autobiography.* New York: Fleming H. Revell, 1937.

Garcia, Hazel Dicken. *To Western Woods: The Breckenridge Family Moves to Kentucky in 1793.* Rutherford, N.J.: Fairleigh Dickinson University Press, 1991.

Gaskins, Avery. "An Introduction to the Guineas: West Virginia's Melungeons." *Appalachian Journal* 1 (Autumn 1973): 234–37.

Gates, Henry Louis, Jr. *Colored People: A Memoir.* New York: Alfred A. Knopf, 1994.

Glen, John M. *Highlander: No Ordinary School.* 2nd ed. Knoxville: University of Tennessee Press, 1996.

Goodrich, Carter, Bushrod W. Allin, and Marion Hayes. *Migration and Planes of Living, 1920–1934.* Philadelphia: University of Pennsylvania Press, 1935.

Gordon, Linda. *Pitied but Not Entitled: Single Mothers and the History of Welfare, 1890–1935.* New York: Free Press, 1994.

Govan, Gilbert E., and James W. Livingood. *The Chattanooga Country, 1540–1976:*

From Tomahawks to TVA. Knoxville: University of Tennessee Press, 1977.

Graff, Orin B. "The Needs of Education." In Ford, *Southern Appalachian Region*, 188–200.

Gray, Robert. *The McGavock Family: A Genealogical History of James McGavock and His Descendants from 1760 to 1903.* Nashville, Tenn.: Bradley Whitfield, 1970.

Green, Archie. *Only a Miner: Studies in Recorded Coal-Mining Songs.* Urbana: University of Illinois Press, 1972.

Greenway, John. "Folksong: A Protest." *Australian Literary Studies* 2, no. 3 (1966): 177–92.

———. "Rejoinder." *New York Folklore Quarterly* 14, no. 1 (1958): 3–5.

Gregory, James N. "The Southern Diaspora and the Urban Dispossessed: Demonstrating the Census Public Use Microdata Samples." *Journal of American History* 82 (June 1995): 111–34.

Griffin, Roscoe. "Appalachian Newcomers in Cincinnati." In Ford, *Southern Appalachian Region*, 79–84.

Groce, W. Todd. "The Social Origins of East Tennessee's Confederate Leadership." In Noe and Shannon, *Civil War in Appalachia*, 30–54.

Hall, Jacquelyn Dowd, James Leloudis, Robert Korstad, Mary Murphy, Lu Ann Jones, and Christopher B. Daly. *Like a Family: The Making of a Southern Cotton Mill World.* Chapel Hill: University of North Carolina Press, 1981.

Halperin, Rhoda H. *The Livelihood of Kin: Making Ends Meet "the Kentucky Way."* Austin: University of Texas Press, 1990.

Hamilton, Virginia van der Veer. *Alabama: A History.* New York: W. W. Norton, 1977.

Hanchett, Thomas W. *Sorting Out the New South City: Race, Class, and Urban Development in Charlotte, 1875–1975.* Chapel Hill: University of North Carolina Press, 1998.

Hardin, Elizabeth. *The Private War of Lizzie Hardin.* Edited by C. Glenn Clift. Frankfort: Kentucky Historical Society, 1963.

Hatley, Thomas M. *The Dividing Paths: Cherokees and South Carolinians through the Era of Revolution.* New York: Oxford University Press, 1993.

Hawks, Francis L. *History of North Carolina.* 2 vols. Fayetteville, N.C.: E. J. Hale and Son, 1859.

Hayes, C. Willard. *The Southern Appalachians.* National Geographical Society Monographs, No. 10, Vol. 1. New York: American Book Company, 1895.

Hayes, Rutherford B. *Diary and Letters of Rutherford Birchard Hayes.* Edited by Charles R. Williams. 5 vols. Columbus: Ohio State Archaeological and Historical Society, 1922.

Holmes, William F. "Moonshining and Collective Violence: Georgia, 1889–1895." *Journal of American History* 73 (September 1986): 591–606.

Hsiung, David C. *Two Worlds in the Tennessee Mountains: Exploring the Origins of Appalachian Stereotypes.* Lexington: University Press of Kentucky, 1997.

Hudson, Charles M. *The Catawba Nation.* Athens: University of Georgia Press, 1970.

Inscoe, John C. *Mountain Masters: Slavery and the Sectional Crisis in Western North Carolina*. Knoxville: University of Tennessee Press, 1989.

———. "Race and Racism in Nineteenth-Century Southern Appalachia: Myths, Realities and Ambiguities." In Pudup, Billings, and Waller, *Appalachia in the Making*, 103–31.

Inscoe, John C., and Gordon B. McKinney. *The Heart of Confederate Appalachia: Western North Carolina in the Civil War*. Chapel Hill: University of North Carolina Press, 2000.

Ireland, Robert M. *The County in Kentucky History*. Lexington: University Press of Kentucky, 1976.

Jackson, Mary Anna. *Memoirs of Stonewall Jackson, by His Widow*. Louisville, Ky.: Prentice Press, 1895.

James, Preston E., Wilford A. Bladen, and Pradyumna P. Karan. "Ellen Churchill Semple and the Development of a Research Paradigm." In Bladen and Karan, *Evolution of Geographic Thought*, 29–58.

Jennings, Francis. *The Ambiguous Iroquois Empire*. New York: W. W. Norton, 1984.

Jensen, Merrill, ed. *Regionalism in America*. Madison: University of Wisconsin Press, 1951.

Johnston, David Emmons. *The Story of a Confederate Boy in the Civil War*. 1914. Reissue (electronic ed.). Chapel Hill: University of North Carolina, Documenting the American South, 1998.

Jones, Diana Nelson. "Appalachia's War: The Poorest of the Poor Struggle Back." *Pittsburgh Post-Gazette*, November 26, 2000.

———. "Looking for Life after Coal." *Pittsburgh Post-Gazette*, November 28, 2000.

———. "A Tale of Two Successes." *Pittsburgh Post-Gazette*, November 27, 2000.

Jordan, Terry, and Matti Kaups. *The American Backwoods Frontier: An Ethnic and Ecological Interpretation*. Baltimore, Md.: Johns Hopkins University Press, 1989.

Karpeles, Maud. *Cecil Sharp: His Life and Work*. Chicago: University of Chicago Press, 1967.

Kegley, F. B. *Kegley's Virginia Frontier: The Beginning of the Southwest, the Roanoke of Colonial Days, 1740–1783*. Roanoke: Southwest Virginia Historical Society, 1938.

Kegley, Mary B. *Wythe County, Virginia: A Bicentennial History*. Wytheville, Va.: Wythe County Board of Supervisors, 1989.

Keller, Kenneth W. "What Is Distinctive about the Scotch-Irish?" In Mitchell, *Appalachian Frontiers*, 69–86.

Kennedy, Joseph C. G. *Agriculture of the United States in 1860 Compiled from the Eighth Census*. Washington, D.C.: Government Printing Office, 1864.

Kephart, Horace. *Our Southern Highlanders*. Rev. ed. New York: Macmillan, 1922. Reprinted as *Our Southern Highlanders: A Narrative of Adventure in the Southern Appalachians and a Study of Life among the Mountaineers*. With an Introduction by George Ellison. Knoxville: University of Tennessee Press, 1976.

Kiffmeyer, Thomas J. "From Self-Help to Sedition: The Appalachian Volunteers in Eastern Kentucky, 1964–1970." *Journal of Southern History* 64 (February 1998): 65–94.

King, Spencer Bidwell, Jr. *Selective Service in North Carolina in World War II.* Chapel Hill: University of North Carolina Press, 1949.

Klein, Rachel. *Unification of a Slave State: The Rise of the Planter Class in the South Carolina Backcountry, 1760–1808.* Chapel Hill: University of North Carolina Press, 1990.

Kodish, Deborah. *Good Friends and Bad Enemies: Robert Winslow Gordon and the Study of American Folksong.* Urbana: University of Illinois Press, 1986.

Kvaraceus, William C., and Walter B. Miller. *Delinquent Behavior: Culture and the Individual.* Washington, D.C.: National Education Association, 1959.

Lacy, Eric Russell. *Vanquished Volunteers: East Tennessee Sectionalism from Statehood to Secession.* Johnson City: East Tennessee State University Press, 1965.

Lane, Mills. *The People of Georgia: An Illustrated History.* Savannah: Library of Georgia, 1992.

Lanman, Charles. *Adventures in the Wilds of the United States and British North American Provinces.* Philadelphia, Pa.: J. W. Moore, 1856.

———. *Letters from the Alleghany Mountains.* New York: G. P. Putnam, 1849.

Latham, Michael E. *Modernization as Ideology: American Social Science and "Nation Building" in the Kennedy Era.* Chapel Hill: University of North Carolina Press, 2000.

Lay, Elery A. *An Industrial and Commercial History of the Tri-Cities of Tennessee-Virginia.* Kingsport, Tenn.: Lay Publications, 1982.

Lee, David D. *Sergeant York: An American Hero.* Lexington: University Press of Kentucky, 1985.

Letwin, Daniel. *The Challenge of Interracial Unionism: Alabama Coal Miners, 1878–1921.* Chapel Hill: University of North Carolina Press, 1998.

———. "The Early Years: Alabama Miners Organize, 1878–1908." In Brown and Davis, *Its Union and Liberty,* 11–37.

Lewis, Helen Matthews. "You've Got to Be Converted: Helen Matthews Lewis, Interviewed by Patricia Beaver." *Appalachian Journal* 15 (Spring 1988): 238–50.

Lewis, Helen Matthews, Linda Johnson, and Donald Askins. *Colonialism in Modern America: The Appalachian Case.* Boone, N.C.: Appalachian Consortium Press, 1978.

Lewis, Ronald L. *Black Coal Miners in America: Race, Class, and Community Conflict.* Lexington: University Press of Kentucky, 1987.

———. "Railroads, Deforestation, and the Transformation of Agriculture in the West Virginia Back Counties, 1880–1920." In Pudup, Billings, and Waller, *Appalachia in the Making,* 297–320.

Lewis, Ronald L., and John C. Hennen Jr., eds. *West Virginia: Documents in the History of a Rural-Industrial State.* Dubuque, Iowa: Kendall Hunt Publishing Co., 1991.

Lewis, W. David. *Sloss Furnaces and the Rise of the Birmingham District.* Tuscaloosa: University of Alabama Press, 1994.

Lichtenstein, Alex. *Twice the Work of Free Labor: The Political Economy of Convict Labor in the New South.* London: Verso, 1996.

MacMaster, Richard K. "The Cattle Trade in Western Virginia." In Mitchell, *Appalachian Frontiers*, 127–49.

Maddox, Robert F. *The Senatorial Career of Harley Martin Kilgore*. New York: Garland, 1981.

Malone, Bill C. *Southern Music, American Music*. Lexington: University Press of Kentucky, 1979.

Mann, Ralph. "Diversity in the Antebellum Appalachian South: Four Farm Communities in Tazewell County, Virginia." In Pudup, Billings, and Waller, *Appalachia in the Making*, 132–62.

———. "Ezekiel Counts's Sand Lick Company: Civil War and Localism in the Mountain South." In Noe and Wilson, *Civil War in Appalachia*, 78–103.

Markusen, Ann, Peter Hall, Scott Campbell, and Sabina Deitrick. *The Rise of the Gunbelt: The Military Remapping of Industrial America*. New York: Oxford University Press, 1991.

Mastran, Shelley Smith, and Nan Lowerre. *Mountaineers and Rangers: A History of Federal Forest Management in the Southern Appalachians, 1900–81*. Washington, D.C.: U.S. Department of Agriculture, Forest Service, 1983.

McCauley, Deborah Vansau. *Appalachian Mountain Religion: A History*. Urbana: University of Illinois Press, 1995.

McCormick, Charles H. *This Nest of Vipers: McCarthyism and Higher Education in the Mundel Affair, 1951–52*. Urbana: University of Illinois Press, 1989.

McDonald, Michael J., and John Muldowney. *TVA and the Dispossessed: The Resettlement of Population in the Norris Dam Area*. Knoxville: University of Tennessee Press, 1982.

McLaughlin, William G., *After the Trail of Tears: The Cherokees' Struggle for Sovereignty, 1839–1880*. Chapel Hill: University of North Carolina Press, 1993.

McNeil, W. K., ed. *Appalachian Images in Folk and Popular Culture*. 2nd ed. Knoxville: University of Tennessee Press, 1995.

McNeill, Louise. *Gauley Mountain*. New York: Harcourt, Brace and Co., 1939.

McNeill, William H. *Arnold J. Toynbee: A Life*. New York: Oxford University Press, 1989.

Meriwether, Robert L. *The Expansion of South Carolina, 1729–1765*. 1940. Reprint. Philadelphia, Pa.: Porcupine Press, 1974.

Merrell, James H. *The Indians' New World: Catawbas and Their Neighbors from European Contact through the Era of Removal*. Chapel Hill: University of North Carolina Press for the Institute of Early American History and Culture, 1989.

———. "Shamokin, 'the Very Seat of the Prince of Darkness': Unsettling the Early American Frontier." In Cayton and Teute, *Contact Points*, 16–59.

Milanich, Jerald T. *Florida Indians and the Invasion from Europe*. Gainesville: University Press of Florida, 1995.

Miles, Emma Bell. *The Spirit of the Mountains*. 1905. Reprint. Knoxville: University of Tennessee Press, 1975.

Milnes, Gerald. *Play of a Fiddle: Traditional Music, Dance, and Folklore in West Virginia*. Lexington: University Press of Kentucky, 1999.

Mitchell, Elisha. *Diary of a Geological Tour in 1827 and 1828*. Introduction and notes by Kemp P. Battle. James Sprunt Historical Monograph No. 6. Chapel Hill: University of North Carolina, 1905.

Mitchell, Robert D. *Commercialism and Frontier: Perspectives on the Early Shenandoah Valley*. Charlottesville: University Press of Virginia, 1977.

———. "Introduction: Revision and Regionalism." In Mitchell, *Appalachian Frontiers*, 1–22.

———, ed. *Appalachian Frontiers: Settlement, Society, and Development in the Preindustrial Era*. Lexington: University Press of Kentucky, 1990.

Moffett, James. *Storm in the Mountains: A Case Study of Censorship, Conflict, and Consciousness*. Carbondale: Southern Illinois University Press, 1988.

Montell, William Lynwood. *Killings: Folk Justice in the Upper South*. Lexington: University Press of Kentucky, 1986.

Montell, William Lynwood, and Michael Lynn Morse. *Kentucky Log Architecture*. Lexington: University Press of Kentucky, 1976.

Mooney, Fred. *Struggle in the Coal Fields: The Autobiography of Fred Mooney*. Edited by J. William Hess. Morgantown: West Virginia University Library, 1976.

Mooney, James. *James Mooney's History, Myths, and Sacred Formulas of the Cherokees*. Edited by George Ellison. Asheville, N.C.: Historical Images, 1992.

Moore, Tyrel G. "Economic Development in Appalachian Kentucky, 1800–1860." In Mitchell, *Appalachian Frontiers*, 222–34.

Morgan, John T. *The Log House in East Tennessee*. Knoxville: University of Tennessee Press, 1990.

Muir, John. *A Thousand Mile Walk to the Gulf*. Reproduced at <http://www.yosemite.ca.us/john_muir_exhibit/writings/a_thousand_mile_walk_to_the_gulf/chapter_3.html>.

Muller, Edward K., ed. *A Concise Historical Atlas of Pennsylvania*. Philadephia, Pa.: Temple University Press, 1989.

Mylott, James P. *A Measure of Prosperity: A History of Roane County*. Charleston, W.Va.: Mountain State Press, 1984.

National Park Service. Southeast Regional Office. *De Soto Trail: De Soto National Historic Trail Study, Final Report*. [Atlanta?]: National Park Service, 1990.

Nelson, Scott Reynolds. *Iron Confederacies: Southern Railways, Klan Violence, and Reconstruction*. Chapel Hill: University of North Carolina Press, 1999.

Newcomb, Harold. "Appalachia on Television: Region as Symbol in American Popular Culture." *Appalachian Journal* 7 (Autumn 1979/Winter 1980): 155–64.

Noe, Kenneth W. "'Deadened Color and Colder Horror': Rebecca Harding Davis and the Myth of Unionist Appalachia." In Billings, Norman, and Ledford, *Confronting Appalachian Stereotypes*, 67–84.

———. "Exterminating Savages: The Union Army and Mountain Guerrillas in Southern West Virginia, 1861–186." In Noe and Wilson, *Civil War in Appalachia*, 104–30.

———. *Southwest Virginia's Railroad: Modernization and the Sectional Crisis*. Urbana: University of Illinois Press, 1994.

Noe, Kenneth W., and Shannon H. Wilson. *The Civil War in Appalachia: Collected Essays*. Knoxville: University of Tennessee Press, 1997.

Norman, Gurney, and Lance Olsen. "Frankenstein in Palestine: Or, Postmodernism in Appalachia. A Dialogue of Sorts between Gurney Norman and Lance Olsen." *Pine Mountain Sand and Gravel* 3, no. 1 (1988): 77–100.

O'Donnell, James H. *Southern Indians in the American Revolution*. Knoxville: University of Tennessee Press, 1973.

O'Donovan, Donal. *The Rock from Which You Were Hewn: A History of the Catholic Church in Lewis County, West Virginia, St. Patrick's Parish, Weston*. Parsons, W.Va.: McClain Printing Co., 1989.

Olmsted, Frederick Law. *A Journey in the Back Country*. 1860. Reprint. Williamstown, Mass.: Corner House Publishers, 1972.

Otto, John S. *The Southern Frontiers, 1607–1860: The Agricultural Evolution of the Colonial and Antebellum South*. New York: Greenwood Press, 1989.

Palladino, Grace. *Another Civil War: Labor, Capital, and the State in the Anthracite Regions of Pennsylvania, 1840–1868*. Urbana: University of Illinois Press, 1990.

Paludan, Philip. *Victims: A True Story of the Civil War*. Knoxville: University of Tennessee Press, 1981.

Pastorius, Daniel Francis. "Positive Information from America Concerning the Country of Pennsylvania by a German Who Traveled There." In Soderland, *William Penn and the Founding of Pennsylvania*, 353–61.

Patton, Randall L. *Carpet Capital: The Rise of a New South Industry*. Athens: University of Georgia Press, 1999.

Pearsall, Marion. *Little Smoky Ridge*. Tuscaloosa: University of Alabama Press, 1959.

Pennsylvania Council of State. *Minutes of the Provincial Council of Pennsylvania*. Vols. 2–10. Harrisburg: Theophilus Fenn, 1838.

Perdue, Charles J., and Nancy Martin-Perdue. "Appalachian Fables and Facts: A Case Study of the Shenandoah National Park Removals." *Appalachian Journal* 7 (Autumn 1979/Winter 1980): 91–100.

Perdue, Theda. *Cherokee Women: Gender and Culture Change, 1700–1835*. Lincoln: University of Nebraska Press, 1998.

Perry, Huey. *They'll Cut Off Your Project: A Mingo County Chronicle*. New York: Praeger, 1972.

Phillips, Ulrich B. *Life and Labor in the Old South*. Boston: Little, Brown, 1929.

Pierce, David S. *The Great Smokies: From Natural Habitat to National Park*. Knoxville: University of Tennessee Press, 2000.

Polansky, Norman A., Robert D. Borgman, and Christine De Saix. *Roots of Futility*. San Francisco: Jossey-Bass Publishers, 1972.

Poole, Cary Franklin. *A History of Railroading in Western North Carolina*. Johnson City, Tenn.: Overmountain Press, 1995.

Puckett, Anita. "On the Pronunciation of Appalachia." *Now and Then: The Appalachian Magazine* 17 (Summer 2000): 25–29.

Pudup, Mary Beth. "Social Class and Economic Development in Southeast Kentucky, 1820–1880." in Mitchell, *Appalachian Frontiers*, 235–60.

Pudup, Mary Beth, Dwight B. Billings, and Altina L. Waller, eds. *Appalachia in the Making: The Mountain South in the Nineteenth Century*. Chapel Hill: University of North Carolina Press, 1995.

Purdy, Jedediah. *For Common Things: Irony, Trust, Commitment in America Today*. 2nd ed. New York: Vintage Books, 2000.

Purvis, Thomas L. "The European Ancestry of the United States Population, 1790." *William and Mary Quarterly* 41 (1984): 85–101.

Quaife, Milo M., ed. *The Preston and Virginia Papers of the Draper Collection of Manuscripts Calendar Series, Volume I*. 1915. Reprint. Owensboro, Ky.: McDowell Publications, 1980.

Rawick, George P., ed. *The American Slave: A Composite Autobiography*. Supplement, ser. 2, vol. 5, *Texas Narratives, Part 4*. Westport, Conn.: Greenwood Press, 1979.

Remini, Robert. *Andrew Jackson and the Course of American Freedom, 1822–1832*. New York: Harper and Row, 1977.

Richter, Daniel K. *Ordeal of the Longhouse: The Peoples of the Iroquois League in the Era of European Colonization*. Chapel Hill: University of North Carolina Press for the Institute of Early American History and Culture, 1992.

Rogers, William Warren, Robert David Ward, Leah Rawls Atkins, and Wayne Flynt. *Alabama: The History of a Deep South State*. Tuscaloosa: University of Alabama Press, 1994.

Romalis, Shelly. *Pistol Packin' Mama: Aunt Molly Jackson and the Politics of Folksong*. Urbana: University of Illinois Press, 1999.

Roper, Peter W. *Jedediah Hotchkiss: Rebel Mapmaker and Virginia Businessman*. Shippensburg, Pa.: White Mane Publishing Co., 1992.

Rostow, Walt Whitman. *The Diffusion of Power, 1957–1972: An Essay in Recent History*. New York: Macmillan, 1972.

———. *The Stages of Economic Growth: A Non-Communist Manifesto*. Cambridge: Cambridge University Press, 1960.

Rothman, Hal K. *Devil's Bargains: Tourism in the Twentieth-Century American West*. Lawrence: University Press of Kansas, 1998.

Royal, Anne Newport. *Sketches of Life, Manners, and Society in the United States, by a Traveller*. New Haven, Conn.: Printed for the author, 1826.

Royce, Charles C. *Indian Land Cessions in the United States*. Washington D.C.: Bureau of American Ethnology, 1884.

Salmond, John A. *Gastonia 1929: The Story of the Loray Mill Strike*. Chapel Hill: University of North Carolina Press, 1995.

Salstrom, Paul. *Appalachia's Path to Dependency: Rethinking a Region's Economic History, 1730–1940*. Lexington: University Press of Kentucky, 1994.

Sarris, Jonathan. "An Execution in Lumpkin County: Localized Loyalties in North Georgia's Civil War." In Noe and Wilson, *Civil War in Appalachia*, 131–57.

Schoenbaum, Thomas. *The New River Controversy*. Winston-Salem, N.C.: John F. Blair, 1979.

Schulman, Bruce J. *From Cotton Belt to Sun Belt: Federal Policy, Economic Development, and the Transformation of the South, 1938–1980*. New York: Oxford University Press, 1991.

Schwarzweller, Harry K., James S. Brown, and J. J. Mangalam. *Mountain Families in Transition: A Case Study of Appalachian Migration*. University Park: Pennsylvania State University Press, 1971.

Scott, Robert. *Footloose in Jacksonian America: Robert W. Scott and His Agrarian World*. Edited by Thomas D. Clark. Frankfort: Kentucky Historical Society, 1990.

Sears, Richard D. *The Kentucky Abolitionists in the Midst of Slavery, 1854–1864*. Lewiston, Ont.: Edwin Mellen Press, 1993.

Semple, Ellen Churchill. "The Anglo-Saxons of the Kentucky Mountains: A Study in Anthropogeography." 1901. Reprinted in McNeil, *Appalachian Images*, 145–74.

Shade, William G. *Democratizing the Old Dominion: Virginia and the Second American Party System, 1824–1861*. Charlottesville: University Press of Virginia, 1996.

Shaler, Nathaniel Southgate. "The Border State Men of the Civil War." *Atlantic Monthly*, February 1892, 245–58.

Shapiro, Henry D. *Appalachia on Our Mind: The Southern Mountains and Mountaineers in the American Consciousness, 1870–1920*. Chapel Hill: University of North Carolina Press, 1978.

Shapiro, Karin A. *A New South Rebellion: The Battle against Convict Labor in the Tennessee Coalfields, 1871–1896*. Chapel Hill: University of North Carolina Press, 1998.

Sharp, Cecil. *English Folk-Songs from the Southern Appalachians*. New York: Putnam, 1917.

Silver, Timothy H. *A New Face on the Countryside: Indians, Colonists, and Slaves in South Atlantic Forests, 1500–1800*. Cambridge: Cambridge University Press, 1990.

Slaughter, Thomas. *The Whiskey Rebellion: Frontier Epilogue to the American Revolution*. New York: Oxford University Press, 1986.

Smith, Betty. *Jane Hicks Gentry: A Singer among Singers*. Lexington: University Press of Kentucky, 1998.

Smith, Merrit Roe. *Harpers Ferry Armory and the New Technology: The Challenge of Change*. Ithaca, N.Y.: Cornell University Press, 1977.

Sobel, Joseph Daniel. *The Storytellers' Journey: An American Revival*. Urbana: University of Illinois Press, 1999.

Soderland, Jean, ed. *William Penn and the Founding of Pennsylvania: A Documentary History*. Philadelphia: University of Pennsylvania Press, 1983.

Sparks, Jim. "ASU Benches Mascot; His Look Raises the Ire of Many." *Winston-Salem Journal*, September 17, 1999.

———. "ASU's Mascot, Yosef, Gets New Look; Students Select Grizzled, Mountain-Man Design." *Winston-Salem Journal*, April 4, 2000.

Spiker, Linda McHone. *Max Meadows, Virginia: Destined for Glory*. Pulaski, Va.: Edmunds Printing Co., 1990.

Starr, Blaze, and Huey Perry. *Blaze Starr: My Life as Told to Huey Perry*. New York: Praeger, 1974.

Stekert, Ellen J. "Focus for Conflict: Southern Mountain Medical Beliefs in Detroit." *Journal of American Folklore* 83 (1970): 115–56.

Stephenson, John B. "Place for Sale: The Search for Fantasy Mountain in Scotland
and Western North Carolina." *Now and Then* 9 (Summer 1992): 26–30.

————. *Shiloh: A Blue Ridge Mountain Community*. Lexington: University Press of
Kentucky, 1968.

Strother, David Hunter ["Porte Crayon"]. "The Mountains." *Harper's New Monthly
Magazine*, December 1871–June 1872, 659–76, 801–15; July–November 1872,
21–35, 347–61, 502–16, 801–16; December 1872–June 1873, 669–81; July–
November 1873, 821–32; July–November 1874, 156–68; July–November 1874,
475–86.

————. "Old Time Militia Musters." *Harper's New Monthly Magazine*, July 1878,
212–21.

————. "A Virginia Militia Training of the Last Generation." *Harper's New
Monthly Magazine*, July–November 1872, 243–45.

————. "A Winter in the South." *Harper's New Monthly Magazine*, July–November
1857, 433–51, 594–606, 721–40; December 1857–June 1858, 167–83, 721–36;
July–November 1858, 289–306; December 1858–June 1859, 1–17.

Sullivan, Charles Kenneth. *Coal Men and Coal Towns: Development of the Smokeless
Coalfields of Southern West Viriginia, 1873–1923*. New York: Garland Publishing,
1989.

Taylor, James W. *Alleghenia, a Geographical and Statistical Memoir: The Strength of
the Union and the Weakness of Slavery in the Highlands of the South*. St. Paul,
Minn.: James Davenport, 1862.

Thomas, John L. *Alternative America: Henry George, Edward Bellamy, Henry De-
marest Lloyd, and the Adversary Tradition*. Cambridge, Mass.: Belknap Press, 1983.

Thwaites, Reuben Gold, and Louise Phelps Kellogg, eds. *The Revolution on the
Upper Ohio, 1775–1777*. Madison: Wisconsin State Historical Society, 1908.

Tichi, Cecilia. *High Lonesome: The American Culture of Country Music*. Chapel Hill:
University of North Carolina Press, 1994.

Tindall, George Brown. *The Emergence of the New South, 1913–1945*. Vol. 10 of *A
History of the South*, edited by Wendell Holmes Stephenson and E. Merton Coul-
ter. Baton Rouge: Louisiana State University Press, 1967.

Toynbee, Arnold J. *A Study of History*. Abridgment of vols. 1–6 by D. C. Somervell.
New York: Oxford University Press, 1947.

Tribe, Ivan M. *The Stonemans: An Appalachian Family and the Music That Shaped
Their Lives*. Urbana: University of Illinois Press, 1993.

U.S. Bureau of the Census. *Seventh Census of the United States, 1850: An Appendix*.
Washington, D.C.: Robert Armstrong, Public Printer, 1853.

U.S. Department of Agriculture. Bureau of Agricultural Economics. *Economic and
Social Problems and Conditions of the Southern Appalachians*. Washington, D.C.:
USDA Miscellaneous Publication 205, 1935.

U.S. Department of Commerce. Bureau of the Census. *Consolidated Federal Funds
Report, 1983–1992*. CD. Washington, D.C.: Bureau of the Census, 1993.

U.S. Department of Defense. Office of the Secretary of Defense, Progress Reports and Statistics Division. *State Maps of Major Military Stations and Active Industrial Facilities Owned and Operated by the Army, Navy, and Air Force.* Washington, D.C.: Government Printing Office, 1955, 1962, 1970, 1980.

———. Washington Headquarters Services, Directorate for Information Operations and Reports. *Atlas/State Data Abstracts for the United States.* Washington, D.C.: Government Printing Office, 1985, 1990, 1995.

Vance, Rupert B. "The Region's Future: A National Challenge." In Ford, *Southern Appalachian Region,* 293–99.

Vance, Zebulon. *The Papers of Zebulon Baird Vance.* Edited by Frontis W. Johnston. Raleigh, N.C.: State Department of Archives and History, 1963.

Vandiver, Frank. *Mighty Stonewall.* New York: McGraw-Hill, 1957.

Wallace, Paul A. W. *Conrad Weiser, 1696–1760: Friend of Colonist and Mohawk.* Philadelphia: University of Pennsylvania Press, 1945.

———. *Indian Paths of Pennsylvania.* Harrisburg: Pennsylvania Historical and Museum Commission, 1993.

Wallenstein, Peter. "'Helping to Save the Union': The Social Origins, Wartime Experiences, and Military Impact of White Union Troops from East Tennessee." In Noe and Shannon, *Civil War in Appalachia,* 1–29.

Waller, Altina L. *Feud: Hatfields, McCoys, and Social Change in Appalachia, 1860–1900.* Chapel Hill: University of North Carolina Press, 1988.

———. "Feuding in Appalachia: Evolution of a Cultural Stereotype." In Pudup, Billings, and Waller, *Appalachia in the Making,* 347–76.

Walls, David. "On the Naming of Appalachia." In *An Appalachian Symposium: Essays Written in Honor of Cratis D. Williams,* edited by J. W. Williamson, 56–76. Boone, N.C.: Appalachian State University Press, 1977.

Ward, James A. *J. Edgar Thomson: Master of the Pennsylvania.* Westport, Conn.: Greenwood Press, 1980.

Ward, Robert David, and William Warren Rogers. *Convicts, Coal, and the Banner Mine Tragedy.* Tuscaloosa: University of Alabama Press, 1987.

Warren, Kenneth. *Triumphant Capitalism: Henry Clay Frick and the Industrial Transformation of America.* Pittsburgh, Pa.: University of Pittsburgh Press, 1996.

Washington, George. *The Diaries of George Washington.* Edited by John C. Fitzpatrick. 4 vols. Boston: Houghton Mifflin, 1925.

———. *The Papers of George Washington: Colonial Series.* Edited by W. W. Abbot and Dorothy Twohig. 8 vols. Charlottesville: University Press of Virginia, 1983–95.

———. *The Writings of George Washington from the Original Manuscript Sources.* Edited by John C. Fitzpatrick. 39 vols. Washington, D.C.: Government Printing Office, 1931–44.

Weidensaul, Scott. *Mountains of the Heart: A Natural History of the Appalachians.* Golden, Colo.: Fulcrum Publishing, 1994.

Weller, Jack. *Yesterday's People: Life in Contemporary Appalachia.* Lexington: University Press of Kentucky, 1965.

West, Carroll Van. *Tennessee's New Deal Landscape: A Guidebook.* Knoxville: University of Tennessee Press, 2001.

West, John Foster. *Lift Up Your Head, Tom Dooley: The True Story of the Appalachian Murder That Inspired One of America's Most Popular Ballads.* Asheboro, N.C.: Down Home Press, 1993.

Wharton School Industrial Research Unit [Carter Goodrich, Rupert B. Vance, et al.]. *Migration and Economic Opportunity: The Report of the Study of Population Redistribution.* Philadelphia: University of Pennsylvania Press, 1936.

Wheeler, William Bruce, and Michael J. McDonald. *TVA and the Tellico Dam: A Bureaucratic Crisis in Post-Industrial America, 1936–1979.* Knoxville: University of Tennessee Press, 1986.

Whisnant, David E. *All That Is Native and Fine: The Politics of Culture in an American Region.* Chapel Hill: University of North Carolina Press, 1983.

———. *Modernizing the Mountaineer.* Boone, N.C.: Appalachian Consortium Press, 1980.

Wilkinson, Silvia. *Dirt Tracks to Glory: The Early Days of Stock Car Racing as Told by the Participants.* Chapel Hill, N.C.: Algonquin, 1983.

Williams, Brett. *John Henry: A Bio-Bibliography.* Westport, Conn.: Greenwood Press, 1983.

Williams, Cratis D. "The Southern Mountaineer in Fact and Fiction." Ph.D. diss., New York University, 1961.

Williams, David. *The Georgia Gold Rush: Twenty-Niners, Cherokees, and Gold Fever.* Columbia: University of South Carolina Press, 1993.

Williams, John Alexander. "Appalachian History: Regional History in the Post-Modern Zone." *Appalachian Journal* 28 (Winter 2001): 168–87.

———. "The Birth of a State: West Virginia and the Civil War." In *True Stories of the American Past,* edited by Altina L. Waller, 216–32. New York: McGraw-Hill, 1995.

———. "Class, Section, and Culture in Nineteenth-Century West Virginia Politics." In Pudup, Billings, and Waller, *Appalachia in the Making,* 210–32.

———. "Counting Yesterday's People: Using Aggregate Data to Address the Problem of Appalachia's Boundaries." *Journal of Appalachian Studies* 2 (Spring 1996): 3–27.

———. "Cultural Intervention in Appalachia: An Historical Perspective." In Bulger, *Promoting Southern Cultural Heritage,* 35–38.

———. "The Politics of Urban Decay." *Review of Politics* 32, no. 4 (1970): 536–42.

———. "Radicalism and Professionalism in Folklore Studies: A Comparative Perspective." *Journal of the Folklore Institute* 11 (March 1975): 211–34.

———. "Unpacking Pinckney in Poland." *Appalachian Journal* 20 (Winter 1993): 162–75.

———. *West Virginia: A History.* New York: W. W. Norton, 1976.

———. *West Virginia: A History for Beginners.* 2nd ed. Charleston, W.Va.: Appalachian Editions, 1997.

———. *West Virginia and the Captains of Industry*. 1976. Reprint. Morgantown: West Virginia University Press, 1997.

Williams, John Alexander, and Alex Hooker. "Southbound on the Hillbilly Highway." Paper delivered at the Appalachian Studies Association annual meeting, Newport, Ky., March 18, 1997.

Williams, John Alexander, and Jessica Kelley. "The Other End of the Hillbilly Highway: What Happened to Appalachian Migrants in the Sunbelt?" Paper delivered at "Down Home, Downtown: Urban Appalachians Today" conference, Cincinnati, Ohio, September 22, 1995.

Williams, Michael Ann. *Homeplace: The Social Use and Meaning of the Folk Dwelling in Southwestern North Carolina*. Athens: University of Georgia Press, 1991.

Williamson, J. W. *Hillbillyland: What the Movies Did to the Mountains and What the Mountains Did to the Movies*. Chapel Hill: University of North Carolina Press, 1995.

Willis, Bailey. *The Northern Appalachians*. National Geographic Society Monographs, No. 1, Vol. 6. New York: American Book Co., 1895.

Zinn, Jack. *Robert E. Lee's Cheat Mountain Campaign*. Parsons, W.Va.: McClain Printing Co., 1974.

Index

Elizabethton, Tenn., 146, 172, 248, 275, 277, 287
Elkins, W.Va., 233
Eller, Ronald D, 362
Elyton Land Company, 237
Embree's Iron Works, 128
Emerson, Ralph Waldo, 80
Endangered Species Act, 353
England, 245
Environmentalism, 349, 352–53
Environmental Protection Agency, 343
Ephrata commune (Pa.), 39–40, 41, 100
Episcopal Church, 99, 201, 282
Erie, Pa., 340, 345
Erie Canal, 147
Ervin, Sam (U.S. senator, N.C.), 375–76
Erwin, Tenn., 233
Estill County, Ky., 128
Ethnic clustering, 39, 46
Ethnicity, 364, 394

Fairfax, Thomas (Lord), 32, 54, 57, 59, 93, 119, 132, 236
Fairfield, Ala., 260
Fairmont State College (W.Va.), 329
Fallam, Robert, 34–35
Fallen Timbers, Battle of (1794), 67
Familism, 322, 325
Family structure, 121
Fannin County, Ga., 165
Farm-and-forest economy, 114–16, 125–26, 135, 153–54, 242, 251–52, 389
Farming, 113–15, 225–26, 314–15. See also Agriculture
Farmington, W.Va., 351
Fatalism, 322–23, 325
Fayette County, W.Va., 347, 388
Fayetteville, W.Va., 388–89, 391, 392–93
Fear: of slave rebellions, 27, 126
Federal Emergency Relief Administration (FERA), 315. See also New Deal
Federal government, 280–81, 284–85,

288–89, 301–2, 312, 340, 347, 348–49, 389–90; and migration from Appalachia, 313–15. See also names of specific agencies, defense expenditures, loan guarantees, military recruitment, and transfer payments
Federal Road, 77–78, 95, 147, 152, 242
Federal Power Commission (FPC), 291–92
Fee, John G., 154–56, 200
Felts, Lee, 197, 287, 392
Felts brothers, 270, 287
Fence laws, 218
"Fenno-Scandian" cultural complex, 31, 49, 88, 104–6
Fentress County, Tenn., 223
Feuds, 192–93, 201, 305. See also Clay County, Ky.: "war"; Hatfield-McCoy feud
Film industry, 199, 223, 301
Fincastle County, Va., 75
Finland, 105
Finns, 31, 88
Fifteenth Amendment, 182
Fire and fire prevention. See Forests; Forest Service
Fish and game laws, 250
Fiske, John, 325
Five Nations. See Iroquois Confederacy
Flannery Fork (N.C.), 42
Flat Rock, N.C., 132, 176
Flatt, Lester, 357
Flat Top Mountain (W.Va.), 164–65, 173, 244, 257
Florida, 2, 24, 77, 83, 394
Floyd, George Rogers Clark, 117–18, 191, 194
Floyd, John (d. 1782), 75, 117, 141–42
Floyd, John (1783–1837), 75, 126, 141–42, 154
Floyd, John B. (1806–63), 75, 141–42, 165, 168
Floyd, John B. (state official, W.Va.), 191
Floyd, Letitia Preston, 141

George III (king of England), 83

George Washington National Forest, 290

Georgia, 13, 46, 114, 297, 311, 347, 350, 384; boundaries of, 69, 144; and Cherokee Indians, 63, 78–81; and Civil War, 158, 163, 174; defense-related spending in, 367–69, 376; forests and forest fires in, 290; government and politics of, 72, 77–80, 142, 285, 368–69; land lottery (1832), 79, 153; military academy, 149; Mountain Area Management Plan, 390; population growth of, 77, 232; railroads, 148–51, 233; roads, 22, 147. *See also* Bartram, William; North Georgia

German Americans, 89, 93, 140

Germans, 26, 38–42, 48–49, 105

Gershwin, George, 210

Gettysburg, Pa., 45

Gettysburg, Battle of, 169, 171

Giardina, Denise, 358, 362

Giles County, Va., 365–66

Gilmer County, W.Va., 317

Gist, Christopher, 54–55

Glacier National Park, 298

Glades, 86, 92

Glasgow, Va., 52

Glen Rogers, W.Va., 258

Globe, the (N.C.), 94

Goad, Dexter, 196

Gold: discovery of, 79

Good Roads movement. *See* Roads and road building

Gordon, Robert Winslow, 210

Government and politics, 134–43, 157–59, 169–70, 180, 187, 191–92

Graff, Orin, 329–30

Grafton, W.Va., 149, 163, 167

Graham, Martha, 308

Grand Canyon National Park, 2, 298

Grandfather Mountain (N.C.), 107, 132, 295, 299

Granville, Earl (John Carteret), 32, 42, 59

Grant, James (colonel), 58

Grant, Lizzie, 110

Grant, Ulysses S. (general, president, U.S.), 169

Graves, Bibb (governor, Ala.), 285

Grayson County, Va., 97, 229

Grazing. *See* Cattle; Livestock industry; Open-range grazing

Great Awakening, 98, 100

Great Depression, 288–89, 306, 314–15

"Greater Pennsylvania," 49, 244, 246

Great Kanawha River. *See* Kanawha River

Great Lakes, 23, 254

"Great migration." *See* Migration

Great Smoky Mountains, 15, 20, 70, 246, 295, 297

Great Smoky Mountains National Park (GSMNP), 9, 295–301, 307, 352–53

Great Society, 348–49, 389. *See also* War on Poverty; names of specific relief agencies

Great Trading Path, 115

Great Trail. *See* Great Wagon Road

Great Valley, 2–11 passim, 20–37 passim, 91, 93, 95, 117, 146; Civil War in, 152, 159; description of, 103; economy of, 119, 143–44, 218, 242, 273, 330; migration and settlement in, 37–38, 48–49, 51, 52–53, 61, 143; as transportation corridor, 33–34, 61–62, 66, 87, 115, 144, 145–46, 154, 242; slavery in, 71

Great Wagon Road, 48–49, 93, 120, 144, 146, 242, 283. *See also* Valley Turnpike; Warrior's Path

Green, Mary Jane, 177

Greenback Labor Party, 263

Greenbrier, The. *See* White Sulphur Springs, W.Va.

Greenbrier Company, 7

slaves and black people, 154–55, 212; description, 116, 134–35, 189–90, 211–12, 229, 250–51, 363–66; loyalties during Civil War, 164–66; in textile industry, 273–74, 275–76, 286–87
Mountains: compared to ocean waves, 83–84, 95, 107
Mountaintop removal, 395. *See also* Strip mining
Mt. Airy, N.C., 385
Mt. Jackson, Va., 151
Mt. Jefferson (N.C.), 106
Mt. Mitchell (N.C.), 132, 296, 392
Mt. Washington (N.H.), 296
Mugler, Henry J., 163
Muir, John, 117, 186
Mumford, Lewis, 293
Murfree, Mary Noailles ("Charles Egbert Craddock"), 198. *See also* Mountaineer: as literary stereotype
Murphy, N.C., 317
Muscle Shoals (Ala.), 115, 148, 215, 291, 293
Music, 227–28. *See also Appalachian Spring*; Country music; Folk music

Nantahala Outdoor Center, 359
Nantahala River, 358–59
Nanticoke Indians, 24
Napoleon I (emperor of France), 149
Nashville, Tenn., 74, 78, 95–97, 148, 149, 152, 168, 232, 303
Nashville basin (Tenn.), 62
National Academy of Sciences, 386
National Aeronautics and Space Administration (NASA), 367, 378
National Banking Act (1863), 180
National Emergency Council, 294
National Folk Music Center, 392
National forests, 17, 290–91. *See also* names of individual forests
National Industrial Recovery Act (NIRA), 279–80, 296

National Institutes of Health, 377
National parks, 17, 295–96. *See also* names of individual parks
National Park Service, 295, 298, 301, 357, 378, 389
National Recovery Administration (NRA), 278
National Road, 202
National Science Foundation (NSF), 311, 326
National Textile Workers Union, 276
Native Americans. *See* Indians
Nat Turner's Rebellion (1831), 126
Navy, U.S., 377
Neely, Matthew M., 284–85, 375–76
Negro League, 240
Negro Mountain ("Nigger Mountain"). *See* Mt. Jefferson
Nemacolin Path, 55. *See also* Braddock's Road
Neonatives, 355, 364, 387, 391. *See also* Residential tourism; Settlers
Netherlands, 39
Nevels, Gertie (fictional character), 322, 366, 398
New Castle, Del., 31
New Deal, 278, 284–85, 289, 312, 315, 316, 323, 375. *See also* Roosevelt, Franklin D.
New Echota (Ga.), 78
New England, 44, 68, 107, 116, 202, 204–5, 218, 275; and "free labor" colonies in Appalachia, 156
New Englanders, 88, 123, 234
Newfound Gap, 296, 299
New Jersey, 31, 48
New Market, Tenn., 351
New Mexico, 328
New Orleans, La., 23, 141, 231, 283
New River (N.C.-Va.), 2, 3, 15, 40, 42, 54, 94, 95, 107, 128, 171, 226, 321
New River controversy, 353, 357, 364
New River Gorge, 2, 3, 7, 86, 292, 359, 388; coal mining in, 345, 347

New River Gorge Bridge, 3, 389
New River Gorge National River, 389
New River valley, 6–7, 10, 34, 45, 106.
    See also North Fork
New South, 251, 286
Newspapers, 236
New York, N.Y., 1, 76, 252, 308, 331
New York (colony), 21, 23, 25, 37, 44, 51
New York (state), 10, 13, 65, 76, 116,
    128, 130, 156, 276, 293; Appalachian
    portion of, 343, 347, 366
Niagara Falls, 23
Niagara region (N.Y.), 25
Nixon, Richard (president, U.S.), 344
Nixon administration, 348
Nolachucky River, 95, 201
Norfolk, Va., 3, 151, 162, 296, 330
Norfolk and Western Railway (N&W),
    3, 193, 196, 229, 232, 237, 246, 292,
    310; as coal carrier, 232, 244, 255,
    258. *See also* Virginia and Tennessee
    Railroad
Norfolk Southern. *See* Norfolk and
    Western Railway
Norman, Gurney, 18, 358, 361
Norris, George W. (U.S. senator, Neb.),
    291, 293
Norris, Tenn., 302
Norris Basin, 302, 305, 307
Norris Dam, 302
North American Land Company, 76
North Carolina (colony), 32, 51; bound-
    aries of, 46, 53–54, 69, 128; Daniel
    Boone and, 49, 56, 60; geography of,
    10, 13, 15, 45; migration to and from,
    25, 48–49; Moravians in, 39, 41–42,
    100; western region of, 30, 42, 49.
    See also Carolina colonies; Carolinas;
    Western North Carolina
North Carolina (state), 74, 76, 292, 311,
    392; Cherokee Indians in, 21, 78, 80,
    105, 144; convict lease labor system
    in, 221, 284; defense spending in,
    367; forests and forest fires in, 290;

geological survey of, 130; government
    and politics of, 71, 134, 135–36, 137–
    38, 139–40, 142, 145, 353; migration
    to and from, 117, 394–95; military
    draft and enlistments in, 384; national
    parks in, 295; Piedmont section of,
    106; "quart law," 119; religion in,
    100–102; resorts in, 347, 395; rail-
    roads in, 148–51, 233; and secession
    crisis, 159, 161; sectionalism in, 71,
    144, 149; and State of Franklin, 94;
    textile industry in, 273. *See also* West-
    ern North Carolina
North Carolina Central Railroad,
    148–51
North Cove (N.C.), 113
Northeastern states, 122, 251, 312
Northern Alabama. *See* Alabama
Northern Ireland, 3, 4, 33, 100; immi-
    gration from, 43–44, 46
North Fork (of New River), 107.
    See also New River valley
North Georgia, 16, 135, 330–31, 377,
    390; and Atlanta, 148, 390; as Chero-
    kee territory, 22–23, 30, 67, 77–78;
    railroads in, 152; resorts in, 132, 347,
    395; travelers' descriptions of, 84, 91
Northwest Ordinance (1787), 71
Nuclear power, 337
Nunn, Sam (U.S. senator, Ga.), 368, 375

Oak Ridge, Tenn., 313, 317, 366
Ocoee River, 358
Oconee County, S.C., 18
Oconoluftee valley, 112
Odum, Howard W., 293
Office of Economic Opportunity
    (OEO), 342, 349. *See also* War on
    Poverty
Office of War Information, 307
Ohio, 13, 25, 64–65, 91, 313, 321, 394;
    Appalachian portion of, 30, 88, 120,
    125, 149, 343, 347, 366–67
Ohio Company, 7, 55

Veterans Administration, 387
Vietnam War, 375, 383
Vincennes raid (1779), 68
Vincent, George, 207
Vinson, Carl, 369
Violence: in lower-class culture, 384;
  in post–Civil War era, 185–97, 223
Virginia (colony), 6, 8, 22, 25, 35, 44–
  45, 49, 52–53, 59; border with Tennessee, 27; and French and Indian
  War, 54–56; Indian relations and
  trade, 23, 31, 35–37, 59
Virginia (state), 14, 16, 45, 63, 65, 66,
  113, 117, 142, 392; agriculture in, 91,
  119–20, 125; boundaries of, 69–70;
  and Civil War, 152, 158–67; coalfields
  in, 318, 345, 391, 395; constitutions
  of, 70–71, 136, 141; and convict lease
  labor system, 221; debt of, 184; defense spending in, 367–69; forests
  and forest fires in, 290; mines and
  miners in, 307; population of, 318,
  345, 353, 392; racial segregation in,
  350; railroads and related debt in,
  148–51; resorts in, 130–32; sectionalism in, 71; social structure of, 73–74,
  140. See also West Virginia; Western
  Virginia
Virginia, University of, 293, 310
Virginia and Tennessee Railroad, 3, 149,
  151, 170, 172, 193
Virginia Central Railroad, 183
Virginian Railway, 229–30, 258
Virginia Polytechnic Institute and State
  University. See Virginia Tech
Virginia Road, 48
Virginias, The (periodical), 184
Virginia Tech, 363, 365.
  See also Blacksburg, Va.
VISTA (Volunteers in Service to Amer-
  ica), 348. See also Poverty workers;
  War on Poverty
Voting, 140–41

Wabash Railroad, 229
Wachacha, Maggie, 249
Wachovia (N.C.), 42, 100.
  See also Moravians
Wagner Labor Relations Act (1935), 280
Wales, 245
Walker, Thomas, 7, 51, 62
Walker County, Ala., 278
Walking Purchase (1737), 37, 42
Waller, Altina, 192–93
WalMart, 346
Waltons, The (TV show), 396
Warm Springs, N.C., 132
Warm Springs, Va., 132, 146
War of 1812, 139
War on Poverty, 342, 348–50, 369.
  See also Office of Economic Oppor-
  tunity; Poverty workers
Warrior's Path, 35, 37, 66, 146, 151.
  See also Great Wagon Road
Washington, Booker Taliaferro, 183
Washington, D.C., 297, 389; as migrant
  destination, 306–8, 320, 347; as na-
  tional capital, 269, 312, 341, 364, 383
Washington, George, 68, 93, 119, 143,
  147, 151; and French and Indian War,
  55–56; as land speculator, 59, 92, 111,
  114
Washington, Pa., 94
Washington College (Washington and
  Lee University), 143
Washington County, Va., 97
Washington County, Tenn., 146
Washington Iron Manufacturing Com-
  pany, 128
Washington Senators (baseball team),
  240
Washington Weaving Corporation, 226,
  238
Watauga County, N.C., 139, 209
Watauga River, 88, 107, 121, 125
Watauga settlements (Tenn.), 66, 94,
  144
Water Power Act (1920), 291

Watson, Arthel ("Doc"), 357
Watterson, Henry, 192
Waxhaws (N.C.-S.C.), 45
Wayah Bald (Ga.), 85
Wayne, Anthony (general), 68
Wayne County, W.Va., 150
Waynesboro, Va., 233
Waynesville, N.C., 170, 184, 209, 212
Weatherford Award, 363, 392
Weeks Act (1911), 290
Weir, Ernest, 282
Weiser, Conrad, 26, 40, 83, 402 (n. 59)
Welborn, John, 288
Welch, Isaiah, 244–45
Welfare capitalism, 260, 265
Weller, Jack E., 325
West, Don, 285, 311
Western and Atlantic Railroad, 148
Western Maryland Railroad, 229
Western North Carolina, 10–11, 16, 98,
    115, 122–24, 250, 366–67, 384; and
    Civil War, 163, 164, 171, 174; econ-
    omy of, 91, 250, 347, 392–93; forestry
    in, 289–90; livestock industry in, 91,
    120; mountain resorts in, 132; trans-
    portation problems in, 115; travelers'
    descriptions and accounts of, 98,
    115–16, 121–22, 250–51; vernacular
    housing in, 107–8; and Whiskey Re-
    bellion (1794), 118
Western North Carolina Alliance, 352,
    386
Western North Carolina Railroad, 221,
    232
Western Virginia, 54, 117, 119, 135, 142,
    156; Euro-American settlement in,
    30, 38, 45, 46; northwest, 66, 69, 73,
    93–94, 125, 141, 155; southwest, 16,
    45, 54, 57, 68–69, 88, 142, 171
West Liberty, W.Va., 97
Weston, W.Va., 177
West Virginia, 88, 221, 245, 278, 306,
    307, 386; boundaries of, 69–70; Civil
    War in, 163, 164, 171–74; coalfields

in, 255, 318, 345, 391, 395, 397–98;
constitution of, 182; defense spending
in, 366–68, 375–76; desegregation
in, 350–51; education in, 328; Euro-
American settlement in, 30; forests
and forest fires in, 290; geography
and environment of, 10–15, 25, 115,
116, 352–53, 398; government and
politics of, 169, 181–82, 234, 261,
281–82, 338–41, 343, 349–50; land
distribution in, 76, 114; military recruitment and service in, 383–85;
mines and miners in, 307, 318, 345–
46; mine wars (1912–27), 266–72,
288; population of, 117, 318, 345–47,
394; railroads in, 229–36; slavery
issue in, 102; statehood movement in,
155, 159, 165–68, 234. See also Coal,
bituminous
West Virginia Central and Pittsburgh
    Railroad, 229
West Virginia National Guard, 383
West Virginia Pulp and Paper Company,
    246–47
West Virginia University, 240, 363.
    See also Morgantown, W.Va.
Wheeling, W.Va., 169, 282; early history
    of, 61, 64, 96, 97, 144, 145, 147, 155,
    158; industries in, 128, 130, 244; and
    West Virginia statehood movement,
    159, 163, 166, 167
Wheeling and Wytheville, diocese of,
    118
Wheeling Intelligencer, 155
Wheelwright, Ky., 353
Whig Party, 140, 161, 166
Whiskey, 93, 95, 118–19, 139, 310.
    See also Moonshine
Whiskey Rebellion (1794), 118–19, 187
Whisman, John, 335, 338
White, Jesse, 344
"White basis" (of legislative apportion-
    ment), 72
White family (Clay County, Ky.), 195